From Basic Needs to Basic Rights:
Women's Claim to Human Rights

Edited by Margaret A. Schuler

From Basic Needs to Basic Rights:
Women's Claim to Human Rights

Edited by Margaret A. Schuler

Women, Law & Development International
Washington D.C.

Production Manager: Yasmin Tambiah
Associate Editor: Charlotte Jones

Design and Layout: Margaret Schuler
Cover Design: Xanthus Design
Printing: PressXpress

Library of Congress Catalog Card Number: 95-79859

Contents

Part III: Religious, Cultural and Ethnic Identity & Human Rights

Part IV: Sexual and Reproductive Rights

Part IV: Activism to Advance Women's Human Rights

Appendix A

Appendix B

Contributors

Index

Foreword

Noeleen Heyzer

This foreword is being written on the eve of the Fourth World Conference on Women. Women have been working to ensure that Beijing affirms the kind of world we want to live in, a world where development processes will empower women in particular, a world in which the promotion and protection of all human rights and fundamental freedoms will be considered an international priority.

We are delighted to be involved in this project, and congratulate the Institute for Women, Law and Development for compiling these thoughtful and provocative pieces in time for the Beijing Conference.

The challenges inhibiting women's full enjoyment of their human rights and participation in development are manifold. Examining them, it is evident that sustainable development will remain elusive unless women can freely and effectively exercise the full range of their economic, social, cultural, civil, and political rights.

There are alarming trends which present key challenges in the areas of development and women's rights:

* *Globally women are still invisible in formal political institutions.* Worldwide, women hold only 10 percent of parliamentary seats. This figure *fell* by nearly three percentage points between 1989 and 1993.

* *In virtually every nation, violence or the threat of violence, constricts the range of choices open to women and girls in almost every area of life, public and private.* UNIFEM entered the human rights arena through its work on violence against women. In 1990, the Fund commissioned a study on the linkages between violence against women, human rights and development and that resulted in the *Battered Dreams: Violence Against Women as a Development Issue.* The study found that, internationally, gender violence is a major obstacle to the achievement of equality, development and peace. It inhibits

women's full participation in society, and creates a climate in which sustainable human development is manifestly impossible.

- *Women are increasingly the specific targets of aggression during wartime.* Systematic mass rape and forced impregnation have been documented as weapons of war and/or ethnic cleansing in many parts of the world. Frighteningly, there is growing evidence that war and civil unrest not only endanger women in the public sphere, but increase the risk of violence against women in the home.

- *Women all over the world perform multiple roles in productive labor, paid and unpaid, that are not reflected in official measures of economic activity.* Their access to family benefits, financial credit, the right to own and inherit property are either nonexistent or are seriously limited by law and/or traditional or religious practices.

- *Women's low status everywhere has been enshrined in law, and women continue to face injustice in virtually every nation solely on the basis of their gender.* Legal traditions and legal systems discriminate against women in many ways. Gender bias may be institutionalized through laws (legislated and customary) which openly discriminate against women. Laws may be passed which are gender neutral on paper but discriminatory in practice. Some tax laws, for example, may require married women to have their husbands signature to validate tax forms.

- *Today millions of women live in conditions where reproductive health is beyond their reach.* Around the world, an estimated 3 million couples do not have access to family planning services. Many societies, according low status to women, accept a high incidence of maternal death as natural and inevitable.

- *In both industrialized and developing countries women and girls suffer the effects of harmful and sometimes life-threatening traditional practices, rooted in long-held cultural assumptions and/or religious beliefs.* These practices include but are not limited to: female genital mutilation, female infanticide, son preference and eating disorders.

Such obstacles to women's equality ensure that the majority of the world's women and girls remain excluded from fully participating in society and from the prevailing vision of "universal," human rights. Women are asking for greater commitment, accountability and resources for the implementation of the results of the various world summits and conferences.

How do we make this possible?

Expanding the current understanding of state responsibility and accountability is a key element in implementing, enforcing, and assessing human rights instruments and laws from a women's human rights perspective. Activists are insisting upon a more expansive and inclusive interpretation of violations of women's human rights, which are not direct actions of the state (i.e., domestic violence) but for which the state may be held accountable.

It is crucial to insist on international recognition of all human rights as universal, interdependent and interrelated. This stresses the indivisibility of civil, political, social, economic and cultural rights, and allows the international community to identify the abuses and denial of rights which are unique to women. For instance, we know that the existence of extreme poverty amongst women inhibits their full and effective enjoyment of human rights, denying their full participation as both agents and beneficiaries in the development process.

Strategies to strengthen the Convention on the Elimination of All Forms of Discrimination Against Women are gathering momentum. CEDAW does not attempt to define rights in gender-neutral terms; rather, it elaborates the meaning of discrimination against women. The Convention is an important tool for the advancement of woman's human rights. Advocates of women's human rights are lobbying to strengthen CEDAW's implementation and monitoring procedures (particularly its investigatory and enforcement powers), to facilitate NGO input to the CEDAW Committee, and to increase its funding.

Finally, the Vienna Declaration articulates the necessity of integrating the equal status of women and the human rights of women into the mainstream of United Nations system-wide activity. It goes further, to assert that "these issues should be regularly and systematically addressed throughout relevant United Nations bodies and mechanisms." Women are pursuing this mandate comprehensively, including the UN's development agendas and peacemaking/keeping programs, in order to combat the persistent and global scourge of violations of women's human rights.

Since the World Conference on Human Rights in Vienna in 1993, UNIFEM's approach to sustainable human development has increasingly integrated activities that support and promote women's human rights. Taking our cue from the international women's movement, UNIFEM has recognized that the pursuit of gender equality is an essential component to human rights and democratic development, and is focusing new attention on the human rights of women.

UNIFEM is the voice and conscience of women within the United Nations. In the interest of the political empowerment of women, UNIFEM advocates for the development of legal and policy frameworks which deal with issues of civil, political, cultural, economic and social rights. We are committed to utilizing a rights-based framework that views the pursuit of sustainable human development as a fundamental human rights issue, consistently relating human rights to the development dialogue.

Situated in the United Nations, UNIFEM is in a unique position to be an advocate for mainstreaming women's human rights in the international human rights arena, and developing strategies at the global policy level to ensure the achievement of women's fundamental human rights.

It is now clear that sustainable development will remain elusive unless women—more than half the world's population—can freely exercise their full panoply of rights. We must fashion a women's development agenda that is based on the principle of social justice, recognizing that neither the paradigm of basic needs nor basic rights will, on their own, speak to the issues impeding women's full participation in society.

Acknowledgments

This was a collaborative project from the start and clearly not the work of any one person. Everyone who contributed deserves sincere gratitude. First and foremost, thanks goes to the contributing authors, whose insights and commitment to women's rights provide an inspired platform for interchange and learning, and to all the participants in the October, 1994 Kuala Lumpur strategy meeting. Their ideas and experience inspired and produced not only this book but the "Kuala Lumpur Agenda," our agenda for action on women's rights.

For the development of this project thanks goes to the project Editorial Advisory Committee and others—especially Roberta Clarke, Shireen Huq, Akua Kuenyehia, Irina Mouleshkova, Naila Kabeer, Athaliah Molokomme, Maureen O'Neil, Rhonda Copelon and Dorothy Thomas—for their thoughtful contribution to framing the issues to be explored and conceptualizing the "From Basic Needs to Basic Rights" Project.

The organization of the project, including the Kuala Lumpur meeting and the actual production of this book required the help of many people, but the contribution of one person, Yasmin Tambiah, deserves special mention. As Project Coordinator, Yasmin's dedication and assistance in every phase of the project, from proposal writing and fund raising, to the organization of the Kuala Lumpur meeting and finally the production of this volume was inestimable. Her patient and persistent communication with paper writers and participants in the project was especially appreciated.

The Kuala Lumpur meeting was, of course critical to the book. We would especially like to thank the International Women's Rights Action Watch/Asia Pacific for co-convening the meeting with us. We are truly indebted to Shanthi Dairiam for making this international collaboration a success. Superlative thanks goes to Rosa Briceño, overall manager and coordinator of the meeting, and to the organizing team, including our Malaysian counterparts, Thilaha

Nalliah and Prema Govindasamy, together with other IWLD staff and volunteers, Hitty Norris and Sameena Nazir.

Thanks for work involved in the production of the book itself is owed to many people. First, appreciation goes to Charlotte Jones, whose editorial assistance was essential to completing the project. Other members—staff and interns—of the Institute for Women, Law and Development also made valuable contributions to the production, especially in the final phases when they gave up weekends and worked long hours into the night. Sheila Gyimah's work on the index was not less than heroic and is most appreciated. Karen Sanzaro's dedication to cleaning up the citations was also critical and we thank her. Appreciation goes again to Rosa Briceño and to Katherine Culliton and Arati Vasan for their willingness to stop other work and help in proofreading and indexing such a large manuscript.

Our gratitude extends to all the donors who supported this project, including those who funded participants to the KL strategy meeting, including the American Council of Learned Societies, DANNIDA, FINNIDA, the Ford Foundation, IWRAW/Asia Pacific, the Knowles Foundation, the Memton Fund, NORAD, the San Francisco Foundation, the Shaler Adams Foundation, SIDA, the Soros Foundation/Open Society Fund, UNDP (Malaysia), and UNIFEM. Without their support, this project would not have been possible.

I would also like to thank my family, in particular, Jim, Bev, Larry, Mary Ann and Rose for their kind hospitality on Anderson Island, which permitted me to focus on the project for an entire six weeks without distraction—except for the spectacular views of evergreen trees, Puget Sound and Mount Rainier.

Finally, I would like to express my special appreciation to Margaret Schink for her encouragement and moral support for this project and for her personal commitment to the promotion and defense of women's human rights throughout the world.

Margaret Schuler
August, 1995

Introduction
From Basic Needs To Basic Rights: Women's Claim to Human Rights

Margaret A. Schuler

Engendering Human Rights

At the dawn of the 21st century, women's rights advocates around the world have achieved a significant victory in asserting that women's rights are human rights and that women are entitled to the protections provided by the international system to ensure the exercise of rights. The 1993 Vienna Declaration and Program of Action recognized that

> the human rights of women and of the girl child are an inalienable, integral and indivisible part of universal human rights. The full and equal participation of women in political, civil, economic, social and cultural life at the national, regional and international levels, and the eradication of all forms of discrimination on the grounds of sex are priority objectives of the international community (para. 18).

Like all victories, however, acknowledgment of women's human rights by the international community represents as much a *commencement* as it does a *culmination* of a process.

The history of human rights since the framing of the Universal Declaration fifty years ago has been one of dynamic struggle to understand and make real the meaning of the rights enshrined therein. What evolved into the "traditional" human rights paradigm did so within an androcentric, patriarchal world dominated by East West polarization and the Cold War. During this period, worldwide economic, social and cultural pressures produced unparalleled technological achievements, economic growth and democracy for some and poverty, environmental degradation and political repression for others. In response to the most clamorous of social changes during this period, great strides were made in recognizing and affirming the concept that *human beings have rights to the minimum requirements of a life of dignity*. Supported by a strong international consensus about the International Bill of Human Rights, the list of recognizable human rights has evolved and expanded over the past fifty years to cover a growing field of vital concerns and threats to human dignity.

The dynamic character of human rights—that is, the interaction of factors such as changing ideas about human dignity (the very cornerstone of the modern concept of human rights), emerging forms of human relationship (and human exploitation), the rise of new political forces and patterns of governance, new economic arrangements and interdependencies, and technological changes, among others—"allows attention and resources to be shifted to threats that previously were inadequately recognized or insufficiently addressed" (Donnelly, 1989, p.26). The interactive quality of the human rights process is what permits new ideas and needs to challenge current thinking and approaches and to articulate progressively new theory and practice.

The source of one recent and significant challenge to the traditional human rights framework is the international women's rights movement.[1] The dynamic nature of human rights permitted women to enter the arena, challenge the current discourse and offer fresh perspectives on both theoretical and practical elements of the debate. Women recognized that the evolving human rights consensus of the late twentieth century was heading in a direction that affirmed the primacy—practically and conceptually—of men's needs over women's, of civil and political rights over social, economic and cultural rights, and the public sphere over the private.

In working at the local level to empower women to change discriminatory legislation, to educate women about their rights and redress grievances, activists and advocates in many parts of the world began to understand the patriarchal character of law and how even the concept of rights was skewed against women. They discovered in daily life the adverse consequences of the public sphere vs. private

---

[1] In reference to a "women's rights movement," I use this term broadly to include groups and individuals at the local and national level as well as regional and international networks working to promote and defend women's *human* rights through a variety of strategies. I prefer not to use the term "movement" in the plural, since similarities and differences abound at every level and separating one movement from another is neither possible nor particularly enlightening. What is important is the convergence developing at all levels as groups progressively learn from one another and forge interactive linkages and common agendas.

sphere ideology which left women little recourse in law. As networks of women's rights advocates began to coalesce—primarily in the global south, in Latin America, Asia and Africa—their struggles, experiences and strategies stimulated a feminist critique of rights, mobilized attention around the more egregious violations of women's rights and opened up a broader debate about human rights. (Schuler, 1986). The work of feminist scholars exposed the essentialist assumptions underpinning international human rights law and produced compilations of human rights law demonstrating that violations of women's rights are violations of human rights. (Smart, 1989; Charlesworth, Chinkin & Wright, 1991; Cook, 1992, 1994, and Romany, 1994).

Over the past fifteen years, this emerging women's rights movement has insisted on reinterpreting human rights traditionally thought not to apply to women (interpreting the right to bodily integrity, for example, to include protection from domestic violence). In doing so, it has expanded to some degree the sphere of state responsibility and very gradually and recently increased the power of international mechanisms to monitor government actions and omissions related to women's human rights. Thus, women's participation in the system and worldwide mobilization under the motto of claiming "women's rights as human rights" have already had a fundamental and transformative effect on the human rights agenda by pushing the boundaries and altering ever so slightly the frontiers of the debate.

On the other hand, women and women's interests are not yet totally integrated within the human rights arena. Women still lack acceptance as full players in the system and as subjects of fully recognized and enforced human rights. Clearly, some progress in both directions has been achieved, exemplified by the assertions in favor women's rights in the Vienna Declaration and the naming of the Special Rapporteur on Violence Against Women among others, but there is still a long road ahead. For this reason, the victories of the Vienna and later the Cairo Conference are significant not only because they mark the successful completion of a dynamic mobilization, but because they mark the beginning of a new and challenging process necessary to complete the task begun a decade ago.

Progress on violence against women occurred because women vigorously engaged the system by requiring it to respond to women's reality, experiences and needs. Engaging the system meant getting its attention, forcing it to listen, requiring it to act on its own principles and insisting on a response. The efforts paid off on violence against women, but *all* threats to women's human dignity call for engaging the system in a similar manner until every woman enjoys the full range of *human* rights—including rights of women as women. Finding effective ways to do this is one of the most critical challenges facing the women's rights movement.

This book, *From Basic Needs to Basic Rights,* is about engendering human rights, that is, pushing the boundaries of the human rights debate, changing the traditional paradigm to cover all threats to the dignity of women's humanity and creating an effective and responsive system for enforcement of women's human rights and redress of violations.

"Engendering human rights" means articulating a gendered concept of human dignity. It means building a new consensus within the entire human rights community about what human rights are, about what the specific rights are that women require to live as full human beings, about how these rights are violated and how their enforcement and enjoyment can be assured. Changing the paradigm means grappling with threats to women's human dignity and the fulfillment of their basic needs. It means naming the human rights of women that are threatened and showing how they can be protected.

At the level of practice, "engendering human rights" means consolidating an interactive relationship between women's rights activism and scholarship to engage the human rights system strategically to listen to women's experience and respond to their demands as legitimate claims. The dynamics of pushing the boundaries require intervention in several ways and at several points in the achievement of three critical targets: expanding the *definition* of human rights, expanding the scope of *state responsibility* and expanding the *effectiveness of the human rights system* to enforce women's rights. To achieve these goals, women's rights advocates must take decisive action in various ways.

- ◆ As women's scholarship and activism achieve the acceptance of a reinterpretation of human rights to address the rights of women previously excluded from the definition, the *definition of human rights* expands.
- ◆ As women articulate states' obligations to respect women's human rights and they engage the state to comply, the *sphere*

of government responsibility for the defense of women's human rights expands.

♦ As women engage the human rights system and require it to take measures to stop, remedy, or otherwise solve problems of violations of women's human rights, the *ability and willingness of human rights system to enforce women's human rights* expands.

The Human Rights Environment

Expanding the scope of human rights does not happen in a vacuum. The act of identifying, exploring and articulating rights takes place in a context of tension where concrete economic, social and cultural changes create new needs that require new perspectives and new answers. Today a complexity of economic and political forces at play in the international arena has created an environment that is adverse to the full and effective realization of human rights and poses a major challenge.

The factors are multiple: changing economic conditions, the interventions of international financial institutions and the processes of global re-structuring of the economy have resulted in the withdrawal of the state from responsibility for providing basic services for their people and an erosion of state accountability to citizens, particularly in relation to the protection of their fundamental rights. The pursuit of free market development models and strategies by states, international financial institutions and transnational corporations which emphasize consumption and the indiscriminate exploitation of natural resources rendering them, thereby unsustainable, has exacerbated the precarious state of the material conditions through which people seek to better their lives.

Women are at the center of these new economic tensions and the impact of economic restructuring on women has been particularly adverse. Women are burdened with the responsibility of meeting the essential needs of family and community in the face of increasing economic hardship; at the same time, the system of structural adjustment also relies on the devaluation of women's work in both the formal and informal sectors to lower direct and indirect production costs. Poor women, indigenous women, disabled women, women living in areas of armed conflict, refugee women, internally displaced women, migrant and immigrant women and women prisoners are often the most harshly affected.

Increased militarization worldwide, as manifested in swollen expenditures on arms and armaments, the upsurge in armed conflicts, and the channeling of investments/expenditures into "national security" systems, contributes to a greater imbalance of power not only between states, but between the state and its citizens. This process is one which is constantly undermining democratic processes by reinforcing authoritarian and repressive forms of government and draining scarce economic resources away from social development. Women are disproportionately affected by this situation.

The growth of religious fundamentalisms, identity-based politics and chauvinistic nationalism based on ethnic and other differences is also contributing to the creation of increased social polarization in many societies. In many parts of the world issues of cultural, religious, ethnic and other forms of identity have become highly politicized. Movements based on identity are acquiring increasing importance. The specific gendered agendas of these movements are oppressive to women and have significant and potentially devastating implications for the human rights of women.

The socio-economic and political climate within which the world's women struggle for the full realization of their rights is therefore profoundly insecure, forcing women throughout the world today to face routine denial of their rights. This denial takes many forms, from the outright violation of fundamental rights of women to the failure by states and the international community more generally to recognize and remedy such violations when they occur. The world community's persistent failure to respect and ensure civil, political economic and social rights for women not only prevents women from fully participating in the civil, political economic, and social life of their countries, but also compromises the principles of universality and indivisibility on which the entire human rights system is based.

It is in this context that women's rights advocates seek to expand the scope of human rights. To assure an adequate response from the human rights system, advocates must take bold action. Unless pressed to do so, the international human rights system will not automatically resolve to take responsive action to new threats to human rights posed by the environment. Nor will states decide to accept fully their responsibility for the enforcement of rights. There are forces at work to deliberately impede the recognition of the rights we seek to define. The burden of leadership in advancing the cause, as advocates of women's human rights know too well, falls upon those who care, upon those whose interests are at stake.

Shaping an Agenda: From Basic Needs to Basic Rights

This book, *From Basic Needs to Basic Rights*, gathers together thoughts and experiences of women's rights activists and thinkers from the international women's rights community in the process of confronting this reality in order to engender human rights. It offers a snapshot in time of their struggle to "push the boundaries," to grapple with contemporary challenges to women's dignity as human beings in order to articulate new interpretations of human rights and new strategies to make the system to respond.

The period between the 1993 Human Rights Conference in Vienna and the 1995 Women's Conference in Beijing provided a unique opportunity for taking stock of the state of women's rights with regard to the issues and agenda addressed and the strategies used to address them. It was an opportunity to identify gaps in theory as well as practice. Linking this assessment to the 1995 World Conference on Women helped clarify early on that the issues to be addressed needed to take into consideration the development framework in addition to that of human rights.

From the beginning of the UN Decade for Women (1975 to 1985) the development perspective played the dominant role in UN activities related to women. Although women remained outside the human rights discourse in the early part of the modern human rights era, they came into the development discourse early on. Not surprisingly, "rights" and "development" pursued independent, and often divergent, tracks. During the UN Decade for Women "WID" (women in development) provided the preponderant framework within which to explore and address women's issues. "Basic needs" was the governing paradigm, although at the Nairobi Conference in 1985 the issue of "violence against women" broke through the WID barrier for the first time.

By 1993, with the impetus provided by the UN Human Rights Conference, a "rights" perspective took on greater importance in consideration of women's problems—however, for many their perspective on rights remained within the "civil and political" framework of traditional human rights practice. Moreover, for strategic reasons, recognition of violence against women as a human rights violation became the most visible issue to be pursued at the Human Rights Conference and targeting women's economic, social, cultural, sexual, reproductive or other rights with the same high profile or degree of energy was not possible.

In organizing for Beijing, with the experience of Vienna as an important benchmark, the need to take a broader view and to develop new links of collaboration between "gender and development" and human rights became apparent. The principles of indivisibility and universality of human rights together with the full range of women's experiences across the globe cried out for a more comprehensive and integrated approach. The imperative was to revisit both development and human rights from a gender perspective with the view to articulating a new vision to bridge the gap between basic needs and basic rights and offering a new paradigm to explore the full range of contemporary challenges to women's advancement. This book contributes to bridging this gap.

During the last week of October, 1994, the Institute for Women, Law and Development together with the International Women's Rights Action Watch/Asia Pacific, convened a strategy meeting in Kuala Lumpur Malaysia. It brought together over 100 women from 47 countries as part of a collective effort to evaluate the progress of the women's rights movement over the past decade, specifically to assess the needs of women to improve their status globally, regionally, and nationally, with special attention to the development/human rights nexus; to determine strategies for advocacy and action that will help refine and bring to fruition women's rights agendas internationally; and finally, to influence the intergovernmental proceedings on women's rights and human rights during and after the 1995 Fourth World Conference on Women in Beijing.[2] The major themes discussed at the meeting include: gender and hierarchy in human rights; making social and economic rights effective for women; challenges to the exercise of women's human rights posed by religious, cultural and ethnic identity; and conceptualizing and defending women's sexual and reproductive rights; and

---

[2] Using the drafts of their papers as a basis for discussion, the participants in the meeting produced the "Kuala Lumpur Agenda," a document, officially entitled *A Women's Rights Agenda for Action* (Appendix B), outlines a set of goals and recommendations for action to be taken at the international, national and local levels in promotion of women's rights by the United Nations, Governments and NGOs.

exploring the strategic dimensions of women's organizing and articulation as a movement.[3]

The 35 papers in this book together with the "KL Agenda," (see footnote 2) represent a cross-section of contemporary scholarship and activism in function of women's human rights. The essays and case studies highlight the thinking and activism that is giving impetus to the growth and effectiveness of the women's human rights movement today. They raise issues that challenge not only the human rights system but the women's rights movement as well. The authors display a common thread of agreement about the identity of the major threats to the enjoyment of women's rights but they also reveal divergent ideas on some aspects of the issues and how to address them. Indisputably the authors share the common goal of ensuring the full realization of women's civil and political rights, of strengthening, promoting and securing the enjoyment of economic, social and cultural rights and of defending and advancing the fundamental principles of universality and indivisibility of all human rights.

Gender and Hierarchy in Human Rights

The first theme covered in this book, which relates to the nature and hierarchy of human rights and their implications for women, touches on challenges to the indivisibility of rights. In addressing it, one question which arises asks whether women's needs *as women* figure in their claim to human rights. Florence Butegwa (pp. 27-40)[4] raises a fundamental concern, asserting that one of the limitations of the current human rights paradigm is an "equality" trap rooted in a "unisex" approach to human rights. Since women are not recognized as having rights that are "unique to their gender and not shared equally with men" they are forced to defend their rights by showing that violations result from discrimination in the law or by the state. Butegwa argues that women have certain characteristics for which there is no equivalent experience for men and thus a legitimate claim to human rights and fundamental freedoms rests on these differences.

---

[3] This book is divided into five sections, corresponding to the major themes of the project. In each section theoretical essays and case studies explore aspects of the theme. It is acknowledged, however, that this approach is a somewhat limited devise. It is useful as a point of departure, but not as a rigid organizing structure.

[4] In this introduction, contributors to the volume will be cited by indicating the name of the author and relevant page numbers in parenthesis.

She then calls for the construction of a specific framework for women's rights that would offer the human rights system effective mechanisms to address women specific issues including reproductive choice and health and violence against women.

Butegwa's notion represents a radical departure from the accepted framework for conceptualizing and defending violations of women's human rights. It will, no doubt spark continued debate and further exploration. In many ways, the papers in this collection are ambivalent about the use of "discrimination" as a foundational element of women's human rights. On the one hand it is a powerful tool and acknowledged to be so. To lose it would be to run a certain risk of marginalization, something most women's rights advocates fear with good reason. None would deny that equality is an important and sustaining principle of the women's human rights agenda. On the other hand, the "rights talk" of many of the contributors imply, if not explicitly state, an agreement with Butegwa about the limitation and inadequacy of the discrimination approach. It is difficult to take a serious look at women's issues and come away without asserting that women have characteristics that are indeed different from those of men and that require a specific framework for adequately addressing them.

A second question that comes to mind in consideration of the nature of human rights is whether it is *possible* to confront the imbalance of the *de facto* rights hierarchy without establishing another or without giving priority to one kind of right over another? Many of the papers in this book attest to the reality of a changing economic and ideological landscape in which the new arrangements of the global market have placed social and economic rights under siege. They insist that this situation together with the ambivalent commitments to the indivisibility of human rights by the international community calls for active disapproval of the hierarchy of rights that privileges civil and political over social and economic rights (Butegwa, O'Neil, Clarke, Lamarche).

While all agree in theory that the absence of rights for women in one sphere could obstruct the exercise of rights they already have in another sphere, Butegwa points out that privileging civil and political rights through the establishment of an optional protocol and other mechanisms that give ICCPR the political clout it needs to be effective has been paralleled by neglect of the ICESCR which has no protocol and lacks political force. She concludes that the resultant undesirable hierarchy of rights must be countered by greater attention to social and economic rights by women, a position shared by many of the writers in this book, whose articles deal in one way or another with redressing the imbalance. Dorothy Thomas (pp. 41-56) responds by cautioning about the potential losses that could be sustained if a "reverse" rights hierarchy were to be established as a result of over-attention to economic, social and cultural rights. She challenges the notion that economic and social rights are more relevant to women's lives than civil and political rights and asserts that by underestimating the potential of civil and political rights, women run the risk of weakening "the basis for women's human rights claims in general and [of reinforcing] the very public/private, civil and political/economic social distinctions that much of women's human rights activism purports to challenge" (p. 45).

Despite differences of emphasis, echoed throughout the book is the view that women's realization of their civil and political rights is linked indivisibly with the fulfillment of their economic, social and cultural rights. Copelon and Petchesky go a step farther and assert that solidarity rights, including the rights to "human-centered and sustainable development, self-determination, preservation of the environment and the common heritage of humankind, disarmament and global security based on peace in all spheres of life" (pp. 345-346) are equally part of the interdependence principle of human rights. In affirming these principles the authors of this book recognize that women's responsibilities in the domestic sphere limit the full exercise of their rights in the public sphere and that women experience particular differential obstacles in accessing and enjoying rights because of gender discrimination as well as other socio-economic and demographic variables such as class, ethnicity, race, age and region (KL Agenda, p. 560). Most would be cautious of Thomas's resounding "no" to the question about whether it is possible to realign the imbalance of rights hierarchy by a swing of the pendulum, but they would share her assertion that the answer lies in "fighting for the recognition of female personhood in all realms [public or private] where its denial continues to occur" (p. 55).

Economic and Social Rights

A second set of issues touches on how political, civil, social, economic and cultural rights can be effectively enforced. Given the new global arrangements, the challenge is to understand how social and economic rights can be made effective for women. What power do the treaties have to counter the changing policy climate toward more privatization and less state responsibility for basic services? Perhaps it is even necessary to reconsider what social and economic rights mean in this environment.

In considering the policy responses of national governments to global economic trends, O'Neil (pp. 59-76) offers a sobering reminder that the benevolent, willing state envisioned in the human rights treaties, committed to providing citizens a range of social protection programs, rarely exists in today's reality. The more likely case is for a state to be unwilling to take energetic action to protect economic rights, since the new economic arrangements and the requirements of the international conventions provide little incentive for them to live up to human rights treaty obligations. Case studies in this volume, covering such varied regions as the Caribbean (Clarke & French), Central and Eastern Europe (Sewall), India (Jethmalani), China (Hom), Colombia (Acosta), Canada (Cameron) and the USA (Crooms), demonstrate dramatically how market-based capitalist states—as well as those in transition—have abdicated their responsibility for social and economic rights owing to prods from class based interests at the national level, pressures from international financial institutions, such as the IMF, the World Bank, and other triggers that are reinforcing unequal power relations of the global market. O'Neil explores the problem of making rights consonant with state policies and policies with state obligations for which they can be held accountable.

Clarke and French (pp. 103-122) highlight the ideological basis for giving primacy to either civil and political or social and economic rights, a concept echoed in Sewall's (pp. 153-166) analysis of the status of rights in the transitional economies of Eastern and Central Europe. Sewall points out that the very conceptualization of rights is conditioned by the economic base. In market economies, rights are framed in relation to "access to the market" since economic and social well-being is derived from participation in the market. In these economies, civil and political rights are privileged. On the other hand, centrally planned economies favor social and economic rights. They delineate rights in direct relation to enjoyment in the goods and services the economy generates rather than participation in the market process as a *means* to the enjoyment of its output.

The case studies amply demonstrate these variances in approach to rights and differences regarding the role of the state in the protection of rights. The transitional economies, where states are withdrawing from their former protectionist role in favor of market demands are a case in point. Lacking a tradition of reliance on civil and political rights to protect workers or citizens from the excesses or wrongs of the free market, the diminishment of state commitments to social and economic rights in both China (Hom, pp. 137-152) and the Central and Eastern European countries calls attention to the vulnerability of people without adequate mechanisms to enforce and protect rights. But whether the setting is a "developed," a "third world" or "transitional" capitalist economy, O'Neil, Clarke & French and Lamarche (pp. 77-102) remind us that states are not exempted from their obligations to protect social and economic rights under international human rights law.

Whether or not social and economic rights are respected depends not only on the will of the state to fulfill its obligations, but on the mechanisms that are available to citizens to defend their rights and make the state accountable. Clarke and French explore the "justiciability" issue with regard to social and economic rights and conclude that while it cannot be strictly said that these rights lack justiciability since some states have adopted citizen entitlements to some economic rights, they concede that the lack of a legal basis for the assertion of rights is an obstacle.

Lamarche goes right to the treaty mechanisms themselves to find ways to guarantee the rights and calls for a new argumentation around the notion of economic and social human rights. Basing her approach on the position of the CESCR Committee, which makes it clear that "development should occur in the context of rights," Lamarche proposes a "principled" approach in which states can be forced to assess the impact of laws and social policies (or their absence) on women's social and economic rights. A right to petition at the international level would be needed to accomplish this supported by a legal forum to determine state liability with regard to social and economic rights. She also proposes that women should "ground their claims on the combined meaning of CEDAW and ICESCR and to use those instruments to argue against any commercial institution or human rights institution which fails to read CEDAW and ICESCR jointly" (p. 98).

Sewall and Clarke and French each reiterate the resistance to such an idea that is likely to be encountered. Sewall suggests that to many nations within the dominant development paradigm, development and social and economic rights are mutually exclusive.

> Successful pursuit of structural adjustment policies demand the subjugation of social and economic rights, while the advancement of economic and social rights, especially for women's employment related rights, is perceived as hindering any chance for development. Framed in such a stark dichotomy, it is difficult to present the argument for social and economic rights, if it will necessarily imply that a country's prospect for development will suffer. Proponents of improving social and economic rights are quickly turned into enemies of development (p. 162).

She suggests that since it is unrealistic to expect policy changes from developing countries within the context of the debt and structural adjustment policies that forced them into this position in the first place, the best approach is to change the policies of the international lending and donor agencies and to change the foreign assistance policies and laws of donor countries.

Activist initiatives targeting international bilateral and multilateral trade accords seem to be increasing in recent years as a strategic choice. Cameron's (pp. 183-195) case study of Canadian women in response to NAFTA (North American Free Trade Agreement) and GATT (General Agreement on Tariffs and Trade) shows that it is not only the women in the developing countries who are affected, but those in the "donor" countries as well. The analysis of the two treaties demonstrates how they reflect "classical liberal notions of rights as the rights of property and freedom from state regulation" (p. 183). She recounts women's efforts to influence interpretation of Canada's Charter of Rights and Freedoms and mobilizations against Canadian trade policy as a counter to their failure to take into consideration social and economic rights. Acosta also describes an international campaign to raise awareness and challenge the national and international policies that so negatively affect Colombian women in the flower industry.

In part, as a result of such mobilizations in response to the negative effects of international finance and trade structures and policies, the use of "social clauses," which place some restrictions on the trade relationship, is common in trade agreements today. However, in Lamarche's view, they are not, *cannot*, be an effective means to ensure economic human rights.

> To put it simply, social clauses can be nothing other than a commodifica-
> tion product of human rights. An accountable state is a protectionist state.
> And to be accountable a state must protect human and labor rights, tasks
> which are contrary to market rules. Controlling social dumping would
> not be a compatible approach in a market system (p. 94).

Cameron's analysis of the GATT and NAFTA show how such accords undermine human rights by requiring fewer obligations to protect workers rights than, for example ILO conventions, and less
stringent accountability mechanisms than are present in the human
rights treaties. Lamarche's concern is that we are accepting, perhaps
willy-nilly, a trade-oriented redefinition of rights. She cautions human right activists to be careful about losing perspective. All their efforts to force international financial institutions to take into account
the negative effects of structural adjustment programs could undermine the need to focus more attention on developing mechanisms to
enforce economic human rights. To her, developing trade-related
rights is less important than reaffirming existing human rights.

Indeed, the goal of human rights work, whether at the international or the national level, is to give legal force to social and economic rights. Ultimately, unless these rights attain the force of law,
they remain vague, probably unattainable, ideals. Several of the case
studies explore work at the national level to give force to social and
economic rights using the tools that are available at that level. They
illustrate the dynamic interdependence between social and economic
rights and civil and political rights in practice. Often a rights' violation can be conceptualized as a civil right and an economic right at
the same time (Crooms, Jethmalani, Hom) and strategies to address
them take into account the means available from both sources.

Jethmalani outlines the developed use of "social action litigation,"
or public interest law, in India to show how the interests of the most
vulnerable social sectors can be defended using innovative legal
strategies at the level of the Supreme Court. This approach has been
effectively used in the cases of criminal law and civil law. In the "Narmada Dam" affair, a recent case that directly pits a community against
"irresponsible and reckless activity in the name of industrial development" (p. 131), it is being applied in the context of social and economic rights. The approach has even been used to challenge the
government on its commitment to CEDAW. While the outcome of
these two cases are still pending, the possibilities of using such an approach in advance of women's rights are promising.

Finally, in response to the question, how can social and economic rights be effectively enforced, Lamarche says that this will depend on the capacity of women to "blame the state for not taking rights seriously" (p. 98). In speaking of China, Hom says "ultimately, it will be the outrage of the *dagongmeis* (working little sisters), and the political negotiations of domestic women's groups and the courage of human rights activists and scholars that will ensure that social and economic rights are realized in the daily lives of women" (p. 151). The strategies described in this book, not only in relation to social and economic rights but to any threat to women's rights, come about as a result of the courage of women to say "enough" in words and in action.

Cultural, Religious and Ethnic Identities

A third theme explores the threat to the universality of rights inherent in the politics of religious fundamentalism and of cultural and ethnic revivalism. The questions that come to mind with this theme confront the universality issue: How can women's sexual equality rights be defended while retaining sensitivity to identity choices women themselves make? What strategies are available to support women whose choices are in alignment with human rights articles but are in opposition to religious and cultural practices which are often invoked by the state or political groups to support their agendas?

Coomaraswamy (p. 213) notes that women are at the cutting edge of the paramount threat to human rights today. One of the tentative achievements of the Vienna Declaration was an affirmation that culture should not be used to deny women's human rights. However, despite the Declaration, wavering commitments to the principle of universality threaten to undermine the gains that have been made and slow the development and power of human rights as the standard bearer and protector of human dignity. Coomaraswamy asks why so many countries throughout the word are willing to accept human rights without the women's rights component. The papers in this section explore the reasons for this situation, the pressures it places on women in various contexts throughout the world and the varied answers they have framed in response to it.

Although women are considered the custodians of culture in the majority of our societies, most religious, cultural and traditional practices are defined on the basis of patriarchal norms. It is in defense of these norms that many states, pushed by fundamentalist and nationalist political movements, pit cultural diversity rights against the universal applicability of human rights. This is easily borne out by the number of countries registering reservations on some of the most essential provisions of CEDAW.

Rajasingham (pp. 233-248) and Coomaraswamy remind us, however, that the challenge to universality is arising not only from conservative sources. Rajasingham explores the conflict from the perspective of a clash between "universalizing formulations" of women's rights and the opposition to this formulation by some third world feminists on the basis of cultural difference. Their concern is that "women's gender/sexual rights and identities have been pitted against their ethnic/national communities in universalizing terms" and that the pressure women are put under when they are forced to choose between their ethno-religious community and their rights as women "necessitates a rethinking of the very idea of 'rights' in a constructive, contextually located and historical way" (pp. 240-241).

Both Rajasingham and Afkhami (pp. 217-232) address the idea of women's "identity" as central to the dilemma and acknowledge the multiplicity of intersecting discourses that come into play and that challenge the validity of individual rights for women. Afkhami's position is to assert that

> [t]he point of women's struggle for rights is cultural change, that is, changing attitudes, behaviors, and laws that have a negative impact on women's human rights. Such a struggle would be meaningless if women did not agree that there are rights beyond those prescribed by the traditional culture and that these rights are nevertheless valid everywhere (p. 225).

The papers in this set directly address struggles that occur between rights and culture (or between rights and culture change) and illustrate varied experiences of resolution. The "Shabanu" case (pp. 242-244) in India demonstrates what Rajasingham calls the "volatile and overdetermined nature of women's rights in multi-ethnic cultures." In this case, the rights of a Muslim woman (with legal implications for all Indian Muslim women) became the point of contention around the issue of minority rights. Shabanu's choice in the end was to abandon her quest for a resolution of her situation, for which she had received a favorable ruling from the Supreme Court, in favor of the demands of her religious group and out of fear of ethnic/religious violence. The Abdel Halim article (249-266) on female circumcision in Sudan reflects the conflict women can experience and the tension that arises when rights are invoked without contextual, cultural understanding.

On the other hand, Coomaraswamy cautions that to "query the human rights tradition from a progressive position is to fall into another trap . . . [and provide] the discourse to movements fighting for political hegemony . . . under the guise of different religions" (p. 216). To her, diversity can only be celebrated on the foundation of international and universal human rights. Sharon McIvor, a member of the Lower Nicola Indian Band, British Columbia, is unambiguous on the issue. She begins her story (267-288) with the affirmation:

> Aboriginal women can successfully seek to have their sexual equality rights recognized without subjugating their struggle to the indigenous struggle for self-determination. It is not necessary for Aboriginal women to put aside their equality rights, and they can simultaneously contribute to the larger struggle for indigenous rights (p. 267).

Siklova's paper (pp. 327-339) about women in the Czech Republic describes a struggle to frame and maintain a unique and culturally specific position about women's status and rights that is in some ways in opposition to Western formulations. While emanating from an entirely different context where rights are (or at least were) highly elaborated, the Czech struggle, nonetheless, echoes the South Asian, post-colonial critique of rights presented by Rajasingham. Wali's paper (pp. 289-303) on the situation of refugee and displaced women dramatically makes the case for universality of rights by highlighting the manner in which women's rights are ignored even as states and ethnic groups use women "as pawns to portray the virtues of male ideology." Although strikingly different, the transitory circumstance of women's experiences as refugees or as citizens in a rapidly changing society brings to the fore issues that may not arise in a more stable environment. The uprooted context of refugees and displaced women brings out the dangers of cultural relativist arguments in a dramatic fashion and the transitional character of the Central European societies today highlights the need to take a critical look at simplistic formulations of rights in the context of reshaping a culture of rights.

Shaheed (pp. 305-326), and Afkhami use the experience of Muslim women to argue for the universality of rights and the dynamic role women can play in reshaping cultural frameworks. Shaheed's thoughtful reflections on women's self-identification in Muslim societies points out how difficult it is for many women (and not only Muslim women) to distinguish between cultural practices and faith. This recognition, however, does not lead her to question universality. Rather, her call to demystify the factors that constrain women's potential and provide support mechanisms for change (p. 312) is a reminder that if there is a conflict between women's rights and culture, the resolution will come in the struggle for change and that the major players will be women themselves.

Afkhami sums up the challenge well when she says:

> Our problem is two-fold: (1) to establish the moral priority of universal rights; and (2) to devise strategies for developing and communicating ways and means of realizing universally accepted women's rights in all countries while upholding and appreciating the diversity of life styles and variety of cultures across the globe. Both points involve moral and ethical issues, but their nature is fundamentally political (p. 222).

Despite the questioning of formulations of women's rights and the validity of the universality of rights arising from both conservative and progressive sources, the consensus of women's rights advocates is clearly in favor of women's ability to choose the human rights framework as a alternate ethical framework.

The KL Agenda (p. 557-572), for example, affirms women's courage in coming forward to challenge the ways in which they have been, and are being, defined by religion, culture and tradition on the one hand, and claiming their right to define and interpret religious, cultural and traditional norms and practices according to their own needs and experiences on the other hand.

As stated in the KL Agenda, in the context of the rapid expansion of all forms of fundamentalist and chauvinist nationalist movements it is necessary to struggle for a process of democratization which will provide women with the space to assert their various identities without fear of reprisal and which will not permit the political usage of religion, culture and tradition to oppress women.

Sexual and Reproductive Rights

A fourth set of issues in this book, *From Basic Needs to Basic Rights,* covers sexual and reproductive human rights and addresses how they can be framed as human rights; what special threats to human dignity are associated with sexual and reproductive choices, practices and policies; and what mechanisms are available to support those rights as human rights. The papers in this section demonstrate how patriarchal laws, institutions, and attitudes limit women's ability to express and enjoy their sexuality both within and outside marriage, to choose their partners, to make decisions whether and when to bear children, to protect themselves from disease (STD's, HIV/AIDS) and violence, and to participate equally in all aspects of economic and social life. Because of this fact, and because sexual and reproductive rights are the least elaborated rights within human rights instruments, the greatest challenge to pushing the boundaries of the human rights paradigm in order to articulate new rights appears to be in this domain. The papers in this section explore the potential of the human rights framework for reinforcing reproductive and sexual rights and challenging abuses offering clear examples of efforts to reframe and reinterpret human rights from a women's perspective.

Building on the language of the Universal Declaration on Human Rights, the other major instruments, and the Draft Platform for Action for the Fourth World Conference on Women (1995), Tambiah (pp. 369-390) offers a definition of sexual rights.

> Sexual rights include the individual's right to have control over and to decide freely in matters related to her or his sexuality, free of coercion, discrimination and violence. They include the right to information, so that informed decisions can be made about sexuality; the rights to dignity, privacy, and to physical, mental and moral integrity while realizing a sexual choice; and the right to the highest standard of sexual health (p. 372).

Copelon and Petchesky (pp. 342-367) analyze the Declaration and Programme of Action adopted at the 1994 International Conference on Population and Development (ICPD) in Cairo to assess progress in achieving a more adequate approach to these rights. While they acknowledge that Cairo moved beyond a debate centered on family planning and population control to one of rights and women's empowerment, they also lament the Programme's weaknesses from the perspective of women's human rights. The final document has no references to "sexual rights," and the narrow definition of "family" fails to recognize and prohibit discrimination against a range of sexual relationships and family forms. It also fails to reassert that human rights take precedence over conflicting cultural traditions (pp. 355-356).

The problem with the notion of sexual rights is that it is not found explicitly in any of the instruments. The Universal Declaration and other conventions, including CEDAW, focus exclusively on marriage and even there the treatment is limited. Sexual rights outside of marriage is a particularly weak concept as far as the instruments are concerned. Tambiah shows that although the right to privacy and the rights to physical and mental integrity have been used to argue successfully against laws opposing homosexual activity, "the fact that sexual rights are nowhere explicitly articulated as such, but dependent upon other conditionalities, such as privacy, make them especially vulnerable to compromise" (p. 386).

On the other hand, Copelon and Petchesky show that the ICPD laid the foundation for interpreting the rights to liberty and security of person to include women's rights to determine and control their sexuality and reproduction as well as protection from abuse. Also, the right of freedom from servitude could be interpreted to include forced prostitution, involuntary motherhood, domestic servitude and violence (p. 357). The same could be said of the right to life and other recognized civil and political rights.

Gita Sen's (pp. 390-399) analysis of the development and availability of reproductive technologies raises critical ethical issues that are only beginning to be framed in relation to human rights. Sen demonstrates how the social and economic context plus gender, class and race biases influence decisions regarding which reproductive technologies will be developed, how they will be tested and who will have access to them. Huq and Azim's (pp. 421-431) case study of Norplant in Bangladesh contextualizes these ethical issues related to availability and freedom of choice in reproduction. Beginning from a perspective that safe contraception is a basic human right, activists in Bangladesh challenged the policy that gave primacy to a provider-dependent method in a context where the service delivery system was unable to safeguard either the safety of the method or the choice of the user. Nwashili's case study (pp. 409-422) illustrates the impact of HIV/AIDS on women's human rights in Nigeria. She calls for new strategies to reinforce women's rights and economic empowerment in order to protect women living with HIV/AIDS, from discrimination in housing, employment, international travel, and access to quality health services.

Taking a firm position on the indivisibility and interdependence of rights, Copelon and Petchesky assert that the exercise of

reproductive rights require the realization of basic economic and social rights as "enabling conditions" for free reproductive choice to
happen. They suggest, therefore, that women can begin to use the
concepts and mechanisms of the human rights system to insist that
states be held accountable for policies, structural adjustment and
other programs that violate human rights of women. Plata and Espriella's (pp. 401-408) case study on using CEDAW to press for a
health program in Colombia that promotes women's sexual and reproductive rights is an example of how this can be done. Through the
activism of a coalition of women's organizations, which pressed for
change in the Colombian Constitution to include principles contained
in CEDAW and other human rights instruments, the new Constitution of 1991 "incorporated some principles and rights which reflect
and strengthen those contained in CEDAW" (p. 401). The establishment of the primacy of human rights international treaties over national legislation and the right to claim protection in any court when
a fundamental right is violated gave women new tools and arguments
to defend and promote women's human rights. Using these new
tools, women successfully lobbied the government to adopt a health
policy which establishes women's rights to participate in decisions related to health, life, body and sexuality.

Activism to Advance Women's Human Rights

The issues addressed in this book collectively give rise to an additional set of considerations related to how women approach the advocacy and activism required to achieve the goals that all pursue. The
final set of papers addresses women's human rights advocacy strategies at various levels exploring what it means to struggle for human
rights at the local level; the political and cultural factors that condition the possibilities for advocacy at different levels; the limits of international instruments and mechanisms; the kind of relationship and
interaction that exists and should exist between national and international advocacy groups and individuals in shaping the agenda and determining the strategy to be pursued and what we can learn from past
experience.

The reality of women's lives in different historical moments is
often the prime factor in determining the kind of strategy that can be
pursued. The papers in this section bring this home forcefully. It is
one thing to "frame the issue" correctly and clearly and another to

assess the context and take action that will make the difference. The importance that conjunctural variables have together with the challenges they pose in asserting human rights are highlighted in Abeyesekera's reflection on women's mobilizing in Sri Lanka (pp. 445-474) during times of conflict. The powerful insights that resulted from reconciling them are useful far beyond the Sri Lankan context. Finding ways to link women's rights issues to broader issues of rights and justice, to rethink and reshape relationships with political parties and movements, to create positive linkages among women at various levels are all challenges the Sri Lanka experience offers to women elsewhere. The circumstance of Chilean women (Matus Madrid. pp. 461-475) during and after the period of dictatorship and state violence is also illustrative of the challenges linked to historical context. Oppression provided the impetus to develop an authentic women's movement as well as a human rights movement. Once the crisis was over, however, the task of restructuring society within a democratic framework shifted the parameters of the rights agenda and demanded new responses by women toward the state, political parties, and the women's movement itself.

Work at the national, regional and global levels to press specific rights agendas, as exemplified by the experience of immigrant women organizing in the USA (Jang and Marin, pp. 495-505), the campaign on Rape as a War Crime in Asia (Sajor, pp. 506-54) or the Global Campaign on Violence Against Women (Bunch and Reilly, pp. 529-541), provide particularly rich illustrations of successful mobilizations to advance women's rights. These experiences make it clear that for such mobilizations to have an impact on breaking the barriers of the human rights paradigm, the violations of women's rights must become "real" to the world. In speaking of the "comfort women" in the Philippines and Korea, Sajor says it is the "bravery of these old women that allows one to recognize the impact of openly vocalizing rape as a war crime. The crime becomes real and the issue is recognized by the international community" (p. 513). The task of building a new consensus on women's human rights requires both the courage of those whose rights have been violated and the leadership of those who have clarity and passion about the message and the capacity to mobilize around it effectively.

However, taking effective leadership on behalf of women's rights is not a simple project as these and other papers disclose. It requires successfully maneuvering over very difficult terrain to avoid getting entangled in the process. It requires facing the thorny issues of leadership, determining not only how a strategy should be articulated, but who should articulate it (Romany, pp. 544-554) and resolving the challenges posed by differences within the movement stemming from geographic, cultural, linguistic, religious, ethnic and class positions. Facing up to these issues means opening up our assumptions to critical scrutiny and honestly allowing dialogue to take place.

The papers in this section remind us that for the women's rights movement to mature and become effective it must simultaneously develop its theoretical and strategic capacities. To deal effectively with the human rights system, it becomes important to resolve differences within in the movement, since it is easy to get trapped in the system on *its* terms. Evading such entrapment requires speaking convictions with audacity, moving from "what is" toward "what can be," boldly exploring new perceptions and approaches and escaping the snares of entrenched modes of doing and thinking about human rights. Dealing with differences and being able to assess one's own efficacy is a stepping stone to effectively challenging the system. Understanding how to be strategic players is an imperative of this crucial dynamic of engendering human rights. The lives of women depend on it.

References

Charlesworth, H., Chinkin, C. & Wright, S. (1991). Feminist Approaches to International Law. *American Journal of International Law*. 85.

Cook, R. (1994). *The Human Rights of Women*. Philadelphia: University of Pennsylvania Press.

Donnelly, J. (1989). *International Human Rights Theory and Practice*.

Romany, C. (1994). State Responsibility Goes Private: A Feminist Critique of the Public/Private Distinction in International Human Rights Law. In R. Cook (Ed.), *The Human Rights of Women*. Philadelphia: University of Pennsylvania Press, pp 85-115).

Schuler, M. (Ed.). *Empowerment and the Law: Strategies of Third World Women*. Washington, DC: OEF International.

Smart, C. (1989). *Feminism and the Power of the Law*. New York: Routledge.

Tomasevski, K. (1993). *Women and Human Rights*. London: Zed Books.

Part I:
Gender and Hierarchy in Human Rights

Chapter 1

International Human Rights Law and Practice: Implications for Women

Florence Butegwa

There appears to be broad agreement that "modern" international human rights law owes its development to the United Nations and its institutions (Buergenthal, 1988; Renteln, 1990; Shelley, 1989). It is becoming increasingly clear that the human rights discourse is central to many multilateral and bilateral policy formulations whether within or outside the framework of the United Nations. Progress in the protection of human rights is a determining factor, at least at the rhetorical level and in certain international political contexts, in shaping international and bilateral political and economic relationships (Shelley, 1989).

In spite of this broad agreement and the significance of the concept of human rights in current politics at the national and international level, the exact meaning tends to be hazy, subjective and clouded by political self-interests of the states. The nature and content of human rights is as controversial today as it was in 1948 when the Universal Declaration of Human Rights was adopted.

This paper examines the concept of human rights, the development of international human rights law and the implications for the human rights of women. The major human rights instruments shy away from a definition of human rights, contenting themselves with an enumeration of the rights that they respectively seek to protect. Despite attempts by scholars to define the concept, it would appear from the formulations of the instruments and the practice of human rights treaty bodies, states and nongovernmental human rights organizations that the content of human rights and the nature and extent of obligations assumed by states is not definitive. It may vary from one historical moment to another. Human Rights is a dynamic concept and this fact has significant implications for women.

If the content of and obligations pertinent to human rights changes with time, are they also influenced by cultural, religious and development specificity? In other words, is the controversy over the so-called universality or relativism of human rights significant to the women's human rights discourse? This paper argues that women's human rights are vulnerable in both theoretical and political positions. While many states and the international human rights bodies have historically promoted the concept of universal human rights, their practices have rarely addressed women-specific violations. Similarly, those states advancing the need for a concept of human rights that is sensitive and responsive to cultural, religious and development contexts have tended to raise their voices more in those issues of specific concern to women.

The development of human rights law and practice also has been significantly influenced by the still controversial concept of indivisibility of human rights. In spite of the Universal Declaration of Human Rights, which treated all human rights stated therein as equal, the practice has been for different states to give preference to either civil and political rights or economic, social and cultural rights. The so-called "Western" and "socialist" or developing country positions can easily be seen from the following excerpts:

> Since human rights and fundamental freedoms are indivisible, the full realization of civil and political rights without the enjoyment of economic, social and cultural rights is impossible. The achievement of lasting progress in the implementation of human rights is dependent upon sound and effective national and international development policies of economic and social development (Proclamation of Tehran, 1968).

By contrast, some legal scholars do rank rights in order of importance. Cassese (1986), for example, argues, "Although it is not possible to rank human rights in order of preference, civil and political rights appear to be of primary importance."

The paper argues that the division of human rights into civil and political rights and the resultant hierarchical importance given to civil and political rights within the United Nations and in the practice of states have slowed down progress in the recognition and protection of women's human rights. They also have restricted the women's human rights discourse and jurisprudence to the framework of equality and discrimination. In this framework the theory, practice and application accept the male as the norm and point of departure (Peterson,

1990). As a result, legitimate concerns of women which lacked a male norm or experience, have been considered irrelevant to the human rights framework until very recently.

The end of the Cold War and the growth of a strong women's human rights advocacy movement have opened up possibilities for international human rights law to be relevant to the majority of the world's women. The progress made as a result of the Second World Conference on Human Rights in Vienna in 1993 needs to be consolidated by the development of jurisprudence and practice in women's rights in the United Nations human rights system, in regional human rights frameworks and in the work of nongovernmental organizations at all levels.

The Concept of Human Rights

Although human rights is a key concept in international law and relations, its precise meaning and content remain as controversial as ever. The Charter of the United Nations, to which the development of human rights law is often attributed, is a prototype. Article 1(3) includes, as part of the purposes of the organization, the promotion and encouragement of a respect for human rights and fundamental freedoms for all, but without defining them.[1] The Universal Declaration of Human Rights also shies away from a definition. Its preamble merely declares that "recognition of the inherent dignity and of the equal and inalienable rights of all members of the human family is the foundation of freedom, justice and peace in the world." The operative articles merely list the rights and freedoms guaranteed by the Declaration. This pattern is repeated in the other major international human rights instruments.[2]

Human rights scholars either have assumed that the concept is universal and requires no definition or have offered definitions which offer little help to a person grappling with the questions of what a human right is and what qualifies something to be a human right. Henkin (1989) states that the idea of human rights is related, but not equivalent to, justice, good and democracy. It is a political idea with

---

[1] See also Articles 55 and 56 of the Charter of the United Nations.

[2] See the International Covenant on Social, Economic and Cultural Rights, the International Covenant on Civil and Political Rights, the Convention on the Elimination of All Forms of Racial Discrimination, the Convention on the Elimination of all Forms of Discrimination Against Women and the Convention on the Rights of the Child.

a moral foundation which defines the relationship that should exist between the individual and society (Henkin, 1989). Cranston (1973) defines human rights as moral rights which all men everywhere at all times ought to have and something which no one may be deprived of without grave affront to justice; something which is owing to every human being simply because he is human. Wasserstrom (1964) outlines the four characteristics which a human right must have:

> First, it must be possessed by all human beings, as well as only by human beings. Second, because it is the same right that all human beings possess, it must be possessed equally by all human beings. Third, because human rights are possessed by all human beings, we can rule out as possible candidates any of those rights which one might have in virtue of occupying any particular status or relationship, such as that of parent, president, or promisee. And fourth, if there are any human rights, they have the additional characteristic of being assertable, in a manner of speaking, "against the whole world." (p. 50)

Stark (1989) sees human rights as internationally recognized norms for behavior of states and other persons in international law; Buergenthal (1988) defines human rights by reference to the law which governs human rights. He refers to "the law which deals with the protection of individuals and groups against violations by governments" (p. 1).

Attempts at defining human rights have not been central to the human rights discourse. There is a surprising and significant assumption, similar to that made by the human rights instrument, that the concept itself is obvious and does not require clarification. A look at the definitions of human rights provided above shows the inherent difficulty of the concept. They range from the very abstract and justification-oriented position offered by Henkin to the limited and pragmatic approach adopted by Stark.

The aim of this section of the paper is not to critique existing definitions, however, but rather to shed some light on the position of women within the human rights discourse. International human rights law has not been effectively used to redress violations of women's human rights (Cook, 1993). Is the problem inherent in the definition and perception of human rights as a concept? Wasserstrom's (1964) understanding of human rights as rights possessed by all human beings equally seems to reflect the notion underlying most human rights instruments. While there is no explicit reference to women in the Universal Declaration of Human Rights, the

International Covenant on Civil and Political Rights (ICCPR) or in the International Covenant on Economic, Social and Cultural Rights (ICESCR), all of the instruments implicitly include women in the "equality" context. The covenants underscore this "unisex approach" by providing that

> each State Party to the present Covenant undertakes to respect and to en-
> sure to all individuals within its territory and subject to its jurisdiction the
> rights recognized in the present Covenant, without distinction of any
> kind, such as...sex... (Tomasevski, 1993).

Because women have not been perceived as having any human rights unique to their gender and not shared equally with men, any claims to entitlement to protection by women had to be framed within the "equality" framework. For women to show violations of their rights as women, they had to show that they were discriminated against in that the law or practices of the state failed to provide women the same protections as men. As a result, scholars and other proponents of women's human rights were forced to argue for recognition of specific women's human rights issues within the discrimination clauses of the international instruments.

It is this assumption of a "unisex" concept of human rights that needs closer attention and analysis. How objective and/or justified is this assumption of a "unisex" conception of human rights? Women and men do share some common aspirations as to fundamental rights and freedoms, but one cannot deny the fact that there are significant differences between men and women. The differences arise from biological differences as well as from the differential roles and vulnerabilities arising out of those biological differences. They may also arise from the socialization process and consequent roles and vulnerabilities associated with those roles.

It is from this perspective that women do have a legitimate claim to human rights and fundamental freedoms due them as women. There are actions and/or omissions which impinge on "the inherent dignity" of women as members of the human family within the context of the Universal Declaration of Human Rights that are not experienced by men. When there is no equivalent category of experience for men, the equality or non-discrimination discourse found in most human rights instruments is inapplicable. The result has been an absence of guarantees for fundamental rights and freedoms when women are the actors most affected. A closer look at the interpretation and actions of various human rights organizations will confirm that despite claims of gender neutrality in human rights instruments, the monitoring bodies and human rights nongovernmental organizations have rarely considered human rights specific to women as worth monitoring and reporting upon.

Similarly, within national constitutions where the concept of gender neutrality has been adopted, interpretation and application tends to leave out women. A notable historical example (unfortunately still replicated in many countries) was the English Representation of the People Act (1867), granting men the right to vote. The term "man" was used in the text of the act. On the basis of the rule of interpretation that words importing the male gender shall be taken to include females, a woman, Mary Abbott, requested that her name be included on the electoral register. Her application was rejected by both the electoral authorities and the courts in the ensuing court case (Tomasevski, 1993).

Acceptance by the international community of the demand for a specific framework for women's rights would give the human rights system effective mechanisms to address women-specific issues, including reproductive choice and health, and violence against women in all its forms, such as the slave-like practices like Ngozi in Zimbabwe or trokosi in Ghana in which young girls are given out (to other families or to shrines) in atonement for "wrongs" committed by their families.

Some encouraging steps toward broadening the language of human rights instruments to protect women have already been taken. In June 1993, the Second World Conference on Human Rights declared that:

> The human rights of women and the girl-child are an inalienable, integral and indivisible part of universal human rights. Gender-based violence and all forms of sexual harassment and exploitation, including those resulting from cultural prejudice and international trafficking, are incompatible with the dignity and worth of the human person, and must be eliminated. (Vienna Declaration and Programme of Action, 1993, p. 33).

The United Nations General Assembly also has adopted the Declaration on the Elimination of Violence Against Women. The United Nations Commission on Human Rights has appointed a Special Rapporteur on Violence Against Women and has called upon other human rights bodies and special rapporteurs to deal with the issue of violence against women within their specific mandates. These advances are welcome but much more needs to be done in reconceptualizing human rights and the mandates and practices of the international community to address women-specific human rights concerns. The safeguarding of people's rights is, and will continue to be, both conceptually and practically, an unfinished task, a permanent challenge to take action to advance the humanization of the world community.

Universality of Human Rights

The magnitude of the horrors of the Second World War and the need to protect individuals from abuses on that scale provided sufficient incentives for states to put their own interests and claims of sovereignty in second place in 1948. States were able to adopt the Universal Declaration of Human Rights as a common standard of achievement for all peoples and all nations. The rights and freedoms guaranteed therein were to have universal validity and application. The concept of universality of human rights has become one of the cornerstones of the international human rights framework reiterated as recently as 1993. The Vienna Declaration and Programme of Action boldly assert that the universal nature of human rights is beyond question. This would appear to be borne out by the practice of states in adopting the principles enshrined in the Universal Declaration of Human Rights into national constitutions and other domestic law or in relying upon it in their relationships with other states and inter-governmental organizations.

In spite of the apparent consensus on universality, however, it cannot be denied that when it suits some states, the idea of universal human rights has been and continues to be questioned and disowned. Demands for a concept of human rights that is sensitive to cultural and religious particularities and values continue to be voiced. Governments in national and international fora that demand cultural and religious hegemony argue that women's dignity is at risk when universal standards are applied in their countries, especially in the arenas of marriage and the family. Even within these spheres, aspects of culture that safeguarded the dignity of women have been largely discarded and/or made inoperable in the modern socio-economic environment.

A look at the Convention on the Elimination of All Forms of Discrimination Against Women may provide a good case study. It is the human rights convention with the most reservations attached. The reservations are not limited to procedural matters, but to substantive provisions, some of which go to the core and purpose of the convention. What is insightful is that some of the states entered reservations on articles they purport to accept in the context of other human rights instruments. It is, therefore, pertinent to ask whether cultural and religious or other relativism in human rights theory and practice are in the interests of the protection of the human rights of women.

Indivisibility of Human Rights

For decades most "western" developed countries have put emphasis and resources on the promotion and protection of civil and political rights. They see these rights as necessary ingredients of good governance and democracy, which are prerequisites to development (Cassese, 1986). Several reasons have been advanced for this preference. Among these is the perceived cost to states of ensuring these rights. Civil and political rights are characterized as negative and cost-free rights in that governments are only required to abstain from activities which would violate them. This is contrasted with economic, social and cultural rights which require governments to do something, thereby committing considerable resources, to ensure individuals the enjoyment of those rights. An additional difference lies in the fact that civil and political rights are relatively capable of precise definition, readily justiciable and susceptible to enforcement (Alston, 1987).

A discussion of whether treating civil and political rights as superior rights is justified is beyond the scope of this paper. It is suffucient to make several observations. Privileging civil and political rights has resulted in significantly advancing those rights over the promotion of economic, social and cultural rights. The ICCPR has an Optional Protocol providing an individual complaints procedure. The right of access by individuals and the resultant interaction between the committee and state parties have given this treaty body the much needed political clout to be taken seriously. The Human Rights Committee has through its General Comments helped develop jurisprudence in the area of civil and political rights. The United Nations Commission on Human Rights has complemented and consolidated these advances through its special procedures. A significant number of nongovernmental organizations have complemented over the decades the work of the Human Rights Committee and the Commission on Human Rights in promoting rights and monitoring and reporting violations.

Indivisibility and the Human Rights of Women

While these developments are welcome, they have created an undesirable hierarchy among human rights. Civil and political rights are now referred to as first-generation rights. More conservative scholars and practitioners regard them as *the* human rights. These developments have had considerable implications for the human rights of women. Although women have made significant strides in the bid to play a key role in the politics of their countries, for the majority of women economic, social and cultural rights still remain a major concern. Women are concerned about enhancing their economic status as a major step in freeing themselves from economic dependence on men. This in turn contributes to ensuring their own dignity and life choices. Consequently, access to property, employment (Arts. 6, 7, ICESCR) and credit are crucial rights. Similarly, women are concerned that adequate housing, food, clothing and overall living standards be assured (Art. 11, ICESCR). Women want to work with the State to realize economic, social and cultural rights. It is crucial, therefore, that they be afforded opportunity for education at all levels (Art. 13, ICESCR). Because culture everywhere has a direct impact on the rights of women to exercise fundamental rights and freedoms, especially in developing countries, it is important that women participate in the definitions of cultural values and content (Art. 15, ICESCR).

Economic, Social and Cultural Rights and Human Development

It is not only in the interests of the human rights of women that greater promotion and protection of economic, social and cultural rights is important. Human development, dignity and security within the prevailing socio-economic order depend on it. The United Nations Human Development Report (UNDP, 1994) puts it in the following terms:

> For a long time, the concept of (human) security has been shaped by the potential for conflict between states. For too long, security has been

equated with threats to a country's borders. For too long, nations have sought arms to protect their security.

For most people today, a feeling of insecurity arises more from worries about life than from the dread of a cataclysmic world event. Job security, income security, health security, environmental security, security from crime—these are emerging concerns of human security all over the world.

A look at human development indicators for a majority of countries will show the urgent need for the international human rights community, individual states, intergovernmental and nongovernmental organizations to give as much emphasis to the promotion of economic, social and cultural rights as is given to civil and political rights. For most countries, standards of living are falling. As countries struggle with economic structural adjustment programs, job security is no longer guaranteed. Government subsidies on health, education and other amenities are dwindling fast, exposing greater numbers to a life without health care and education. Malnourishment in children and adults in the developing world is an increasingly serious problem.

The Way Forward

There is an increasing sense of urgency and consensus that economic, social and cultural rights must be promoted and protected with greater zeal and efficiency than ever before. The Second World Conference on Human Rights resulted in the consensus that "all human rights are universal, indivisible and interdependent and interrelated. The international community must treat human rights globally in a fair and equal manner, on the same footing, and with the same emphasis" (Vienna Declaration, 1993, para. 5).

The Second World Conference further encourages the Commission on Human Rights, in cooperation with the Committee on Economic, Social and Cultural Rights, to continue the examination of optional protocols to the ICESCR (Vienna Declaration and Programme of Action, 1993, para. 75). Several other developments are also notable, including the appointment of a thematic working group on the right to development, which the Second World Conference affirmed as an inalienable fundamental right.

There is an urgent need on the part of the Committee on Economic, Social and Cultural Rights, the Commission on Human Rights, other human rights bodies and nongovernmental organizations to make concrete proposals for the effective implementation of the ICESCR. It is true that state parties to the Covenant enter into legally binding obligations to:

> take steps, individually and through international assistance and cooperation, especially economic and technical, to the maximum of its available resources, with a vie to progressive realization of the rights recognized in the ... Covenant...

An analysis of this provision indicates that it was never envisaged that states would do nothing. Rather, states must take steps in accordance with their resources to ensure progressive realization of these rights. The steps may include legislative action to remove barriers to realization of rights or may involve creating an environment conducive to the realization of the rights (Alston, 1987). To facilitate a definition of what steps might be adequate for compliance with the overall obligations in the Covenant (thereby assisting states parties in their reporting), there is need to look at minimum standards in each area covered by the Covenant. In the field of health, for instance, what is the absolute minimum that states parties in the least developed countries group can do to comply with the obligations in the Covenant? The Covenant recognizes that the realization of rights has to be progressive and the pace is dependent on the resources available to the states. Unless attempts are made at more specific and quantifiable ways of measuring progress there is a real danger of states feeling overwhelmed by the task and just dismissing the entire Covenant as a mere statement of ideals rather than creating legal obligations.

The women's rights movement can play a key role in this process. As indicated earlier, economic, social and cultural rights are important in the struggle for equality and dignity for women. The Commission on the Status of Women, the Committee on the Elimination of All Forms of Discrimination Against Women and the various women's rights advocacy groups around the world need to take the issue of indivisibility of human rights seriously. Lobbying for a faster pace in the development of an optional protocol to the ICESCR is one aspect of the challenge ahead. Articulation of jurisprudence and concepts that define more concretely the obligations of the states is another and perhaps more crucial aspect. Lobbying for the strengthening of the Committee on Economic, Social and Cultural rights is the other aspect. Lobbying so-called mainstream human rights groups to address economic and social rights as an integral part of their mandates also is a means of adding pressure on states to act.

Conclusion

In conclusion, I refer to the words of Merek Thee (1993) that the pursuit of human rights is far from complete. It requires constant attention with a view to greater precision, amplification and actual incorporation in national and international law.

For the world's women, this observation is true. The international human rights community has a long way to go to guarantee the dignity of women. The challenge is to reconceptualize human rights to include the human rights of women and to extend beyond the dictates of equality to cover concerns particular to women as women. Related to this is the challenge of looking at culture, religion and other tenets of group identity as tools for the dignity of the group and for individuals rather than as a millstone to keep them in servitude and suffering human indignities. Another challenge is addressing economic, social and cultural inequities women suffer by promoting and protecting more effectively economic, social and cultural rights.

References

Alston, P., & Quinn, M. (1987). The Nature and Scope of States Parties' Obligations Under the International Covenant on Economic, Social and Cultural Rights. *Human Rights Quarterly, 9.*

Buergenthal, T. (1988). *International Human Rights.* St Paul, MN: West Publishing.

Cassese, A. (1986). *International Law in a Divided World.* Oxford: Clarendon Press.

Cook, R. (1993). Women's International Human Rights Law: The Way Forward. *Human Rights Quarterly, 15.*

Cranston, M. (1973). *What are Human Rights?* New York: Taplinger.

Henkin, L. (1989). *International Law* [chapter on human rights]. St. Paul, MN: West Publishing.

Peterson, V. S. (1990). Whose Rights?: A Critique of the Givens. *Alternatives.*

Renteln, A. D. (1990). *International Human Rights: Universalism Versus Relativism.* Newbury Park: Sage Publications.

Stark, B. (1989). International Human Rights and Family Planning: A Modest Proposal. *Denver Journal of International Law and Policy.*

Shelley, L. I. (1989). Human Rights as an International Issue. In W. Marvin (Ed.), *Human Rights in the World.* Philadelphia, PA: American Academy of Political and Social Sciences.

Thee, M. (1993). The Philosophical-Existential Issues of the Human Rights Project: Challenges for the 21st Century. *Human Rights in Developing Countries Yearbook* 1993. Nordic Human Rights Foundation.

Tomasevski, K. (1993). *Women and Human Rights.* London: Zed Books.

United Nations Development Program. (1994). *United Nations Human Development Report.* New York: Author.

The Vienna Declaration and Programme of Action, World Conference on Human Rights. (1993). New York: UNDPI.

Wasserstrom, R. (1964). Rights, Human Rights and Racial Discrimination. *Journal of Philosophy.*

Eine Welt. (1993). The Universality of Human Rights in Theory and Practice. *Human Rights and Development.*

Chapter 2
Acting Unnaturally: In Defense of the Civil and Political Rights of Women

Dorothy Q. Thomas

Introduction

After many years of a largely hierarchical approach to human rights within mainstream human rights practice, an approach that privileged civil and political rights over economic, social and cultural rights and the public over the private sphere, the primacy of civil and political rights and their long-standing association to the public realm has come under increasingly provacative criticism. The emergence of a women's human rights movement worldwide has considerably advanced this trend. Women's human rights activists have posed a powerful challenge to the traditional rights hierarchy in both respects, exposing it as fundamentally gender-biased. Their efforts have significantly energized the call for the promotion and protection of an interdependent and indivisible approach to human rights in all spheres of human life.

While these efforts are crucial, they may carry also certain risks. One of these is the risk of reestablishing a rights hierarchy in reverse, i.e. one that asserts the primacy of economic and social rights and of the private sphere over civil and political rights and the public realm. Another is the suggestion, implicit in such a reverse hierarchy, that both economic and social rights and the private sphere are "more" relevant to women's lives. And a third is that by virtue of such "re-privileging" the continued struggle to achieve civil and political rights in women's public lives in underestimated and the degree to which these rights need to be both recognized and reconstructed is obscured.

This article examines several examples of contemporary women's human rights theory for their treatment of women's civil and political rights. It briefly outlines some positive aspects of the feminist challenge to the primacy of these rights and of the public sphere and then discusses some of possible drawbacks of this same challenge. The remainder of the article attempts to strike a somewhat different balance between so-called first and second generation rights and between the public and private realms. In particular, it examines the degree to which women's assertion of their individual person-hood, as expressed in the exercise of their civil and political rights in the public sphere, remains a key and highly contested women's hu-man rights issue. It then concludes that inattention to this issue could pose a formidable obstacle to women's private and economic and so-cial empowerment and to the struggle to secure a truly interdepend-ent and indivisible approach to human rights. By necessity, this discussion invokes precisely the same rights hierarchies that it seeks to overcome, but attempts to do so in a manner that reflects their on-going transformation.

Challenging the Rights Hierarchy

In general, the feminist critique of the primacy of civil and po-litical rights has pinpointed the deep, structural reliance of this ap-proach on the subordination of women and, in particular on the construction of and women's relegation to the private sphere, out-side both the realm of recognized civil and political activity and the reach of the state. Celina Romany, among others, has persuasively ar-gued this point (Romany, 1994). She notes that traditional notions of civil and political rights assume the existence of a free, prototypically male, individual derived from historical concepts of the "rights of man" against the state. This traditional concept of civil and political rights not only protects political rights but presumes the existence of a private sphere of individual liberty free from arbitrary government intervention. While in theory the principle of equality protects these political rights and private liberties for all human beings, in fact social and legal norms deny women public personhood and consign them to the private sphere, not as free individuals but as what amounts to pri-vate property subordinate to the largely unregulated authority of men in that realm.

The critique of this public/private distinction and thus of the gendered character of traditional concepts of civil and political rights, challenges the historical primacy of these rights as well. That is, the challenge to the public/private distinction is ultimately a critique of the civil and political emphasis on individual male action in the public realm, seemingly free from government constraint or community responsibility beyond that which is minimally required by law. The promotion of economic, social and cultural rights counteracts this notion (at least to a certain extent) with the concept of an individual that exists in community and of a state responsible not only for protecting individual political freedoms, but also for strengthening all people's capacity to access and enjoy those freedoms through the progressive realization of their economic and social rights.

One immediate practical result of this overall feminist critique of current human rights practice has been the gradual erosion of public/private distinction and the assertion of state responsibility of varying kinds for gender-based abuses occurring in the so-called private sphere. Thus not only domestic violence but also trafficking in women for sexual, marital or domestic service and other forms of private actor violence (and even some forms of private discrimination) are seen to fall within the realm of state responsibility and the protection of international human rights law. Moreover, as this civil and political protection has been extended to the private sphere and women's experience has become more publicly visible, so has the degree to which their economic and social subordination is a key impediment to the realization of their full human rights.

The obvious need to challenge the gendered construction of civil and political rights as traditionally exercised by men in the public sphere (often to the detriment of the general public's economic and social well-being) has produced a long overdue emphasis on the need to extend civil and political rights to women in the private sphere and to prioritize their economic and social empowerment. Yet, in course of this "re-visioning" of human rights, the struggle to insert female actors into civil and political rights activity in the public realm is at constant risk of being either downplayed or dismissed outright. As the following examples suggest, current women's rights discourse tends to deem the public sphere as somehow less relevant to women's lives than the private realm and to see civil and political rights as less crucial to women than their economic, social and cultural counterparts.

For example, Hillary Charlesworth in her recently published article "What Are Women's International Human Rights," (1994) notes that "[t]he primacy traditionally given to civil and political rights by western international lawyers and philosophers is directed towards the protection of men in public life, their relationship with government. But these are not harms from which women most need protection." In her recent article on state responsibility for violations of women's human rights, Rebecca Cook points out the "[f]eminist analysts are skeptical of the legal distinction between public and private sectors of life, since the distinction has resulted in the abandonment of women where their interests and rights are most at stake." Celina Romany notes that a primary objective of the women's human rights struggle is to reach those "legislators and adjudicators whose blinders do not let them see that women's civil and political rights in the private sphere are systematically abused...." Butegwa (in this volume) notes that "although women have made significant strides in the bid to play a key role in the politics of their countries, for the majority of women economic, social and cultural rights remain a major concern."

Reclaiming Civil and Political Rights for Women

All of these writers evince a healthy suspicion of traditional human rights hierarchies and practice. However, they also betray to a greater or lesser degree a diminishment of women's civil and political action, particularly in the public sphere, and a subordination of civil and political rights to economic, social and cultural rights. Such an imbalance if left unaddressed could potentially hinder the shared attempt to craft a truly indivisible theory and practice of women's human rights. To shy away from inserting women into the heart of traditional human rights law and practice (i.e. the assertion in the public sphere of civil and political rights), is to neglect an important site for the radical transformation of that law and practice. It is also to abandon women who suffer abuse in this sphere and can still find little or no acknowledgment or redress.

The identification of civil and political rights with men, and the identification of the public realm of the civil and political with male activity, is neither inherent nor accurate. As such, women's struggle to claim these rights presents a radical challenge to male authority, both in fact and as it has been enshrined in human rights law and practice. The struggle to dethrone the male prototype at the heart of traditional civil and political rights practice is nothing less than the assertion of individual female personhood, both in fact and before the law, an assertion that, unfortunately, has yet to be widely accepted in the world. To downplay this struggle, or these rights for women, is in my view to cede this highly contested political turf, to weaken the basis for women's human rights claims in general and to reinforce the very public/private, civil and political/economic and social distinctions that much women's human rights activism purports to challenge.

I recognize, as Radhika Coomaraswamy has pointed out, that an emphasis on women's exercise of their civil and political rights in the public realm privileges "the free, independent woman as an individual endowed with rights and rational agency (1994, p. 40)." While she associates herself with this view of female personality (as do I), she notes that it is not widely agreed upon in the world and argues that its universality cannot be assumed. In underscoring this point, she identifies a formidable challenge for those seeking both to demonstrate the relevance of civil and political rights to women's lives and to ensure that women's exercise of these rights does not replicate the excesses of individual legal privilege that were a central focus of the feminist human rights critique in the first place. In my view, meeting this double challenge may require less the absolute acceptance of the free, independent, individual, rational model of female personality per se, than it does the universal recognition of a woman's right to assert such a personality should she choose to do so, whether as a solitary individual or as, Petchesky and Copelon point out in this volume, as an equal participant in community life.

To some authors, however, the challenge posed by Coomaraswamy is virtually insurmountable, particularly given the limits of contemporary human rights discourse. That is, the assertion of individual female personhood, if ratified through existing human rights protections, will not "feminize" the concept of personhood, but simply establish that women are persons "like men." Thus, to the extent that women are not like men, they will not be protected, and the whole traditional rights hierarchy will reassert itself all over again. In an argument along these lines in a recent article in the *Australian Yearbook of International Law*, Shelly Wright states that where women are "least subservient, least structured into private domesticity, reproduction, nurturance and servitude is where they, like many privileged Western women, including most feminists, are most like men." She goes on to state that women such as these "can rely on 'men's rights' because they have...achieved the equality with men's values expressed in those rights."

The purpose of this paper is not to dispute Wright's claims, nor those of Charlesworth, Romany, Butgewa and Cook mentioned above, but to caution against throwing the baby out with bath water. The effort to overturn the traditional rights hierarchy or even to

reject the current human rights discourse all together, need not necessarily come at the expense of women's enjoyment of their civil and
political rights in the public realm nor need it simply cede these
rights to men. As the remainder of this paper will show, the exercise
by women of civil and political rights in the public realm helps fuel
the struggle to assert female personhood that is a driving force behind
the entire women's human rights endeavor. Women's exercise of
rights in this sphere does not simply replicate or "equal" the male
model of political activity, but counter-balances that model with the
appearance of a female political actor. This development has the potential to transform the traditional, masculine rights prototype and
has profound ramifications not only for human rights theory and
practice but also for women's everyday lives. To be sure, such transformations will be hard won, but it is this very difficulty which speaks
to the necessity of ensuring that the attempt to secure women's full
civil and political rights is not lost in the effort to transform human
rights overall.

The Female Actor: The Application/Expansion of Civil and Political Rights

This section focuses on case-specific efforts to reclaim women's
civil and political rights in the public realm with particular attention
to the rights to bodily integrity, to privacy and to equal protection of
the law. It tracks the various successes that have been achieved in
making such claims, their potentially transformative effect on human
rights law and practice and on women's lives and the degree to which
those changes continue to be contested and profoundly
circumscribed.

A. Bodily Integrity

Human rights work on violence against women has been one of
the most fruitful areas for challenging the public/private distinction
and extending the scope of state responsibility with respect to civil
and political rights into the private realm. My own work as director
of the Human Rights Watch/Women's Rights Project (WRP) began
in collaboration with women's rights activists in Brazil on a report
that considered the Brazilian government's international human
rights obligations to prevent and remedy violence against women in
the home. (Human Rights Watch, *Criminal Injustice: Violence
Against Women in Brazil*). In the winter of 1994, WRP released a

second report on this subject in collaboration with women's rights activists in Russia (Human Rights Watch, "Neither Jobs nor Justice: State Discrimination Against Women in Russia") and we released a third report on domestic violence in South Africa in the summer of 1995. These reports are only one reflection of the efforts of women's rights activists all over the world to apply international human rights standards to violence against women in the home, the combined effect of which has led the United Nations Special Rapporteur on Violence Against Women to focus her 1995 official report on this issue.

In addition to domestic violence, women's human rights activists have also challenged the effective "privatization" of other forms of violence against women which do not necessarily occur in the home or at the hands of private individuals, whether in the community, in custody or in conflict situations. Thus, for example, women's rights activists in Peru and in Kenya have fought to change rape laws that conceive of such abuse as a violation of family or community honor, rather than an abuse of the woman's bodily integrity. Activists in the United States and India have fought expressly to outlaw sexual intercourse and sexual touching by officers of prisoners in custody, an abuse that predominately affects women, and that is often accepted (except in the most extreme cases of severe physical force or harm) as an "inter-personal" exchange between officer and prisoner. Women's human rights activists in internal and international conflicts in Europe, Latin America, Africa, and Asia have transformed the traditional interpretation of rape and other gender-specific abuse in war from a personal or sexual activity incidental to conflict, into a legal and social understanding of such abuse as a crime of war.

These efforts have achieved more than the extension of the state's obligation to protect civil and political rights into the actual or perceived "private" sphere of women's experience. They have also brought women's experience into public light and forced the official recognition of female personhood before the law and in the eyes of society more generally. This development has at times, although not always, involved not only the application of seemingly gender-neutral law to violence experienced by women, but also the creation of new law that is at least facially more responsive to women's particular experiences and needs. Thus, the Brazilian constitution expressly outlaws violence occurring in the home and the new South African government has pledged to focus on the "reconstruction of family and community life by prioritizing and responding to the needs of ...women and children who have been victims of domestic and other forms of violence." (The Reconstruction and Development Programme, African National Congress, 1994.) In addition, the international community is beginning to recognize that forced impregnation constitutes a distinct abuse that should be encompassed by international human rights and humanitarian law.

The potentially transformative effects of these efforts on the traditional concept of public, political personhood are profound in both legal and political terms. Where it was once extremely difficult for women's basic humanity to be publicly or privately recognized as a matter of international human rights law or practice, women are now increasingly laying recognized claims to their civil, and political right to bodily integrity not only in the home, but also in the community, in custody and in war. This fact is effecting their status as persons in both the public and private spheres, even as it challenges that distinction, and reflects, in Carol Smart's words, the efforts of a female person "with dignity demanding a just outcome according to widely accepted criteria of fairness" (1989).

This is by no means to suggest that women's efforts to claim their civil and political right to bodily integrity wherever and however it is threatened do not confront limits. In fact, these persistent limits are this article's principle concern. They are perhaps most evident with respect to women's sexuality and reproduction, the gender-specificity of which are not easily encompassed by male-biased law. However, even in areas where the content of a woman's civil and political right to bodily integrity is more readily established, for example with respect to violence and/or sexual and physical degradation (particularly when committed directly at the hands of agents of the state), considerable and entrenched legal and political constraints on women's capacity to exercise this right, and thus express their individual, female personhood, continue to arise.

A brief review of women's human rights work with respect to violence reveals an interesting trend in this regard. While states continue vigorously to resist the extension of civil and political rights protection to women in the private sphere, it is when women attempt to exercise these rights in the public sphere that they are apt to meet with equally profound resistance. Thus, for example, legislatures increasingly adopt laws criminalizing violence against women in the home, but they are rarely enforced by the police or courts. When women present themselves to public authorities they are often told literally or figuratively to "go home." This and similar treatment of women around the world clearly reflects not only the states' continued misapprehension of domestic violence as a "private matter" but also profound official unwillingness to recognize women's personhood in the public realm as well. A woman in Russia reported going to the police with a domestic violence claim and being asked by the officer "what do you want from me?"

It is worth considering that women's exercise of their civil and political rights in the public sphere is an outcome as profoundly troubling to the status quo as is their exercise of these rights in the private realm. This fact might account for states' increasing willingness to extend public protection to women the private sphere, but their persistent unwillingness publicly to enforce such protections. It might also shed light on an interesting aspect of South Africa's domestic violence law which, while it extends civil and political rights protection to women in the home, exempts from its coverage women not currently or at one time in a marital or proximate marital relationship with their abuser. Women outside a marital or semi-relationship being abused, for example, by a non live in male or female sexual partner would not be covered under this law. In other words, seemingly more independent female persons would not merit public protection.

Now a careful or perhaps even a cursory reader of this section may conclude that I have disproved my own point. In other words, by showing that women's public personhood remains largely unrecognized and that the private application of civil and political rights has little public expression (and may in fact be occurring in part because their private exercise will still be in the purview of male control) proves that human rights discourse simply cannot accommodate female political personhood, whether conceived of as similar to or different than that of men. However, I believe that this conclusion would be premature and confuses what is with what might be. To put it another way, the limits on women's exercise of their civil and political rights in the public sphere are clearly there, but so are the transformative effects of their attempts to do so, both on the enjoyment of the rights themselves and on the effort to reconceptualize them.

B. Privacy

The degree to which these potential transformations continue to be resisted (both in daily life and in the discourse of human rights) is nowhere more evident than in the struggle to assert women's civil and political right to privacy. The collapse of the public/private distinction has in many respects exposed the way in which the right to privacy historically worked to protect the male public actor from state accountability for abusive (or other) acts committed in private. In this context, a woman's right to privacy was fairly meaningless, amounting in effect to little more than her privatization by men. A man's historical right to beat his wife without any fear of state intervention, persistent arguments that rape is by definition an extramarital offense, and man's traditional and entrenched control of a woman's sexuality and reproduction all reflect the degree to which the exercise of the right to privacy—particularly as expressed in the promotion of the family as the fundamental social unit—has often meant the obliteration of female personhood under the guise of the woman's protection.

However, while the emphasis on the collapse of the public/private distinction may have ameliorated women's status in the male dominated private sphere, it has not necessarily advanced women's claim to a private sphere of individual liberty of their own, free not only from male control, but also from public intervention.

I have recently encountered this problem in a profound way with respect to work with women's rights activists in the United States on sexual and other abuse of women in that country's state prisons. Because the United States has ratified the International Covenant on Civil and Political Rights, it is bound to uphold the right to privacy contained therein. The UN Human Rights Committee, which has responsibility for reviewing state compliance with the Covenant, has interpreted that right to protect prisoners from inappropriate body searches and visual surveillance by officers of the opposite sex. The United States has argued to the Committee that it has in fact put in place relevant laws and procedures to protect against such abuse. In fact, nothing could be farther from the truth. We investigated eleven women's prisons in five states and the District of Columbia and without exception the female prisoners reported being inappropriately searched, groped and viewed by male officers during strip and pat frisks and while they were dressing, in the toilet or in the showers.

Such surveillance was often accompanied by lewd remarks and gestures.

The officers' willingness to engage in such activity with respect to the female prisoners reflects the fact that in the public realm, women still have no recognized privacy rights. This is, in this case, partly because they are prisoners, and is true of prisoners generally in the United States. But it is also because they are women and because the notion of women as full persons with privacy rights carries at best disputed social and legal value. The officers are more likely to view and refer to the women as "bitches" and "whores" and to treat them like a form of sexual currency, than they are to treat the women as individuals with a recognized right to privacy. In fact, in the officers' eyes the international obligation to guarantee such treatment is almost laughable. Unfortunately, this view is often adopted by the women themselves who are considerably less likely to challenge privacy violations than are their male counterparts and who commonly accept such abuse as a condition not only of their incarceration, but of their daily lives in the outside world. Again, women laying claim to their right to privacy, like their right to bodily integrity, rests as much on the reclaiming public personality as it does on extending these rights into the private sphere. The two efforts need constantly to inform and accompany each other in both directions, but in much women's human rights theory and practice the movement is all one way, from the public into the private realm. The potentially detrimental effects of this approach are already surfacing in the attempts to lay claim to women's reproductive and sexual autonomy absent the secure recognition of a concept of personhood that encompasses these gender-specific functions. This problem is at the heart of the current threat to women's privacy-based abortion rights in the United States.

Nonetheless, women have engaged in efforts to claim their right to privacy in direct connection to the assertion of public personality that are yielding some potentially transformative results. In Turkey, for example, the women's rights struggle against compulsory virginity control examinations as a violation of women's rights to both bodily integrity and privacy has been directly linked to a discussion about women's public personality, in particular as reflected (or not) in the law. The suggested legal reforms do, by and large, focus on establishing female public personality on the basis of sameness with (rather than difference from) men. But the Turkish women's success in arguing that neither female nor male adult sexuality should be directly regulated by the state in this manner has put a stop to some potentially invasive practices, including the empowerment of public education officials to order such virginity exams for school-age girls. These successes cannot be underestimated and only contribute to the recognition of female personhood and of an associated right to privacy that may ultimately help lay the ground work for a more explicitly gender-based protection of women's reproductive and sexual autonomy.

C. Equal Protection of the Law

When all else fails, equality purports to be the great transformer, what is imbalanced in life will become balanced through the equal protection of the law. Yet again and again we confront the reality in women's lives that the principle of equality does not necessarily take into account the fact of women's structural subordination, a subordination which is not just a matter of the gender-biased application of the law, but which is imbedded in the architecture of the law itself. Thus efforts to establish women's legal equality in the public realm often come up against women's legal relegation to the private sphere and to economic and social dependency, even if that relegation is not always superficially discernible in the law.

Moreover, even if equality is achieved, it is on the basis of sameness with men, and thus apparently will not remedy those deprivations that are unique to women. As Florence Butegwa points out in this volume, while women and men do share similar aspirations with respect to their rights and freedoms, "one cannot deny the fact that there are significant differences between women and men." On this basis, she goes on the state that where women's experiences have no corresponding parallel in the experiences of men "the equality or non-discrimination discourse found in most human rights instruments is inapplicable." In these cases she concludes that "the result has been an absence of guarantees...when women actors are the most affected."

I largely share this assessment of the current conception of equality as a major stumbling block in the women's human rights struggle, but would guard against an either/or approach to the problem. It seems to me that women's efforts to secure their rights on the basis of equality with men have yielded meaningful results for the recognition and protection of individual female personhood and women's rights in both the civil and political and economic and social areas. Whether it's in the challenge, for example, to sex-discriminatory nationality laws in Botswana or Egypt, or to non-prosecution of violence against women in Brazil or South Africa, or to gender-based employment restrictions in Russia or Mexico, this struggle has brought about not only changes in the lives of individual women, but the official recognition by states of women's legal personhood which has the potential to affect the lives of women as whole.

Moreover, the work in Russia and Mexico in particular with respect to women's employment rights, has demonstrated that the equality principle within existing human rights discourse may be able to accommodate more difference than previously imagined. In a recent mission to Mexico, for example, WRP, in collaboration with Mexican women's rights advocates working in the *maquiladoras*, found that women workers in these areas are frequently subjected to pregnancy exams as a condition of employment. On some job applications women are directly asked if they are pregnant. One potential employee whose menstruation was late told us that she was asked to return only when it arrived. In most *maquiladoras* it is forbidden as a matter of informal regulation to become pregnant during the first year of work. In many cases, the women's reliance on the factory income led them to comply with this rule. In cases where they did not, they were compelled to "resign."

In both Mexico and Russia (where similar abuses occur although for different reasons), women's rights activists are arguing that employment bias based on the capacity to bear children constitutes gender-discrimination, even though men do not possess similar child-bearing capacity. Women in both countries are challenging such abuse under article 11(2) of the Convention on the Elimination of All Forms of Discrimination Against Women which prohibits discrimination on the basis of pregnancy or motherhood and requires states parties to prohibit dismissal on either ground. This argument implicitly recognizes that the women' equality is based not only on the presumption that they are similar to men, but on the recognition of their distinct characteristics.

To be sure, this protection is limited, in this case to the area of employment, and needs a great deal more examination and development. But it does suggest that the notion of individual personality implied in international human rights law need not be prototypically male nor does equality always have to be advanced on the basis of sameness with men. It is possible that human rights discourse could accommodate both the sameness and difference approaches, a possibility that as Romany, Copelon, Petchesky and Abeyesekera all point out, is also being put to long overdue test within the women's human rights movement itself.

At a minimum, the fact that women's exercise of their rights based on the all too established criteria of sameness with men is still so far out of reach, speaks powerfully to the need not only to pursue an articulation of rights that reflects the essential differences between women and men, but one that opens up the existing rights discourse to accommodate the expression of female personality on whatever grounds. It is for this reason that I see the continued struggle to advance women's civil and political rights in the public arena, once an exclusively male province, as key, whether with regard to bodily integrity, to privacy, to equal protection or to other civil and political rights.

Conclusion

There can be no doubt that the traditional human rights focus on the primacy of civil and political rights has come at the expense of the promotion and protection of economic and social rights. Nor can there be much argument that efforts to promote women's rights, particularly in the early stages, were biased in favor of civil and political rights. As this bias has been challenged on both fronts, it has become clear that women's exercise of their civil and political rights in the public sphere depends not only on equity in the private sphere, but also on their economic and social advancement in all walks of life, and that women's full enjoyment of their human rights depends on an indivisible and interdependent approach to their realization. The Mexico example, and others like it all over the world, makes the need for such an approach abundantly clear.

However, the promotion of economic, social and cultural rights, while it is often posed as a remedy for the past imbalance in human rights practice and as a speedy road to indivisibility, shares at least one problem with its civil and political counterpart: the potential denial to women of their individual personhood, whether in the private or the public sphere. Thus, as Shelly Wright points out, the distinction between these two generations of rights is false not only because the attempt to privilege one over the other possesses little merit, but also because the exercise of these two distinct sets of rights has in common the presupposition of individuality, whether expressed in a solitary or a collective manner (1994).

Wright notes that both civil and political and economic, social and cultural rights are "predicated on the notion of the accessibility of these rights to individuals through States or international agencies, either to protect specific political freedoms, or to enhance economic or social position." She goes on to state that both States and international institutions tend to ignore women's problems in relating to such rights that "make no allowance for the primary role women are expected to play in most political and social structures, i.e. to give up their own 'individuality' in the care and service of others." She concludes that "[c]are and service to others makes most civil and political rights simply inapplicable, as if they were accorded to a different species, and most social and economic rights practically unattainable."

Ultimately, as this article amply demonstrates, I do not share Wright's fairly bleak assessment and feel that current human rights discourse is much more dynamic and flexible than her remarks might suggest. Nonetheless, I wholeheartedly share her preoccupation with the worldwide failure to recognize women's individual female personality, whether in the civil and political or economic, social and cultural arenas, in the public or private sphere or on the basis of sameness with or difference from men. Efforts by women's human rights activists to overcome this problem will not be much advanced by substituting the struggle for one set or sphere of rights with the struggle for the other, but must rely instead on fighting for the recognition of female personhood in all realms where its denial continues to occur.

References

Abeyesekera, S. *Conceptualising Women's Human Rights: Questions of Equality and Difference.* Unpublished Masters Thesis, November 1994.

Charlesworth, H. (1994). What Are Women's International Human Rights? In R. Cook (Ed.), *The Human Rights of Women.* Philadelphia: University of Pennsylvania Press.

Coomaraswamy, R. (1994). To Bellow Like a Cow: Women, Ethnicity and the Discourse of Rights In R. Cook (Ed.), *The Human Rights of Women.* Philadelphia: University of Pennsylvania Press.

Cook, R. (1994). State Responsibility for Violations of Women's Human Rights. *Harvard Human Rights Journal, 7,* 125-175.

Human Rights Watch/Women's Rights Project. (1991). *Criminal Injustice: Violence Against Women in Brazil.* New York: Human Rights Watch.

Human Rights Watch/Women's Rights Project. (1995). *Neither Jobs nor Justice: State Discrimination in Russia.* New York: Human Rights Watch.

Romany, C. (1994). State Responsibility Goes Private: A Feminist Critique of the Public/Private Distinction in International Human Rights Law. In R. Cook (Ed.), *The Human Rights of Women.* Philadelphia: University of Pennsylvania Press.

Smart, C. (1989). *Feminism and the Power of the Law.* New York: Routledge.

Wright, S. (1994). Economic Rights and Social Justice: A Feminist Analysis of Some International Human Rights Conventions. *Austrailian Journal of International Law.*

Part II
Social and Economic Rights

Chapter 3
Economic and Policy Trends: Global Challenges to Women's Rights

Maureen O'Neil

Framework for Social and Economic Rights

Human rights are born of struggle. Women's social and economic rights, those rights which should permit women to move from fate to freedom, from dependency to dignity, are negotiated by individual women around the world every day in households, in workplaces, on the streets and in parliaments.

The international conventions are important in this struggle not because they embody timeless policy or legal prescriptions but because their essential message is that policies and laws should not disadvantage women. If policies and laws leave women poorer, sicker, less able than men to move about freely, then they should be changed. International agreements make it clear that these issues of fairness are not just the dreams of some feminists but have been agreed to, at some level, by the international community. The success of the International Conference on Population and Development in Cairo is testimony to the existence of an international women's movement capable of taking action and indeed triumphing over culturally prescribed rules for women's behavior. Although progress has been slow, women are better educated today than a decade ago. Women also have more political power today both as elected officials and as members of the international women's movement which has equipped women to mobilize for the rights defined by the conventions.

Economic and social rights as defined in the international human rights instruments include a mixture of standards for developing specific laws, regulations and policy prescriptions at the national level. At the time of their negotiation, these rights were expected to reduce economic deprivation, strengthen individual dignity and result in a more equitable sharing of a nation's resources.

In 1963, three years before the adoption of the International Covenant on Economic, Social and Cultural Rights (ICESCR), the United Nations proposed a Declaration on the Elimination of All Forms of Discrimination Against Women in a General Assembly resolution. The Convention on the Elimination of All Forms of Discrimination Against Women (CEDAW) was not passed until 1979. The ICESCR and CEDAW are the two international instruments, along with the International Labor Organization (ILO) conventions, whose provisions address most directly the economic and social rights of women. Women's economic and social rights enshrined in these documents set standards for mediating women's participation in the economy and in society. The individual conventions outline the legal prerequisites and policy approaches most likely to permit girls and women to live independent lives with dignity. The actual language of the conventions reflects ideas about appropriate policy at the time of the convention's negotiation.

There has been incredible change in our world since then. I will argue that it is the spirit which underlies the conventions that is more important than particular policy prescriptions. The spirit of the conventions is that public policy should work for women, not against them. The benchmark for judging public policy then becomes as simple as that. The simplicity of the idea requires that we rethink most aspects of public and private action. We should not be discouraged that the transformation has taken longer than the two decades between Mexico City and Beijing.

In addition, the language of these conventions presupposed an active role by the state in the economy. This is no longer the view of most governments today. Against a backdrop of significant changes in the functioning of national governments and of the world economy, women seeking change have to confront these realities and begin the arduous task of imposing their experience on ideas about how economies and states should function.

Key Social and Economic Conventions

The ICESCR, which came into force in 1976, states that women and men have the right to work, that is "freely chosen and accepted." The Convention lays down the benchmark for judging economic policy by demanding that states ensure "policies which will achieve steady economic, social and cultural development; policies which will produce full and productive employment under conditions safeguarding fundamental political and economic freedoms to individuals." The norms for labor market policies are clear as well, enshrining "just and favorable conditions of work." This includes technical and vocational training, equal pay for women and men, a "family wage," that is, enough money for wage earners to support their families, safe and healthy work places, limitations on working hours, paid vacations and the right to seniority. Rights to social security and social insurance, care for dependent children, maternity benefits, food, clothing, shelter, health care and education are also guaranteed.

The drafters of the convention recognized that these changes to policies and laws would not come automatically. Economic interests and the political interests which support them are often served by preventing increases in wages, safe working conditions, or equal pay for women, particularly when the state is autocratic. That is why it was important to secure space to dissent without fear of intimidation or death. Trade union rights and the right to associate freely are protected in this convention. However, unlike the International Covenant on Civil and Political Rights which binds states not to infringe on the rights granted, the ICESCR only requires states to take steps "to the maximum of available resources" (Commonwealth Human Rights Initiative, 1991).

In 1979 CEDAW was adopted by the UN General Assembly. CEDAW is the most comprehensive code of women's rights in international law with its focus overwhelmingly on social and economic rights. This convention builds a solid foundation for women to achieve personal dignity and independence. CEDAW requires that women's legal protection be identical to that of men in civil matters, the administration of property, court procedures and tribunals. CEDAW also guarantees women the freedom to choose where they live, when they move, whether to marry, whether to have children and guarantees their continuing right to those children.

CEDAW also sets standards for judging public policy and protects political space for women to carry on the struggle to obtain their right to enjoy such standards. According to the Convention, women have a right to be in public life as officials or elected representatives, or as diplomats or employees of international organizations and nongovernmental organizations (NGOs). As Kathleen Mahoney (in press) writes, "The concept of equality in CEDAW clearly extends beyond specific inequalities." This is evident in those provisions which require fully shared responsibility for child rearing by men and women. The link is explicitly drawn between women's participation in public life and the availability of child care as well as protection for the right to have children and income replacement for maternity. CEDAW states unequivocally that women have the right to reproductive choice. However, CEDAW does not specify a time-table to spur states to action. It is the lack of a specific timetable for action, combined with the fact that many states have weakened their ratification of CEDAW by attaching reservations, which is its greatest weakness.

World Economic Trends: Challenges for the Conventions

The provisions of the conventions imply that governments will intervene in the market to create fairer social conditions. By defini-tion, the state that is willing to fulfill its obligations under ICESCR and CEDAW is not completely trusting of the invisible hand. Quite the contrary. The imaginary state in the minds of the drafters is con-cerned about providing better social protection through social secu-rity programs, health and safety regulations, day care centers and accessible health care. In ratifying the ICESCR, a state agrees to be judged internationally on whether living standards are continuously improving. The state even agrees to educate men to become better fathers. This state is committed to clearing away barriers to people who want to make their political views known. In fact, it will en-courage opposition to the traditional supporters of the status quo be-cause it has committed itself to reduce the stranglehold that culture has on women. This truly would be an amazing state.

The covenants spell out what governments ought to do, both in terms of policies and laws, to ensure that women move toward greater autonomy and control over their lives, but these changes are extremely difficult to obtain. For one thing, states often are unwill-ing to act because they simply don't agree with using their power to improve women's lives. For another, the transformation of the world economy as a result of new technology has changed the nature and location of jobs and has facilitated the unimpeded flow of investment. This combination of changed ideas about the scope of the state's re-sponsibility to its citizens, together with the increased capacity of pri-vate business to organize itself and operate on a world scale, has limited a state's ability to act and has increased the difficulties facing women in achieving the goals set forth in the conventions. States sign these agreements in response to pressure from domestic women's groups as well as out of concern for their international reputation. Both the ideology and the economy look much different today than when negotiators hammered out the terms of the conventions. By contrast, the present nation-state, self-weakened, has given up considerable ground to private actors in the world economy. All but stateless, corporations—for the moment—have the upper hand with governments. National governments are engaged in a competitive struggle to attract increasingly mobile capital. At the same time, companies are shifting jobs from country to country in response to more favorable wage rates and more flexible regulatory frameworks. In countries carrying a high public debt load, there is a struggle to cut back public expenditures so that the choosy international investors, whom these economies need, do not lose confidence in them.

Governments in both developed and developing countries need investment to create jobs and to maintain existing social programs. Organization for Economic Co-operation and Development (OECD) countries, struggling with generally low growth rates and high unemployment, are in no mood to expand equality enhancing measures that require public investment. Developing countries that are successfully manufacturing goods for the export market are capitalizing on relatively lower wage rates and lower labor standards. At least in the short term, raising women's wages and safeguarding their health and safety through more regulation does not seem to coincide with overall government strategy. Nonetheless, some women in rapidly growing economies will see their economic and social situation improve particularly if they are working in export sectors. However, women working in these sectors may have short-lived benefits. If they organize successfully to raise their wages and improve working conditions, investors can move easily to a country with even lower wage rates and labor standards.

Policy Responses to World Economic Trends

For those countries whose lack of economic success drove them into the arms of the International Monetary Fund (IMF) and the World Bank stabilization and adjustment programs, the last 15 years have been fraught with well-documented difficulties. The best intentions of a ratifying government have been diverted to the management of public finances via economic policies that too often do not favor redistribution, new standards to protect economic rights, or improvements in housing, health and education. Rather, there has been a slide in the opposite direction.

In considering women's economic and social rights, close attention must be paid to trends in the world economy and the policy responses of particular national governments to those trends. Work everywhere is highly gender-specific. As employment shifts from one sector of the economy to another, men and women will be affected differently. The current situation has been well described in a recent ILO paper from which the following observations are drawn (International Institute for Labour Studies, 1994).

The first trend is that the formal sector (and hence jobs in that sector) will continue to change in response to the exigencies of the global recession, of international competition, of trade liberalization and, in some of the developed parts of the world, the use of advanced technology. The "economies in transition," including the states which comprised the former Soviet Union and Eastern Europe, are phasing out of heavy industry and are rebuilding or reorienting to light industry. Women in those countries make up a large portion of the growing unemployed. In other economies in transition, including China, there is a loss of enthusiasm for women workers because benefits such as maternity and child care must be provided by the employer. (This does not seem to be true of Vietnam.) In developing countries now attracting foreign direct investment, women may get the majority of jobs, although the numbers are small and long-term viability uncertain. Women are increasingly competing in the overcrowded and precarious informal sector.

Within the formal sector, women have predominated in both the service and the public sectors. Now the rationalization of the service sector through the use of computers is beginning. Developed country jobs in this sector will move off shore or be absorbed by new technology. In Central and Eastern Europe, it appears that training is not gender-neutral and women risk being segregated or segregating themselves into exactly the lower level clerical and service jobs that seem to be disappearing in the western market economies. In developed and developing countries, women have been affected by cutbacks in the public sector, both as workers and as consumers of services for their children and themselves. In developing countries women frequently are working longer hours to pay for previously subsidized services. Sometimes services simply disappear, as with child care and maternity protection in Central and Eastern Europe. In developed countries, women have been seriously affected by management restructuring within a corporate ethos that less and less considers affirmative action a part of good corporate behavior.

The second trend is the emergence of a dynamic intermediate sector identified as a high growth area where women may have opportunities. This sector, based on high technology, is serving the needs of a myriad of small, highly-skilled service enterprises in areas such as accounting, insurance, legal and financial consultancy and marketing and computer analysis, and may hold out hope for well-educated women who, in less turbulent times, might have settled into a large corporation, parastatal or government ministry. The rising numbers of women starting their own businesses suggests this is already happening. As the ILO paper notes, "The greatest challenge may lie not in the acquisition of technical skills but in the acquisition of the necessary entrepreneurial skills" (International Institute for Labour Studies, 1994).

The third major trend is the dramatic growth of the informal sector and the blurring of lines between it and the formal sector with "deregulation, casualization and the growth of subcontracting, outsourcing, homebased work and self-employment in both developed and developing countries." The first challenge is to find ways of making women's precarious lives in this sector easier, whether through micro-coops or organizations like the Self-Employed Women's Association (SEWA) of India. The second challenge identified by the ILO is to find a way of legislating social protection for those workers. However, since real economic interests are served by not protecting workers, it will require considerable pressure and ingenuity to define standards, modes and agents of implementation. Women will have to elect governments who actually want to see these protections in place.

The fourth trend is the continuing interest in workforces that are "flexible" and workplaces not encumbered by regulation. On the positive side is the quest for the best educational tools for workers in this frighteningly unprotected marketplace. It is always good to enhance an individual's capacities. Unfortunately, flexibility has usually meant rolling back legally established frameworks of rules and collective agreements:

> The great majority of workers with non-standard contracts (such as part-time workers, temporary and casual workers, home-based workers and the growing "self-employed") are women and while such forms of work may facilitate their family responsibilities, they do not carry the same benefits, legal protection, career prospects and training opportunities as full-time jobs and work to the long-term disadvantage of many women workers. (International Institute for Labor Studies, 1994, p. 47)

These are issues of particular attention to urban women, whether in developed or developing countries.

Women in rural areas, particularly in the developing countries and Central and Eastern Europe, are affected by the impact of the macro-changes on agricultural production. It, too, is being transformed, both by the shifts in economic policy away from a heavy state presence and by technological developments. The latter have been of greater benefit to larger farms. Women have suffered because they still do not have sufficient land rights, a particular problem when land they have been working is privatized in the name of their husband. Wives are left with the sole responsibility for children as husbands seek work elsewhere. Survival through small-scale trading and production is frequently no more than hand-to-mouth.

These trends are forcing governments to evaluate labor market policies and, where they exist, approaches to social security. That is why the approaches implicit in the provisions of the conventions may have to be rethought. They were the tools to achieve greater equality when most jobs in the developed countries were in one formal sector; most jobs in the former Soviet Union were in the state sector; and, in some developing countries, the public sector, too, was dominant. Labor market and social security policies are the dominant policy lever in the convention. Their application will be challenged by these trends.

Trends in Social Security: The Undermining of CEDAW and ICESCR

The ICESCR and CEDAW are replete with examples of social programs that should be guaranteed, including the right to employment at a fair wage, which is, after all, the best protection against poverty. Although it is not really possible for government to legislate jobs for all, it is feasible for government to assess the effectiveness of its national and international economic policies by whether high levels of unemployment persist. In ratifying the ICESCR, states imposed on themselves the obligation to ensure that economic policies produce full and productive employment.

Both ICESCR and CEDAW refer to the importance of maternity benefits and to the right to an adequate standard of living. CEDAW refers explicitly to the right to social security, particularly in the cases of retirement, unemployment, sickness, invalidity and old age and incapacity to work, as well as the right to paid leave. It also encourages states to provide social services to enable parents to combine family obligations with work responsibilities and participation in public life, particularly through the establishment of child care centers.

Social security programs are now under threat in developed countries and are barely present in developing countries. The unsettling and frequently destructive impact of current economic trends has resulted in a variety of schemes intended to help the poorest population. Initially, these safety nets were not meant to alleviate poverty. Rather they were to prevent further immiseration as a result of the "short-term" dislocation of adjustment programs. The clear expectation was that these programs would be unnecessary after adjustment had taken place. Now the social programs are more likely to be seen as semi-permanent policy shifts. Too often they are collections of projects with the emphasis on visibility to increase the political saleability of adjustment. In developed countries social security includes social assistance ("welfare"), unemployment insurance, children's benefits, old age pensions, school loans and grants. In developing countries, however, there has been insufficient attention to the creation of safety nets.

There are also questions about the applicability of developed country models of social security in poor countries. Valentine Moghadam (1993) addresses these issues in her paper, *Social Protection and Women Workers in South Asia*. She writes:

> Social security systems in developing countries cover only a small part of the economically active population, and even a smaller part of the female economically active population because most women are not engaged in regular formal sector employment and, therefore, are not beneficiaries of social insurance. Where voluntary insurance is available, non-wage earners, including the vast majority of women, simply do not have the means to finance the cost of their social protection. The necessary funding, therefore, would be forthcoming only if there were a strong sentiment of national solidarity or if governments reorganized their priorities to generate employment and thereby expand the tax-base or to reallocate expenditure from, say, the military sector or high interest debt repayments, toward social insurance (p. 44).

If the developed-country model of social security is not transferable, what then? It has been suggested that in poor countries, the idea of appropriate social security should move from the current "protection" model—protection from medical bills, from unemployment, from loss of income due to old age— to "promotion" of programs to reduce deprivation and improve health (Burgess & Stern, 1991).

Access to Socal and Economic rights

Evidence from the United Nations Research Institute for Social Development's (UNRISD) studies on structural adjustment point to male bias in the schemes (Vivian, 1995). Although women may benefit from some components such as nutrition interventions, they are less likely than men to find work through the employment programs. Jessica Vivian (1995) has surveyed the literature and draws on the UNRISD work. For example, in Bolivia, 99 percent of those employed by the social fund were men. In Honduras, 75 percent of the jobs created went to men. In India, only 16 percent of jobs in India's rural employment program went to women. In Mexico, although a micro-enterprise development component of adjustment that targets women is included in the safety net program, few women's projects are actually funded. The situation is similar in Zimbabwe where out of a sample of 30 small enterprise development projects that had reached the funding stage, only one came from a woman. In Ghana, only one percent of the disbursed funds was earmarked for women's projects. Beyond that, no attempt was made to reach women and no data on gender were collected.

Buvinic (1993) argues that this male bias is neither accidental nor incidental, but is built into the structure of safety net schemes: participatory or "demand driven" social investment funds tend to provide employment to men and social assistance to women. They do not reach women with employment because they have no explicit gender policy and because they depend on executing agencies to carry out the projects. These agencies are generally much better equipped to provide relief than to challenge traditional gender roles. In addition, the political function of safety net programs increases the likelihood that the standard assumptions about the nature of the household as being a cooperative unit with a central male breadwinner will be made. Because of their basically populist orientation, safety net programs are likely to assert their commitment to uphold traditional "family values" (Midr, 1992; Buvinic, 1993).

As these examples show, in most developing countries there is a considerable distance to go in reasserting social expenditure as a priority. As the United Nations Development Programme (UNDP) Human Development Report has shown, since 1990 there really are no good excuses, even in poor countries, for avoiding budget restructuring in this direction. Often the resources can come from excessive military spending. In developed countries, adjustments must ensure that workers in the emerging sectors are protected. This requires thinking and restructuring of social security programs. The UN conventions were developed 20 years ago with developed country models very much in mind. As women push for more social spending to meet their needs, we can expect different program emphases in different countries. However, whatever form these programs take, they must be tailored to the needs of the poorest women and be consistent with the current economic trends in the particular country.

Strategies for Change

Ideas about the role and scope of governments in relation to the economy have shifted substantially since the covenants guaranteeing economic and social rights have come into force. Technology has created new opportunities for the global production of goods and services and the sharing of information. Public policy has downplayed, if not outright rejected, the central tenets of the welfare state. At the very least policy experts deem it unaffordable. At the same time, there is a worldwide call to respect democracy and human rights including women's rights. In some unhappy regions cultural and religious xenophobia vitiates those hopes.

There is an inscription on a statue of Kwame Nkruma in Accra which reads, "Seek ye first the political kingdom, and all things shall be added onto it." Women are making very slow progress in entering this political kingdom with power. They are seriously under represented in legislatures and at cabinet tables. The Nordic countries are the shining exception to this practically universal rule. In most countries women also are under represented at senior levels of the administration. National machineries, the agencies created to focus the policy apparatus of the state on equality issues, are frequently compromised by insufficient authority and resources. While some countries have advanced women's rights without women's strong presence in government, women are most likely to enjoy social and economic rights in the Nordic countries where there has been consistently high investment in social programs within the context of a market economy. The durable presence of women in politics there serves to reinforce the legitimacy of the continual examination of policies to reduce inequalities and change social relations.

The overthrow of authoritarian regimes has not increased the presence of women in government. It did not happen in Latin America nor in the states of the former Soviet Union. In some cases, even the validity of women's struggle has been called into question. The language of equality reverberated too closely with the nostrums of the old regimes in Eastern Europe. In countries like Poland where the Roman Catholic church was such a strong force in the collapse of the Communist regime, the church has become the enemy of women seeking their rights. However, more political space means more room to raise the issues crucial to women's social and economic equality, even if this means fighting for rights that previously had been established.

At the national level, political action is the only way in which economic and social rights are translated into laws, policies and programs. Engaging in political action is dangerous business in many countries. It would be difficult, if not impossible, in those states which do not respect the provisions in the International Covenant on Civil and Political Rights. This convention describes the protections required to create space for the political debate which is a necessary prelude to change. These include protection from arbitrary arrest, the requirement of proper court procedures, freedom of speech, the right to assemble peacefully, to take part in public affairs, to vote, and to be elected. It also will be hard to make headway if courts are not independent and there is no way to make the ubiquitous equality provisions of constitutions come to life.

There is considerable interaction between strategies for change nationally and internationally. States sign these agreements in response to pressure from domestic women's groups as well as out of concern for their international reputation. The agreements then provide ammunition for domestic women's groups which aim to hold those same governments accountable for their commitments.

The Interaction of Scholarship and Activism

National movements to achieve women's social and economic equality have profited from the rigorous critique by feminist scholars of the law and how it is applied to women. That scholarship is international. Country by country, activists transformed the ideas to nourish national strategies. The sharing of ideas and approaches are essential to change even though tactics will differ from country to country. An example of this is the success in moving issues of violence against women higher on both the national and international agendas. It is important to remember that at international tables 15 years ago, there was virtually no recognition of its primacy in women's lives.

Over the years women have lobbied for a familiar set of programs to increase their economic bargaining power. This lobbying agenda was directly reflected in the provisions of the conventions. However, the current mismatch between these provisions, government policy orientations and trends in the world economy have precipitated fundamental questioning of the principles of economics by the growing number of feminist economists. This is reminiscent of the critique women brought to law as they moved into that discipline. Their work will shape the future strategies to attain economic and social rights for women.

The International Covenant on Economic, Social and Cultural Rights commits ratifying states to continuous economic progress and reduction of poverty for women and men. Holding states to their commitments requires good research to show that the policies now followed are not producing these results for women. Understanding how different macroeconomic choices affect women is still in its infancy. The relevant questions were not even posed until feminist economists with the desire for change emerged. As Diane Elson (1994) writes:

> Feminist critical economics argues that the operation of economic reform at micro- meso- and macro- levels is male-biased, serving to perpetuate women's relative disadvantage, even though the forms of that disadvantage vary between different groups of women and are disrupted and changed in the course of policy reform. Most economic theory, whether orthodox or critical, is also male-biased, even though it appears to be gender-neutral.

The North-South Institute organized an Expert Group Meeting to propose ways in which this issue of uncovering male bias generally considered gender- neutral could be reflected in documents for Beijing. As Diane Elson (1994) said then, "We need a two-pronged strategy where we think both in terms of access to and transformation of the productive structures." Elson spoke about the "care economy" (usually the domain of women either at home or at work) and the "commodity economy" (the sector where most goods and services are produced). The narrow focus of the private sector does not see the externalities that are involved in the care economy. The family, where most caring is done, needs transformation too. "If women continue to have the major responsibility in the care economy, they are never going to be able to compete on equal terms with men in the commodity economy" (Elson, 1994).

The uncovering and explaining of male bias in economic policy may seem arcane in the face of women's poverty. The feminist critique of issues of criminal justice was "domesticated" by activists with very particular injustices before them. Soon it will be possible to do the same with issues of economic policy. Our understanding of the economy and government's role in relation to the market have shifted considerably in the last 30 years and will continue to do so. After all, Milton Friedman, one of the architects of neo-classical economics, must have felt shut out of policy circles in the 1960s.

Women aren't waiting for theories to be straightened out as the struggles of trade unionists demonstrate. However, as the formal economy is eroded, there are new approaches. The Self Employed Women's Association (SEWA) of India is an excellent example (Kerr, in press) of women in the informal sector gaining some control over the conditions in which they live and work. In the informal sector, casual workers will have no voice unless they organize. SEWA has a membership of more than 30,000, most of them illiterate, poor women whose income is derived from petty trading, homework or selling their service labor. According to Jhabvala (1993), SEWA's goals are to:

> increase income; provide assets; provide security of work; provide access to the social security services of health, child care and housing and access to developmental services such as training, communications and banking; build solidarity and cooperation among workers; strengthen democracy; bring the self-employed women into the mainstream of national life; and be equal partners and equal beneficiaries in the process of economic development (p. 130).

According to Rowbotham and Miller (1993), SEWA has achieved so much where the mainstream, male-dominated trade unions could not because:

1. it has been able to make the hidden workers of the industrial sector visible to the national and international policy makers;
2. with a female membership it has been able to address women's specific needs, such as child care;
3. as both a trade union and a cooperative it can lobby government and at the same time receive funds; and
4. it can mobilize casual workers who are not accustomed to organization [and who] often become disillusioned when a union fails to accomplish dramatic change.

The example of SEWA reinforces the theme running through this chapter; that rights are established through struggle, usually one issue at a time.

Conclusions

The provisions of the ICESCR and CEDAW describe women's economic and social rights. Sometimes these can be protected by laws. However, the overall approach of government economic policy and the priorities for public spending determine the shares of the national budget devoted to the social sector, to health (including women's reproductive health), to education, to maternity benefits and to child care. The extent to which government supports a strong regulatory framework to ensure equal pay or healthy and safe working conditions is also key. Public policy both acts on and is influenced by trends in the world economy. In democracies it is ultimately influenced by voters, by women's ability to mobilize public opinion in favor of their issues.

Women can take no institution of society for granted. Gradually all institutions must change, from the bedroom to the courtroom, from the classroom to parliament, from the factory floor to the cathedral and the mosque so that women win economic and social rights. The ICESCR together with CEDAW make clear that international principles of justice are offended if the movement to transform women's lives is delayed, ambushed or stopped.

References

Burgess, R., & Stern, N. (1991). Social Security in Developing Countries: What, Why, Who and How? In E. Ahmad (Ed.), *Social Security in Developing Countries*. Oxford: Clarendon Press.

Buvinic, M. (1993). The Feminization of Poverty? Research and Policy Needs. In *Poverty: New Approaches to Analysis and Policy*. Symposium conducted at the International Institute for Labour Studies, Geneva.

Commonwealth Human Rights Initiative. (1991). *Put Our World to Rights*. London: Author.

Elson, D. (1994). Micro, Meso, Macro: Gender and Economic Analysis in the Context of Policy Reform. In I. Bakker (Ed.), *The Strategic Silence: Gender and Economic Policy* (p. 38). London: Zed Books.

International Institute for Labor Studies. (1994). Women Workers in a Changing Global Environment: Framework for Discussion. *International Forum on Equality for Women in the World of Work: Challenges for the Future*. Geneva: Author.

Jhabvala, R. (1993). Self-Employed Women's Association: Organizing Women by Struggle and Development. In S. Rowbotham & S. Miller (Eds.), *Dignity and Daily Bread: New Forms of Economic Organizing Among Poor Women in the Third World and the First*. London: Routledge.

Kerr, J. (in press). Transnational Resistance: Strategies to Alleviate the Impacts of Restructuring on Women. In *Changing Spaces: Gender and State Responses to Restructuring in Canada*. Toronto: University of Toronto.

Mahoney, K. (in press). *International Strategies to Implement Equality Rights for Women: Overcoming Gender Bias in the Courts*. Philadelphia: University of Pennsylvania Press.

Midr, G. (1992). Bread or Solidarity? Argentine Social Policies, 1983-1990. *Journal of Latin American Studies, 24*, 343-373.

Moghadam, V. M. (1993). *Social Protection and Women Workers in South Asia*. Helsinki: WIDER.

Rowbotham, S., & Miller, S. (Eds.). (1993). *Dignity and Daily Bread: New Forms of Economic Organizing Among Poor Women in the Third World and the First*. London: Routledge.

United Nations Centre for Human Rights and United Nations Institute for Training and Research. (1991). The Convention on the Elimination of All Forms of Discrimination Against Women. In *Manual on Human Rights Reporting Under Six Major International Human Rights Instruments* (pp. 153-176). New York: United Nations.

Vivian, J. (1995). Social Safety Nets and Adjustment in Developing Countries. In U. Kirdan & L. Silk (Eds.), *People: From Impoverishment to Empowerment* (p. 319). New York: New York University Press.

Women and Global Economic Restructuring: Towards Solutions. (1994). In J. Kerr (Ed.), *Expert Group Meeting on Women and Global Economic Restructuring: Final Report* (pp. 7-11). Ottawa: The North-South Institute.

Chapter 4
Women's Social and Economic Rights: A Case for Real Rights

Lucie Lamarche

Social and Economic Rights and the ILO

Too often it is forgotten that social and economic rights are a century old in international law, at least with respect to some labor rights. The International Labour Organisation (ILO) was created in 1919, but the practice of states enacting conventions concerning labor and work conditions began in 1905. The context in which the ILO was created is important to analyzing and defining women's social and economic rights. The ILO was established in response to the objective living conditions of new industrial workers and to the political pressures of the socialist movement and pioneering sociologists. The creation of a level playing field with regard to standards designed to improve workers' living conditions was one of the key objectives of the ILO. The concern with improving the quality of life for workers was linked to the issue of fair trade practices by some industrialists who argued that competing industrial states must protect themselves from unfair production costs based on low or non-existent labor standards.

In the early 1900s, the definition of both work and workers was then specific to the newly industrialized European context. The worker was a male industrial laborer responsible for supporting his wife and children. The ILO, reflecting the traditional values of the larger culture, saw its role as one of shielding women from the work place, thereby allowing women to assume their primary role as stay-at-home mothers. In the view of the ILO, women were drawn into the labor market because of the inadequate wage structure for men. The appropriate place for women, however, still was considered to be in the home. The first social security standards established in the relevant ILO conventions reflected a traditional gender bias in workers' rights norms.

The first generation of labor rights, reflecting new developments in domestic labor law, institutionalized a three-party labor contract involving the state, the employer and the worker. From the start, the state was seen as an active and responsible player with regard to social and economic rights. The first generation of international labor rights established state protection for workers in four areas: the conditions of work (which included reasonable limits on working hours and a day off each week), social security, protection of income and prohibition of forced labor. This last category was a response to the strained North-South relations that were a legacy of the colonial era.

The states, through the introduction of social and economic human rights into international law, subjected themselves to some form of international control. First, according to the ILO Constitution, it is the obligation of a state member to report on the reasons why a convention adopted by the International Labor Conference has not been ratified. Second, it is the obligation of a ratifying state to report on the means of implementation of a convention. Only ILO Conventions (98) and (87), which guarantee the freedom of association and the right to bargain collectively, use a distinct form of international control. This modest form of international control where states are governed through reporting obligations is today still the prevalent mode of control of the ILO conventions.

For the most part, these first generation norms were to be implemented through the adoption of domestic legislation. The legislation was to be designed to prohibit certain categories of persons (such as children) from entering the work place or to regulate the conditions of the work setting on behalf of workers.

The group of states that created the ILO made it relatively easy for its first conventions to be ratified and implemented (with the exception of social security conventions that were never extensively ratified). Until the post-World War II period, ILO conventions concerned mainly one type of work (industrial) and one type of worker (the male industrial worker) as a framework for normative action.

The Post-War East-West Compromise and the Welfare State

In 1944, the ILO adopted the Philadelphia Declaration and restructured itself as a specialized institution in the new framework of the United Nations. Although the Declaration is not an instrument of normative content, it changed the ILO mission in a significant way.

The Philadelphia Declaration broadened the mission of the ILO to include the protection of all workers, not just industrial workers. Also, while the ILO Constitution never addressed the right to work, the Philadelphia Declaration did. It declared that ILO member states shall adopt policies dedicated (1) to work that respects labor standards; and (2) to the promotion of full employment. Politically speaking, the Declaration created a new balance between every person's obligation to work and every person's right to work which relied heavily on state commitment. Legally speaking, the Declaration opened the way for what we now call programmatic entitlements or claim rights. In other words, the Declaration created rights to something, such as the right to work, to health or to education.

In 1962, the Convention (122) on employment policy was adopted. This Convention originally was designed for underdeveloped countries, but it evolved until the final draft had universal application. The Convention (122) clearly defines every person's right to work. This right includes the positive obligation of a state to take active measures dedicated to the attainment of full employment. Many scholars and states took issue with the programmatic right to work because it had been adopted primarily as a result of pressure from Eastern bloc states. Western critics of Convention (122) argued that its provision for a right to work reflected and adopted socialist political and economic structures. Some critics argued that there could not be a legal right to work because it would be too contextual and flexible to be universally implemented.

The debate over an international and universal right to work has further significance. A few years after the adoption of the Philadelphia Declaration, the Universal Declaration on Human Rights was adopted in 1948. It is a typical East-West compromise. The Universal Declaration is legally considered a body of customary, universal human rights to be respected by every country. The idea that it is universal means that every country, whether or not it has ratified the international treaty, must respect and defend the rights contained in the Declaration. The Declaration contains many programmatic rights including the right to education, to health and to work. However, because the level of precision granted to the entitlements found in the Universal Declaration is not exhaustive, the entire debate on programmatic rights is left open.

In 1966, the Universal Declaration was split into two covenants or treaties: the International Covenant on Civil and Political Rights

(ICCPR) and the International Covenant on Economic, Social and Cultural Rights (ICESCR). Although these two covenants are considered still to constitute an "International Bill of Rights," many states have only ratified and agreed to abide by the obligations of the ICCPR while the ICESCR has remained under-ratified and its legal mandates considered optional. Generally, states in the West believed that programmatic rights such as the right to work, which were codified in the ICESCR, referred only to rights of people in Eastern bloc states.[5]

In fact, it was on political, rather than legal grounds, that the states split the original Universal Declaration of Human Rights into two covenants. Neither the Western nor the Eastern bloc was willing to put the domestic implementation of social and economic human rights under international surveillance. The Western bloc contended that social and economic rights were not universal rights but could be granted only through ratification as well as moral commitment by the states. The eastern bloc deeply resisted a breach of the principle of national sovereignty and opposed any international control of rights.

Therefore, whereas a consensus rapidly developed around the idea of an Optional Protocol for the enforcement of civil and political rights, this was not the case for the ICESCR. States limited their commitment to a procedure of reporting on progress of implementation. A review of the preparatory work during the last drafting period of the covenants demonstrates that neither the fundamental state commitment provided for in Section 2 of the ICESCR nor the control of its implementation generated serious debate.

In sum, the status of social and economic rights at the end of the 1960s was such that neither their internationalization nor their universalization through the ICESCR opened the way to serious and effective mechanisms of accountability. Implementation was not foreseeable and therefore was not the major concern of either the Experts Commission of the ILO or the Economic and Social Council

---

[5] Western critics argued that programmatic rights only applied to states that were set up to establish a universal right to work and that an international right to work was designed to accomplish standards of a growing welfare state. Many western states with substantial influence in the international political arena, such as the United States, stated that programmatic rights did not legally apply to them. Therefore, the international right to work was relegated to a lower status than civil and political rights and its meaning became vague and practically unenforceable.

(ECOSOC) of the United Nations. The major concern was to create and maintain what was called a constructive dialogue with the ratifying states. The intimate and historical relationship between the ILO and the United Nations as to social and economic rights makes it clear that the adoption of the ICESCR was much more a project for the universalization of those rights than one dedicated to create a superior level of state accountability. Again, among international labor rights, only rights of freedom of association and collective bargaining were enacted with a strong mechanism for enforcement and state accountability. The great majority of international social and economic rights only require that states take measures towards their progressive implementation.

The model of implementation reserved for most of the social and economic rights is a model where the state's role is to advocate for its people. By contrast, the model adopted by the United Nations for implementing civil and political rights positions the people against the state. This overall philosophy of rights distinguished social and economic programmatic rights (such as the right to work) as positive rights in contrast to civil and political rights (such as the right to freedom from arbitrary imprisonment) which were negative rights. However, developments in the 1970s demonstrated that the positive/negative distinction was a false distinction.

The 70s and the Emergence of the Right to Development

From its adoption in the 1960s, implementation of the ICESCR took a back seat to other issues. The crucial importance legitimately given to the right of peoples to self determination and to the construction of a person's right to development overshadowed the implementation and international control of social and economic rights. Furthermore, mainly southern states argued that other rights, including the right to development and peace, were prerequisites to an effective implementation of the first (civil and political) and second (social and economic) generations of rights. On the international political agenda, the quest for a right to development lay somewhere between the march for peoples' self-determination and the recognition of third generation rights that had yet to be codified and recognized including indigenous people's rights and other collective, "group" rights.

This is exactly where, chronologically, an important shift took place from a rights perspective to a needs perspective. At the time, the accepted international legal reasoning described above resulted in the conclusion that the implementation of the majority of rights in the ICESCR could only be enforced by "progressive implementation" standards.[2] Thus it is understandable that the immediate aspects of the recognition of a person's right to development and to the satisfaction of one's basic needs superseded interest in utilizing international legal mechanisms to advance social and economic rights.

The tension between a rights and a needs perspective produced theoretical confusion in assessing functions and international legal obligations of states. For example, the commitments by states to peace and equity are undertaken through Article 55 of the United Nations Charter, which takes a needs perspective. Their commitments to advance social and economic rights are codified in the ICESCR which takes a rights perspective.

Several questions added to the uncertainties concerning the legal standing of programmatic social and economic rights. For instance, is the right to development a person's individual right or a people's group right? What are the elements that constitute a person's right to development? How are third generation, so-called collective rights, which are interdependent with the right to development, defined? Is enforcement of these rights limited by the lower status, "progressive implementation" mechanisms of justiciability that are already in place? Unfortunately, there were not enough powerful voices to help resolve these issues on the side of the ICESCR.

It was not until 1976 that ECOSOC created a sessional working group to control the implementation of the ICESCR. The working group was bombarded with so many complaints that no serious progress was made toward implementing the ICESCR before 1985 when the Covenant Committee of Independent Experts was finally created.

At the same time, the preoccupation with development inundated the work of the ILO and created an important shift away from

---

[2] That is, the language of the ICESCR requiring that states "take all measures necessary" to implement social and economic rights was interpreted to mean that states should try their best, without much international oversight, to someday achieve the goals of the Convention. Under the interpretation that was then dominant, if states believed they did not have the resources to implement the Convention's rights, the fact that they asserted an inability to comply generally excused their inaction.

the promotion of and respect for codified labor and economic rights towards the satisfaction of basic human needs as a political target. The 1976 Declaration and Action Plan for social progress, actualized in 1979, is a clear illustration of this. Labor rights are not mentioned in the Declaration, which focuses instead on the satisfaction of basic human needs. No mechanisms of state accountability are present in the Declaration, even in nascent form. The satisfaction of human needs cannot be evaluated by reference to legal standards unless the methodology for such an evaluation is framed in terms of rights.

The absence of mechanisms of state accountability is understandable in a context where millions of people were not in a position to capture the sense and merits of the universality of human rights. But it is a fact that the North was delighted to not hear about social and economic rights for a while. As was shown above, the North profited from the opportunity to rhetorically lower social and economic human rights standards. Social and economic "rights" were then reduced to "human needs" or the even more vague and minimal "basic human needs." Some Northern countries also felt that they were above any requirement to enact, defend or comply with the normative content of international social and economic rights. However, their declining economies showed the need for globally addressing social and economic conditions. New forms of Northern poverty and exclusion from the international economy emerged around 1972. In response to global changes, Northern economic conditions continued to worsen throughout the decade.

Prior to the era of globalization, programmatic social and economic rights, and even more objective labor rights, never developed to the point that they seriously demanded state accountability. A major reason for this was their lack of justiciability, or the lack of an enforcement mechanism, but that certainly could have been developed later.

About the rights themselves, two other factors slowed progress. First, the presence of the right to development became a competing value and tensions between the rights/needs approaches hindered enforcement. Second, the institutions in this specific field of human rights collaborated with financial institutions in the field of international trade without protesting the hegemonist attitudes present in those institutions. NGOs also bear a measure of blame. NGOs kept the international human rights focus exclusively on civil and political rights for too long. As a result, the states were left alone to fundamentally restructure and transform the welfare state, which is intimately linked to social and economic rights, into the trade state as a facilitator for international business. Many states had little choice but to follow the dramatic changes in the global, essentially North-South economy. However, some of the damage of the 1970s was arguably avoidable. Generally speaking, the international community had not seriously considered a defensive strategy of social and economic rights.

The Economic, Social and Cultural Rights Committee

It was not until 1985 that the ICESCR Independent Experts' Committee got a mandate from ECOSOC to assume the monitoring of the Covenant. The committee was created in the context of the globalization of the market. This was a period marked by the emergence of international trade agreements and new policies of structural adjustments. These developments were to transform notions regarding a person's obligation to work and his or her right to decent living conditions.

The recent work of the ICESCR Experts' Committee has given a legal meaning to social and economic rights, especially to those that can be described as programmatic. The Committee's work basically resolves definitional problems of the past and demonstrates that social and economic rights are new universal rights. Because the Committee's official observations regarding the ICESCR state that its rights apply to "persons," the rights are shown to be much more than general goals to be progressively implemented by willing states. The use of the word "person" shows that social and economic rights are human rights. If they are universal human rights, then surely they must apply to women.

Trade and Social And Economic Rights

Under the modern international legal regime, women's social and economic rights will be affected by international trade issues. Human rights have always been trade-related. Examination of either the creation of the ILO or the relevant factors that led to the creation of the Bretton Woods institutions demonstrates that human rights have always been linked to trade.

In April 1994, in Marrakech, Morocco, the General Agreement on Tariffs and Trade (GATT) General Secretary Sutherland declared that the Uruguay Round (the most recent in a series of general agreements on tariffs and trade) was to be the GATT of employment. The Uruguay Round of GATT was adopted by international agreement among the world's prominent trading partners but is still in the process of national ratification, debate and implementation. The Marrakech announcement meant that employment policies could from then on be considered as trade-related and not human rights-related. Commodification of human rights in the international commercial sphere would be a profound but questionable transformation of human rights.

Under the rules of the 1994 GATT, labor rights, in order to be submitted to international control, must affect trade in a detrimental way. The consequences of this new management of human rights means (1) a redefinition of labor rights, often referred to as labor standards within commercial agreements; (2) a lowering of labor rights content and a reduction of the labor and economic rights, which from then on are recognized as the aforementioned labor standards of commercial agreements; and (3) the creation of competing spheres, one being trade-oriented and the other person-oriented.

Competing means bargaining and this is exactly the strategy adopted by the ILO at its 81st session of 1994. The director of the ILO, in discussing the role of the ILO in a new global economy, did not reject the idea that the normative mission of the ILO might move toward a soft and supportive mission in world trade. Perhaps another arm of the ILO, to be created by member states, could control the human rights dimensions of international trade or at least address the core of the existing legal standards such as freedom of association or the ban on child labor. It is not yet clear whether the ILO would then be addressing human rights or trade-related human standards.

This discourse of cooperation is alarming because it is obvious that human rights "management" or social clauses in commercial agreements implies the commodification of social and economic rights. How can we fight this move toward commodification given that the stage has already been set? It seems that human rights have now been redefined as a matter of development through a needs-based approach. The question remains whether human rights activists and southern states have inadvertently created the problem by emphasizing a needs-based theory of social and economic rights.

We should underscore the fact that the ICESCR is doing much more than affirming every person's right to the satisfaction of his or her essential needs. The ICESCR is committed to the progressive development of all social and economic rights, which, although not limited to basic rights, at least includes them. Even if we are used to living with trade-related human rights, it does not mean that those rights should no longer be related to persons and controlled as such in their own sphere. This assumes, however, that we are talking about normative contents and not mere human aspirations.

Gender Equality Perspective in Social And Economic Rights

"A woman should not be discriminated against because she is a woman ..."

The principle is so easy to state. As we review the first generation of gender-based anti-discrimination standards offered by the international law of human rights, we discover the premises on which they were based. Quite simply, it was presumed that women were in a similar social position to men and that it was sufficient to correct the gender variable to attain equality. Of course, it was accepted that some affirmative action measures were required, specifically in the fields of employment and education. The assumption was that women, with a bit of help and protection from affirmative action measures, would gain an equal footing with industrial male workers in developed countries. Put another way, all women's problems were going to be solved if we created a normative framework dedicated to bringing women into the formal work sector. Entering the sphere of formal work would, in itself, guarantee women social security by assuring decent living conditions.

This working model of equality has been misleading although it has some utility. Let us take as examples the *Zwaan-de Vries* (1987) and *Danning* (1987) decisions of the ICCPR Human Rights Committee. In those cases, the Committee concluded that it was against the equality guarantees provided by the ICCPR to deny or lower the benefits of a social security scheme to married women either because they were women or married women. How much progress can we accomplish with this classical approach to equality? To tell the truth, very little.

Women's Exclusion in the Global Economy

To understand this situation, one has to take into account what women's social and economic exclusion is all about. For sure, it is about being kept powerless at all levels: in the family, through violence, through invisible domestic work, in the informal work sector and in the formal work sector but without protection, through the absence of fertility control, and through exclusion from public processes of decision making, whether *de facto* or *de juris*. All these elements taken together preclude women from attaining equality with men. The particular configuration of oppressive circumstances varies, of course, from one group of women to another. But the basis of the oppression is the same everywhere: it is the simple fact of having been born female.

Substantive equality is about taking into account the causes and consequences of women's social exclusion. It is about naming, stopping and correcting the mechanisms of exclusion. It is not about simply integrating women into society without attention to social structures. Equality concerns structural adjustment as well as domestic production. It concerns the so-called reorganization of work in the North and a push for microenterprises as a means for women's survival in Latin America.

Some states, including Canada, have taken a principled, "substantive equality" approach in their constitution. However, in the field of social and economic rights, the Canadian norm of equality is having trouble guaranteeing more than the right to be equally poor. What occurs is that once litigation gets to the heart of public policy in social and economic matters, Canadian courts refuse to put substantive equality into practice. In socio-economic rights cases affecting Canadians, the courts have refused to apply constitutional equality principles and instead deferred to the legislature. Therefore, in the case of women, socio-economic rights are a "wall" that prevents their practical enforcement.

One major conceptual problem with the welfare state approach to equality is its incapacity to integrate the interdependence of all human rights. Equality is a norm of equity to the benefit of persons who, aside from being women, are similarly situated in the social and economic world. This highly individualistic approach to equality is certainly in accordance with the logic of civil and political rights. But it does not take into account that social and economic rights were framed by the principle of mutuality and solidarity. Unfair class differences and economic tensions were recognized and resolutions sought through social and economic rights.

Women are at the heart of new economic tensions. Twentieth century international trade is counting on women to manage poverty and the essential needs of family and community in countless ways (in the North as well as in the South). Commonly, international trade also relies upon the devaluation of women's work (in the formal and informal sectors) as a means to lower direct and indirect production costs. The structuring of a two-tiered civil society (rich and poor) is, in fact, the structuring of a many-tiered society (and differentiated by the socio-economic situation of rich and poor, male and female). Among the poor, women are adversely affected by structural changes and expected to assume new responsibilities to respond to the so-called need for structural adjustment. Cultural, religious and sexual forms of discrimination and exclusion are factors in this new restructuring of women's exclusion. The singular claim for the integrity and respect of women's civil and political rights won't do it. The principle of mutuality needs to be redefined in legal terms to ensure women's equality. We must then contribute to the process of legally shaping women's equality in a global economy.

Interdependence of Rights: a Model for Substantive Equality

The adoption of the Convention on the Elimination of All Forms of Discrimination Against Women (CEDAW) was certainly a move in the right direction. It is imperfect, however. It can even be argued that its Preamble is not clear in its objectives. But it remains a valid example and standard of substantive equality for women. Basically, CEDAW integrates the principle of the interdependence of women's rights as human rights. It gives logic to the numerous affirmations of this principle taken by the UN General Assembly. CEDAW affirms that women count and that their legal claims have valid foundations. It proposes a principled approach to equality that suggests a new reading of women's social and economic rights in the actual context. It can be summarized, from an economic perspective, by the following three affirmations: (1) women must not be adversely affected by economic change because they are women (i.e., economic decisions must not rely for social peace on women's invisible or devalued work either in the market or at home); (2) women should be protected from any manifestation of physical commodification (i.e., women are not goods that can be sold in the market through institutions of prostitution and networks which traffic in women); and (3) states have the burden of proof to demonstrate that they are effectively taking into account women's right to substantive equality in any decision affecting the enjoyment of their social and economic programmatic rights (i.e., the right to health, education and work).

CEDAW is a proper legal standard for such an interpretation. First, it recognizes that the sources of exclusion are public (the state is gendered) and private (society is gendered). Second, because CEDAW, like most of the human rights normative instruments, relies heavily on state commitment, it forces an analysis of the adverse effects that the privatization of the social sphere have on women. CEDAW requires more from the state than the attitude of a good government. It requires the government to be responsible for the achievement of women's equality.

One major dimension of CEDAW's philosophy is the need for the interdependence of all human rights including social and economic programmatic rights. Perhaps the best example of this is the recent work of the ICESCR Experts' Committee, which did not hesitate to take into account the prejudicial effects on women of some manifestations of social exclusion. In matters such as rights that can be guaranteed through not only legislation but also policy, this interdependence between CEDAW and the ICESCR is of fundamental importance. It is no coincidence that in both cases serious discussions are going on as to the need for an Optional Protocol that would guarantee a right of petition to individuals or groups of individuals.

States Parties Obligations According to the ICESCR

Let's face it. Few people want to hear nowadays about the ICESCR Experts' Committee. Furthermore, there are few voices in favor of serious efforts to frame the debate surrounding social development in terms of rights. Since the eighth session of the Committee (1993), the World Bank, for example, has declined invitations from the Committee to discuss the effects of structural adjustment policies on social rights. The UN General Secretary also seems to have forgotten about the existence of the ICESCR and its Experts' Committee when organizing the Vienna and Copenhagen Conferences. Even the Vienna Declaration is a weak model with regard to the principle of the interdependence of all human rights and social and economic rights themselves.

At its 10th session (1994), the ICESCR Experts' Committee, partly to disprove an emerging consensus that the Committee was defunct, decided to organize a General Debate. The Committee chose the theme of social security concerns as a means of protecting economic rights confronted in the context of major structural adjustments policies. Interestingly, the debate, which included the ILO, the United Nations Development Programme (UNDP) and the United Nations Research Institute on Social Development (UNRISD), focused on the question of finding the appropriate place for social and economic rights in the process of shaping human development. This question is of crucial importance because, as underlined by Committee member Bruno Simma of Germany, it is unclear whether social and economic rights are a condition or a presumed consequence of human development.

The position of the Committee is quite clear. Human rights are not negotiable. Henceforth, respect for human rights should be a fundamental condition of any structural adjustment policy or economic model. This implies that (1) state obligations are primary and states should not be forced to deal (directly or indirectly) with international agencies which neglect human rights and (2) a state cannot rely on globalization arguments to ignore the level of development of the national social and economic rights. In the same manner, and even if they are not bound by the Covenant, NGOs involved in the field of international cooperation or assistance should develop a principled approach based on preliminary guarantees with regard to social and economic rights and not one based on assumptions that the accomplishment of such rights would occur as a consequence of the NGOs' presence or assistance. This proposed approach is based on the interpretation of Section 2(1) of the ICESCR that is provided by General Observation No. 3 of the ICESCR Experts' Committee.

The General Observation No. 3 contains five pages of rich interpretation demonstrating that the language of the ICESCR mandating "progressive implementation" of social and economic rights has some teeth to it. The major directives include: (1) means for implementation of the ICESCR shall be taken immediately following the ratification of the Covenant; the lack of resources is never a good excuse for inaction, although the action will be proportionate to the available resources; (2) means include adopting appropriate legislation, including legislation to prohibit or correct discrimination; legislative intervention is often not only conceivable but highly expected; (3) means should be appropriate. The Experts' Committee, when proceeding to the implementation report submitted by a state, may not only look for the existence of means for implementation but may also examine whether the means are appropriate; often, the Committee will be in a position to conclude that adopting laws is an appropriate means but, also, that such a law will be appropriate only if a recourse is made available; and (4) the ICESCR may be implemented through means other than legislation or through legislation that sets principles that cannot so easily provide openings for individual recourses.

The state cannot deliberately cut back resources for implementing economic, social and cultural rights including, for example, the right to health or to work unless those cutbacks are justified by the need to use those resources for the implementation of other rights guaranteed by the Covenant. Progressive implementation of these rights never means that the implementation of basic or core social and economic rights can be denied. Or, in other words, the satisfaction of basic rights must be immediately implemented. A state that alleges that it cannot even implement basic rights must demonstrate to the Committee that every effort has been made to use the full resources available in order to respect that minimal and immediate obligation.

The international community, according to the general principles of the UN Charter, is bound by the ICESCR. Accordingly, it should not make, directly or indirectly, any support to the weaker states conditional to adjustment standards that are not compatible with such an interpretation. Therefore, foreign aid programs, foreign development and foreign investment must not be made either directly or indirectly conditional to any standards less than ICESCR standards.

How Women's Rights Can Transform Socio-Economic Rights

As we can see, the Committee developed, through its General Observation No. 3, a principled approach to evaluate state parties' compliance with the general obligation of the Covenant. That methodology should be enriched by the right to equality. This is the first application of the interdependence principle. Accordingly, women's social and economic rights can be said to force the state to assess the impact of laws and social policies (or the absence of needed laws and policies on women's equality). This principled methodology of social and economic rights applies to basic rights, as well as to cases in developed countries involving the dismantling of economic programs and social rights that adversely affect women. It is not only principled but universal as well.

Such an approach sets aside the old debate about the justiciability of programmatic social and economic rights. The implementation of those rights is not about defining their objective and immutable content. The sanction of denying such rights is not about damages. The maturity of social and economic rights should provide any group of persons with the ability to denounce, in a formal international forum, the adversarial effects of any related national policy. Social and economic rights also should civilize the international law of human rights. The principle of interdependence requires that a treaty body or judicial committee take into account the entire body of law relevant to the dignity of the person. It should not confine itself to the instrument that created it. Ultimately, the justiciability of programmatic social and economic rights is about forcing the state not to implement any law or policy that constitutes a reduction or a denial of any person's rights. It is about stopping the state from adjusting to globalization while forcing it to adopt or comply with the law of international social and economic rights, which includes the more positive labor rights.

This general principle is of great significance for women's right to equality. In the arena of social development, women are seen as an economic variable that international financial institutions must factor into their proposals. Any economic model of adjustment must take into account the adverse effects on women and must adjust the model to ensure protection of women's social and economic rights. This approach is not the legal standard of either CEDAW or the ICESCR. Criticisms of structural adjustments or economic strategies for change are to be addressed by an accountable state before their implementation. Structural adjustments or economic strategies are one thing. Respecting human rights and their implementation is another. Human rights should not be sacrificed to structural adjustment. The justiciability of social and economic rights is then necessary to shape the process of adjustment (in the North and the South) with respect to women's rights and, more specifically, to women's right to equality, which is a requirement for any generation of rights. We should stop considering social indicators and social development as legal standards. Methodologically, this approach to development contradicts states' commitment to economic rights. Basic rights as well as social and economic rights may vary from one country to another not only because of the available resources but also because of states failure to implement these rights, which in turn has adverse consequences for women. The ICESCR makes clear that development should occur in the context of rights. The most we can probably expect from managers of international financial institutions and others concerned with social development is a statistical calculation of the price for social peace in a world comprised of trade states. We need the multiple functions of human rights, especially the protective ones, but also the political ones, against that trade state.

The Implementation of Economic Rights: A Matter of State or of Trade Accountability?

As the generation of economic rights has emerged, the state has been assigned the role of promoting and protecting the social and economic dimensions of human dignity. Yet it is the states themselves that are opposed to any mature form of accountability in the field of economic human rights. The states want to restrict the emergence of mature economic rights that would be expressed through a right of petition at the international level. Instead the states want to meet a narrower requirement to report on their progress with regard to the implementation of social and economic rights. The legal definition of a right and the maturity of that right are not the same thing. Indeed, accountability has much more to do with its maturity than with new mechanisms dedicated to the recognition and implementation of new economic rights. Trying not to be bound by existing rights, states, within the tiny scope of their remaining sovereignty that has not been decimated already by new market rules, are actually looking for new limits and new core definitions of economic rights. States want to introduce new and limited definitions of economic rights into the commercial field to protect themselves from the consequences of the human rights field as it matures.

We believe that the implementation of economic human rights is, above all, a matter of states accountability in the socially oriented perspective of the Universal Declaration on Human Rights. Accountability mechanisms must be person oriented and not trade oriented. Consequently, we consider that the persons' struggle for state accountability in the field of economic human rights has, as a prerequisite, struggle for the rehabilitation of state sovereignty. As we are fighting for this goal, political pressure and lobbying also should be exerted on the United Nations and the ILO to define an operative means to respect the interdependence of all existing human rights. In addition, pressure should continue for the adoption of additional protocols granting persons and groups of persons a right of petition at the international level in the field of economic human rights.

Social Clauses in Trade Agreements

The idea of social clauses in commercial international agreements is not new. For example, in 1948 at the conclusion of the Bretton Woods Agreements, Cuba insisted on a trade agreement that contained language protecting social and economic rights. However, the Bretton Woods agreement failed. And similar efforts will fail in the future because social clauses are not an effective means to ensure economic human rights.

To put it simply, social clauses can be nothing other than a commodification of human rights. An accountable state is a protectionist state. And to be accountable a state must protect human and labor rights, tasks which are contrary to market rules. Controlling social dumping would not be a compatible approach in a market system. If we accept this globalization argument, we must then look for another operating principle designed for social peace.

The concept of fundamental rights has surfaced recently as a means of protecting rights in an age of globalization. But fundamental rights is a puzzling expression. Although fundamental rights have some specific consequences with regard to international law principles, the problem is that the reference to some rights as more fundamental than others creates a hierarchical organization of human rights. Furthermore, according to the general principles of international law, few rights would be really fundamental.

In addition, there is more than one perspective on fundamental human rights. The ILO itself, through its numerous working groups on labor standards, always maintained its own hierarchy that recognizes some fundamental rights, which include the interdiction of forced labor, protection against discrimination and the right to associate and bargain collectively. Establishing a hierarchy has some logic for the ILO. The ILO has to set priorities to make it clear to member states that some rights are not negotiable. Other rights are not ranked as fundamental rights. For example, the right to benefit from a national employment policy, as expressed in Convention

(122) on employment policy, never attained the importance of a fundamental right.

Currently, the recourse to fundamental rights in international commercial institutions and agreements is determined by trade customs, which historically have been oriented much more to economics than to social or human concerns. The United States and the European Community rely on the use of fundamental rights to attach some conditions to their bilateral and multilateral aid programs. The conditions, broadly defined, require a good government, which means a democratic state, albeit one designed around commerce. Matters such as wages, social security, health, education and citizenship (not solely designed through the industrial model of unionized participation or participation in free elections) are not included in the list of fundamental rights.

The wording of the North American Agreement on Labor Cooperation, otherwise full of mysteries with regard to labor cooperation, speaks for itself. In a state-to-state complaint procedure, an Arbitral Panel is *rationae materiae* limited to the following matters: occupational safety and health, child labor, minimum wage and technical labor standards in trade-related matters which have shown a persistent pattern of failure. Several caveats weaken the operative aspects of that short list. It is worth identifying two of them. First, a party can defend against complaints by demonstrating that the failure to enforce a requirement of labor law results from a bona fide decision to allocate resources to enforce other labor matters considered higher priorities. But this contradicts Article 2(1) of the ICESCR which requires states to use "the maximum of its available resources, with a view to achieving progressively the full realization of the rights recognized in the present Covenant . . . ." Second, the definition of technical labor standards, as provided in Section 49 of the North American Agreement on Labor Cooperation, states that the setting of all standards and levels with respect to minimum wages and labor protection for children and young persons are not subject to obligations under the Agreement. Each party to the Agreement sets its own standards on the general minimum wage and age limitations on child labor. There is, in effect, a large gap between the obligations set forth in some major ILO conventions and the level of commitment required by the terminology of the Agreement.

With regard to the North American Free Trade Agreement (NAFTA) side agreement on labor it can be said that (1) clauses referred to as social in NAFTA are having a negative impact on the construction and definition of economic human rights and (2) the NAFTA Labor Side Agreement is a perfect example of the commodification of economic human rights in the sense that any dispute has to be based on the allegation that a persistent pattern of failure is trade related. Although state parties seem to be satisfied with such an agreement, it is worth asking whether these new trade-related labor rights should be submitted to a more operative form of control or accountability that would provide state parties (and not persons) with guarantees of compliance.

The ILO has an answer for that. Why not create some form of secular arm of the ILO that could control the implementation of such agreements? Again, we can take the NAFTA side agreement on labor as an example of commercial trade agreements potentially weakening international labor rights. Some of the most fundamental ILO rights are not construed in the Agreement for the purpose of arbitration as technical labor standards. On one hand, it has been said many times that the NAFTA social clause is nothing more that an exploratory model for the United States in the field of international trade. On the other hand, it is also reasonable to assume that the general idea of social clauses in commercial agreements, as announced recently in the context of creating the World Trade Organization, also represents a serious departure from human rights objectives and standards. In addition, we can safely presume no international commercial institution will ever feel forced to comply with more than the new core rights guaranteed in NAFTA or any other trade agreement. The problem is much more complex as we consider women's economic rights. Social clauses in commercial agreements are commodifying economic human rights while women's economic rights are being decommodified in many circumstances. Women's input in productivity is increasingly either invisible or discounted.

Operative Aspects of Social Clauses and the Maturity of Economic Human Rights

To reiterate, we are facing a serious problem in the field of labor and economic human rights. That is, most of those rights are immature because of the states' collective wishes to preclude any serious mechanisms of accountability. However, this problem must not be confused with the rhetorical one regarding the legal meaning of such rights. After all, what is the difference, in terms of certainty, between the right to freedom of speech and the right to work? Both are flexible, submitted to limits and variable according to different constitutional contexts. Both are submitted to a principled approach regarding means of implementation which are binding on states. While good governments admit that approach with regard to the right of freedom of speech, that is not the case for economic rights. The Experts' Committee of the ICESCR established a principled approach to the implementation of social and economic rights, but it has been rejected by state members. What we are currently offered is a trade-oriented approach to economic rights, a framework which offers a soft approach to rights and that is supportive of trading states. It is as though no other possibility exists.

We need now more than ever to discover means to take advantage of the principled approach developed by the ICESCR Experts' Committee. The task is not to submit trade and cooperation agencies to a principled human rights approach designed for commercial purposes but rather to force states to respect, in a principled way, economic rights. What we need is a right to petition at the international level. We must then fight attempts by the United Nations and the ILO to transform economic human rights into trade-related economic rights, even if there is a strong temptation to focus on the operative aspects of social clauses in commercial agreements. This strategy inevitably takes for granted the need for new trade-related rights instead of reaffirming existing economic human rights.

This simple affirmation requires much more discipline from human rights activists than it would seem at first glance. So much energy has been invested recently in work dedicated to social development instead of human rights. So much work has been directed at forcing international financial institutions to take into account the prejudicial effects of structural adjustment policies and free-trade agreements on people's rights rather than directing attention to developing mechanisms that would make economic rights mature rights. We must ask ourselves if we believe in economic rights? Or are we ourselves trapped in the utopian discourse on economic rights?

Preconditions for Implementing State Accountability Mechanisms

The first precondition is rehabilitation of the state. A sovereign state is the operative concept in human rights and it must regain its stature. The globalization of the market is operating against the human rights of individuals in two major ways. First, globalization of the market tends to assume the existence of a good faith state and the state is allowed to ignore acting on the best interests of individuals. Second, globalization provides a rationalization for the state to avoid allocating resources in the people's best interests.

Women's interests are doubly neglected in the process because (1) states' limitations affect women more seriously and (2) in the process of allocating or reallocating resources, a state relies on women's invisible contribution to the family, to the cohesion of society and to social needs. The principled and flexible approach to equality for women with regard to economic rights is determined by women's capacity to blame the state for not taking their rights seriously, in the North as well as in the South.

The second precondition is acceptance of the interdependence of all human rights. It is time for the human rights community and NGOs to provide the world of human rights institutions with practical models of human rights interdependence. We are talking about a simultaneous reading of both CEDAW and ICESCR. Both CEDAW's and ICESCR's Committees have started such work. It is time now for NGOs and women's groups to adopt this dual approach in their dialogues in international events. Any infringement of women's right to physical and psychological dignity has an economic meaning in the actual context of restructuring a new global economic order. Any infringement of women's economic rights has a gendered explanation.

Gender-based discrimination and oppression as well as economic-based exclusion of women are interrelated. We should fight against the pattern of generations of rights. The most practical approach to interdependence is for women to ground their claims on the combined meaning of CEDAW and the ICESCR and to use those instruments to argue against any commercial institution or human rights institutions which fail to read CEDAW and the ICESCR jointly. Our best strategy is to depart from the Copenhagen approach to social development and to work instead for the adoption of an Optional Protocol to the ICESCR, not as a secondary target but as an immediate objective. This strategy supports a short-term commitment for a legal playing ground in the field of human rights.

Optional Protocols to CEDAW and the ICESCR

Both the Parliamentary Assembly of the European Council and the ICESCR Experts' Committee have produced recent work on the issue of a right to petition with regard to social and economic rights. It is not necessary to reiterate the legal grounds for a right to petition. Our objective is simply to draw attention to some interesting aspects of a right to petition. First, a right to petition allows the petitioner to exhaust internal remedies. The requirement that the petitioner exhaust remedies has been viewed, in certain circumstances, as an obstacle in matters related to civil and political rights. However, in the case of social and economic rights, the requirement is no obstacle with regard to rights that can be nationally implemented through policies or programs. The petitioner will need to and should engage domestic remedies. Most of the standards for creating legislation that determine such policies and programs no longer even affirm a person's right to health, education, employment, social security or social services. Accordingly, the modern state is more vulnerable than ever to such an international right of petition.

Second, neither the ICESCR Experts' Committee nor the European Council have excluded the idea that such a petition right could be available to groups of persons affected in a patterned way by national policies and programs or social and economic legislation. Thus, women as a group could take advantage of such a legal space, all the more because their claim to social and economic equality is often based on the identification of some exclusion or prejudicial effect of a government policy, program or legislation. Contrary to a constitutional right of action, which is often conditioned by the existence of legislation, this international recourse privileges the examination of programs and policies. Such an examination is governed by all human rights principles and conditioned by state obligation to take into account the exclusionary effects on groups of persons of any of its decisions or its failure to protect economic human rights.

Such a forum could provide women a means to conceptually construct, at the universal and international level, their right to social and economic equality. In the specific field of labor rights, this right of petition also would force the ILO to contribute, according to its own existing legal standards, to the meaning of women's labor rights in the actual context of decommodifying women's work. This contribution then could be used as a counterweight to the ILO's institutional strategy in the sphere of international trade. Without creating undesirable distinctions between the interests of unions and those of people, it is worth noting that a community group would have access to this right to petition. This is not the case in the ILO perspective due to a historical tripartism that reserves the persons' representation for unions.

Of course, the final issue concerns the output or result of a right to petition. Considering the weak operative guarantees offered by the social clauses approach in the field of trade and its excluding effect on persons, it seems that the primary objective should be the creation of a legal forum to define state liability with regard to social and economic rights. Ultimately, what we can expect as a result of a right to petition is a recommendation from the international community to invalidate states' decisions, programs, legislation or policies that would negatively affect people's social and economic rights.

The political impact of a human rights forum that could conclude, for example, that the allocation of resources to the military, the nuclear industry or even tax exemptions for companies denies the right to equality of women and other groups that are victims of exclusion is not negligible. Suppose that the investigation of a complaint shows that structural adjustment policies constitute an obstacle to the education or health care systems. The committee responsible for such a protocol could conclude that structural adjustment policies are affecting people's right to education or health. The finding of the international economic rights forum would, in turn, put pressure on the commercial international community. We need such a legal forum simply because not too much can be expected from domestic tribunals in this regard. Furthermore, an international right to petition in regard to social and economic rights provides a remedy that is needed to defend against international trade interests.

Conclusion

This paper is about strategizing in the actual context of women's social and economic rights. We have tried to demonstrate the need for a new focus and argumentation around the notion of social and economic human rights. For some of us, economic rights are still new rights or not yet even developed rights. The distinctions and similarities between labor rights and economic rights may still have to be noted in some cases. But surely what we are actually accepting against our will is a trade-oriented redefinition of those rights. If we can come to a common understanding of the factors influencing this development, then we can begin to draw on social and economic human rights to constitute a real and operative obstacle to the commodification of these important rights.

References:

Constitution of the International Labour Organisation. (1946). C.T.S. 48

Danning v. The Netherlands. Communication No. 180/1984, UN Doc. A/42/40 (1987).

Declaration Concerning the Aims and Purposes of the International Labour Organisation. (1946). (UN Doc. No. 62 Stat. 3485, 15 UNTS 35).

General Agreement on Tariffs and Trade. (1994). (UN Doc. No. UNTS 187).

International Labour Organisation Declaration and Action Plan for Social Progress. (1945). O.B., Vol. LX, 1977, ser. A, no. 2.

International Labour Organisation Convention 87. (1950). *Concerning Freedom of Association and Protection of the Right to Organise.* (UN Doc. No. 68 UNTS).

International Labour Organisation Convention 98. (1950). *Concerning the Application of the Principles of the Right to Organise.* (UN Doc. No. 96 UNTS).

International Labour Organisation Convention 122. (1965). (UN Doc. No. 569 UNTS).

North American Agreement on Labor Cooperation. (1993). Pub. L. No. 103-182, 107 Stat. 2057.

United Nations Charter. (1945). (UN Doc. No. 59, Stat 1031).

World Conference on Human Rights. (1993). (UN Doc. No. A/Conf. 157/DC/1 Add.1).

Zwaan-de Vries v. The Netherlands. Communication No. 182/1984, UN Doc. A/42/40 (1987).

Chapter 5
Issues in the Enforceability of Human Rights: A Caribbean Perspective

Roberta Clarke & Joan French

Introduction

Differences in the character of rights enumerated under the International Covenant of Political and Civil Rights and the International Covenant on Economic, Social and Cultural Rights have been discussed extensively. Some argue that the existence of the two covenants is only significant from the point of view of the nature of the implementation of those rights. Political and civil rights require for their enforcement only a state recognition of these rights and a corresponding commitment of noninterference by the state in so far as interference or limitation is not reasonably justifiable for the collective good. On the other hand, social and economic rights have been considered as "needs-based" rights whose realization require positive action on the part of the state in providing the conditions for access to, for example, health, housing, education, social security and employment.

Of course this dichotomy, like most, whilst useful in highlighting essential differences, is really not accurate. Many political and civil rights do require positive state action and not mere noninterference, particularly in relation to the provision of judicial, administrative and security mechanisms sufficient to give citizens remedy or redress when political or civil rights are threatened.

There has also been a significant counter debate that the classification of the two types of rights reflected in the two covenants is meaningful beyond mere differences in implementation procedures. The dual classification has allowed for the selective prioritization of state responsibility for guaranteeing citizens' access to these two categories of rights.

Why Social and Economic Rights Are Not Implemented

Philosophical or ideological concepts on the role of the state in civil society very much determine the emphasis given to state action in fulfilling obligations on social and economic rights or political rights. By way of example, reference can be drawn to the experience in the Caribbean. In countries with capitalist-oriented economies, notwithstanding a certain "welfareism" in the post-independence period, primacy has been given to the protection of civil and political rights as opposed to economic rights. On the other hand, where we see an emphasis on social and economic rights, it has been in countries with a stated and/or actual commitment to socialist provision of basic needs, for example, Cuba.

The Caribbean's history is one of denial of fundamental rights and freedoms under the slavery and colonial experiences. It is only in the 1940s that universal adult suffrage became a reality. Out of the independence movement there grew a strong sense of post-colonial governments' responsibility to correct historical social and economic inequalities in the access to basic social services, to education, housing and health care in particular. But to the extent that provision of these basic needs by the state were articulated not so much as rights, but as gifts attendant on political patronage, this paper will argue that the withdrawal of state responsibility in meeting social and economic rights has been relatively unhampered by an organized popular resistance which utilizes the language of rights and state responsibility and accountability.

The paper will therefore argue that the first impediment or variable affecting the extent to which states comply with the international norms around the provision of social and economic rights is an ideological question on the role of the state in economies which are driven by market forces.

Within the dominant ideological discourse privileging the market over economic planning, civil and political rights continue to be given much greater prominence in human rights practice. Importantly, while political rights are justiciable, social and economic rights (beyond labor rights protected by ILO conventions) tend not to be grounded in national level legislations and therefore tend to be non-justiciable. More importantly, the scale of nonsatisfaction of these rights, and indeed the reluctance even to view them as rights, as opposed to normative standards, reinforce their secondary level of importance to political and civil rights.

Other barriers impeding the realization of a wide access to social and economic rights include the structure of economies, structural adjustment programs and debt, political will and a popular consciousness of human rights.

The structure of the economy determines to some extent the level at which states can guarantee enjoyment of basic social and economic rights in the Caribbean. The economies are largely characterized by their open and independent nature. Insofar as the consumption patterns are out of balance with the patterns of production, the region has experienced increasingly severe balance of payment crises. The consequences of these crises for many countries has been a move towards entering into structural adjustment programs (SAPs) with the IMF and World Bank.

For the countries which have entered into agreements, conditionalities imposed and accepted have included a withdrawal of state responsibility for the provision of social services, including social security, health and housing.

The developments and consequences attendant upon entering into agreement with the IMF are not unique to the Caribbean. Indeed, the Special Rapporteur on Social and Economic Rights in his 1992 report draws out very clearly that structural adjustment programs advocated by the international financial institutions have had and continue to have a negative impact on the realization of these rights, and in particular rights to work, food, housing, health, education and development (Turk, 1992).

The inclusion now of "social safety nets" in the rhetoric and practice of the IMF agreements in fact only serves to highlight the marginalization of state responsibility for the realization of a broad access to social and economic rights.

Class inequalities as expressed in severe income distribution inequalities have also served historically as an impediment in the realization of social and economic rights. Again the report of the Special Rapporteur on Social and Economic Rights reveals that in countries as diverse as Jamaica, Costa Rica, Colombia, Malaysia, and Guatemala amongst others, economic systems are maintained where the richest 20% of the population possesses more than a 50% share of total household income, whilst the poorest 20% of families hovers around 4% (Turk, 1992).

The imposition of structural adjustment programs, whose primary focus is the paying off external debt, has been accompanied by a growing impoverishment of the population. As the growing unequal income distribution has also been accompanied by the resistance of the rich to the provision of social services, such provision requiring as it does progressive measures of taxation and policies leading towards income distribution.

Associated with the structural adjustment programs has been a conscious policy of states towards the privatization of social services and therefore the privatization of social and economic rights. As has been pointed out repeatedly by several authors, economic planning with its reference to meeting basic needs has now been replaced in the era of SAPs with a reliance on market forces for regulating the economy (Turk, 1992). Examples of this development include the removal of price controls and subsidies of medicines and food, privatization of key productive sectors, cutbacks in social services, imposition of user fees for previously free services, etc. The effect of this withdrawal of state responsibility has been devastating for people in countries where SAPs have been vigorously applied.

An absence of a popular appreciation of the indivisibility of human rights also constitutes a barrier to the attainment of social and economic rights. Rights are not definable solely by reference to their justiciability. Rights can be understood as those conditions which are due to a people irrespective of legal provisions. In essence then, it is contended that when people understand viscerally the positive role of the state (the state as the distillation of the social collective) in ensuring and maintaining national people-centred development, it is less easy for states to avoid meeting the normative standards expressed under the Covenants without suffering a political price. Whereas on the other hand if social services were extended in the form of patronage or a privilege, such "rights" can more easily be violated. In the developed world, although social and economic rights are largely not enshrined in legal provision, norms have developed around the necessity of state provision of social services to the extent that they cannot readily be withdrawn.

Linking Basic Needs to Rights

In the historical experience of the Caribbean the social and economic rights which most need to be recognized are the rights to employment/income, education, health, land, housing, care of infants, youth and the elderly, food and nutrition, the right to representation/recognition and to participate in the decision making about development directions and programs at all levels.

In relation to all of these social and economic rights, issues of adequacy and quality arise. It is not enough to provide employment or opportunities for earning and income if these cannot satisfy the basic needs of the employed/income earners, or if the conditions of employment/income earning violate other basic rights such as the rights to health and the rights of the child.

For example, the income of women workers in Free Trade Zones often require that they work 2-3 shifts on a regular basis in order to meet the minimum needs of their families. The absence of provisions for child care and the inability of the income of the women to cover the provision of adequate care while they themselves are occupied at the treadmill violates the rights of the child. The absence of provisions for the control of dust and lint which cause lung diseases and respiratory complications is a violation of the right to health.

The history of the Caribbean is replete with struggles around these basic rights, from the time of slavery to the present. The assertion of these rights by the rebellious practice and popular action of Caribbean people has been evident in the resistance and position to colonial laws which sought to prevent the accession these basic social and economic provisions by slaves, indentured laborers and their descendants who comprised the basic fabric of Caribbean society. In the slave period, slaves ignored colonial laws which sought to prevent them from producing and marketing their own goods for their own benefit. The slaves subverted the system where the slavemasters supplied them with provision grounds so that they would be rid of the responsibility to feed them, and used these grounds to produce, in addition, ground provisions and other agricultural commodities for marketing, from which slaves were prohibited by law. They established markets and engaged in trading even though the colonial authorities established a myriad of laws and a violent system of punishment to prevent such activity. In the post-emancipation period the ex-slaves became squatters to assert their right to land, despite the fact that this was illegal and that they were often forcibly removed or lost their lives in violent confrontations with the repressive institutions of the state. At that time, the state was more inclined to support, validate and promote the rights of large plantation holders than to promote the rights of small producers.

Similar struggles were waged in all other areas of social and economic rights. Slaves, indentured laborers and their children gradually moved by their struggle from the total denial of the right to education to the right to basic (only basic) education. They moved from a situation where their health was regarded as unimportant since they were replaceable goods easily available on the market, to a recognition that rising costs and increased rebelliousness of slaves and indentured laborers required their preservation as commodities and their pacification through the provision of minimal health care for themselves and their offspring. Similar struggles were waged in relation to housing, increased access to land, food and nutrition, representation/recognition, and recreation in accordance with a cultural heritage evolved on the basis of a variety of cultural influences, but particularly those of Africa and India.

In recent times the struggle around basic social rights has manifested itself in protest at huge land concessions to foreign companies and the concurrent neglect of the land needs of small farmers, indigenous people and other nationals. The struggle challenges state policies that reduce unemployment in the social sectors, seek to expand employment in the low-wage sector as the strategy for employment creation, harass the small trading sector which has expanded tremendously in response to the contraction in formal employment, and reduces the social protection of workers and the population in general to ensure the payment of debt to international financial institutions (IFIs).

In the area of housing, the establishment of squatter communities on available land without regard to the legal ownership of land has become a major problem for countries such as Jamaica and Trinidad where the rural/urban population drift, combined with a spiraling cost of living, inadequate income and growing levels of poverty, has forced the poor into radical solutions. In some states, the organized and spontaneous mobilization of civil society has forced a quasi-legal recognition from the state which has collaborated with nongovernmental organizations in programs to improve access to basic facilities in these communities. The struggle around the right to food has manifested itself in a variety of forms ranging from aggressive mendicancy, through praedial larceny and theft, to protests against the decline of state support for basic nutrition, such as the removal of subsidies on basic foods, cutbacks in school feeding programs and decline in nutrition standards in hospitals. In education there have been protests against declining state support, diversion of taxes designed to support education, creation of partnerships with the private sector in an attempt to stem the erosion of the quality as well as the quantity of education provided, and the placing of support to tertiary level education as an electoral issue. In the area of participation/recognition, struggles are being waged by NGOs and community-based organizations around participatory and consultative approaches to government (i.e., change from mere government to governance) and the formal recognition of the institutions of civil society as partners in decision-making. The private sector and trade unions (whose formal recognition in the Caribbean preceded that of the more recent developmental NGOs) are seeking to advance the interests of their constituencies despite a hostile, global economic and social environment prone to depriving workers of their rights and prioritizing the interests of multinational companies over those of the local population, including the local business sector, particularly the manufacturing sector.

In the area of culture, the historical marginalization of the popular culture with its Afro- and Indo-Caribbean base, is mirrored in the current period by the priority given to North American soap operas, music and interpretations of events in the public media. Even here, however, this is contested by attempts to assert the validity of Caribbean culture, particularly in the areas of music, dance and the visual arts and even sporadically in teledrama. The establishment of a Caribbean-wide television network, the Caribbean Broadcasting Union, and a radio network, the Caribbean News Agency, have contributed in significant measure to advancing this alternative trend.

Development, Debt and Structural Adjustment

The limitations on social rights in the Caribbean has been historically linked to the imposition of a model of development serving the interests of external agents rather than those of Caribbean people and especially the marginalized in Caribbean society. There have been various phases. The direct rape and plunder of physical resources and marketing of people to service that plunder were the means of operation in the slave period. This gave way in later times to national, political institutions at the same time as colonial powers maintained control of the highest levels of production and the processing of primary commodities, to whose production ex-slaves and ex-indentured laborers were for the most part confined. To the extent that these populations were involved in manufacturing and technological enterprise, it was mainly a cheap labor performing tasks whose value was determined by the dominant partner in a continuing neo-colonial relationship. These dominant partners were primarily white Europeans or North Americans, although later Asians—particularly the Japanese, Taiwanese and Koreans—came to play a significant role either as brokers for European and North American interests, or in their own right.

In the current phase, the limitations on social rights are integrally related to the structural adjustment policies of the International Monetary Fund, the World Bank and related institutions and mechanisms such as the Inter-American Development Bank and the General Agreement on Tariffs and Trade. The ideological symbol of the thrust represented by these institutions and mechanisms is the doctrine of "free trade," which on closer examination shows itself to be the proposed freedom of multinational corporations from the North to open up the commodity and labor markets of the South to their needs. Concurrently the Northern countries from which these multinationals emanate are protecting themselves by a variety of mechanisms from any "excessive" entry into their markets of goods from the South. The promise of the doctrine is "growth" which increasingly translates into the garnering of huge profit while workers are replaced by technology and populations are deprived of the basic services they need for survival and development. The situation has become so generalized that the term "jobless growth" has been coined to describe this feature of the current phase of capital accumulation.

Under structural adjustment policies the state is expected to become primarily a stimulator and promoter of private enterprise rather than a guarantor and promoter of social equity, equal opportunity, and basic social and economic rights. External financial obligations are prioritized over local needs. Social services, regarded as "non-productive," are contracted so that resources can be allocated to the stimulation of foreign private investment through infrastructural and promotional support and to the payment of the external debt,

Since this debt is due not only to internal distortions in expenditure and resource allocation, but more significantly to distortions in international trade and power relations which place southern countries, particularly ex-colonial ones, at a particular disadvantage, the debt syndrome has become endemic despite increased levels of production in primary commodity and service economics.

In this situation the doctrine of privatization of state enterprises and the withdrawal of the state from the economic sector becomes a quick-sale auction-type activity in which the more profitable state enterprises are sold to the highest bidders in a desperate short-term and short-sighted attempt to honor debt obligations and reduce debt levels.

The rescheduling of debt, which is now increasingly accepted as necessity by the IFIs, eases the immediate crisis by extending it into the future to become a millstone around the necks of future generation. As the struggle around these issues intensifies, debt equity swaps and debt cancellation are becoming more acceptable in relation to bilateral and commercial debt. However, the debt owed to multilateral agencies, which constitutes the majority of Caribbean debt, is not currently eligible for either debt equity swaps or cancellation.

The hard fact is, however, that even if all the debt were to canceled, we would still be faced with the challenge of restructuring power relations in international trade to ensure equity of opportunity and real free entry to global markets. Failing this, the distortions which led to the creation of the debt in the first place will incline towards a reconstruction of the old situation. This is especially so since the opening up of southern markets and the removal of the protection for local industry and agriculture, which are proposed under SAPs, tend towards the destruction of local economies that are unable to compete on equal terms in the open market since there is not, in fact, a "level playing field" in relation to available resources, technological expertise, educational and social infrastructure, capital access or market opportunities.

Structural adjustment policies and the millstone of debt translate at the local level into a denial of basic social and economic rights. They result in wage cutbacks, lay-offs and redundancies in the public sector and the social services in particular, cuts in government spending on social services, devaluation of local currencies and spiraling increases in the cost of living, removal of subsidies and price controls aimed at guaranteeing access to basic needs, increased interest rates, reduction in real wages, threats to the sustainability of local manufacturing and agriculture, the selling out of key areas of the economy to foreign interests and the erosion of local control, the development of a "take-it-or-leave-it" attitude by governments to people's demands, and a subjecting of local needs to the macroeconomic accounting needs of the International Monetary Fund and other international financial institutions. Jamaica's experience between independence and the early 1970s is a striking testimony to the dangers of this approach. While GDP grew at 4.4% per annum, unemployment rose from 14% in 1960 to 23% in 1972—a clear example of "jobless growth."

Under structural adjustment policies Jamaica has suffered significant decreases in per capita income and increases in the numbers and percentages of persons living in poverty. Frightening social disintegration, evident in rising rates of crime and violence (including violence against women) in Guyana and Trinidad and Tobago, provide another clear example of the negative impact of SAPS in these respects. These phenomena are present to a greater or lesser degree in all territories undergoing SAPs, whether the policies have been implemented as part of official IMF agreements or whether they have been applied by ideologically persuaded governments without formal agreements .

The manner in which SAPs are decided upon and implemented is contrary to the most fundamental tenets of democracy and popular participation and the right to representation. Governments democratically elected at the national level proceed to make agreements with IFIs which fundamentally contradict the expressed will and mandate of the people who have elected them. For example, in Jamaica in 1976 the vote for the government of Michael Manley was widely understood as a rejection of the IMF path. The government, however, had cold feet and decided that the alternate was too difficult and the IMF path was therefore inevitable, thus ignoring the mandate of the people. In Barbados, the government of Erskine Sandiford implemented wage cuts in line with IMF demand despite the massive protests of workers and their offers of alternative solutions. In Guyana a plan for ministerial consultations with, and accountability to, organizations of civil society on a regular basis was rejected by the World Bank as an example of "state centralization."

Structural adjustment policies also require the contraction of expenditure in the social services in the context of prioritizing support to private enterprise (mainly foreign) and the payment of debt. The social services themselves are increasingly privatized in the process. This has resulted in increased shortages of health personnel, increased inaccessibility of health services as clinics are closed and services "rationed," and fees are established for previously free services in public health facilities. Medicines are priced out of reach by devaluation of the local currency and taxation, while the range of medicines and services available is reduced to the point where they become unavailable to many who need them, and there is increasing dependence on private fundraising for the maintenance and improvement of equipment.

In education, primary level provisions have deteriorated as a result of these policies in several countries of the region, and the class origin of those accessing tertiary education has become skewed in favor of the upper middle and upper classes. Free education (i.e., tuition), designed to create non-stigmatized access for all who had the ability to benefit from both primary and tertiary level education, is under pressure as the cost of books, shoes, clothing and food make it more difficult for parents to keep children in school. This, of course, is true also at the tertiary level as the University of the West Indies increasingly institutes measures for cost recovery from the individual student, even in the one area where free education operated, i.e., the payment of tuition fees by some governments for their nationals. There have been declines in real per capita government recurrent expenditure on education in Jamaica, Guyana, Trinidad and Tobago and most other territories. This has resulted in declining ratios of trained teachers to total teachers at all levels in several territories. In Jamaica, pass rates for students in secondary-level examinations declined from 58.8% to 34% in English and from 36% to 13% in Mathematics between 1975 and 1988. Per capita expenditure on education declined from US$84 to US$58 and on health from US$44 to US$25 between 1986-87 and 1992-93.

There have been significant decreases in per capita income since 1970 in the major territories under structural adjustment (Jamaica, Guyana, Trinidad and Tobago), as well as exchange rate depreciation (devaluation), marked consumer price inflation (price increases), and rising unemployment rates. This has translated into growing poverty even where unemployment is reported to be decreasing. This reflects the fact that such employment as is being created is mainly of the low-wage subsistence kind and that there are high levels of income inadequacy among the working population. The situation highlights the phenomenon of the working poor and has particular disadvantages for women who operate primarily in low-income categories relative to men and also bear the main responsibility for the satisfaction of basic needs, including the care of children, young people, the elderly and the infirm.

The high levels of poverty combined with escalating prices as a result of devaluations, increased taxation, and high dependence on imported inputs for both agriculture and industry has made the access to quality nutrition more difficult.

Adequate housing and basic facilities, such as light and water, have become increasingly inaccessible both as a result of escalating prices and the decline in the state's ability to act as a broker to ensure availability to low income groups, given the insistence of the IFIs on "real market rates," private sector led development, and their opposition to subsidies.

The Justiciability of Social and Economic Rights

How can these basic social and economic rights which are currently being denied or eroded be made justiciable? What initiatives have there been in the Caribbean in this regard?

Several countries in the Caribbean have not ratified or acceded to the International Covenant on Social, Economic and Cultural Rights.[7] However, all Caribbean states have signed and ratified the Women's Convention and the Children's Convention both of which contain substantial provisions on social and economic rights in relation to women and children respectively.

Apart from acceding to the International Conventions which in essence signify the state's commitments to implement measures aimed at realizing these rights for their citizens, only very few countries can be said to have recognized the state's obligations to realize social and economic rights in their constitutions. In the Commonwealth Caribbean, constitutional recognition of social and economic entitlements, where these exist, are to be found in the preambular statements in the Constitution. The Grenada Constitution for example refers to the right to work. The Trinidad and Tobago Constitution[8] commences with the lofty affirmation that the people of that state "respect the principles of social justice and therefore believe that the operation of the economic system should result in the material

---

[7] The countries which have signed and ratified the Covenant are Barbados, Trinidad and Tobago, Guyana, Jamaica, St. Vincent and the Grenadines, Dominican Republic, Grenada and Suriname.

[8] The 1976 Constitution of Trinidad and Tobago.

resources of the community being so distributed as to subservice the common good."[3] Chapter II of the Guyanese Constitution entitled "Principles and Bases of the Political, Economic and Social System" sets out a list of social and economic rights including the right to work, free education and medical care. The Guyanese Parliament has subsequently declared that the Chapter is without binding legal consequence.

In none of these territories, therefore, are social and economic rights on their own terms justiciable except where they may also be derived from civil and political rights.

The absence of self-executing language around social and economic rights in the Caribbean Constitutions, however, does not negate the fact that in some areas states have legally accepted the citizen's entitlement to certain economic rights.

In Trinidad and Tobago for example, the question of access to land and security of tenure was addressed in the Land Tenants (Security of Tenure) Act which effectively protects the relevant tenants from eviction from lands upon which dwelling houses have been erected. Similarly, the Tenantries Freehold Purchase Act enacted in Barbados in 1980 entitled many tenants of land lots in numerous tenantries to purchase the freehold of the lot.[4] This Act makes it a term of every relevant tenancy that the tenant may make this purchase as of right and at her/his option. The enactment of this piece of legislation was very much within the context of an appreciation of the historical social and economic inequalities of plantation society in Barbados.

In some countries recognition of the state's obligations to provide a level of social security is reflected in the enactment of national insurance legislation. In Jamaica, Barbados and Trinidad and Tobago for example, the relevant legislation provides pecuniary payment for such matters as invalidity, old age and death arising from injury sustained on the job.

In the area of labor law, significant legislation has been enacted in Trinidad and Tobago[5] aimed at protecting workers from unfair dismissal and this legislation provides for the reinstatement of workers who have been dismissed by employers in circumstances that are

---

[3] Land Tenants (Security of Tenure) Act Chapter 59:54.
[4] Tenantries Freehold Purchase Act No. 53 of 1980.
[5] Industrial Relations Act, Chap. 88:01.

harsh and oppressive or not in accordance with the principles of good industrial relations practice.

Further, it can be argued in relation to the right to education that legislative provisions on compulsory schooling for children under the prescribed age which obtains in most countries in the Caribbean is also a recognition of the state's obligation to provide education at least at the primary level.

Whilst therefore it would not be accurate to speak of non-justiciability of social and economic rights in blanket terms, it is true that the fundamental problem of the lack of a legal basis for the assertion of most of the social and economic rights enunciated at the international level has meant that such efforts at their defense (as have been made) have been either through political action and mobilization of civil society or through "exemplary" challenges by individuals to actions against the social and economic rights of groups.

In the first category the current period has seen demonstrations and public protests in Jamaica, Barbados, Trinidad and Tobago and in the case of Guyana major public mobilization to end a dictatorship which was imposing a particularly destructive version of structural adjustment.

In most cases, however, broad political mobilization has been hampered by the lack of a clear common critique and a coherent alternative strategy allied to concrete policy proposals which take into account the need to move concurrently in an integrated way on the economic and social fronts.

Elements of such a strategy and some concrete proposals have begun to emerge at the sectional levels of the private sector, the trade unions and other specific constituencies. It is in the NGO sector, however, where comprehensive, integrated, holistic alternative development strategies are being most consistently developed. In this regard women's organizations such as the Caribbean Association for Feminist Research and Action and the DAWN Third World women's network have been playing a leading role. The emerging analysis advocates a holistic approach which takes into account power relations and the structure of power from household through national and regional levels, to the area of relations between states and groups of states at the international level. Here, issues of gender relations and the implications for women's political and economic power are an integral part of the analysis. The plan of action includes sensitization and corrective measures on the issue of women's unpaid labor and excessive responsibility for reproductive work at the household level and in the domestic related areas outside the home.

Political mobilization around an alternative direction is increasing as civil society asserts itself against the neglect of the state This is evident in the series of protests around the region which have come from teachers, nurses, trade unions and the public. Their uncoordinated but relatively concurrent character speaks to their response to a set of common circumstances throughout the region. However, the development of this into a movement capable of sweeping away the current order will depend on increasing clarity in its articulation, increasing coherence and holism in its analysis, and currency at the level of the public media and opinion-makers in the various territories. This will emerge from a process already afoot—a process of drawing on the analysis of experiences of current policies from the household right through to the international level, on reflecting on where we want to go as compared to where these policies are taking us, and designing and implementing the strategies that will take us in the direction in which we want to go despite the existence of contrary forces with which we must contend.

In the category of exemplary challenge by individuals to action against the social and economic rights of groups, there have been some examples in the Caribbean. A recent case in point, directly related to SAPs, was the challenge by Ms. Gladwin King of the Barbados Worker's Union to the implementation of a 7% wage cut for public sector workers by the Erskine Sandiford government which was responding to pressures from the IMF. The case illustrates the way in which such individual challenges can support and advance group and societal mobilization. While Ms. King brought the case as an individual, the society understood it as a challenge on behalf of a group and in defense of a principle which affected their rights as citizens. Though Ms. King lost the case, the matter became a major public issue which contributed to the relatively speedy downfall of the Sandiford administration and to the restoration of the 7% to the wages of public servants by the new administration which has also taken a more independent stance in relation to the IMF and in defense of the national interest.

Beyond these types of initiatives, but somewhat allied to the political mobilization approach, are the increased attempts by communities at direct representation of their interests to the state at community, local government and national levels. Examples of such action by community-based organizations (CBOs) and nongovern-mental organizations (NGOs) exist in every territory from Belize to French Guyana. In this regard, while these organizations see a role for themselves in addressing these needs, they are not inclined to ab-solve the state of the fundamental responsibility for the protection of social and economic rights. Their perspective is therefore in direct contradiction to the role prescribed for the state by the IFIs.

Proposals to Make Social & Economic Rights Legally Enforceable

The enforcement of social and economic rights (of which justicia-bility is but one mechanism) will not become a reality until and un-less this thrust of civil society achieves their enthronement in the law with adequate provisions for redress.

The 20/20 Proposal advanced by UNICEF moves in this direc-tion. It proposed the allocation of percentage norms of social expen-diture, as well as social development aid from developed to developing countries. It should not be difficult to move conceptually from this to legal provisions and the mechanisms for redress in which either individuals or groups could bring charges and seek redress.

The idea of justiciability of social and economic rights needs to gain currency, and experiments at legal entitlement need to be em-barked on as a matter of urgency. This is the clear message from the World Summit on Social Development which constituted a recogni-tion that, within the current dominant development model poverty, unemployment and social disintegration have increased at the same time as capital accumulation has become increasingly concentrated. Nothing shows more clearly the failure of the current model and the need for urgent attention to the justiciability of social and economic rights.

Such justiciability needs to be supported by data collection on the key social and economic indicators which relate to the most urgent rights to be protected. This data collection needs to be generalized, and the data disaggregated by gender, race, class, generation and ability and disability, and the indicators need to be monitored over time. In this regard the following recommendations of a Caribbean Symposium on Social Development held in March, 1995, merit attention:

> Notwithstanding present policy trends associated with the diminution of the role of the state, governments have an inescapable responsibility for

social development policy and planning, for the setting of goals and standards, and for the provision of basic services. CARICOM governments
should therefore seek to establish a set of minimum standards in these areas as a basis for negotiating with international financial institutions (IFIs)
in structural adjustment and macroeconomic programs....

In view of the crucial role of social development and the central-
ity of governments, each CARICOM government should seek to establish a system of social indicators which have equal importance and
prominence as the well-known economic indicators of GDP, inflation, trade and balance of payments. Initially five basic indicators of
social development are recommended as a matter of priority by the
Caribbean Symposium on Social Development:
1. the rate of unemployment;
2. the proportion of the population living in absolute poverty;
3. the rate of infant mortality (0-1 years) paying special attention to
   the problem of underreporting of prenatal mortality (infant
   deaths at or around the time of birth);
4. the proportion of the child population aged 0-8 years without
   adequate child care; and
5. the proportion of children leaving primary school who have attained an appropriate level of competence in literacy and numer-
   acy skills.

These indicators should be broken down by sex, social and economic group, ethnic group (where appropriate), and geographic
area, and should include qualitative assessments (e.g., for education)
as well as quantitative measurement.

Assuming the existence of adequate data bases and effective mobilization of civil society, the mechanism of redress by individuals,
households, groups, sectors and nations will have to be established
and given the authority to enforce compliance or institute sanctions
no on states which do not comply with internationally agreed
standards.

Even while calling for the justiciability of social and economic
rights, it is important that other mechanisms of enforcing or implementing measures guaranteed to realize the popular access to basic
rights be articulated and strengthened.

In the context of liberal democratic societies, the judiciary can
only be expected to extend social and economic rights if there exists
clear legislation setting out state obligations. Certainly the liberal
democratic government is characterized by an acceptance of the

concept of separation of powers, that the functions of the judiciary, executive and legislature should be kept separate and distinct. Policy formulation and implementation are tasks for the executive and the legislature. Judicial reluctance, often noted by commentators,[6] to assume responsibility for the budget and fiscal priorities of the state is mirrored in the linguistic conventions of the International Covenant on Economic Social and Cultural Rights itself under which states are rarely obliged to implement these rights progressively to the maximum of their available resources. This formulation gives states a wide margin of appreciation in deciding the extent of their obligations under this Convention.

Extra-Legal Mechanisms of Enforcement

Short, therefore, of any clear legislative language at the national level on the content and meaning of social and economic rights, enforcement of these rights must also be ensured through extra legal mechanisms aimed at catalyzing popular awareness of state responsibility and accountability with regard to the protection and promotion of social and economic entitlements.

Building a popular appreciation of the notion of social and economic rights requires a number of strategic initiatives by human rights organizations working in close collaboration with developmental NGOs. As has been advocated elsewhere, strategic action campaigns around issues such as child labor, sex tourism and deforestation can not only build the potential for solidarity, but also have important, value-formation dimensions (Dias, n.d.).

Nongovernmental organizations in the Caribbean have for sometime been concerned with developmental alternatives particularly at the community level. The intensification of these efforts and the sharing of these alternatives and experiences where they exist can help establish in the public consciousness that people-centred development is indeed possible.

The point to be made is that rights are not definable solely by reference to their justiciability. Arguably, where people expect and require governments to act positively in ensuring access to social and economic rights, it would be most difficult for such governments to violate these rights without suffering a political price. It is also

---

[6] See the review of cases in Beatty (1994).

undeniable however that justiciability would strengthen community demands for state accountability around social and economic rights.

It is beyond dispute that ensuring state compliance with international standards with regard to social and economic rights is a thorny and complex issue. The barriers to the realization of these rights are internal to states and are also externally generated. The barriers are philosophical, legal, economic and political in nature. For all states in the Caribbean, their margin of flexibility in meeting their obligations is severely hampered by the workings of international concern and geopolitical order in which developments countries are inserted in a highly inequitable matter. The difficulties that some states have in meeting their obligations under the Covenant is caused in part by the diversion of substantial portions of their national incomes in servicing the external debt. No more stark example of the potency of the external forces in limiting the parameters of state action around economic rights can be drawn than that of Cuba in the contemporary period.

The challenge in enforcing social and economic rights requires firstly that all governments in the Caribbean region ratify the International Covenant on Economic, Social and Cultural Rights. At the international level, greater pressure must be bought to bear upon states to comply with their reporting obligations under the Covenant. In this regard further consideration needs to be given to strengthening the supervisory mechanisms at the international level. Minimum standards need to be developed which take account of regional inequalities and which are also taken into account by international financial institutions and governments in developing and implementing fiscal and developmental policies.

Emphasis must also be placed by the NGO section on consistent monitoring and documenting of policies which violate the minimum standards of state compliance and which serve to roll back popular access to social and economic entitlements.

Monitoring of violations of economic rights must also be accompanied by systematic monitoring of violations of political and civil rights since the denial of the latter category of right in and of itself constitutes a barrier to the realization of social and economic rights. Where a citizenry, or significant section of it, are prevented from participating in the political process public policy often does not reflect their needs and will, in fact, often sharply conflict with the interests of the politically excluded groups.

By way of historical example, it is clear that it was not until Caribbean people attained universal adult franchise that some level of mass provision of health care and education became a reality. And similarly, having won in part the battle for freedom to associate, workers and trade unions ensured less inequitable relations in the workplace. The attainment of these political rights was greatly contested by the economic elite and this contestation has never ceased.

Human rights are indivisible, interdependent and mutually reinforcing not only in their realization but also in their breach and it must be the task of human rights and development organizations to constantly make the linkages between the political and civil rights on the one hand and social and economic rights on the other.

REFERENCES

Antoine, R-M. (1995). *Securing Economic, Social and Cultural Rights for Women Workers in the Commonwealth Caribbean, With Particular Reference to Structural Adjustment.* Paper presented at the conference organized by CAFRA and Caribbean Rights on Critical Perspectives on Human Rights in the Caribbean, Trinidad and Tobago, 26-28 January, 1995.

Beatty, D. (Ed.). (1994). *Human Rights and Judicial Review: A Comparative Perspective.* Boston, MA: Dordrecht.

Caribbean Development Bank. (1993). *Social and Economic Indicators of Borrowing Member Countries, 1986-1991, 1992.* Barbados: Author.

Caribbean Policy Development Centre. (1994). *Economic Education Resource Kit for the Caribbean.* Barbados: Author.

Caribbean Symposium on Social Development. (1995, March). *Report.* Cosponsored by UNICEF, CARICOM, and the Consortium of Graduate Studies, University of the West Indies, Mona.

Dias, C. (n.d.). *Relationships Between Human Rights, Development and Democracy: South/North NGO Solidarity in Fostering Popular Participation.* Unpublished manuscript.

Thomas, C. (1995). *Social Development and the Social Summit: A Report on Guyana, Jamaica, and Trinidad and Tobago.* Guyana: University of Guyana.

Turk, D. (1992). *The Realisation of Economic, Social and Cultural Rights* (Special Rapporteur's Report: UN Economic and Social Council, E/CN:4/Sub.2/1992/I63 July, 1992). Geneva: United Nations Commission on Human Rights.

United Nations Development Program. (1994). *Human Development Report.* New York: Author.

Chapter 6
Public Interest Litigation in India: Making the State Accountable

Rani Jethmalani

With the collapse of communism and the end of the cold war, the United Nations became the symbol of a New World order and countries united in their commitment to a global agenda based on respect for human rights. For the developing countries of the South this imposes greater obligations on state action, increased accountability and an urgency to create new avenues for access to justice and minimum basic needs.

For India, the world's most populous democracy, the task of distributive justice and participative democracy poses an even more daunting challenge. With a population of 900 million, which will exceed China's by the year 2001 (Census of India, 1991); with 29.9 percent of the people living below the poverty level; with 39.42 percent female literacy; with 452 abortions in every one thousand births; with 44 million children engaged in backbreaking labor (Centre of Concern for Child Labour, 1995); with 51.56 percent male employment (Economic Survey, 1994/1995); with 22.69 percent female employment (Economic Survey, 1994/1995); and a per capita income of about 60 US dollars a year,[1] the task appears overwhelming and formidable.

Vast disparities in income coupled with a deeply entrenched feudal and patriarchal order makes the struggle for survival more painful and arduous for 50 percent of India's population—its women. Professor Amartya Sen points out that women have been reduced to the "missing or vanishing" factor in demographic studies due to maltreatment and neglect in providing food, nutrition and health care (Sen, 1990). The invisibility of women (even though paradoxically some of them occupy high positions of public office) makes the struggle for justice an unequal and impossible battle. The constitutional promise

[1] Information from Indian Broadcasting Ministry.

of equality for 50 percent of the population, i.e. its women, has not yet filtered down to them.

Constitutional Basis for Public Interest Litigation

India's constitutional and plural democracy has stood the test of time except for a brief aberration between 1975-76 when Mrs. Gandhi imposed an illegal emergency and suspended fundamental rights. Curiously, Mrs. Gandhi introduced a constitutional amendment before the Copenhagen International Decade for Women to legitimize her rule during the illegal emergency in 1975, adding a new chapter to the Indian Constitution, i.e. the 42nd Amendment, 1976, consisting of Part 4A Fundamental Duties Article 51A Clause (e), which is as follows:

> [It shall be the duty of all citizens to] (e) promote harmony and the spirit of common brotherhood amongst all people of India transcending religious, linguistic and regional or sectional diversities, to renounce practices derogatory to the dignity of women.

While there is a separation of powers among the legislature, executive and judiciary, the courts, by a creative use of the constitutional provisions of the writ jurisdiction under article 32[14] and 226[15] of the Constitution, assumed the role of checking the violation of rights and repression of the disadvantaged and vulnerable section of society. Article 14[16] of the Constitution of India guarantees equality

---

[14] Article 32 : "Remedies for enforcement of rights conferred by this Part (1). The rights to move the Supreme Court by appropriate proceedings for the enforcement of the rights conferred by this part is guaranteed. (2) The Supreme Court shall have power to issue directions or orders or writs, including writs in the nature of *habeas corpus, mandamus,* prohibition, *quo warranto* and *certiorari,* whichever may be appropriate for the enforcement of any of the rights conferred this part."

[15] Article 226: "Power of High Courts to issue certain writs (1) Notwithstanding...article 32(3), every High Court shall have power, throughout the territories in relation to which it exercises jurisdiction, to issue to any person or authority, including in appropriate cases, any government within those territories, directions, orders or writs, including (writs in the nature of *habeas corpus, mandamus,* prohibition, *pro warranto* and *certiorari,* or any of them, for the enforcement of any of the rights conferred by Part III and for any other purpose.)"
These two rights comprise the "writ jurisdiction" of the Court.. "Writs" are orders issued by the court. Article 32 is a fundamental right, i.e. it is in the chapter on fundamental rights. Article 226 is a constitutional right in the Constitution.

[16] Article 14: "The State shall not deny to any person equality before the law or the

men and women, while Article 15(3)[5] provides for affirmative action by the State for women and children. Both Articles 14 and 15 are Fundamental Rights. Article 38[6] and 39[7] of the Constitution, which are Directive Principles of State Policy, are not enforceable but lay down policies and guidelines for the State to secure a social order in which social, economic and political justice informs all institutions of national life.

The Supreme Court of India explained the development of Public Interest Litigation (PIL) in the *People's Union for Democratic Rights v. Union of India* (1982) case, stating:

> The rule of law does not mean that the protection of the law must be available only to a fortunate few or that the law should be allowed to be prostituted by the vested interests for protecting and upholding the status quo under the guise of enforcement of their civil and political rights. The poor too have civil and political rights and the rule of law is meant for them also, though today it exists only on paper and not in reality. If the sugar barons and the alcohol kings have the fundamental right to carry on their business and to fatten their purses by exploiting the consuming

---

equal protection of the laws within the territory of India."

[5] Article 15(3): "Nothing in this Article shall prevent the State from making any special provisions for women and children."

[6] Article 38 directs the State to secure a social order for the promotion of welfare of the people: "(1) The State shall strive to promote the welfare of the people by securing and protecting as effectively as it may a social order in which justice, social, economic and political, shall inform all the institutions of national life. (2) The State shall, in particular, strive to minimize the inequalities in income and endeavor to eliminate inequalities in status, facilities and opportunities, not only amongst individuals but also amongst groups of people residing in different areas or engaged in different vocations."

[7] Article 39: "The State shall, in particular, direct its policy towards securing—(a) that the citizens, men and women equally, have the right to an adequate means of livelihood; (b) that the ownership and control of the material resources of the community are so distributed as best to subserve the common good; (c) that the operation of the economic system does not result in the concentration of wealth and means of production to the common detriment; (d) that there is equal pay for equal work for both men and women; (e) that the health and strength of workers, men and women, and the tender age of children are not abused and that citizens are not forced by economic necessity to enter avocations unsuited to their age or strength; (f) that children are given opportunities and facilities to develop in a healthy manner and in conditions of freedom and dignity, and that childhood and youth are protected against exploitation and against moral and material abandonment."

public, have the chamars belonging to the lowest strata of society no fundamental right to earn an honest living through their sweat and toil?

With rare sensitivity the court went on to point out:

Civil and political rights, priceless and invaluable as they are for freedom and democracy, simply do not exist for the vast masses of our people. Large numbers of men, women and children who constitute the bulk of our population are today living in sub-human conditions of abject poverty; utter grinding poverty has broken their back and sapped their moral fiber. They have no faith in the existing social and economic system. What civil and political rights are these poor and deprived sections of humanity going to enforce?

The only solution for making civil and political rights meaningful to these large sections of society would be to remake the material conditions and restructure the social and economic order so that they may be able to realize their economic, social and cultural rights. There is indeed a close relationship between civil and political rights on the one hand and economic, social and cultural rights on the other and this relationship is so obvious that the International Human Rights Conference in Teheran called by the General Assembly in 1963 declared in a final proclamation "since human rights and fundamental freedoms are indivisible, the full realization of civil and political rights without the enjoyment of economic, social and cultural rights is impossible."

Of course, the task of restructuring the social and economic order so that social and economic rights become a meaningful reality for the poor is one which legitimately belongs to the legislature and the executive. However, mere initiation of social and economic rescue programs by the executive and the legislature would not be enough. It is only through multi-dimensional strategies, including public interest litigation, that these social and economic rescue programs can be made effective.

In *People's Union for Democratic Rights v. Union of India* (1982), a challenge was brought on the grounds that the fundamental right in Article 23 (4) of the Constitution, which prohibits "begar," i.e. forced labor and traffic in human beings, had been violated. The case arose as a result of the award by the Delhi Administration and local authorities of contracts for construction works relating to the Asian Games. The contractors employed workers from different parts of the country through middle men or sub-contractors. Acting on reports of the exploitative conditions of poor workers, the People's Union for Democratic Rights (PUDR), a social and political organization, sent a letter to the court alleging violation of the laws. This letter was treated as a writ petition under Article 32 of the Constitution, which is the fundamental right to move the Supreme Court when there is a violation of any fundamental right. Notice was issued to the Government of Delhi to explain its transgression of labor laws. The court held by interpretation that "begar" was committed not only when the worker is forced to work against his will but also when such persons are exploited and paid less then the minimum wages.

The PUDR case demonstrates the methodology by which the court asserts itself to advance the rights of disadvantaged and vulnerable groups at the behest of any bona fide person with an interest in the public good. Professor Upendra Baxi, who has termed Public Interest Litigation (PIL) as "Social Action Litigation," attributes this remarkable development to the post emergency winds of freedom when the Court became energized and transformed into a "pro-people's" court. Its preoccupation with the fundamental right of property[8] of the rich landlords in the early years after the enactment of the Constitution had given the Supreme Court a class complexion, and its dismal role in upholding the suspension of fundamental rights during the emergency had been a betrayal of people's hopes and expectations.[9]

The constitutional power of intervention was possible because of the Chapter on Fundamental Rights[10] in the Constitution. Judicial review of all laws is a function of the courts. The role of the courts in PIL is to insist on the law being followed, i.e., when there is a failure to implement the law either through acts of commission or omission. Article 13 (2)[11] of the Constitution prohibits the state from taking any action which violates fundamental rights.

"Letter Jurisdiction" and the Role of the Court

Acting on the basis of a letter or a postcard written to the court PIL has come to be known as the "epistolary" jurisdiction (i.e., letter

---

[8] Article 31. The Fundamental Right to Property has been deleted. It is now a Constitutional Right only, i.e., Article 300-A.

[9] See *A. D. M. Jabalpur v. Shivkant Shukla* (1976). This was a habeas corpus case.

[10] Part III of the Constitution. These are enforceable rights available against the states.

[11] Article 13(2): "The state shall not make any law which takes away or abridges the rights conferred by this Part and any law made in contravention of the clause shall, to the extent of this clause, be void."

jurisdiction). This has made struggles for justice to advance the human rights of women and the poor, who otherwise would have been marginalized, less cumbersome in view of the relatively easier procedure adopted for PIL. In a country in which female literacy is low, it is left to public spirited citizens, NGOs and women's organizations to take initiatives. The Supreme Court has responded sensitively to women's issues even though this has often been paternalistic (*Indian Federation of Women Lawyers v. Smt. Shakuntala & Ors.,* 1986).[12] In this process, the Court has also been sensitized.

To ensure swift and speedy justice the court has enlarged the strict rules of *locus standi*. Normally, the court entertains petitions when a person is aggrieved because his or her fundamental rights are directly violated, except in the case of *habeas corpus* petitions when persons are detained in illegal custody and any person on his behalf, though not an absolute stranger, can move the court. In *S.P. Gupta v. Union of India* (1981) the Court stated:

> We must hasten to make it clear that the individual who moves the court for judicial redress in cases of this kind must be acting bona fide with a view to vindicating the causes of justice and if he is acting for personal gain or private profit or out of political motivation or other oblique consideration, the Court should not allow itself to be activised at the instance of such person and must reject his application at the threshold, whether it be in the form of a letter addressed to the court or even in the form of a regular writ petition filed in court. We must be careful to see that the member of the public, who approaches the court in cases of this kind, is acting bona fide and not for personal gain or private profit or political motivation or other oblique consideration.

By enlarging the rules of *locus standi* in the court, the doors have been thrown wide open to undertrials, convicted prisoners, women in protective custody, slum and pavement dwellers, children detained as juveniles, tribals and many more to whom otherwise the courts are virtually inaccessible. In the same case, with regard to the rules of pleadings and procedure for moving the court in Article 32 of the Constitution, the Court stated:

> It is true that there are rules made by that court prescribing the procedure for moving this court for relief under Article 32 and they require various formalities to be gone through by a person seeking to approach the court. But it must not be forgotten that procedure is but a handmaiden of justice and the cause of justice can never be allowed to be

---

[12] See concluding paragraphs for observations of the Court.

thwarted by any procedural technicalities. The court would therefore un-hesitatingly and without the slightest qualms of conscience cast aside the technical rules of procedure.

With the lifting of emergency in 1977, the first opportunity to do so was presented to the Supreme Court in 1979 when a newspaper account in the Indian Express reported that several undertrials, including women and children, in various prisons in Bijar had been awaiting their trials for years. The period of imprisonment undergone by many of them was more than the maximum sentence due for their alleged crimes. They were unable to arrange either a lawyer or obtain bail. A Supreme Court lawyer acting on behalf of the public interest on the report moved a *habeas corpus* petition.[25] Acting on the petition the court swiftly passed orders while releasing the unfortunate undertrial prisoners in batches. The court held that a speedy trial is the fundamental right of every person and was included in the Right to Life and Liberty, i.e. Article 21.[26]

Wide publicity was given to these cases. The court insisted on monitoring the conditions of the undertrial prisoners. It asserted that no procedure which does not ensure a quick trial can be regarded as "just, fair and reasonable" if it violated Article 21 of the Constitution. While free legal aid is not a fundamental right in the Indian Constitution, Article 37A makes social justice and free legal aid a directive principle.[27] The Supreme Court held that the right to free legal aid was implicit in the fundamental right of Article 21, i.e., Right to Life and Liberty. The court's expanding jurisdiction in this area has strengthened the rights of prisoners in several subsequent petitions pertaining to them.[28]

In *Munna v. State of U.P.* (1982), the Supreme Court dealt with the case of a young offender who had been detained with adult prisoners in violation of the Juvenile Prison Act and prison rules. A petition was made by social activists on the basis of newspaper reports. The court asked the Superintendent of Jails to explain the circumstances under which the children were detained and then hurriedly released. Similarly, on the basis of a petition filed by a journalist, the

[25] See All Indian Reporter (A.I.R.), SC 1360 (1979).

[26] Article 21: Protection of life and personal liberty. No person shall be deprived of his life or personal liberty except according to procedure established by law.

[27] Directive Principles are contained in Part IV of the Constitution. They are not enforceable but are important guidelines for state action.

[28] See A.I.R. SC 1579 (1980) and A.I.R. SC 1747 (1991).

court dealt with torture and ill-treatment of women in police lock-ups.[17] Several of them had been assaulted and treated with indignity. The court issued notice to the Director of the College of Social Work, Bombay, to visit the jail and interview the prisoners to ascertain the truth. A notice was also issued to the state government and the Inspector General of Prison. The court upheld the right of the women to free legal aid. The court also directed certain safe measures for women prisoners and directed that the jail authorities and the state government provide special lock ups for women in reasonably good localities; that women constables guard the women; and that interrogation of women should only be done by female police officers.

The court's attention was drawn to the inhuman conditions in protective homes for women. Acting on news reports two professors of Delhi University in *Upendra Baxi v. Union of India* (1983) sent a letter to the court to examine the conditions in such homes. The court turned the letter into a writ petition. The government resisted the litigation. The court appointed a judicial magistrate to inquire into the condition of the inmates and the facilities provided in the protective homes. The court passed several orders from time to time and asked the Superintendent of Jail to provide sufficient numbers of toilets and bathrooms for inmates and draw up a scheme for vocational training and rehabilitation.

In Laxmikant Pandey's case (1986) a report appeared in the papers of a racket by unscrupulous mercenaries pertaining to the sale and "export" of orphaned children without any safeguards about their future destinations. An activist lawyer was prompted to involve the court to investigate such malpractices. After hearing the Indian Council for Social Welfare and several NGOs dealing with childcare and adoptive facilities and after examining all the laws pertaining to guardianship and adoption, the court laid down elaborate guidelines to prevent the exploitation of children.

The court's concern for ensuring the basic needs of the poor who have no shelter was highlighted in *Olga Tellis v. State of Maharashtra* (1985). A Constitution Bench had to deal with the plight of those who live in slums and big cities. The petition was filed as a public interest litigation by a journalist, Olga Tellis. In her petition she asked whether by living on the streets in inhuman conditions the slum

---

[17] See 2 Supreme Court Cases (S.C.C.) 96 (1983).

dwellers had not acquired a right to live there. Could they be evicted overnight by a Corporation? Were they entitled to alternative accommodation? Ms. Tellis was moved by the pathetic insecurity of the homeless who come to big cities for their livelihood. The roads and pavements were the only shelter available to them. After arguments which went on for months the court held that though they had no right to live on pavements they had a right to livelihood. The government's policy of eviction was upheld and no relief was given to these unfortunate persons. Yet the court requested the government to make policies to ensure alternative accommodation.

The courts in PIL cases use the skillful strategy of making the state comply with its laws and thereby gives redress to the persons aggrieved. Its method is justice in collaboration with the executive rather than in opposition to it. Adverse strategies invite resistance. PIL invites compliance and responsibility.

The uncaring policies by successive governments undertaking large projects in the name of promoting tourism and industry with no concern for damage to the environment is a matter that has engaged the court in several cases brought by public spirited citizens.[18] Without a safe environment and conservation of resources, tribals and people dependent on natural resources have no avenues for their livelihood, thus exposing them to insecurity and hunger. This was amply demonstrated in Narmada Bachao Andolan v. Union of India (1994).[19] This writ petition was filed by an organization of tribal and non-tribal people of the Narmada Valley affected by a project which is the biggest undertaking in the country with the largest irrigation network in the world, known as the Sardar Saravar Project on the river Narmada. The project affected a large number of people, especially tribals.

At least 150,000 people and their families in 245 villages would have been affected by the submergence of their land and would have displaced several lakhs [1 lakh= 100,000] of people from their homes and their livelihoods. The petition was filed to protect their human and democratic rights. They were the most marginalized section of the population. The petitioner organization had, by non-violent and peaceful means over a period of time, highlighted issues relating to

---

[18] An activist lawyer, M.C. Mehta his brought several cases to the court. See 2 S.C.C. 1746 (1986).

[19] The movement has been spearheaded by a social activist Medha Patkar. She has received wide-spread popular support for her unflagging commitment.

development, particularly the rights of people who had been displaced from their land for the purpose of the project. The project had
been cleared by the Ministry of Environment and the Planning Commission. The World Bank had cleared the project. The petitioners
complained that their fundamental rights under Article 14 and 21 of
the Constitution were violated.

The matter is now pending before the Supreme Court where the
petitioners have asked for stoppage of the construction of the dam.
An application has been moved by the Union of India and the state of
Gujarat that some construction activity to safeguard the dam from
floods be permitted. The court's interim measures from time to time
act as a deterrent against irresponsible and reckless activity in the
name of industrial development. It makes the government answer-
able and accountable where public monies are utilized in the name of
people and progress.

From these and many other cases, it is evident that the court's
sweeping jurisdiction has made it virtually a third chamber of Parliament supervising all administrative acts and has transformed the role
of the judiciary. It has made the PIL movement into one of checking
the government's lawlessness and profligacy.

Indira Sawhney v. Union of India (1992), known as the Reservation case, was an important watershed in the PIL movement. Then-
Prime Minister, Mr. V.P. Singh, and his government issued a notifi-
cation to implement the Mandal Commission recommendations for
reservations[20] for backward castes. On behalf of the government it
was stated that castes were equivalent to classes and that there were
socially, educationally and economically backward classes. Those arguments were repelled by meritorious students on the ground that
caste was a constitutionally impermissible criterion and such a policy
violated Article 14 and Article 16 (2)[21] of the Constitution. This issue
saw a divide between the forward and backward castes. It was a turbulent period in India's history.

The initiation of the case by a public spirited lawyer was followed by similar petitions by almost 91 other organizations. Political

---

[20] Reservations are equivalent to "quotas." This is compensatory justice to those
who, in an inequitable caste system, have been kept out of the tangible benefits of
society for thousands of years because they were considered to be of low caste.
The caste system was justified on the grounds of religion. The Constitution addresses these inequalities.

[21] Article 16(1)(2)(3)(4). These are fundamental rights to public employment.

parties also submitted arguments before the court. These went on for almost a year. Finally a nine-judge Constitution Bench of the Supreme Court delivered a judgment of over 1,000 pages, in which it examined several issues while upholding reservations.

The majority of the court upheld the reservation policy. The Court asked the government to set up a commission to identify the backward classes. The Mandal case demonstrates the judicial power of diffusing a highly explosive political situation through public interest litigation.

Public Interest Litigation and Criminal Law

Another significant development of PIL has been in the area of criminal law. Criminal law is adversarial in nature. The state prosecutes the accused. Yet resort to PIL has been achieved in two ways: by use of the writ jurisdiction and by using the ordinary law of the penal code to file private complaints with the assistance of public interest organizations such as NGOs and women's organizations. With the growing atrocities against women, novel and unique ways were developed to use PIL strategies to assist relatives of victims in filing private complaints. These strategies were later extended to women's organizations filing cases on behalf of the victims directly.

The lawlessness and collusion of witnesses, doctors, police, prosecutors, and the lower judiciary have led to a serious travesty of justice. In these circumstances, in *Neelam Varma and Ors. v. Union of India* (1983), seven dowry victims and two women's organizations moved the Supreme Court of India alleging that their rights under Articles 21 and 14 of the Constitution of India had been violated. They submitted that the police authorities had not complied with their statutory obligations under the criminal procedure code and the Constitution, by refusing to register their complaints regarding dowry harassment and by not carrying out the necessary investigations enjoined upon them under the Criminal Procedure Code. It was contended that the right to life included the right to live with human dignity. In several cases pertaining to dowry death similar pleas have been advanced by women's organizations.[22]

---

[22] See A.I.R. SC 2060 (1987).

Dowry death: (1) Where the death of a woman is caused by any burns or bodily injury or occurs otherwise than under normal circumstances within seven years of her marriage and it is shown that soon before her death she was subjected to cruelty or harassment by her husband or any relative of her husband for, or in con-

In *Satya Rani Chadha and Ors. v. Subhash Chander and Ors.* (1981) the complainant mother of the deceased, whose daughter had been burnt for dowry, filed a private complaint with the assistance of women's organizations. She later appealed to the Supreme Court for an expeditious hearing of her case. This method has enabled women through PIL to raise public consciousness, lobby for changes in the Dowry Law and, what is more important, obtain direct supervision of the highest court to thwart possible manipulation by unscrupulous police officers and dishonesty from the accused. It has made the subordinate judiciary aware of the need for taking suffering seriously and disposing cases expeditiously.

While the Supreme Court permitted women's organizations to appeal in the Sudha Gotl dowry death case[35] against the acquittal by the High Court of the accused, in Shalini Malhotra's case (1990)[36] the right claimed by women's organizations to intervene in public interest in criminal trial has been challenged. A petition to hear this important issue is pending in the Supreme Court. Women's organizations have not been rendered helpless by this decision. Instead, at their request the government has either appointed lawyers of their choice as Special Public Prosecutors or the courts have permitted representative lawyers of women's organizations to assist the Public Prosecutor.

---

nection with, any demand for dowry, such death shall be called "dowry death," and such husband or relative shall be deemed to have caused her death.

Explanation: For the purposes of this sub-section, dowry shall have the same meaning as in Sec. 2 of the Dowry Prohibition Act, 1961 (28 of l961).

(2) Whoever commits dowry death shall be punished with imprisonment for a term which shall not be less than seven years but which may extend to imprisonment for life (S. 304B I.P.C.)

Dowry is the giving and taking of money, commodities etc. at the time of marriage from a spouse in exchange of marriage. It is normally the girl for whom a "price" is paid b y her parents to the groom and his parents. According to official figures there were 5.,817 "dowry deaths" in 1993 and 4,277 in 1994.

[35] See State (Delhi Administration) vs. Laxman Kumar and others, and Indian Federation of Women Lawyers & Ors. v. Smt. Shakuntala and others (A.I.R. SC 250, 1986).

[36] SLP Criminal pending in the Supreme Court. Special Leave Petitions are made under Article 136 of the Constitution of India: "Notwithstanding anything in this Chapter, the Supreme Court may, in its discretion, grant special leave to appeal from any judgment, decree, determination, sentence or order in any cause or matter passed or made by any court or tribunal in the territory of India." This is by way of an appeal.

Public Interest Litigation has enlarged the frontiers of criminal jurisprudence to give justice to victims. The emphasis on legal aid for the accused had eclipsed the rights of these who needed it most, i.e. vulnerable and disempowered victims. This has been redressed through PIL.

Public Interest Litigation and Personal Laws

Another highly emotional issue in which several public interest litigation cases are pending in the Supreme Court is in the area of personal laws. These laws have been justified on the ground that they are associated with the fundamental right of freedom of religion. In a Hindu dominated pluralist and secular state, any attempt to reform discriminatory personal laws is seen as an encroachment on the rights of religious minorities. Despite Article 14 of the Constitution, which guarantees equality before the law to both men and women, the dilemma of reconciling Article 14 and Article 25 of the Constitution has been a frustrating and difficult exercise. In a recent case, *Smt. Sarla Mudgal President Kalyani and Ors. v. Union of India and Ors.* (1994)[25] the Supreme Court held that conversion to Islam by a Hindu husband to escape his first marriage to a Hindu woman could be bigamous and subject the person to penal consequences. The Court made important observations on the need to enact a Uniform Civil Code, and stated as follows:

> Therefore, a unified code is imperative both for protection of the oppressed and promotion of national unity and solidarity. But the first step should be to rationalize the personal law of the minorities to develop religious and cultural amity. The government would be well advised to entrust the responsibility to the Law Commission which may in consultation with the Minorities Commission examine the matter and bring about the comprehensive legislation in keeping with the modern day concept of human rights for women.

The court's decision witnessed a predictably adverse reaction from fundamentalist organizations. In a petition filed by WARLAW[26] in public interest (1994), the government's "declaration" in the CEDAW (Convention to End All Forms of Discrimination Against

---

[25] Judgment dated 10th May, 1995. In Writ Petitions, the Petition originates in the Supreme Court under Article 32 and in the High Court under Article 226 of the Constitution of India.

[26] Women's Action Research and Legal Action, A Charitable and Public Trust to advance the cause of women's human rights.

Women), which is, in fact a "reservation," has been questioned. Notice has been issued to the government by the Supreme Court on how it proposes to implement its declaration. The declaration states that while the government is committed to the basic principles of CEDAW, it will initiate change only at the request of communities desiring change. The petitioners wanted the government to disclose who would be involved in the process of ascertaining the need and desire for change and reform of inequitable, discriminatory laws both amongst the Hindus and other minorities. Would this be confined to religious leaders alone or include women directly affected? The government's reply is awaited.

With the expanding scope of PIL, several judges have advised caution from time to time. In *Sudeep Majumdar v. State of M.P.* (1983) the court paused to reconsider the scope and procedure of PIL. When the matter came up before the Supreme Court, only this year the court took the view that judicial proceedings in the case should be manageable. The court was not inclined to issue a public notice to invite intervention from public interest groups. Instead it asked the counsel for the Public Interest Legal and Research Centre (PILSARS)[27] to coordinate with social action groups to elicit their view on the questions presented to the Court. Accordingly, PILSARS sent a questionnaire to NGOs and public interest groups inviting a response.

When the matter came up again this year the court adjourned the matter. The wisdom of laying down precise parameters within which PIL must fit in has to be carefully considered. Any strait-jacketing of a mechanism and movement for justice may only hinder and retard its future development.

Obviously, interest in PIL is sustained as long as there is faith in the judicial system and awareness that there is no instant remedy or instant solution. Court calendars are clogged with numerous cases. Often the court keeps a case in cold storage after referring it to a Constitution Bench to activate it at an appropriate stage when issues are pressing. This has happened in the petition pending before the Court on the question of personal laws.

The court provides the healing touch by giving interim compensation as it did in the Bhopal case (A.I.R. SC 1069, 1989), in which

---

[27] PILSARS is a Public Interest Society. Its dynamic director, Dr. Rajeev Dhawan was appointed *amicus curia* to the court in this case. Several important cases have been filed by PILSARS.

about 3,000 people perished as a result of the world's largest industrial disaster caused by the escape of poisonous gas. In several other cases, the court has awarded compensation to persons detained illegally in jail. The remedy of filing a civil suit in addition is always available, yet the court in exercise of its jurisdiction under Article 32 awards some compensation.

The court is aware of its own limitations. For every 1 lakh litigants there is only one lawyer available in paid cases. In public interest litigation, in which there is no payment to lawyers by way of fees, and sometimes even costs are borne by the public interest litigant. The number of lawyers is woefully inadequate.

In Sheila Barse's case (1988), the court lamented that scornful impatience can only wreck a mission. In a long and important judgment the court did not permit the petitioner, an activist journalist, from withdrawing from the case, but instead asked the Legal Aid Committee to pursue it under directions of the court.

By involving lawyers, social action groups, and experts to draft schemes, the Court has advanced human rights. Collaboration with the courts is the medium through which to monitor the progress of implementation of the Courts' orders. Many newspapers have shown an awareness to service consumers on developmental and public interest issues. Reporting on these issues has become a regular feature of many leading newspapers.

Through PIL, the Court intends to ensure that "freedom does not suffer atrophy and that activism, which is essential for participative public justice, is encouraged" so that the public are not deterred by the courts and that they offer their services gratuitously to society, thereby strengthening the commitment to actualize basic human needs as basic human rights.

REFERENCES

Barse, S., 1 S.C.R. 210 (1988).

Baxi v. Union of India, 2 S.C.C. 308 (1983).

Baxi, U. (1988). Taking Suffering Seriously: The Social Action Litigation before the Supreme Court of India. In U. Baxi, (Ed.), *Law and Poverty: Critical Essays*, (pp. 387-415). New Delhi.

Census of India. (1991). New Delhi: Ministry of Home Affairs.

Center of Concern for Child Labour. (1995 June 5). *The Hindustan Times*.

Chadha & Ors. v. Chander & Ors., SLP Criminal No. 2034 (1981).

Gupta v. Union of India, Suppl. S.C.C. 87 (1981).

Indian Federation of Women Lawyers v. Smt. Shakuntala & Ors., A.I.R. SC 250 (1986).

Jabalpur v. Shukla, A.I.R. SC 1207 (1976).

Kalyani & Ors. v. Union of India & Ors., Writ Petition Civil No. 1079 (1994). Judgment reported in S.C.C. Criminal, part 6, 569 (1995, June).

Majumdar v. State of M.P., 2 S.C.C. 258 (1983).

Malhotra, S., S.L.P. No. 410 (1990).

Munna v. State of U.P., 1 S.E.C. 1747 (1982).

Narmada Bachao Andolan v. Union of India, Writ Petition No. 319 (1994).

Pandey L., A.I.R. SC 272 (1986).

People's Union for Democratic Rights v. Union of India, 2 S.C. 253 (1982).

Sawhney v. Union of India, Suppl. (3) S.C.C. 217 (1992).

Sen, A. (1990, December 20). More Than 100 Million Women are Missing. *The New York Review of Books*.

Tellis v. State of Maharashtra, 3 S.C.C. 272 (1985).

Varma & Ors. v. Union of India, Supreme Court Writ Petition Crl. No. 51068-1076 (1983).

WARLAW v. Union of India & Ors., Writ Petition No. 684 (1994).

Chapter 7
Economic Reform and Social and Economic Rights in China: Strategy Brainstorming Across Cultures

Sharon K. Hom

Introduction

After a decade of social chaos and the destruction of education, law, and other stigmatized institutions during the Cultural Revolution, China embarked upon a series of pragmatic legal and economic reforms beginning with the historic Third Plenum of the Thirteenth Party Congress in 1978. In this post-Mao era, economic reform policies aim to move China away from its former "Soviet-type" of centralized planning and to reopen China to the outside world. Despite the fact that China's leadership may not currently be of a single mind with respect to the pace and direction of reforms, it continues to implement reforms in the areas of enterprise management and finance to allow for greater local autonomy in decision-making, ongoing price incentives for agricultural production, housing reforms to increase apartment rents in the cities, the expansion of areas for foreign investment to the service sectors, and the expansion of the preferential investment policies from the coastal areas to the interior of China (Jefferson, 1993, pp. 35-39).

Western observers present shifting assessments about the extent of the success of these early and ongoing economic policies, and although they note serious social and economic problems such as inflation, unemployment and underemployment, crime and corruption, the human and environmental costs, and the impact on women (when this is addressed at all), they generally applaud the move towards market reforms and speak with awe, enthusiasm, and admiration, or at least qualified respect for China's domestic economic growth and the way in which China has become a "key player" in the international arena in less than a decade. These western

commentators generally point to macro-economic quantitative indicators such as the annual expansion rate of 10 percent of the economy, the doubling of living standards and consumption, the tripling
of foreign trade, and the place of China as the 13th largest exporter
in the world as indicators of this "success" (see e.g., Hardt & Kaufman, 1991). However, in Post-Mao China, economic reform is also
characterized by a bifurcation from political reform, by an implicit
resourcist view,[1] and an explicit acceptance of uneven development
as a stated policy. Despite some academic debates, the Chinese government views the uneven development that is resulting from the
current policy of "allowing some people and some areas to get rich
first" (*rang yibufenren, yibu fendiqu xianfuqilai*), as a necessary policy
that will result in the benefits of prosperity eventually flowing down.

The role of Chinese women in contemporary China has consistently been articulated by shifting Party lines as part of a broader
national/Party agenda. Whether as part of the productive forces joining in the industrialization of the country, or as mothers ensuring the
future of 'Socialist spiritual civilization,' or as obedient workers returning to the home in the face of a surplus labor problem (Gao,
1994, Li X. 1994), Chinese women are viewed as instrumentalist
tools for the collective enterprise of China's modernization and reform. Throughout contemporary Chinese history, Chinese women
are often rhetorically referred to as holding up half the sky to suggest
the significant role they play in building the new China. What is the
impact of China's economic reform policies on Chinese women holding up half the sky and more in the current modernization efforts?
Does uneven development also result in gender specific uneven development? The difficulties of assessing the gender implications and
impact of these reforms are partially due to the focus and methodology of much of economic policy research,[2] the diversity of Chinese
women's situations and experiences, and the enormous regional

---

[1] Despite the increasing evidence from twentieth century history that current models of development have resulted in increasing inequality of incomes, staggering
Third world debt, rampant militarism, and the devastation of the natural world,
the Chinese government has also adopted a high growth model of development
that reflects this same resourcist view of the world, that is, a vision of constant
growth as desirable.

[2] As one prominent Chinese researcher pointed out, "[T]here has been a lack of
specialized research and measured analysis of the improvement in rural women's
familial status" (Gao, 1994, p. 90).

differences in terms of demographics, economic status, and policy implementation.[3]

As a context for a "strategy brainstorming" exercise, I will first briefly discuss the economic reform policies initiated by China since the late seventies and examine the status of Chinese women under these reforms. By "strategy brainstorming," I mean a provisional thinking-out-loud about implementation "lessons" and insights from the Chinese experience as an invitation to challenge conventional wisdom about what is appropriate or what "works," for example, in human rights advocacy. Some questions I will address are: What are some of the domestic responses to the negative consequences of these policies? What do they suggest about the strengths and limits of domestic initiatives to address gender justice demands? What roles do and can Chinese NGOs play in current and future implementation strategies? What is the role of Chinese law in advancing women's economic and social rights given the present Party regime? What roles, if any, can international women's human rights groups play in addressing these questions? How does the international women's rights agenda play out in China?

In an effort to negotiate approaches that avoid both an imperialistic universalism and a politically disempowering nativism, I also explore foreground issues implicated in developing appropriate roles for different agents of reform and social change. As a Chinese-American legal scholar and law teacher working in the material West, my own perspective is partially situated in what Tu Weiming has described as "Cultural China," that is China as inclusive of three symbolic universes, the mainland China, Taiwan, and Hong Kong; Chinese communities overseas; and scholars elsewhere in the world interested in China (cited in Chu & Ju, 1993, p. 321). Although I do not share Tu's optimism that these periphery sites outside China might serve an alternative reference points for the mainland Communist system nor as sites for the development of an autonomous

---

[3] Given the diversity reflected in the intersections of class, ethnicity, geography, urban/rural location and the shifting of these categories, it is reductionist to refer to Chinese women as a monolithic whole. This diversity of Chinese women's situatedness has implications for any effort to assess the impact of economic reforms on women and underscores the need for diverse strategies to address the range of problems facing women in the cities, the newly developing townships and villages outside urban areas, or in the remote interiors of the mainland.

intellectual force within China, I do view the expansion of the symbolic imagined communities as a hopeful strategy for negotiating the increasingly porous cultural, economic and political boundaries of nationhood.

Economic Reform: Trickle Down with Chinese Characteristics

Instead of the shock treatment approaches adopted by Eastern European countries, China adopted an incremental gradualist policy of economic reform. Post-Mao domestic economic reform eliminated the life security offered by the "iron rice bowl" employment system and returned production to the household unit under the household responsibility system (HRS). The shifting mixed economy is characterized by the appearance and fast growth of private enterprises, the growth of a private sector, and the reform and privatization of state owned enterprises. Rural modernization is marked by a process of industrialization of the countryside resulting from the rise in town and village enterprises. Special economic zones (SEZs) along the coastal areas, such as Zhuhai and Shenzhen, were constructed and given preferential treatment in terms of tax advantages, greater flexibility to attract foreign investment, and the role of experimental "windows" in taking the lead in reform and modernization.[4] The growth in local special development zones has been enormous, from 117 at the end of 1991 to 10,000 at the end of 1992 (Christine Wong, 1994, p.49).

Although the economic liberalization policies aim to decentralize economic decision making, they also attempt to maintain some central regulatory control over the provinces and autonomous municipalities straining away from Beijing. As China adopts market approaches carefully qualified with adjectives, e.g. Socialist market economy, planned commodity market economy, regulated market economy, mixed system, it has been argued that "[a]s long as the current leadership is in power, China will seek the impossible: a market-based system within a socialist planned economy in a one-party state" (Hardt & Kaufman 1991, p. xiv). The key values underlying Post-Mao reform policies under Deng Xiaoping, are articulated in the

---

[4] In 1993, for example, Shenzhen's exports amounted to $8.335 billion, ranking first in the country (Yuan, 1993).

ideological slogan, "reform, development and stability" (*gaige, fazhan, and wending*),[5] primacy assigned to stability, particularly in the face of a deep Chinese cultural revulsion of *luan* (chaos). Although the violent use of armed force by the Chinese government against its own people on June 4, 1989 to quell "an internal civil disorder," does not appear to have seriously affected China's position in the global market and the geopolitical arena,[6] the political legitimacy of and domestic faith in the Communist Party has clearly been further undermined.[7] Lurking in the near future as the octogenarians now in power inevitably pass on, the political succession maneuvering among protectionist conservatives and reformers in the Party and the final power transfer will determine whether a peaceful transfer of power occurs and the impact on the future of the developing rule of law.

There is also increasing domestic dissatisfaction and unrest resulting from problems that economic reforms have engendered or contributed to, including the resurgent problem of inflation, employment for the growing working-age population, the visible reemergence of prostitution and the sale of women and children, the pervasive rising materialism and focus on money (Chu & Ju, 1993, pp. 103, 279-282), serious environmental degradation and health hazards (Smil, 1993) and the impact of uneven development between the coastal and interior areas, between the urban and rural areas.

Although recognizing that women's liberation is still not "complete," domestic and foreign assessments of the improvements in the status of Chinese women since liberation in 1949 have been clearly

---

[5] See e.g. the editorial, "Gaige, fazhan, and wending: queyibuke," 1994.

[6] Direct foreign investment in China continued to grow after 1989 from 5,779 investment projects pledged in 1989 to 48,791 projects in 1992. By the end of 1992, China had absorbed foreign capital investment worth $35 billion (Pearson, 1994).

[7] See Alford (1992) for a thoughtful discussion of the complexities of interpreting the events of June 4 and the pro-democracy movement in China. Alford suggests that the monolithic picture presented by the Western media of the pro-democracy forces runs the danger of "merely hearing one's own voice in its words" (67) and points out the race, class, and gender biases of the students involved in movement. See also Hom (1992a, pp. 287-290) for a critique of the engendered rights discourse reflected in the leadership structures, decision-making, and personal leadership styles of the student movement.

positive. The decrease in infant and maternal mortality rates, the abolition of arranged marriages, concubinage, and other feudal vestiges of women's oppression, and the increase in literacy and improvement in health care for women clearly indicate the improvement in the lives of women today when compared to pre-liberation China. Yet, recent official reports and assessments also acknowledge the persistence of gender-based inequalities and violence in the social and economic spheres in Chinese society today. Despite great changes for women, e.g., the movement of large numbers of women into the productive sector, economic reforms for women have not necessarily resulted in improvements in the overall position of women in the economic or social hierarchy. For example, in the rural areas, economic changes have been characterized by differences in distribution of men and women in jobs created by industrialization, the concentration of women in labor-intensive, low-skilled, low-pay jobs, and unequal pay for equal work for women. Although women's incomes in some areas have increased, there are large disparities between women's incomes, and a gap between most women and men's incomes (Gao, 1994, pp. 90-91). In noting the persistence of extensive rural poverty, Smil (1993) points to the growing income disparities between poor and rich provinces (37 percent in 1988) and the millions of rural households in Guizhou, Gansu, or Shanxi that could not extricate themselves from dire poverty.

> Taking rural per capita income of less than 200 rmb in 1987 as an indicator of abject poverty, no fewer than 8.3 percent of peasant households, or over sixty million people, were below that line, and it is unlikely that the total dipped below fifty million by 1990. For these people a well padded coat, a well-heated room, or a well-built chair are still beyond reach. Elevating these families-a population equivalent to a large European nation-at least to the level of bearable subsistence will not be done easily (Footnotes omitted). (Smil, 1993, pp. 97-98)

In addition to poverty, rural women and girls face additional problems resulting from high illiteracy and school drop out rates, domestic violence, and the persistence of patrilocal residence and patrilineal inheritance traditions that result in the valuation of boys more than girls (*zhongnan qingnu*).[8] In early 1994, I participated in a

---

[8] The fact that the majority of the babies and children in the orphanages in China are female underscore the lower value placed upon girls.

legislative drafting workshop involving ten provinces in China. I asked the 100 or so participants to identify a specific case that reflected a typical problem in their province. Almost all ten groups identified a problem involving domestic violence or gender-based violence. However, when I was teaching in Shanghai in the summer of 1994, I asked a number of women, including a journalist, several lawyers and researchers, and some cadres from the Shanghai Women's Federation whether violence against women was a problem. They all responded that they did not think violence against women was a "real" problem at all in the urban areas. I cite these discussions as anecdotal evidence of the different perspectives and sensitivity of women and men situated in very different Chinese realities regarding the problems facing different Chinese women.

In contrast to rural women, women in Shanghai are hailed in China as a "preview of what a majority of Chinese women will be tomorrow and in the future" (Wu, 1992). As one of the nation's largest industrialized cities, Shanghai has the highest concentration of female workers and well-educated women in strong economic positions. With a significantly higher percentage of the work force (42.53 percent in 1989 compared to the nation average of 37 percent), Wu suggests that the wide range of jobs held by women, the seniority of their positions, their equal wages, the humorous reputation of Shanghai husbands as "henpecked," and the widespread participation of husbands in housework all provide evidence of the special (read modern) equal status of Shanghai women.

However, this class-based (and biased) assessment, even for Shanghai, is incomplete and ignores the realities facing the majority of Chinese women who live in the still predominantly poor rural areas, or for the large numbers of women from the rural areas flowing into the cities to work in the SEZs, or for female college graduates facing sex discrimination in job assignments or employment opportunities, or in the industrializing areas outside of the urban centers. Concentrated in light industries like textiles, electronics, toys, and plastics, these "*dagongmeis*" (working little sisters) constitute the majority of the work force in the SEZs and in some cases 90 percent of the work force in some factories (Woo, 1994, p.287). The plight of these "working little sisters" include facing sexual harassment in the work place, low pay, poor and dangerous working conditions, long hours, and poor crowded housing conditions. Yet, these working little sisters in China are not silent either about what they perceive as the injustices of their situation and the fact that the fruits of their bitter hard labor accrue to the boss. They ask, "Why not become a boss one day," and complain, "I'm not a ball to be kicked around," and assert their hopes that one day they'll be able to successfully escape the net they find themselves in.[9]

The causes generally cited for the persistence of the range of gender-based and class-based injustices and abuses include the persistence of feudal values and ideology, the necessary first long stage of China's Socialism, the cultural impact of modernization and "spiritual pollution" resulting from reopening to the West, and the "weak psychological" aspects or low consciousness of women themselves. Yet, these causes are related to fundamental, structural economic and social inequities that require radical change, not reformist tinkering. As in Southeast Asia and other parts of the world, development is being carried out by environmentally mortgaging the future and on the backs of the cheap labor of women.

In the face of the privileging of quantitative macro-economic indicators cited in assessments of China's reform efforts, it is time for a critical reassessment of the adequacy and appropriateness of the continued acceptance of current indicators of development progress or success. As Vaclav Smil argues in his carefully documented and passionate analysis of China's environmental crisis, the quantitative surrogate indicators that we rely upon to measure human well-being and intangible qualities such as health, affluence, security, intellectual capability, social integration, quality of the environment, and aesthetic satisfaction may not be faithful imprints of the larger realities. They approach human being from the negative aspects (e.g., measuring death, infant mortality as indicator of improvements in life) and are uncertain as categories of analysis (1993, pp. 75-78).[10] As we explore a range of roles that human rights organizations and activists can play, we need to interrogate the assumptions of current research

---

[9] See *Shanghai Jingjiyanjiu*, (1994, January), p. 47.

[10] In the context of China, this may mean the critical interrogation of accepting short term gains at the cost of massive deforestation and land degradation caused by unsustainable farming techniques (inadequate crop rotations, imbalanced use of synthetic fertilizers and diminution of arable land resulting from takeovers for housing and industries) (Smil, 1993).

methodologies and push for the development of more inclusive, human-based data bases that will inform development policy decisions.[11]

Strategies for Multiple Futures: "Brainstorming" Across Cultures

As a case study of a country that is characterized by a huge population,[12] geographically diverse land, a predominantly rural society, and an authoritarian one-Party political regime, China's experience might offer comparative insights into future approaches for other developing countries adopting market approaches for modernization and economic development. As the host for the Fourth World Conference on Women in 1995 and as a focus for human rights criticisms for its repression of political dissidents (Asia Watch, 1992), its Tibet policy, and use of prison labor, China is also a significant actor and focus in international human rights debates and practice. For women's rights activists and scholars, what are some ideological and pragmatic issues arising from attempts to "network" across this sensitive and difficult terrain?

As a general strategy approach, the models pursued so effectively by international human rights advocates to address civil and political rights violations on behalf of individuals (Claude & Weston, 1992, pp. 364-370), may not be as effective when addressing structural systemic obstacles to the full realization of economic and social rights. Keeping in mind the dangers and opportunities of working across systems, I suggest that we need to expand domestic and international strategies to develop multiple and simultaneous points of intervention for activists within and outside China. In the limited space here, I will examine the role of law in China as an example of the importance of the larger legal framework in advancing rights; and the role of the All China Women's Federation (ACWF) as an example of NGO issues in the China context.

[11] See Hom (1994) for a critique of the marginalization of gender and women's issues in the field of Chinese legal studies in the United States.

[12] China's population of about 1.13 billion people in 1990, constitutes 21 percent of the world's population and fully 28 percent of the population of developing countries. Although its population growth rate is only 1.47 percent a year on average, this has meant an additional 126 million people from 1982-1990 (Bannister 1991: 236). In addition to the Han majority, China has 55 ethnic minority groups that account for approximately 7 percent of the total population.

The Role of Law

In its official report prepared for the 1995 World Conference, the Chinese government points to the full equal legal status Chinese women now enjoy with men in marriage and family, economic, political, and social spheres (State Council of the PRC, 1994). The extensive legislation that has been promulgated to protect the legal interests and rights of Chinese women since liberation include 1982 constitutional provisions that guarantee the equal rights of women with men in all spheres of life, and that the state "protects the rights and interests of women, applies the principles of equal pay for equal work to men and women alike, and trains and selects cadres from among women."[13] China also is an early signatory (1980) of the United Nations Convention for the Elimination of All Forms of Discrimination Against Women (CEDAW).[14] In addition, in 1992, China promulgated the Law for the Protection of Women's Rights and Interests[15] that was intended to coordinate and guarantee, not expand the existing rights in existing laws and regulations. These laws collectively set forth principles of equality between men and women in the areas of political, cultural, educational, and economic rights, marriage rights of the person, and family rights.[16] Despite the promulgation of extensive legislation that sets forth this normative formal equality, the reality for most Chinese women is a gap between stated legal and policy goals and implementation (Gao, 1994; Hom, 1992a, 1992b; Woo, 1994).

In the area of labor regulation affecting Chinese women workers in the urban areas, Woo has argued that a regime of protective legislation has resulted in the "biologization" of women's issues (1994). Labor regulations intended to protect the health of women and to

---

[13] Constitution of the People's Republic of China (1982), art. 48, trans. in Laws of the PRC, 1979-1982 (Beijing: Foreign Languages Press, 1987), p. 14.

[14] For an analysis of China's implementation of the Convention, see Mckenzie, (1992).

[15] Translated in FBIS-CHI, April 14, 1992, pp. 17-20.

[16] Yet in a recent volume that focuses on domestic law reform in Post-Mao China that has an editorial selection guideline which chose to include those "sectors where the potential for expanded autonomy appears to be the greatest" (Potter, 1994, p.xii), there is no discussion of the PRC Law for the Protection of the Rights and Interests of Women, or the framework of labor regulations, the 1982 Constitutional provisions, or Marriage Law provisions.

enhance the "quality of the nation" impose limits on the types and conditions of work that women can perform during the five periods of a woman's life when she must be accorded special treatment (menstruation, pregnancy, delivery, nursing and menopause). Although these regulations arguably represent advances in addressing the health needs of women, as Woo argues, they also reinforce the stereotype that the primary role for women is reproduction, and in fact act as disincentives for employers to hire women in the first place given the additional costs of benefits that must be provided to women.

In contrast, the Chinese government has claimed gains and progress for China's 56 million women workers. In a sample survey conducted among 2,000 enterprises, the government claimed that 80 percent of the women in these enterprises were fairly treated during pregnancy and while on maternity leave.[17] However, no one disputes, at least off the record, the fact that women are laid off in generally higher numbers then men or that women continue to face discrimination in the work place.

Nevertheless, Woo's argument underscores the complexity and double-edge dangers of protective legislation that accords different treatment for women without adequate economic and structural supports for implementation. The recent development of a unified state social fund to spread the cost of benefits for women on maternity leave in state enterprises may be an example of one such structural approach. However, in the context of state enterprises facing enormous problems of low productivity, inefficiency, competition in the emerging market economy, and serious problems of funding and managing income and social security programs (Liu, 1991), it remains to be seen to what extent these state sector approaches will be persuasive as models for other enterprises, such as foreign-funded, or township-run enterprises.

Problems of implementation of economic and social rights also implicate the broader complex problem of developing a rule of law in China in light of China's history of rule by man, bureaucratism, authoritarianism, and preference for informality (Woo, 1993, p.81). Given the constitutional protection for the supremacy of the Party

---

[17] See "Labor Minister Reports Gains for Female Workers," *Xinhua*, July 21 1993, (reported in FBIS-CHI July 22, 1993, p. 40).

and the subordination of law to Party policy, the development of law as a source of enforceable economic and social rights for women still is an open question contingent upon the political reform kept tenuously at bay by the present regime.

The Role of Chinese Women's Groups and NGOs with Chinese Characteristics

As the mass organization arm of the Party that acts to implement Party policies and to inform Party decision-making on the needs and interests of women, the All China Women's Federation (ACWF), *Fulian*, occupies a difficult position. The ACWF serves as the propaganda arm, the "service" counseling arm, and as advocate for women, for example, in cases of domestic abuse and violence. One of the current challenges facing the ACWF is the articulation and development of a role for itself as an "independent" women's NGO despite its Party affiliation. In this process, the ACWF is negotiating the perceptions of international NGOs, the diverse perspectives and roles of provincial and local *fulians*[18] and the theoretical assessments emerging from the growing number of Chinese women's studies centers (Tao, C. 1993; Tao, J., 1993), and its own relationship to the various organs of state power. At the same time, it is increasingly clear to outside observers that the ACWF does not speak with a monolithic voice for "Chinese women," nor is it free from internal criticism (Li, X., 1994; Hom, 1993).

The role of the ACWF within China and in the international arena, particularly in light of its visible key role in the Chinese planning for the 1995 Conference, also implicates issues regarding the role and existence of Chinese NGOs. A recent study of the rising number of Chinese foundations suggests that a range of NGOs with Chinese characteristics is emerging and that these NGOs will contribute to the development of an autonomous civil sector, but they will need to develop more transparency and accountability in its financing structures, processes, and funding decisions. (National Committee on U.S.-China Relations, 1994). I have suggested that in efforts to

---

[18] For example, the Shanghai *fulian* has recently developed its own set of enterprises (a clothing boutique store, a hotel, and conference facilities) as an independent source of income that might support expanded activities (Hom, S. K. 1994, July interview with Shanghai fulian).

develop alliances across different political and cultural systems, we need to understand the context, obstacles, and opportunities facing Chinese NGO or human rights/women's advocates attempting organizational strategies situated within a politically authoritarian regime (Hom, 1993).

When the priorities defined by the male dominated leadership are in tension with the interests of women, historically the "women's" issues have been subordinated to some other project, e.g., nationalism and modernization, or labeled divisive (Hom, 1992a, 1992b). The question of potential conflict between the modernization agenda as defined by a patriarchal Party leadership and gender-based justice goals is foreclosed by the reality of an authoritarian one-Party regime that clearly will not allow dissent that questions its leadership. But ultimately, it will be the outrage of the *dagongmeis* (working little sisters), the political negotiations of domestic Chinese women's groups, and the courage of human rights activists and scholars, that will ensure that social and economic rights are realized in the daily lives of Chinese women. International human rights NGOs and activists can contribute to this difficult process by being open to the development of new alliances and simultaneous strategies (Hom, 1993), strategies that resist the seduction of the geo-political power games of governmental bodies, and that stake out an independent substantive human rights agenda that avoids cultural imperialism and the privileging of nativism claims.

REFERENCES

Alford, W.P. (1992). Making a Goddess of Democracy from Loose Sand: Thoughts on Human Rights in the People's Republic of China. In A. An-Na'im (Ed.), *Human Rights in Cross-Cultural Perspective: A Quest for Consensus* (pp. 65-80). Philadelphia: University of Pennsylvania Press.

Asia Watch. (1992). *Anthems of Defeat: Crackdown in Hunan Province 1989-1992*. New York: Author.

Chu, G. C., & Ju, Y. (1993). *The Great Wall in Ruins: Communication and Cultural Change in China*. Albany, NY: SUNY Press.

Claude, R. P., & Weston, B. H. (Eds.). (1992). *Human Rights in the World Community: Issues and Action*. Philadelphia: University of Pennsylvania Press.

Gaige, fazhan, and wending: queyibuke (Reform, development, and stability: all are necessary, or literally, cannot lack one). (1994, April). *Shanghai Jingjiyanjiu* (Shanghai Economic Review), p. 1.

Gao, X. (1994). China's Modernization and Changes in the Social Status of Rural Women. In C. Gilmartin, G. Hershatter, L. Rofel, & T. White (Eds.), *Engendering China: Women, Culture, and the State* (pp. 80-97). Cambridge, MA: Harvard University Press.

Hardt, J. P. & Kaufman, R. F. (1991). Chinese Model for Change: Prospects and Problems. In Joint Economic Committee, Congress of the United States (Ed.), *China's Economic Dilemma in the 1990s: The Problems of Reforms, Modernization, and Interdependence* (pp. ix-xiv). Armonk, NY: M.E. Sharpe.

Hom, S.K. (1994). Engendering Chinese Legal Studies: Gatekeeping, Master Discourses, and other Challenges. *Signs, 19,* 1020-1047.

Hom, S. K. (1993, Winter). Listening for Diversity: Broaden Debate Among Rights Groups in the Round-Up to 1995. *China Rights Forum,* 12-15.

Hom, S. K. (1992a). Female Infanticide in China: the Specter of Human Rights and Thoughts Towards (An)other Vision. *Columbia Human Rights Law Review, 23,* 249-314.

Hom, S. K. (1992b). Law, Ideology, and Patriarchy in the People's Republic of China: Feminist Observations of an Ethnic Spectator. *International Review of Comparative Public Policy, 4,* 173-191.

Information Office of the State Council of the People's Republic of China. (1994, June). *The Situation of Chinese Women.* Beijing: Author.

Jefferson, G. (1993). The Chinese Economy: Moving Forward. In W.A. Joseph (Ed.), *China Briefing, 1992* (pp. 35-53). Boulder, CO: Westview Press.

National Committee on U.S.-China Relations, Inc. (1994, May). *The Rise of Nongovernmental Organizations in China: Implications for Americans.* (National Committee China Policy Series, No. Eight). New York: Author.

Orleans, L. A. (1991). Overview: Social and Human Factors. In Joint Economic Committee, Congress of the United States (Ed.). *China's Economic Dilemma in the 1990's: The Problems of Reforms, Modernization, and Interdependence* (pp. 227-233). Armonk, NY: M.E. Sharpe.

Li, X. (1994). Economic Reform and the Awakening of Chinese Women's Consciousness. In C. Gilmartin, G. Hershatter, L. Rofel, & T. White (Eds.). *Engendering China: Women, Culture, and the State* (pp.360-382). Cambridge, MA: Harvard University Press.

Liu, L. (1991). Social Security for State Sector Workers in the People's Republic of China: The Reform Decade and Beyond. In Joint Economic Committee, Congress of the United States (Ed.), *China's Economic Dilemma in the 1990's: The Problems of Reforms, Modernization, and Interdependence* (pp. 270-289). Armonk, NY: M.E. Sharpe.

Mckenzie, P. (1992). China and the Women's Convention: Prospects for the Implementation of an International Norm. *China Law Reporter, 7,* 23-60.

Pearson, M. (1994). Foreign Investment and Trade. In W. A. Joseph (Ed.), *China Briefing*. Boulder, CO: Westview Press.

Ross, L (1988). *Environmental Policy in China*. Bloomington and Indianapolis, IN: Indiana University Press.

Potter, P. (Ed.). (1994). *Domestic Law Reforms in Post-Mao China*. Armonk, NY: M.E. Sharpe.

Smil, V. (1993). *China's Environmental Crisis: An Inquiry into the Limits of National Development*. Armonk, NY: M. E. Sharpe.

Tao, Chen. (1993). Zhongguofunujiefangyundung Zhauchienlema? (Is the Chinese Women's Movement Moving Forward?). *Tansuoyuzhengming, 6,* 23-27.

Tao, Jianmin. (1993). Shehuijinbu yu Funujiefang (Social Progress and Women's Liberation). *Tansuoyuzhengming, 6,* 28-32.

Wong, C. (1994). China's Economy: The Limits of Gradualist Reform. In W. A. Joseph (Ed.), *China Briefing*. Boulder, CO: Westview Press.

Woo, M. (1993). Courts, Justice and Human Rights. In W.A. Joseph (Ed.), *China Briefing, 1992* (pp. 81-102). Boulder, CO: Westview Press.

Woo, M. (1994). Chinese Women Workers: The Delicate Balance Between Protection and Equality. In C. Gilmartin, G. Hershatter, L. Rofel, & T. White (Eds.), *Engendering China: Women, Culture, and the State* (pp. 279-295). Cambridge, MA: Harvard University Press.

Yuan. M. (1993, June 25). Special Views on Strengthening Special Economic Zones Construction. *Renmin Ribao*, 2. (Translated in FBIS-CHI-94-127, July 1, 1994, pp. 30-33.)

Chapter 8
Reconstructing Social and Economic Rights in Transitional Economies

Rebecca P. Sewall

Summary

Today, a woman's right to work, the nature of her work, the amount of her wages and the conditions under which she works are increasingly determined by international forces. The fully documented erosion of women's economic rights is a direct consequence of larger shifts in the global economy. These shifts are being "managed" by the World Bank and the International Monetary Fund (IMF) together with the United States of America which promote a structural, rather than a social adjustment model. In promoting the shift from a social to a structural adjustment model, the international financial institutions and the U.S. have failed to recognize the need for a concomitant shift in the legal infrastructure protecting women's employment-related rights. As will be shown below, women's economic rights are determined by the shape of the economic system in which they are articulated. In the shift from one economic system to another, women will continue to suffer disproportionately until changes are made in the legal structures that protect their employment-related rights.

Women's social and economic rights are not separate entities unto themselves, but instead exist as principles that take their form through laws and policies. Traditionally, it has been through labor and employment-related laws that women's social and economic rights have been articulated. Although employment-related rights have been universally used to protect women's social and economic rights, the rights these laws serve to uphold vary greatly among nations and economic systems. As the first section of this paper will demonstrate, what constitutes a woman's social and economic right is determined by the economic system of which she is a part. In the free-market economies of the industrialized West, where social and economic rights are defined within the context of the market, employment-related rights are largely limited to granting women equal opportunity to access the market. In command economies throughout the world, where social and economic rights are defined in terms of goods and services, employment-related rights have been the means through which these goods and services are disbursed.

Today, throughout the world, command economies are being eclipsed by market economies through a process known as structural adjustment. While the "social adjustment" models of the 1950s and 1960s viewed the provision of social and economic rights as a means towards achieving development, the abolishment of these very same rights was the initial requisite for the success of the structural adjustment models of the 1970s and 1980s. As a result, the protective labor rights that once safeguarded women's social and economic rights have now become viewed as "rigidities" and impediments to economic growth (Standing, 1989). The second section of this paper will explain why and how the successful pursuit of a structural adjustment strategy required the subjugation or abandonment of employment-related rights that protected women's social and economic rights in a command economy, and will explore two trends in women's labor-force participation that have transpired as a result of this supply-side shift.

The shift from one economic system to another signals the need for a redefinition of women's social and economic rights, and new employment-related legal mechanisms to uphold these rights. But as the third section of this paper will bring to light, while the mechanisms of a free-market economy may be taking form in many countries, the basic laws protecting women's social and economic rights within a free market are not yet in place, or have not been enforced.

This global economic shift is being "managed" by the World Bank and the IMF together with the US. While the US has been active in leveraging structural adjustment reforms (which require the subordination of certain employment-related rights in the command economy), it has also made many of its foreign assistance and trade programs conditional upon the observance of specific rights aimed to protect workers in a free-market economy. Although these "workers' rights" provisions may protect some workers, they fail to provide women with the most basic employment-related rights necessary for them to actualize their social and economic rights in a free-market economy. The fourth section of this paper will suggest specific actions that can be taken to correct this oversight. Specifically, it suggests including the right to equal opportunity and treatment as a workers' right in U.S. foreign assistance and trade policies as a means to protect women's economic rights. The fifth and final section of this paper will briefly discuss some of the current debates surrounding this approach.

Social and Economic Rights in Free-Market Economies

In the free-market economies of the industrialized West, social and economic rights are defined within the context of the market; the most basic premise being that each individual has the right to formulate his/her own economic destiny within a free market. The market is therefore the vehicle through which social and economic rights are actualized — without it the realization of social and economic rights would be impossible.

Within this paradigm, the notion of equality is expressed in terms of granting all persons equal access to the market. From then on, they are left largely on their own. Accordingly, the most fundamental social and economic right provided by the state to individuals is the right to access the market. In most Western free-market economies, this right has been extended by laws granting individuals the right to freedom from discrimination and the right to equal opportunity.

In most Western industrialized nations, laws granting the freedom from discrimination and equal opportunity are the major (and in many situations, the only) employment-related rights specifically geared to protect the social and economic rights of women. Over the past thirty years, these laws have become the vital protectorate of women's social and economic rights.

It is important to note that in many free-market economies, and in the US in particular, these laws grant women access to the labor force, but do little beyond that. They do not, in themselves, provide the legal mechanisms often required to sustain women's continued labor-force participation. If a woman chooses to leave the labor force to bear and raise a child (which would jeopardize her job and earnings), she must then bear the consequences. She has no "right" to her forfeited earnings.

Social and Economic Rights in a Command Economy

In command economies, social and economic rights are conceptualized differently. The redistributive welfare state is the ultimate
goal of the command economy and is carried out through the state-
run public sector (Standing, 1989). Within these economies, social
and economic rights are defined as a basket of goods and services (i.e.
each individual has a right to adequate housing, health care, old-age
care etc.). While in the West, individuals have the right to access the
market through which they may or may not acquire the basket, in
command economies, individuals are granted the right to the goods
within the basket. The public-sector work place is therefore the
means through which the basket is disbursed.

Within this paradigm, the protection of women's economic
rights did not require laws granting women equal opportunity or
freedom from discrimination as long as they received the same basket. Gender discrimination within certain professions was rampant,
but its actual consequences were minimal and did not jeopardize
women's social and economic rights as long as they were provided
with a host of goods and services roughly equivalent to that received
by others.

The Economic Shift and Labor Deregulation

Recent changes in the global economy and in the world system of
production have precipitated a major shift in the predominate strategies for development. Over the past two decades, "social adjustment"
strategies have been replaced by those favoring supply-side forces and
structural adjustment. While the "social adjustment" models of the
1950s and 1960s viewed the provision of social and economic rights
as a means towards achieving development, the abolishment of these
very same rights was the initial requisite for the success of the structural adjustment models of the 1970s and 1980s. As a result, the protective labor rights that once safeguarded women's social and
economic rights have now become viewed as "rigidities" and impediments to economic growth (Standing, 1989). The erosion of
employment-related rights has been an unfortunate consequence of
this new development strategy, prompting one observer to label the
1980s "the decade of labor deregulation" (Standing, 1989, p.1077).

Since the early 1980s, the US has been active in promoting the
adoption of structural adjustment policies by providing cash grants or

commodity transfers to host countries to leverage the adoption of these reforms. It also has various programs conducted through numerous U.S. government agencies (USAID, Commerce, the Export-Import Bank, OPIC and Treasury etc.) that provide financial incentives for U.S. producers to invest and/or relocate their production overseas—a movement otherwise known as "that giant sucking sound."

Structural adjustment consists of a number of economic measures aimed to correct "existing imbalances" and make economies more market oriented. In World Bank parlance, these measures are designed to correct "markets distorted by inappropriate regulation and price supports" by deregulating state support (GAO Report, 1993, p.60). Generally, these measures are aimed towards increasing exports, promoting private and direct foreign investment, privatizing public-sector enterprises and cutting back on state provided social and welfare services. Virtually all of these components require the dismantling of previously existing labor rights.

Countries with a high premium on export-led production, and/or those reliant on attracting direct foreign and/or private investment for the success of their strategy, must offer a host of incentives to encourage investment in, or relocation to, their country. Although these incentives vary from one country to another, they usually include tax holidays, subsidized credits, customs exemptions and unrestricted remittances of profits. Because the primary motivation for foreign firms to invest or relocate is the availability of cheap labor, host countries deregulate wage legislation in an effort to provide foreign/private firms with low labor costs. Many countries, particularly in Asia and Latin America, have witnessed the proliferation of export processing zones. These zones are designated areas for export production where investment laws and labor standards are less restrictive than prevailing national standards. In some countries, labor costs are artificially low as countries are competing against other countries with even lower labor costs to attract this type of investment.

Feminization

While the 1980s have been dubbed the "decade of labor deregulation," they may as aptly be labeled the "decade of labor feminization." Accompanying this shift has been an increased demand for female labor in many parts of the world that are heavily reliant on export-led growth, and critics are quick to argue that this is no slight coincidence. As governments remove or weaken wage legislation and institutional safeguards, there has been an enormous proliferation of low-wage jobs paying an individual, rather than a family wage. Casual and short-term laborers have replaced full-time salaried workers, reducing fixed labor costs for employers, and income and security for workers. As minimum wages are eroded, employers substitute high-cost male labor with lower-cost female labor. In virtually all countries that have established successful export-led production, there has been both an absolute and relative growth in the use of female labor. In some cases, the rates for women have increased, while the rates for men have decreased.

But while women's labor-force participation rates in many parts of the world have increased, their wages and job security have decreased. The types of jobs that have been relocated are low-skilled, low-paying jobs that can easily be learned in a short period of time. Most often they are dull, repetitive jobs with little room for advancement that would be associated with high turnover anywhere in the world. Usually they involve the assembly of light articles such as toys, electronics, and garments.

As the primary motivation for enterprises to relocate is access to cheap labor, they will take advantage of the cheapest available labor within these countries. In nearly every country, it is women who constitute the cheapest source of labor. Most efforts to explain why women, rather than men, accept these jobs point to socio-cultural factors which inhibit women's levels of productivity. That is, women are one of the cheapest available sources of labor (next to children) because patriarchal, socio-cultural factors outside of the labor force make them temporary and adjunct members of the labor force and secondary wage earners in the family. Women's primary role as wife and mother means families are less likely to invest in their education and skill training. With little education and few marketable skills, women are more likely to resort to low-skilled and low-paying jobs. Since women in most countries are viewed only as secondary wage earners, they are more likely than men to accept jobs paying individual rather than family wages. Employers are also more likely to hire women for jobs paying low wages, because they believe that when men are paid individual wages, they respond by reducing their effort.

As a result of the stereotypical attributes of nimble fingers and near-divine patience that are associated with women, they are perceived as better suited for performing jobs which in many nations are traditionally thought of as "ladies' jobs." Perhaps most importantly, women's perceived docility and compliance makes them the preferred employees for employers whose goal it is to maintain a constant supply of cheap labor.

In these global factories, young women perform low-skilled repetitive tasks with minimum or no job security. In efforts by employers to maintain a cheap and compliant labor force, women are usually fired when they marry, or are forced to leave due to debilitating health conditions caused by factory work, just at a time when they would be commanding higher wages.

In most situations, employment in these factories has done little to help integrate women into their national economies in any meaningful way. To the contrary, critics argue that this type of employment has only subjected them to "super-exploitative" conditions and furthered the patriarchal, social conditions that relegated women to these jobs in the first place (Lim, 1983).

Perhaps more disturbing is the fact that because a nation's prospect for development has become reliant on the low-wage work of women, female workers have been increasingly subjected to repressive national policies to preserve their compliance. In many countries, union formation is prohibited for a specific period of time, or outlawed all together. In other countries, where the right to unionize may be on the books, severe "informal" pressure may serve as a sufficient deterrent to union participation. The presence of state guards and para-military forces to enforce compliance is commonplace in countries where the deprivation of employment-related rights has resulted in little more than forced labor (Enloe, 1989).

Marginalization

While the 1980s witnessed a huge increase in the use of female labor in countries heavily reliant on export production, the 1990s are witnessing a dramatic decrease in the use of female labor in economies in which women once played a vital role. The whittling away of protective labor policies has been a vital component of the economic restructuring currently taking place in the former Soviet Union and East Central Europe, as they make their transition from a command to a market economy.

State policies of full employment—once the hallmark of the socialist state—have been abandoned. Employment is no longer

considered a right, but for many, it has become a luxury. State resources have been channeled into the development and expansion of
private-sector enterprises, while the public sector has been left to fal-
ter under its own weight. For a region of the world that once privileged social and economic rights above political and civil ones, the
loss of these rights has been particularly disrupting.

Recent evidence reveals that as enterprises are forced to make
redundancies in response to the recessionary constraints, or in preparation for privatization, women are more subject to layoffs than are
their male counterparts. This is evidenced by higher rates of female
unemployment in many parts of the region. Additional research reveals that women's unemployment rates are not solely a function of
their labor-market position, but that discriminatory layoff practices
play a determinant role (Sewall, 1992).

But the problem for women not only lies in how the old economy is being dismantled, but also in how the new economy is being
assembled. In the socialist economy that privileged workers in heavy
industry, women, who dominated jobs in the low-paying commercial
and service sectors, were placed at an economic disadvantage. Today, however, it is precisely these sectors that are considered the
most viable for the region's economic future. Due to recent economic reforms and the subsequent influx of direct foreign investment, the sectors of the economy that women once dominated have
assumed greater importance in the new market economy. Many of
these once low-paying jobs have almost overnight become prestigious
jobs paying salaries often three to ten times more than before. Unfortunately, now that these jobs have become high-paying, prestigious
jobs in the private sector, women are no longer being hired for them
even though they are more qualified. A masculinization of jobs is occurring. Men are replacing women in jobs women have traditionally
held.

Gender-biased hiring practices that exclude women from new
jobs in the private sector will likely result in the economic dislocation
of a substantial proportion of the current labor force and will have
dire consequences both for women and for the inchoate economies of
the region. Before the fall of communism, women's labor-force participation rates in the region were among the highest in the world.
Given the region's dismal economy, women's wages are vital both
for themselves and for the economic survival of their families. Demographic considerations such as high divorce rates and high rates of

male mortality only underscore the need for women to earn their own wages.

If women are denied access to the formal private sector, it is not unrealistic to expect that the faltering public sector will become increasingly feminized. As men continue to dominate the higher-paying private sector and as women are relegated to the lower-paying public sector, wage differentials between men and women will widen drastically. As men leave the public sector for higher-paying jobs in the private sector, women will assume a greater proportion of public-sector workers. Public-sector enterprises currently have two fates: to become private, or to collapse. Whatever the outcome, women are likely to lose. Those enterprises that become private are unlikely to retain much of their female labor. Those that eventually collapse will move a greater proportion of women into the ranks of the unemployed.

If women are unable to get jobs in the private sector, it is also not unrealistic to expect that they will be pushed into the informal sector where wages are low and security is minimal. U.S. initiatives in the area may actually be encouraging this trend (see below).

If women continue to be excluded from the private-sector labor force, it is likely that the next few years will witness their remarginalization from the labor force. If steps are not taken to prevent their remarginalization now, there is little chance that women will ever be able to regain the labor-market position they once held. Without preventative measures, women as a social group will become economically vulnerable. Before the economic reforms, the consequences of gender discrimination were minimal as women were guaranteed the rights to a host of goods and services. Today, with the loss of these goods and services, the consequences of gender discrimination are and will continue to be devastating.

Women's Social and Economic Rights in the Shift

While mechanisms of a free-market economy are taking form in many formerly command economies, the basic laws protecting women's social and economic rights within this type of economic system are not yet in place, or have not been enforced. As a result, women have been denied their basic social and economic rights in both types of economies. While the loss of the previous social and economic rights has caused women to suffer disproportionately, they have not been legally or actually granted the employment-related rights upon which the actualization of their social and economic rights in the free market depend.

Options for Action

Within the current development paradigm, development and the actualization of social and economic rights are mutually exclusive. The successful pursuit of structural adjustment policies demands the subjugation of social and economic rights, while the advancement of social and economic rights, especially women's employment-related rights is perceived as hindering any chance of development. Framed in such a stark dichotomy, it is difficult to present the argument for social and economic rights, if it will necessarily imply that a country's prospect for development will suffer. Proponents of improving social and economic rights are quickly turned into enemies of development.

This either/or dynamic was made painfully apparent at the recent World Trade Organization (WTO) meetings in Rabat. While the US and France pressed for the inclusion of "workers' rights" on the WTO agenda, developing nations chose to view these actions as nothing more than veiled protectionism, arguing that enforced compliance with "workers' rights" would strip them of their competitive edge and thwart any prospect for their development.

It is unrealistic to expect that developing countries will change their development tactics without changes in the situational factors (i.e. debt) that forced them to adopt these policies in the first place. Therefore, changing the policies of international lending and donor agencies (World Bank and the IMF) and changing the laws governing foreign assistance and trade policy of donors and trading partners of these countries may be a worthwhile approach to moving this stalemate beyond the current paradigm and altering the conditions that surround the continued depravation of social and economic rights.

The World Bank and the IMF are the most obvious targets for this type of action. However, it is important to keep in mind that until mechanisms are established for their accountability through NGO pressure, they are still only accountable to their country membership. The most expedient approach then, may not be an all-out assault on these institutions, but continued pressure on the countries that comprise their membership.

The next logical step in this approach would be to target the laws regulating foreign assistance and trade policies of the countries that are the biggest donors, and to whom the greatest percentage of trade is directed. The U.S. is uniquely positioned for this type of action both because of its role as a donor and trade partner, and because of its leverage in the international community.

While the U.S. has been active in promoting structural adjustment policies which require cut backs in employment-related rights, it has also made many of its foreign assistance and trade programs conditional upon the observance of specific workers' rights to protect against the worst abuses in the free market. These laws require countries receiving foreign assistance or trade benefits from the U.S. to take steps to provide the following workers' rights known as "internationally recognized workers' rights" (IRWRs): freedom of association, freedom to organize and bargain collectively, prohibition of forced labor, minimum age for employment and the right to acceptable conditions of work. These provisions fail to include an antidiscrimination provision that would provide women with the most basic right in a free economy—the right to equal opportunity and treatment.

These workers' rights provisions are derived from two of the three categories of fundamental workers' rights delineated by the International Labor Organization (ILO). The ILO has recognized "fundamental" or "basic" human rights as (1) freedom of association (including freedom to organize and bargain collectively), (2) freedom from forced labor, and (3) equality of opportunity and treatment (including equal remuneration and freedom from discrimination). To date, the right to equality of opportunity and treatment, or an antidiscrimination provision, though recognized by the ILO as a IRWR, remains conspicuously absent from U.S. provisions (Travis, 1992).

Even though the legislative history of section 502(a)(4) of the Trade Act of 1974, which defines these rights in U.S. legislation, states that "the underlying intent in promoting these internationally recognized rights of workers is to ensure that the broadest sectors of the population benefit from trade and development" (USAID G.N., 1994) the U.S. fails to make any distinction between male and female workers in these "workers' rights." Although these provisions may help some women, most are excluded from the areas of employment where they might be able to benefit from them (Travis, 1992). Without the freedom from discrimination, or absent a job, women can not benefit from the right to organize. One way to alter the conditions that surround the deprivation of women's social and economic rights would be to include an antidiscrimination provision in the list of workers' rights already recognized by the US in its trade and foreign assistance policy.

Because the Trade Act of 1974 is cross-referenced into other laws, if an antidiscrimination provision were included in the Act, it would extend to several other laws governing U.S. foreign assistance and trade policies. Such a provision in P.L. 102-391 would prohibit the use of appropriated funds for financial incentives to U.S. firms and enterprises to invest or relocate overseas, if these projects would discriminate. These changes in OPIC would prohibit it from insuring projects that maintained discriminatory employment practices.

Several major U.S. preferential trade programs also link trade benefits to workers' rights. The inclusion of an antidiscrimination provision would also be crossed referenced into several major programs including the Generalized System of Preferences (GSP), the Overseas Private Investment Corporation, the Caribbean Basin Initiative, and the Omnibus Trade Act of 1988. The potential of these programs to leverage changes in host countries' legal codes should not be underestimated. Duty-free imports to the US under the GSP alone totaled $11.1 billion in 1990 (Travis, 1992, p. 182).

If such a provision were included in the Trade Act, then it could easily be cross-referenced into the Multilateral Investment Guarantee Agency Act (MIGA) and start to exert significant influence at the World Bank. MIGA is a World Bank organization that provides investment insurance and technical assistance to developing countries. The MIGA Act requires the U.S. Director of the Agency to adopt policies that would ensure that MIGA does not guarantee any investments in countries that are not taking steps to afford the above-mentioned workers' rights.

Debates Surrounding This Approach

There are, however, very real short-term and long-term consequences to be considered in pursuing this approach with regard to U.S. foreign assistance and trade policies specifically, and to workers' rights-linked trade laws in general. Opponents of such an approach are quick to argue that attaching such a condition to U.S. foreign assistance and trade-related programs is not only a case of veiled protectionism, but may, in fact, hurt the very women these provisions are designed to protect. Will the successful pursuit of women's economic rights through an antidiscrimination provision in U.S. foreign assistance and trade policies discourage investment and ultimately curtail the job prospects available to women? Would it have the effect of pushing them into even less desirable jobs with lower pay and worse conditions? Opponents also argue that investment should be encouraged rather than discouraged as wages and working conditions are expected to improve with increased investment.

Observers of such arguments point out that this line of reasoning, though entirely valid in the short term, might be overly naive when it comes to the protection of women's economic rights in the long term. They argue instead, that although wages and conditions may improve for men, there is little to indicate that, without protective legislation, they will also improve for women. And, if wages and conditions do start to improve for women, what will be done to ensure that they improve for women vis-a-vis men? Occupational segregation and stubbornly persistent wage gaps in countries where wages and conditions have improved across the board only underscore the need for action in order to achieve long term goals.

Furthermore, arguments against pursuing such an approach pose a particular dilemma for U.S. women who, as a matter of principle, want to see their government uphold the right of equal opportunity and treatment on the same level it upholds the right to collective bargaining. Many American women would also not take kindly to the notion of their tax dollars, in the form of foreign assistance and preferential trade programs, going to countries that overtly or tacitly condone discrimination against women.

Perhaps one of the most compelling arguments against undertaking such an approach is presented by Lamarche in this volume. In championing workers' rights-linked foreign assistance and trade policies, do we risk jeopardizing human and workers' rights as basic international principles, or would we risk, as she aptly puts it "the commodification of human rights in the international commercial sphere?" Or, as some might argue, might it be to our advantage to advance these provisions wherever we can, especially given that with very real economic consequences, these provisions may be more apt to encourage compliance?

These are difficult issues with which women worldwide must start to contend. But as the "benefits" of free trade are premised upon women's lack of economic rights, one point of common ground from which to start addressing these concerns may be the undisputed need to demand space for women and women's NGOs in the institutions and processes that regulate it.

REFERENCES

Enloe, C. (1989). Women Textile Workers in the Militarization of Southeast Asia. In J. Nash (Ed.), *Women, Men and the International Division of Labor* (pp. 70-89). New York: State University of New York.

Lim, L. (1989). Capitalisms, Imperialisms and Patriarchy: The Dilemma of Third-World Women Workers in Multinational Factories. In J. Nash (Ed.), *Women, Men and the International Division of Labor* (pp. 70-89). New York: State University of New York.

Sewall, R. (1992). *A Tenuous Movement: Women and Economic Reform in Hungary* (Report). Budapest, Hungary: Budapest University of Economic Sciences.

Standing, G. (1989). Feminization Through Flexible Labor. *World Development, 17,* 1077-1095.

Travis, K. (1992). Women in Global Production and Worker Rights Provisions in U.S. Trade Laws. *Yale Journal of International Law, 17*(1), 173-194.

U.S. Public Document 20. (1994). *USAID/General Notice* (PPC 01/10/94).

* Partial support for this paper came from the Health and Development Policy Project. Thanks are given to Shawn MacDonald and Sydney Smith for assistance and comments.

Chapter 9
Flowers That Kill: The Case of the Colombian Flower Workers[1]

Gladys Acosta Vargas

"I worked five years in flower growing and I wasted all my youth and beauty in a pigsty of a flower plantation." (A flower worker) (Silva, 1982)

I first became involved with the situation of the Colombian flower workers after coming into contact with activists working to improve the quality of life of these workers. I agreed to help raise awareness about the need for international, regional and national strategies to improve the working conditions for employees in the expanding and profitable flower industry. In 1992, I became acquainted with a European campaign, begun in 1990, to call attention to the serious situation of the workers in the flower industry. ("What is the Flower," 1993, p. 1). In July, 1993, the European Parliament's enactment of a resolution on Human Rights, Democracy and Development, produced an immediate response from the Colombian government and the Colombian Association of Flower Exporters (*Asocación Colombiana de Exportadores de Flores* or *ASOCOLFLORES*).

The resolution requested the European Commission to study the importing of products manufactured in the so-called re-education fields of China, products made by children, and flower and fruit produced under subhuman conditions that threaten workers' health in Central America, Colombia, Peru, Kenya and elsewhere. The resolution asked that the European Commission petition the Council to stop the importing of these goods produced under conditions that violate human rights.

---

[1] This article is the result of a collective effort by staff members at *La Federación Nacional Sindical Unitaria Agropecuaria*, at the Inter-Institutional Flower Commission and, in particular, Lucy Alvarez Benítez, who patiently gathered information from women who work in the flower industry.

The resolution had serious implications for an export item as important as flowers. The public, thanks to the media, began to find out what was happening in those open, plastic-covered parcels of land that have changed the face of the Bogotá Savannah. The timing was perfect for uncovering the real interests at issue. Even the Colombian organizations supporting the public campaign denouncing the treatment of workers said they would refuse to boycott flower sales abroad ("What is the Flower," 1993, p. 3).

Framework for Globalization

The last 30 years have seen accelerated changes in the global economic system. We are in an important phase in the historical cycle of capitalism and we must ask how to incorporate our countries into the so-called "globalization." Who are the workers? How do they work? Under what conditions? Who are the beneficiaries? What jobs are open to women and why? The flower industry is a good example of an industry that is dominated by women workers and integrated into a globalized chain of production.

Today, more than ever, it is possible to contrast the states which constitute the centers of economic power from those on the periphery and to see how the latter are disadvantaged in accessing world markets. The flower industry so far has been profitable, but the market for flowers remains extremely volatile. In this sense, the flower industry shows us the fragility that surrounds the insertion of peripheral countries into the world system.

So far the flower industry has been able to overcome barriers imposed by State health policies regulating use of fungicides and pesticides. But there are other types of barriers that pose more difficult obstacles. Before the congressional elections of 1994, the United States, the largest buyer of flowers, passed protectionist legislation against the "dumping" of Colombian roses. California rose growers, who have much higher production costs than Colombian growers, exerted pressure during the pre-election campaign to recover their market position. Similar protectionist movements around the globe have closed markets for bananas, coffee and other products. The result has been to weaken the working conditions in those industries in peripheral countries, as in the case of the flower industry in Colombia.

The Flower Industry and the Emergence of the Flower Worker

Perhaps some of the readers of these pages have seen shop displays in New York or Amsterdam of gorgeous Colombian flowers and have wondered about the women workers who tend these exotic blossoms—symbols of love and friendship—which somehow manage to maintain the appearance of being freshly cut even after their transoceanic journey. In this article the focus is not on flower conservation but on the deteriorating social and economic rights of workers (who are predominantly female) in the flower industry. The descriptions that follow identify the concrete elements that must be analyzed in order to bring about legal actions to safeguard the social and economic rights of workers.

Flower production in Colombia began in the 1960s in the Bogotá Savannah, a region that holds several advantages over North American and Dutch competition: a stable climate, an inexpensive female workforce, nearby air transport, state policies that foster export-oriented investment and the possibility of acquiring land at bargain prices. These are all comparative advantages for the Colombian flower industry. American flower growers have formed partnerships with Colombian investors and moved production to Colombia rather than maintaining production in the United States where production costs are much higher.

Currently, there are about 450 companies in the Colombian flower industry with a total crop area of 3,655 hectares (9,031.55 acres) of land. Ninety percent of the total flower crop is located in the Bogotá Savannah at an altitude of 2,600 meters (8,530 feet) above sea level, where temperatures range from 14 to 20 degrees centigrade (57 to 68 Fahrenheit) during the day and 4 to 8 degrees centigrade (39 to 46.5 Fahrenheit) at night. The remaining 10 percent of the crop is grown in Valle and Antioquia.

The flower industry generates about 140,000 jobs. A total of 80,000 of those jobs are in the flower industry itself (70 percent of those employees are female). The other 60,000 jobs are indirectly tied to the flower industry through firms which supply plastics, packaging materials, pesticides and other products and services related to the flower industry ("Conclusions of First Forum," 1991, p. 1)

The flower industry produces very high revenues. Of the top 100 exporting companies in Bogotá, 22 are in the flower industry (*El Espectador*, 1994 June). According to *ASOCOLFLORES*, between

1975 and 1980 flower exports grew at a rate of 30 percent per annum. In the 1990s the growth rate hovered around 16 percent per annum. In 1991 the value of exports reached US $267.3 million which corresponds to 101,000 tons of flowers. The main market for Colombian flowers is North America (United States, Canada and Puerto Rico) which absorbs 79.75 percent of the total flower exports (US $213.1 million for 83,097 tons of flowers). The United States alone receives 80.54 percent of the flower exports to North America, or US $184.3 million. (*"La Floricultura,"* 1993, p. 6).

Recruitment Patterns for Women

Several factors shape the patterns of recruitment for female workers. Most importantly, female labor is much cheaper than male labor. Women also leave and re-enter the labor market because of childbirth, which decreases the payment of social benefits. By contrast, men tend to have unbroken periods of employment and permanent jobs which allows them to rise up the vocational ladder to higher paying jobs. Women overwhelmingly are trapped in the lower paying jobs related to the production process as well as in the subsequent preparation of flowers for air transport. These jobs require a high level of discipline and skill in the delicate handling of plants, skills which are prevalent in the female workforce.

At the end of the 1960s, the workforce was recruited from towns in the vicinity of flower plantations in Tabio, Tenjo, Nemocon and Suesca. In those early years of the flower industry in Colombia, employers could satisfy their labor needs with part-time rural women from the countryside (Silva, 1982, p. 34). With the accelerated growth of agribusiness, however, employers found it necessary to recruit urban women who were transported from Bogotá, by bus or truck, to the fields.

The Labor Contract, Maternity Benefits, Wages and Company Profits

According to Silva's study, the female workforce is recruited principally from two groups: young, single women who have not had children and women who are at least 35 years old and not interested in having more children. Through these hiring policies, employers try to reduce their liability for maternity leave and to avoid accommodating pregnant workers by changing job assignments.

Most flower workers are recruited from the same sector of the workforce as housekeepers. Salaries are below the minimum wage and working conditions are almost slave-like. In spite of joining a labor system that is subject to very demanding standards, the flower worker has "advantages" over the housekeeper in terms of her personal freedom because at least she knows what time of day she will get off work.

This industrial sector shows with clarity that the female labor force, when incorporated into the most modern and profitable sectors, does not automatically imply progress in improving the quality of life for women (Medrano, 1982, pp. 53-54). However, women need jobs with salaries where there are better opportunities to negotiate working conditions. Instead women are employed through contracts which are for a fixed period of time and many are written as subcontracts for piecework.

These varied contractual arrangements and different categories of employees impede all efforts to organize male and female workers. Many companies are not directly responsible for layoffs or contract termination. The subcontractor is the direct employer and acts as an intermediary in labor relations.

Yet despite job insecurities and poor working conditions young women with small children prefer to work under these conditions rather than face the prospect of total starvation. It is not an exaggeration to say that there is a "reserve army" of females with no professional experience who are willing to accept low wages. Wages for these women exceed the minimum wage established by the Colombian government by about 20 percent and, according to Silva's (1982) study, the wage scale is structured to give the better paying jobs to men.

Some managers believe that mothers with several children are very efficient and responsible and make better employees than either single or married men. Yet hiring practices prevent working mothers from getting the better jobs even though their work history should weigh in their favor.

Not only is getting a job difficult, but keeping a job is equally difficult. Because of the way work is organized, it is very easy to replace members of the workforce. In the flower industry, for instance, workers tend to be rotated frequently so that it becomes difficult for workers to form stable relationships. Resistance is punished with dismissal, which is what women who head households fear the most.

Some workers who were interviewed said that some companies who send representatives to recruit workers in the working class areas of Bogotá ask women to take a pregnancy test. The tests are performed in laboratories that send the results directly to the company. When the results are negative, the chances of getting hired improve significantly.

The Division of Labor in the Flower Industry

The process of producing flowers is divided into management tasks, supervisory tasks and manual tasks (where the production process itself takes place). Flower production requires a very well-defined sequence of steps. The ground has to be prepared in order to guarantee a high yield at harvest time. The ground is sterilized, disinfected with steam and undergoes a fumigation process. Male workers are the most active during this step because this is hard physical labor. Many of the men complain of irritation in their eyes because of the potency of the chemicals being applied. Women workers irrigate the flowers (in the midst of high humidity), harvest the flowers and prepare them for storage. Planting in March produces flowers for the European market. During planting season women work on their knees, quickly setting out the seedlings which come from the United States, Germany and Holland. The planting is monitored by computer and must be carried out by a specific time. Irrigation is very important because it prevents flower "stress." Then, there is weeding which women also perform on their knees. Some flowers are grown under artificial light in greenhouses to accelerate the growth of varietals. The greenhouses and their corresponding facilities are built by groups of men. Men do the fumigation and women workers care for the flowers (Medrano, 1982, p. 50).

Tending the flowers is labor intensive and involves several steps. These steps include netting (stringing wire, string or sisal netting into squares to support the plants as they grow), pinching (removing lateral buds from the plant to ensure the growth of a single, central bud of maximum size), covering (placing a plastic strip on each of the buds to prevent early blooming), combing (examining each plant to ensure vertical growth) and cutting (even cutting the flowers is very specialized and technique varies based on the type of flower). Selection and classification is done flower by flower. Flowers of lesser quality are held for the Colombian market (Silva, 1982, note p. 35).

Almost the entire female workforce is concentrated in the most monotonous manual tasks associated with flower production. Very few women are in supervisory roles and none in management. Men perform the jobs which require more physical strength (fumigation, opening of water channels and irrigation) and they are better paid than the women.

The location of the flower crops in the Bogotá Savannah raises some concerns which merit analysis. One concern is the concentration of land holdings and the escalating value of that land. Another element of equal importance is that the flower industry occupies the most fertile and productive lands in the region, rapidly displacing agricultural production and other crops to hillsides ("Conclusions of First Forum," 1991, p. 1). Each type of crop requires enormous amounts of water. Drawing huge amounts of water from underground often has a destabilizing influence above ground and can cause the collapse of roads among other problems. In addition, the rivers of Bogotá are severely contaminated by chemicals used on the land and are displaying signs of decomposition. The water supply for the people living in the vicinity is affected because water is diverted to the irrigation of flower crops.

The Use of Chemicals and the Health of Those Who Work in the Fields

Flowers of export quality require a single characteristic: the total absence of insects or disease, or in agronomic terminology: "zero pests, zero diseases." Sanitary controls at customs in the United States and Europe are very demanding on this point, forcing employers to be extremely careful in this regard. Errors could mean that customs officials refuse an entire shipment of flowers because they do not meet required sanitary standards. Flowers which do not pass inspection are burned at the point of entry. This explains the intense use of chemicals throughout the production process (about 95 chemicals are used by the flower industry). These include fertilizers, dyes, pesticides, fungicides and insecticides. Specialists have evaluated the chemical composition and toxicity of these products for humans. For 60 of those products, it is said that 95 percent of the toxicity is absorbed through the skin, 86 percent orally, 73 percent through the respiratory system, and 31 percent through the eye membrane. The workers themselves, environmentalists and others want to ban the most toxic chemicals from use in Colombia. While it is essential to use fungicides, pesticides and insecticides, there is a growing feeling that workers should at least be protected from the most dangerous chemicals that have been banned. (Aldrin, Dieldrin, Endrin, Clordano/Heptachloro, Parathion, Aldicarb and Paraquat).

Workers in the fields suffer from many health problems. Among the most common problems are severe respiratory afflictions due to exposure to temperature changes and high levels of humidity inside the greenhouses. The dust from fumigation seems to have an impact as well and can cause headaches, dizziness, cramps, weakness and fainting. Muscle pains in the back and arms and pain in the kidneys also are very common.

Other health problems stem from the type of activity itself. For example, the classification of flowers must be done standing at a rate of 1,500 flowers per hour. Those who are pregnant or who suffer from varicose veins are the most affected. Occasionally, out of sympathy, supervisors may change the job of a pregnant woman, although making exceptions for pregnant workers is not standard policy. What those in the flower industry call "intoxication" can result from the by-products of fumigation which may be absorbed if recently fumigated flowers are placed against the body or if dust from fumigation is inhaled once the product dries out. Sometimes, "intoxication" of the intestines, ovaries, and eyes have led to hospitalizations. Many observers believe there have been cases of mortality, spontaneous abortions and fetal death for the same reason although these are claims which are difficult to prove. The most serious threats to health risks are from insecticides which affect the nervous system. Insecticides have caused some cases of paralysis of limbs that have required neurological treatment and long periods of recovery.

The advocacy campaigns so far have not produced tangible results. However, a Health Committee of Flower Workers is forming in Colombia and is involved in discussions with the Ministry of Health so that officials can carry out the relevant inquiries and assist the claims of workers. There has been even less progress with respect to compensation that companies must grant to those who are severely injured and unable to return to work.

Limitations Imposed on Trade Union Activity

Although *ASOCOLFLORES* publications reiterate the industry's respect for "freedom of assembly and union participation," less than 20 percent of the workers in the flower industry belong to unions. Workers who do organize in defense of their rights do not have job security. The likelihood of dismissal is so great that very few men and women dare take the risk for fear of losing their income. Many workers feel that they are not safe even when attending church. They report that they believe they are being followed and fear being investigated by the company and possibly fired. Among the existing unions, moreover, many are sponsored by the employers, which gives the appearance of representing the interests of both male and female workers. But truly autonomous unions still are repressed and those who want to unionize face the possibility of layoffs.

The Inter-Institutional Flower Commission

In 1991 research centers, human rights groups, activist groups linked to the trade union movement and academics attended a forum called the Impact of the Flower Industry. Out of the forum came the Inter-Institutional Flower Commission comprised of the National Union of Farm workers (*Sindicato Nacional de Trabajadores de la Industria Agropecuaria* or *SINTRAINAGRO*), the National Unitarian Federation of Farm Trade Unions (*la Federación Nacional Sindical Unitaria Agropecuaria* or *FENSUAGRO*), the Workers' Pastoral Commission of the *Diocese of Facatativá (la Comisión Pastoral Obrera de la Diócesis de Facatativá*), the National Trade Union Institute (*el Instituto Nacional Sindical* or *INS*) and the National Center of Health and Labor (*el Centro Nacional de Salud y Trabajor* or *CENSAT*).

The mandate of this Commission is to create a "sphere of coordination and a push for the organization of male and female workers in the floricultural industry and initiatives to transform their current living and working conditions." ("What is the Flower," 1994, p. 3). The challenge is one of how to develop educational and research initiatives affecting the lives of those individuals who have been working day after day in this profitable industry. The Commission, in conjunction with the *Universidad Nacional de Colombia*, is conducting research on the floral sector and the results will be released soon.

Members of the Inter-Institutional Commission invited me to talk to legal advisors who provide legal counseling in one of the so-called "Support Houses" where workers may submit complaints and request the assistance of legal advisors in their case. A lawyer told us that most of the cases he discusses with administrative labor officials involve complaints lodged by workers who have been affected by the systematic policy of dismissals witnessed in the floral sector.

Other cases involve workers who would like to retire but want to ensure that they will receive their social benefits once they stop working. The legal advisors said there has been very little success in dealing legally with health problems or discrimination against women. They also said that the flower industry likes to recruit mothers because they have proven to be responsible workers, but they are unwilling to grant paid maternity leave or to adopt work policies to accommodate nursing mothers.

The Constitution of Colombia (1991) contains an article that addresses maternity benefits and expressly prohibits discrimination. Article 43 states that, "Women and men have equal rights and opportunities. A woman may not suffer any type of discrimination. During pregnancy and after childbirth, she will be entitled to special assistance and protection from the State and receive food subsidies if she is unemployed or destitute. The State will support a woman who is the head of the household." Based on this mandate, one can discuss the legal rights of the female flower worker.

There exist definite problems in the interpretation of the law, above all, when both sides of the dispute enjoy legal protection. The Labor Code of Colombia guarantees paid leave for women around the time of childbirth for all types of labor contracts, including those without a fixed salary (piecework or by task). However, problems arise when one examines the law more closely. Although it is true that "no worker may be dismissed due to pregnancy or nursing" (Art. 239), it is possible for employers to obtain an authorization from the Labor Inspector to dismiss the woman or, if there is no Inspector in the region, from the Mayor. If the employer does not obtain this authorization, he may still dismiss the worker as long as he gives the worker compensation equal to 60 days of wages in addition to any indemnification or benefits accrued as part of her contract. She is entitled to 12 weeks of paid maternity leave. If the worker has a fixed-time contract, or if termination coincides with pregnancy or with the months following childbirth, the worker has the right to receive social security benefits (the employer is responsible for registering her). But the worker cannot stop her employer from terminating the labor contract.

It is very important to determine the type of contract that governs labor relations between the worker and the contracting company because everything rides on it. Problems ensue if the worker starts working without formalities (some women have told us that they were not even asked to show identification) and, only later when they are immersed in their job, they sign the work contract without any direction or guidance. In several cases workers have signed their dismissal without realizing what they had signed. These cases are practically impossible to resolve in the worker's favor. There is no favorable culture with respect to workers' rights and the legal system is increasingly reluctant to attend to the rights of workers. This is especially noticeable with women's rights.

Importance of Legal Protection: *La Acción de Tutela*

So far there have not been any legal battles sufficiently influential to produce changes in the unfavorable conditions of flower workers. Workers need more protection in negotiating with employers. It also is essential to sensitize all levels of the judicial administration.

La acción de Tutela, instituted by Article 86 of the Constitution, may be a very important source of power for workers. Thanks to this mechanism for safeguarding constitutional rights, any person can file a claim before a judge, at any time or place, through a summary and speedy procedure, in his/her own name or by someone acting in his/her name, for the immediate safeguarding of basic constitutional rights when these are violated or threatened by the action or omission of any public authority. This legal action may be used against individuals who are in charge of providing a public service or whose behavior seriously and directly affects the collective interest or who have a relationship of subordination or defenselessness with the claimant.

This last situation is the one that seems important to us. In this type of labor relations, it can be proven that a state of subordination or, in some cases, of defenselessness exists. The structure of the judicial administration is so complex and the mechanisms of access so removed from the average workers' abilities that a true collective effort is required to undo the numerous barriers which come up once a claim or denunciation is filed.

Strategies to Achieve Respect for Flower Workers's Rights

The international advocacy campaigns always state that what is desired is a "clean flowers" industry. That there has never been strong opposition to the flower industry can be explained by the fact that the growers hire many workers and especially large numbers of females. The issue revolves around how to overcome the present incompatibility between respecting the human rights of flower workers while maintaining a highly profitable export-oriented industry.

The constitution is not the only form of protection for workers' rights in Colombia. Colombia also has signed all the major human rights treaties and the covenants of the International Labor Organization which are required to cover denunciations and the rights of male and female workers. There are also specific regulations that pertain to water conservation and preservation. The standards applied to the Guarantee of Medical Attention and Physician Care for those who are in contact with pesticides, as well as anything related to occupational and industrial health in the Ministry of Health and Industry, require the knowledgeable application and supervision of labor organizations.

The precarious organization of workers inhibits the possibility of making demands for existing rights. This lack of organization also explains the near absence of negotiations over working conditions between employers and workers even where a framework for negotiation already exists. For instance, international standards pertaining to the use of chemicals may be a necessary and useful paradigm for improving working conditions provided there are trade union organizations or associations that can negotiate with corporate representatives and State officials.

Strong worker representation is therefore needed to protect workers on a variety of issues. The participation of Colombian officials is likewise essential to establish adequate regulations to protect the health of those who handle the toxic substances that must be used in this type of crop. And given that the educational level of the flower workers and of workers in general is low, the company too must agree to teach workers about the hazards involved in handling toxic products.

An issue of major importance to women are safe working conditions for pregnant workers and mechanisms for addressing unwarranted dismissals of women which might occur because the employer has verified that a worker is pregnant. With respect to other forms of discrimination against women, it is necessary to document the differences in recruitment policies, job assignments and pay between men and women in order to focus on possible claim actions. The top priority must be to improve the organization representing workers and to broaden the potential for negotiation with employers. Next, individual cases must be submitted to the judicial branch. After the rulings are retained at the local or national level, it is possible to think about bringing cases to international bodies.

In the meantime, given that this economic activity transcends borders, it is important not only to pursue advocacy campaigns to demand "zero pests, zero diseases" with regard to the sanitary condition of flowers but also to be concerned with respecting the human rights of workers. This is what is meant by the slogan of producing "clean flowers," and this is the type of export that can best benefit our countries.

Conclusion

As an international system of protection, human rights must face the social costs of global development. Flower workers in Colombia are integrated into the global system and the respect of their rights depends on a clear vision of how to use the international mechanisms for protection.

An interpretation of human rights is not acceptable if it relies on the limitations of the capitalist market. The challenge today is to confront the basic contradiction between private appropriation vs. social accumulation. It is obvious that, if we look at concrete cases of *"maquiladoras"* and other corporate structures which employ a high proportion of female labor, we likewise encounter varied forms of exploitation. This is part of the modern world. Investors seek to prevent a decline in profits by reducing wages and this is what happens in countries at the periphery of the core of world power.

Samir Amin has argued persuasively that it is not possible nor is it desirable to stop the globalization process of the world economy. Globalization is an inexorable process and one that can be viewed as a positive development. It certainly would be regressive to return to agricultural economies. Still, globalization is causing great suffering for many workers and women are especially vulnerable to exploitation by employers who scan the globe for cheap labor and limited regulatory measures. Now is the time to develop global strategies to protect workers against increasing exploitation. Our task is to discover the concrete ways of putting them into action.

References:

Amin, S. (1994). La Nouvelle Mondialisation Capitaliste: Problemes et Perspectives. *Alternatives Sud, 1,* pp. 19-44.

Conclusions of the First Forum of Flower Industries. (1991, October). Bogotá, Colombia. Unpublished manuscript.

European Parliament (1993, June). Minutes of the meeting held on June 13, 1993. (PE 174.417).

Inter-Institutional Flower Commission. (1994, May). *Flowers: Wealth, Life and Death.* Bogotá: Author.

Inter-Institutional Flower Commission. (1993, February). *What is the Flower Campaign in Europe?* Bogotá: Author.

La Floricultura en Colombia. (1993, September). Asociación Colombiana de Floricultores. Subgerencia Económica.

Medrano, D. (1982). Desarrollo y Explotación de la Mujer: Efectos de la Proletarización Femenina en la Agroindustria de Flores en la Sabana de Bogotá. In M. León (Ed.), *I. La Realidad Colombiana. Debate Sobre la Mujer en América Latina y el Caribe.* Bogotá: ACEP.

Silva de Rojas, A., & Corredor de Prieto, C. (1980). *El Doble Papel de la Mujer en la Reproducción de la Fuerza de Trabajo Familiar.* Unpublished manuscript. (Archived in the Fondo de Documentación sobre la Mujer, Universidad Nacional de Colombia, Bogotá.)

Silva, A. E. (1982). De Mujer Campesina a Obrera Florista. In L. Magdalena (Ed.), *II. La Realidad Colombiana. Debate Sobre la Mujer en América Latina y el Caribe,* (pp. 28-42). Bogotá: ACEP.

Silva, J. *Flores, Mujeres y Pesticida.* [Film]. (Archived in the Fondo de Documentación sobre la Mujer, Universidad Nacional de Colombia, Bogotá.)

Chapter 10
NAFTA, GATT and the Rights of Women: the Case of Canada

Barbara Cameron

This article examines the conception of rights and of the role of the state found in the North American Free Trade Agreement (NAFTA) and in the General Agreement on Tariffs and Trade (GATT) and contrasts these to the ideas of the Canadian women's movement. It shows that NAFTA, to a far greater extent than GATT, reflects classical liberal notions of rights as the rights of property and as freedom from state regulation. It argues that a rejection of these conceptions was central to the opposition of Canadian women's organizations to NAFTA and that rejection provides the starting point for the search for a feminist strategy for intervening in the politics of trade, both nationally and internationally.

NAFTA, Rights and Regulation

The conception of rights and the role of government found in NAFTA reflects classical liberal notions in a number of respects. Like classical liberalism, NAFTA treats rights as belonging to a private sphere free from state regulation and recognizes a very limited role for the state in regulating the private sphere. In both the classical liberal framework and in NAFTA, the rights being protected are the rights of those who own property. Equality in classical liberalism is a formal, contractual equality that ignores the real inequalities in resources and power, for example, of the worker entering the employment contract or the woman entering the marriage contract. Similarly, the member states of NAFTA are all formally equal as all are bound by the same basic provisions, but this formal equality masks the underlying inequalities in economic and political power and the different political traditions of the countries that are members of it.

In the discussion which follows, the rights granted in NAFTA are described as the rights of transnational corporations or the rights of capital unless it is clear that what is being affirmed is the right of a state to regulate. The reason for this is that trade can no longer be thought of primarily in terms of trade among countries. Rather, trade today is increasingly trade within and between transnational corporations as the example of the United States illustrates. The United Nations Center on Transnational Corporations estimates that 80 per cent of the external trade of the United States (exports plus imports) was undertaken by transnational corporations in 1989, with one third of exports and over two fifths of imports being intra-firm transactions (United Nations, 1992). As the discussion below shows, the rights to move capital, goods and services (and, in certain cases, labor) across international boundaries as guaranteed in NAFTA are essentially rights for transnational corporations to be free of state regulation. When the role of the state appears positively in the Agreement, it is as an advocate for a corporation located within its territory in the disputes resolution procedure or as an exception to a general rule of state deregulation.

The Rights Guaranteed by NAFTA

NAFTA significantly expands the rights enjoyed by corporations in previous multilateral trade agreements by extending the principle of national treatment beyond goods to include investment capital and cross-border trade in services. National treatment means a state is obligated to treat the goods, services, capital, or labor (depending on what is covered by the agreement) in the same way as it treats its domestically produced equivalents. There are three corporate rights which are related to the principle of national treatment: the right of establishment, the right of non-establishment and the right of commercial presence.

The right of establishment means the right of a foreign investor, whether a corporation or an individual, to set up a facility in a domestic jurisdiction (Grey, 1990). In NAFTA, this right is recognized in article 1102, which guarantees a foreign investor national treatment "with respect to the establishment, acquisition, expansion, management, conduct, operation, and sale or other disposition of investments."

The right of non-establishment means the right of the owner of goods and services to have access to a foreign market without establishing a branch, affiliate or subsidiary through an investment (Sauvant, 1986). In NAFTA, the "right of non-establishment" is recognized with respect to goods in article 301, which guarantees national treatment for goods entering a domestic market of a NAFTA country, and, with respect to services, in article 1205 which prohibits a NAFTA member state from requiring a service provider of another NAFTA member "to establish or maintain a representative office or any form of enterprise, or to be resident in its territory as a condition for the cross-border provision of a service."

The right of commercial presence means the right to maintain a "presence," which is something less than an investment in a facility, within a country for purposes of selling or repairing a service. This right is important to cross-border service providers and could take the form of an office, an "instant teller," a laptop computer (Grey, 1990). In NAFTA, the right of commercial presence is guaranteed through a combination of articles 1202 ("National Treatment") and 1201 ("Scope and Coverage"), which together guarantee a cross border service provider a "presence" in the territory of another NAFTA member country.

In addition to the rights derived from the principle of national treatment, a variety of other rights are guaranteed to corporations in the Agreement. These include the right of foreign investors "to compensation at fair market value" in cases where a member state of NAFTA nationalizes or expropriates an investment or takes measures "tantamount to nationalization or expropriation" (Canada, 1992, article 1110, 11-8); the right of holders of intellectual property rights to enjoy a monopoly on the exploitation of innovations and inventions for a period of twenty years (Canada, 1992, article 1709 (12), 17-11); the right of foreign investors to transfer any profits, dividends, interest, capital gains, royalty payments or other returns derived from an investment out of the country where they were earned (Canada, 1992, article 1109, 11-7); and the right of a financial institution to transfer information in electronic or other form into and out of the territory of a NAFTA member state for data processing (Canada, 1992, article 1407 (2), 14-5). There is a general, and quite sweeping, right for a member state of NAFTA to challenge measures taken by another NAFTA state even when these measures are not inconsistent with the provisions of the Agreement. This is granted in the "Nullification and Impairment" provisions which state that a party to the Agreement may have recourse to the dispute settlement procedure if the benefits that it expected to accrue under key sections of the Agreement are being "nullified or impaired as a result of the application of any measure that is not inconsistent with this Agreement" (Canada, 1992, Annex 2004, 20-14).

Limitations on the State

NAFTA guarantees other rights to transnational corporations indirectly but no less effectively through explicit restrictions placed on state activity. By limiting the sphere of state activity, NAFTA carves out and guarantees an enlarged sphere of private commercial activities.

The investment chapter reinforces national treatment of foreign investment in article 1106, which contains a long list of proscribed "Performance Requirements" (which are essentially trade-related investment measures). These prohibit a state from imposing any requirements regarding the percentage of goods or services that must be exported, the percentage of production that must be produced locally, or the purchase of domestic goods or services or the transfer of technology. Article 1107 prevents a government from placing any requirements on foreign-owned enterprises located within its territory regarding the nationality of senior managers. The financial services chapter prevents a NAFTA state from restricting the right of a consumer of financial services from purchasing such services from a cross-border financial service provider (Canada, 1992, article 1404(2), 14-3). The telecommunications chapter of NAFTA is devoted to enumerating what a state must and, especially, may not do in the regulation of its telecommunications industry (Canada, 1992, articles 1302, 1303 and 1304, 13-2). Many other examples could be cited of restrictions NAFTA places on state regulatory measures.

Enforcing the Rights of Capital

NAFTA provides bilateral and trilateral institutions to enforce the rights of capital against regulatory measures introduced by a NAFTA member state. None of the trilateral or bilateral bodies established by the Agreement are directed at instituting at the supranational level the regulation of corporate activity which NAFTA prohibits at the level of the national state. There are three basic procedures in NAFTA through which the rights guaranteed to transnational corporations can be protected: a general procedure for dealing with all disputes among governments arising from the Agreement except those related to trade in goods; a separate procedure for covering disputes between governments related to trade in goods; and a special procedure to allow corporations to directly challenge certain measures of a NAFTA member state as inconsistent with the Agreement. (Mexico obtained a specific exemption from this provision.) (Canada, 1992, Annex 1120. 1, 11-26).

The rights guaranteed to owners of capital in NAFTA are in sharp contrast to the rights guaranteed to working women and men in the North American Agreement on Labor Cooperation, which is a parallel agreement to NAFTA. The parallel Agreement merely requires a NAFTA member state to enforce its own laws with respect to occupational safety and health, child labor or minimum wage technical labor standards. These are subject to enforcement only when they are trade-related and when a persistent pattern of failure of effective enforcement can be demonstrated (Canada, 1993, articles 27 and 36, 17, 22). A more comprehensive list of labor principles is included in Annex I to the Agreement on Labor Cooperation and three are even stated as rights: the right to organize, the right to strike, and the right to bargain collectively (Canada, 1993). However, there is no mechanism provided to enforce these rights and principles or even to ensure that a NAFTA member state enforces its own legislation concerning these.

The sole recognition of women's rights in NAFTA comes in Annex I to the Agreement on Labour Cooperation. These are expressed as principles, such as the elimination of employment discrimination on such grounds as race, religion, age, or sex, and the very weak principle of equal pay for equal work in the same establishment (Canada, 1993). Like most of labor's rights, these are not subject to any effective enforcement.

NAFTA's Formal Equality

Under NAFTA, the member states are formally equal, all exercising the same rights and all bound by the same rules. But just as the classical liberal notion of equality ignores the differences in access to resources of workers and employers and of women and men, NAFTA's formal equality glosses over the differences in economic power and in national traditions of the member countries. The most glaring example of this is that nowhere does NAFTA acknowledge the huge differences in living standards and level of economic development between Mexico and the other two NAFTA countries. Any protections which Mexico managed to obtain are included in the Agreement in annexes, essentially as non-conforming measures. Throughout the Agreement, state measures, such as "performance requirements" related to foreign investment, or state ownership and state regulation are either prohibited or restricted. In general, these are measures which have traditionally been used by the Canadian or Mexican government and not by the United States government. At the same time, the Agreement recognizes national sovereignty when it comes to the use of domestic trade laws for deciding disputes related to trade in goods. It is widely believed in Canada that U.S. domestic trade laws have been interpreted in a way that is highly protective of the U.S. market for manufactured goods.

GATT, Rights and Regulation

The Agreements resulting from the Uruguay Round of GATT negotiations represent a significant extension of the rights of capital through the provisions on services, trade-related investment measures and intellectual property rights. The gains made in the NAFTA negotiations by the most powerful transnationals, particularly those in the service sector, provided important precedents for the GATT negotiations. Probably because of the larger presence of developing countries in the negotiations, the rights of the private owners of property are much less completely recognized in GATT than they are in NAFTA. These can be shown through a comparison of the provisions of the two agreements governing trade-related investment measures (TRIMS) and trade in services.

The GATT Agreement on Trade-Related Investment Measures prohibits regulations concerning domestic content or requirements which relate the volume of exports to domestic production, as NAFTA does (GATT Secretariat, Trade Negotiations Committee, 1993, II-A1A-7, 1). But GATT does not contain the other restrictions on TRIMS found in NAFTA, such as the right of a foreign investor to freely transfer profits, dividends, interest, capital gains, royalty payments and other returns from an investment out of a country (Canada, 1992, article 1109, 11-7). Nor does GATT recognize the right of foreign investors to compensation at fair market value in cases of nationalization or expropriation or government measures "tantamount to nationalization or expropriation" (Canada, 1992, article 1110, 11-8) or the right of corporations in their own right to take a case against regulations of a member state, as NAFTA does (Canada, 1992, articles 1116 and 1117, 11-11). Furthermore, GATT does not include the very broad national treatment clause found in the investment chapter of NAFTA requiring each member state to treat investors of the other NAFTA countries the same as its own investments "with respect to the establishment, acquisition, expansion, management, conduct, operation and sale or other disposition of investments" (Canada, 1992, article 1102, 11-2).

The GATT General Agreement on Trade in Services provides a greater recognition than does NAFTA of the role of government and a more limited recognition of the rights of corporations in the service sector. The preamble to the Agreement specifically acknowledges "the right of Members to regulate, and to introduce new regulations on, the supply of services within their territories in order to meet national policy objectives . . ." (GATT Secretariat, Trade Negotiations Committee, 1993, II-A1B, 3). The GATT Agreement on Trade in Services permits a member state to distinguish between domestic and foreign service providers by requiring that all member states offer other GATT members Most Favored Nation (MFN) treatment (as distinct from national treatment) to foreign service providers. MFN treatment requires that all foreign service providers who are members of GATT be treated in a like manner. In the new GATT General Agreement on Trade in Services, national treatment is only available in those areas which a member state specifically designates (GATT Secretariat, Trade Negotiations Committee, 1993, Article XVII, II-A1B, 18).

Another significant difference between GATT and NAFTA is the formal recognition within GATT of the differences in economic resources between developed, developing and least developed countries. This appears throughout the text of the different agreements, such as the Agreement on TRIMS (GATT Secretariat, 1994, II-A1A-7 2) and the Agreement on Safeguards (GATT Secretariat, 1994, II-A1A-14 5). This formal recognition, unfortunately, does not always mean that the recognition in practice will be sufficient, as for example the provisions in the Agreement on TRIPS (trade-related intellectual property rights) (GATT Secretariat, Trade Negotiations

Committee, 1993, II-AIC p2, 28). The distinction between developed, developing and least developed countries also appears in dedicated documents, such as the "Decision on Measures in Favor of Least-Developed Countries" (GATT Secretariat, Trade Negotiations Committee, 1993, III-1 1) and the "Decision on Measures Concerning the Possible Negative Effects of the Reform Program on Least Developed and Net Food-Importing Developing Countries" (GATT Secretariat, Trade Negotiations Committee, 1993, III-6, 1).

NAFTA, GATT and the Rights of Women

Many of the demands of the Canadian women's movement have called for state intervention either to regulate private markets, through measures such as equal pay for equal value or affirmative action legislation, or to provide social services such as child care on either a public or non-profit basis. Feminist legal activists seeking to influence the interpretation of Canada's Charter of Rights and Freedoms, introduced into the Canadian Constitution in 1982, have argued for a view of rights as involving not only the absence of discrimination but a more positive notion of equality of results measured by such things as pay and opportunity (Razack, 1991). The basic perspectives of Canadian feminism on the role of government and the nature of rights is incompatible with the conceptions underlying NAFTA. The specific concerns Canadian women's organizations have about NAFTA can be illustrated by examining the possible impact on policies important to women's equality regarding some of the rights of capital outlined earlier.

Canadian feminists have been strongly opposed to the strategy of privatizing public and social services which has been underway in Canada for the past decade and a half. The "national treatment" provisions of the investment chapter of NAFTA raise the concern that privatized social services now will be open to investment from U.S.-based service corporations. A particular worry is the expansion of transnational insurance companies into the Canadian market as government cost-cutting exercises lead to more and more medical services being excluded from the services covered under Canada's public system of medical insurance (known as medicare).

The fears of women's organizations have been increased, rather than alleviated, by the reservation on social services that the

Canadian government included in Annex II to NAFTA. This reservation reads:

> Canada reserves the right to adopt or maintain any measure with respect to the provision of public law enforcement and correctional services, and the following services, *to the extent that they are social services established or maintained for a public purpose*: income security or insurance, social security or insurance, social welfare, public education, public training, health and child care (Canada, 1992, Annex II, II-C-9).

Since the term "social services" is not defined in the Agreement it is not clear what the underlined phrase means. The fear is that the clause will lead to increased pressure to open up to competition from commercial interests, including non-Canadian ones, any activities not considered "core" social services, such as cafeteria, janitorial and even management services.

The Canadian system for delivering social services is based on a mixture of public, non-profit and commercial services. The Canadian women's movement has campaigned for services important to women's equality to be provided on a non-profit or public basis. This demand conflicts with two rights which NAFTA guarantees to foreign investors: the right to compensation at fair market value in situations "tantamount to nationalization or expropriation" (Canada, 1992, article 1110, 11-8) and the right to compensation in cases where the benefits which an investor expected to derive from NAFTA have been nullified or impaired (Canada, 1992, Annex 2004, 20-18). The Canadian reservation in Annex II does not exempt social services from coverage of these provisions. Two examples important to feminists will illustrate the problem: child care and medical services related to new reproductive technologies.

In Canada today child care services and medical services related to new reproductive technologies, like other social services, are offered through a combination of public, non-profit and commercial services. The child care movement has campaigned against government funding for commercial child care centers and for the creation of a publicly funded system of universally accessible, quality child care composed of public and non-profit services. Similarly, a recent Royal Commission on New Reproductive Technologies (NRT) has recommended that many of the NRT-related medical services be offered only in non-profit or public clinics (Royal Commission on New Reproductive Technologies, 1993, 1022-1033). The fear is that the removal of the government funding currently enjoyed by commercial operators in the area of child care, including some U.S.-based corporate chains, or prohibiting the making of a profit from new reproductive medical services would open the way to claims for compensation under either the "tantamount to nationalization" or the "nullification and impairment" clauses of NAFTA (Cameron, in press).

The strong protection of the right of non-establishment in NAFTA has given rise to fears about women's employment. In the manufacturing sector, these fears are accentuated by the experience of Canadian women and men with the Canada-U.S. Free Trade Agreement. Beginning immediately after the coming into effect of CUFTA in January of 1989, many branch plants in the manufacturing sector were closed as U.S. parent companies opted to serve the Canadian market from already existing or new facilities in the United States. The expectation of women's organizations is that the loss of manufacturing jobs, particularly the labor intensive jobs in the garment and electronics manufacturing industries, will increase with the extension of the free trade area to include Mexico.

The very large majority (85 percent) of Canadian women in the paid labor force are employed in the service sector, rather than goods producing industries. Twenty-nine percent of women working for pay are employed in clerical occupations, which are essentially devoted to the processing of information. Canadian women's organizations just now are becoming aware of the implications of the current revolution in information technology for the contracting out and outsourcing of data processing work. Once information processing is separated out from what are considered the core activities of an organization and performed by another organization it is often as easy for the work to be done outside a country as it is across a city. The cross border trade in services and telecommunications provisions of NAFTA tie the hands of any Canadian government which might wish to prevent this loss of women's employment (Canada, 1992, chaps. 12-13). Even in the area of financial services, where the rights of foreign service providers are less fully recognized, NAFTA guarantees foreign banks the right to process data outside the country (Canada, 1992, 14-5). Furthermore, the Canadian government failed to include data processing among the government data services it exempted from coverage of the government procurement chapter (Canada, 1992, Annex 10001. 1b-2, 10-43).

Canadian women's organizations strongly support the current public medicare system in Canada and have opposed efforts of conservative governments to weaken it. The intellectual property rights recognized under NAFTA, and now under GATT, will have a significant impact on the cost to governments of medicare by eliminating the competition transnational pharmaceutical corporations faced in the Canadian market from domestically controlled generic drug manufacturers. The government of Ontario, Canada's most populous province, has estimated that the protection of the intellectual property rights of pharmaceutical companies will increase the costs of the province's drug plan by $80 million to $100 million a year (Canadian Centre for Policy Alternatives, 1992). Increased cost pressures will result in further reductions in the medical services covered by medicare and in the amount and quality of the staff in medical institutions. This would pose problems for the women employed in these institutions and for women whose burden of unpaid labor in the household is increased when services providing care for the sick or elderly are cut.

The involvement of Canadian women around the Uruguay Round of GATT negotiations came through general constituency organizations, such as farm organizations and unions, rather than through the autonomous women's movement. For farmers, including farm women, a major concern was the protection of Canada's agricultural supply management system, which involved quotas on both domestic production and imports in order to ensure a stability in the supply of food. The Canadian government was unsuccessful in protecting the import quotas essential to Canada's agricultural supply management system. The 1994 GATT provision says that the only border measures allowed will be customs duties (GATT Secretariat, Trade Negotiations Committee, 1993, II-AIA-3). As these customs duties are progressively reduced, the Canadian government will lose the capacity to regulate the Canadian market for agricultural products. For unions in the clothing industry, where the majority of workers are women, the negotiations to integrate the Multi Fibre Arrangement (MFA) into the General Agreement on Tariffs and Trade was a matter of interest but not for political mobilization. It was generally recognized that the MFA had not achieved the objective of protecting the domestic clothing market of developed countries from competition from imports from countries with lower wages and that the insistence of some developing countries on an end to the MFA as a condition for discussing trade in services meant that renewal was not a realistic option.

The Future

An important consequence of feminist mobilization against the Canadian government's free trade strategy has been an increased commitment of feminists to international solidarity. Canadian feminists were instrumental in the creation of a tri-national solidarity network *Mujer a Mujer* (Woman to Woman) which united women in Mexico, Canada and the United States. The recognition that NAFTA reflects the rights of transnational corporations and limits the capacity of national governments to regulate in the interests of achieving equality has been important to building this solidarity. Canadian feminists have understood that they have much more in common with the women of Mexico and the United States than they have with the transnational corporations based in Canada which campaigned so actively and so publicly for both the Canada-U.S. and then the North American Free Trade Agreements. The fight against free trade made the connection for many Canadian women between the corporate agenda of privatization and deregulation which they had been fighting at home with a global corporate agenda.

While GATT, as it emerged from the Uruguay Round of negotiations, is less a "bill of rights" for corporations than NAFTA, women in Canada are recognizing that they cannot simply rely on multilateral rather than regional fora for trade negotiations. Instead, women's organizations have begun to explore the possibility of intervening in the politics of trade by promoting international agreements in which trade and social development are linked. In a February 1993 submission to the Canadian government, the National Action Committee on the Status of Women (NAC) endorsed a proposal for a trade and development agreement which would affirm a continental social agenda directed at providing employment and decent living standards (NAC, 1993). The proposal originated in a tri-national meeting of Mexican, Canadian and U.S. non-governmental organizations held in Mexico in January 1993. For Canadian women, finding a way to make trade agreements respect human rights represent a new and promising approach both to international solidarity and to the promotion of women's economic and social rights.

References

Cameron, B. (in press). Brave New Worlds for Women: NAFTA and New Reproductive Technologies. In J. Brodie (Ed.), *Women in Canadian Public Policy*. Toronto: Harcourt Brace.

Canada (1992). North American Free Trade Agreement Between the Government of Canada, the Government of the United Mexican States and the Government of the United States of America. Ottawa: Minister of Supply and Services Canada.

Canada (1993). North American Agreement on Labor Cooperation, Between The Government of Canada, the Government of the United Mexican States and the Government of the United States of America. (Final Draft, September 13, 1993).

GATT Secretariat, Trade Negotiations Committee (1993). *The Final Act Embodying the Results of the Uruguay Round of Multinational Trade Negotiations*. Geneva: GATT Publication Services.

Grey, R. de C. (1990). *Concepts of Trade Diplomacy and Trade in Services*. (Thames Essay No. 56). London: Trade Policy Research Centre.

National Action Committee on the Status of Women. (1993). *NAC Brief to the Sub-Committee on International Trade*. Toronto: NAC.

Razack, S. (1991). *Canadian Feminists and the Law. The Women's Legal Education and Action Fund and the Pursuit of Equality*. Toronto: Second Story Press.

Royal Commission on New Reproductive Technologies. (1993). *Proceed with Care: The Final Report of the Royal Commission on New Reproductive Technologies*. Ottawa: Minister of Government Services Canada.

Sauvant, K. P. (1986). *International Transactions in Services. The Politics of Transborder Data Flows* (The Atwater Series on the World Information Economy, No. 1). Boulder, CO: Westview Press.

United Nations. (1992). *Transnational Corporations as Engines of Growth* (World Investment Report). New York: United Nations.

Chapter 11

The Rhetoric of Welfare Reform: A Case of Gender Discrimination in the United States

Lisa A. Crooms

> It was not the failure of the United States federal and local governments to equally entitle and equally protect all of its citizens, but it was the failure of black families to resemble the patriarchal setup of White America that explained our unequal, segregated, discriminated-against and violently hated black experience of non-democracy, here. We were...[the] problem (Jordan, 1992, p. 67).

Over the past three decades, the official poverty discourse in the United States has portrayed poverty as a largely urban, black and female phenomenon. According to the rhetoric, the availability of public assistance causes single motherhood, which causes black inner-city poverty. The pundits claim that black women and their children are disproportionately poor because public assistance encourages them to have children without the benefit of economic support from employed male breadwinners. Policy makers conclude that responsible social welfare policy must end single motherhood and encourage these women to marry and to bear children properly, i.e. within the confines of the traditional two-parent family. This explanation of black inner-city poverty, however, does not derive its strength from the extent to which it accurately reflects reality. Rather, its status as "truth" is strengthened by the extent to which it comports with the socially-constructed reality on which social order depends. Professor Patricia Williams makes the following observation about this relationship between "truth" and reality:

> Truth, like a fad, takes on life of its own, independent of action and limited only by the imagination of a plurality of self-proclaimed visionaries; untruth becomes truth through belief, and disbelief untruths the truth. (Williams, 1991, pp.175-176)[1]

---

[1] See also Gramsci (1971), identifying the "juridical problem" as "the problem of assimilating the entire grouping to its most advanced fraction is the problem of

In this way, the circular analysis which posits that public assistance begets single motherhood and single motherhood begets poverty is supported by the extent to which it follows the official poverty discourse's socially-constructed story about poor black women and the communities in which they live. As long as black women head the majority of families living in poverty, the "truth" remains legitimate while the untruthed truth goes ignored.

What follows is a critical examination of what the current consensus about welfare reform asserts is a causal relationship between public assistance, single motherhood and poverty. My central thesis is that what appears to be a neutral debate about poverty is an effort to force poor women to modify what has been identified as their poverty-causing behavior, central to which is bearing children outside the confines of the traditional two-parent family. The consensus relies on a sex-gender system (Chodorow, 1979),[2] as well as an earlier poverty discourse under which such childbearing is socially-constructed conduct identified with black women. Therefore, the current consensus and its proposed welfare reforms are based on gender stereotypes about black women. This violates both U.S. civil rights and international human rights norms.[3]

The first part of this paper provides a brief overview of the main U.S. welfare program, Aid to Families With Dependent Children,

---

education of the masses, of their 'adaptation' in accordance with the requirements of the goal to be achieved" (p. 195).

[2] "[T]he sex-gender system, [as first used by Gail Rubin in her essay 'The Traffic of Women,'] includes ways in which biological sex becomes cultural gender and gender-organized social worlds, rules and regulations for sexual object choice, and concepts of childhood" (pp. 83-97). As used in this article, the sex-gender system does not treat whiteness as representing a race-neutral position. Rather, the way in which the sex-gender system constructs gender necessarily depends on the race of the individuals to be gendered. Simply put, white women's gender is different from black women's gender because of the way race operates within the sex-gender system. This, however, is not meant to suggest that black and white women are the only groups for whom gender is so constructed. This observation about gender as constructed by the sex-gender system is applicable to all women, but for the purposes of this article, the discussion is limited to white and black women.

[3] Both U.S. civil rights and international human rights norms prohibit most government discrimination on the basis of race and sex. See, e.g. U.S. Constitution, Amendments V and XIV; Universal Declaration on Human Rights and the Conventions on the Elimination of All Forms of Racial Discrimination and of Discrimination Against Women; see generally Van Dyke (1970).

and the poverty discourse. It then examines the rhetoric of the current welfare reform consensus. The paper goes on to analyze the gendered meaning of the facially-neutral rhetoric and illustrates how stereotypes about black women drive the current consensus. The final part of the paper discusses how these gendered reforms constitute gender discrimination on the basis of race and sex which violates both U.S. civil rights and international human rights norms.

Economic Rights, "AFDC" and the Poverty Discourse

The U. S. Constitution does not recognize a positive right to economic subsistence. The government has the discretion to distribute its largesse as it sees fit, provided that it does not abridge the constitutionally protected rights of the beneficiaries of this distribution (e.g., *Goldberg v. Kelly,* 1970; *Shapiro v. Thompson,* 1969). Although there may be a moral obligation to assist the poor, this does not translate into a legally enforceable right to public assistance. Any rights and duties arising from this moral obligation are further limited by the desire to avoid providing workers with an alternative to low-waged employment. Social welfare policy attempts to mediate the tension between these two competing objectives by distributing public assistance through categorical programs and setting benefit levels far below the income available from low-waged work. In this way it makes public assistance less attractive than low-waged employment for the limited pool of individuals who meet the program's eligibility requirements.

Aid to Families With Dependent Children (AFDC), the main U.S. public assistance program, provides cash benefits for eligible single parent households with dependent children under 18 years old (Social Security Act of 1935; see generally *King v. Smith,* 1968). The program is facially neutral, and benefits are available to any eligible parent irrespective of sex. The sex-gender system, however, creates an expectation that women function as the primary caretakers for children. Consequently, virtually all of the families receiving AFDC are headed by single mothers.

Originally enacted in 1935 as part of the Social Security Act and the New Deal, the federal government used the program to provide economic support for poor widows and their children, virtually all of whom were white (Handler, 1987-88). With eligibility limited in this way, all other poor single mothers were denied benefits and expected to work for wages to support their children. Their single motherhood evidenced their failure to abide by the sex-gender system's conventions governing marriage and the traditional two-parent family. Their anti-patriarchal conduct rendered them morally responsible for their poverty and justified the government's refusal to provide them with assistance.

As society changed, however, so too did the make-up of the AFDC rolls. These changes accompanied a poverty discourse which became increasingly focused on gender roles in the black community. In 1965, the U.S. Department of Labor identified the prevalence of matrilocal families within black communities as one of the major causes of black inner-city poverty (Moynihan, 1965). To prove the "truth" of this assertion, they pointed not only to the numbers of such families within this community but also to the fact that these families were disproportionately poor. They ignored, however, both cultural differences and economic realities which might better explain this phenomenon. Rather, they embraced the idea that the economic salvation of blacks was contingent upon the establishment of a proper patriarchy.

This sentiment was echoed by the National Advisory Commission on Civil Disorders [hereinafter Kerner Commission]. In its 1968 report, the Kerner Commission concluded that the urban rebellions of 1963-67 were caused by high levels of both black male unemployment and black single motherhood. Therefore, it was thought that responsible social welfare policy required measures to increase black male employment, which would increase the numbers of black traditional two-parent families. If black men were employed, then they would be able to assume their positions as economic providers within the confines of traditional two-parent families. If black women were removed from the labor market to tend to their domestic caretaking responsibilities, then they would be primed to be economic dependents of employed black patriarchs. Consequently, social welfare policy makers enacted programs which targeted unemployed men and provided public assistance for single mothers and their children. These programs were designed to permit poor black men and women to assume their proper roles as dictated by the sex-gender system.

These efforts failed, and black urban poverty persisted. Social welfare policy decision-makers re-evaluated their policy initiatives, but they ignored the historical context within which black, inner-city poverty developed as well as the hostilities faced by actors in a market economy based on white supremacy and patriarchy. They continued to cling to their constructed and deceptively simplistic story which blamed single motherhood for this poverty. It was against this backdrop that the Welfare Queen replaced the black Matriarch as the "truth's" scapegoat.

The poverty discourse constructed the Welfare Queen as a single black mother who first became pregnant as a teenager. Her sexual irresponsibility enabled her to drop out of school and to join the AFDC rolls. Rather than marry the child's father and make the best of the situation, she chose to remain single, to collect AFDC and to have many more children by as many different fathers. Her choices were driven by an AFDC program that rewarded her for remaining promiscuous, single and prolific. Her sexual irresponsibility placed her at the beginning of a chain which ultimately ended with an impoverished and dysfunctional community.

The social welfare policy pundits claimed AFDC was responsible for the Welfare Queen's culture of intergenerational dependency, irresponsible reproduction and consumption. The government was named her partner in poverty because its AFDC program had created a twisted set of incentives which paid the Welfare Queen to have children without the benefit of either marriage or a male breadwinner. Accordingly, it was thought that responsible social welfare policy should remove this financial incentive in the interest of creating conditions conducive to the establishment of a proper black patriarchy. AFDC had to encourage marriage and traditional two-parent families and discourage single motherhood.

This socially-constructed story of poverty as a problem of black single motherhood failed to consider evidence which established that the availability of AFDC was not a significant factor in determining if black women will become single mothers. Moreover, it ignored studies which showed that the prevalence of matrilocal families within the black community was, in large part, attributable to that community's historical privileging of the mother-child relationship over the husband-wife relationship. In addition, it dismissed the fact that there was no evidence to suggest that there was any significant relationship between the number of children born to poor women on AFDC and the level of benefits available. Despite indications to the contrary, the poverty discourse continued to hold fast to its "truth" about the relationship between AFDC, black single motherhood and poverty. Consequently, it continued to advocate welfare reform proposals designed to end this anti-patriarchal childbearing on the part of the Welfare Queen and the women she came to represent.

"Ending Welfare As We Know It"

During the 1992 presidential campaign, Bill Clinton pledged "to end welfare as we know it." This promise spurred an intense national debate about AFDC and other public assistance programs. Out of this debate emerged a consensus which articulated themes embraced by conservatives and liberals alike. According to the consensus, welfare dependency must be tackled, and AFDC must be changed from a way of life to a temporary program to assist individuals as they move from poverty to economic self-sufficiency.

The consensus stresses themes which drive virtually all welfare reform proposals being considered at both the federal and state levels. These themes include the following: (1) replacing welfare with waged work in the market economy; (2) discouraging single motherhood; (3) remedying fatherlessness; and (4) increasing state discretion to implement experimental programs which will address the particular problems faced at both the municipal and the state levels. As welfare reforms seek to change these themes from normative pronouncements to positive realities, it is believed that poverty and the social ills stemming from the alleged pathologies of welfare dependency will be eliminated.

Current Consensus: The Gendered Rhetoric of Reform

The current welfare reform consensus resembles much of the poverty discourse of the previous thirty years. It constructs a story about poverty central to which are the "truths" that AFDC encourages single motherhood, undermines traditional two-parent family values and creates an underclass which is chronically dependent on welfare. Statistics showing that, despite the government's efforts, black women and their children remain disproportionately poor bolster the legitimacy of these "truths." The consensus claims these statistics prove there is a causal nexus between public assistance, single motherhood and poverty.

The current consensus, however, departs from the previous poverty discourse in at least one significant way. The rhetoric has become neutral and has abandoned the gendered language of the earlier debate. This change does not reflect an altered poverty paradigm no longer concerned about the pathologies allegedly caused by black single motherhood. Most recognize the political costs of using explicitly racial terms outweigh any benefits derived from such language. More importantly, the socially-constructed meanings of the poverty discourse's rhetoric make the current consensus' use of explicitly gendered language unnecessary. If "the welfare dependent single mother [has become]...the synecdoche, the shortest possible shorthand, for the pathology of poor, urban, black culture" (Lubiano, 1992, p. 323), and welfare has become "a fourth generation code word for [black]" (L. E. White, 1993, pp. 1961-1966), then there is no need to talk about black single mothers on AFDC in explicitly racial terms.

The facially-neutral rhetoric, however, remains focused on the alleged relationship between AFDC, single motherhood, and poverty. Indeed, current proposals include measures explicitly intended to end the threat to social order posed by single motherhood, particularly among white teenagers. Since AFDC causes single motherhood, welfare, as reformed, must break this cycle and remove the financial incentive of AFDC.

Both the poverty discourse and the sex-gender system constructed the single motherhood responsible for poverty as black women's conduct. This is conduct in which all women may engage but which remains associated with black women whose womanhood is constructed largely as a function of sexuality and reproduction. Considered in this way, all poor single mothers are penalized for their anti-patriarchal, irresponsible childbearing which means they are punished for acting like black women. Conversely, responsible social welfare policy must encourage them to stop their pathological reproduction and observe the conventions of the sex-gender system which mandate proper childbearing within the confines of the traditional two-parent family. In this way, the proposed reforms attempt to modify this behavior based on its socially-constructed meaning as stereotypical black women's conduct.

This social construction of black women's conduct is rooted in the historical meaning of black womanhood, central to which are sexuality and reproduction. Part of this historical meaning is derived from U.S. slavery, which socially constructed race so as to privilege whiteness as the norm and to devalue blackness as the "other" (Wallace, 1990, p. 53). The sex-gender system's "othering" of black women was used to justify their treatment without compromising true, socially-constructed white womanhood.

Two of the images used to accomplish this "othering" of black women were Jezebel and the breeder. Jezebel was sexually promiscuous and her lasciviousness both rendered her un-rapeable and guaranteed her sexual accessibility (Austin, 1989; Roberts, 1991; Genovese, 1974; Tushnet, 1981; D. G. White, 1985). The breeder was the most extreme reminder of the female slaves' status as property. She was fecund and discharged her obligations by reproducing as many children as possible to increase her owner's property holdings. These images, which survived the abolition of slavery, remained central to the sex-gender stereotypes about black women. Within the context of the poverty discourse, these images made the "AFDC causes single motherhood causes poverty" explanation seem logical and appear to be "true." Moreover, the current consensus' rhetoric is infused with these images which make the "AFDC begets single motherhood begets poverty" formula legitimate and justify the proposed welfare reforms.

U.S. Welfare Reform As A Violation of U.S. Civil Rights and International Human Rights Norms

The Fourteenth Amendment of the Uniteed States Constitution provides, in pertinent part, that "[n]o state shall make or enforce any law which shall abridge the privileges or immunities of citizens of the United States; nor shall any State deprive any person of life, liberty, or property, without due process of law; nor deny to any person within its jurisdiction the equal protection of the laws."[4] The Equal Protection Clause of this amendment has given rise to an analysis which mandates three different degrees of judicial scrutiny for state legislation. Strict scrutiny is invoked where either a suspect classification such as race, or a fundamental right is involved. Under strict scrutiny, the legislation involved must be not only narrowly tailored, but also necessary to achieve a compelling state interest. Intermediate or heightened scrutiny is invoked where a quasi-suspect classification such as sex is used. Under intermediate scrutiny, the legislation will fail if the discriminatory means used are not substantially related to the achievement of an important governmental objective. The

---

[4] The Fifth Amendment of the U.S. Constitution imposes the same limits on the scope of permissible actions of the Federal Government.

rational basis test is invoked in all other cases, such as those involving wealth-based classifications, and only requires that the classifications involved be reasonably related to legitimate government objectives.

Problems arise with respect to Fourteenth Amendment jurisprudence on at least three different levels. First, under the rubric of substantive due process, courts have attempted to delineate the fundamental rights protected by the Constitution.[5] Although there is little debate about the fundamental nature of rights, such as the right to vote and the right to interstate travel, identifying additional fundamental rights protected by the Constitution has not been as simple. For example, in the area of reproductive rights, the right of a woman to an abortion within the first trimester of pregnancy has been deemed part of the fundamental right of privacy (*Roe v. Wade,* 1973). This right, however, has not been interpreted to impose on states a constitutional duty to fund abortions for indigent women (*Maher v. Roe,* 1977; *Harris v. McRae,* 1980). The Fourteenth Amendment merely requires states to avoid unduly burdening women's ability to exercise their fundamental right to privacy, which, in this context, guarantees women nothing more than the right to be free from unjustified and direct state interference with their personal autonomy.

Second, the Equal Protection Clause's three different tiers of scrutiny create a problem for individuals who wish to pursue claims on the basis of their membership in two or more groups that are subject to different levels of scrutiny. For example, poor black women who wish to challenge proposals based on the current welfare reform consensus are theoretically attempting to pursue a claim of gender discrimination that recognizes gender, as constructed by the sex-gender system, as a function of race, sex and class. Traditional Fourteenth Amendment jurisprudence, however, permits courts to characterize such a claim as one based on class and to assess the constitutionality of such state welfare reform proposals using the lowest level of review, i.e. the rational basis test. Accordingly, this

---

[5] Since *Lochner v. New York* (1905), substantive due process has been looked upon with disfavor by the courts. This view, however, seems not to have had a negative impact on substantive due process as it relates to non-economic rights such as marriage (*Loving v. Virginia,* 1967), procreation (*Skinner v. Oklahoma,* 1942), contraception (*Eisenstadt v. Baird,* 1972), family relationships (*Prince v. Massachusetts,* 1944), and child rearing and education (*Pierce v. Society of Sisters,* 1925; *Meyer v. Nebraska,* 1923).

state legislation would pass constitutional muster as long as the classification was reasonably related to a legitimate government objective.

Third, Fourteenth Amendment jurisprudence is not flexible enough to recognize the injuries of sub-groups that possess characteristics of more than one of the constitutionally-recognized classifications. Its reliance on formal equality requires all who are similarly situated to be afforded similar treatment, while it permits those who are dissimilarly situated to be treated differently without violating the Fourteenth Amendment. Failure to recognize the position of individuals who are simultaneously members of more than one constitutionally-recognized class, which is deeply ingrained in U.S. law, leaves their injuries unremedied (Crenshaw, 1989).

This inability to recognize the legitimacy of the existence of those at the intersection of more than one constitutionally-protected classification is evidenced by the words of the late Justice William Brennan, who made the following observation in his 1973 opinion in *Frontiero v. Richardson*:

> [Our] Nation has had a long and unfortunate history of sex discrimination. Traditionally, such discrimination was rationalized by an attitude of "romantic paternalism" which, in practical effect, put women, not on a pedestal, but in a cage. As a result of notions such as these, our statute books gradually became laden with gross, stereotyped distinctions between the sexes and, indeed, throughout much of the 19th century the position of women in our society was, in many respects, comparable to that of blacks under the pre-Civil War slave codes. Neither slaves nor women could hold office, serve on juries, or bring suit in their own names, and married women traditionally were denied the legal capacity to hold or convey property or to serve as legal guardians of their own children. And although blacks were guaranteed the right to vote in 1870, women were denied even that right [until] adoption of the 19th Amendment half a century later.

According to Justice Brennan's vision, women and blacks are distinctly different groups oppressed in similar but fundamentally different ways. Justice Brennan's observations evidence a paradigm in which oppression is a parallel phenomenon rather than an intersectional one. As such, the dictates of formal equality render black women similarly situated with neither women nor blacks, which means they cannot successfully pursue a gender discrimination claim to redress their complex, multi-axis injuries. Unless the rights of the entire class, as recognized by constitutional jurisprudence, are implicated, then the law will not recognize a constitutional violation on the basis of membership in that class. In other words, if the whole group is not similarly injured, then the injuries of the portion of the group impacted will be neither recognized nor redressed.

In the area of international human rights, there appears to be a danger that the short-comings of U.S. constitutional jurisprudence will be duplicated. This has particularly troubling implications for those who, like black women in the U.S., suffer multi-axis discrimination. For these groups of individuals, their injuries would be neither recognized in the context of, nor remedied by, international human rights law.

The Charter of the United Nations and the Universal Declaration of Human Rights include general pronouncements about the basic human rights to which all individuals are entitled. The specifics about the nature and scope of those general human rights are left to documents such as the International Covenants on Civil and Political Rights and on Economic, Social and Cultural Rights. These instruments evidence an international human rights regime in which civil and political rights are considered first generation human rights, while economic, social and cultural rights are deemed second generation rights. By conceptualizing these rights in this way, international human rights law appears to use an analysis which is analogous to the three-tiered Equal Protection Clause jurisprudence that has developed under the U.S. Constitution. This approach not only ignores the interconnectedness of the so-called first and second generation rights, but also posits that civil and political rights can be both fully realized and meaningful, absent economic, social and cultural rights. Such an analysis fails to correspond to the ways in which most women, particularly poor black women in the U.S., experience oppression and the multi-axis injuries they suffer as a result of such oppression.

Furthermore, the promulgation of separate International Conventions on the Elimination of All Forms of Racial Discrimination and of All Forms of Discrimination Against Women appears to support an analysis which conceptualizes discrimination as a parallel phenomenon rather than a multi-axis, intersectional phenomenon. The dangers posed by this type of analysis are the same as those which have arisen under U.S. constitutional law, which fails to recognize the complex injuries suffered by those who stand at the intersection of race, sex and class. This danger is exacerbated by the ability of member states either to ratify the Conventions with reservations, or to ratify one Convention while opting not to ratify the other. In such a case, an aggrieved group, such as poor, black women in the U.S., has no legally recognized international human rights that protect them from gender discrimination, as gender is constructed through the sex-gender system as a function of race and sex.

Conclusion

The current consensus about welfare reform is invested in the socially constructed "truth" of black inner-city poverty advanced by the official poverty discourse. It fails, however, to examine the erroneous propositions on which the "AFDC causes single motherhood causes poverty" formula are based. Unless social welfare policy makers challenge these underlying assumptions, the debate about the nature of poverty in the U.S. will continue to blame poor, single mothers for the poverty of their families and the communities in which they live. Making them scapegoats limits the official poverty discourse to a one-sided, acontextual diatribe about welfare dependency which incorrectly identifies these women as morally blameworthy for their poverty because of their anti-patriarchal childbearing.

The faulty "AFDC begets single motherhood which begets poverty" formula relieves the government of any responsibility for the conditions which create the need for public assistance. It also permits both the poor to be held morally responsible for their poverty and the government to continue to ignore the need for a legally enforceable right to economic subsistence. Moreover, the government is allowed to exploit public ambivalence about the poor which not only is supported by the idea that the poor are poor because they are morally deviant but also justifies the government's refusal to provide recipients with adequate income to support their families in the interest of not providing a feasible option to low-waged work. If the consensus continues to cling to the socially-constructed "truths" on which its analysis rests, then any potential the poverty discourse has to move beyond a narrow and misguided discussion of welfare dependency will be compromised and the issue of poverty will be neither addressed nor remedied.

References

Austin, R. (1989). Sapphire Bound! *Wisconsin Law Review,* 539.

Chodorow, N. (1979). Mothering, Male Dominance, and Capitalism, *Capitalist Patriarchy and the Case for Socialist Feminism.*

Crenshaw, K. (1989). Demarginalizing the Intersection of Race and Sex: A Black Feminist Critique of Antidiscrimination Doctrine, Feminist Theory and Antiracist Politics. *University of Chicago Legal Forum,* 139.

Eisenstadt v. Baird, 405 U.S. 438 (1972).

Frontiero v. Richardson, 411 U.S. 677 (1973).

Genovese, E. (1974). *Roll, Jordan, Roll: The World the Slaves Made.* New York: Vintage Books.

Goldberg v. Kelly, 397 U.S. 254 (1970).

Gramsci, A. (1971). In Q. Hoare & G. N. Smith (Ed. and Trans.), *Selections from the Prison Notebooks of Antonio Gramsci.* London: Lawrence & Wishart.

Handler, J.F. (1987-88). The Transformation of Aid to Families With Dependent Children: The Family Support Act in Historical Context. *New York University Review of Law and Social Change, 16,* 457-460.

Harris v. McRae, 448 U.S. 297 (1980).

Jordan, J. (1992). *Technical Difficulties: African-American Notes on the State of the Union .* New York: Pantheon Books.

King v. Smith, 392 U.S. 309 (1968).

Lochner v. New York, 198 U.S. 45 (1905).

Loving v. Virginia, 388 U.S. 1 (1967).

Lubiano, W. (1992). Black Ladies, Welfare Queens and State Minstrels: Ideological War by Narrative Means. In T. Morrison (Ed.), *Race-ing Justice, En-gendering Power: Essays on Anita Hill, Clarence Thomas and the Construction of Social Reality.* New York: Pantheon Books.

Maher v. Roe, 432 U.S. 464 (1977).

Meyer v. Nebraska, 262 U.S. 390 (1923).

Moynihan, D. P. (1965) *The Negro family: The Case for National Action.* Washington, DC: U.S. Department of Labor.

National Advisory Committee on Civil Disorders. (1968). *Report of the National Advisory Committee on Civil Disorders.* Washington, DC: Author.

Pierce v. Society of Sisters, 268 U.S. 510 (1925).

Prince v. Massachusetts, 321 U.S. 158 (1944).

Roberts, D.E. (1991). Punishing Drug Addicts Who Have Babies: Women of Color Equality and the Right of Privacy. *Harvard Law Review, 104.*

Roe v. Wade, 410 U.S. 113 (1973).

Shapiro v. Thompson, 394 U.S. 618 (1969).

Skinner v. Oklahoma, 316 U.S. 535 (1942).

Social Security Act of 1935 (current version at 42 U.S.C. Sections 601-622).

Tushnet, M. (1981). *The American Law of Slavery 1810-1860: Consideration of Humanity and Interest.* Princeton, NJ: Princeton University Press.

Van Dyke, V. (1970). *Human Rights, the United States and the World Community.* New York: Oxford University Press.

Wallace, M. (1990). Variations on Negation and Heresy of Black Feminist Creativity. In H.L. Gates, Jr. (Ed.), *Reading Black, Reading Feminist: A Critical Anthology.* New York: Meridian.

White, L.E. (1993). No Exit: Rethinking "Welfare Dependency" from a Different Ground. *Georgetown Law Journal, 81,* 1961-1966.

White, D. G. (1985). *Ar'n't I a Woman: Female Slaves in the Plantation South.* New York: Norton.

Williams, P. J. (1991). *The Alchemy of Race and Rights: Diary of a Law Professor.* Cambridge, MA: Harvard University Press.

Part III

Religious, Cultural and Ethnic Identity & Human Rights

Chapter 12
Diversity, Universality and the Enlightenment Project

Radhika Coomaraswamy

An Introduction

The women's question in recent years has become the cutting edge with regard to the international debate on the universality of human rights. The argument for universality has always placed international human rights as the main item on the international agenda. In addition many women have argued that women's rights are human rights and that therefore they should be given the same universality of treatment as other rights outlined in the Universal Declaration of Human Rights.

For third world women living in the West or in the developing countries this dilemma is not a conceptual issue. It is a question of interrogating certain traditional belief systems and making them compatible with international human rights. This act of interrogation does not come easily. Often, such interrogation requires a catalyst from outside the tradition which will force men and women to focus on certain aspects of their tradition which they have felt to be important. Each continent has some issues, but the most popular and most controversial has been the question of female circumcision. In many contexts, female circumcision is not even considered violence, and its articulation as violence is seen as an international imposition on national culture.

Why are women's rights at the cutting edge of the universality of international human rights? Why is it that countries throughout the world are ready to accept human rights without the women's rights component? In the work of the United Nations Special Rapporteur on Violence Against Women this dichotomy among the governments is particularly strong but also hypocritical.

In December 1994, the General Assembly passed by consensus the Declaration on the Elimination of Violence Against Women. There was complete agreement on the wording. What are the universal international principles of women's rights as specifically linked to violence that are spelled out in the Declaration, i.e., what is this universal consensus?

The Declaration recognized that violence against women is a universal reality and that its eradication required international attention. It is clear and unambiguous in its terminology and because it received the consensus of all the countries of the General Assembly, we can conclude that violence against women is an international phenomenon, recognized as universal by the international community and requiring international action and intervention.

The Declaration is a call to action of all the states to recognize violence against women and it states quite clearly that states should not invoke custom, tradition or religious considerations to avoid their obligations with regard to eradicating violence against women. This consensus implies that, at least with regard to violence, diversity is not an acceptable excuse in international fora. Eradication of violence against women is more important than nation states preserving the diversity among states and civilizations.

This joint action with regard to violence against women, however, is not present in other aspects of the international agenda dealing with women's rights. If you take the Convention on the Elimination of All Forms of Discrimination Against Women, very few countries have ratified the international standards set for marriage, divorce and what are called personal laws. Even countries that have ratified the Convention are not ready for a uniform civil code which gives all women equal rights.

So we have a dualism at the international level. With regard to eradicating violence against women, there seems to be a strong consensus, at least at the formal level, which cuts across societies and culture. But in other areas of women's rights there is a desire to make compromises to allow diversity to flourish from nation state to community. Violence is the bottom line. Beyond that, collective rights prevail in most societies around the world, especially in Asia and Africa, where different communities have argued passionately for a recognition of collective rights over the rights of individual women.

For human rights activists this dilemma poses a problem. On the one hand, there is the position of the Enlightenment crusader. It is argued that human rights was the most positive contribution of the Enlightenment. In the Enlightenment context, man was placed at the center—today along with women—and seen as being endowed with reason and dignity. The Enlightenment personality gives luster to the human rights project and it has become the standard bearer of human dignity. Although one may argue that human rights are worth fighting for and are present in the spirit of all the world's religions, not every society has gone through the Enlightenment experience and is not as genuinely attached to its ideals as others. It is in this context that the argument between universality and diversity acquires added meaning.

There are many individuals in the world today who are against violence and for women's rights but who are also against the victory of the Enlightenment project as an international political agenda. Post-structuralists and sub-altern studies are all schools of thought that come from the alternative progressive traditions which will wield such an analysis. None of them have directly challenged human rights, but they are deeply skeptical of the mechanisms both at the national and international level which have been set up to implement these rights. Sub-alterns want diversity and marginality to flourish while at the same time expecting that injustice and intolerance will disappear.

It is in this context that the women's question emerges. Isolated within the human rights tradition, it becomes a crusading call which has increasingly been seen as an imposition of the western colonial project. Although the human rights tradition has emerged victorious in the area of violence against women, many activists are confronted with a broad cultural critique of the western colonial project in their own society. This critique comes from the conservative elements which refuse to accept universality over their diverse cultures. But it also comes from the more progressive writers who want to know whether special rapporteurs and human rights activists realize that they are instruments of the Enlightenment, a project which they feel led to colonialism. For these writers human rights is the benign face of the colonial encounter.

This same dichotomy also is present in the dialogues between expatriate activists and national activists. While in the Third world activists have taken human rights as a banner, the well-known writers from Said to Foucault force us to question this banner and to see it not as end in itself but only as an instrument of international struggle.

For human rights to be truly successful requires that they be accepted as a value premise or an ideal. But there are those who argue that human rights must be perceived only as an instrument and be subjected to the same type of critique that we give to other political action. To answer this critique, we have to ask the question, what is the alternative to a democratic, human rights-oriented political order? Is there anything that will bring more liberation to our women and our populations at large? Is there another alternative at the level of the macro political? Though a critique of human rights is possible at a conceptual level, there really can be no world or national order without a strong human rights tradition if it is to bring peace, freedom and social justice to its people.

To query the human rights tradition from a progressive position is to fall into another trap, especially when it comes to women's rights. This is to become an ally, in part, of the project of fundamentalism which has become an important force in many political parties, especially in Asia and Africa. To argue against the mainstream Enlightenment project from the point of view of the colonial encounter may in some sense provide the discourse to movements which are at the moment fighting for political hegemony in West and South Asia under the guise of different religions. Unless we are careful, the same discourse which questions the Enlightenment project as an international project will give strength to forces which insist on using women's issues as the banner of their collective rights.

I therefore feel that if we are to fight for women's rights in our societies, not only in the area of violence but across the full range of rights, the universal, mainstream Enlightenment view of human rights is one of the major instruments we have to do battle. Human rights is not only a product of the Western Enlightenment. It was also a result of the horrors of World War II and all nations at that time were united in their commitment to defend human rights. This is the 50th anniversary of the Universal Declaration and it is important to re-accept the principles of human rights as being truly universal and to realize that diversity must be celebrated on a firm foundation of international human rights. It is only then that we will remain united and bonded by our "humanness." It is that bond which will allow human rights and women's rights to receive the allegiance of diverse communities around the world.

Chapter 13
Identity and Culture: Women as Subjects and Agents of Cultural Change

Mahnaz Afkhami

Introduction

In a preface to Ruth Benedict's *Patterns of Culture,* Margaret Mead gives a casual definition of culture as the "systematic body of learned behavior which is transmitted from parents to children" (Benedict, 1959, p. vii). Comparing Malinowski (1944), Firth (1971) and Bottomore (1962),[1] Chris Jenks (1993) concludes that "the concept of culture implies a relationship with the accumulated shared symbols representative of and significant within a particular community, what we might describe as a context-dependent semiotic system" (p. 121). For Jenks, culture as concept is "at least complex and at most so divergent in its various applications as to defy the possibility, or indeed the necessity, of any singular designation" (p. 1).

Identity also is a complex subject defying any singular designation. Charles Taylor (1989) broaches the concept as follows:

[T]he question is often spontaneously phrased by people in the form: Who am I? But this can't necessarily be answered by giving name and genealogy. What does answer this question for us is an understanding of what is of crucial importance to us. To know who I am is a species of knowing where I stand. My identity is defined by the commitments and

---

[1] Malinowski defines culture as "inherited artifacts, goods, technical process, ideas, habits and values" and also "the organisation of human beings into permanent groups." Firth distinguishes between social structure and culture and defines the latter as "the component of accumulated resources, immaterial as well as material, which a people inherit, employ, transmute, add to and transmit; it is all learned behavior which has been socially acquired." Bottomore defines culture as "the ideational aspects of social life, as distinct from the actual relations and forms of relationship between individuals; and by a culture the ideational aspects of a particular society."

identifications which provide the frame or horizon within which I can try to determine from case to case what is good, or valuable, or what ought to be done, or what I endorse or oppose. In other words, it is the horizon within which I am capable of taking a stand (p. 27).

In this paper I will discuss culture and identity within a feminist context by suggesting the following: (1) Women's modern search for their identity is historically mandated and has now become a universal phenomenon; (2) even though cultures differ and strategies for gaining rights will have to be reflexive and adaptive, central values of the search are common to all searchers; (3) women's achievement of identity is geared to cultural change, that is, the need that launches women on a search for identity drives them logically and practically to a politics of cultural change; and (4) the intellectual mechanism to promote the process is a kind of global feminism based on the concept of unity in diversity in which women from the south must play a leading role. I will conclude with some observations on the condition of women in the Muslim world and some strategies for empowering them as agents of change.

Culture and Women's Identity in Traditional Settings

Individuals acquire identity as they become socialized over time in norms that are defined and determined by the prevailing culture, that is, values, beliefs and aesthetics[2] that together constitute the perceptive medium by which individuals or societies communicate with their environment. In principle, traditional cultures, that is, cultures of old societies that have remained more or less unchanged over long periods, assign the individual to a particular position in the social hierarchy which is generally accepted as legitimate. In this formulation, every person is supposed to know who she is and where in the maze of social relations she stands.

The question of a search for identity does not arise, or is not critical, in the traditional setting since the identity is already known. The picture here is that of a community where everyone is serenely content with his or her lot. Contradictions are minimal. If they should arise, it is the function of the culture to resolve them through systems of admonitions, rituals, laws, and rewards and punishments.

[2]   This notion of culture has been derived from the work of Max Weber as interpreted by Talcott Parsons. It is useful to this discussion because it allows for the introduction of a criss-cross of contradictions in and among the components over time (see Parsons & Shils, 1951).

Government and society work hand in hand, king and priest being the two arms of the same legitimate ruling order. Everything functions to maintain the system.

The traditional setting assigns women to the lower positions in the social hierarchy. Women are accorded value as mothers and wives under the jurisdiction of fathers, husbands, and sons. Their main function in the family is that of procreation and childrearing. They are denied the kind of education that confers social prestige and power. Their sexuality is geared to the needs of man and family, including the need for assuring the authenticity of the patriarchal lineage. Even though they work harder than men and their work is indispensable to the well being of the family, the village, and the tribe, they usually do not control the fruits of their labor or participate in its disposition and distribution. Many reasons have been adduced to explain this phenomenon, ranging from differential availability of brute force to subtler ways of social and intellectual manipulation and domination. It may be, as Katherine K. Young (1987) suggests, that patriarchal societies and patriarchal religions are predicated on a correlation of historical, psychological, sociological, and biological stress points. In this view the rise of kingdoms is associated with a particular stage of child development which is in turn associated with man's tyranny over women and children as a reflection of the king's power and

> male ambiguity regarding chastity and sexual license. If the world religions grew out of a situation of extreme stress and were, in part, formed by this milieu, they also responded to this stress syndrome by searching for a new order and vision of harmony. Focal to this order was a stable family structure and careful definition of gender roles, which reflected the male's dominance of the age but also tried to tame it by ensuring economic and physical protection of women. (Young, 1987, p. 32)

In the traditional culture women are silent, but the culture is not silent about women. On the contrary, it is quite vocal as myth, ritual, religious text, and aphoristic male wisdom. Beginning with prophets and early philosophers, Aristotle for example, and continuing up to our time in patriarchal circles in practically all countries, this wisdom suggests that there must be a union of male and female, for they cannot exist without each other, that man is the master and lord as ordained by God, because man can foresee with his mind, is the soul of the union and therefore, by nature, superior. Woman, in contrast, is body, cold, receiver, and naturally inferior.

Interestingly, the originary myth usually treats man and woman more equitably. The Buddha, for example, taught his male and female disciples the same doctrine; women, however, were systematically kept out of the society of the male monks. In the Gathas, the Yashts, and other early Zoroastrian texts, as well as in Iranian epics, woman is treated with respect, but by the middle of the Sasanian period she had lost many of her rights and privileges under a dominant Zoroastrian clergy (Afkhami, 1994, chap. 1). Abrahamic societies also present the same pattern. In Genesis, Eve appears the more resourceful of the first pair. The Israelite woman, however, received her identity from her father and husband. Christ appears to have treated women in manners that shocked Jewish and Roman male sensibilities. Paul, however, placed women in the custody of men and, among other things, forbade them to speak in the church, where religion took shape and power (Sharma, 1987). The same may be said of Islam. Muslim women played their most important roles at the dawn of Islam. Khadija, Aisha, Hind, Zainab and a host of other women were instrumental in the shaping of Muslim society and politics before, during, and after the Prophet's announcement of his message. Indeed, there were several strains of male/female relationship in the Arab tribal society from which a positive prescriptive pattern might have been drawn and according to which the revelation might have been interpreted (Mernissi, 1987). Patriarchy, however, insisted on the one least favorable to women's freedom. The rest has been, more or less, a history of silenced and invisible Muslim women.

Women's struggle to define an identity has been in part a struggle to become visible to themselves and to others, to participate in the definition and solution of "the world's problems," and to help develop an order of priorities and relationships that is different from the patriarchal order. This is now beginning to happen in many parts of the world. Our epoch is progressively tuned to the idea that women have entered the political arena and will remain there in the future. Our politics focus on women's rights. As we become increasingly involved in the economic, social, cultural, and political fields, our interests, that is, the foci of our rights, spread over the entire range of human concerns.

Autonomy and Authenticity as Common Conditions of Women's Identity and Rights

The rise in women's awareness of their identity has not been accidental. It is part of a historical process in which all individuals, men and women, have increasingly appropriated their "selves." The form of appropriation differs from culture to culture, but the essence is commonly shared. Thus, diverse modes of consciousness converge on the idea of human autonomy and personal authenticity (Taylor, 1989). The philosophical axis around which the idea of autonomy takes shape is the move from the concept of natural law (the condition of obeying the rules already given) to that of natural right (the condition of participating in making the rules).

The moral problem of much of humanity, but particularly of women in the developing world, is how to make the transition from law to right while forging and maintaining an identity that is psychologically rewarding and morally acceptable. This is a tangled proposition because it involves every aspect of a woman's personal life—belief in God, religious ritual, family relations, sexuality, friendships, position in society, peer opinion, economic sufficiency, etc—and is directly related to one's idea of self respect. These tensions are exacerbated by the division of the world into north and south and the loyalties that are engendered as a result of racial, ethnic, religious, and national solidarities. Thus the transition is always difficult and probably never complete.

Questions about women's identity are often posed in psychological and ethical terms, but they are also sociological, that is, they are time-bound, geared to levels and complexities of consciousness resulting from historical change. Although the immediate connecting point of identity is moral and psychological, women's identity depends particularly on the changing properties of political culture, i.e. values, beliefs, and aesthetics that have to do with the dispositions of power in the community. Given their powerlessness throughout history, whenever women have become self-conscious as individuals with rights of their own, they have had to search for an identity other than the one assigned to them by the social order—an identity that defines them as authentic human beings. Authenticity, in turn, puts them at odds with the social order. Self-search among women, therefore, is inevitably a moral odyssey in the realm of the political. A modern woman, regardless of geography or culture, seeks an authentic self and finds it mainly in terms of political consciousness.[3] To be effective, this consciousness will have to be informed by the ethical and psychological powers of the myths that nourish the indigenous culture. The idea is to reinvest the myth with positive feminist meaning.

We have come to accept and promote the complex of human rights as stated in the UN Universal Declaration of Human Rights, and most women activists accept the Convention on the Elimination of All Forms of Discrimination Against Women (CEDAW) as an appropriate document for promoting women's human rights. Nevertheless, we need to face the problem of implementation in the face of the challenge posed not only by the patriarchal power structure, but also by the philosophical and moral underpinnings of cultural relativism. Our problem is two-fold: (1) to establish the moral priority of universal rights; and (2) to devise strategies for developing and communicating ways and means of realizing universally accepted women's rights in all countries while upholding and appreciating the diversity of life styles and variety of cultures across the globe. Both points involve moral and ethical issues, but their nature is fundamentally political.

To establish the moral priority of universal rights we must demonstrate the primacy of the individual as human being. It may be argued, as implied in some relativist positions, that there is no way that this can be done if a society chooses, for example, a fundamentalist interpretation of a religion. It should be noted, however, that fundamentalism also is a modern phenomenon—it emerges at a time when society has moved objectively beyond the complex of values and rituals that the fundamentalists wish to enforce. As such, fundamentalism is faced with the same doubts and trepidations that result from the inexorable passage from a world determined by an intelligible cosmic

---

[3] The term "modern" is somewhat problematic and requires a comment. When used in non-Western contexts, modern often connotes Western. Western, in turn, conjures up all kinds of orientations—from a positive feeling of social progress, political freedom, and economic and technological development to a host of negative ideas, including colonial subjugation, economic and political exploitation, moral decadence, and religious torpor. Here I use the term modern neutrally as in the dictionary sense of contemporary or belonging to present. In this sense modernity is the normal condition of women living at the end of the 20th century. The salient characteristic of culture and identity for these women is contradiction and change, rather than stable and unchanging values. To be confused about one's identity is a condition of being a conscious modern woman.

order, in which the human position is clearly defined, to a world in which the cosmic order is mediated by human beings.[4] This mediation is a heavy burden, conferring enormous responsibility which not everyone can carry.[5] Fundamentalism, therefore, is always a reaction and hence an unauthentic rendition of religion because, by opting for a forceful implementation of religious doctrine and rites, it transforms a moral question into a power issue.[6] One cannot be a fundamentalist if the society has not already transcended the "traditional" values.

The drive for autonomy and authenticity affects all issues that interest women across cultures, among them pre-puberty marriage and forced marriage, control over one's relations in the family, control over one's body, having a room of one's own and freedom of movement. In the final analysis it is the respect for the self and others that will render a change in law and behavior necessary by rendering patriarchy's traditional ways no longer cost-effective. I have already suggested that this process is historically mandated, though not necessarily in the forms and with the consequences that have come about in the West. Exaggerated individualism, over-emphasis on technology, and consequent limitations on freedom have been identified in the West as worrisome for the future of human civilization (Taylor, 1991). Authoritarian secular and religious patriarchies point to rampant crime, unbridled consumerism, poverty in the midst of plenty, sexual license, and other malaise in the West to justify their own patterns of rulership and social organization. As mentioned earlier, they use the present unequal dispensation of economic and technological power as well as political and cultural influence in the world to exploit women's sense of national and/or ethnic allegiance. Evelyne Accad (1993) remembers a debate in which African women sided with African men attacking her for having referred to excision as mutilation. In the evening, she says,

> I had sung one of my compositions on genital mutilation and the pain it causes in women. Some of the African women present there had tears in

---

[4] Max Weber called the process a historical passage resulting in the "disenchantment" of the world.

[5] This is the central issue of existentialist thought from Dostoyevsky and Nietzsche to Heidegger, Camus and Sartre.

[6] In Iran all major ayatollahs were opposed to the Khomeini brand of Islam not because they disagreed on esoteric and substantive matters but because of the method which necessitated the use of force.

their eyes and came to thank me after the performance. They told me the reason they had sided with their men in the morning was because they had to be loyal to them. In front of the West, loyalty was more important than truth, but I was right in denouncing the practice. (p. 9)

It is also important that issues that are relevant to the historical conditions of Western societies do not become an excuse for the abuse of women in the non-Western world. An example is when an otherwise correct emphasis on the value of multiculturalism in Western societies is projected as a nebulous and contradictory concept of cultural relativism that functionally justifies abuse of women based on cultural norms. Obviously, every multicultural society ought to respect the variety of its constitutive cultures. But no culture should be condoned if it misuses the internationally recognized rights of its women, children, racial and religious minorities, or other disadvantaged groups. Attention to this point is particularly important because of an implicit misunderstanding that sometimes produces sinister effects. In the West, individuals are assumed to enjoy basic rights including the right to differ. These basic rights, however, are not predicated on cultural relativity. On the contrary, cultural relativity in the West presupposes individual human rights. In the absence of individual protection based on universal human rights, cultural relativism can easily deteriorate into an apology for otherwise heinous practices against women. It should not be difficult to see that in such cases neutrality about values, regardless of the context, is not a morally acceptable position (Bloom, 1987).

Women's modern quest for identity needs to be highly articulate and structured. The reason is that everywhere women have to provide a reason for the rights they seek, no matter how small, innocuous, or obvious they may be. The search, however, is at its beginning. "Truthfulness anywhere means a heightened complexity," writes Adrienne Rich (1984):

> But it is a movement into evolution. Women are only beginning to uncover our own truths; many of us would be grateful for some rest in that struggle, would be glad just to lie down with the shreds we have painfully unearthed, and be satisfied with those. Often I feel this like an exhaustion in my own body. The politics worth having, the relationships worth having, demand that we delve still deeper (as quoted in Spretnak, 1982, p.347).

To uncover our own truth is to rediscover ourselves in the course of a new genesis, to recreate ourselves in images that relate to a politics that is morally worth having. In the introductory essay to *Sisterhood Is Global*, Robin Morgan (1984) writes:

> Because virtually all existing countries are structured by patriarchal mentality, the standard for being human is being male—and female human beings per se become "other," and invisible. This permits governments and international bodies to discuss "the world's problems"—war, poverty, refugees, hunger, disease, illiteracy, overpopulation, ecological imbalance, the abuse and exploitation of children and elderly, etc.—without noticing that those who suffer most from "the world's problems" are women, who, in addition, are not consulted about possible solutions (p.1).

The point of women's struggle for rights is cultural change, that is, changing attitudes, behaviors, and laws that have a negative impact on women's human rights. Such a struggle would be meaningless if women did not agree that there are rights beyond those prescribed by the traditional culture and that these rights are nevertheless valid everywhere. The focus of contention on the first point, therefore, is political, that is, it has to do with power and strategies of empowerment. Power, however, is a concept women have been conditioned to eschew, partly because patriarchal culture looks down on women's seeking of power and partly because of its gross misuse by men. To defend its own power the male-dominated society has held that nothing

> is more ridiculous than a woman who imitates a male activity and is therefore no longer a woman. This can apply not only to speaking and writing, but also to the way a woman looks, the job she does, the way she behaves sexually, the leisure pursuits she engages in, the intellectual activities she prefers and so on ad infinitum. Sex differentiation must be rigidly upheld by whatever means are available, for men can be men only if women are unambiguously women (Cameron, 1985, pp. 155-156).

On the second point, power does not need to be construed as traditionally observed in patriarchal societies. The values of women differ significantly from "masculine" values, as Virginia Woolf stated in 1929. Women's empowerment as both concept and process may be conceived in ways that are qualitatively different from the hitherto known history of power. Women experience life as an interconnected chain of relationships. Autonomy and authenticity in the case of women do not suggest separateness, crass individualism, a Darwinian struggle where only the fit survive. In the words of

psychologist Carol Gilligan (1982), women have "a different voice."[7]
Nonetheless, power is essential to women's cause and needs to be redefined in non-patriarchal terms as a concept that agrees with essential feminist values. "The true representation of power," writes
Carolyn Heilbrun (1988),

> is not of a big man beating a smaller man or a woman. Power is the ability
> to take one's place in whatever discourse is essential to action and the
> right to have one's part matter. This is true in the Pentagon, in marriage,
> in friendship, and in politics (p. 88).

To seek feminist power is, in itself, an exercise in cultural
change.[8]

---

[7] In a perceptive article on recent scholarship on women, Anastasia Touflexis
(1990) summarizes part of the findings: "Relationship colors every aspect of a
woman's life, according to the researchers. Women use conversation to expand
and understand relationships; men use talk to convey solutions, thereby ending
conversation. Women tend to see people as mutually dependent; men view them
as self reliant. Women emphasize caring; men value freedom. Women consider
actions within a context, linking one to the next; men tend to regard events as
isolated and discrete."

[8] Elsewhere I have written that the discourse of empowerment must transcend the
boundaries of any particular culture, religion or ideology:

> It will be feminist rather than patriarchal, humane rather than ideological,
> balanced rather than extremist, critical as well as exhortatory. The global
> feminist discourse recognizes that the problem of women constitutes an
> issue in its own right, not as a subsidiary of other ideologies, no matter
> how structurally comprehensive or textually promising these ideologies
> seem to be. Since "traditional" concepts are by definition founded in pa-
> triarchal discourse, global feminism must be skeptical of those who pre-
> sent them as liberating. This feminism is not anti-man; rather, it sees the
> world in humane terms, that is, it seeks a redefinition of social, economic
> and political principles on the basis of non-patriarchal models. Realizing
> that such a feat cannot be accomplished without or against men's partici-
> pation, it does not hesitate to engage men politically in favor of the femi-
> nist cause.

> The global feminist discourse rejects the notion that "East" and "West"
> constitute mutually exclusive paradigms; rather, it looks at life as evolv-
> ing for all and believes that certain humane and morally defensible princi-
> ples can and should be applied in the West and in the East equally. The
> point, of course, is not that, for example, Middle Eastern women should
> forget the problems that are obviously "Middle Eastern" and intensely
> present. It is, rather, that unless they think globally, they will neither be
> able to mobilize world opinion for their cause, nor succeed in breaking
> out of the boundaries of patriarchy on their own, and, therefore, they

Globalization of Women's Search for Identity: the Case of the Muslim Women.

What I have said so far applies equally to women in Western and non-Western societies. There are, however, differences that arise as a result of the colonial experience. The spread of women's consciousness of rights and their fight for a new identity are made inevitable by the evolving structure of world relationships and the development of modern technology, particularly the communication revolution. This in turn creates tensions between an authentic drive for self realization and a perception of national, ethnic, or religious solidarity in face of a threatening hegemonical world order. In almost all cases, patriarchal regimes use international tension to deflect demands for freedom and equality for women. This process ranges from purely political strains on human rights, which are the hallmark of secular autocratic regimes, to more encompassing systems of constraints rooted in ideology or traditional culture and enforced either directly through governmental fiat, as in China or the Islamic Republic of Iran, or indirectly as a result of organized religious pressure on government, as in Algeria and Egypt.

At present women are particularly under pressure in Muslim countries, where approximately 500 million women live, a majority of them in south and southeast Asia, facing a resurgence of religious fundamentalism that threatens their limited but hard-earned rights. In certain Muslim countries the struggle for women's rights has now become decidedly life threatening. Algerian women have been threatened with physical mutilation and death for objecting to fundamentalist propositions to curtail their rights. In Sudan, Egypt, Morocco, and Pakistan women are increasingly under attack. In Bangladesh Taslima Nasrin, a 32 year old feminist author, was forced into hiding for fear of her life. A fundamentalist leader has "offered a $2,500 reward to anyone who kills her" (Anderson, 1994). In Iran, Homa Darabi, an academician and teacher of psychology, destroyed herself publicly in protest to the apartheid practiced against women in Iran.

However, Muslim women are subject to different interpretations of the shari`a, depending on the prevailing traditions and customs as well as the nature and extent of socio-economic change in their countries. Women's rights are particularly strained in the Middle East and

will likely fail to address their problems in a way that will lead to their solution. (Afkhami, 1994, pp. 16-17)

North Africa, where women have been targets of extreme and vociferous attack. Part of the reason is that the more traditional patriarchies are pressured by the exogenous forces they cannot control, the more they revert to their fundamental structures and concepts. In modern times most aspects of life in Muslim societies have been bent to the requirements of modern international forces and, consequently, to the dictates of secular law. Only family laws, which affect the position of women most intimately, have remained relatively impervious to the forces of modernization. Wherever the law has changed, it has triggered a vociferous reaction among the patriarchal vanguards—the conservative religious leaders and their allies in the traditional economic, social, and cultural domains. The veil, the vehicle for the symbolic and actual segregation of woman in a world dominated by man, becomes the emblem of male control of women's spaces and movements (Mernissi, 1987; Moghadam, 1994). Thus, Muslim women's seeking and achieving modern kinds of identity becomes a central point of conflict between the forces of modernity and the forces of reaction. It ought not to be difficult to see why, for fundamentalist movements, the most transparent reason for being is so often to stop the tide of change in the status of women.

Nevertheless, even in societies where at present fundamentalism appears particularly strong the situation begins to turn strategically to women's advantage. The reason is that despite the existing obstacles an increasing number of women have become conscious of themselves as authentic individual human beings independent of their kinships and community relations and increasingly insist that others acknowledge this fact. For example, over the past decades Muslim women, as well as women in other parts of the non-Western world, have successfully penetrated learning and other communicative institutions, creating a potential for achieving political power. There now exist in all Muslim countries clusters of women who have the ability to create, receive, interpret, and expand feminist thought and to translate it to political and economic leaders on one hand, and to the masses of women, on the other. According to 1988 United Nations Educational, Scientific and Cultural Organization (UNESCO) statistics, women constituted 27 percent of faculty in Egypt, higher than in France (24%) and in the USA (24%). The 1993 United Nations Development Programme (UNDP) Human Development Report states the percentage of women in technical and scientific fields as 43% for Kuwait, 24% for Syria, 31% for Saudi Arabia, 28% for Iraq,

24% for Tunisia, 31% for Algeria, 25% for Morocco, 26% for Egypt, and finally 27% for Sudan.

A woman who possesses information is capable, in principle, of appropriating herself. She has eaten of the forbidden fruit and what she has learned cannot be unlearned. Patriarchy may subdue her by force, but it cannot win her over. The experience of Iranian women under the Islamic Republic helps us understand the acerbity of the conflict between women who have evolved historically beyond the confines of the patriarchal order and a government that forces them to conform to a particularly restrictive patriarchal blueprint. Prior to the revolution and after decades of struggle, Iranian women had succeeded in creating an atmosphere that was receptive to the notion of gender equality. They had made important strides in economic, social, cultural, and political fields. They were visible in positions of leadership. In 1978, just before the Islamic revolution, there were 22 women in the House of Representatives and two in the Senate. There were five mayors, two governors, one ambassador, one cabinet minister, and three undersecretaries, among them undersecretaries of Labor and Mines and Industries. More importantly, they were present in large numbers in institutions of higher learning, especially in non-traditional fields. Women's organizations were spreading throughout the country. The fundamentalist leadership proposed to undo what women had accomplished by replacing the secular vision, from which women had drawn the moral and political force of their arguments, with the Islamist model, which rendered the feminist position irrelevant. Women, however, fought for their rights and made the enforcement of the new propositions costly. Step by step the regime has been forced to retreat. Women are still made to wear the veil in public places, but, significantly, the Islamic Republic has failed to resocialize them in fundamentalist norms. The Iranian case shows that once women forge a new identity for themselves they create a new set of historical realities that can no longer be easily dislodged. This, in fact, is where women are now in the greater part of the world.

The experience of women's human rights movements across the globe strongly suggests that the lead for the study and implementation of strategies of women's empowerment in the non-Western world should be taken by non-Western women themselves. In the case of Muslim women, certain steps have already been taken in this direction in many countries, including Jordan, Morocco, Egypt,

Pakistan, Turkey and Iran (Sisterhood is Global Institute, 1994). The idea is to address the strategic possibilities, among others, for (1) interpreting the Qur'an and the *hadith*; (2) educating the political elite and providing them with new interpretations that can be used as a basis for legislation and implementation of change; and (3) mobilizing grassroots support and establishing dialogue between people at the grassroots on the one hand, and the national and international decision-makers on the other. The goal is to modify traditional mores and laws to accommodate the requirements of women's freedom, equality and human rights.

Clearly, grassroots populations ought to gain access to the aspirations and agreements of the international community on women's rights. An important mechanism for raising women's consciousness at various socio-economic levels is a women's rights literacy program. There are several specific international declarations and conventions that address women's problems. These documents can form the basis for an international grassroots campaign. They need to be rewritten in local dialect and reinterpreted in a way which makes sense to grassroots populations. Indigenous images, events, myths, and ideas must be incorporated to relay the basic messages of the universal principles. Muslim feminist activists, as cultural intermediaries, have the connections and the pre-established trust necessary to communicate these ideas to the general population.

The women's rights literacy campaign should also help women unlearn certain harmful ideas and practices. There are many cases where an anti-woman behavior is falsely attributed to a religious mandate. An example is female genital mutilation (FGM) which affects 90 million girls and women. Many Asian and African women who practice FGM suppose that the practice is mandated by an Islamic injunction, although no such injunction exists in the Qur'an or Muslim law. A human rights literacy campaign would provide a simple and clear justification for why FGM is unnecessary.

Equally important, cultural intermediaries can simultaneously communicate the needs, priorities, and the points of view of the masses to the political decision makers. They are in the best position to integrate the international rights documents into the national consciousness and the national agenda. It is imperative that this reservoir of ideological and political power be activated and reinforced by the international human rights community.

In the preface to *Philosophy of Right*, Hegel has written "As the thought of the world, [philosophy] appears only when actuality is already there cut and dried after its process of formation has been completed . . . The owl of Minerva spreads its wings only with the falling of the dusk." This is only partially true in the case of feminist philosophy and the human condition of women in the non-Western world. It is true in the sense that a consciousness of authentic identity, set in motion by the requirements of our time, is already there, both actual and potential, irreversible, waiting to be discovered and understood. On the other hand, it is an idea that must be theorized, given shape, and realized as concept and process. It presents all kinds of possibilities—unknown now, probably unknowable now, but possibilities that nevertheless exist, and in which we must believe.

> "I can't believe that," said Alice.
> "Can't you?" the Queen said in a pitying tone. "Try again: draw a long breath, and shut your eyes."
> Alice laughed. "There's no use trying," she said. "One can't believe impossible things."
> "I dare say you haven't had much practice," said the Queen. "When I was your age, I always did it for half-an-hour a day. Why, sometimes I have believed as many as six impossible things before breakfast." (Carroll, 1992).

References

Accad, E. (1993, Fall). Third World Women and the Family. *Al-Raidam, 10,* 63.

Afkhami, M. (1994). Women in Post-Revolutionary Iran: A Feminist Perspective. In M. Afkhami & E. Friedl (Eds.), *In the Eye of the Storm: Women in Post-Revolutionary Iran.* Syracuse: Syracuse University Press.

Anderson, J. W. (1994, June 17). In Bangladesh, Militants Seek Writer's Death: Islamic Radicals Call Feminist Blasphemer. *The Washington Post,* p. A21.

Benedict, R. (1959). *Patterns of Culture.* Boston: Houghton Mifflin.

Bloom, A. (1987). *The Closing of the American Mind.* New York: Simon and Schuster.

Bottomore, T. (1962). *Sociology.* London: Allen and Unwin.

Cameron, D. (1985). *Feminism and Linguistic Theory.* London: Macmillan.

Carroll, L. (1992). *Alice in Wonderland: Alice's Adventures in Wonderland and Through the Looking Glass.* Chicago, IL: J.G. Ferguson.

Firth, R. (1971). *Elements of Social Organisation.* London: Tavistock.

Gilligan, C. (1982). *In a Different Voice: Psychological Theory and Women's Development.* Cambridge, MA: Harvard University Press.

Hegel, G. (1965). *Philosophy of Right.* Oxford: Clarendon Press.

Heilbrun, C. (1988). *Writing a Woman's Life.* New York: W.W. Norton.

Jenks, C. (1993). *Culture.* London: Routeledge.

Malinowski, B. (1944). *A Scientific Theory of Culture.* Chapel Hill: University of North Carolina Press.

Mernissi, F. (1987). *Beyond the Veil: Male-Female Dynamics in Modern Muslim Society.* Bloomington: Indiana University Press.

Moghadam, V. M. (Ed.). (1994). *Gender and National Identity: Women and Politics in Muslim Societies.* London: Zed Books.

Morgan, R. (Ed.). (1984). *Sisterhood Is Global.* New York: Anchor Books.

Parsons, T. & Shils, E. (Eds.). (1951). *Toward a General Theory of Action.* Cambridge, MA: Harvard University Press.

Sharma, A. (Ed.). (1987). *Women in World Religions.* Albany, NY: SUNY Press.

Spretnak, C. (Ed.). (1982). *The Politics of Women's Spirituality.* New York: Anchor Books.

Taylor, C. (1989). *Sources of the Self: The Making of Modern Identity* Cambridge, MA: Harvard University Press.

Taylor, C. (1991). *The Ethics of Authenticity.* Cambridge, MA: Harvard University Press.

Touflexis, A. (1990). Coming from a Different Place. *Time,* 64-66.

Tucker, J. E. (Ed.). (1993). *Arab Women: Old Boundaries, New Frontiers.* Bloomington, IN: Indiana University Press.

United Nations Development Programme. (1993). *Rapport Mondial sur le Developpement Humain.* New York: United Nations.

United Nations Educational, Scientific and Cultural Organization. (1988). Chart 23/7: Enseignement du troisieme degre: Personnel enseignant et etudiants par type d'establissement, *L'Annuaire Statistique de l'UNESCO, 1988,* pp. 3-169. New York: United Nations.

Young, K. (1987). "Introduction" in A. Sharma (Ed.), *Women in World Religions.* Albany, NY: SUNY Press.

Woolf, V. (1929). *A Room of One's Own.* London: Hogarth Press.

Chapter 14
On Mediating Multiple Identities: The Shifting Field of Women's Sexualities within the Community, State and Nation

Darini Rajasingham

In the past two decades optimism about achieving gender equality within the framework of the modern nation-state has waned in the face of persistent old and new forms of women's cultural and sexual subordination. Deep historical patterns of patriarchal control over women's sexuality within the structure of the family and the state persist, or have emerged in new forms in the world's more successful secular democracies where the struggle for women's rights as such has a long history. This has been the case despite the availability of advanced birth control devices and new reproductive technologies which have enabled women to take unprecedented control over their bodies and sexual lives, and despite women's greater participation in the political and economic spheres in a majority of Euro-American countries.[1]

Struggles for gender equality have taken different forms in the post-colonial nation-states of the third world. Resurgent cultural and ethnic nationalist movements and state sponsored religious fundamentalisms have undercut gains made by women's greater political activism and participation in national economies. At the same time, many third world women who participated in anti-imperial post-colonial nationalist movements have been caught in the currents of nationalist religious and cultural revivals which circumscribe their sexual autonomy and independence.

---

[1] For example, the debate over women's right to abortion which took place in the late eighties in the US and Britain reflected the dominant societal belief that women's choices with regard to birth control can and must be overseen by the state. The state, though officially secular, acted in conformity to dominant Christian beliefs regarding the sanctity of life and unborn fetuses.

The reasons for these contradictory trends are complex and might be sought in the history of post-colonial nationalisms and global, uneven economic development. As several scholars of nationalism (Chatterjee, 1990; Jayawardene, 1986) have noted, the majority of anti-imperial, post-colonial (ethnic) nationalisms which have redefined national culture in terms of archaic religious traditions, ideologies, and customs have impinged on women's lives in contradictory ways. These scholars have also pointed out that post-colonial nationalisms which harken back to a pure pre-colonial past constitute a riposte to the cultural penetration, domination and modernization program of European imperialism.

In any event, within the dialectics of post-colonial nationalism, women have figured as the idealized preservers of pre-colonial culture and tradition. They are seen to be: a) untainted by colonialism; b) the bearers and nurtures of custom, tradition and culture within the household (a space untouched by colonial rule in many parts of Asia); c) the mothers of the nation who literally reproduce and maintain the purity of the ethnic/racial/national community. The powerful idealization of the role of mother as reproducer of the ethnic community and national culture, has fundamentally configured and circumscribed the definition and realization of women's sexual choices and reproductive rights in post-colonial nation-states.

At the same time, many third world women have been active participants in anti-imperialist nationalist movements which legitimate patriarchal scrutiny and control over women's sexualities by emphasizing their reproductive responsibilities to the nation. The tension between women's activism and the constricting role of mother and nurturer has often been resolved in time, when as Jayawardena has noted in her study, *Feminism and Nationalism in the Third World* (1986), women political activists have been pushed back into the "private" arena, or household in the post-independence period. This was the case with Iranian women who took an active role in the anti-imperialist struggle against the Shah and made the veil into a symbol of resistance. Later, they found themselves relegated to the roles of wives and mothers alone. Their freedom was severely circumscribed when in the post-Shah period, the 'chador' became a legally binding requirement, the age of marriage was reduced to 13 years, and divorce became nearly impossible.

As participants in anti-imperialist struggles for cultural autonomy, independence and self-determination, women have also sometimes inadvertently contributed to the mythology that they are the keepers and guardians of national culture and ethnic/racial purity. It is therefore difficult if not impossible to deny that they have subscribed to strongly patriarchal ideologies in order to fight for community and nation, more often than not in situations of ethnic and/or nationalist competition, tension and conflict, such as Northern Ireland, Palestine or Sri Lanka. At the same time, many nationalist women have creatively used and manipulated the symbolism of motherhood to fight state oppression and violence against themselves, their families and ethnic communities. In doing so they have challenged and extended the definition of the culturally sanctioned role of "mother", and have both appropriated and subverted the nationalist ideologies that circumscribe their sexual choices. Taken as a whole, the experiences of nationalist women and their lives complicate any attempt to see women's sexuality and sexual identities as separate from their ethnic and national identities.

This paper highlights the paradoxical imbrication of women in post-colonial nation-states and nationalist movements, which preach women's reproductive and cultural obligations to the nation and ethnic community. It brings a site of present and future struggle for gender equality into focus, even as it tries to show how gender identities are multiply mediated.

The paper draws from recent critical rethinking about women's identities and experiences in the post-colonial state, ethnic community and nationalist struggles. It explores how the state and/or nationalist ideologies and conflicts both impinged on women's lives and bodies, and have been manipulated and subverted by women. It argues that women's sexuality has been increasingly domesticated via reproductive technologies and population policies which both enlarge their choices and give impersonal forces greater access to and control of women's bodies and subjectivities. It briefly touches on women's resistance to patriarchal state regulation, as well as their appropriation of the symbols of the nation/ nationalism to contest and subvert communal attempts to control their lives and sexuality. In so doing, I challenge the simplistic view that women have been and are merely passive victims of States, nationalist movements and/or their ethnic communities, or that women's subjectivities are singular. The attempt is to explore women's experiences in their multiplicity and complexity, and to recognize the various cultural factors that configure gender roles and identities. While the paper focuses primarily on the complex and contradictory experiences of Asian women living and working in contexts of post-colonial ethnic and nationalist struggle, it grapples with the general problematic of defining and implementing a set of universally applicable women's rights as such.

A Brief History of Women's Reproductive Roles in the State and Nation

The persistence of gender inequalities despite women's greater participation in the economic sphere, has problematized the nineteenth-century Euro-American feminist project, which posited that incorporation of women in national politics and economics would lead to liberation.[73] Many early feminists believed that women should and could be recognized as equal partners with men if and when they were able to enter the public sphere and the state in large enough numbers. They therefore focused on blurring the distinction between the "private" and "public". Yet recent research on the impact of women in the development process has made clear that women's incorporation into national economies and state bureaucracies, as well as advances in reproductive health have brought contradictory benefits to women. Women have had to carry the double burden of wage labor and house work, and in many less developed countries where labor regulations are weak or nonexistent, they have often been propelled from restrictive family and kinship structures to equally structured and restrictive factories and work environments controlled by international capital interests and/or the state. This fact has been noted by many socialist feminists as well as by critics of modernization.

Jayawardene (1986) and Chhachhi (1988) for instance, have pointed out that special programs for women's employment and skills training have often been supplemented by the passing of restrictive laws in line with regressive tradition and religious fundamentalist positions in many South and South East Asian countries. The greater control of sexuality appears to go hand in hand with the provision of opportunities for women to work outside the household. Economic and political gains are thus off-set by the imposition of other cultural

---

[73] Early Euro-American feminists had argued that women's incorporation into the public sphere, coupled with recognition of household labor as paid labor, would release women from bondage to the household, family and kin group, while facilitating their autonomy and independence. For a similar, more recent approach to the question of gender (in)equality see Heyzer (1986) and Young et al. (1981).

and religious strictures which are explicitly aimed at the greater control of women's sexuality and reproduction. Chhachhi has pointed out that economic liberalization and fundamentalism constitute two sides of the same coin, "the imperative to control and direct women's labor, fertility and sexuality to suit both capitalist and patriarchal interests" (1988, p. 3). Here it should be noted that in many postcolonial less developed nations the state has actively furthered the dual process of reinventing cultural traditions and ideologies which emphasize women's role as keepers of national tradition, mothers and wives, even as they follow open economic policies which impel women to reach beyond the household economy, and the culturally prescribed role of "mother" and "wife".

Early feminist struggles for sexual/gender equality were premised on the assumption that the modern nation-state could and would constitute an ally in the struggle for gender equality. While in the Euro-American world the state might have played the role of uneasy ally and forms of gender inequality shifted, women in the postcolonial world have more often than not lacked the support of the state in their fight for equality. This is particularly the case in countries where the state openly plays ethnic politics. In these contexts the proliferation of medical and scientific knowledges and technologies has enabled greater state and/or communal control of women's reproductive and sexual lives in the interests of the nation. Women in nationalist contexts have suffered diminished control over their bodies and lives in real and relative terms.

The uneasy and ambivalent position of women within the modern state and nationalist cultures is not a recent phenomenon. Virginia Woolf, for instance, argued very early on that women have never been considered full citizens of the patriarchal state which disenfranchised and discriminated against women and their offspring if they married or conceived outside the ethnic community, while it accepted men who married and fathered children outside the ethnic community (Mackey & Thane, 1986). She went as far as suggesting that women could not and should not participate in Britain's imperialist and nationalist projects. While the issues that Woolf highlighted have been redressed in England, where laws of nationality and citizenship for English women's spouses and children have been altered to compare with those of men, patterns of national/ethnic discrimination based on patriarchal and patrilineal kinship and descent structures remain in many parts of Asia, Africa and Latin America. Often, sexist immigration restrictions are also the residue of colonial racism and fear about miscegenation.

The interpellation of racial and gender based discrimination with regard to who is or is not a legitimate citizen provides insight into the deep anxieties of nationalisms. It also points to the manner in which anxieties regarding racial/ethnic purity have been projected onto women who come to bear the responsibility of maintaining national/ethnic purity as the literal reproducers of the nation. In this context it is hardly surprising that the imagery of ethnic, racial and nationalist conflict has historically been replete with sexual stereo-types, and that the speeches of nationalists are peppered with refer-ences to "violation of our sisters and mothers", and exhortations for the men of the community to prove that they are in fact men.

Arguably, an extreme and obverse aspect of nationalist idealiza-tions of women, is state-sponsored religious fundamentalism, na-tionalist violence, and state policies which are aimed at controlling women's fertility, sexuality and reproduction. The rhetoric of com-munalism and nationalism has historically been full of the increase in numbers of "other" communities and the excessive breeding of the "lesser races". For instance, recently the Hindu nationalist Vishva Hindu Parishad, produced a pamphlet which argued that due to po-lygamy, by the year 2000 Muslims would outnumber Hindus in In-dia—a statistical impossibility. In Sri Lanka there are reports that ethnic minority Muslim women are being pressured to stop the use of contraceptives and to produce more children in the contested East coast provinces. Similarly, in Singapore where the state openly plays race and class politics, wealthy Chinese women from the dominant ethnic community have been reprimanded for betraying the nation since birth rates of ethnic Chinese have declined. The former Singa-porian Prime Minister, Lee Kuan Yew, went as far as leveling an ex-traordinary charge against the nation's mothers by accusing them of them of "imperiling the country's future by willfully destroying pat-terns of biological reproduction" (Heng & Devan, 1992, p. 344). Similar attempts to channel women's fertility are evident in countries such as Sudan, Nigeria, Egypt, Malaysia, Bangladesh, Pakistan, where fundamentalist forces have state support. Iran offers an extreme ex-ample of the implication of this phenomenon for women.

The flip side of state and nationalist attempts to protect and maintain national reproductive success, is state promotion and en-forcement of rigid birth control policies in countries like China and

to a lesser extent India. In both these Asian nations ruthless population reduction policies have been enforced through forced steriliza-
tions and/or government removal of family subsidies and persecution
and harassment of women who have more than one child. These
strictures combined with cultural prescriptions that value male children have made for high levels of female infanticide.

In such situations, ironically, the availability of new reproductive
technologies and/or technological innovations like amniocentesis and
sonograms has proved to be mixed blessings. While enabling the
screening and selection of unborn infants these technologies have
raised new social and moral dilemmas for Indian and Chinese
women. Women facing societal pressures for a boy child often end
up aborting girl children in the hope of producing a male child sometimes at great emotional, physical and psychological cost to themselves (U.S. Department of State, 1994). While these technologies
provide greater selectivity for women—i.e. the ability to select the
gender of their children—they have also brought about extraordinar-
ily levels of female infanticide and unbalanced sex ratios in China and
India. The availability of such screening technologies has arguably
furthered direct or indirect societal and state pressure on women by
enabling communal scrutiny and intervention in hitherto inaccessible
aspects and processes of women's reproduction. In a majority of poor
post-colonial nations, where population policies rather than women's
health and well being are the criteria for what kinds of birth control
and or reproductive technologies are available, the more useful and
safer contraceptive and reproductive technologies are often inaccessible to the women who need them.

What seems clear in all of this is that in most parts of the world,
including economically advanced nations, women's sexuality has become the subject of unprecedented scrutiny, research and control by
States, medical institutions and other impersonal powers. This has
been partly enabled by developments in reproductive health and science as well as by population policies. Thus even as scientific and
medical developments in the field of fertility and reproduction have
enabled women to take greater control over their bodies and biological cycles they have also become the subjects of increased scrutiny
and attempts to control their fertility by the state. For women living
in highly patriarchal societies, advances in birth control methods and
new reproductive technologies have indeed provided mixed blessings. While they have been freed from endless pregnancies by the

wide availability of the pill and other birth control devices, areas of their bodies and sexualities which were not hitherto within the purview of state and communal scrutiny have been opened. Following Foucault (1980) we might then argue that the bounds of sexuality have been expanded.

The result has been that the female body has become increasingly articulated within the public sphere for state regulation. More often than not such regulation takes place on the grounds that their offspring are members of the national community. This has been evident in recent debates regarding women's rights to abortion, the debates as to how abortion might be sanctioned, and the period of time in which abortions might be legally carried out.

In both the first and third world, for different reasons it is then arguable that there has been a shift from a familial and kin based pattern of patriarchal control over women to that of state and/or collective communal regulation of women's sexual lives and choices in the past decades. In many less developed countries this shift has occurred with the redefinition of female and feminine sexuality in terms of women's biological role as reproducers of a social group, the ethnic community or nation.

Post-Colonialism, Community and the "Women Question"

Given that contraceptive and new reproductive technologies have extended the field of human sexuality (particularly women's reproduction), as well as the means for increased medical, scientific, societal, communal, and state scrutiny of women's bodies and sexualities, it is not surprising that the issue of balancing women's rights against the community and family has reemerged as a central issue in international feminist forums, such as CEDAW, over the last two decades. Yet it is arguable, following Foucault, that the idea of sex/sexuality, and its boundedness, is historically and culturally particular to the Anglo/European construction of the human body and identity, which treats a person's sex/sexuality as if it were separable from other aspects of that person's cultural/communal identity.

Feminist scholars and academics from the post-colonial world have suggested so much in critiquing universalizing tendencies in the feminist movement and in human rights discourses from a variety of positions. In particular, these critics have highlighted how women's gender/sexual rights and identities have been pitted against their ethnic/ national communities in universalizing terms, even as they acknowledge the complex ways in which women are marginalized by their communities. This post-colonial critique draws from the contradictory experiences of women in the post-colonial nations of Asia, Africa and Latin America, to challenge what they see as a false dichotomy between (women's) individual rights and the community. A corollary nationalist feminist critique of "human rights" discourse is the argument that the idea of "rights" is trapped in Anglo-European constructions of personhood and individual entitlement, which uses a biologized construction of women to posit cross-cultural commonalities as the basis for universal laws.

Other feminist critics have challenged the notion of universal progress, and the idea that rights constitute protection from previous and colonial forms of inequality. The concept of equality is seen to consist of a reductive denial of difference while being yet another attempt to reassert western hegemony, this time in the form of "human rights." The latter position sometimes dovetails with that of post-colonial nationalism, but is arguably the more serious critique of the universalizing aspects of human rights discourses which flatten or treat cultural differences as epiphenomenal.

One productive strand of the post-colonial feminist critique has focused on reconstituting the struggle for gender equality by framing the issue of "women's rights" as "human rights" in a manner that is sensitive to the dilemmas which women from relatively impoverished and conflict ridden nations face. The difficulties that women who have deep allegiances to their religious and ethnic communities experience when they are forced to choose between their ethno-religious community and their rights as women as such, they note, necessitates a rethinking of the very idea of "rights" in a constructive, contextually located, and historically situated way (Hensman, 1989; Spivac, 1987).

The rest of this paper then draws from post-colonial feminist critiques of universalizing and relativizing discourses in the literature on South Asia to explore how and if women's rights discourses might be reconciled with the multiple identities which women straddle and live. For, it is indeed arguable that the universalizing aspects of rights discourses flatten differing cultural conceptions of women's bodies, subjectivities, and possibilities of action. Further, in the context of heightened nationalist conflicts, emphasis on women's rights which pit women against their ethno-religious communities can result in great violence against women and men. In such contexts negotiating a third space between universalizing (feminist) human rights discourses and relativist post-colonial nationalist discourses is a strategy for survival for most women.

The post-colonial feminist critique begins with analysis of orientalist constructions of the Asian societies. It challenges the frequently made equation between (Eastern) religion, culture, tradition and gender inequality/oppression, against (Western) secular modernity, gender equality, and civilization. Such an equation posits that non-Euro-American peoples and cultures are traditional, ahistorical, and bound by hierarchical religious traditions and superstitions which are fundamentally oppressive to women. Rather, it is arguable that secularism is itself not culture blind but merely masks the national hegemony of dominant groups while eluding the issue of cultural difference and other modes of being. This point might be extended to the failures of modern secular western democracies to contend with racial/ ethnic and cultural minorities and their differences.

The post-colonial critique also attempts to get beyond the dichotomy between "nation/community" and "individual" that both the liberal discourse and the post-colonial nationalist discourse are caught in, by foregrounding the ambivalences that women live. The well known Shabanu case in India illustrates the point.

The Shabanu case became the focus of national debate and violence in the eighties when the Indian Supreme Court first ruled that Muslim women could file for divorce and maintenance under Section 125 of the secular Criminal Procedure Code, which is far more favorable to women than Muslim law, but subsequently reversed the decision stating that they were subject to Muslim personal law. What was curious was that Shabanu herself subsequently asked that the court overturn the first judgment in her favor, even though she stood to lose by having her case heard under Muslim personal law. Later following protests by Muslims throughout the country (the Bombay protests alone numbered over 100,000 people and included many Muslim women) she had said, "If there is going to be bloodshed, then let the judgment be withdrawn," and signed her name to the petition calling for her defeat (Hensman, 1990, p. 25).

Shabanu asked for the withdrawal of the judgment because she feared the threat of communal violence between Muslims who claimed that their minority rights were being infringed, and Hindus who claimed that Muslims should conform to secular law which privileges Hindu custom. Circumstances had forced her to make an impossible choice. What emerges from the Shabanu episode is the highly volatile and overdetermined nature of the issue of "women's rights" in multi-ethnic cultures where the question of the status of women is already prefigured though a history of colonial discourses and ethnic antagonisms. In India the question of the status of women, whether Hindus or Muslims, cannot be treated in isolation from the Indian post-colonial nationalist riposte to how the European coloniz-ing powers constructed "Islam" and the "women question", as well as the history and current conflict between Muslims and Hindus.

The dominant liberal colonial discourse constructed Asian and particularly Muslim women as victims of their culture, while positing that gender equality was a Western feminist project and a mark of civilizational superiority. It is as a post-colonial riposte that we must read the response of many Indian nationalists, men and women, who deny that women are oppressed by Hindu and Muslim religious tradi-tion and law. In the post-colonial phase of nation building the ques-tion of women's rights is highly problematic because of the difficulties that addressing the issue poses to the nation attempting to construct its genealogy on the basis of a valorized past, glorious cul-ture, history and heritage of which women were viewed as the moth-ers and keepers. The problem of constructing what Benedict Anderson (1984) has termed the "antiquity of the modern nation" is a fundamental aspect of the woman question in India and many South Asian nations. The issue of women's rights is inseparable from ethno-national identity formation.

And it is this light that we might also understand the Indian gov-ernment's initial refusal to sign the Convention on the Elimination of All Forms of Discrimination Against women (CEDAW) even as we might critique it. When CEDAW became available for ratification in 1981, the Indian government registered a qualification against the Article of the convention which required States parties to modify so-cial and cultural patterns and the laws of marriage and family rela-tions (Articles 5 [a] and 16[1]) . The Indian government declared that it would abide by this article only "in conformity with its policy of non-interference in the personal affairs of any community without its initiative and consent."[3] In other words, Indian constitutional

---

[3] Extract from comment on the Convention, in multinational treaties deposited with the Secretary General of the United Nations, United Nations, New York (Goonesekere, 1991, p. 3).

guarantees which authorize ethnic and religious (minority) communities to oversee the exercise of personal/ customary/ family law could not be altered under any circumstances, including CEDAW. What is interesting is that the Indian constitutional guarantee of personal law to its minority communities which goes a great deal further than that of most Anglo-European secular democracies toward a genuine multiculturalism raises the most difficult stumbling block for the enhancement of women's (a different sort of minority) rights. Rather, when the constitutional guarantee of gender equality came into conflict with other constitutional guarantees to respect the cultural and religious autonomy of minorities, the issue of women's equality was rendered secondary.

Our choice is not however that of dismantling constitutional guarantees to protect ethnic minorities in order to enforce CEDAW, but rather to work with Muslim personal law towards gender equality from within the community in a manner that does not fuel already polarized ethnic tensions. The project should be to reform Muslim personal law in a way that such reforms might be made a reality for Muslim women and result in a positive outcome rather than the backlash against Muslim women that Shabanu feared. Given the reality of ethnic conflict and violence, and the effects that such conflict has and might have on women it is difficult to dismiss the initial reluctance of governments of countries such as India to sign CEDAW as merely cynical disregard for the status of women.[4] Rather, the hesitation of nations like India (which subsequently signed CEDAW), which encompass a diversity of ethnic communities, to ratify the treaty on the grounds of respect for the cultural boundaries of ethnic, religious and national minorities pose a challenge to attempts to formulate and implement a set of universal women's (reproductive) rights. Several governments which declined to sign CEDAW or signed it with reservations have done so on the explicit or implicit grounds that "women" are subject first to the personal or customary laws of their ethno-religious communities, and that women's status and rights are therefore communally governed and mediated. The reticence of many third world countries to ratify CEDAW might also be explained in terms of a more general perception that the discourse of "human rights" in practice, whether when applied to women, ethnic, and religious minorities or children, has been used by first world

---

[4] CEDAW had been signed by 130 countries as of 1994.

countries in recent times as an excuse for justifying unequal trade relations, and the maintenance of the global status quo.

What emerges from the arguments for and against CEDAW is
the fact that attempts to formulate a universal set of rights on the basis of women's perceived biological, sexual, or natural commonality
breaks down at many different levels and sites, also because women's
nature or sexuality is culturally mediated and inseparable from other
facets of identity and experience. This is particularly evident with regard to women who have strong allegiances to their ethno-national
communities and/or in situations of ethno-national conflict. These
women are often asked and forced to make here, what Spivac has
termed in a different but related context, "impossible choices," between their ethnic/ religious/ cultural communities and their individual (women's) rights, as such. Like Shabanu, women who have
allegiances to their communal, ethnic and religious communities, and
feel the onus of maintaining ethnic peace, often cannot articulate
their individual (gendered) needs and desires in terms of human
rights, when human rights entails identification with the enemy community. Both nationalist claims that women, in exercising their rights
as women, betray their nation, and human rights discourses, which
dichotomize between the claims or ethno-religious communities and
women's rights, structure this dilemma.

Conclusion: Women's Sexuality and Reproductive Rights vs. the National Community

Feminine sexuality is a field where science, culture and myth
have been and continue to be confusingly and seamlessly merged.
Women's sexuality has been historically the focus of magico-religious
belief about impurity and danger, as well as various forms of cultural
and moral denigration and regulation. Women's sexuality has been
increasingly redefined through scientific research, political debates
over women's reproductive roles and "rights," and the invented traditions of modern national cultures. Women have been both the
agents and victims in the proliferation of scientific and pseudoscien-
tific discourses on their sex, sexuality, and its ideological elaboration
and practice.

What is distinctive about the present is the elaboration and proliferation of discourses, knowledge and policies vis-a-vis women's
sexuality and reproductive roles and the opportunities that science

and new reproductive technologies have opened to the state, and other impersonal powers as well as extended families to monitor, scrutinize and control domains of women's sexual lives and bodies that once seemed outside their purview. Thus, this paper has traced how medical innovations and policy discourses have reconstituted the field of women's sexualities and enabled the development of new forms of patriarchal control. At the same time I have argued that women's sexual identities take different contours in different parts of the world because they are constituted through multiple intersecting discourse of identity, such as ethnicity, religion and language. Broad similarities in women's biological and reproductive roles are in this scenario undercut by cultural particularities and peculiarities.

In particular, I have focused on how women's perceptions and experiences of their sexual identities are interpellated by ethnic, communal, national and cultural difference. Human rights discourses, as well as feminist discourses, have often ignored this fact and pitted women against their ethnic, religious and cultural communities with scant attention to the violence that such dichotomization does to women who have strong allegiances to their national identities and religious communities even as they are oppressed by aspects of communal ideologies.

At the same time, I have tried to explore the current conflict between universalizing formulations of the woman question and one strand of third world feminist critique of this formulation on the basis of cultural difference. Thus the issue of gender equality has been framed within the broader problematic of post-colonial nationalism, east and west. Understanding the challenges that patriarchal nationalisms pose to a general formulation of women's rights entails also recognizing other existing economic and political hierarchies, differences and difficulties that colonialism and post-colonial nationalisms pose to women. This difference intersects with and problematizes universalizing formulations of women's rights, responsibilities and needs, particularly given the present history of Euro-American cultural hegemony and dominance.

Abstract legal strictures and state level interventions such as CE-DAW need to be supplemented by community level mobilization for women's equality in local situations. As shown by the Shabanu case in India, often, where other issues intersect with the "women question", feminist community and grass roots activism is the only way to proceed. The formulation of women's rights must be sensitive to the multiplicity of discourses which intersect and determine the outcome of such controversies and, more importantly, the contradictory realities of women's lives.

References

Anderson, B. (1984). *Imagined Communities*. London: Verso.

Chatterjee, P. (1990). The Nationalist Resolution of the Women's Question. In K. Sangari & S. Vaid, (Eds.), *Recasting Women: Essays in Indian Colonial History*. New Brunswick, NJ: Rutgers University Press.

Chhachhi, A. (1988). *The State, Religious Fundamentalism and Women: Trends in South Asia.* (Working Paper: Subseries on Women, History and Development: Themes and Issues - No. 8).

Foucault, M. (1985). *The History of Sexuality (Vol. 1).* (R. Hurley, Trans.). New York: Vintage Books.

Goonesekere, S. *The UN Convention on Women (1980) and the Sri Lankan Legal System.* Colombo, Sri Lanka: Centre for Women's Research (CENWOR).

Heng, G. & Devan, J. (1992). State Fatherhood: The Politics of Nationalism, Sexuality and Race in Singapore. In A. Parker, M. Russo, D. Sommer & P. Yaeger, *Nationalisms and Sexualities.* New York: Routledge, Chapman and Hall.

Hensman, R. (1990, November/December). Oppression within Oppression: The Dilemma of Muslim Women in India. *The Thatched Patio.* Colombo, Sri Lanka: International Center for Ethnic Studies.

Heyzer, N. (1986). *Working Women in South East Asia: Development, Subordination and Emancipation.* London: Open University Press.

Jayawardena, K. (1986). *Feminism and Nationalism in the Third World.* London: Zed Books.

Mackey, J. & Thane, P. (1986). The Englishwoman. In R. Colls & P. Dodds, (Eds.), *Englishness: Politics and Culture, 1880-1920.* London: Croom Helm.

Spivac, G. (1987). Can the Sub-Altern Speak? In C. Nelson & L. Grossberg, *Marxism and the Interpretation of Culture.* London: Macmillan.

United States Department of State. (1994). *Country Reports for Human Rights Practices for 1993.* Washington DC: Author.

Young, K., Wolkowitz, C., & McCullagh, R. (Eds.). (1981). *Of Marriage and Markets: Women's Subordination in International Perspective.* London: CSE Books.

Chapter 15

Rituals and Angels: Female Circumcision and the Case of Sudan

Asma Mohamed Abdel Halim

> It is only in understanding the practice, its meaningfulness for the women
> who undergo it, and its embeddedness in the village culture, that those
> who are presently committed to its eradication might approach the prob-
> lem with the sensitivity it demands (Boddy, 1982, p. 681).

"Female Circumcision," "Excision," "Female Genital Mutilation"
and "Infibulation" are used to indicate traditional practices in which
all or part of the external female genitalia are removed. A controversy over the use of these different terms is threatening to derail the
debate over Female Circumcision (FC).[1] In the heat of the debate,
accusations of racism and misunderstanding—usually directed by Africans at Western activists—continue to escalate. Misunderstanding
of the tradition of FC among westerners has put some Africans on the
defensive. Westerners sometimes have seemed, to some Africans, to
imply that the African women's movement is legitimating the practice of FC. The use of the word mutilation also has contributed to defensive reactions among some Africans who have argued that FC is
not always mutilative and who have stressed that there are different
types of FC. As a result of futile cultural feuds and a belief among
some Africans that Western activists tend to distort FC, Africans have
begun to claim singular legitimacy in addressing the issue.

The purpose here is to discuss the practice of FC in Sudan and
the ongoing effort by activists and others to eradicate the practice.
The first part of the article discusses the history of activism to eradicate FC in Sudan and the complex and seemingly intractable cultural
context in which FC is embedded. The latter section examines the
debate over appropriate legal and activist strategies for eradicating

[1] I chose the term female circumcision because it is the name used in the Sudan by
the grassroots activists. For a definition of the various forms of FC, see (Toubia,
1993).

FC in Sudan and ways to use the rights discourse to strengthen the campaign for eradication of FC.

Historical Background of Eradication Efforts

The earliest attempts to eradicate female circumcision (FC) started in the Sudan almost 50 years ago. Educated Sudanese women and British women who lived in the Sudan began to talk about the tradition. The first attempts at challenging the custom were greatly hindered by taboos surrounding sexual behavior and by a broad resistance to education. At that time even convincing people to send their daughters to school was difficult. Parents feared that daughters would be exposed to a foreign education that would adversely affect or disrupt their stable and familiar social life. Successive Sudanese governments only paid lip service to supporting efforts to eradicate FC and, overall, remained passive and indifferent to the tradition, viewing it as a socially harmful custom that would disappear on its own.

The most daring campaign against FC, which challenged the practice as a health hazard, was launched by the Sudanese Women's Union during the late 1950s and the 1960s. The Union's magazine, *Sawat al-Mara'a* (Woman's Voice), reported medical and religious discussions about the practice. The Women's Union, as a pioneer in promoting women's rights, had some experience in tackling difficult issues. The magazine targeted a written campaign to literate women in the urban areas. Local members of the Women's Union, elementary school teachers and nurses gave talks to the people in rural communities. Finally, the Women's Union used radio programs and relied on religious leaders and physicians as spokesmen.

Despite the efforts of the Women's Union, the campaign did not attract widespread public attention. Many Sudanese thought the campaign addressed a private issue that should not be discussed in the media. Still, the campaign did help bring the tradition of FC out in the open for discussion. Unfortunately, the Women's Union campaign to eradicate FC was interrupted by the political upheavals that have plagued the Sudan since independence in 1956. The Sudanese Women's Union was banned for a total of 18 years between independence in 1956 and 1989 (although the organization continued to work underground during times when it was officially illegal) when the nongovernmental Women's Union was replaced by a government organization called the Woman's Union. The women's groups

that were affiliated with political parties which were formed after independence have tended to give FC a low profile out of fear that advocating for eradication of the practice would become an explosive
political issue that could tilt the outcome of elections. Several
women's chapters have formed in the political parties during the
democratic era in Sudan, but none has undertaken a serious effort to
make eradication of FC a visible issue in an election campaign.

In the last 15 years, however, Sudanese nongovernment organizations (NGOs) have taken steps to elevate the visibility of the issue
of FC. Sudanese NGOs have hosted three African conferences directed at eradication of FC, in 1979, 1984 and 1993. The Ahfad University for Women, the Physicians' Association, the Sudanese
Women's Union and the Babiker Badri Society for Research on
Women were active in the first two conferences. The Inter-African
Committee, based in Sudan, convened the most recent conference in
Khartoum in November, 1993. However, none of the recommendations from the three conferences or from other inter-African conferences on FC have been implemented.

The Cultural Debate

What sometimes gets lost in the debate is an appreciation for the
dynamics of the practice in the context of family life. Female circumcision is performed in the presence of and with the support of female
family members who are concerned about the safety of the child. A
child undergoing circumcision is believed to have the protection of
angels. It is a widely circulated belief in Sudan that a circumcised
child, a bride and groom, and a woman who has just given birth all
are guarded by angels for 40 days.

In the event of life-threatening complications from the procedure, rituals which invoke a mix of religious and superstitious elements (including some non-Muslim elements) are performed.
Mushahara are rituals performed as an antidote to some unknown
source of evil believed to be causing the complications in the child.
The cross, a Christian symbol, might be placed under the bed of the
child. Or the child might be taken to visit the river Nile. The *jirtig*
ritual involves wearing jewelry such as a British sovereign and beads
around the neck and jewels shaped in a half moon or crescent which
are attached to a cloth and affixed to the forehead. It is often only

after these powerful rituals fail that a child who is critically ill after the operation will be taken to the hospital.

The circumcision itself is almost always exclusively a family affair and the practice is seldom handed over to outsiders (Boddy, 1982, El Dareer, 1988, and Abdel Halim, 1992). The practitioner is frequently the only person in attendance who is not a family member. The operation may be performed at home, usually with aunts and female cousins supervising the circumcision and comforting the child. Female members of the family also are present if the child is instead taken to the practitioner's house and the child is brought home immediately after the procedure. This support from the family combined with the fact that the child looks forward to the event does not, however, eliminate the child's fear.

The child herself usually is not given specific information about what the operation entails, although she may know that it involves cutting and removal of some body parts. As a rule, therefore, the child looks forward to the event as a special occasion and she may ask members of her family when she will have it done. Family members see their role as one of helping the child cope with the fear and the pain associated with the operation. For the family members involved in the circumcision, the rituals and symbols which are a part of the operation serve to protect the child. It might also be argued, however, that the rituals function more as a protection for family members than for the child. That is, the rituals are seen to serve as a safety net to protect the parents and other family members from the heavy burden of responsibility that they might otherwise feel for the suffering the act causes the child.

FC cannot be understood as an act carried out by individual actors but rather is best understood as a product of group dynamics. In their view, FC is a "group act" which leaves little space for individuality. The individual thus becomes a representative of the social values of the group. One cherished group value in Sudan is the suppression of sexual desires in women. The suppression of sexual desire among the female population is often cited as one of the primary goals of FC. By dampening female sexual desire in women, FC places the focus on fertility. Boddy, a western anthropologist, has argued that female circumcision functions as a means of enhancing femininity and fertility by de-emphasizing sexuality.

> By removing their external genitalia, women are not so much preventing their own sexual pleasure (though obviously this is an effect) as enhancing their femininity. Circumcision, as a symbolic act, brings sharply into focus the fertility potential of women by dramatically de-emphasizing their inherent sexuality (Boddy, 1982, p. 687).

In men fertility and sexual capacity remain linked together. But for women only fertility counts. As Boddy rightly points out, fertility is the bargaining power for women in Sudan (1989). The fertile woman gains status both in the marriage and in the community.

The women in the village she studied told Boddy that they do not like to sleep with their husbands and encourage them only when they want to get pregnant (Boddy, 1982). The women also told Boddy that they do not mind if their husbands have girlfriends (Boddy, 1989). However, the women's views on their own sexuality is more complex than Boddy was led to believe. It is more accurate to argue that the women do not disengage from their sexuality but rather consciously inhibit the outward expression of sexuality because of social norms against appearing "lustful."

In the villages that form the town of Kaboshia in the Sudan where Boddy did her research, women often gather at midday when the men are away tending their farms. The women can be observed spending hours together grooming themselves for their husbands. As part of the grooming, women take smoke baths and use perfumed dough (*dilka*).[2] At this all-female gathering, women frequently express their eagerness to meet their husbands. However, the women agree that they will not openly express sexual feelings with their husbands because of the social value that requires "respectable" women to not appear "lustful." Indeed, girls are taught to inhibit the expression of sexuality as they prepare for marriage. Thus, the inhibition of the expression of sexual desire in women, although cited as a key factor in sustaining the practice of FC, is more a function of learned behavior than of FC itself.

Closely related to the social value of inhibiting female sexual desire is the value placed on virginity before marriage. The community believes that in delivering a virgin bride to the husband, the

---

[2] Aromatic wood is burned during a smoke bath. The woman sits over the fire that is burning either in a small pit dug into the ground or in a small container. She is covered with a woolen blanket that causes her to sweat and leaves a pleasant smelling yellow residue on her skin. The *dilka* is dough made of flour and perfume and is used to massage and smooth the skin.

community has preserved its honor. FC is seen as necessary both because women cannot be trusted to protect their virginity and because the community does not have the means to watch over them all the time. Controlling virginity in girls before marriage is probably the reason most often cited for the practice of circumcision in Sudan. But once again the intent behind the practice of FC and its effect are not necessarily the same. There is irony in the fact that FC is practiced primarily to assure virgin brides and yet the practice itself can be used to deceive. A woman who is no longer a virgin can "restore" her virginity by being recircumcised. Because the skin tissue to be penetrated is thick, the man cannot tell whether the woman is a virgin or not.

FC also is legitimated by the social value placed on "covering" women. Covering of women is a term used both literally and metaphorically. In the literal sense of the term, women wear clothes that cover them. They are also covered when they remain enclosed in houses (Boddy, 1982). In the figurative sense, men are encouraged to "cover" the women in their immediate family network through marriage rather than marrying outsiders. If a man attempts to marry outside the family when marriageable cousins are available, the man may be admonished to cover his own "pots" rather than other people's. Covering women through marriage is seen as the responsibility of men. FC also is seen as a cover for women inasmuch as it serves to prepare and protect girls for marriage.

In addition to controlling female sexual desire, preserving virginity and covering women, FC often is cited as necessary for a wide array of other reasons as well. Some adherents have argued that FC is necessary for the sexual pleasure of men. Some proponents have argued that FC is linked to cleanliness. In the Arabic language, *Tahara* or *Tahoor* literally means cleanliness or immaculateness. A final source of support and, perhaps the most ominous development on the horizon, is the growing support for the practice of FC among Islamic clerics and other interpreters of Islam who shape the legal and cultural debate concerning FC in Sudan.

The Legal Debate

As long as the law is not enforced it (female circumcision) will not stop. You know, in China they said, 'Stop binding the feet of your children.

Otherwise you will be shot.' That was it. Because probably a few parents have been shot ("Tearing Off," 1993, p. 156).

These are the words of the French prosecutor Linda Weil-Curiel. She has been prosecuting FC cases in France since the 1980s. Weil-Curiel appears to advocate the most severe penal laws against parents who subject their daughters to FC. She implies that shooting a few parents might be good public policy to speed the eradication of FC. But Weil-Curiel expresses greater confidence in the law than is warranted. The law without question has an important role to play in the crusade for eradication, but it is not the only factor. The law has to be effectively employed and made accessible to women. The fact that the law has not been used in the past should not stop women from using it in the future. It is also true that awareness of the law, coupled with the knowledge that FC is not mandated by religion, is a legal strategy that could aid the move toward eradication, especially now that Sudan has a religious state that claims that all laws are Islamic and that society will be reconstructed according to the tenets of Islam.

Although a patriarchal view of Islam often has been used to justify the practice of FC, there is very little evidence that Islam explicitly mandates FC. While Islam does clearly mandate circumcision for boys, there is at best only shaky evidence that Islam supports FC. Even the shaky evidence that some Muslims find in the *Sunna* (which includes the traditions and sayings of the Prophet Mohammed) is not tantamount to a clear order regarding circumcision for women. The Koran itself makes no mention of circumcision for either sex. Indeed, the prevalent view among Islamic scholars is that FC has nothing to do with Islam. Moreover, the tradition of FC predates Islam and did not survive in Arabia, the cradle of Islam, nor in other Islamic countries. Among the predominantly Islamic countries, FC has survived only in Egypt, the Horn of Africa and West Africa (as well as in other African countries which are not predominantly Islamic).

Attempts to outlaw the practice of FC by forces outside the culture, however, have produced a backlash from the Islamic leaders in Sudan. When the Anglo-Egyptian colonial power introduced an amendment to the Penal Code of 1925 to the effect that the practice of infibulation or what is known as Pharaonic circumcision would be punishable, even those who were outspoken against the practice participated in demonstrations against the government. The nationalists saw the amendment as interference by the British dominated government and as an attempt to manipulate the lives of the Sudanese people.[3]

The law has played a limited role as a tool of eradication in Sudan for three reasons. First, the cumbersome legal procedure made it extremely difficult and time consuming for anyone to pursue an FC case. According to the Criminal Procedure Act, complaints by family members had to be lodged with the commissioner of the province who had to give his approval before the police could begin the criminal procedure. The complicated procedure made the law inaccessible to the women activists who were ready to take action and who would have been willing to press the judicial system into enforcing the law. Second, those charged with enforcing the law—the commissioner of the province, the police and the judge—had their own daughters circumcised and, therefore, were part of the social machinery upholding the tradition. Third, the law was conceived as a part of the Penal Code and called for a prison sentence for those practicing FC. No one wanted family members sent to prison for committing an act which has strong cultural legitimacy and one considered completely acceptable by social measures.

Contrary to a widespread belief that the Sudan still has a law that punishes FC, there is no current law that punishes the practice per se. In 1983 a new penal code, introduced as part of Islamic legislation, did not include Section 248.d that existed in its predecessors (the 1925 and 1974 Penal Codes) and punished FC. Nor does the 1991 Criminal Act, the second of the Islamic legislation era, include a section on the prohibition of FC. Despite a commitment by the different Sudanese governments to pursue eradication, no action has yet been taken to deal effectively with the practice.

Outside the Sudan, enforcing the law against the parents also has proven to be difficult, even for a French prosecutor for whom FC was a practice "without a value, a marking of inferiority, a mutilative wound, without foundation and . . . a lucrative practice" (Verdier, 1992). Although the French prosecutor, Commaret, could find no reason or excuse for the practice, she found it unjust to deprive the children of their parents by sending the parents to jail. In requesting a

---

[3] Jomo Kenyata, the leader of the Mao Mao movement for independence and later president of Kenya, used the British law against FC to mobilize the Kenyan people against the colonizer.

suspended sentence, Commaret argued, in the Criminal Court of Paris,

> On the other hand, I come not to ask you to cut the Coulbalys (the parents) off from the social fabric but to support their acculturation. They let their six daughters be mutilated because they had not been sufficiently convinced of the uselessness and harmfulness of excision. (Verdier, 1992, p. 3)

The French lawyer, who saw the law as the only tool for eradication, believed there was evidence of intent, on the part of parents, "to hurt." Yet, after prosecuting several cases, the prosecutor could not help but bring the cultural debate into the legal one. By contrast, the African woman who is deeply immersed in the culture and who probably underwent the operation as a child, does not see any intent to hurt the child. An intent to harm is the important ingredient that is needed to render the procedure a criminal act. If the parents' intent "to hurt" is absent, the act of FC lacks the important ingredient that turns it into a criminal act.

The law then becomes a dividing issue because the only type of law available to curb or prevent the practice is the criminal law. What is needed is a shift away from the paradigm that holds up criminal law as the only type of law that can be effective. The debate may take a new turn if other legal measures, such as civil law,[4] the law of torts and constitutional law, are considered, where the harshness and the scandal of criminal procedure are absent. The cultural debate will continue to derail the legal debate as long as the only operative remedy or deterrence is criminal law.

Public opinion is another important factor that directly affects the implementation of the law. In France, the prosecutors have no difficulty lobbying French public opinion against the tradition. In the Sudan, however, the public has been struggling over change and eradication for the past 50 years with minimal results. It should be noted that efforts at eradication were not taken seriously until women came to the forefront as active advocates and injected their arguments into the public arena. A new law will be effective only when women demand it, for at that time there will be no doubt in anybody's mind that women also will use it.

---

[4] For example, a child might use the civil law to sue the practitioner when she is older

The arguments that call for legalization of the less severe form of FC, in order to protect children by preventing the occurrence of infection and disease, may sound comforting and acceptable to those who would like to keep the practice (Verdier, 1992, and Ogiamen, 1988). Earlier Sudanese law only prohibited infibulation while legalizing the less severe Sunna type of FC to be practiced by licensed midwives. Yet the practice of infibulation continued and the dangers were not lessened because the practitioners were licensed.

The Sunna type of FC provides an acceptable substitute for those people who are convinced of the harmfulness of infibulation and for those who have lost their faith in circumcision altogether but who find themselves pressured by society to conform to tradition. As well meaning as the above argument may be, it is deceiving to suggest that the practice should be legalized so as to assure hygienic conditions. The very adoption of hygienic methods allows proponents of FC to continue the practice by addressing the argument that unhygienic practices are responsible for the damage caused by FC. Any law that condones the practice expressly or implicitly will slow the process of eradication.

The Universal Versus the Relativist

So far, discussion of Sudanese women's rights, even within women's groups, does not seem to include FC. However, the debate about FC has only begun to position the tradition within the rights discourse—or to be more exact—to bring the issue of rights into the debate about FC. The strategy to forge a link between traditional practices and women's rights emanates from an approach that views women's subordination as the common thread that links women's suffering worldwide. While the debate on FC in the Sudan seems to be developing into a debate about women's rights, FC has yet to be incorporated into the mainstream rights debate.

Recently African women have begun to deal with the practice of FC as a human rights issue and as a violent act against women. (Graham, 1985; Abdel Halim, 1992; Toubia, 1993). They insist, however, that identifying the practice as a violation of the rights to bodily integrity and control over one's body be accompanied by efforts to address the larger issue of the subordinate status of women in African societies.

The problem with calling attention to the human rights violated by FC is that African societies do not recognize the right of women to control their own bodies. However, many activists hope that by dealing with FC and other basic rights simultaneously, it will make the right of women to control their own bodies visible and identifiable. It is equally necessary to combat the violations of the woman's right to choose her husband, to contract her own marriage and to the right of enjoyment of marital life, including sexual enjoyment. Restricting the concept of marriage to the husband's right to enjoyment—or, even more narrowly, to ownership—of his wife's body, amounts to saying that *society* determines the destiny of a woman's body, regardless of the direct harm it may cause her.

Furthermore, bringing men into the debate, not in their capacity as doctors or religious leaders but as husbands and fathers, may verify that men are equally trapped in a tradition that requires them to prove their virility. It is conceivable that men do not necessarily want to have women's bodies altered by FC. Using an approach that identifies universal rights will fully defeat the relativist argument that is based only on the hollow purpose of preserving society as it is.

The relativist position holds that women who live in different cultures do not share the same rights. This argument, however, may be defeated by premises derived from the very cultures it claims to preserve. For example, the Islamic religion that is cited as upholding FC claims universality and sets standards of conduct for all human beings regardless of their culture. Islam provides for equal rights for all people.

The universalist approach also is useful for engaging the UN to support local programs of eradication. After the United Nations Special Rapporteur for Human Rights in the Sudan came across materials from the conference on FC that took place in 1993, he was willing to include in his report a statement about his desire to see this practice disappear (Special Rapporteur, 1994). Unfortunately, as a result of the special rapporteur's comments on the Islamic penal code, the whole report came under fire from the government because, in the words of the Sudanese Attorney General, it was blasphemous in its dealing with Islamic laws in the Sudan. The controversy over the religious issue and the overall human rights situation in the country did overshadow the remarks on FC. But the fact that the special rapporteur cited FC as a human rights violation that should be eradicated is an important step forward in the battle to bring FC to the fore in the debate over universal rights.

Obviously, there is more the special rapporteur could have done within his mandate. He could have undertaken a special investigation on FC. He was satisfied merely to express his concern over the issue. It is well within his mandate to address the need for specific eradication efforts, but he made no recommendation for dealing with FC in the report. He did include, however, a recommendation that Sudan sign on to the Convention on the Elimination of All Forms of Discrimination Against Women (CEDAW). Unfortunately, the Sudanese government attacked the whole report. The government considered it blasphemous because of the comments made about the Sudanese penal law.

The general failure of the UN to support FC eradication through its health or education programs has been reported in the media. On September 20, 1993, the American television network ABC aired a "Day One" report on Female Genital Mutilation, in which James Grant, the executive director of United Nations International Children's Emergency Fund (UNICEF), acknowledged that of the $922 million budget of UNICEF, not even $1 million—less than 0.1 percent—is spent on FGM (Women's Action, 1993).

In The Eyes of the West

Sudanese women often are offended by Western scholars or activists who address the practice of FC. The West generally sees FC as a barbarous act that cannot be justified. Unless FC is understood as one version of a feminization process that is manifested in different forms the world over—including in Western cultures—the transformative change that feminists are crusading for will be obstructed.

People in the West seem to be offended by the comparison between FC and other painful practices for "beautifying" the body, such as breast implants or the relatively new practice of tattooing permanent eyeliner to replace daily use of a cosmetic, which can cause irrevocable damage. Sudanese women find these Western practices incredible. In their view, breast implants are a mutilation of a sensitive part of the body that is held, in most African cultures, as the symbol of womanhood .[5]

---

[5] A go-go dancer who appeared as a guest on the Phil Donahue show July 18, 1994, reported that she started earning more money as a dancer after having breast im-

Reactions are similar across cultures to mutilation or surgical changes to parts of the body in keeping with cultural norms. Whether western women are reacting to FC or Sudanese women to western "beautification" practices, there is misunderstanding and disbelief. Cultures which do not practice male circumcision view the circumcision of men as "a barbarous practice" that leaves males disfigured. This is much the same view that an American might have toward female circumcision in some cultures" (Harris, 1985 p. 34).

Boddy, one of the rare westerners who has come to understand the cultural roots of FC, started out from where many westerners did. She studied the practice in a village in the northern part of Sudan where the practice prevails. Describing her experience, Boddy said, "Initially I felt numbed by what appeared to be the meanlinglessness of the custom; yet as time passed in the village, I came to regard this form of female circumcision in a very different light" (Boddy, 1982, p. 1). Similar sensitivity is lacking in much of the work of other Westerners who isolate the social and religious aspects from the whole issue of gender relationships in Africa and launch an attack on the practice as torture (Walker, 1993).

Addressing the issue of FC under the rubric of violence against women is useful in eradication efforts only when it can be shown that FC is not integral to religious or customary canon. To convince those who practice FC about the rights or violations involved, the argument must make sense from within the cultural framework. Clearly, those within the culture are better equipped to develop such an analysis and, therefore, better able to use the universal approach. Understanding the "meaningfulness" of FC for those who practice it does not amount to legitimating the tradition. Rather it is a means for developing the strategy that is most likely to result in eradication of FC.

Some Westerners have seen the practice of FC as a policy issue and a political matter that should be solved by governments and human rights organizations (Rosenthal, 1993). Calling for the elimination of aid money to countries that allow FC to continue and rebuking human rights organizations for not dealing with the issue is a facile strategy for those who fail to understand that the practice is neither government imposed, nor expressly encouraged. Failure to

plants. It appears to African women that Western women are often too willing to conform to male standards of beauty regardless of the pain, health hazards and expense involved.

deal seriously with eradication is part of the society's failure to address women's issues in general.

Strategies

The difference between the strategies developed in the West and
those developed in Africa reflects a difference in the perspective that
each side has of the target. On the one hand, Africans, taking aim
from a very close distance and from within, are cautious about the repercussions of any action they take. They are concerned that eradication efforts could make the little girls they are trying to protect even
more vulnerable. Those persons within the culture who are intent on
preserving the practice of FC are likely to step up the pace of performing FC and may begin to lower the age at which the operation is
usually done once they become aware of serious efforts to legally ban
FC. African activists also fear that eradication efforts increase the vulnerability of women in the communities who stand to lose their support systems if they take a stand against FC. In Africa today there is
no satisfactory alternative to the security of belonging to the community. Any woman who is ostracized from her community has few
places to turn to for support.

On the other hand, for some Western cultures the practice of FC
is like a dangerous animal which has arrived from a far away place.
People do not feel safe unless it is behind bars in a zoo. Their strategy
aims at preventing FC from taking place in their country and at sav-
ing the medical system from additional medical costs that result from
FC. Some western nations, such as The Netherlands, have instituted
successful and progressive laws against FC. The Netherlands has outlawed the practice of FC but, at the same time, has established programs for its eradication among those communities who practice it.
(Minister of Foreign Affairs, personal communication, February 25,
1993). Realizing that the problem cannot be dealt with as just a
health issue any longer, the Sudan is pioneering a new approach that
was reflected in the papers presented at the 1993 conference. The
gist of that approach may be summarized as follows:

The phenomenon of FC has to be considered in the wider context of women's social status and within the general human and constitutional rights set forth by the UN and other international and
regional organizations. An assessment of the past efforts of eradication should be made with particular emphasis on the religious beliefs

which impeded the efforts. The medical approach should be restructured and incorporated into a socio-cultural approach. Social groups and institutions who are ready to be active in the eradication of female circumcision should be identified and supported. Research on female circumcision should be undertaken by research teams whose work is complementary and policy oriented (A. H. Khier, A. O. Siraj, I. S. Hassan, & A. El Safi, 1993).

It is important to change our strategies for eradication of FC. The approach that demands that the target group simply comply with the changes is not based on a workable strategy but simply is a belief in the moral and political correctness of its position. This approach has proven to produce minimal effects.

> We have to bear in mind that society does not intend to cause harm to itself, it is the closed absolutist type of cultural education that ignores the social, economic, and political change around it that are responsible (Doleeb, 1993, p. 8).

Because the tradition is a group practice and individuals are subject to the control and punishment of the group if they do not conform, the method of eradication should be one that addresses the practice as a group practice affecting the group, as such, and not just individuals in the group (Doleeb, 1993). Other customs that were deemed valueless have been eradicated in Sudan through the dynamics of the group. The customary long mourning periods following a death in the family, which took time and financially burdened the family, were quick to disappear when a group decision was made to shorten the mourning period. The effort was successful because of the group control and punishment of the individuals who did not conform with the change. Thus the same strategy that was used to keep the custom going was used to eradicate it. Psychologically, this leaves individuals at ease because they can achieve the change without being ostracized.

Strategies that include legal literacy programs and human rights education at the grassroots level are needed. Only by giving women power and control over their lives and by asking them to take off the blindfolds will they see that their bodies only belong to themselves and not to others. Through education and conversation women will come to see the practice of FC as valueless and maintained solely for the purpose of enforcing the "right" of the man to a virgin wife.

Infibulation, the practice that gave female circumcision or excision the name, "Female Genital Mutilation," is on its way to disappearance in the Sudan. In the urban areas a different and less invasive type of operation has been in use since the 1950s. The fact that healthier and safer methods of circumcision have become available has made many people more comfortable with the thought of continuing FC in Sudan. New methods which involve the use of anesthesia during the operation address the issue of the pain caused during the operation. This move towards a less harmful, less mutilative, or even non-mutilative form of FC represents measurable progress for the advocates of eradication. A widespread recognition in Sudan that infibulation is unnecessary and can be replaced by less harmful and disfiguring forms of FC is the first step towards an eventual awareness that the practice of FC is unnecessary in any form. It is important to stress again that this cultural shift toward the practice of less severe forms of FC should not be accompanied by any new legislation which legalizes the less severe forms of FC. Any legislation which legalizes the practice of FC in any of its forms is a step backward for eradication efforts. As argued earlier, any legislation which legalizes FC will serve to reinforce the practice, including its most harmful forms.

The weakening of support for the practice of FC in Sudan is occurring concomitantly with the linkage of FC to a rights discourse. The latest conference that took place in Sudan, in November, 1993, the NGOs Preparatory Conference on Harmful Practices, focused mainly on the issue of FC as a violation of rights. The recognition of FC as a rights issue is a victory for those who have worked for years to anchor the issue of FC within a rights discourse.

Interviews with about 85 Sudanese women living in the United States revealed an overwhelming opinion against the practice. It is interesting to note that two women said that they did not have their daughters circumcized (their daughters are now past the age of 20) because of religious reasons. One of them quoted the *Hadith* that prevents any change in the body of women. Even wearing a wig is thought to be in contravention of the *Hadith*. One of the women said she had to lie and tell her family that she circumcised the girls in Egypt during one of her vacations there.

All the women said that they will not circumcise their daughters because they would be ridiculed in the United States for adhering to the practice as much as they would be ridiculed for not following the tradition in Sudan. It is hoped that the 1990s will witness continued changes in the urban centers that will have positive repercussions in rural areas.

REFERENCES

Abdel Halim, A. (1992). Claiming our Bodies and Our Rights: Exploring Female Circumcision as an Act of Violence. In M. Schuler (Ed.), *Freedom From Violence: Women Strategies From Around the World.* (pp. 141-156). New York: OEF International.

Boddy, J. (1989). Wombs and Alien Spirits: Women, Men, and the Zar Cult in Northern Sudan. Madison: University of Wisconsin Press.

_____ (1982). Womb as Oasis: the Symbolic Context of Pharaonic Circumcision in Rural Northern Sudan, 9, 682.

Conference on Harmful Practices. Strategies for Participation in the Inter-Africa Conference in Konacry, 1994.

Doleeb, T. (1993). Al-abaad al-igtisadia wal igtimaieia wal nafsia limanhagiat al adat ed dara. Sudan National Committee on Harmful Traditional Practices Affecting the Health of Women and Children   (pp. 1-3). Khartoum, Sudan.

El Dareer, A. (1982). *Woman, Why Do You Weep?* London: Zed Books.

Graham, S. (1985) Female Circumcision: Women as Victims of Outmoded Patriarchal Traditions. *Third World Affairs.*

Harris, C. (1985). The Cultural Decision Making Model: Focus Circumcision. *Health Care of Women International,* 6, (25-43).

Khier, A. H., Siraj, A. O., Hassan, I. S. & El Safi, A. (1993). *Sudan National Committee on Harmful Traditional Practices Affecting the Health of Women and Children* (Report). Khartoum, Sudan, Mogadishu, Somalia.

NGOs Preparatory Conference on Harmful Practices Strategies for Participation on Inter Africa Committee (IAC) Conference, Khartoum, Sudan, November 15-17, 1993.

Ogiamen, T. (1988). Legal Aspects of Female Circumcision. *Proceedings of the International Seminar on Female Circumcision (*pp. 57-69).

Rosenthal, A. On My Mind: Female Genital Mutilation (1993, December 24). *New York Times,* p.A27.

Special Rapporteur Report on Human Right in the Sudan. UN Doc. No. E/CN.4 (1994)/48.

Female Genital Mutilation (FGM): UNICEF's Failure to Fund Efforts to Stop FGM. (1993, November). Equality Now. Women's Action 5.1. Distributed by Women Living Under Muslim Law.

Tearing Off the Veil. (1993, August). *Vanity Fair.* pp. 150-158).

Toubia, N. (1993). *Female Genital Mutilation: A Call for Action.* New York: The Population Council.

Verdier, R. (1992) The Excise Use in Criminal Court: the Trial of Soko Aramata Kieta. *Passages , 3.*

Walker, A. (1993, November). Derek McGinty Show. National Public Radio.

Chapter 16
Native Women's Rights as Aboriginal Rights

Sharon Donna McIvor

Introduction

Aboriginal women can successfully seek to have their sexual equality rights recognized without subjugating their struggle to the indigenous struggle for self-determination. It is not necessary for Aboriginal women to put aside their equality rights, and they can simultaneously contribute to the larger struggle for indigenous rights. The Native Women's Association of Canada has used a court strategy and political lobbying to achieve their objectives, even though this has at times been met by consternation from other male Aboriginal leaders and governments.

In July 1993, the Native Women's Association of Canada (NWAC) received recognition by federal, provincial and territorial governments as the fifth national Aboriginal organization. The NWAC was given its own seat at the negotiating table with the federal, provincial and territorial ministers of Aboriginal Affairs, along with the Assembly of First Nations, the Metis National Council, Inuit Tapirisat of Canada and the Native Council of Canada (now, Congress of Aboriginal Peoples). Louise Bouvier and I represented NWAC, supported by technical adviser, Teressa Nahanee. In August 1993, the NWAC was the fifth recognized national Aboriginal group to sit with premiers of the provinces of Canada in Bedeck, Nova Scotia. In May 1994, the NWAC had its own seat at the Ministers of Aboriginal Affairs and National Aboriginal Leaders' Conference held in Quebec City, Quebec. It has been a long, lonely, rocky road to that negotiating table.

The Native Women's Movement: Origins

The native women's movement began in 1967, two years before the rise of Aboriginal men's national organizations representing chiefs of Indian band governments. It began with elder, Mary Two Axe Early, a native of the (then) Caughnawaga Indian Band in Quebec, Canada, who had married a non-Aboriginal American man, now deceased. When her husband died in the United States, Mary moved back to Caughnawaga (now called Kahnawake). She discovered, as did thousands of Indian women after her, that she had lost her rights by law to live within her own community. Two years later, Jeanette Corbiere Lavell challenged this loss of rights in the courts (*Lavell v. Attorney-General of Canada,* 1971), and in 1974, lost her case in the Supreme Court of Canada (*Lavell v. Attorney-General of Canada,* 1974). Jeanette was the first Indian woman in one hundred years to contest her loss of rights. Under the law only Indian women, and not Indian men, lost their right to be an Indian upon marriage to a non-Indian (section 12(1)(b), Indian Act, R.S.C., 1970). In law, the non-Indian wives of Indian men gained Indian status and band membership. The right of Indian women to retain their birthright to membership and Indian status fired the women's movement from 1967 to 1985.

Indian men and Indian women were destined to clash over sexual equality rights because Canada threatened to take away Indian status and rights from everyone. In 1969, the Canadian government published the "White Paper Policy," threatening to abolish Indian rights, the federal Indian Act, and the federal Department of Indian Affairs and Northern Development. The government of Canada refused to recognize the existence of Aboriginal rights, and denied Indians their rightful claim to thousands of square miles of land in British Columbia, Yukon, the Northwest Territories, Quebec, parts of Ontario and the Atlantic provinces. This denial of rights and the government's attempt to shift responsibility for Indians to the provincial governments fired the chiefs' movement from 1969 to the present.

The chiefs have always believed that the struggle for sexual equality by Indian women has dampened their own struggle for what became known as "self-government." The Indian women pushed themselves onto center stage and insisted their issue be placed on the political agenda. The position of the chiefs has consistently required the Indian women to put their sexual equality issues on the back-burner while the men fought for self-government and self-determination.

In almost every arena, nationally and internationally, the Aboriginal women have entered every door to get to the table to achieve sexual equality rights. To a degree, the Indian women have been successful. In 1985, the government of Canada amended the Indian Act to bring it in line with section 15(1) of the Canadian Charter of Rights and Freedoms. That section of the Canadian Constitution calls for sexual equality in all laws in Canada. The amendments were designed to end sex discrimination in the Indian Act. After April 15, 1985, Indian women no longer lost status and band membership for marrying non-Aboriginals; the law was amended to allow up to 120,000 Indians to regain status; and Indian bands and communities were given control of the membership provision of the Indian Act.

In 1983, the Indian women were successful in having the Constitution Act, 1982, amended to add section 35(4), which guarantees Aboriginal and treaty rights equally to men and women. The women successfully lobbied premiers and Aboriginal leaders to have those amendments brought forward even though the women were not officially at the table. The Aboriginal women gained some measure of sexual equality by constant political and legal action and have made more gains than the other Aboriginal leaders. Their struggle has now shifted to participatory rights, for example the right to participate in self-government discussions.

Why are Aboriginal women struggling to have their right to participate recognized? Why not sit back and let the men do the fighting for self-government and reap the rewards of our Aboriginal and treaty rights alongside the men? I think Canadians wonder why we, as Aboriginal women, have a struggle separate from Aboriginal men.

Our movement started in 1967 and accelerated through the courts in 1969. It was not a very popular movement. When our women would go out to speak to other women (we had a very small group of women who took this on), they were physically thrown out of community halls. They were met with rifles. Their lives were threatened. They jeopardized their safety each time they went out to speak. It was very difficult to get the message out, to get any kind of support, because the women on the reserves who were suffering knew that they could not speak without repercussions.

Even women who were single, who needed their housing or social assistance or education funds, could not speak out because the minute they did the Band Council could take all of that away. That is still happening today. I have had conversations with women in Saskatchewan very recently whose lives, income, homes and educational allowances for their children have been threatened because of the political activity that they have undertaken. The Aboriginal women's movement came out of a need to have some kind of balance, to have some kind of fair treatment. That is our goal.

The Native Women's Association of Canada has been involved in the constitutional processes since 1982. The kind of involvement we have had is very superficial. We have been told that we cannot have our own participation, that we have to work through the other Aboriginal organizations: the Native Council of Canada; the Metis National Council; Inuit Tapirisat of Canada; and the Assembly of First Nations. We have lobbied ministers of past governments asking for our own seat at the constitutional discussions. The government response has always been: "No, you cannot have your own participation. Go to the other organizations and see what kind of participation they will give you. We will give you some money, but that money has to be funneled through those organizations."

The Political Struggle

In 1982 we had no voice at all. We spoke to the other organizations. The Assembly of First Nations (AFN)—the most powerful organization—had always been opposed to any of the sexual equality issues. Section 35(4) in the Constitution Act, 1982, is the equality section which covers Aboriginal rights. The AFN opposed that amendment. It took a very powerful lobby, not only of ourselves but other non-Aboriginal women's groups, to bring section 35(4) into effect.

When Jeannette Lavell initially won her case at the Court of Appeal level, it was appealed by the federal government. Many—if not all—male dominated Indian organizations, as well as the National Indian Brotherhood [forerunner of the Assembly of First Nations] intervened against Lavell. In this latest round of constitutional talks leading to Charlottetown, it was difficult to go in and negotiate or talk to these groups who have traditionally opposed anything to do with women's rights.

Several things happened prior to the constitutional round, which started in June of 1991. Jane Gottfriedson is a friend whom I have worked with in the BC Native Women's Society for a long time. She has always had Indian status. We had made some preliminary approaches to both the Assembly of First Nations and the Native Council of Canada. We asked if we could have a substantial role in this new round. Jane and I went on a retreat to her place at Keremeos, BC, way out in the bush. We discussed the frustration in dealing with the government, the other Aboriginal groups and with the whole constitutional process. Our work seemed futile.

This new constitutional round was the same story. Jane and I discussed what we could do. We knew the Metis National Council had not initially been one of the four recognized groups. Jane's recollection was that they had threatened a lawsuit and before it reached the courtroom, the government decided to recognize and include the Metis. We believed that if we threatened a lawsuit, we would get the same treatment as the Metis National Council. The idea of the case was born. But we had other major problems.

In June of 1991, the new constitutional process started. There were four of us who did the majority of work for the Native Women's Association of Canada. Many of us did it on a volunteer basis. For example, my life for a number of years has been to go back to BC, practice law for three months, get enough money so I could do volunteer work for three months, go back to BC, make sure that I had enough to pay my rent, make sure my kids were taken care of, and then go do my volunteer work. It has been a pretty hectic time.

On June 16, 1991, we went forward with our request to the government of Canada to participate as equals at the table and be funded. We met with the Right Honorable Joe Clark, former Prime Minister (1979), and then Minister for Federal-Provincial Relations (in 1991-1992). The Minister refused our request. Minister Clark approved funding for the Native Women's Association of Canada but he would not give it to us directly. He said that he would give it to the Native Council of Canada and the Assembly of First Nations and they would direct it to us. Eventually, over a two-year period, the Minister provided up to $23 million to the four groups, and $560,000 to the Aboriginal women. The Metis (mixed blood) women were refused funding.

We had many problems that arose because of the burdensome funding process established by the government of Canada. The Native Council of Canada tried to make us sign contribution agreements. We could not get our money. These were critical times for Aboriginal women and the government had subjugated our voice to the whims of two other national Aboriginal organizations: the Assembly of First Nations and the Native Council of Canada. We could not get the money to do the work that we wanted to do, to go out and attend the meetings. We went for many months living in a deficit, borrowing to make sure that we made the meetings. We eventually received our money, but long after it was useful to us.

There was a First Ministers' Conference in Whistler, BC in August of 1991. That was our first political attempt to try to get involved. We wrote a letter to then Premier Rita Johnston and asked if we could be invited as one of the Aboriginal groups. She responded in writing stating that NWAC was not recognized because we were not one of the four national Aboriginal groups invited to similar meetings in the past. We went to Whistler uninvited.

When the ministers were meeting in Whistler, the Assembly of First Nations and Native Council of Canada attended the meeting. Each had six passes to get into the premiers' meetings. We asked if we could have one of the passes. It was an interesting meeting because they did not want to refuse publicly, but they did not want to give us a pass. I was the one designated to ask for the pass. I stood up in the middle of the meeting and I asked the National Chief, "Can the Native Women's Association of Canada have a pass to the premier's meeting?" Ovide Mercredi told us of the many people he had at the meeting and stated that he had only a few passes. I asked, "Are you saying 'no'?" He explained the process that his Assembly used to select people to go to the meeting. He never did say "no." What I needed was a "no" for the record. I could not get a "no," but the end result was that we did not get a pass. We were treated very badly. But we did get a pass to go to the reception with the premiers after everything was all over.

Towards the end of the constitutional process the governments established what they called Multilateral meetings. At the technical level, the Aboriginal organizations, provincial and territorial officials and federal officials met to put together proposals for consideration by ministers. Technicians met apart from the ministers. Badges or tags were required by all participants. When the ministers met, only those persons recognized as ministers and Aboriginal leaders were allowed into the room. The Native Women's Association of Canada was barred from every meeting. Technicians were allowed into the meeting if they had colored badges. The Native Women's Association of Canada, not considered to be technicians or advisers to anyone, were never given colored badges to go to the ministerial meetings. The purpose of these meetings was to attempt to reach a consensus among the various parties to enable governments to start drafting the new amendments.

During that period of time, the Native Council of Canada and the Assembly of First Nations had their own parallel process. Each organization had a process where a commission went to meet with the people—what they called the grassroots people—to get input from them and then draft a report. The two organizations invited the Native Women's Association of Canada to participate in their respective processes. I participated with the Assembly of First Nations on what the AFN called the First Nations Circle on the Constitution. Jane Gottfriedson participated with the Native Council of Canada.

The First Nations Circle on the Constitution started on October 15, 1991, and ended on March 15, 1992. During that period of time we visited 80 Aboriginal communities across Canada. We held open hearings in the communities and listened to the many concerns of the people.

The stated intent of the Circle on the Constitution was to draft a report following the hearings to give to the chiefs. The chiefs would then use it as a basis for their participation in the Constitutional negotiations. What actually happened was that the report was drafted in-house by the Assembly of First Nations after March 15th and reflected very little of what we heard. Since my association with the Assembly of First Nations—like the other commissioners who attended the hearings—stopped on March 15th, we did not participate in the preparation of the report. The process with the Native Council of Canada was basically the same. They made the attempt to go out and talk to the people but when the report was drafted no one who was actually involved in the hearings drafted or reviewed it. I was unable to endorse the final report for the Assembly of First Nations. Although superficially it looked as if we were involved, in reality nothing we heard and nothing we wanted to be included was reflected in the Report.

We had solicited several opinions on the applicability of the Charter because it was such a controversial issue. The people we heard did not say, "Yes, I want the Charter to apply," or, "No I do not want the Charter to apply." What they did say was that there needed to be some checks and balances. They said, "We need some kind of control. We don't trust our leadership. We need our leadership to have some ethics. We can't have them in control." For us that translated into some kind of Charter, something that would bring checks and balances with it and something that would serve as a form of protection. The final report stated that the people told the Commissioners that the Charter should not apply. It was many of the Assembly of First Nations' own ideas and own positions that went into the final report. They then tried to assert that the people who made presentations at the hearings had said these things. That is not true.

As part of my participation in the First Nations' Circle on the Constitution, I had an opportunity on several occasions to talk to the National Chief. We talked about the applicability of the Charter and the position taken by the AFN that, as a European document, it should not apply in our Aboriginal communities. Ovide said, "Let us deal with self government and then we'll take care of women's issues." I told Ovide of the many women who asked for our help and asked, "What do we tell them when they come and tell of the violence and discrimination in their communities? Wait? Many are life-and-death issues. I cannot tell them to get out of their community. They have no place to go. They have no money. They are stuck. I cannot with a clear conscience say 'The National Chief told me to wait and when they get self-government then they will see about working on your issues'." Ovide was unable to answer me. He was unable to offer any solutions.

At this time three things were happening. We went to the multi-lateral meetings, we were negotiating with the government for more input, and we were discussing the court case. We obtained three separate opinions on the case. We were also looking for a lawyer. We had no experience with Charter litigation and had no idea who had the expertise we needed. Someone suggested Mary Eberts. We asked Mary to give us an opinion on the case. In December, case-development funding was approved by the Court Challenges Programme.

The Legal Strategy

By March of 1992, we had not been able to negotiate representation at any level. Our Board of Directors was finally convinced that we would have to try another course of action. Two of the three legal opinions on the potential legal action suggested that we had a fairly strong case. After much discussion the Board of Directors agreed to proceed. We hired Mary Eberts. Eberts advised us that the Native Women's Association of Canada may not have standing to bring this type of a challenge as it was unclear whether an association is entitled to the freedom of speech protection of the Charter. Eberts also suggested that we have an individual named as a plaintiff. The logical person was Gail Stacey-Moore, the Speaker of the Native Women's Association. Gail agreed. When the Statement of Claim and affidavits were complete she was apprehensive and afraid to go on by herself. I agreed at that time to put my name forward to be included as a party to the litigation. As it turned out, Gail's fears were well-founded.

The affidavits outline the 100-year history of discrimination against Indian women in Canada. Gail's affidavit was very substantial. Teressa Nahanee researched and compiled all of the information for it. We had everything ready to start the court action. We needed a decision from our 22-member Board of Directors. They wanted us to make one last effort to see if we could get some participation without going to court.

On March 16th, 1992, we had a meeting with Minister Clark, our executive members, our Toronto lawyer, Mary Eberts and her assistant. We asked Mr. Clark if we could have our own seat at the table and separate funding to participate. He said, No, it would complicate his life too much. It was quite a long meeting and he was very upset with us. He made snide remarks about our "Bay Street lawyer," Mary Eberts. When one of our members talked about the discrimination that goes on in the communities and the plight of the women and the children in the communities he stood up from the table, pushed his chair back, and said, "Just don't get on me about women and children!" He then poured himself a coffee and settled down. He kept asking "Well, what do you want?" And we kept saying, "We would like a seat at the table and our own funding." He said, "Well, we're not going to get anywhere if you just keep on like a broken record." He refused our requests. The next day we filed our documents in Federal Court. Our Board of Directors was finally convinced that we could not use the political route.

Those words about women and children did come back to haunt Joe Clark. In NWAC's referendum case, Mary Eberts filed that conversation as part of the court documents. He was very upset about it. He stopped her at the Ottawa Airport and chastised her for it. Joe told Mary that he did not recall saying that. She responded that she takes very good notes and puts verbatim notes in quotation marks. She said that statement was in quotation marks.

Joe Clark also said at a later date, "Well, if we knew you were going to court, we may have done things differently." Once we filed the court documents we were met with a lot of hostility.

We were still having meetings where we were in the same room with the Assembly of First Nations and the Native Council of Canada. We had multilateral meetings going on where the groups met and we still had to go begging for passes. We could not get our own passes. We could have passes to go into technical meetings, which meant we could go sit in the back of the room and listen, but we could not have passes to go into the ministerial meetings, even though all we would have been allowed to do is sit in the back of the room and listen. We do not know what criteria the chiefs used for denying us access to the room. In very many instances the hostile environment erupted into yelling, shoving and threats.

We were in Toronto in May, 1992. Law Professor Anne Bayefsky acted as Constitutional Adviser to the Native Women's Association of Canada along with myself. Anne knew many of the people—mostly lawyers and law professors—around the table. Professor Bayefsky teaches international human rights law and is author of a text on international human rights law and co-author of a book on the Charter, with lawyer Mary Eberts. The year we retained her she was on sabbatical, having received the Bora Laskin Award. Anne was helpful in negotiating our position with many of the government participants. The representative from Canada, Fred Caron of Justice Canada, brought forward an Aboriginal women's issue and was challenged by the Assembly of First Nations. "Are you speaking for the Native women?" He said, "No." The issue was dropped.

Anne Bayefsky also lobbied the government of Nova Scotia's representative to bring forward another issue on Section 33, the notwithstanding clause. The Native Women's Association of Canada did not want the notwithstanding clause to be available to the Aboriginal governments. Nova Scotia was very quickly silenced by Assembly of First Nations advisor, Mary Ellen Turpell. She stood up and pointedly remarked to the Nova Scotia representative "Well, other governments can have notwithstanding but us savages can't have the notwithstanding clause."

After that no one would speak up. It was a brutal process and a difficult one for us to gain any allies or understanding. Government representatives would not bring our concerns forward. It was a strange situation because of the intimidation that went on in the closed meetings. No one, other than us, had the courage to take a stand on sexual equality for Aboriginal women. They were all afraid of the controversy our issue raised.

The multilateral process continued in Toronto in June of 1992. Major amendments were being drafted. We took part in a group which looked at Section 35(4), the gender equality section, as it relates to the Aboriginal rights. We spent two days in a room with representatives from Saskatchewan, the Native Council of Canada, Inuit Tapirisat, Pauktuutit, the Assembly of First Nations and lawyers trying to get an agreement on gender equality. We did come up with an agreement. It came to the table as Item No. 16. After Item No. 15 the National Chief stood up and left. He said he had to go to his daughter's recital in Ottawa. Joe Clarke then adjourned the meeting. Item No. 16 was not tabled. Even though we had spent two and-a-half days drafting it, it was never tabled. I believe there was never an intention to table it. They would humor us for two and-a-half days, but the intent was never to bring it to the table.

We received other not-so-subtle messages. For example, I spent about half-an-hour in the lobby of the hotel being screamed at by two members of the Native Council of Canada. They were very angry and yelling about the court case. They told me how horrible we were to say that they discriminated against women and that they were chauvinists. I had not met this kind of confrontation before. I did not know what to do. I had the options of crying, which I felt like doing, talking back or just turning and leaving. While I was making my decision—I am a very slow decision-maker—I just stood there and looked at them, back and forth, as they were yelling. This continued for about 20-25 minutes. Teressa Nahanee came along. I had no idea what she was doing or where she was going. I said "Oh, there you are, I have been waiting for you. Sorry guys, I've got to go."

We endured this kind of treatment until August, 20, 1992. The decision on August the 20th made quite a difference. In March 1992, the Board of Directors of the Native Women's Association of Canada, of which I was an Executive Member, made a brave decision to go to the Federal Court-Trial Division to force the government of Canada to include Aboriginal women at the constitutional table. At that time, we were demanding a right to participate as women in constitution-making. We claimed a democratic right to participate as women and as equals in a process leading to Aboriginal self-government. It was our belief that unless we participated, gender equality would be swept off under the constitutional table.

The initial court case, which we lost at the Federal Court-Trial Division, was based on sexual equality guarantees in the Constitution Act, 1982, namely sections 15, 28, and 35(4). Section 15 guarantees men and women equality before and under the law, including benefit of the law. Section 35(4) is a gender equality provision guaranteeing Aboriginal and treaty rights equally to Aboriginal men and women. Section 28 is a sexual equality provision applying to men and women, which overrides everything in Part I of the Constitution, including legal rights and other human rights. What was unique in the NWAC case was an interpretation on the right to freedom of political expression, section 2(b) of the Constitution. Under our interpretation, freedom of political expression is guaranteed equally to male and female persons, particularly when coupled in a legal, constitutional argument with section 28.

The Federal Court of Appeal agreed with our interpretation and held that Canada had violated our constitutional right to freedom of political expression. The Court was not so clear on whether this meant the Native Women's Association of Canada could take a seat at the constitutional table. The Court wavered on interpreting the constitutional process as a policy-making process or a legislative process. If being at the constitutional table was legislative, the Court believed it had no jurisdiction to impose upon the government an obligation to give us a seat. The Native Women's Association of Canada went to Charlottetown and was refused a seat despite the August 20th decision. That decision was later appealed by Canada and is now before the Supreme Court of Canada.

I mentioned that Gail Stacy-Moore was fearful of being left "holding the bag" when this matter went to court, and for that reason I joined her as a party, along with the national association. In the fall of 1993, the National Chief, Ovide Mercredi, filed an Affidavit to intervene in our case at the Supreme Court of Canada. Up to that point the National Chief's organization was not involved and, in fact, had refused to intervene during the constitutional process. By the fall of 1993, the Canadian constitutional process was dead, and the Native Women's Association of Canada had the only action in town. We were perched on the Supreme Court's steps. The National Chief contended that his organization, representing 665 chiefs and band

Councils, had supported the Aboriginal women throughout the constitutional process.

Fearful of being cross-examined by Mary Eberts, the National Chief pressured members of the Native Women's Association of Canada into reversing their position on the case. Some board members lobbied successfully to ensure that the National Chief was not cross-examined in December, 1993, by Mary Eberts. Other Members successfully lobbied board members to get out of the case altogether. Gail Stacey-Moore and I were the only ones left to bring the case to the Supreme Court of Canada. Mary Eberts filed papers on our behalf to continue the case, and the National Chief and Assembly of First Nations got to the Supreme Court of Canada without being questioned on their affidavit or intervention. It was only at the last minute that the Native Women's Association of Canada decided to leave their name on the case and had their name inscribed. The National Chief and his lawyers came extremely close to side-lining the Aboriginal women's case at the Supreme Court of Canada.

We have been criticized over and over again, that the Native Women's Association of Canada is being influenced by the National Action Committee on the Status of Women (NAC) and white feminists of Toronto. Each time that someone asks one of the Assembly of First Nations' representatives or other male groups, "What about the Aboriginal women?" The response is "You don't have to listen to them because they are being too influenced by the white feminists. We have to talk about tradition, we have to talk about our own communities, we cannot be influenced by the feminists."

We have not had a lot to do with the National Action Committee on the Status of Women. We met with them about our Constitutional position and our right to participate in constitution-making. We said we believed we should have 52 percent representation because we, as women, make up 52 percent of the population. We also stated that we would not settle for anything less than our entitlement. NAC said we were much too radical. Their women would settle for 15 percent. We said we would compromise and would settle for 50 percent. They said, "No, that was too radical."

When we tried to negotiate for certain changes to the equality sections of the Constitution we were met with a certain "game" format. We put forward the changes we needed for protection. The other organizations would put forward a position with significantly less protection. We would say, "No, these changes are what we really need. We need this kind of protection." They would alter their position and come back with a slightly better position, and we would come back and say, "No, this is what we really need." After about three or four moves on their part, they said, "But you have not moved at all. We have given you this much, and you have not given us anything." We said, "No, this is what we really, really need." They could not understand that we were not playing the game. We were not negotiating. We were telling them what we really needed in order to get the protection that we felt that our women were entitled to. We were unable to negotiate with them because they did not understand that style. It happened not only with the other organizations, it also happened with the government. They seem afraid of the certainty of our position. We know what we do not want. We know what kind of protection our women want, need and deserve. I think it is clear we are playing by our own rules and the government and our men do not understand those rules. Those rules have to do with a sense of sharing, caring, fairness and justice for Aboriginal women.

We are not, as women, making power grabs or seeking to take for ourselves more than we need or deserve. We are seeking control of our lives, of our bodies. We want security of the person. We want respect for our bodily integrity. We want protection. Yet, none of the constitutional actors has any idea of what we were fighting for in the constitutional talks. As women we understand the rules the men play by and we choose to ignore them. We do not support patriarchy or paternalism. If men say, We represent you, we do not accept that. If they say, We will protect you, we will not accept that. We want to be there, at the table, representing and stating our own viewpoint. As Aboriginal women leaders we never met with the individual Aboriginal male leaders alone. We set up one meeting and Ovide Mercredi brought in some Prairie Aboriginal women so as not to meet us alone. The Native Women's Association of Canada invited the National Chief to our annual general meeting and he refused to attend. In his term of office, the National Chief never met with the Native Women's Association as "the leader." Not once. The chiefs were afraid to talk to Aboriginal women as a group.

What became evident throughout the process is that the white male governments and our male leaders play by the same rules and it excludes women and women's voices. The NWAC court cases are about freedom of political expression and the equal right of women to represent their own viewpoint and speak with their own voices.

The men of government and our men cannot understand these court cases. They have called us every name under the sun for those cases and for the actions of the Aboriginal women with respect to equality. From our view those rules have to be changed, and until they are changed women will not be able to have a voice in their own futures.

The Inherent Right to Aboriginal Self-government: Collective and Individual Rights

Aboriginal peoples, collectively and individually, have an inherent right to self-government and the right to self determination. In plain language, women and men have the collective and individual right to govern themselves, including their land, people and resources. Much ado about nothing has been made of the inherent conflict between collective and individual rights when speaking of Aboriginal self-government. The right to government is an individual right exercised when individuals decide to live as a group and be governed by rules of social, moral, political and cultural behavior upon which they agree. In their testimony before the Penner Committee, the Assembly of First Nations took the position that the "problem of discrimination against Indian women in the Indian Act was a symptom of the non-recognition of the collective rights of the Indian community, which include the right of the men and women together to decide their own form of government" (House of Commons, 1980-82, p. 9).

While collective and individual rights are inherent, they are also protected in the Canadian Constitution (Assembly of First Nations, 1994). The federal Canadian Human Rights Commission has stated that the foundation of group rights is individual rights. That is a fundamental principle (House of Commons, 1980-82, p. 20). This foundational principle of individual rights, even in the face of organized government, has been found among traditional Aboriginal societies. While individuals may appoint a leader it is not necessarily agreed that this individual has power over anyone but himself or herself. Such a leader may be powerful only in that he or she is eloquent. He or she may be a good speaker, but that leader is not revered (Etienne & Leacock, 1980). It is accepted that, in matrilinear societies, women had important and accepted roles in selecting or appointing leaders. In the predominantly hunting societies, women had various roles which were not subservient. On the contrary, in hunting societies political decision-making tended to be collective or by consensus, elevating neither man nor woman in the political process (Krosenbrink-Gelissen, 1991).

The Aboriginal position is clearly that collective and individual rights coexist in domestic and international law, including the right to self-government and the right to self-determination (Krosenbrink-Gelissen, 1991). There is clearly a linkage of rights in domestic and international law which cannot be ignored by Aboriginal peoples. In the exercise of the right to self-government, Aboriginal peoples who make that decision are also deciding the larger question—the definition in domestic law of their international right to self-determination. While the Canadian government may deny that Aboriginal peoples have the right to self determination, there is increasing recognition internationally that as "peoples" the right exists:

> Indigenous groups are unquestionably 'peoples' in every political, social, cultural and ethnological meaning of this term....It is neither logical nor scientific to treat them as the same 'peoples' as their neighbors, who obviously have different languages, histories and cultures....The United Nations should not pretend for the sake of a convenient legal fiction, that those differences do not exist. (Daes, 1993, p. 8)

Women and men had and retain traditional political, social, economic and cultural roles within Aboriginal societies. According to Etienne and Leacock (1980), women had domestic power in that men respected decisions made by women. Where property was held by women and passed to women, the man, upon marriage, moved in with the wife. In those cases, as in matrilinear societies, the wife decided on "the choice of plans, of undertakings, of journeys or wanderings," not the man. Women's worth was well appreciated and her advice and counsel were accepted and acted upon. In some Aboriginal societies women could inherit chiefly titles or offices, they being wives or sisters of male leaders. As keepers of the family treasures, women often dictated terms (Etienne & Leacock, 1980). Even where women selected male political leaders, the leaders had position, but it was the women who had and exercised political powers (Krosenbrink-Gelissen, 1991). Women not only selected leaders, but could depose them as well. These rights are protected within the inherent right to self-government.

The traditional roles of men and women are protected in section 35(1) and those rights are subject to a gender-equality right contained in section 35(4). The traditional role of Aboriginal women is one in which women play a leadership role in all matters of governance. Such roles include: negotiators, advisors, diplomats, teachers and keepers of the family (Canada, Department of Justice, Draft Report, 1994). Women as well as men "share the same wish for self-government" (Canada, Department of Justice, Federal Issues, 1994, p. 7).

The scope and content of the inherent right to Aboriginal self-government has yet to be set out in the Canadian constitutional and legal framework. There has been a reluctance by all governments and Aboriginal leaders to commit principles to paper which will govern the implementation of the right to self-government. There has been an absence of trust by governments and Aboriginal peoples (Siross, 1994, p. 3), so today there is nothing written explicitly in the constitution or in laws which helps to decipher the meaning of self-government in practical terms. This does not mean, however, that because it is not in writing it does not exist. It exists. It is important to note, as well, that the powers and jurisdiction of Aboriginal governments are not only those that operated in the Stone Age or in the pre-European world. Culture, traditions and values change with time and these changes must be taken into account (*Simon v. The Queen*, 1985). Because the present cannot be ignored in favor of the past, what is needed is a balance between past and present in terms of tradition and culture (Canada, Department of Justice, Draft Report, 1994.) Culture is, after all, a living thing, like a constitution, for it is ever-changing. It is this characteristic of culture which allows a people to survive, to evolve, and to change with their circumstances.

Gender Equality and the Inherent Right

In many aboriginal languages, there is no distinguishing between "he" and "she." Both are seen as being the same (to the extent that they are equal). In 1841, a commission was established to investigate the condition of Indians in Upper and Lower Canada. It reported in 1847 that Indian women were the primary providers for their families. Indeed, the notion of egalitarianism in Aboriginal societies was not restricted to the Iroquois. Robert Campbell of the Hudson Bay Company reported in 1838 that the Chieftainess of the Nahany, a hunting tribe in the Yukon Territory, "commanded the respect not only of her own people, but of the tribes they had intercourse with..." (Isaac & Maloughney, 1993, p. 455).

The inherent right brings forward the participatory rights of Aboriginal women in traditional matriarchies, and indeed brings forward matriarchal governments. Women's right to participate politically, socially and militarily is part of the custom and tradition brought forward within the existing right to Aboriginal self-government. This balance between men and women, and the right of men and women to participate in government-making is inherent and brought forward in time. The Indian, Inuit and Metis women have individual rights that abridge the collective rights according to custom, tradition and historical practice (Canada, Department of Justice, Draft Report, 1994). This includes restoring the gender relations that existed between First Nations men and women since time immemorial. To restore this balance will require throwing aside women's obedience and men's sexual powers over women, getting rid of patriarchy and bringing harmony back into human relations in the home and the communities (Krosenbrink-Gelissen, 1991).

Within traditional Aboriginal societies there is a notion of equally respected roles of men and women. For example, today "Inuit women [have] stressed the importance of equality between men and women. They must be given equal access to the same opportunities" (Canada, Department of Justice, Draft Report, 1994, p. 2). Traditionally, Aboriginal women were involved in decision-making. The concern for involvement today is tempered by a number of factors, including "the level of violence they [women] experience, the inability of communities and their leadership to deal with this issue, and their own lack of involvement to date in discussions for change" (Canada, Department of Justice, Federal Issues, 1994, p. 7). The almost complete destruction of Aboriginal women and their role within Aboriginal societies must be healed (Krosenbrink-Gelissen, 1991).

This modern-day quest by Aboriginal women to be involved in decision-making that affects their future and that of their children is reflective of their immediate past. As one author noted, "One thing is clear—that to be born poor, an Indian and a female is to be a member of the most disadvantaged minority in Canada today, a citizen minus. It is to be victimized, and utterly powerless, and to be, by government decree, without legal recourse of any kind" (Jamieson, 1978, p. 92).

The Road to Self-Government

Between 1913 and 1930 the Administration of Indian Affairs followed a rigid policy of forced assimilation. Traditional practice such as the Sundances and Potlatch were prohibited and traditional languages were suppressed. The Assistant Deputy Superintendent of Indian Affairs, Duncan Campbell Scott, in explaining the rationale for changes to the legislation in 1920, said:

> Our object is to continue until there is not a single Indian in Canada that has not been absorbed into the body politic and there is no Indian question, and no Indian Department. That is the whole object of this Bill. (House of Commons, 1980-81-82, p. 9)

Today Aboriginal peoples are embarking upon a road less-traveled in government-Aboriginal relations. I say it is a road less-traveled because there is a lot of brush on this road. There is our oppressive past and our murky present. In recent months we have heard governments—federal and provincial—state that they recognize the "inherent right to self-government" as contained in section 35(1). They do not explain the meaning of these words and as Aboriginal leaders we accept those words as if they have meaning.

We have heard the federal Minister of Indian Affairs and Northern Development state that he is dismantling the department and devolving its programs and services to Indian bands. This process has been on-going for twenty years. Political accords have been signed between ministers and Aboriginal leaders on Indian programs and services; on gaming; on land claims; and on a plethora of other services. In this context, it is left to us, as men and women of the First Nations, to determine the government's agenda. As women of the First Peoples we have to be concerned about the impact of these activities upon women and future generations. National, provincial and local women's groups must be involved in the day-to-day negotiations on implementing the self-government rights. Historically women have been excluded from the national, regional, tribal and band government organizations. That is why a conscious effort must be made to include women and their organizations (Jamison, 1978).

Conclusion

As women of the First Nations, as Metis women and as Inuit women we have the freedom to exercise our right to self determination within our nations. We, too, have the right to self-government.

As a group, since 1971, we had a vision. It is a simple vision where we see ourselves standing united with our own people, on our own lands, determining our form of self-government and deciding the rules for membership in our nations and deciding who will live on our lands. That is the vision. We see ourselves home, among our own people—that place from which we and our mothers, and our aunts and our sisters and some of our grandmothers were banished by law. We see ourselves back there. So when the road is lonely and dark, and we are cold from the reception we receive when we speak of our right to participate, of our right to be at the negotiating tables, and of our right to vote in our communities even when we live in the cities, that is the vision that will sustain us.

References

Assembly of First Nations. (1994). *The Crees, Self-determination, Secession and the Territorial Integrity of Quebec.* A paper tabled by the Assembly of First Nations at the Federal-Provincial-Territorial Meeting of Ministers Responsible for Native Affairs and Leaders of National Aboriginal Organizations in Quebec. (Document: 830-507/016).

Canada, Department of Justice. (1994, May 24). *Draft Report on the Role of Aboriginal Women in Justice Reform.* Ottawa: Department of Justice.

Canada, Department of Justice. (1994, May). *Federal Issues Document on Violence Against Women.* Ottawa: Department of Justice.

Daes, E. I. (1993). Explanatory Note Concerning the Draft Declaration on the Rights of Indigenous Peoples. (UN Doc. E/CN.4/Sub.2/1993/26/Add.1.). Geneva: United Nations, Commission on Human Rights.

Etienne, M., & Leacock, M. (1980). *Women and Colonization.* New York: Praeger Publishers.

House of Commons. (1980-81-82). Minutes of Proceedings and Evidence of the Standing Committee on Indian Affairs and Northern Development Respecting Report on Sub-Committee on Indian Women and the Indian Act and Appointment of Sub-Committee to Review the Status, Development and Responsibilities of Band Governments on Indian Reserves as well as the Financial Relationship Between the Government of Canada and Indian Bands Including the Sixth Report to the House (Report of the Sub-Committee on Indian Women and the Indian Act). First Session of the Thirty-second Parliament, (Chair: Keith Penner), Issue No. 58.

Isaac, T., & Maloughney, M. S. (1993). Dually Disadvantaged and Historically Forgotten? Aboriginal Women and the Inherent Right to Aboriginal Self-government. *Manitoba Law Journal, 21,* 453-475.

Jamison, K. (1978). *Indian Women and the Law in Canada: Citizens Minus.* Ottawa: Indian and Northern Affairs Canada/Supply and Services Canada.

Krosenbrink-Gelissen, L. E. (1991). *Sexual Equality as an Aboriginal Right: The Native Women's Association of Canada and the Constitutional Process on Aboriginal Matters, 1982-1987.* Saarbrucken, Germany: Verlag Breitenback.

Morin, G. (1994, May 17). (Speaking Notes for a Meeting of the Federal-Provincial-Territorial Ministers Responsible for Native Affairs and

Leaders of National Aboriginal Organizations in Quebec). Ottawa: Metis National Council.

Simon v. The Queen, 24 D.L.R. (4th) 390 at 410-412 (S.C.C.), (1985).

Siross, C., Minister of Natural Resources and Minister Responsible for Native Affairs. (1994, May 17). (Notes for a Speech to the Federal-Provincial-Territorial Meeting of Ministers Responsible for Native Affairs and Leaders of the National Aboriginal Organizations in Quebec).

Chapter 17
Women in Conditions of War and Peace: Challenges and Dilemmas

Sima Wali

Overview:

The historic maltreatment of women and girls has very much defined their subservient position in male-dominated societies. Although women have achieved some progress in socio-political arenas, there is little dispute that the quality of life for a majority of women and girls, especially uprooted females, has rapidly declined in what remains a male-defined and male-oriented world. The absence of war does not necessarily advance the status of women and girls. Several years ago, in recognition of this reality, the United Nations issued the following statement:

> While women represent half the world's population and one-third of the labor force, they receive one-tenth of the world income and own less than one percent of the world property.

This paper will analyze the double jeopardy of female victims of war and conflict—as women and as war victims. It will further the position that sustainable socio-political change benefiting female war victims will occur only when corrective action is based on a recognition of the inherently negative attributes of patriarchal values and structures—that is, the values and structures that constitute the very underpinnings of displaced and refugee women's lives.

The experience of being uprooted, crossing borders under perilous conditions and living in sub-human refugee camps has life-long repercussions for both male and female refugees. However, refugee and displaced women and girls are in double jeopardy owing to their gender, which heightens their vulnerability to the most pervasive and egregious forms of human rights abuses. The status of such women is further complicated by socio-political processes and historical societal attitudes that view women and girls as war-booty. It is becoming increasingly evident that governments, as well as male-led resistance and liberation movements, irrespective of their socio-religious backgrounds, resort to the pillage of women in war. In this age of massive internal and external displacement, abuse of women and girls can no longer be considered the by-product of warfare, but part of its calculated strategy.

During war, forcibly uprooted women and girls lose the minimal standards of protection, identity and access to established socio-political systems accorded to them in times of peace. When a woman or girl crosses a border in search of a safe haven she is stripped of everything: her identity, citizenship, even the basic right to survival and a humane standard of living. Lacking the protection of her own State, a refugee is completely reliant upon and at the mercy of the host country and the international community to safeguard her against human rights abuses.

The international community and the United Nations High Commissioner for Refugees (UNHCR), the entity of the UN mandated to provide refugee care and assistance, must rely upon States for invitations to intervene and conduct humanitarian activities. UNHCR activities (including monitoring human rights abuses and the behavior of States and State Parties and implementing refugee protection, care and assistance) can only be carried out when UNHCR is invited by a State to operate inside its territories. Fortunately, the implementation of UNHCR's mandate is expedited when refugee-receiving countries are signatories of the 1951 Convention on the Status of Refugees and its 1967 Protocol. As a result, to date, there has been no significant precedent by States to inhibit UNHCR access to people in distress and in need of humanitarian assistance.

Over the years, a large body of literature and information on refugee and displaced people has been developed. However, an examination of the international refugee regime (in particular, UNHCR), which defines and governs refugee relief and assistance, reveals a dearth of information on gender issues. This paper highlights the problem of refugee and displaced women and its interconnectedness to historical, political and economic factors. It addresses the following themes from a gender perspective:

- Refugee institutional framework, language and law.
- State sovereignty: refugee and displaced women's protection.

- Historical, political and cultural roots of gender violence during conflict.
- Gender in the context of liberation, resistance and nationalistic movements.

Refugee Institutional Framework, Language and Law

It is ironic that the perpetration of violence against refugee women and girls occurs while they are under international protection (Rogers, 1993). The forms of abuse common to refugee and displaced women and girls include rape, forced prostitution, trafficking in women and children, domestic violence, sexually-related torture and murder, abduction and the demand of sexual favors in exchange for basic relief items such as food, water, fuel, documentation and transportation to relief centers (Wali, 1993a). Cognizant of these abuses, UNHCR has on several occasions placed the question of refugee and displaced women's protection before the Executive Committee because "the problem of sexual violence against refugee women continues and, in certain States, appears to be worse than ever" (UNHCR, 1993, p. 5).

Although a growing body of literature and advocacy identifies gender as a compounding factor in forced migration, the international refugee regime and its instruments have been designed with little regard to refugee demographics and without particular attention to gender issues. Despite the fact that a majority of refugees are women and girls with significant needs, they are accorded no particular attention. In neglecting to make a distinction between male and female refugees, the international refugee instruments are in fact gender-biased (Johnsson, 1989).

The 1951 UN Convention on the Status of Refugees and accompanying 1967 Protocol to the Convention constitute the primary sources of international refugee law stipulating refugee status (Article 1A[2]).

The Convention on the Status of Refugees defines a refugee in the male gender as follows:

(A person who) owing to a well-founded fear of being persecuted for reasons of race, religion, nationality, membership of a particular social group or political opinion is outside the country of his nationality and is unable or owing to such fear, is unwilling to avail himself of the protection of that country; or who, not having a nationality and being outside the country of his former habitual residence or, owing to such fear, is unwilling to return to it.

Furthermore, Article 33 of the Convention states:

No contracting State shall expel or return a refugee in any manner whatsoever to the frontiers of territories where his life or freedom would be threatened on account of his race, religion, nationality, membership of a particular social group or political opinion. (quoted in Johnsson, 1989, p. 222)

The language of this international instrument relating to refugees is a stark reminder of a patriarchal system whose institutions accord scant attention to the needs of women and girls. Anders Johnsson further reports that although women make up more than half the world's refugees, no single woman plenipotentiary was present or consulted in the drafting of this seminal international instrument conceptualized in Geneva in 1951. Furthermore, the UNHCR *Handbook on Procedures and Criteria for the Determination of Refugee Status* makes no reference to the female gender.

In fact, the last 100 years of treaty-making of direct relevance to refugees and their protection, which can be said to have started when the 1889 Montevideo Treaty on Penal Law established the inviolability of asylum from political persecution, is exclusively male-oriented. (Johnsson, 1989, p. 1)

The institutional gender bias of the refugee regime conveys direct consequences for women refugees. For example, adherence to the concept and practice of cultural relativism by the international relief and development agencies is a systemic problem created when men make decisions on behalf of women, especially in cultures alien to the West. The Afghan situation is a case in point demonstrating the marked regression of the status of women and girls in exile where cultural norms and practices take precedence. In this case they were kept from access to education, training, community organizing and capacity building efforts. More importantly, the system for distribution of food rations, designed by those believing they were upholding cultural traditions, resulted in a program which benefits men rather than women, despite the fact that a majority of the refugee population is widowed, handicapped and female.

The world view that men are the targets of political persecution has led to misperceptions and under-recognition of the gendered nature of asylum. Correction of these perceptions is a recent phenomenon. Particular attention was paid to the situation of refugee women late in the United Nations Decade for Women. In 1985, UNHCR spearheaded a landmark effort to address such concerns, resulting in a resolution on refugee women's protection.

Recently, dialogues, discussions and expert group meetings have been organized to focus attention on refugee women and girls. Most recent UNHCR successes include the creation of the office of a Senior Coordinator for Refugees in Geneva and the development of the 1991 UNHCR Policy on Refugee Women, as well the 1991 Guidelines on the Protection of Refugee Women.

Moreover, the applicability of the Convention to women who flee gender-based persecution is currently under debate. Of note is the creation of the "Women-at-Risk" program with the underlying objective of removing women and girls from intolerable conditions and granting them asylum in the West. To date, Australia, New Zealand and Canada have subscribed to the "Women-at-Risk" program. Furthermore, the European Parliament's 1984 effort, which calls upon States to extend refugee status to women and girls, supports asylum provisions for those seeking asylum on the basis of gender in European countries. The UNHCR, upon pressure from the European Parliament, undertook the responsibility through its Executive Committee to seek identical recommendations from other member states. The Executive Committee failed in its efforts because some States issued protests over "criticism of certain religious beliefs or social or cultural practices." The efforts ended with a compromise agreement whereby the Executive Committee simply recognized that States, in the exercise of national sovereignty, are free to adopt the interpretation that women asylum-seekers who face harsh or inhuman treatment due to having transgressed the social mores of the society in which they live may be considered a "particular social group" (Davar, 1993).

The granting of refuge and asylum does not cover the totality of "refugee rights." In fact, refugee and displaced women's rights extend beyond the granting of asylum to the right of survival, protection, access to food and relief supplies, development assistance, voluntary return, the right to own and operate their own businesses and to social and political participation and nation-building. Too often the rights of refugees have been interpreted to mean only those defined by the 1951 Convention and its accompanying Protocol without adequately exploring foundational human rights instruments and their applicability to refugee women. In particular, the Convention on the Elimination of All forms of Discrimination Against Women (CE-DAW) has yet to be applied to refugee and displaced women. Other human rights instruments may also serve as tools to safeguard uprooted women from all forms of abuse and discrimination.

State Sovereignty and the Protection of Refugees

In general, refugees and forced migrants are the products of governments. States regularly perpetuate mass violence against their own citizens, causing large population displacements. Government policies that induce hunger and starvation, as well as land and property confiscation policies, are also factors that lead to forced migration. Moreover, States use torture, rape and other sexual violence against women to obtain information on the whereabouts and/or resistance activities of male relatives. Thus, governments create refugees and displaced people, sanction violence against their citizens and provide asylum when it best fits their national security interests. At the same time, the international structures and systems established to monitor state actions and human rights abuses against their citizens are also created by nation states.

The international entity entrusted with the protection of refugees is the UNHCR. In the absence of effective social entities in their own countries responsible for their protection, displaced women have also become reliant upon the UNHCR. However, the UN has only recently begun to respond to the plight of the internally displaced. The concepts of "territorial integrity" and "national sovereignty" were used to justify non-intervention on behalf of people displaced within the borders of their own countries. Recognition of the national sovereignty of States has consistently superseded international intervention.

The concept of state sovereignty has until recently limited the international community to humanitarian action on behalf of uprooted people who have managed to cross international borders. No international agency was charged with the protection of people caught in war-like conditions inside the borders of their countries. Owing to the inviolable integrity of nation states, no international alliance has managed to challenge the issue of state sovereignty before the UNHCR. However, the case of Iraqi intervention did raise the issue of national sovereignty and territorial integrity for consideration.

There is an on-going debate concerning the stage at which international intervention should occur. Should the UNHCR function in its traditional role of protection and relief assistance when refugees have crossed borders? Or should its mandate be extended to provide humanitarian assistance to internally displaced people as well? "The United Nations Charter upholds sovereignty by forbidding intervention in matters 'essentially within the domestic jurisdiction' of states" (Van Rooyen, 1993, p. 4). Critics of the UNHCR charge that it is powerless to protect the rights of people since it is itself a creation of member states. Moreover, the temporary mandate accorded to the UNHCR, coupled with its archaic definition of the term "refugee," hinders its leverage in a changing world.

Roots of Gender Violence During Conflict

Because of the breakdown of law, order and social and cultural sanctions during times of conflict, forcibly-uprooted women and girls are especially likely to be victims of human rights abuses. And yet, almost no society or culture demonstrates compassion for female victims of sexual assault. Social codes of conduct, norms and attitudes toward female victims of sexual assault reflect society's disdain toward women. This attitude is carried to an extreme in many cultures which justify "honor killings," of women, designed to blame and punish a female victim for a crime committed by men.

At no stage of their lives are women and young girls more vulnerable **en masse** to sexual violence and gender-related persecution than when they are forcibly uprooted. For a majority of refugee and displaced women the experience of rape is neither a one-time abuse, nor is it committed by one perpetrator. It is systematically extended over a prolonged period, occurring in cramped refugee camps or along escape routes or in the presence of family members.

Although no statistical data fully documents the extent of rape, rape-related torture, abduction, domestic violence or trafficking in refugee and displaced women and girls, these practices are recognized as common occurrences during war. It is becoming increasingly clear that systematic gender-related human rights abuses exist when women and girls are victims of forced migration. During the mid-1990's, reports of the mass rape of Bosnian Muslim women and girls in an organized war campaign of ethnic breeding and ethnic cleansing galvanized international attention to this atrocity. Such events are sometimes erroneously viewed as a newly-emerging form of human rights abuse. It is an historical fact that women in flight have always been victimized through rape and sexual violence.

During the height of the exodus from Vietnam, reports of the systematic rape of Vietnamese refugee women and girls by Thai pirates led to a $2.4 million per year anti-piracy program funded by the international community to arrest and convict Thai perpetrators (Forbes, 1991). Beginning in 1983, Refugee Women in Development (RefWID), Inc., an international non-profit agency in Washington, DC established to support the institutional development efforts of refugee and displaced women, began reporting on the rape of Cambodian, Central American, Ethiopian and other refugees in its "Alerts" in an effort to draw policy makers' attention to the widespread abuse of women in flight. Furthermore, RefWID called for the recognition of rape as a form of political torture against refugee women and girls at the First International Conference on the Treatment of Victims of Violence, held in France in 1989. In 1990, the World Health Organization (WHO), in collaboration with UNHCR, developed "Refugee Mental Health Manual," a demonstration tool that includes a chapter on "Helping Victims of Rape" intended for use with front-line relief workers in refugee camps administered by the UN.

RefWID further reports that domestic violence-related incidents among refugee communities that have resettled in the United States are consequentially linked to rape trauma ("RefWID Protection Program Findings"). Refugee men who have witnessed the rape of their wives during flight and in refugee camps accumulate a heightened vulnerability to not having been able to protect them, as stipulated by their traditional cultural mores. Upon resettlement, this male vulnerability manifests itself, adding to the many pressures caused by resettlement in a new culture.

One of the most difficult changes confronting refugees, the majority of whom have fled traditional societies, is the changing role of women in a new and modern society. Upon resettlement, women are often forced to work outside the home to help support the family. Men who have been acculturated to serve as the sole breadwinners are unaccustomed to their wives assuming work outside the home and are, once again, left feeling helpless and confused. Such feelings are often acted out in the form of spousal abuse. Furthermore, the loss of country, identity, family members and the ensuing trauma of flight prompts men to replace their multiple losses by exerting more control over their wives. The rapid acculturation of refugee children in western societies and the resulting generation gap further contribute to the phenomenon of spousal abuse among refugee families in the United States.

Another factor which distinguishes the rape experience of refugee and displaced women is that the perpetrators of sexual violence against uprooted women are often the very men assigned to their "protection." Cultural relativity and established societal norms and attitudes toward female victims of sexual assault bear direct relevance to their prolonged suffering in silence (Wali, 1993b). In large part, the international community actively involved in refugee relief and development assistance perpetuates this phenomenon by deferring the needs of women and girls to male refugees. It must also be noted that the staffs of such agencies, although effective in providing assistance to refugees, are not representative of refugee populations. This same pattern holds true for UNHCR and host country nationals.

Physical protection and safety from sexual violence must constitute the core of the international community's responsibility toward refugee and displaced women and girls (Forbes, 1991). In 1985, in preparation for the UN World Conference on Women and the NGO Forum, RefWID interviewed refugee, entrant and undocumented women from Vietnam, Cambodia, Afghanistan, El Salvador, Guatemala, Nicaragua and Haiti who had sought asylum in the United States. Sexual violence was unanimously identified as a priority concern for these women who, despite the social stigma against rape victims, agreed to address this issue publicly on videotape (RefWID, 1985).

Although Islam, as well as other religions/cultures, recognizes and advocates societal norms and practices to support the particular needs of war widows, orphans and the elderly, such support generally does not extend to female victims of sexual violence. Thus, female rape victims bear the added burden of their particular ethnicity and cultural and religious affiliation during war and civil upheaval. A contemporary example is the "ethnic breeding" of Bosnian-Muslim women by Serb military troops. Other incidents of ethnically focused multiple rapes during war and conflict occurred in the Bangladesh War, in which as many as 400,000 women were raped (Brownmiller, 1975, p. 78). The rape of Vietnamese women and girls by Thai pirates is also an illustration of ethnic-driven hatred. Age-old historic enmities between the Thai and the Vietnamese provide an added dimension to the rape of Vietnamese women and girls. These violations often occurred while male family members were present to witness the brutal act. The act of rape is thereby justified as a "get-even" policy with the enemy—a form of war reparation even more potent than killing the male war victim.

A majority of the world's refugee and displaced women and girls are concentrated in traditional male-dominated societies in which their position as women is repressed even prior to flight. Traditional male-dominated societies have little regard for gender equality. Wherever there are hunger, poverty, starvation, illiteracy, health or mental-health problems, uprooted women and girls suffer most due to society's disregard for its female citizens. In addition, social stigma attached to rape and sexual violence, in effect, displace blame back to the victims. Gender-biased cultural mores serve as a severe deterrent to the psycho-social well-being of women and girls and help perpetuate the trauma of rape and sexual violence.

Gender in Resistance and Nationalistic Movements

Another illustration of the vulnerability of women in times of war is the status of Afghan women under the Communist regime as well as Afghan women living in asylum under the control of the "mujahedeen" or "Islamic warriors." Controlling scarce resources during the war became the primary objective of Afghan male decision-makers. Moreover, during the war, Afghan's most valued members, its male soldiers or resistance fighters, were accorded the greatest share of power and resources. Any focus on "women's problems" was seen by both the "mujahedeen" Resistance Movement and the Communist Soldiers as a diversion of attention from the primary objective of the war. The situation in Afghanistan exemplifies how a war is maintained by keeping more than half of the Afghan refugee and displaced population—its females—subservient and defenseless. Foreign supporters of the war bought into this Afghan male political agenda by financially maintaining its most ardent leaders. Fifteen years later, Afghan refugee and displaced women and their female children continue to suffer from the diversion of relief and development resources, although they constitute at least 80% of the refugee and displaced population.

Afghan female victims of war displaced internally within the borders of Afghanistan, as well as those who have crossed international borders, are both used as pawns to portray the virtues of male ideology. This ideology has exerted itself in the guise of Islamic or communist practice.

The debate and argument over the status of women and girls, erroneously focused on the status of women in Islam, must shift to that of societal attitudes toward women in male-dominated societies. This debate becomes critical when male members of a society en masse lose power and control and are forced into exile. Since power and control are the traditional domain of men, when their status is lost or threatened, men in exile exert misdirected control over "their women."

An illustration of this phenomenon is the resurgence of the "Islamic practice" of veiling and seclusion of Afghan women in refugee camps. Although Afghans were guided by and practiced Islam for centuries, Afghan women's and girls' mobility in refugee camps has been severely restricted (Wali, 1993a). Through campaigns of public violence women have even been restricted from participating in social service delivery programs. "Fetwas" (religious decrees) during Friday prayer sessions are being used to provoke public violence against Afghan women who disobey socio-religious mores. In 1990, the violence reached its height in Pakistan when the Afghan refugee widows' camp in Peshawar was burned down (Wali, 1993a). Religious leaders cited the corruption, rape, and trafficking of young Afghan women by host-country nationals and the international community as the reason for its destruction. Since corrupt foreign men previously had unlimited access to the camps, the burning of the widows' camp was meant to send a profound message to foreign male perpetrators. At the same time the destruction was carried out without regard to the camp's inhabitants, Afghan widowed women and their orphaned children. Thus, in incidents such as these, male domination should be addressed rather than placing blame on religion or culture.

Cultural Mores in Muslim Societies

In the Muslim world, tensions heighten during discussions of policies and practices concerning women's issues. "Islamists" mistakenly perceive women's liberation as a western concept alien to

Muslim cultures. The belief that Islam is necessarily "fundamentalist," anti-feminist and undemocratic arises when the definition of democracy, human rights and gender issues are developed by male-led populist movements with the sole objective of consolidating their own power. Women in the Muslim world are working to challenge this notion and to define Islamic history as well as Islamic principles from a gender perspective. Female Muslim jurists and scholars contend that such misperceptions are based on inequitable systems of patriarchy and polity based on the male world-view rather than on Islamic principles.

These issues are especially relevant for the large majority of the refugee and displaced population that originated from and/or have sought asylum in Muslim nations. Women and girls constitute a significant segment of uprooted Muslims who are of interest to male-led populist, nationalist, liberation and resistance movements.

The "Islamic extremist" policies did not abate following the withdrawal of the Soviet Union's forces from Afghanistan. An added feature of male political leadership following the Soviet withdrawal is best demonstrated by the religious "fetwas" issued during the takeover of the Islamic government. One "fetwa" reclaimed Islam as a State religion and commanded the immediate withdrawal of Afghan women from governmental and non-governmental posts. This directive is particularly notable since throughout the 15 years of warfare, Afghan women, especially war widows, had to take employment outside the home as they found themselves heads of households. Although centuries-old Afghan traditions supported by Islamic principles call for the protection and caretaking of widows and orphaned children, little regard was given to these factors. With the new "fetwa," female wage-earners were ordered to stay home and resort to the practice of public veiling. This policy served as a powerful tool to make jobs available to the estimated 1.5 million returnees (US Committee for Refugees, 1993), the majority of whom were men. Once again, priority access to resources and employment as payback for political participation in the liberation movement has led to large numbers of women living in hunger and poverty.

Conclusion

This paper has advanced the position that any program or policy devised on behalf of refugee and displaced women must take into consideration the larger economic, political and societal context. Such policies must also be responsive to the lack of real partnership between refugee/displaced women and girls themselves and the larger multilateral relief and development institutions, human rights agencies and mainstream women's organizations. The empowerment and sustainable development of uprooted women can only occur when programs and policies are designed to address the inherent powerlessness of uprooted women and girls.

In this regard, it bears repetition that the post-cold war environment is characterized by massive population displacement and demographic shifts which have acute implications for national as well as international security. Refugee and displaced people are direct products of war, civil strife and human rights abuses. Women and their children constitute a large majority of the entire refugee and displaced populations and bear a disproportionate share of sexual violence and other human rights abuses. Simply being female in a war situation is a risk factor. This risk is complicated by a woman's ethnicity, culture and religion. Viewed in this context, refugee and displaced women and girls merit special protection assistance due to the organized nature of abuses committed against them and the severity and life-long impact of sexual assault on both victims and their larger communities.

Lastly, global economic and political restructuring, exaggerated myths that asylum seekers and immigrants drain domestic economies and misperceptions about the Muslim world have contributed to a skewed western view of asylum seekers. Tensions in the West, especially in American and European countries, have grossly swayed the larger public toward xenophobic attitudes that threaten the very principle of asylum. Furthermore, such misperceptions have negatively affected refugee and displaced women's asylum claims on the basis of gender persecution.

The development of universal humanitarian policies responsive to the needs of uprooted women as well as men, irrespective of political and economic considerations, has never been more critical. Ultimately, understanding the underlying male-oriented social and institutional norms is essential to developing effective resolutions and strategies aimed at rectifying existing gender imbalances in the area of forced migration. Recent legal, legislative and policy guidelines concerning refugee women seem more concerned with changing the *intent*, rather than the *consequence*, of gender inequity. Policies and programs aimed at change will be ineffective unless refugee and displaced women—the critical link—are included as active partners in the process. To be successful, challenging male power structures at the community, national, international and larger societal levels requires the active involvement of women refugees themselves.

References

Brownmiller, S. (1975). *Against Our Will.* New York: Simon & Schuster.

Davar, B. (1993). *Rethinking Human Rights, Development and Humanitarianism: A Gender Specific Response.* Manuscript submitted for publication.

Executive Committee of the High Commissioner's Programme. (1993). *Note on Certain Aspects of Sexual Violence Against Refugee Women,* (Report, 12 Oct. 1993, A/Ac. 96/822, GE. 93-03298). New York: United Nations.

Forbes, M. S. (1991). *Refugee Women.* London: Zed.

Johnsson, A. B. (1989). The International Protection of Women Refugees. A Summary of Principal Problems and Issues. *International Journal of Refugee Law, 1* (2).

RefWID. (1985). *The Quilting Bee.* Washington DC: Author.

Rogers, R. & Copeland, E. (1993). *Forced Migration Policy Issues in the Post-Cold War World.* Medford, MA: Fletcher School of Law and Diplomacy.

United Nations Department of International Economic and Social Affairs (UNDIESA). (1991). *The World's Women: Trends and Statistics 1970-1990.* New York: United Nations.

United Nations High Commissioner for Refugees (UNHCR). (1993). *Report on the Forty-fourth Session.* Geneva: Author.

United States Committee for Refugees. (1993). *World Refugee Survey.* Washington DC: Author.

Van Rooyen, R. (1993). *Challenges and Opportunities in the Decade of Repatriation: The Role of NGOs.* Washington, DC: Georgetown University.

Wali, S. (1993a). *Uprooted People: Third Annual Report on the State of World Hunger.* Washington, DC: Bread for the World Institute on Hunger & Development.

Wali, S. (1993b). *How to Address Rape Among Refugee Women.* Washington, DC: RefWID, Inc.

Women's Commission for Refugee Women and Children. (1990). *Afghan Refugee Women: Needs and Resources for Development and Reconstruction* (Report of Delegation to Pakistan). New York: Women's Commission for Refugee Women and Children.

Chapter 18
Linking Dreams: The Network of Women Living Under Muslim Laws[1]
Farida Shaheed

[I]t's as good a thing to remember as anything. I never went like you to school but I know it. No two things are exactly alike. In odd days like these—snow comes too early, the gypsy bear too late—people study how to be all alike instead of how to be as different as they really are. (Shannon, 1993)

Introduction

One of the greatest advantages that networks have over organizations is their fluidity. They provide a vehicle for individuals and organizations to share information, analyses and strategies without trying to either homogenize the diversity of those they link or to control their autonomy in matters of political or personal choices. People can learn from the sharing of experiences and information and decide for themselves what appears most relevant in their own contexts.

Networks are also a viable alternative to the either/or discourses of dominant groups. For women, redefining gender is not only a matter of changing definitions; it is about changing women's lives. Of necessity, this implies parallel redefinitions of all those markers of identity important to individual women. For some it may be class, for others religion or culture, for yet others one's profession. There is no logical reason to assume that each marker is equally important at all times for all women. Maintaining that feminism can only be defined in secular terms or that women can only operate in the religious framework equally give credibility to the dichotomy of choice

---

[1] Of necessity, this paper draws on previous writings on the WLUML network. In particular, parts of the analysis appear in Shaheed (1994). I would like to express my thanks to Cassandra Balchin for helping me edit this into shape.

defined by politico-religious (and other identity-based political elements) to further their own ends. Neither seems to respond adequately to the needs of women as a whole. Avoiding the dichotomous logic of dominant male discourse, networks provide a channel through which women can learn of different alternatives and be free to make their own autonomous choices.

A serious challenge for feminist groups is that definitions of the female gender shared by women across class and ethnicity tend to be those of limitation and oppression. This distinguishes gender from identities of community (whether defined in ethnic, religious or other terms) that allow women to share in myths of greatness and strength, and not just oppression. A community's promise (whether spoken or not) to look independently after their own is beyond the scope of women's groups whose promises for improved conditions usually depend for implementation on state structures which, in much of the Muslim world, have been unable to deliver on promises made. By itself, networking may not be able to develop a shared identity of strength for women, but it does at least give women access to some stories of women successfully mobilizing for change. Less obviously, a strong network also provides an alternative reference point for women and legitimacy for change.

To redefine gender in the spheres of the personal as well as the public undoubtedly requires a multi-pronged strategy. At the level of national policies, effective lobbying and advocacy strategies must be devised and initiatives pursued. The discourse of politico-religious groups must be consistently and loudly opposed at all levels, local, national and international. Local initiatives need to be strengthened through linkages at the national and international levels, and strategies must be evolved to address, effectively respond to and modify the contextual constraints within which women are obliged to live their lives. No single women's group can adequately assume such diverse roles. However a multitude of autonomous groups effectively networking may achieve the critical mass needed to transform women's struggles for survival into workable strategies for bringing about a gender-equitable society, whether in the Muslim world or elsewhere.

This said, networks do not materialize out of nothing. They have to be created with a specific aim in mind and, if they are to survive and grow, need constant nurturing. They face a range of challenges: of communications and logistics, channels of interaction and structure. Networks also have to address conflicting viewpoints within the network, the varying strengths of networking groups and individuals and the different levels of inputs. Networks often start with a small group of dedicated women (sometimes a single woman) whose personal commitments cannot be measured in terms of mere time and energy input. To take root and flower, a network has to fire the imagination of the myriad groups and individuals it hopes to link.

The Creation of a Network

In 1984, four apparently unconnected incidents took place in different parts of the Muslim world. The link between these events was that each involved a denial or violation of women's rights through the application of laws considered "Muslim." Three Algerian feminists were arrested, jailed without trial and kept incommunicado for seven months. Their crime was to have discussed with other women the contents of a new set of personal laws (Code de la Famille, 1984) that would severely reduce women's rights. That same year, an Indian Muslim woman challenged the application of religious minority law, arguing before the Supreme Court that this denied Muslim women rights guaranteed all citizens under the Constitution of India. Meanwhile in Abu Dhabi, a pregnant Sri Lankan woman was tried and found guilty of adultery. She was sentenced to be stoned to death two months after giving birth. In Europe, a group of women divorced from Algerian men ("Les Meres d'Algers") sought custody or access to their children.[2] Except for the woman condemned to death by stoning, in each case those concerned sought support both within their countries and internationally.

Amongst those who responded were nine women from the Muslim world who happened to be attending a Tribunal on Reproductive Rights in Amsterdam (July, 1984). The group of women (from Algeria, Bangladesh, Iran, Mauritius, Morocco, Pakistan and Sudan) used the opportunity to exchange experiences and do some collective

---

[2] In Algeria, the three feminists were released; however, the new Family Code was enacted in 1984, negatively affecting women. In India, the Muslim Women (Protection of the Rights on Divorce) Act 1986 allowed Muslim minority law to supersede the Constitutional provisions, depriving Muslim women of rights enjoyed by others. In Abu Dhabi, after a strong international campaign of numerous groups, the woman was repatriated to her own country, Sri Lanka. After several years the governments of Algeria and France signed a treaty providing for visiting rights to divorced mothers of Algerian children.

thinking and strategizing. They came to several conclusions. First, that while the existential realities of women in the Muslim world differed from one cultural, socio-political, economic and historical context to another, the commonality lay in the fact that

> women's lives were shaped, conditioned or governed by laws, both written and unwritten, drawn from interpretations of the Koran [sic] tied up with local traditions and that generally speaking, men and the State use these against women, and have done so under various political regimes. (WLUML, 1986)

Second, that the geographically scattered incidents of 1984 were symptomatic of a much wider problem confronting women in the Muslim world. In the struggle for political power and preeminence, political forces (in and out of office) are increasingly formulating and justifying by reference to Islam, legal, social or administrative measures that militate against women's autonomy and self-actualization. Third, that women have actively struggled (as individuals and as groups) against both the traditional restrictions and the newly imposed ones, but that they have usually been obliged by circumstances to carry out their struggles in isolation. This isolation amplifies their vulnerability and is one of the factors that may constrain effective intervention and narrow the impact of their struggles. The question the group asked itself, therefore, was not how women affected by Muslim laws could be mobilized so much as how to support women in their on-going struggles. The consensus was for the formation of an Action Committee of Women Living Under Muslim Laws. The success of its first campaigns, the support received from women and human rights groups and activists in the Muslim world, and their expressed desire for linkage provided the impetus for this Action Committee to coalesce into a permanent network. In 1986, the network formulated its first Plan of Action.

The network's name was chosen with care, with the emphasis placed on women and their relationship with laws in the Muslim world. The plural in the word "laws" is critical, indicating both the complexity and diversity of women's realities. Not only do the laws classified as Muslim vary from one country to another, each country has at least two parallel legal systems: the formal codified statutes, and informal customs and traditions—the latter considered by the network to be uncodified laws. "Muslim laws" therefore extend well beyond legal rights in personal matters to govern the relationship of individuals with the socioeconomic and political environment in which they are concentrically located. Practices, customs and laws are synthesized into one cohesive whole in which no distinction is made between laws actually derived from Islamic doctrine and those borrowed from outside. In each society this corpus of formal and informal laws in large measure defines in women's everyday lives what is possible and what is improbable (not to say impossible) at the personal, community and national levels.

In some aspects the formal law may be more important, in others the uncodified "laws" internalized by women may have a greater impact. A few countries have, for instance, imposed a formal dress code, banned women's access to specified educational and employment fields, denied women the right to operate bank accounts or codified the limits of a woman's mobility. Yet, in each of these areas women's lives are circumscribed by a socially sanctioned behavior code which is internalized through the socialization process, finds reflection in societal attitudes and practices and ends up being obeyed either automatically through self-censorship or out of fear of physical or other forms of reprimand. Moreover, a number of countries have two formal laws: civil and religious (e.g. India, Philippines, Senegal). These multiple systems of law are the key to understanding women's lives and activism. Irrespective of the historical specificity giving rise to both written and unwritten laws, and regardless of the particular contents of the law and the sources for this, the whole is accepted as being "Islamic." A less obvious concern that went into the choice of name is that women affected by Muslim laws may not be Muslim, either by virtue of having a different religion or by virtue of having chosen another marker of political or personal identity. The emphasis in the title and in the network is therefore on the women themselves and their situations and not on the specific politico-religious option they may exercise.

WLUML's initial "Plan of Action" clearly states that "its purpose is simply to facilitate access to information and to each other. Its existence therefore depends on our links and not on the specific activities undertaken or positions held by any group or individual involved in this process" (1986, p. 1). As a network, WLUML extends to women living in countries where Islam is the state religion as well as those from Muslim communities ruled by religious minority laws, to women in secular states where a rapidly expanding political presence of Islam increasingly provokes a demand for minority religious law as well as to women in migrant Muslim communities in Europe, the Americas, and Australia, and further includes non-Muslim women who may have Muslim laws applied to them directly or through their children.[3]

Propelled by concrete, on-the-ground issues rather than the outcome of merely theoretical discourse, WLUML's strategy is based on a process of collective analysis rooted in diverse experiences that starts from the premise that women's lives are situated in a complex web of cross-cutting influences that derive from personal and political developments, cultural and structural environments and local, national and international concerns. It is in the light of their knowledge and experience of these multiple factors that women have devised their strategies for survival. Women's activism and self-assertion is therefore dependent on the types of resources available to them and on their ability to analyze and understand these factors.[4] Second, while the essential components of patriarchal structures in a Muslim society are the same as elsewhere (with women's subordination occurring at multiple levels: in the structures of family and kinship, in state policies and programs, in the discourse of dictatorial and populist ideologies and in the politics and policies of the new world order)[5] some of the contextual constraints shaping women's strategies for survival and well-being are specific.

One of the most important common constraints is the impression that there exists one homogeneous Muslim world. In fact, this is a myth deliberately nurtured by vested interests for, while some similarities may stretch across cultures, classes, sects, religious schools, and continents of the Muslim world, the diversities are at least equally striking. Interaction between women from different Muslim societies indicates that the reality experienced by women ranges

---

[3] A few feel that WLUML should only be a network of Muslim women, excluding all those who fall outside such a definition (whether individuals, groups or other networks).

[4] Recognizing the need to focus women's attention on ways of dealing constructively with differences (of race, religion, ethnicity, class, power and resources), WLUML is collaborating with INFORM (a human rights organization based in Sri Lanka) on a workshop on this theme at the World Conference on Women (Beijing, 1995). The workshop will look at strategies used by women in specific situations to manage their differences and work in solidarity and respect.

[5] For a more complete discussion on the subject of the cultural articulation of patriarchy, see Shaheed (1986) and Kandiyoti (1989).

from being strictly closeted, isolated and voiceless within four walls, subjected to public floggings and condemned to death for presumed adultery (which is considered a crime against the state) and forcibly given in marriage as a child, to situations where women have a far greater degree of freedom of movement and interaction, the right to work, to participate in public affairs and also exercise a far greater control over their own lives. (WLUML, 1986)

This is hardly surprising. The communities and states that make up the Muslim world have widely divergent cultures, social structures and histories, and while it is frequently claimed that any given state, society or community is "Islamic," it is in fact not Islamic (implying something ordained by religious scriptures), only Muslim (i.e. comprised of people who adhere to Islam).

This distinction is particularly important today when religious idiom is increasingly coloring the political discourse in so many Muslim communities where ever more strident claims and counter-claims of being the only true mantle-bearers of Islam clash in a tussle for popular support and political power. Whether Islam has been used by those in power or by those seeking it, by right-wing elements or, less frequently, by progressive forces, it has been invoked in a bid for political power: for consolidating support or legitimizing force (Mumtaz & Shaheed 1987, p. 1).[6] The increased religious idiom of the political arena has a direct bearing on women's activism. In the second half of the twentieth century, the political use of Islam has almost inevitably militated against women's self-realization, undermining women's ability to assume control over their own lives by locating both the discourse and decision-making in an area that has long excluded women, i.e. religious scholarship. Of equal importance is that politico-religious groups find it convenient to cite so-called Islamic laws already being applied in different Muslim countries in support of their own demands for more stringent, essentially undemocratic or discriminatory "Islamic" laws. For their part, when women can cite examples of positive legislation or their demands are supported from within the Muslim world (though not necessarily from within a religious framework), their effectiveness is strengthened.

If the dominant political discourses posit uniformity, the actual diversities in structures, norms and cultures visible in the Muslim

---

[6] Though the statement was made with reference to the specific context of Pakistan, it is generally applicable to other parts of the Muslim world (Mumtaz & Shaheed, 1987).

world reflect the degree to which the assimilation of Islamic doctrine depended on a particular society's understanding of Islam on the one hand, and the grafting of this understanding onto prevailing structures, systems and practices on the other. Nor are women an inactive and undifferentiated mass defined exclusively by gender. Within and across societies women are distinguishable (and often divided) by factors such as class, race and ethnicity. These factors moderate women's interaction with each other, the state and religion and, together with personal and political preferences, they have led to a plethora of feminist responses in the political arena that range from the exclusively secular to the exclusively theological, from the reformist to the radical, from the local to the international.

In their attempts to redefine the contours of their lives, women confront the obstacle of a social code that is presented—and commonly internalized—as having religious sanction. In reality, the frequency with which customs having nothing to do with religion, and sometimes in contradiction to the doctrine, are practiced by communities supposedly religious,[7] are visible proof that attitudes towards and practices flowing from religion are determined as much by collective memories, existing social structures and power relations as by doctrines. Most individuals do not, however, distinguish customs, practices or attitudes from their faith and self-identification. As a result, for the many women whose religion is a living reality, improving everyday reality is to a large extent conditional on their ability to distinguish their religious faith from the social customs that have become its symbolic representations.

Women's groups and networks can facilitate mobilization and strengthen women's struggles by demystifying the factors that constrain women's potential and by providing support mechanisms for change. In the Muslim world, demystification needs to focus on three issues: the premium placed on gender roles and family/personal laws as a means of Muslim identity, the myth of one monolithic world of Islam bolstered through political discourses, and the isolation in which many women in the Muslim world have been obliged by

---

[7] This is borne out by the empirical findings of the country projects of the Women and Law in the Muslim World Programme initiated by the Women Living Under Muslim World network in 1992. The 21 country projects initiated (out of 26 planned) are all at different stages of implementation. Research has been completed in both Pakistan and Bangladesh, partial information is also available from several others.

circumstances to conduct their struggles. In networking it is important to remember that women's experiences depend on multiple factors, including class, socio-cultural environment and political
preferences and that these disparate factors have varying influence on
women. For example, although religion may be of paramount importance for one woman, it may be of no consequence for another. The
net result is a broad spectrum of choices and strategies adopted by
women in their personal and public lives such that, if it is to be effective, a networking strategy must not only recognize but accept.

In much of the world, a community's Muslim identity appears almost exclusively hinged on how the community regulates family and
personal matters.[8] In most parts of the Muslim world, Muslim jurisprudence and the application of shari`ah is limited in its scope to cer-
tain fields. In most countries, the vast majority of laws implemented
in the field of commerce, revenues/taxes, administrative matters,
public service or other public sectors, such as banking, standing armies or political structures, for instance, have either been inherited
from the ex-colonial power or have been adopted from elsewhere. In
sharp contrast, the laws governing personal and family matters are
regulated almost universally through Muslim jurisprudence and justified by reference to Islamic injunctions.

Specific laws governing personal and family matters delineate the
boundaries within which a Muslim woman can hope to define her
own identity. Precisely because personal/family laws are so consistently labeled "Muslim" and justified with reference to Islamic doctrine or culture, in each particular—and often highly
varied—cultural context, the identity/space defined for women is
put forward as that of a "Muslim woman." A person who challenges
any aspect of law relating to family or personal matters is therefore
deemed to be refuting—or at the very least challenging—the very
definition of Muslim womanhood in her own setting.

Further complicating the issue of identity is the interweaving of
traditional customs, mores and beliefs into ethnically defined or geographically specific frameworks outlining the parameters of a Muslim
woman's identity. Perhaps the most striking illustration of this is the
case of female genital mutilation (FGM) (circumcision) that originates and is most widespread in parts of Africa, but is shocking to the

---

[8] This is neither new nor restricted to the Muslim world. For an analysis of the
gender question in the context of Hinduism see Mani (1989). For an historical
perspective in the Muslim world see Ahmad (1992).

rest of the non-Shafi'i Muslim world.[9] Yet this interlocking of customs and religion is such that the average Muslim woman in Sudan, Somalia and parts of Egypt cannot conceive of being able to retain her Muslim identity if she rejects this practice.[10]

The condemnation of any challenges to existing "Muslim" laws as rejections of both Islamic injunctions and the very concept of Muslim womanhood is a very potent formula for maintaining the status quo, as it implicitly threatens challengers with ostracism. (The same argument is used to maintain ethnic or national control.) The fear of being pushed beyond the collectivity of one's nation, religion and ethnic group—of losing one's identity—is a strong disincentive to initiating positive action for change. Under these circumstances, questioning, rejecting or reformulating "Muslim" laws is indeed a major undertaking and one that women are ill-equipped to face—isolated as they are and collectively the least powerful social group, not just in terms of socio-political and economic structures, but also in the vital fields of jurisprudence and Islamic scholarship. WLUML contends that to challenge effectively the corpus of laws imposed on them, women need to start assuming the right to define for themselves the parameters of their own identity and stop accepting unconditionally and without question what is presented to them as the "correct" religion, the "correct" culture or the "correct" national identity. To dream of different realities, women will have to unravel the strands of identity in which they are enmeshed so as to find the space in which to conceive of new self-definitions.

Dreaming of an alternative reality is not simply a matter of inspiration, but to a large extent depends on accessing information on the

---

[9] In 658 AD a split occurred in the Muslim world over the selection of the fourth caliph into Sunnites (the followers of the Prophet's tradition) and Shi'ites (those who accept only the traditions of the Prophet's family). Both follow specific texts of *fiqh* (religious knowledge) as sources of the shari'ah. Additionally, Sunni Islam has four major schools of law, developed on the basis of interpretation of theology and law during the first century of the introduction of Islam: Hanafi, Maliki, Shafi'i and Hanbali. The Hanafis are located in Turkey, Sudan, Egypt, Syria and Central and South Asia; the Malikis are dominant in North and West Africa; the Shafi'i school is found in Indonesia, Malaysia, Lower Egypt and parts of the Arabian Peninsula, Central Asia and East Africa; and the Hanbalis are mostly in Saudi Arabia. On the question of women's rights, status and role, the four schools agree in principle. The differences between them relate to details of legal procedures.

[10] It is important to recognize that where FGM is practiced, non-Muslims as well as Muslims consider this an integral part of their collective identity.

sources of law and customary practices and on the political and social forces that determine women's current reality. Equally important is information about the strategies and struggles of other women in the Muslim world and the discussions and debates that flow from these. Beyond this is the need to belong to a social collectivity. The fear of being cut off from one's collective identity militates against women challenging "Muslim laws." Women therefore find it easier to take steps against such laws if they are certain of having the support of some collectivity that functions as an alternative reference group. The existence of an alternative reference point may also help women redefine the parameters of their current reference group(s). In this, contacts and links with women from other parts of the Muslim world (within and outside national boundaries)—whose very existence speaks of the multiplicity of women's realities within the Muslim context—is an important source of inspiration. Likewise, information on the diversity of existing laws within the Muslim world gives material shape to alternatives. Both encourage women to dream of different realities—the first step in changing the present one.

Methodology of WLUML

To achieve its basic purpose of increasing the autonomy of women affected by Muslim laws, WLUML has had to address different types of challenges. At the level of analysis the challenge has been how to encourage women to analyze and reformulate the identity imposed on them through the application of what are deemed to be Muslim laws in their own contexts. At both an emotional and practical level, the issue has been how to build a system of support and solidarity that engenders a feeling of belonging and allows women to act as a meaningful reference point for others. In terms of both conceptualization and action, WLUML has had to devise means for breaking the isolation of women struggling for change in the Muslim world. And, finally, the network has faced the question of how to evolve a structure and working methodology that is, itself, respectful of women's diverse realities and the choices they make.

The strategy evolved by the network has been (a) to collect and disseminate systematically information through regular and irregular publications, as well as more informally by responding to requests from individuals and groups; (b) to promote interaction and linkages consciously between women from Muslim countries and communities, on the one hand, and between them and progressive and feminist groups at large, on the other; (c) to build a mutual support system by responding to violations of human rights and undertaking other solidarity activities; and (d) to carry out common projects identified by and executed through network participants.

1. Information and Exchanges

For WLUML, the importance of making information available lies in its capacity to give material shape to the diversity in the Muslim world, not just in terms of existing laws, but equally important, in terms of women's lives, struggles and strategies. Mindful of the different types of women linked through the network (from academicians to grassroots activists), the network publications range from academically-oriented articles and information on relevant publications, research and events (Dossiers, Special Bulletins), to the collation of news items and articles (Newsheet).[11] Other information packages are developed around a specific theme in response to an identified need (e.g. *The Delegated Right of Divorce (Talaq-e-Taweez), Ex-Yugoslavia, Women in the Qur'an)*. Additionally, many of the networking groups produce materials under their own names. Finally, a number of new publications are being generated through the research and common projects undertaken by the network.

WLUML was among the first networks to recognize that information exchange should feed into action, and exchanges should evolve into common or collective actions. Therefore, from the very beginning, in addition to sharing written information, WLUML has promoted face to face interactions between women from the Muslim world who normally do not have a chance to travel and meet with women from other, culturally diverse, Muslim societies.

---

[11] Dossiers are currently produced in English and French by the WLUML Coordination Office. Articles are also translated into local languages such as Bahasa, Urdu, Bangla and Tamil. The Regional Coordination Office for Asia brings out a Newsheet (in English and Urdu), collates news items and articles of particular interest to Pakistan and links international and national concerns. Special Bulletins are also produced by the Regional Office. Titles include: The Erosion of the Judiciary and Human Rights through Legislation (Pakistan); Fundamentalism and Secularism in South Asia, Blind Justice for All?: Parallel Legal Systems and the Implications for Justice; The Woman Not the Womb; and Women's Political Participation in Pakistan. Special Bulletins are increasingly printing new research material in Pakistan relating to women and laws.

A cross-cultural exchange program organized in 1988 by WLUML in collaboration with a sister organization, ISIS-WICCE, enabled eighteen women from fourteen countries who normally do not have the opportunity to interact with women from different cultural contexts to spend three months living in a Muslim, but vastly different, environment from their own.

2. Solidarity and Support

In some sense, WLUML's solidarity work (initiating and responding to appeals for support in instances of human rights violations) remains its most important activity. Requests for solidarity action automatically supersede other activities of the WLUML Coordination office(s). Campaigns do more than provide immediate support to specific women and groups, they also convey to women struggling for their rights that there are many, many women and groups—scattered both within and outside the Muslim world—who are sympathetic to their cause, appreciate their struggle and are willing to support their initiative, as defined by them.

Solidarity work includes support for collective issues, such as the repeal of discriminatory legislation, the end of oppressive practices and the enactment or enforcement of legislation favorable to women. Solidarity support also covers individual cases, for example, where inhuman sentences have been given, where women are forcibly married against their will (often kidnapped for this purpose), where husbands have abducted their children or where women's very lives are threatened. As a general policy, unless it is unlikely that the person herself could initiate action (such as the death sentence given to the woman in Abu Dhabi), WLUML does not initiate campaigns on behalf of others but responds to requests from local groups or individuals. It recognizes that there are situations where external support may either undermine the local struggle or actually endanger the concerned women. Therefore the network relies on the judgment of those affected in requesting support. Further, recognizing that different groups or individuals concerned with a particular situation may—and often do—differ in their analyses and positions on a particular issue, WLUML simultaneously circulates all the requests it receives on that issue. This ensures that those connected through the network can decide for themselves which position they may agree with most. (With respect to family laws in India, for example, WLUML circulated the requests of those national groups seeking one common civil law for all Indian citizens as well as those of groups seeking reform within Muslim personal laws in India.)

Solidarity work in support of individuals entails more than mobilizing national and international support through letter campaigns and includes contacting lawyers, identifying support groups, providing shelter, mediating between parties, lobbying with governments and the like. WLUML is also called upon to provide documentation concerning women whose lives are threatened by either the laws or the prevailing social customs of their country. This may be requested by lawyers involved in political asylum cases or by the potentially affected persons themselves who need to know the possible repercussions of actions or decisions they may be contemplating.[12]

The most critical lesson learned by WLUML in its solidarity work has been the importance of establishing solid working linkages, both within and outside the Muslim world. Many of the cases could not have been successfully handled without multiple levels of resources, information and linkages that have grown through networking. Needless to say, the support must be reciprocal, and WLUML regularly participates in appeals and actions initiated by other human rights organizations throughout the world from Peru and Ireland to Kenya and Australia. Clearly, positive outcomes are the result of multiple actors working in concert and the network sees itself only as an enabling mechanism for rapidly mobilizing support and activating the right connections as needed.

3. Resource Centre

Through its multiple activities, WLUML has built up a growing roster of women's organizations, lawyers, human rights and advocacy groups, feminist scholars (including theologians) and individual activists. Its capacity to function as an effective resource center has grown, ensuring that it is able to put people and groups in touch with other people, information or institutions they need for legal cases, research or advocacy initiatives. WLUML's networking is not limited to either the Muslim world or to women alone. It recognizes the

---

[12] A number of solidarity actions have culminated in the granting of political asylum for women who would be in physical danger if they returned home; in other cases timely referrals to legal aid groups in specific countries has resulted in women being granted custody of their children. In yet others, legal cases have been dropped or proceedings suspended due to international pressures.

need to build and strengthen links with feminist groups in the non-Muslim world and especially to learn, not just from organizations and networks focused on women and the law in their own contexts, but also from those working in the field of human rights, providing legal aid services and running shelters, as well as from grassroots organizations. In turn the strengthened networking and resource base of the network as a whole has facilitated the implementation of "common projects."

4. Common Projects

Common projects are activities that people and groups linked through the network identify and work on collectively. One constraint, however, is that the materialization of any given project is dependent on groups and individuals within the network assuming responsibility not only for conceptualization and logistics but also for sharing with the Coordination Office(s) the task of raising the material resources required. A further constraint is that, so far, WLUML has only been able to undertake one collective project at a time. This is partly due to the limited resources of the network, and partly due to the amount of energy women linked by the network can spare from their other commitments to devote to a common project.

The speed, efficiency and capacity of groups/individuals to act determines which collective project WLUML carries out at a particular time. For example, the group of women who met in 1986 identified as needed projects a cross-cultural exchange program, an action-research project on women and laws in the Muslim world, and a very large meeting of women from the Muslim world. Of these three, the exchange program materialized first. It was clear from the start that the sheer size and geographical dispersal of the women and law project would require a consolidation of the network prior to implementation. The large meeting did not materialize simply because the group that was to arrange this was unable to do so. The exchange program was facilitated in part by the support of ISIS-WICCE which agreed to run their next exchange for women living under Muslim laws in collaboration with WLUML, and to raise funds and train women within the WLUML network. The collaboration was very positive for both networks and reaffirmed the need and potential for international solidarity in the women's movement and that this can operate beyond boundaries that may separate women in other spheres.

Identified as a common project in 1986, the Women and the Law in the Muslim World Programme (W&L) formally began in 1991-92 and, extending into 26 countries, is by far the most ambitious collective undertaking of the WLUML network. Designed to document and analyze the disparate laws (codified and uncodified) that govern the lives of women in the Muslim world and the circumstances, forces and strategies underlying both positive and negative trends, the project is intended to provide grassroots and other activist women tools for understanding the multiple forces that define the parameters of their lives. An integral part of each national project is an outreach program to extend networking within each country, promote legal awareness and strengthen local initiatives. National projects are developing teaching materials, animation programs (such as dramas, videos, plays, songs, etc.) and manuals on prioritized aspects of law and women's struggles.

Challenges and Responses

Today over two thousand women in several continents are linked through WLUML. These women have diverse professional and academic backgrounds, organizational frameworks and political perspectives but share a commitment to expanding women's autonomy. Most are actively involved in the women's movement in their countries or place of residence. In addition, many are engaged in general advocacy initiatives.

In the first few years growth was a slow process because the WLUML network did not want to grow artificially according to any preconceived blueprint for expansion. Instead, the network developed organically through its support and information services, common projects and interactions with others. The original galvanizing force consisted of the 1984 women's human rights campaign. During the course of these campaigns, international support was mobilized and numerous individuals and groups participating in the campaigns from the Muslim world established a web of connections. Alerts remain an important catalyzing force in expanding the network, but in terms of consolidation, the greatest catalyst has been face-to-face meetings that allow for discussion and an understanding of the rationale for another's difference in location and choice. WLUML's publications and information services have been another important and growing means of expanding and consolidating contacts. Particularly important in linking scholars and researchers, published materials also act as an outreach mechanism through which activists come into and maintain contact with the network. For those who network, linking up and sharing information becomes second nature—a constant exercise carried out both formally and informally—so that linkages are made in the course of forums and gatherings organized by other networks and organizations; at international meetings and over dinners and chance encounters. Currently and increasingly, people themselves initiate contact.

Having chosen to deepen and strengthen ties instead of pursuing often unstable geographical extensions, it is clear that the process of consolidating linkages and activities was facilitated first in those regions where networking already existed. This, for instance, is the case in South Asia where the presence of earlier linkages amongst human rights activists, environmentalists and women's groups facilitated the growth of the WLUML network by helping to identify interested individuals and groups. The network—with strong links in South Asia and substantial ones in South East Asia—only began to consolidate its linkages in Africa and the Middle East in 1994. The existing situation, therefore, has influenced the geographical spread of a network.

Another factor determining growth is language. All international networks face this question. Those who, like WLUML, work with women affected by Muslim laws are obliged to operate in at least three different international languages: English, French and Arabic—in which only the last is a national language, the former two being accidents of colonial history. At the national level, just between India and Nigeria, the WLUML network encompasses hundreds of languages and dialects. Under these circumstances, working languages and translations are a major challenge in which choices are made or imposed by circumstances. From the beginning, all WLUML meetings (even when only nine women met in 1986) have been conducted in French, English, and Arabic—often with at least one more language being used—and translated back and forth. The process is time-consuming and exhausting for bilingual participants since almost inevitably, adequate translation facilities are not available. Either the funds or the facilities are not available, or the skills of those unfamiliar with the network or the situations in the Muslim world have left much to be desired. This time-consuming and expensive problem is not limited to face-to-face interactions but extends to all work: publications, communications, common projects and alerts. Quite apart from costs, whichever language becomes the "first" working language of the network has its own repercussions in terms of consolidation/exclusion. For many years, through a series of accidents relating to those who initially took on responsibility, the primary working language gravitated towards English. Consequently, a first consolidation of contacts and connections emerged among those who were at ease communicating in English. Translations into local languages, on the other hand, have highlighted the absence of equivalent terminology in some languages, pointing to the need for women activists to develop and enrich the local language of feminism.

WLUML's own strategies and actions have developed through a process of exchanging and reflecting upon the experiences of multiple and distinct groups and individuals in the Muslim world linked through the network. These range from Marxist groups to feminist theologians, but most are located somewhere in between. Trying to reconcile such divergent tendencies would be impossible for an ideological or political organization, but a network such as WLUML can provide linkages between them, the means for mutual support and space for each to evolve and change. Because the essence of networks lies in linkages, interactions and mutual support that bring together different groups and individuals with varying priorities and participation levels, the overall direction and image of the network in a given period will be influenced by whichever groups or individuals are more active at that particular point.

An issue raised fairly frequently in the initial years of WLUML relates to how the network defines its ideological parameters, particularly with respect to the controversial question of Islam. Currently, throughout the Muslim world women's movements are sharply divided on the question of whether a Muslim feminism exists (or should exist) separately from feminism in general and on whether the struggle is to be located in a religious or secular framework. Because those linked through WLUML vary in their positions on these issues, the network can simultaneously be seen as being "too Islamic," and as not Islamic enough (or of consisting of people who "go about Islam in the wrong way"); in addition, from outside the network, a few feel that WLUML's activities (especially the human rights Alerts for Action) contribute to a negative image of Islam and Muslims or of a particular country. At some level, there seems to be a general resistance to the idea that, by its nature, a network does—and should—have divergent opinions and positions, and that this is a strength and not a weakness.

To evolve a common understanding or position, a substantial number of those linked through WLUML need to participate in the process. Only rarely, e.g. on women's human rights and reproductive rights, have those in the network managed to develop a collective statement, and even this is not binding on any networking group or individual for, in the words of WLUML, it functions in a manner intended to ensure that

> each group/individual is fully autonomous in analyzing its own situation and developing strategies according to their own objective conditions and circumstances.

Consequently, while friction undoubtedly exists, WLUML maintains that each of the divergent trends in the women's movement, spread across the more than one billion strong Muslim world, can learn from the other, and accordingly, the WLUML coordination offices consciously promote exchanges and inter-flow of information. In practical terms, this poses its own set of issues.

All networks face the challenge of evolving an operational structure that maximizes participation, collective decision-making and space for diverse opinions, while retaining the ability to be responsive and effective. Networks cannot and should not determine either the nature or the parameters of activities carried out by those they link, as this would defeat the very purpose for which they are created. On the other hand, for coordination purposes there has to be a secretariat responsive to priorities and suggestions within the network. With its growing institutional memory and data-bank, the Coordination Office plays an important role in all of WLUML's activities. It continues to carry the major responsibility for ensuring that the relevant people are meeting, strategizing, planning and acting at the right time. Somewhat like a central nervous system, the Coordination Office is most likely to know at the international level who can help in which situation, whether it is a request for information, the setting up of a project or an alert. Responsibilities are shared with a Coordination Group that brings together women responsible for coordinating various aspects of WLUML (solidarity work, common projects and networking). The network's desire to decentralize tasks and share responsibilities is conditional on certain practical considerations such as the institutional base of groups, language and time-availability, but also other considerations, such as personal security. In certain countries the functioning of formal groups is not officially allowed, in others it may actually be dangerous. Under such circumstances, specific individuals may function as coordination points. Alternatively, although affiliated with a particular organization, a person may prefer to separate her networking from the framework of a formal organization. Consequently, not all those who may be willing to function as coordination points for the network can assume this role.

Though this structure allows for both flexibility and collective responsibility, it does not solve the complicating factor of coordinators being dispersed throughout the world and many of them having to do daily battle with inadequate and inefficient communication facilities simply in order to coordinate and respond to (often urgent) requests. WLUML for example, constantly faces such communication problems and, often enough, communications within South Asia or between one geographical area and another have to be (or, after numerous abortive efforts, end up being) routed through the WLUML Coordination Office based in France. As so many other issues, the dispersal of responsibilities raises the question of resources, since coordination points/offices need to have financial support in order to function.

While questions of finance have to be addressed by all women's groups, networks seem to have a harder time making support institutions understand the concept of a network. Networks can spend considerable time and energy in negotiations/discussions with donor agencies that center around what donors conceive networks to be and how women define these for themselves. With its fluid structure and rejection of hierarchies, WLUML has probably had more than its fair share of such discussions, and has had to actively resist suggestions to redefine itself in terms more easily understood by others (e.g. membership, executive boards and governing bodies). It has also had to struggle with the task of raising funds for different geographical points of the network while ensuring that the institutional strength of the WLUML Coordination Office continues to grow in step with expanding demands from the network. Also, in the context of network-donor relationships there is a tendency on the part of the latter to demand quantitative evidence of the network's impact. However, while networks are as anxious as others to know their usefulness, solidarity and support, which frequently stretch over international boundaries and indefinite time periods, these do not lend themselves to simplistic quantification. There is a further question. Where on the one hand, networks and groups, particularly in the area of human rights, consciously seek and need to share actions for which they believe they have a collective responsibility, donors, on the other hand, appear uncomfortable with the lack of a clearly defined division of input for each contributing institution. WLUML, for its part, has insisted that international solidarity actions are, by their very nature, indivisible.

Today, conceptually if not yet materially, the network Women Living Under Muslim Laws has become sustainable. It has filled a gap by becoming the first network linking so many and such diverse women affected by Muslim laws, and it has certainly surpassed the expectations—though not dreams—of the nine women who catalyzed the process in April 1986 by drafting the first WLUML Plan of Action. The very fact that WLUML has expanded to its present strength, with each day bringing new women—and men—into the network, testifies to its being a response to a felt need. Until recently, WLUML's responsiveness to requests for solidarity action, internationally and locally, attracted women who saw in it a potential safety net, a reassurance that should a woman or group need international support this can be achieved by activating the network. However, with the development of the Women and Law Programme, the network appears to have entered a new phase in which a common project has merged with solidarity action and networking. Through this program, the groups involved on a day to day basis have multiplied, links have been extended and strengthened, and analysis has deepened. Systems for mutual support are no longer only activated in instances requiring urgent responses, but have started operating on the more mundane level of the everyday activities of the groups linked. The net result has been a qualitative change in the feeling of solidarity and belonging that has become more tangible and carries a sense of permanence. It is this that suggests that WLUML has become sustainable in that the networking, if not the network, will survive.

References

Ahmad, L. (1992). *Women and Gender in Islam*. New Haven, CT: Yale University Press.

ISIS-WICCE. (1989). *Women's World Issue on Women Living Under Muslim Laws, 21-22,* Geneva.

Kandiyoti, D. (1989). Women and Islam: What are the Missing Terms?, *Dossier* 5/6, December 1988-May 1989, 5-9. Grabels, France: WLUML.

Mani, L. (1989). Contentious Traditions: The Debate on *Sati* in Colonial India. In K. Sangari & S. Vaid (Eds.). *Recasting Women: Essays in Colonial History*. New Delhi, India: Kali for Women.

Mumtaz, K. (1993). The Changing Status of Women in Muslim Societies, Special Report: Anthropology. *1993 Britannica Book of the Year,* p. 95. Chicago: Encyclopedia Britannica Inc.

Mumtaz, K. & Shaheed, F. (1987). *Two Steps Forward, One Step Back? Women of Pakistan*. London: Zed Books.

Shaheed, F. (1986, Spring). The Cultural Articulation of Patriarchy: Legal Systems, Islam and Women in Pakistan. *South Asia Bulletin, 6*(1), 38-44.

Shaheed, F. (1994, Summer). Controlled or Autonomous: Identity and the Experience of the Network, Women Living Under Muslim Laws. *SIGNS, 19,* 997-1019.

Shannon, M. (1993). *Dobry*. London: Puffin Newbury Library.

WLUML (1986). Plan of Action-Aramon.

Chapter 19
Women's Identity in a Transitional Society: The Czech Republic

Jirina Siklova

The post-communist countries remain isolated from the rest of the world as a result of more than 40 years behind the iron curtain. Although we often use the same words as western and other feminists to describe our experience, our cultural differences often shade the definitions. This is especially true in discussions of feminism and concepts of identity. Too often social scientists view the Soviet bloc countries as homogeneous. But that is far from the case. There always have been and continue to be major differences among the countries in the region, which are now collectively called post-communist. Several factors have shaped the current economic and political context of each country in the region, including the pre-World War II traditions, how closely and for how long the country was tied to the former Soviet Union and the ethnic and religious makeup of the country.

Socialism or communism as a system of centrally planned or command economies did not succeed in the Czech Republic or in any other country of Eastern Europe. Even the fertile Ukraine, often called the "corn basket" of Europe before World War II, could not produce enough wheat to feed its own population. Today socialism is widely condemned in the Czech Republic as a failed experiment. But the Czech people also are disillusioned with the economic and political systems offered by the Western democratic countries to shape a "New Europe." For many years, the censored communist newspapers wrote about social conflicts within the capitalist countries, but this was assumed to be lies and propaganda. Today, however, the widespread poverty, unemployment, homelessness and racism is all too apparent.

The disintegration of the communist system disrupted the continuity of our lives and thrust our country into a painful period of economic and political reform. Even now the present disillusionment is great, although we are in a good economic position relative to some other countries in the region.

The Czech Gross Domestic Product (GDP), which fell by 22.3 percent from 1990 to 1993, began to recover in early 1994. Clearly, the Czech-Slovak split January 1, 1993, had a negative effect on the Czech GDP of 1993; it declined 0.3 percent. By the first quarter of 1994, however, the economy had begun a strong turnaround and the GDP rose by 3.5 percent. Real industrial production in the Czech Republic fell by 44.8 percent from 1990 to 1993, but estimates for 1994 predict zero growth in industrial production (Czech Republic, 1993), as opposed to further declines.

Throughout the period of transition, inflation in the Czech Republic has remained among the lowest in the region of East and Central Europe. After the considerable decline in 1992, when it dropped to 11.1 percent, annual inflation rose again in 1993, reaching 20.8 percent. However, during the first four months of 1994 inflation was very low and in April, 1994, monthly inflation was only 0.4 percent. Predictions for annual inflation in 1994 range from 10 to 11 percent.

Since the fall of communism in the Czech Republic, unemployment also has remained remarkably low. Unemployment peaked at 4.4 percent in January, 1992, and has since fluctuated between 2.5 percent and 3.8 percent. It is expected to be between 5 percent and 6 percent by the end of 1995. Many critics of the Czech style of economic reform view the unemployment rate as too high and as a negative sign. They say that it shows that significant parts of the economy have yet to be restructured.

The Czech government's policy on wage control has affected both unemployment and inflation. By the fourth quarter of 1993, the average monthly wage was 6,832 crowns (US $238). That monthly wage was considerably lower than in Poland and Hungary and only 1/15th of the average industrial wage in neighboring former German Democratic Republic. By limiting the growth of wages, the government hoped to keep layoffs low and to prevent spiraling inflation, while at the same time boosting production by making exports more competitive.

When the "Velvet Revolution" took place in Czechoslovakia in November, 1989, the country had virtually no private sector. The large-scale privatization of large state-owned firms started in February, 1992, and was based mainly on the "voucher" program devised by Vaclav Klaus, who was the Czechoslovak minister of finance at the time. Klaus is now prime minister and the leader of the right-wing Civic Democratic Party in the Czech republic. The Czech government was intent on accelerating the pace of privatization and, in that regard, the privatization program has been successful. By the fourth quarter of 1993, 67 percent of the Czech economy had been privatized. The country's privatization program is expected to be completed by the end of 1996. The state expects to retain only 10 percent of all property.

Although the basic economic indicators look positive for the Czech Republic, the country's transitional period is not over yet. Large-scale restructuring has not yet taken place and many sectors, such as banking, are troubled. To a large extent, the social stability in the country has been created through carefully controlled policies that limit unemployment and promote a general consensus for reforms through programs such as coupon privatization.

The employment rate of women in Czechoslovakia was among the very highest in the region and the Czech Republic still has one of the highest percentages of women in the workforce. Almost 97 percent of women of working age were employed during the socialist period; and even now almost 90 percent of 4.4 million women of working age are employed. The degree of female employment reached a saturation level in 1968 when 45 percent of the total workforce was comprised of women (Cermakova, 1993). In 1990, 46.2 percent of the total workforce was made up of women. In 1994, the figure was 43.2 percent. Almost all of these women work full time.

The high employment rate of women was primarily the consequence of economic pressures and communist work policies, and only in part a result of women's need for self fulfillment through work. Emancipation for women during the Soviet years was synonymous with the duty to work. The roots of Czech women's attitudes today toward feminism and emancipation have been shaped, in part, by these years of forced employment under the Soviet system.

Feminism as an ideology and political movement remains unpopular in the Czech Republic and similar negative attitudes towards feminism are predominant in the other post-communist countries of Eastern and Central Europe. The relatively high level of solidarity between men and women in the Czech Republic can be traced to the 19th century when the Czech nation initiated its political revival in opposition to the German-speaking population of the Austro-

Hungarian monarchy. The monarchy provided men and women with a common "enemy." This enhanced the cohesion of all those regarding themselves as Czechs. Men supported the education of women as well as their civil rights, including the right to vote. Women were men's allies against the Hapsburg monarchy. Any conflicts over gender, or battles against patriarchy, were subsumed under the battle against the external enemy (Davic-Fox, 1991; Johnson Freeze, 1985).

A somewhat similar historical scenario was repeated in the next century. After World War I, when many other European women were struggling for their civil rights, women in Czechoslovakia were spared from a similar battle by the first president of Czechoslovakia, T.G. Masaryk, who advanced a policy of women's equality (Skilling, 1991). Masaryk helped women. He clearly placed the women's question above issues of nationality. Under Hitler and then the communists, however, Masaryk was forbidden to articulate his position on women. Recently he has been "rediscovered."

During World War II, once again both genders were forced to join ranks against a common enemy—this time Nazism. Men and women suffered equally in forced labor and concentration camps during the German occupation. The oppressive conditions of occupation and war were not the breeding grounds for gender discrimination and patriarchy. Men and women suffered an equally low status during the war years.

In the post-war period, it was the Soviet Union that was the oppressor. During the communist era, businesses were nationalized, including even the smallest ones such as barber-shops and small farms. As a result, the state, rather than men, became the employer of women for the next 40 years. Both genders were equally oppressed by the Soviet-controlled political system. In general, men's work did have more value in the eyes of the state than did female labor. Male labor, especially in the army and heavy industry, was viewed as "productive" labor and was more highly valued ideologically and better paid than female-dominated sectors of the workforce.

Thus, it was in the post-war context that the workplace began to show signs of patriarchy. Not only was male labor more highly valued than female labor, but male representatives of the communist party assumed senior positions in the workplace and in unions. Both men and women employees rebuked such a reality, but still women did not frame the problem as one of "patriarchy." Although Czech women have experienced gender bias and even hostility in the work setting, most of them do not identify with the notion of "patriarchy."

The number of employed women increased dramatically within a few years. Just after World War II women represented merely 22 percent of the labor force. Fifteen years later the number rose to 48.6 percent, which meant that 97 percent of women in Czechoslovakia were employed. Women have been employed in the health care, education and services sectors, but there have been few attempts to challenge this "ghettoization" of female occupations within a feminist critique that is common currency in the West.

By comparison to other regions, there is a relative lack of emphasis on careers as a source of personal fulfillment in the post-communist countries. Undoubtedly, this important cultural factor has inhibited the growth of feminist consciousness in the Czech Republic and elsewhere in the region. Women have viewed the dual role of work and homemaking/motherhood as burdensome and undesirable. During the socialist period, two generations of women became convinced that they could not fulfill parallel professional and household roles (Vodakova, 1992). Combining full-time work with motherhood and housework has been a source of permanent frustration for Czech women. And for large numbers of Czech women, professional achievement in the workplace has not been gratifying. There are no grounds for solidarity between Czech women and feminists in the developed world. Czech women feel that they already have equal access to the labor market, a battle that feminists in the West and elsewhere are still fighting (Šiklová, 1993; Busheikin, 1993; Scott, 1974; Corin, 1992).

The ideology of the Communist Party and its variant of Marxism was itself another damper on the growth of feminism in the former Soviet bloc. The official ideology of the party regarded feminism as a bourgeois ideology whose goal was to split the unified struggle of the working class against the class enemies and capitalism. The Communist regime, relying on russified Marxism, "nationalized" the means of production. Women were not expropriated by men (patriarchy), but by the state, personified as an omnipotent Communist Party.

As they had done in earlier times, men and women joined ranks to fight the external enemy. During the 1960s and 1970s, men and women were united in their aversion to the communist economic and political system. Once again, the problem was not a matter of male privilege and power, but rather Soviet oppression. Men and women alike suffered under the system. One woman, the lawyer Milada Horakova who was also the founder of the Czechoslovak Women's Council, was sentenced to death and executed in 1949 at the beginning of the Communist terror. Hundreds of other women were put in concentration camps (Šiklová, 1992). Women also played an important role in the opposition movement as dissidents, especially during the last two decades of socialism. They were signatories and speakers of Charter 77 and comprised the majority of the Committee of Unjustly Persecuted. They were tried in political trials. They wrote, translated and copied texts which were published in samizdat and exile publishing houses. By means of western broadcasting, these texts influenced the political situation in Czechoslovakia. A high level of cohesion between men and women was needed to conspire against the regime.

Certainly, one could discover a division of labor between men and women among the Czech dissidents who were fighting the Soviet regime. In general, men created programs and concepts while women copied, edited and translated documents. But during the battle against Soviet domination, issues of gender bias were perceived as unimportant or a "subtle pseudo-problem" in the face of the larger dissident cause (Mozný, 1991).

Women who lacked an interest in politics under the Soviet regime tended to escape into the private and relatively uncontrolled sphere of the family. Because work was unfulfilling for many people during the Soviet period, greater interest was placed on private relationships. The family was an important source of status for Czech women during socialism. Czech women's perception that the private realm of the household is somewhat devalued by feminists in the developed world places Czech women on the defensive.

Many Czech women today look back on the double roles they incurred during the Soviet era and see that they have endured terrific stress. Still, many of those same women will admit that succeeding in the twin roles of worker and homemaker inspired great confidence in their own capabilities. There is the sense among middle-aged Czech women today that they "managed it all." Under socialism, women showed that they could work as well as men. Simultaneously, however, women lost the illusion that their professions and economic independence would solve all of their problems. For many women, work for the family unit had undisputed value (Cermakova, 1991), whereas work for society often seemed senseless.[1] Family became the means of escape from an oppressive public realm for both men and women. This private realm of the home, which often served as a haven from an oppressive public realm, was largely the construction of women.

The generation of Czech women who are middle-aged today were placed in kindergartens in the 1950s when their mothers were involuntarily recruited, for the most part, into a labor force that underpaid women. If anything, the daughters of these women are even less inclined toward feminist ideology. The daughters see their mothers as having had broad opportunities for employment under socialism. The daughters see that, despite their careers, their mothers were disappointed with their lives. Further, the socialist system, with its proclamations of equality, fell apart.

The character of the economic system under socialism also contributes to the lack of feminist sentiment in the region in another way. The Marxist and socialist feminists who live in the West identify patriarchy with capitalism. Czech women, by contrast, did not have a capitalist system for more than 40 years. Western feminism, which is most often a reaction to male economic, sexual and ideological power under capitalism, must necessarily take different forms in the Czech republic. Women under communism did not experience themselves as suffering under real patriarchy even when their boss was a man. Rather, the socialist boss was seen as a tool of the political regime. He had to conform to his superiors, and his prestige and power were granted to him in exchange for his obedience to higher ranking officials in the party.

Women, in large numbers, were not interested in leadership within the work setting or in the political party. Women often used the second "household shift" as a way to excuse themselves from petty political functions.

Women in the Czech Republic today are unfamiliar with the full range of feminist thought. So far, Czech women have been exposed to the most strident and least nuanced feminist voices from the West and elsewhere. The result has been to provoke an a priori resistance

---

[1] Although women declare within sociological research that they would like to leave work and stay home, they are definitely not doing it. The total number of employed women was 45.2 percent in 1990 and 43.6 percent in 1993, a drop of only 1.6 percent (Czech Republic, 1994).

to an ideology with which we are as yet unacquainted. At this juncture women in post-communist countries are impatient with feminists who long for global solutions and who believe that transforming
the antagonism and power differential between the genders will
change the world.

The post-communist world is not prepared to embrace this feminist conceptual framework because it does not fit with perceptions of
women in post-communist societies. The resistance is not only to
feminism as it has developed in the West and elsewhere, but it is also
a reaction to our own recent past. Women theorists in the post-
communist regions have already begun to write their own history of
women in the region. Feminists and historians of feminism who have
been writing the history of women in Eastern Europe include Nan-
nete Funk, Sharon Wolchik, Barbara Einhorn, Valentine M.
Moghadam and Marilyn Rueschemeyer, among others (Castle-
Kanerova, 1992; Wolchik, 1993; Einhorn, 1993; Paukert, 1993).
Their books and other writings are unfortunately not widely available
in the post-Communist countries, and are even less accessible outside
the region.

During this painful period of economic reform, which has made
women "emigrants in their own country" (Siklova, 1993), we have
had the tendency to look for simplified solutions. It is probably fair to
say that we have overestimated the economic reform as a means of
improving the quality of life in our region. We have placed our faith
in an omnipotent market and a renewal of capitalism. For us, it is
Marxism turned upside down. Rather than "the means of production
resulting in class struggle," we have "private property relations, market and monetarism." We hope the market will liberate us and, by
changing the economic base to a market economy, that our biggest
problems will be solved, including our own version of gender problems. In this critical phase, we do not want to hear, because of our
own uncertainty about the path we have chosen, criticisms by western feminists and others regarding the dangers of an unchecked market economy.

While everything around us is changing, the essential paradigm
of our history remains unchanged. Once again, the conflicts between
the sexes are, to a large degree, being subordinated to the higher
goals of transforming society. There is an undercurrent of belief that
the gender conflicts we have will be solved once the Czech Republic
is securely anchored to Europe.

Czech women today need time to fashion a domestic variant of feminism that fits our experience and temperament and reflects a new economic and political era. Socialist-oriented feminism cannot take the lead during this transformation to a market economy without seeming naive and confusing. Western leftist feminists continue to urge women from post-communist countries to fight to retain the best elements of communism, such as long maternity leave, parental leave policies to care for sick children, and state-supported day care and preschools. But there is a fear among Czech women that such demands may, in fact, handicap women as they are forced to compete in an all new labor market. Labor laws are being written and trade commissions as yet lack expertise and influence. It is difficult to know how best to lobby for the concerns of women in the workplace without making women less competitive in a competition-drive labor market.

So far women are taking far less risk in private enterprise than men. A total of 74 percent of working women are still employed in the state sector. This hesitation to take risks will affect women's ability to gain a footing in entrepreneurial enterprises. As the state sector undergoes transformation, women may face new labor difficulties, which could lead to a growth in feminism. But right now the relatively strong economy and the low level of unemployment is inhibiting feminism.

If economic reform has not fueled a rise in feminism in the Czech Republic, neither have cultural factors, which have contributed to the women's movement elsewhere. The church, for example, is not the unyielding bastion of patriarchy that it is in other settings. Religiosity in the Czech Republic is low (only 31 percent of the population is formally Catholic). The church also is relatively tolerant of abortion and divorce. The Parliament has passed a strong law legalizing abortion. Abortions are relatively affordable (costing less than 50 percent of the average monthly wage) and contraception is now available and affordable to most couples. Because of new awareness of contraception, the demand for abortions has decreased by one third since 1990.

In the Czech Republic there is a high tolerance for alternative sexual behavior. Therefore, we do not have to deal with one of the problems which feminists encounter elsewhere. Lesbian lifestyles are accepted and the lesbian community even receives state subsidies for its publications. Nor is feminism used as a shield to protect minority women as it is elsewhere. The minority population in the Czech Republic represents only about 4 percent of the population and the largest group, Romany women or gypsies, live a life far removed from feminist currents of thought.

Feminists elsewhere blame Czech women for the fact that they are not represented adequately in the Parliament or in the leadership of the political parties, and are often urged to advocate for a quota system. But the quota system incites adverse reactions in the Czech Republic. It was discredited when the Communist Party set quotas on the number of workers, farmers or women who should participate in party activities. It is a little known fact, even in the Czech Republic, that women dominate the nongovernmental and nonprofit organizations in the so-called third sector, which many women consider the grassroots of real democracy (Siklova, nd).

Czech Women and Human Rights

The Czech Republic has a strong set of laws protecting the rights of women. Women have the right to vote, hold elected office, work in government administration, sit on boards of companies, control their own economic investments, own property and enter any profession. These laws pertain to both married and unmarried women. Thus the communist era has bequeathed strong legal protection for women's rights. And, at this juncture in the transition to a market economy, the strong legal protection for women remains intact.

Still, there is no room for complacence. The culture in the Czech Republic, as is the case elsewhere in former communist countries, contains some regressive forces which are attempting to redefine women's roles in traditional terms. It is social attitudes, not an absence of protective laws, that threaten Czech women today. What is needed now is bold thinking regarding the future for women in both the public and private sector. Today many Czech women do not even realize that a number of occupations and political posts that are now held by men could be opened to women as well. Similarly, women have not yet questioned why they alone are the sole caretakers of children.

In this period of political and economic transition, there is much debate and uncertainty regarding what is "suitable" for women. Political parties, which campaigned on a platform to "return the woman to her family and her children," have failed to gain support thus far.

Increasingly it will be necessary for women to organize politically as a means of defining for themselves how they wish to live in an increasingly capitalist society. The women's political party, which was started in the Czech Republic following the communist period, did not survive after the first year. Czech women traditionally have displayed little interest in politics and the sphere remains "reserved" mostly for men at present. But Czech women must realize that as capitalism progresses, they will face the same problems as women elsewhere in capitalist societies. Czech women need to arm themselves to compete against men in a market economy.

Already there appears to be some loss of equality for females in the educational sector. Even though under socialism the quality of the educational process was poor and ideological, education was free of charge for all. Private schools of better quality are being started. But parents must pay for private school. There is some evidence that parents are electing to send sons, rather than daughters, to these better schools when there are financial constraints in the family. Czech women today have high qualifications for competing in the labor market, but if women do not defend their rights to equal education they will not be competitive with men in the future.

There is also an abdication of female equality in the field of private enterprise. There is a trend toward wives giving up careers to work for their husbands as accountants or managers. There is not nearly enough entrepreneurial activity on the part of women in the transition to a capitalist economy and this will be an economic setback to women in the future.

The Revolution shattered the society but, in the end, the new political regime adopted many of the same traits as the old one. That is the way history works. Traditions, laws and norms are deeply rooted in every society and cannot be changed easily. Post-communist feminism has just begun to take shape. It will be different from feminism elsewhere and will reflect our past. We have to move from totalitarianism and state paternalism to find our new identity. In this journey we will need to draw on the language and culture of rights in the international women's movement to assure women's rights in every sphere of life. The further we travel from our own communist past, which brought legal equality for women in many areas of life, the more we will need to link ourselves to the international women's movement. We will have to develop new criteria to evaluate our status in a new political and economic system that is likely to pose increasing challenges to the rights of women.

References

Busheikin, L. (1993). Is Sisterhood Really Global? Western Feminism in Eastern Europe. In L. Busheiken & S. Trnka (Eds.), *Bodies of Bread and Butter: Reconfiguring of Women's Lives in the Post-Communist Czech Republic* (pp. 69-76). Prague: Gender Studies Centre.

Castle-Kanerova, M. (1992). Superwomen and the Double Burden. In S. Rai, H. Pilkington, & A. Phizacklea (Eds.), *Women in the Face of Change: The Soviet Union, Eastern Europe and China* (pp. 97-124). New York: Routledge.

Cermakova, M. (1991). *Women in Czechoslovakia and their Reflections on Human Rights.* Unpublished Paper. Prague: Institute of Sociology, Czechoslovak Academy of Sciences.

Cermakova, M. (1993). *State and Perspectives of Research on the Economic Status of Women in the Czech Republic.* Paper presented at the Labor Process Conference, Blackpool, UK.

Corin, C. (Ed.). (1992). *Superwomen and the Double Burden: Women's Experience of Change in Central and Eastern Europe and the Former Soviet Union.* London: Scarlet Press.

Czech Republic. (1994). *Macro-Economic and Social Indicators of the Czech Republic.* Research Institute of Labour and Social Affairs, 4.

Czech Republic. (1993). *Statisticka Rohenka 1993.* (Statistical Yearbook 1993), Prague: Author.

Davic-Fox, K. (1991, Fall). Czech Feminists and Nationalism in the Late Habsburg Monarchy. *Journal of Women's History, 3,* 2.

Einhorn, B. (1993). Chapter 2. In V. Moghadam, (Ed.), *Democratic Reform and the Position of Women in Transitional Economies.* New York: Oxford University Press.

Johnson Freeze, K. (1985). Medical Education for Women in Austria: A Study in the Pol. In S. L. Wolchick & A.G. Meyer (Eds.), *Women, State and Party in Eastern Europe.* Durham, NC: Duke University Press.

Mozny, I. (1991). *Proc tak Pozde a Proc tak Snadno? Studie o Pricinach Prevratu v Listopadu 1989* [Why so Late and so Easy? Sources of the Revolution of November, 1989]. Prague: Nakaladatolstva SLON.

Paukert, L. (1993). Chapter 11. In V. Moghadam, (Ed.). *Democratic Reform and the Position of Women in Transitional Economies.* New York: Oxford University Press.

Scott, H. (1974). *Does Socialism Liberate Women?* Boston: Beacon Press.

Siklova, J. (n.d.). *The Role of NGOs During the Transition from a Totalitarian Society to a Civil Society.* START Foundation project, "Social Costs of the Economic Transformation in Central Europe," organized by the Institut fur die Wissenschaften vom Menschen, Institute for Human Sciences, Vienna Spittelauer Ldnde.

Siklova, J. (1992). *Women in Politics in the CSFR.* Paper presented at the Women in Leadership, Politics and Business Conference, John F. Kennedy Institute of Government, Harvard University, Cambridge, MA.

Siklova, J. (1993). McDonalds,Terminators, Coca-Cola Ads and Feminism? Imports from the West. In L. Busheiken & S. Trnka (Eds.), *Bodies of Bread and Butter: Reconfiguring of Women's Lives in the Post-Communist Czeck Republic* (pp. 7-11). Prague: Gender Studies Centre.

Skilling, H.G. (1991). T.G. Masaryk: A Radical Feminist. *Cross Currents: A Yearbook of Central European Culture,* 10.

Vodakova, A. (1992). K Filosofii Zenske Pracovni a Zivoini Dvourole [Towards a Philosophy about Women's Dual Role in Work and Health], *Filosoficky Casopis, 40*(5), 769-780.

Wolchik, S. L. (1993). Chapter 1. In V. Moghadam, (Ed.), *Democratic Reform and the Position of Women in Transitional Economies* (pp.248-279). New York: Oxford University Press.

Part IV

Sexual and Reproductive Rights

Chapter 20
Toward an Interdependent Approach to Reproductive and Sexual Rights as Human Rights: Reflections on the ICPD and Beyond

Rhonda Copelon & Rosalind Petchesky

During the 1990s, regional and global coalitions of women's rights activists have been focusing on a series of United Nations conferences to lay the foundation for a new integrated approach to human rights. This approach challenges the piecemeal categorizations and formalistic strategies that have characterized the human rights field in the past. Instead, it emphasizes the linkages between rights, needs and social contexts as well as redefining human rights from the perspective of women's needs.

Women are everywhere socially subordinate and marginalized, even while they are primarily responsible for social and biological reproduction and the maintenance of community life. As women develop a consciousness of having rights, define them from their own needs and experience, and feel empowered to demand them, women's human rights become more than an academic and legal abstraction, but rather a powerful vehicle for social transformation. Through mobilization of a global human rights constituency, women have won recognition of "private" gender violence as a human rights violation, successfully challenging the traditional impunity provided by the public/private dichotomy. A combined health and human rights constituency has eroded the androcentrism of the traditional human rights paradigm in winning recognition of applicability to women's sexual and reproductive rights as well as bringing the principle of gender equality from the margin to the center of international concern. Only through broader mobilization—in which women are today the most creative force—will accountability to human rights become applicable to the "private" market forces that are currently operating with impunity and defining "values" and public policies throughout the globe.

Human Rights and the Interdependence Principle

The new approach to human rights rests on the principle of inter-dependence applied among four intersecting axes:

1. the view of individuals as self-determining as well as connected with the diverse families, networks, communities, societies and states in which they live;

2. the dissolution of traditional boundaries between "public" and "private" domains of normative enforcement, so that human rights become applicable to intimate relations and ultimately to market actors previously excluded from their reach;

3. the indivisibility of the three generations of human rights in international law—political and civil; economic, social and cultural; and "solidarity" rights, including the right to equitable and sustainable development, self-determination, a sound and healthful environment, security and peace; and

4. the recognition of women as full subjects of human rights and full participants in their definition and implementation.

This paper argues that the Declaration and Programme of Action adopted at the 1994 International Conference on Population and Development (ICPD) in Cairo moves toward a more expansive recognition of these aspects of the interdependence principle, particularly with regard to reproductive and sexual rights. We discuss the role of women's non-governmental organizations (NGOs) in transforming the Cairo agenda as well as both the political opponents and the political limitations of this transformation. We go on to examine the ethical bases of reproductive decision-making and health rights and their integration with a wide range of enabling conditions—also part of an integrated concept of human rights—necessary for women to realize their right to decide about childbearing.

Following this, we analyze the positive aspects of the ICPD Programme, insofar as it replaces a debate centered on family planning and population control with the foundation for a broader framework of reproductive and sexual self-determination and health rights and women's empowerment. Analyzing these advances as both significant and partial, we also find severe shortcomings and silences, particularly on the issues of alternative approaches to development, financial resources and mechanisms for implementation. These failures, we argue, inevitably weaken the human rights perspective in the Cairo document. Finally, we explore some of the possibilities for interpretation and implementation of the human rights principles achieved in Cairo and highlight the need to press the women's human rights, development and environment agendas further in the context of the World Women's Conference in Beijing and beyond.

The Ethical Bases of Reproductive and Sexual Rights

Three critical, ethical concepts, indispensable to women's empowerment and full citizenship, underlie the women's human rights agenda as it applies to the range of issues debated in Cairo.[1] First is the significance of bodily integrity and self-determination, including health, wellness and sexual pleasure, not as individualistic concerns, but as inseparable from women's full and equal participation in all aspects of social life.

Second is the principle of equality, a centerpiece of which is the recognition that women's ability to make decisions over their sexuality and fertility is an essential ingredient of equality as persons and equal participation in all spheres of life.

Third is the necessity of enabling conditions or social rights, demonstrating the connection between economic, social and cultural rights and the larger global issues of sustainable and equitable development, environmental preservation and peace.

Through their concern with such issues as domestic violence, rape, sexuality, access to primary and reproductive health care and technologies, and an end to abusive medical and family planning practices, women's groups have brought questions of personal security and bodily integrity squarely to the center of human rights debates. Rejecting traditional dichotomies between "private" and "public," or between "society" and "individual," women insist that affirmative rights pertaining to individual persons and their bodies, applicable to private as well as official invasions, are necessary prerequisites to full participation as community members and citizens.

Women have stressed as well the equality dimensions of human rights, insisting that equality be understood on the one hand in light of gender and, on the other, in light of the diverse identities and conditions which shape women's lives. The former calls for a reconceptualization of human rights, including, as we have said, a new

---

[1] This framework is developed more fully in Correa & Petchesky (1994). See also Correa (1994) and Petchesky (1990).

appreciation of the role of bodily integrity, security of person, empowerment and social status as predicates to women's equal enjoyment of human rights. The latter calls for recognition that many conditions, for example, race and ethnicity, economic class, culture, sexual orientation and geopolitical and urban/rural or indigenous status, bear on the definition and realization of equality for all women. In other words, the equality principle envisages the universal applicability of human rights to women at the same time as it requires recognition and respect for the diversity among women. As such, the ethic of equality addresses the dangers of formalistic universalism through attention to social context and to concrete results.

At the same time, reproductive and sexual rights are inseparable from a broader framework of enabling conditions. These include the responsibility to assure other basic economic and social rights, such as food, shelter, education, basic health and livelihood, in order to create an environment conducive to free choice. From an ethical standpoint, such enabling conditions imply correlative obligations on the part of governments and international organizations to treat basic human needs, not as market commodities, but as rights. The realization of these rights is, in turn, dependent upon larger structural changes, such as the elimination of poverty, violence in all its forms, harsh structural adjustment programs, trade inequities and unsustainable production and consumption patterns and environmental degradation. In other words, reproductive and sexual rights ultimately require a radical shifting of priorities toward expenditures that serve social welfare and the quality of life and away from market incentives, private profit and militarism.

The translation of these ethical concepts into international human rights converts fundamental principles and desirable policies into state obligations and lays the foundation for state accountability. The human rights framework is an embracing and multi-layered one that must be further developed to respond to new challenges to state responsibility and international cooperation presented by globalization of the market and the interconnectedness of human survival. Sexual and reproductive self-determination and health requires the protection of "first generation" political and civil rights as well as steady progress in the realization of "second generation" economic, social and cultural rights. They are, in turn, inseparable from the urgent need for new international commitments to ensure the "third generation" of solidarity rights, including human-centered and sustainable development, self-determination, preservation of the environment and the common heritage of humankind, disarmament and global security based on peace in all spheres of life.

Until recently, however, women have been excluded from or marginalized by the traditional human rights paradigm. Responding to a global mobilization of women, the 1993 World Conference on Human Rights at Vienna recognized the need to transform the paradigm so as to encompass the needs and experience of women. The Vienna Declaration recognized that gender violence, inflicted by both state officials and private persons is a violation of women's human rights. Vienna also called for the integration of gender concerns into all the work of the human rights system as well as for the development of special mechanisms to advance this process. It opened the door to confronting the ways the public/private dichotomy shields husbands, partners, fathers, medical institutions and doctors, religious and cultural adherents, for example, from responsibility. In so doing, Vienna laid the foundation for expanding the human rights perspective in relation to population and development issues to embrace state and international responsibility for national and multinational corporations and other private sector actors. Before turning to an assessment of the results of the ICPD at Cairo, we examine briefly the preparations of the women's movement and the positions of the opposing forces.

The Political Context of Cairo

The formation of an international women's coalition to influence the Cairo Conference was a risk. Some women opposed involvement in the official process while many entered this terrain with concern about the possibility of co-optation. However, there was a very broad sentiment that women, as primary victims of target driven population control programs and male-centered development initiatives, had to transform the Cairo agenda and the role of women from objects to subjects of population and development programs.

A meeting of some 200 women from all regions of the world, held in Rio de Janeiro in 1994 (Reproductive Health and Justice: International Women's Health Conference for Cairo '94, January 24-28, 1994, Rio de Janeiro), was an important milestone. It signaled unity, across regional and political differences, in participants' emphasis on the impossibility of separating development issues and a critique of global economic trends from the issues of reproductive and sexual decision-making and health rights and gender equality (International Women's Health Coalition, 1994). This breadth of approach also characterized the work of the various task forces of the Women's Caucus, which drafted and lobbied for considerable revision of the draft Programme of Action during the ICPD preparatory process and the conference.

Women working to transform the outcome of the Cairo meeting had to face two distinct and powerful constituencies. On the one hand, as reflected in their media approach up to and through the Conference, the population and environment groups that have dominated this field for decades maintained their single-minded focus on population growth—and primarily on women's fertility—as a major cause of environmental degradation and poverty. In Cairo, however, the population and environment constituency did not openly oppose the women's agenda for sexual and reproductive rights and health and women's empowerment. In part, their acquiescence (and in some cases active support) in this aspect of the women's agenda flowed from the acknowledgment that women around the world are rejecting unsafe and coercive family planning methods, and that fertility control depends on women having access to education, literacy and basic resources to promote their empowerment and broader participation in social and economic life.

Yet considerable difference remains between the views of population groups and the women's movement as regards women's empowerment. On one level, this difference is reflected in the Cairo document's limited reallocation of resources between family planning and reproductive and primary health. On a deeper level, it is reflected in the contrast between treating women's health and empowerment as instruments of population control or as women's inherent right as human beings. So long as environmental preservation is separated from social justice, women's fertility (as opposed to unsustainable patterns of production and consumption, maldistribution and militarism), will remain the primary focus for population and environment groups.

The second challenge to the women's human rights movement at Cairo was an unprecedented coalition of religious fundamentalists, forged between the Vatican, its predominantly Catholic satellite governments, and some of the Muslim fundamentalist states,[2] that sought to impose a rigid pronatalist agenda on the Conference. This coalition opposed any terms that might suggest the acceptability of abortion, sexual pleasure, education and services for adolescents, lesbian and gay existence as well as rights, or any form of family or union outside a traditional heterosexual form. It also attempted persistently to elevate religion and traditional cultures as constraints on the implementation of human rights.

While claiming solidarity with the South on the issues of development, the Vatican and its allies held the Conference hostage to what was publicized as the abortion issue. In this way, it was ensured that there would be no time to grapple with broader issues of development involving global economic structures and power imbalances. The United States was a major opponent of the attack on reproductive rights; but its interest, along with that of other Northern countries, in avoiding serious discussion of sustainable human-centered development and economic redistribution was also served by this focus on abortion.

Assessing Cairo

The result of the encounter in Cairo—the ICPD Programme of Action—reflects one of the most powerful statements to date of the interdependence principle, as well as the structural and political barriers to its full articulation and accomplishment. However, while women did succeed in transforming the rhetoric and principles underlying population and development programs, we were able only to scratch at the surface of the underlying causes of inequality, poverty, unsustainable and profit-driven development and environmental degradation. Nonetheless, in recognizing the importance of women's health, rights, equality and empowerment and in placing population and development programs within an integrated human rights framework, Cairo represents a critical step forward in the process of translating basic needs into basic rights.

The Strengths of Cairo

The ICPD Programme advanced the Vienna approach, as well as the notion of interdependence outlined at the outset of this article, in a number of respects. The Principles which frame the Programme

---

[2] Such as Argentina, Benin, El Salvador, Guatemala, Honduras and Iran.

explicitly incorporate all the human rights recognized in the Universal Declaration of Human Rights (Princ. 1). This encompasses political and civil as well as economic, social and cultural rights. The Principles specifically articulate rights to equality and non-discrimination and to life, liberty and security of person (Princ. 1); to an adequate standard of living and to development (Princs. 2 & 3); to gender equality (Princ. 4); to the enjoyment of the highest attainable standard of physical and mental health (Princ. 8) and to education (Princ. 10); and the rights of children (Princ. 11) and migrants (Princs. 12 & 13). By quoting the first article of the Universal Declaration—"All human beings are born free and equal in dignity and rights," the Principles also negate the Vatican's effort to claim rights for the fetus and make clear that all human rights are contingent on birth.

In addition, the Principles identify responsibilities of the world community, and particularly of the North (Princ. 15), to achieve sustainable development "as a means to ensure human well-being, equitably shared by all people" (Princ. 5), to eradicate poverty (Princ. 7), and to eliminate unsustainable patterns of production and consumption (Princ. 6). Population policies are seen as an integral aspect of development policies designed to improve the well-being of all people (Princs. 5 & 6), while coercion in reproductive health programs is forbidden (Princ. 8).

The chapter on reproductive rights and health accepts, almost intact, as the "basis for action," the World Health Organization's (WHO) definition of reproductive health, which includes sexual health.[3] It also applies the human rights framework explicitly to

---

[3] The amendment to the WHO definition, based on the Vatican's objection that "fertility regulation" includes abortion, is underlined for identification.

Para. 7.2 provides: Reproductive health is a state of complete physical, mental and social well-being and not merely the absence of disease or infirmity, in all matters relating to the reproductive system and to its functions and processes. Reproductive health therefore implies that people are able to have a satisfying and safe sex life and that they have the capability to reproduce and the freedom to decide if, when and how often to do so. Implicit in this last condition are the right of men and women to be informed and to have access to safe, effective, affordable and acceptable methods of family planning of their choice, as well as other methods of their choice for the regulation of fertility *which are not against the law,* and the right of access to appropriate health-care services that will enable women to go safely through pregnancy and childbirth and provide couples with the best chance of having a healthy infant. In line with the above definition of re-

reproductive health concerns.[4] This far transcends the often reiterated "right of individuals and couples to decide freely and responsibly the number and spacing of their children and to have the information and means to do so." This right, which first entered international parlance in a more limited form in 1968 as a means of overcoming southern resistance to the US-led fertility control initiatives, has been slowly transformed, through the influence of women's NGOs, into a basis for protection of women's control over not only their fertility but also all aspects of their reproductive and sexual health and well-being. The Programme emphasizes the importance of bodily integrity, women's ability to control their fertility and the necessity of enhancing male respect for women and responsibility for sexuality and reproduction.

There is little doubt that the concerns of many delegations, particularly from sub-Sahara Africa, about the devastating health and social consequences of HIV/AIDS did far more than the women's movements ever could have to bring sexual health (though not sexual self-determination) into the document. One does not want to overstate this; nowhere did freedom of sexual expression or sexual orientation gain recognition as a human right. Yet the extent to which "a satisfying and safe sex life" as an affirmative and not only disease-preventive goal appears as an integral component of reproductive health and rights in the Cairo Programme (para. 7.2) is surprising. Chapter 7 urges governments to provide adolescents with a full array of sexual and reproductive health services and education "to enable them to deal in a positive and responsible way with their sexuality."

---

productive health, reproductive health care is defined as the constellation of methods, techniques and services that contribute to reproductive health and well-being through preventing and solving reproductive health problems. It also includes sexual health, the purpose of which is the enhancement of life and personal relations, and not merely counseling and care related to reproduction and sexually transmitted diseases.

[4] Para. 7.3 provides: . . . [R]eproductive rights embrace certain human rights that are already recognized in national laws, international human rights documents and other relevant United Nations consensus documents. These rights rest on the recognition of the basic right of all couples and individuals to decide freely and responsibly the number, spacing and timing of their children and to have the information and means to do so, and the right to attain the highest standard of sexual and reproductive health. It also includes the right to make decisions concerning reproduction free of discrimination, coercion and violence as expressed in human rights documents . . .

These services should include "the education of young men to respect women's self-determination and to share responsibility with women in matters of sexuality and reproduction." While "voluntary abstinence" is offered as one means toward this end for adolescents and others, so too is condom use. These provisions, while heterosexist in their orientation, are not, however, expressly limited to heterosexuals, nor to married couples.

The indivisibility of human rights is reflected in the Programme's articulation of a broad range of affirmative obligations of states, NGOs, and the world community with respect to women's health and education. To assist in the realization of the maximum attainable standard of health, reproductive health initiatives must transcend the narrow focus on family planning and be placed in the context of primary health care. The Programme disclaims the use of demographic targets or coercion of any kind, although it does not unequivocally forbid the use of incentives. It calls for increased prevention and treatment of sexually transmitted diseases including HIV/AIDS, giving priority to sex education, especially for adolescents, to "enable them to deal in a positive and responsible way with their sexuality" (para. 7.3). Recognizing the serious health consequences of gender violence, the Programme outlines legal as well as educational measures to punish and prevent it. It also reiterates the importance of safe motherhood initiatives and sets goals for the reduction of maternal mortality. During conference deliberations, the Vatican attempted to bracket the term "safe motherhood" and ultimately blocked language that would ensure the safety of abortion and call for its decriminalization. But while anti-abortion forces succeeded in securing adoption of the statement that "abortion should in no case be a method of family planning," the Programme for the first time urges that all levels of government "deal with the health impact of unsafe abortion as a major public health concern..." and ensure access to quality services in response to complications.

Unlike the two previous world population conference documents, the ICPD Programme contains an entire chapter devoted to "Gender Equality, Equity and Empowerment of Women." It recognizes the empowerment of women as an end in itself and as central to their ability both to enjoy sexual and reproductive health rights and to participate in (and transform) development and environment initiatives. Although it fails to critique women's exclusion from and exploitation in development or provide alternative visions, it offers a vehicle for change in the commitment to advance women as full and equal participants at all levels of social life and to engage them in all aspects of population and development program planning, implementation and review. Indeed, by giving prominent attention to addressing women's equality and empowerment, and emphasizing the education and health needs of women and girls as well as the cultural impediments to equality and self-esteem, the Cairo document has the potential to convert the principle of equality contained in the Convention on the Elimination of All Forms of Discrimination Against Women (Women's Convention) into a working program. This advance over previous conferences reflects the strength and impact of the women's movements globally since the Nairobi women's conference in 1985. And it acknowledges women's empowerment as an indispensable link in the interdependence thesis.

The Deficiencies of Cairo

Yet the Cairo Programme's weaknesses and omissions are as troubling as its advances are encouraging. While it states at many points that population growth is the symptom as much as the cause of poverty, environmental degradation and social inequalities, it fails to address these "root causes" in any meaningful way. It urges the indispensable integration of population and development concerns, but development gets short shrift. Here and there the Programme mentions such problems as the link between environmental degradation, widespread poverty and unsustainable patterns of production and consumption, the harsh impact of Structural Adjustment Programs (SAPs) on social services, the need for debt relief, and the inequitable distribution and flow of resources between north and south as well as between the military and social sectors. Nowhere, however, does the Cairo Programme address these as global structural crises requiring radically alternative economic and social solutions before reproductive and sexual rights—or any human rights —can be fully realized.

The ICPD circumvented the demand of the Women's Caucus and the development NGOs to commit to concrete steps. It explicitly deferred the 20:20 formula for redistribution advanced by the United Nations Children's Fund (UNICEF) and the United Nations Development Programme (UNDP) to the World Social Summit on Development (WSSD) in Copenhagen in March 1995.[5] In direct

---

[5] The 20:20 proposal calls for allocating 20 percent of bilateral and multilateral development aid to the social sector in return for national governments pledging 20

contradiction to the substantive emphasis on a broad, comprehensive model of reproductive and sexual health care and its integration with primary health care, the Cairo Programme directs two-thirds of the United Nations Population Fund (UNFPA) budget identified in that document to family planning, leaving everything else—primary health care, "social and economic sector goals," HIV/AIDS treatment and prevention, obstetrical care, sex education, etc.—to await "additional resources." While offering new opportunities for the future with regard to NGO "partnership" in development, monitoring and implementation, it provides no allocation at all for women's education, empowerment or the facilitation of NGO participation and rejected virtually all of the Women's Caucus' proposals for explicit implementation measures.

Not only are the document's references to financial and enforcement arrangements weak; they also contradict the main principles and goals related to reproductive health, reproductive rights, and development of "the social sectors." At the same time as it urges increased public expenditures for social services and SAPs that are "responsive to social concerns," the Programme also aims to promote "increased involvement of the private sector" in producing and marketing contraceptives and providing reproductive health services, as well as "the selective use of user fees" and "social marketing" techniques. At the same time as it advocates that such commodities and services be "of high quality," "socially responsible" and "culturally sensitive," it encourages governments to lift regulations "that unnecessarily prevent or restrict the greater involvement of the private sector in efficient production of commodities for reproductive health, including family planning and in service delivery." In other words, the Cairo document promotes the very privatization, commodification and deregulation of reproductive health services that, by its own admission, have led to diminished access and increasing mortality and morbidity for women who constitute "the most vulnerable groups" in both developing and developed countries.

But if the private market is to remain the dominant mechanism for determining whether and what "additional resources" will be allocated to the entire health care and social development sectors; if states are not required to shift budgetary priorities from militarism and debt servicing to social expenditures, particularly health; and if

---

percent of national resources to the social sector.

strong enforcement and accountability procedures representing women are not set up to counter abuses, then it is difficult to see how the ICPD's broad vision of reproductive health and rights, women's empowerment and gender equality will ever materialize. For that vision to become a reality would require the commitment of the United Nations and its agencies and member states to an alternative model of development, one that places the quality of life and necessary investments in social capital over economic growth, militarism and market incentives. "Development" in ICPD is not absent, but rather stuck within neo-liberal, capitalist priorities.

Despite its strong affirmation of gender equality and reproductive health and rights, the Cairo document is deficient from a women's human rights perspective, not only in its equivocation on abortion (see above), but also in its conservatism with regard to human sexuality. The Vatican-led religious fundamentalists succeeded in eliminating all references to "sexual rights" and diluted the clear and consistent recognition of diverse family forms in the pre-Cairo draft by retaining some references to "the family"—meaning the heterosexual, nuclear form—as the "basic unit of society." Homophobia drove these decisions, which resulted in the failure to recognize and prohibit discrimination against lesbian and gay relationships along with women-headed households, less formalized partnerships and extended, more communal family forms prevalent in different parts of the world. The document's silence on these matters weakens, though it does not negate, its positive affirmation of the value of a "satisfying and safe sex life" which contains no limitation based on sexual orientation or age.

Another significant gap in the Programme is its silence on racism and the needs of racial and ethnic minorities—except in the context of migration (as though all victims of racial and ethnic discrimination were "aliens!"). It is also weak on both the right to self-determination and the contributions of indigenous peoples, whom it refuses to recognize as "peoples" in their own right. Instead, such groups are referred to as "people," implying a lack of common identity and sovereignty relative to those represented by the nation state. Finally, the refusal to recognize a right to family reunification for migrants underscores the hypocrisy of the "pro-family" position.

Finally, the ICPD Programme reflects a strong tension between the integrative or interdependent approach and deference to national sovereignty and religious and cultural traditions which various parties

asserted in Cairo specifically to counter women's sexual and reproductive rights and health (as if countries would collapse if women had
these rights!). Backtracking from the Vienna agreements, it fails to
assert unequivocally that human rights take precedence over conflicting traditions. And, rejecting the demand of the Women's Caucus
for concrete accountability mechanisms at the level of the UN, the
Programme simply acknowledges the need for such mechanisms and
contains scattered, vague directions to states.

Human Rights As an Implementation Strategy

Despite its limitations, the ICPD Programme provides unprecedented emphasis on the integration of human rights, and particularly
of women's human rights, in this area of programmatic UN work and
opens up a range of potential implementation strategies for the future. While there are many avenues for implementation of the ICPD
Programme, we focus here on how the Programme's recognition of
human rights can be used in women's advocacy, particularly in the
area of reproductive and sexual rights. Indeed, in a Programme of
Action that lacks formal accountability mechanisms, the human rights
framework provides a crucial vehicle for insisting upon principled
implementation of population and development policies.

The affirmation in Cairo that women's basic needs in the area of
sexual and reproductive health are human rights provides the basis
for challenging the abuse of women as objects and non-participants in
population policies and for implementing positive measures to advance women as full citizens. The human rights perspective, adopted
in the ICPD Programme, emphasizes that this is not just a desirable
policy but rather an ethical and legal imperative. Human rights constitute limitations on the sovereignty of states and principles to which
donors, providers, intergovernmental organizations, and, ultimately,
the private economic sector, must be held accountable. The human
rights framework provides concepts and strategies—formal and informal—that women can shape in light of diverse needs and contexts
to challenge abuses, promote positive programs, and, at the most
fundamental level, empower women in their daily lives (Copelon &
Hernandez, 1994).

Interpreting Human Rights in Light of the Cairo Conference

The ICPD Programme did not create new rights (as our opponents argue), but rather called for applying traditional human rights

concepts in light of the realities and needs of women.[6] Even though the Vatican and its allies succeeded in excluding abortion and sexual rights from the list of human rights recognized in the Cairo document, it cannot freeze the human rights concept in time. Human rights are evolving, not static. Just as the Vienna Conference took a major step in identifying both public and private gender violence as a human rights violation, the Cairo Programme accelerated the process of reinterpretation by illuminating the significance of human rights for the realm of reproduction and sexuality.

Thus, for example, in the sphere of civil and political rights, the right to liberty and security of the person, found in most international and regional instruments, has been traditionally linked with freedom from arbitrary arrest and protection from harm while in detention. The ICPD Programme lays the foundation for recognizing what feminists have argued for some time, that the concept of detention encompasses the broader limitations on liberty suffered by women, and that the concept of security of person embraces women's right to determine and control their sexuality and reproduction as well as their protection from abuse.[7] Along with security of person, the common prohibitions on torture and cruel, inhuman and degrading treatment and on non-consensual medical or scientific experimentation enable women to insist on informed consent and equal treatment in all medical contexts as well as in the testing of new contraceptive and reproductive health measures. We can also apply the right to be free from involuntary servitude, as well as the protections against torture and inhuman and degrading treatment, to forced prostitution, involuntary motherhood and domestic servitude and violence, all too common in women's lives. The requirement of the Convention on the Rights of the Child that states must protect children from all forms of maltreatment, including sexual abuse, and provide education and access to family planning, also underpins the

---

[6] The full implications of applying the human rights framework to reproductive health care and rights are beyond the scope of this article. They have been thoughtfully elaborated in Cook (1994); Cook (1993); Cook (1992); Freedman & Isaacs (1993); and Hernandez (1991).

[7] In addition to the sources cited in note 6, for example, the Canadian Supreme Court has interpreted the right to security of the person, contained in Canada's Charter of Rights and Freedoms, to encompass the right of women to choose abortion. See *R. v. Morgentaler* (1988) [see opinions of C. J. Dickson, J. Beetz, and J. Wilson (the woman justice)].

commitments of Cairo. The right to conscience and to freedom from religious intolerance and discrimination is applicable to private as well as state violators,[8] and has direct relevance to issues of reproductive and sexual decision-making. While the absence in the ICPD document of any explicit recognition of sexual rights is deeply problematic, it does not prevent the human rights bodies from continuing to protect a right of sexual self-determination.[9]

The indivisible nature of the political, civil, economic, social and cultural rights is also particularly noteworthy in the Cairo Programme. There are essentially four approaches to indivisibility, all of which are embodied in and strengthened by the Cairo consensus. First, even with respect to political and civil rights, states have an obligation not only to respect (to not do harm) but also to take positive measures to ensure their enjoyment. For example, the Human Rights Committee has identified the reduction of maternal mortality as an aspect of the right to life. The Cairo consensus provides a basis for applying the right to life to HIV transmission, reproductive cancers and gender violence. In detailing the steps that governments should take to ensure access, empowerment and participation of women in policy-making, the Cairo Programme elaborates the positive measures needed to ensure the right to participate in public life.

The second foundation for indivisibility is the Programme's explicit linkage of gender equality to reproductive rights and respect for

---

[8] The Declaration on the Elimination of All Forms of Religious Intolerance and Discrimination Based on Religion or Belief (1982) defines this as "any distinction, exclusion, restriction or preference based on religion or belief and having as its purpose or as its effect nullification or impairment of the recognition, enjoyment or exercise of human rights and fundamental freedoms on an equal basis." The opposition to women's human rights in Cairo reflected the alliance of Muslim crusaders against women identified as feminist or as resisters to subordinating orthodoxies and the Vatican-led opposition to fertility control, diverse family arrangements, same-sex partnerships and information and services related to sexuality and reproduction. All these are manifestations of religious intolerance as well as violations of basic civil and political rights of women.

[9] Several human rights treaty bodies have recognized the right to be free of discrimination based on sexual orientation and to determine one's sexuality without interference by the state. Post-Cairo, the Human Rights Committee, in its comments on the US report, criticized the US for permitting criminal laws against same-sex sex. These decisions are technically binding on the states parties to the treaties and eventually, as these interpretations gain broader consensus, they too become part of customary human rights norms.

(hetero)sexual relations. Lack of control over sexuality and fertility plays a profound role in perpetuating women's unequal status in society. Sexual violence, coercion and the unacknowledged perpetuation of heterosexuality as a norm constitute gender discrimination, profound denials of selfhood, and bitter lessons in subordination. Moreover, equality is not limited to identical treatment. Because only women can be pregnant and, as a social matter, bear disproportionate (if not exclusive) responsibility for childrearing, the equality principle requires that women have ultimate power and full ability to consent to childbearing.[10] The Cairo Programme concretizes the Women's Convention's endorsement of positive measures to advance gender equality by emphasizing the necessity of directing resources toward reproductive health, education and empowerment of women.[11]

Despite the general opposition of the North, particularly the United States, to the third approach—direct implementation of social and economic rights—the right to make childbearing decisions has been an exception. It has encompassed access to "information and the means to do so" precisely because fertility control and not self-determination was the goal. The instrumentalist origin of the right, however, made it relatively easy in Cairo to insist on the indivisibility of reproductive decision-making and access to reproductive and primary health care and education. This is also a step toward expanding the concept of "means" to include such economic and social rights as

[10] The Committee on the Elimination of All Forms of Discrimination Against Women (CEDAW), Recommendation No. 21 (1994) clarified this in interpreting the potentially ambiguous provision of the Women's Convention which guarantees women, "on a basis of equality of men and women.... the same rights. . ." to make reproductive decisions. Recognizing that women's responsibilities affect their development and participation in society, CEDAW concluded: "Decisions to have children or not, while preferably made in consultation with spouse or partner, must not nevertheless be limited by spouse, partner, parent or Government."

[11] The Women's Convention requires that states take measures to "ensure the full development and advancement of women, for the purpose of guaranteeing them the exercise and enjoyment of human rights and fundamental freedoms on a basis of equality with men" (art. 3). This includes temporary measures aimed at advancing the de facto status of men and women as protections of maternity, which are excluded from the definition of discrimination (art. 4), as well as measures designed to modify social and cultural patterns and stereotypes which disadvantage women (art. 5).

food, shelter, work and basic security as well as the right to development, all of which constitute enabling conditions for reproductive
and sexual rights to become realities. Moreover, the ICPD document
provides a basis for understanding the need for women-centered research and health care, the impermissibility of withholding fertility
regulation measures such as RU-486, and the involvement of
women's health NGOs in reproductive research as aspects of the
right to enjoy the benefits of scientific progress protected by the International Covenant on Economic, Social and Cultural Rights
(ICESCR) (Cook, 1994). While much work needs to be done to
make economic and social rights meaningful, the Cairo Programme
makes an important conceptual and programmatic advance.

With respect to cultural rights, the Cairo Programme is typically
ambivalent. On the one hand, it calls for "full respect" for religious
and cultural traditions as a general matter; on the other, the action
program recognizes the need to undo cultural norms and practices
that perpetuate inequality and denial of reproductive and sexual
rights. This is reflected in its emphasis on affirmative steps to advance
equality and mutual respect in sexual, reproductive and family life
and to eliminate harmful traditional practices and gender violence.

Finally, the Cairo Programme's emphasis on the participation of
women's NGOs and beneficiaries at all levels of decision-making implicates the mandate of the Women's Convention that women be ensured an equal right to "participate in the formulation of government
policy and the implementation thereof and to hold public office and
perform all public functions at all levels of government" (art. 7).[12]
Though participation is classically understood as a civil and political
right, it is a crucial vehicle for advancing the interdependence of government and civil society and thereby implementing the integrated
concept of rights recognized in the Programme. Yet participation can
be a double-edged sword, insofar as it requires women's groups to
navigate cautiously between the two dangers of exclusion on the one
hand and co-optation, or assuming the responsibilities of governments and international organizations, on the other.

The weakest link in the interdependence thesis involves the critical "third generation" of solidarity rights to development, self-
determination, protection of the environment, culture, peace and

---

[12] See also art. 25 of the International Covenant on Civil and Political Rights
(ICCPR).

security. While the Cairo Programme reaffirms that economic development is an individual right and that women must be full participants in the development process, it creates no new mechanisms of accountability.[13] Moreover, the ICPD declined the Women's Caucus' demands to reconsider external debt and to develop mechanisms to redirect structural adjustment policies and the international financial institutions (IFIs) and transnational corporations (TNCs) that increasingly control the global economy.

Nonetheless, women can begin to use the concepts and mechanisms of the human rights system to insist that states refuse certain structural adjustment policies and discipline private economic actors when they undermine the rights and status of women. Despite the fact that some states are pressured by their external debt and financial vulnerability into accepting SAPs and agreements with multinational corporations that violate the rights of workers, states should nonetheless be held accountable for resulting human rights violations. Thus women's groups and other NGOs can begin to use human rights to challenge indirectly the policies of the IFIs and TNCs. Yet, without the creation of new models of development that reallocate resources from militarism and private profit to the social sector; and without new, positive mechanisms that hold IFIs and TNCs accountable under human rights norms, the commitments of Cairo are illusory. The human rights strategies accelerated by the ICPD are, however, a vehicle for demanding broader change.

Using the Human Rights Concepts and System

Notwithstanding these gaps, the recognition that the Cairo Programme is based on the full range of human rights opens up numerous informal and formal implementation strategies. Since the goal of the human rights system is local enforcement, let us start there. On the national and local levels, the Cairo Programme represents non-binding but good faith commitments to reorder priorities and develop new programmatic initiatives and criteria with significant attention to the advancement of women. That these commitments are based on human rights rather than simply desirable social policy adds force vis-a-vis governments, donors, providers, inter-governmental and non-governmental organizations. Women can use human rights

---

[13] Declaration on the Right to Development, GA Res. 41/128 (4 December 1986). Though technically binding upon all states, unlike a treaty it contains no implementation mechanisms.

362 **Rhonda Copelon & Rosalind Petchesky**

concepts whether or not their country has ratified a pertinent treaty. Human rights advocacy generally precedes ratification and widely endorsed, or "customary" human rights norms apply to all states.

Thus, on the national level, human rights arguments support translating the commitments of Cairo into legislation or administrative policies. In Anglo-American systems women frequently turn to litigation and the possibility of bringing public interest claims to the courts is expanding in non-Anglo systems (Plata & Espriella in this volume). Many legal systems incorporate international law into domestic law; in others, arguments based on human rights and international commitments such as the Cairo Programme can lay the foundation for a more humane jurisprudence and/or public policy. For example, Isabel Plata (1994) analyzes how, even before Cairo, the women's movement in Colombia used the Women's Convention as the basis for a ground-breaking, women-centered public health policy. Moreover, the demand for adherence to human rights principles can influence certain non-governmental and private actors who may fear legal accountability or public embarrassment, or find in the human rights/Cairo approach support for ethical practices.

Where national initiatives fail or are futile, implementation of the Cairo commitments needs to be brought before various human rights bodies. The Cairo commitments provide a basis for calling upon the treaty committees to use the ICPD Programme to measure state progress in fulfilling relevant treaty obligations in the context of their consideration of periodic state reports.[14] Where a treaty

---

[14] For example, the Human Rights Committee can examine classic abuses, including punishment for dissident expression or political activities, and violations of physical and mental integrity through coercive medical practices, experimentation or medical care conducted without informed consent. It can also ask states to report their efforts to reduce gender violence, HIV transmission and maternal mortality (including their commitment in Cairo to deal with the health impact of unsafe abortion), as a measure of the state's commitment to ensuring the right to life, security of person and freedom from torture and ill-treatment. Most of the treaty committees have authority to examine gender-discriminatory policies. CEDAW has the most detailed and extensive mandate, which encompasses all of the gender-specific aspects of the Cairo Programme. The question of the reordering of economic and social priorities is primary for the Committee on Economic, Social and Cultural Rights (CESCR), which enforces that Covenant's obligations to take steps progressively to enhance these rights. The Committees should be used to challenge structural adjustment policies since they are agreed to by states. Documenting the cutbacks in social-sector spending dictated by SAPs raises ques-

committee functions independently and has feminist members, and where NGOs are significantly involved in the preparation and/or critique of state reports, requiring a state to answer to an international body and international opinion, as well as to an internal constituency, can help to galvanize the NGO critique as well as spur a state to change its approach.

The human rights system also provides various possibilities for individual or group petitions requesting investigations and interventions to publicize and stop abuses. A relatively small number of states have acceded to the authority of the treaty committees (where recognition of that authority is optional) to hear individual petitions.[15] The complaints procedures are one of the most effective means for groups and individuals to challenge state policies. These mechanisms have no formal power to *require* states to challenge their policies or to compensate victims because there is no international enforcement mechanism. Rather, human rights advocacy relies primarily on publicity and shaming. Thus the international mechanisms can be a vehicle for building solidarity, internally and internationally, and, where countries are sensitive to international criticism, they can be used to generate domestic reform. Using them generally requires that domestic remedies be tried or be futile. The proposal to create a petition process in the Committee on the Elimination of All Forms of Discrimination Against Women (CEDAW) is particularly important because the Women' Convention gives it jurisdiction over inequality in economic and social—such as access to health care and education—as well as political and civil matters and specifically requires states to take measures to end private discrimination.

---

tions for the CESCR, just as documentation of the disproportionate impact of these policies on women would also come within the purview of CEDAW.

[15] Some treaties create an individual petition process that states may decide to recognize. In the UN system, for example, the Committee Against Torture and the Committee to Eliminate Racial Discrimination have this power. The European and Inter-American systems give their human rights commissions the power to hear complaints against all members, but allow states to agree to the jurisdiction of their human rights courts. The Human Rights Committee, which enforces the International Covenant on Civil and Political Rights, hears complaints against those states which have ratified the optional protocol (amendment to the treaty), which created the individual petition procedure. Currently there are efforts to approve similar optional protocols to enable the Committee on Economic, Social and Cultural Rights (CESCR) and CEDAW to hear individual complaints.

Other investigative mechanisms—the working groups and special rapporteurs of the Human Rights Commission and its Sub-Commission on Prevention of Discrimination and Protection of Minorities[16]—are less formal but more accessible. They can be invoked by any person anywhere in the world, since the Human Rights Commission is a creature of the UN Charter. By seeking the intervention of the rapporteurs, for example, domestic groups can bring recalcitrant governments under international scrutiny and build the basis for broader condemnation in the international system.

To be successful, all these approaches require documentation of abuses, follow-up and outreach to solidarity networks and governments. In addition, by collectively documenting abuses not within the mandates of the existing rapporteurs or working groups, women can insist on their expansion or creation of new mandates.

The human rights system is, however, currently weighted toward scrutiny of violations of political and civil rights, as opposed to economic and social rights. The most effective mechanisms are those geared largely toward negative abuses—state violence and other violations of civil and political rights. But, even with regard to the former, to date little or no attention has been paid to the abuses of women's reproductive and sexual rights, with the exception of rape in war or detention. Women need to critique state reports and use the petition and investigative machinery to generate action against denial of or coercion against reproductive and sexual rights, as well as with regard to state failures to ensure the protection of these rights through positive action. With regard to economic and social rights, as suggested earlier, we can use the human rights system, particularly CEDAW, the CESCR and the sub-commission on protection of minorities, to address exploitation and discrimination against women in national laws and practices and as a result of SAPs and multinational corporate policies.

At the most basic level, women's human rights will never transcend rhetoric to become lived realities until women themselves feel a sense of entitlement. Understanding one's needs and wants as human rights, and subordination and discrimination as wrongs, is the

---

[16] Among the relevant bodies are the Special Rapporteur on Violence against Women, its Causes and Consequences, the Rapporteur on AIDS, on Religious Intolerance, and on Torture. The Sub-Commission has a rapporteur on Traditional Practices Affecting the Health of Women and Children and a working group on Modern Forms of Slavery.

fundamental basis for both personal and social change. As Shanthi Dairiam (1994) says, "human rights transforms women from mere beneficiaries to claimants." The Cairo Programme, like the Women's Convention, provides tools whereby women on the ground can begin to see their needs and experiences reflected in universal principles and, in turn, redefine those principles out of their particular experience and contexts (Toro, 1995). Women-centered human rights education, including reproductive and sexual rights, should be integrated into education, health care and development programs. Women must know they have rights and must feel entitled to make claims not only against blatant abuses, but also for the positive services and social supports they and their families need to live decent and enriching lives. But such knowledge is subversive and provokes dangerous backlash against women on many levels.[17] Without women conscious of their rights and organized and empowered to demand them, "women's human rights" will remain an academic, legal abstraction or, worse yet, result in even greater repression.

Conclusion

Cairo was a step in the process from the United Nations Conference on Environment and Development (UNCED) in Rio de Janeiro to the World Women's Conference in Beijing. It illustrates the power of women's participation to change the dominant discourse of international politics and law, as well as the crucial need for follow-up action and mobilization, particularly at the local level.

The ICPD Programme and the new vision of reproductive and sexual rights it reflects are the outcome of a process of debate in which women's movements have forcefully opposed the treatment of women as objects, whether of pronatalist motherhood policies or anti-natalist population control policies. But the danger remains that "human rights" and "women's empowerment" will be used as legitimizing rhetoric or as an instrument of male-dominated agendas to reduce or augment fertility, to promote religious or nationalist ideologies or to advance the hegemony of global market forces.

---

[17] For example, subsequent to the ICPD, an Egyptian woman was killed in an argument with her husband over equality and the Egyptian government stepped back from its commitment to end genital mutilation and promulgated a new regulation permitting its performance in hospitals.

We are particularly concerned about this danger in light of the gaping holes in the Cairo document, especially its failure to address the economic and political problems of privatization and unregulated "economic growth," escalating racism, sexism, homophobia and the need for alternative approaches to "development." Women's groups will have to be extremely vigilant over the coming decade if we are to transform the new rhetoric of human rights into concrete political action that benefits the most marginalized and impoverished, and not just the already empowered. But the Cairo Programme is nonetheless an important and potentially transformative step in a new direction. Its significance is underscored by the fact that, as this is written, the same forces that cast their reservations to the Cairo Programme are working hard to eliminate any "Cairo" influences from the platform to be debated in Beijing. In this sense, the ICPD story illustrates that new language, while insufficient in itself, is a critical step toward real political and social change.

References

Cook, R. J. (1992). International Protection of Women's Reproductive Rights. *New York University Journal of International Law and Politics, 24*, 645.

Cook, R. J. (1993). International Protection of Women's Reproductive Health. *Studies in Family Planning, 24*, 73-86.

Cook, R. J. (1994). *Women's Health and Human Rights.* Geneva: World Health Organization.

Copelon, R. & Hernandez, B. E. (1994). *Sexual and Reproductive Rights and Health as Human Rights: Concepts and Strategies—An Introduction for Activists.* New York: University of New York Law School, International Human Rights Law Clinic.

Correa, S. (1994). *Population and Reproductive Rights: Feminist Perspectives From the South.* London: Zed Books.

Correa, S., & Petchesky, R. (1994). Reproductive and Sexual Rights: A Feminist Perspective. In G. Sen, A. Germain, & L. C. Chen (Eds.), *Population Policies Reconsidered: Health, Empowerment and Rights* (pp. 107-126). Cambridge, MA: Harvard University Press.

Dairiam, S. (1994, September). Using the Human Rights System to Advance Reproductive Health and Rights. In *The Human Rights Dimensions of Reproductive Health.* ICPD NGO Forum conducted in Cairo, Egypt.

Freedman, L., & Isaacs, S. (1993). Human Rights and Reproductive Choice. *Studies in Family Planning, 24*, 18-30.

Hernandez, B. E. (1991). To Bear or not to Bear: Reproductive Freedom as an International Human Right. *Brooklyn Journal of International Law, 17*, 309.

International Women's Health Coalition. (1994). *Reproductive Health and Justice: International Women's Health Conference for Cairo '94, January 24-28, 1994 Rio de Janeiro.* New York: Author.

Petchesky, R. (1990). *Abortion and Women's Choice: The State, Sexuality and Reproductive Freedom* (2d ed.). Boston, MA: Northeastern University.

Plata, M. I. (1994). Reproductive Rights as Human Rights: The Colombian Case. In R. Cook (Ed.), *Human Rights of Women: National and International Perspectives* (pp. 515-531). Philadelphia: University of Pennsylvania Press.

R. v. Morgentaler, S.C.R. 30 (1988).

Toro, M. S. (1995). Popularizing Women's Human Rights at the Local Level: A Grassroots Methodology for Setting the International Agenda. In J. Peters & A. Wolper (Eds.), *Women's Rights: Human Rights: International Feminist Perspectives* (pp. 189-196). New York: Routledge Press

Chapter 21
Sexuality and Human Rights[1]
Yasmin Tambiah

Discussions of human sexuality and sexual behavior often give rise to a series of complex considerations and responses. This is particularly true when female sexuality is under scrutiny. While sexual interactions are a fundamental reality of social relations, the actual experiences of sexuality by girls and women are determined by a number of permissions and restrictions which seldom apply equally to boys and men. Such permissions and restrictions not only determine the expressions of female sexuality, but through sexuality influence all other aspects of the lives of girls and women.[2]

As the movement pressing for recognition of women's rights as women's human rights has gained increasing visibility and support worldwide, issues concerning sexuality have been pushed to the foreground. Not surprisingly, extreme contention has frequently accompanied this process. In the course of recent international fora and events, the debates and concerns that marked the generation of the Programme of Action of the International Conference on Population and Development (ICPD) in Cairo exemplify this. While the controversies and negotiations in Cairo and the implications of decisions that emerged there have been discussed thought-provokingly by Copelon and Petchesky in this volume, offered below is an example from the Cairo Programme of Action (henceforth the Cairo Document) to underscore the nature of the complications surrounding discussions on sexuality.

The Cairo Document recognizes the right to reproductive and sexual health as follows:

---

[1] My thanks to Ali Miller and Grace Poore for their thoughtful suggestions.
[2] Throughout the text I have referred either to both girls and women or to girls and women separately depending on the context. In some cases, girls are implicit in the term "women."

Reproductive health is a state of complete physical, mental and social well-being, and not merely the absence of disease or infirmity, in all matters relating to the reproductive system and to its functions and processes. Reproductive health therefore implies that people are able to have a satisfying and safe sex life and that they have the capability to reproduce and the freedom to decide if, when and how often to do so.... [Reproductive health care] also includes sexual health, the purpose of which is the enhancement of life and personal relations, and not merely counseling and care related to reproduction and sexually transmitted diseases (Chap. VII, Para. 7.2, Programme of Action, ICPD, 1994).

Based on definitions of health proposed by the World Health Organization[3] and in fundamental rights expressed in major international human rights instruments,[4] the Cairo Document is indisputably one of the most progressive statements acknowledging sexual activity as a positive aspect of human society to emerge recently through global consensus. However, it is evident that, although reproductive rights were acknowledged (even if after close and rancorous contestation) sexual rights per se and the obligations of states parties to guarantee the enjoyment of such rights remained extremely tentative.

The reservations concerning the express articulation of sexual rights appear to have been played out within the Cairo Document. In Chapter VII, Paragraph 7.2, the draft of the Document (1994) carried the bracketed statement: "Sexual and reproductive rights embrace certain human rights that are already recognized in various international human rights documents and in other documents reflecting international consensus." In the same paragraph, references to "sexual and reproductive health" were also bracketed. In the final Document, "reproductive rights" was retained while "sexual rights" was deleted; the language concerning the relationship between reproductive rights and other human rights was refined to include

---

[3] Constitution of the World Health Organization, opening principles:
"Health is a state of complete physical, mental and social well-being and not merely the absence of disease or infirmity...
The enjoyment of the highest attainable standard of health is one of the fundamental rights of every human being without distinction of race, religion, political belief, economic or social condition."
These were re-affirmed in the Declaration of Alma-Ata (International Conference on Primary Health Care) in 1978. The International Covenant on Economic, Social and Cultural Rights also recognizes the right to "the enjoyment of the highest attainable standard of physical and mental health" (Art. 12).

[4] See definitions of sexuality and sexual rights below.

national laws.[5] References to "reproductive and sexual health" were also retained (Chap. VII, Para. 7.4). Taken contextually within the final Document it appears that sexual health is inseparably linked with, and despite assertions to the contrary even subordinated to, reproductive health and parenthood. The language deletions also evince the reluctance and even opposition of most states parties to refine and retain the concept of sexual rights and to deal with the consequences of this retention. Such reservations, in turn, reflect the volatility of issues focusing on sexuality and sexual rights, especially for women.

Events at the ICPD consequently underscore the reality that sexuality is not a "private" matter. They also impress upon us that the definition of sexual rights and how the definition of such rights would affect the lives of girls and women must necessarily be accompanied by consideration of how the state currently influences the articulation and expression of female sexuality. This consideration is necessary to ensure that such rights, once articulated, are respected and realized by the state. It is also critical to consider how community[6] and family, independently of and in relation to the state, inform female sexuality. This paper examines the social organization of female sexuality and its consequences for girls and women, the role of the state in regulating female sexual behavior, and the uses and limitations of current human rights instruments in relation to female sexuality. Finally, it makes recommendations for the development and realization of sexual rights for women.

Defining Sexuality and Sexual Rights

The very definition of sexuality poses a challenge, not in the least because the term evokes a number of possibilities. For this paper, I suggest the following as a working definition: Sexuality is the wide range of erotic feelings and experiences, whether in relationship with the self or in interaction with others, where such interaction may take place between persons of similar or different biological sexes. Sexual activity is engaged in for pleasure (both solitary and mutual),

---

[5] Conditional upon paragraph 7.2, the text in the final Cairo Document now reads: "[R]eproductive rights embrace certain human rights that are already recognized in national laws, international human rights documents and other relevant United Nations consensus documents." (Ch. VII, Para. 7.3, Programme of Action, ICPD, 1994).

[6] Community may be ethnic, religious, cultural, class-determined, etc.

procreation or gendered social control, the last including prostitution, compulsory heterosexuality and other forms of coerced sexual behavior. This definition of sexuality informs the working definition of sexual rights.

As a working definition of sexual rights I have adapted bracketed language from the Draft Platform for Action for the Fourth World Conference on Women (1995):[7] Sexual rights include the individual's right to have control over and to decide freely in matters related to her or his sexuality, free of coercion, discrimination and violence. They include the right to information, so that informed decisions can be made about sexuality; the rights to dignity, privacy, and to physical, mental and moral integrity while realizing a sexual choice; and the right to the highest standard of sexual health.

This language has its roots in the Universal Declaration of Human Rights (UDHR) and the International Covenant on Civil and Political Rights (ICCPR), which affirm human dignity (UDHR Art. 1) and guarantee security of the person (UDHR Art. 3, ICCPR Art. 9); in regional conventions, such as the American Convention on Human Rights (Art. 5), that assure the rights to physical, mental and moral integrity; in the rights to privacy (ICCPR Art. 17), freedom of thought (ICCPR Art. 18) and to information (ICCPR Art. 19); and in the Cairo Document for the right to sexual health (see above). The working definition is framed by the recognition that the realization of economic rights for women are intimately linked with the realization of their sexual rights. To address the issues surrounding the articulation of, and the respect for, sexual rights the social organization of female sexuality needs to be examined.

The Social Organization of Female Sexuality

The social organization of female sexual behavior, along with reproductive behavior, is an area of intense contestation and reflects the formidable challenges girls and women face in their efforts to realize their sexual desire both as individuals and as members of

---

[7] Sexual rights include the individual's right to have control over and decide freely in matters related to her or his sexuality, free of coercion, discrimination and violence. Equal relationships between women and men in matters of sexual relations and reproduction, including full respect for the physical integrity of the human body, require mutual consent and willingness to accept responsibility for the consequences of sexual behavior. (Section C, Para. 97. Draft Platform for Action of the Fourth World Conference on Women, 1995.)

community. Women's attempts to assert their sexual autonomy are frequently opposed by family, society and the state, which seek to control it. The direction and outcome of such struggles are influenced by the material relationship between women and men, which is often one where girls and women are materially dependent on men. Women themselves engage in the contests for the control of their sexuality either as subjects, actively determining sexual behavior (whether or not in conformity with socially acceptable norms), or as objects of repressive social and state programs. While class status, ethnic, religious and cultural identity, age and citizenship, among other factors, profoundly affect the options available for girls and women to articulate and experience their sexuality, some generalizations are possible to highlight the tensions inherent in realizing female sexual agency.

The permissions and restrictions on female sexuality, whether they are experienced within the family, the community, or in relationship to the state, affect women from girlhood. It is therefore difficult to discuss sexuality meaningfully without addressing the impact of socio-sexual constructions on the female child. While the specific treatment of girl children varies depending on class and cultural context, in many communities, both rural and urban, a girl child's birth is heralded with fear. In a world where the preference for male children, influenced by patrilinear inheritance patterns, is still paramount, a girl child's arrival devalues the status of her mother within the larger family and compromises her father's virility. Simultaneously, her birth generates anxiety if family honor centers on the daughter's sexual conduct. This in turn is linked with the social and material implications for the rest of her family when (or if) she marries. The sexualizing of the female child begins, then, at birth and continues through childhood.

Socialization of the girl child is determined by the expectation that she will become a cooperative member in a society that is generally organized to ensure normative heterosexual behavior. In order to ensure such behavior, a society does not impose equal expectations (or restrictions) on both its female and male constituents. Male sexual desire and its satisfaction are frequently considered natural, legitimate and privileged while female sexual desire and its satisfaction are just as frequently considered unnatural, problematic, and fearful. These realities cut across class, ethnicity, religion and nationality (for example, Ogden, 1994; Thorbek, 1994; Atputharajah, 1990; Biale,

1984). The fear of female sexuality is responded to with attempts to contain, distort, and/or suppress autonomous female sexual desire through varying degrees of coercion, including violence.

Domestication[8] is an important means to contain female sexuality, and a process in which the family plays a key role. To this end the girl child is subjected to a series of contradictory messages. She is instructed to devalue her own body lest she be responsible for inciting unwarranted male attention. Simultaneously she is expected to cultivate the ability to hold male attention as a desirable wife. She is kept ignorant about her body because it is alleged that the less she knows about it, the less likely she is to explore her sexuality and therefore compromise her virginity. At the same time, however, she is expected to develop a healthy and knowledgeable attitude towards motherhood. Sometimes such forced ignorance may extend to extreme physiological distortions, such as female circumcision, intended to mute any possibility of sexual curiosity and expression (see Abdel Halim and Nwashili in this volume).

These contradictions and forced ignorance can result in serious consequences. For instance, a girl or young woman who is curious about her body and who wants to express her erotic desire with a male partner but who, having little knowledge about the consequences of heterosexual intercourse, has sex without appropriate protection, may risk pregnancy or infection with a sexually transmitted disease. In addition, in several cultural contexts, she would risk extreme censure and even death by her family members for her self-chosen pre-marital sexual activity (Hawkins & Meshesha, 1994; Heise, Moore & Toubia, 1995). In contrast, while a boy or young man who is curious about heterosexual sex may run the same risk regarding sexually transmitted diseases, pregnancy and its consequences are not an issue. Societal expectations of male sexual behavior, while acknowledging positively his pre-marital (and sometimes extra-marital) sexual experiences, may go so far as to absolve him of the responsibilities of impregnation and fatherhood (Corona, 1995).

Forced ignorance about the female body also allows for silence around sexual violation of female children.[9] A girl who is sexually

---

[8] I.e. the confining of female productive and reproductive labor, sexuality, intellectual and psychological development etc. to the needs of the domestic unit or environment, including care of children and males of different ages.

[9] Sexual abuse of the girl child occurs globally. In their study Heise, Pitanguy and

abused often cannot discuss the violation with her mother or other adult women because she is compelled to feel that it is her fault. This is aggravated if discussing sexual matters or obtaining information about the female body is taboo, which in turn may prevent a girl from fully understanding what she has experienced and the consequences of that experience even though she may instinctively grasp that she has been violated. If she does divulge what happened, she risks disbelief and a complete negation of her experience, or punishment by her elders, including death, for dishonoring her family (examples from Asia Watch, 1992, and Human Rights Watch, 1994; Hawkins & Meshesha, 1994).

When a society is organized so that heterosexuality is normative, rather than one of several viable choices, all other possibilities are consequently marginalized or suppressed. This organization has an impact on the sexual awareness of all girls and the legitimated choices available to them. It has special implications for the girl child or young woman who is a lesbian. First, the deliberate withholding of (unbiased) information on alternatives to heterosexuality, such as auto-sexuality,[10] homosexuality and bisexuality, is usually intrinsic to maintaining a situation of mandatory heterosexuality. This action denies any girl child (or woman) the conceptual space and imaginative tools to develop an informed understanding of the spectrum of her sexual desire and how she can express it. For the young lesbian the lack of means to validate her growing sexual awareness, including the extremely limited or non-existent social support for her choice, often translates into severe self-doubt that is manifested as isolation, depression, self-destructive behavior such as alcohol or drug addiction, and attempted suicide (NCLR Newsletter, 1995 Spring; Dorf & Careaga, 1995). Second, in cultural contexts where (girl) child marriage is still the norm, the girl child is again compelled into heterosexuality, being denied the opportunity to develop an understanding of her sexuality and eventually to exercise an informed, autonomous choice, whether this choice is to be heterosexual, homosexual, or other. The psychological and physiological traumas that accompany forced sexual activity intrinsic to such early marriage places the girl child/young woman at enormous risk, both personally and socially

---

Germaine (1994) cite data from Peru, Malaysia, Mexico, Papua New Guinea, USA, Nigeria, and Barbados.

[10] An erotic/sexual relationship with the self. This may be part of, or separate from, a sexual relationship with a partner.

(Nwashili in this volume). Third, the range of penalties for engaging in activity other than heterosexuality are also aimed at preempting challenges to the sexual status quo. A young lesbian's attempts to resist participation in a heterosexually organized community are frequently met with opposition, ranging from a lack of support and harassment by peers in age, to efforts at coercive change from guardian adults. Attempts to heterosexualize her may range from electroshock, drug and other types of "corrective" therapy (NCLR Newsletter, 1994 Spring and Fall; Dorf & Careaga, 1995) to forced marriage. In India, for example, young women who are to be forcibly married, whether or not their families suspect or know that they are intimates, have attempted suicide together to preempt separation.[11]

While girl children are particularly vulnerable to constraints upon the development of their sexuality, adult women face a series of choices and challenges with regard to exercising an informed, autonomous choice about their sexual activity. The respect accorded to women socially is frequently marked by their sexual behavior, real or imagined. While men also may be marked by their sexual behavior, the social repercussions are not identical. For example, a woman who has several male friends may be identified as a "slut" while a man with female friends is called a "ladies' man;" a woman who actively enjoys sex may be called a "nymphomaniac" while a man is deemed "virile;" and a woman who does not wish to make herself sexually available to men may be termed "frigid" while a man in a parallel situation may simply be considered "shy." The consequences of such naming inform marriage options for women, and have implications within marriage itself.

Society is usually organized such that (heterosexual) marriage and motherhood are the markers of social responsibility and respectability. These arrangements provide legitimized social space for particular types of sexual activity. Sex with one's spouse is expected and, in societies where an unmarried woman may be closely monitored to ensure that she does not engage in transgression that could be interpreted as sexual, even to the point that any privacy is denied, marriage secures for a woman both validated (hetero)sexual activity as well as some semblance of socially acknowledged privacy within which to realize her desire. For a woman who has had the

---

[11] Information from Sakhi, the lesbian resource center in New Delhi, India; and *Anamika* (Vol. 1 #3), a South Asian lesbian newsletter which has ceased publication.

opportunity to make an informed decision about her choice of male partner and who enters marriage without coercion or material dependency and without compromising a range of other rights,[12] it provides the space to develop a mutually satisfying sexual relationship. The need for a married woman's sexual satisfaction independent of pregnancy is even recognized explicitly as a right by some religions, notably Judaism (Biale, 1984) and Islam (Musallam, 1983).

Marriage, however, also brings with it danger. Women may be denied the space to negotiate the occasions and conditions for sexual activity and, by extension, sexual safety and pregnancy. Because several communities still assume that marriage gives a man automatic sexual access to his spouse, many women around the world continue to be subjected to marital rape (Heise et al., 1994) and have no recourse either in communal support or in law (IWLD, forthcoming).[13] In contexts where extra-marital male sexual activity is tolerated, a woman's insistence that her male partner wear a condom may be met with violence, either because it is perceived that, by this request, the woman is "insinuating her infidelity" (Heise et al., 1994, p. 27), questioning the man's rights to multiple relationships, or interfering with his physical pleasure (which the condom is viewed as restricting).

Societies that construct the institution of marriage as the only legitimate venue for sexual intimacy de-legitimize other choices many women actually make about their sexual lives, irrespective of whether or not such sexual activity outside marriage is carried out in socially responsible ways. For instance, a women who chooses to cohabit with a male partner without marriage may be subjected to disparaging treatment by her community, and face graver risks than her partner because of the association between female sexual behavior and female honor, and by extension the honor of her family and

---

[12] Marriage does not always carry privileges for women. Married women, for example, can lose their rights to nationality (see McIvor in this volume; IWLD, forthcoming), to contractual capacity, and to make decisions concerning employment and birth control without spousal approval (IWLD, forthcoming).

[13] The IWLD survey notes Brazil, Croatia, Japan and Turkey, among others, as states that have not criminalized marital rape; India considers it criminal only if the female partner is under 15 years. According to the National Clearinghouse on Marital and Date Rape (USA), 31 states in the USA have yet to legislate that marital rape is a crime under all circumstances where a woman does not explicitly exercise her choice to have sex with her spouse.

community in relation to the rest of society. An even harsher communal reception frequently awaits a woman who chooses to live openly with a female partner.[14] This may range from complete denial of the nature of the relationship because lesbian sexual activity is unimaginable, to hostility manifested as job discrimination and loss of employment, to overt violence such as assault, rape and murder because a lesbian relationship explicitly defies the stereotype of female sexual subordination to the male.[15]

Some human rights advocates and feminists have been complicit in perpetuating societal homophobia (fear of homosexuality), and have marginalized or silenced lesbians within and outside their organizations.[16] Others have been reluctant to raise issues of sexual rights in general, and lesbian rights in particular, claiming that to raise such issues in public fora would jeopardize the women's movement in their countries (Anu & Aziz, 1988), or implying that the need of lesbians to live with dignity, free from coercion into heterosexuality, is insignificant when compared with other fundamental needs such as food and shelter.[17] Creating a hierarchy

---

[14] Some societies, especially those that are "homosocial" (i.e. where boys and men socialize almost exclusively with each other and girls and women with each other) may accommodate homosexual activity as long as it is neither publicized nor politicized. In such societies heterosexual marriage remains the only legally acknowledged and socially accepted domestic unit and site of sexual activity, with the result that homosexual activity is considered, at best, secondary to heterosexual marital activity and, at worst, an aberration that needs to be cured or punished.

[15] Dorf and Careaga (1995) cite examples from Russia, Peru, Mexico, USA and elsewhere.

[16] In a recent example, two women in a lesbian relationship were fired from a human rights organization in the Philippines when their relationship was made public. Several women's rights advocates have protested this and are assisting the two women to bring their case to court (International Gay and Lesbian Human Rights Commission, 1994).

[17] See, for example, Chandra Muzaffar's article, *Setting Western Standards for Human Freedom* (1992). Criticizing the 1991 UNDP Human Freedom Index for not reflecting Third World priorities, Muzaffar highlights the right to "homosexuality between consenting adults" to underscore his point. He has no issue with freedoms such as the rights to peaceful assembly, unrestricted religious practice, independent courts, independent radio and television networks, and freedom from torture or coercion being important in the Third World, even though, as he points out, freedom from hunger, disease, illiteracy etc. are excluded from the Index. But it is homosexuality that signals to him the "Western cultural bias" of the Index. Muzaffar plays on the homophobia of certain Third World communi-

among fundamental rights such as the rights to basic material needs and the rights to life and to physical and mental integrity results in a disservice to *all* women, and compels us into choices that undermine the enjoyment of human rights in the full spectrum of their indivisibility.

The problematic perceptions of female sexuality and societal attempts to control it are also influenced by and reflected in processes that compel a woman to exchange her capacities for sexual pleasure (and motherhood) for material maintenance by a male, regardless of how she may actually wish to express her sexuality. Girls and young women are frequently discouraged from furthering their education or job-training skills because their families and communities believe that marriage and childbearing, defined as inevitable, make such education extraneous. In addition, it is sometimes believed that sending a girl to school after she attains puberty may place her in situations where her virginity risks compromise. Not only is it expected that a daughter/daughter-in-law/wife will dedicate her time and energy exclusively to her family, but also that her education, which may herald independent thinking and action, would challenge the authority of her husband. In particular, there is the fear that her economic independence would translate into opportunities for extra-marital sexual encounters.

The relationship between economic independence and marital status also has serious ramifications for the unmarried woman. Because a "single" woman is read as sexually unfettered, unmarried women are debilitated in several ways. In South Asia, for example, an unmarried woman has great difficulty finding housing to live independently of her parents or other chaperones. Her "single" (or "spinster") status determines the jobs she can get. For a career women, it also determines the places she can be posted to and thus affects her chances for professional advancement. Women who exercise economic independence by working away from home, whether or not they are married, may also risk sexualized violence, such as sexual

---

ties to indicate that homosexuality is a "Western" matter and thereby to negate the struggles of lesbians and gay men, in both the West and the Third World, for the human rights to dignity, freedom from discrimination and from violence. In addition, his critique takes into account neither the gendered experience of human rights violations, nor that women frequently have been excluded from the enjoyment of the Third World "communal" rights that he posits in opposition to the "individual" rights of the West.

harassment and rape, experiences that are used to justify their confinement to the domestic unit. When coupled with a range of systemic inequalities, including gender-determined wage disparities, and compounded by communal and national dictates (such as high levels of unemployment and the consequences of structural adjustment programs), the express denial of opportunities for women to develop economic independence is closely linked with the sexual choices they may be able to exercise. Where opportunities for economic independence are limited marriage, like prostitution, may become compulsory, and the exchange of female productive and reproductive labor (including sexual activity) for male material maintenance becomes explicit.

Sexuality and the State

The communal organization and policing of sexuality frequently finds its counterpart in the state, whether in the process of state-formation or in the maintenance of an established one. Given that colonial and neo-colonial processes are intimately linked with the reformulation of gender relations, and consequently with sexuality, nationalist and revolutionary movements have in turn had an impact on the possibilities and realities of the sexual behaviors of its participants. With few exceptions, such movements have circumscribed female sexual agency, confining it to "mothers of the nation," i.e., domesticated procreation (e.g. Davies, 1983; Moghadam, 1992) or to the (unmarried) female fighter who is expected either to be asexual or sexually available to her male counterparts (e.g. Davies, 1983; Kannabiran & Lalitha, 1990). Nationalist men, in their opposition to the colonizer, may strive to neutralize or to control the perceived threat by pro-active female sexuality, while nationalist women may attempt to use the spaces opening up through political participation to explore the possibilities for change in their lives, both sexual and otherwise. These contests are played out in heterosexualized terrain, i.e., while there is recognition of women's desire for men and vice-versa, however problematically this may be articulated, there is little room for the lesbian in the "new" state (Tambiah, 1993).

An established state continues to influence the sexual behavior of its citizens. A government may legislate sexual behavior in a number of ways. It may do so indirectly through the social and economic policies it endorses. For example, it may give special tax breaks to

married heterosexual couples but not recognize other domestic partnerships for this privilege; it may automatically allow a husband and
wife to travel abroad or immigrate together but disallow this option
for other types of partnership. Or the state may legislate sexual behavior directly by alleging concerns for public morality and health,
e.g., by criminalizing homosexuality or by regulating prostitution.[18]
Such legislation on sexuality results in legalizing some types of activity, notably that which is directed at procreation and engaged in
within marriage, while making others illegal, notably that which is
non-procreative and pleasure oriented (Alexander, 1994), thereby
directly determining who qualifies to be a citizen and, by extension,
who is deserving of protection by the state. Consequently, such
actions by the state bring into question the experience of "privacy" in
relation to sexual activity. Examples that highlight the tensions between the rights to sexual activity and privacy on the one hand, and
what the state perceives as its interests on the other are the virginity-
control tests in Turkey, consequences of the *Hudood* ordinances in
Pakistan, the persecution of lesbians (and gay men) in Romania and
Iran (Amnesty International, 1994), and the debates and legislation
on sexual behavior within and outside marriage in Trinidad and Tobago in the mid-1980s. Some of these are discussed below.

The virginity control examinations in Turkey exemplify how the
state colludes with familial and communal values concerning female
sexuality and its regulation, and serves its own needs while contra-
vening both the constitutional rights and human rights of its female
citizens.[19] The tests are usually conducted by state doctors at the behest of parents and other community authorities to determine if a
girl's or woman's hymen is intact when her social behavior is regarded as suspect. This is justified on the basis of social and legal arrangements where female sexual behavior is intimately linked with
family honor,[20] and by extension, it would seem, with the honor of

---

[18] In the case of prostitution, the state may even act covertly to gain material profit
from the regulation of female sexuality while simultaneously violating fundamental human rights. This is exemplified by the instances of forced prostitution of
girls and women across national boundaries with the complicity of state officials
(Asia Watch, 1993).

[19] The details of this example are from Human Rights Watch (1994).

[20] Sexual crimes against women in Turkey are legally classified as "Felonies Against
Public Decency and Family Order." In comparison, other assaults are classified as
"Felonies Against Individuals" (Human Rights Watch, 1994, p. 7).

the state. A woman who has compromised her virginity compromises her family, her chances of marriage and, if she does marry, her treatment by her husband. So intrusive is this procedure and so hostile the possible consequences that young women forcibly subjected to these tests have sometimes committed suicide.

State agents have also used this milieu of sexual suspicion against women who are perceived as politically and socially disruptive. Virginity exams have been performed by the police on female political detainees, allegedly to protect the police from charges of sexual abuse. They have also been performed on women suspected of engaging in "illegal" prostitution.[21] In the latter instance, women engaged in social activities without acceptable male chaperones have been harassed by the police. In a society where it is believed that any woman not closely monitored by (male) authority must necessarily be engaged in illicit sexual activity, even though consensual sex between unmarried heterosexual adults is not illegal in Turkey, any independent activity by a woman (whether dining at a restaurant with women friends or driving a car alone late at night) becomes suspect. The commission of virginity exams by the Turkish state explicitly violates women's rights to equal protection under the law, to physical and mental integrity, to security of the person, and to privacy.

The Pakistani case of the *Hudood* ordinances exemplifies the consequences when the dictates of fundamentalist religious movement, characterized among others by the need to control closely female sexual behavior, influence the definitions and practice of the state's obligations towards its female citizenry. The *Hudood* ordinances, which were put into effect as part of the increasing islamization of Pakistani society in the late 1970s, have had a profound impact on the definition and experience of sexuality for women, both within and outside marriage. Most critical here is the crime of *zina*, illegal sexual activity such as adultery and fornication. Under this new law a girl or woman victimized by rape may find herself charged and punished as a co-participant in *zina*. She may be unable to obtain a conviction of her assailant if she fails to demonstrate to the court that she defended herself with the requisite amount of force, or if the court deems her a woman of "easy virtue" (Mahmood, 1989). Simultaneously, given that four male witnesses are required to convict a perpetrator of rape, an alleged rapist can have his charge reduced to a

---

[21] Legal prostitutes are registered as such in Turkey.

lesser offense or even be acquitted. There are examples where the victim of rape has been punished for *zina* on the basis of her pregnancy by that rape, while the offender has been freed due to lack of evidence (Asia Watch, 1992). In addition, under the new law, marital rape is no longer recognized. Consequently, while it precludes premarital sexual activity between consenting adults and confines sex to marriage, this law also effectively denies married women both the space to negotiate their sexual activity and protection from the violation of the right to physical and mental integrity.[22]

The last example points to a more subtle delineation of normative sexuality and state protection. In 1986, the government of Trinidad and Tobago engaged in a series of debates and enacted a consolidated body of legislation, the Sexual Offenses Act, on unlawful sexual behavior. In this process it defined what constituted normative sexuality for its citizenry. The clearest example lies in the move by the state to intervene in domestic violence, where marital rape, defined as the act whereby any "husband" had forceful intercourse with his "wife" without her consent, was criminalized for the first time[23] (Alexander, 1994, p. 8). Simultaneously the state, also for the first time, explicitly criminalized lesbian sexual activity, defining it as "serious indecency" punishable by five years in prison (Alexander, 1994, p. 8). By placing lesbian sexual activity in the same category as marital rape, the law equates lesbians with husbands who rape their wives. It removes lesbians from the group of citizens who qualify to be protected by the law, i.e., married women and heterosexuals (ostensibly anyone whose sensibilities would be violated by the "serious indecency" of lesbians), and therefore from citizenry itself. Other categories of sexual behavior listed under the Sexual Offenses Act include prostitution and gay male sexual activity, both of which had been criminalized under British colonial rule. Ironically, in re-criminalizing homosexual activity the post-colonial state,[24] reluctant to reckon with the histories of indigenous homosexual behaviors and anxious to define homosexuality as a colonial import or

---

[22] Families too, especially male relatives, have used the *Hudood* Ordinances to curtail women's rights in areas such as the freedom of movement, choice of marriage partner and rights at divorce (Asia Watch, 1992).

[23] This came at the end of a bitter parliamentary and public debate about the sexual definition of marriage, especially whether marriage existed to provide men with sex on demand, irrespective of spousal consent (see Alexander, 1994).

[24] A post-colonial state is one that was formerly a colony.

consequence, chose to retain or re-work colonial laws to condemn supposedly colonial behavior.

A very recent example of the sexual ordering of the post-colonial state is evident in the uproar surrounding the use of the term "gender" in the Draft Platform for Action for the Fourth World Conference on Women ('Gender' a fighting word, 1995). While the term "gender" has long been used in formal United Nations documents, some Southern government delegates argued that gender is being used to refer to homosexuality, lesbianism and bisexuality, rather than simply "men and women" in the Draft Platform. Taken together with references to "permissive" European societies (the opposition to which, ironically, become "repressive" societies, such as Honduras and Sudan which collapsed 'gender' with 'homosexuality') it is evident that authorities in some post-colonial states rely on a mixture of anti-Northern sentiment, homophobia and fear of any autonomous female sexuality to deflect attention away from issues that are critically important to the vast majority of women in the South. Through lesbian-baiting, the definition of "gender" is made into a Northern agenda, and consequently relieves certain Southern governments of their obligation to honor the Platform for Action and meet their commitments to their entire female citizenry.

The above examples delineate some of the ways in which state actions block the rights of women to realize their sexual needs in an informed, secure and independent manner. The final section of this paper briefly examines how useful international human rights instruments and laws are in guaranteeing choice and protection for the realization of autonomous female sexuality.

Human Rights Instruments and Women's Sexual Rights

Given the reservation and reticence of most states regarding the express articulation of matters concerning sexuality, it is not surprising that most international human rights instruments, while they formally address rights that cover critical areas of human life and interaction, make no explicit commitments to the right to, or protection of, sexual activity, whether of the self or between informed and freely consenting partners. Convention articles that touch upon this aspect of human relationships focus exclusively on marriage. For instance, Paragraphs 1 and 2 of Article 16 of the Universal Declaration of Human Rights assert that women (and men) of "full age" have the right to enter into marriage and to found a family. Marriage is to be entered into of their own free and full consent, and equal rights are to prevail during and at the dissolution of marriage. While the rights articulated in this instrument can be used to strengthen the struggles for fair treatment for a married woman, including the right to express and satisfy her sexual needs within marriage, the language of articulation offers no recognition to intimate social arrangements outside marriage, whether such arrangements are heterosexual or homosexual. In fact, taken together with Paragraph 3, which recognizes the family as "the natural and fundamental group unit of society" and entitles it "to protection by society and the state," the married heterosexual couple are elevated as the twin poles of the so-called primary building block of society to the exclusion of other pervasive realities, such as single mothers, female-headed households, lesbian parents or other familial and domestic arrangements that are not premised on the heterosexual nuclear model. (Unmarried heterosexual parents or partners living together sometimes find themselves subsumed under "marriage,"[25] but do not have a universal guarantee of such recognition.) The non-recognition of other arrangements also signals that states, while they are willing to protect the family as the fundamental social unit, are often unwilling to support the initiatives women themselves take to organize their lives, intimate relationships and communal responsibilities, including their families, in ways that women, given their life conditions, determine to be the most satisfying.

The UDHR's rights in marriage are echoed in Article 16 of the Convention on the Elimination of All Forms of Discrimination Against Women (CEDAW), with not insignificant elaborations. At points (d) through (f), marital status is declared secondary to the responsibilities of motherhood, and point (e) explicitly recognizes the right to education and other means for reproductive regulation. However, CEDAW too does not make any significant attempt to recognize alternatives to the coupled (or spousal) heterosexual unit and related family.[26]

Such limitations notwithstanding, human rights instruments have been used as a basis for arguing for the right to informed and consensual sexual activity outside heterosexual marriage, and advocates for

---

[25] I.e. common law marriage. See Helfer, 1991.

[26] See CEDAW, Article 5 where the reference to "common responsibility" for child rearing presumes again a coupled heterosexual unit.

women's sexual rights, whether within or outside marriage, would find the processes instructive. It is not surprising that the most significant of these cases have focused on challenging national laws that have declared homosexuality illegal and justified the persecution of lesbians and gay men (Helfer, 1991; Amnesty International, 1994). Critical to these efforts is Article 12 in the Universal Declaration of Human Rights, which is Article 17 in the International Covenant on Civil and Political Rights (ICCPR), which guarantees an individual the right to protection from arbitrary interference in privacy, family, home and correspondence. Based on this right to privacy, and provisions such as the right to physical and mental integrity as evinced from the European Convention for the Protection of Human Rights and Freedoms (Art. 3), human rights advocates have successfully challenged legislation that opposes consensual homosexual activity in most member states of the European Union. (Helfer, 1991; Ermanski, 1992).

Basing the articulation of the right to sexual activity outside the perimeters of heterosexual marriage on the right to privacy has, however, revealed the limitations of this strategy. The right to privacy (especially as articulated in the European Convention), like Article 19 in the ICCPR, which is the right to freedom of expression and the seeking, receiving and imparting of information and ideas, is conditional upon the rights of others and upon national security, public order, public health and morals. While this condition does not empower the state to act arbitrarily, but rather according to international human rights law, the fact that sexual rights are nowhere explicitly articulated as such, but dependent upon other conditionalities, such as privacy, make them especially vulnerable to compromise. (Privacy, for instance, is not an actual experience for many people globally, whether on account of very limited separate physical space or of social norms that do not value privacy, especially for women.) Given the often severe circumscription that female sexuality is already subjected to, women are more likely than men to have communal and state concerns for public order, public health and morals used against them, as demonstrated in the example of Turkey above.

Conclusion

For the majority of women and girls around the world, developing a healthy awareness of sexual needs and exercising sexual choice with dignity, integrity and safety remain a significant challenge. This is particularly true if a woman or girl decides to live her sexual life in an arrangement outside heterosexual marriage. Most families, communities and states are opposed to empowering women to make autonomous decisions about their sexual lives, whether alone or in partnership, whether in marriage or outside it.

If the attainment of the highest quality of life is a fundamental right, then no woman or girl should be compelled to compromise her sexual rights so that she can exercise her other rights as a member of a community or a citizen of a state. Women's human rights advocates internationally need to make a powerful argument for sexual rights on the basis of existing human rights instruments. If this struggle is to merit legitimacy equal to other initiatives for civil, political, economic, social and cultural rights for women, then it requires the explicit articulation of sexual rights without masking these rights with other language or subordinating them to other conditionalities. It may even require a new convention. And that may be the final battle in the human rights arena.

Some recommendations

1. Girl children and women should have the right to education about their bodies, including sex education. The latter should include the right to information about different types of sexual behavior presented objectively. The right to such education can be based on the Convention on the Rights of the Child, CEDAW, Article 19 of the UDHR, and the Cairo Programme of Action.
2. Women need to guarantee to each other, and to girls they are guardians to, the right to choose their sexual partners without coercion. As much as possible, they should provide each other with the security to realize their sexual desire in an informed manner without threat to their health or to their bodily and mental integrity.
3. The meanings and experiences of marriage, and the relationships between marriage, material support and women's sexual autonomy need to be thoughtfully assessed by women in different cultural and political contexts. Such assessment may help women

clarify both what is gained and what is lost through marriage, and awareness about what constitutes women's sexual rights within marriage and outside it.

4. NGOs should organize campaigns aimed at outlawing attempts to regulate female sexuality by means such as electro-shock and "corrective" therapy, whether administered by private individuals or the state.

5. NGOs should facilitate fora where girls and women can conscientize and organize themselves in order to challenge attempts to control female sexuality by communal authorities, local governments and states that use the rationale that women who do not conform to normative heterosexuality and related domestic arrangements (such as women in prostitution, lesbians, and single parents) are the root cause of societal disintegration.

6. Women's rights advocates need to reinterpret current human rights instruments to cover sexuality as well as lobby appropriate international bodies, either to amend existing instruments or to generate a new convention, so that sexual rights are explicitly defined and guaranteed as inalienable fundamental rights.

References

Alexander, J. (1994, Autumn). Not Just (Any) Body can be a Citizen: The Politics of Law, Sexuality and Postcoloniality in Trinidad and Tobago and the Bahamas. *Feminist Review*, 5-23.

Amnesty International. (1994). *Breaking the Silence: Human Rights Violations Based on Sexual Orientation*. New York: Author.

Anu & Aziz. (1988, March). Lesbianism: A Political Issue. *Trikone, 3*(2), 4-5.

Asia Watch & Women's Rights Project. (1992). *Double Jeopardy: Abuse of Women in Pakistan*. Washington DC: Human Rights Watch.

Asia Watch & Women's Rights Project. (1993). *A Modern Form of Slavery: Trafficking of Burmese Women and Girls into Brothels in Thailand*. Washington DC: Human Rights Watch.

Atputharajah, V. (1990). *Sexual Behaviour of Women in Singapore*. Singapore: PG Publishing.

Biale, R. (1984) *Women and Jewish Law: An Examination of Women's Issues in Halakhic Sources*. New York: Schocken Books.

Brownlie, I. (Ed.). (1992). *Basic Documents on Human Rights* (3rd ed.). Oxford: Clarendon Press.

Corona E. (1995/1). Teen Sexuality and Development Paradigms. *Women's Health Journal, Latin American and Caribbean Women's Health Network,* 51-53.

Davies, M. (1983). *Third World, Second Sex.* London: Zed.

Dorf J. & Careaga Perez, G. (1995). Discrimination and the Tolerance of Difference. In J. Peters & A. Wolper (Eds.), *Women's Rights, Human Rights: International Feminist Perspectives* (pp. 324-334). New York: Routledge.

Draft Platform for Action of the Fourth World Conference on Women. (1995). [U.N. Doc. A/CONF.177/L.1 May 1995]. New York: United Nations.

Draft Programme of Action of the United Nations International Conference on Population and Development. (1994). [U.N. Doc. A/CONF.171/L.1 13 (1994)]. New York: ICPD Secretariat, United Nations.

Ermanski, R. (1992, Winter). A Right to Privacy for Gay People Under International Human Rights Law. *Boston College International and Comparative Law Review,* 141-164.

"Gender" a Fighting Word to UN Female Delegates: Talks Turn Rancorous Over Definition of Term. (1995, April 8). *The Washington Post,* p.1.

Hawkins, K. & Meshesha, B. (1994). Reaching Young People: Ingredients of Effective Programs. In G. Sen, A. Germain & L. C. Chen (Eds.), *Population Policies Reconsidered: Health, Empowerment and Rights* (pp. 211-222). Boston: Harvard University Press.

Heise, L., Pitanguy, J. & Germain A. (1994). *Violence Against Women: The Hidden Health Burden.* Washington DC: World Bank.

Heise, L., Moore, K. & Toubia, N. (1995). *Sexual Coercion and Reproductive Health: A Focus on Research.* New York: The Population Council.

Helfer, L. (1991, Fall). Lesbian and Gay Rights as Human Rights: Strategies for a United Europe. *Virginia Journal of International Law, 32*(1), 157-212.

Human Rights Watch, Women's Rights Project. (1994). *A Matter of Power: State Control of Women's Virginity in Turkey.* Washington DC: Human Rights Watch.

Institute for Women, Law and Development. (Forthcoming). *Gender Aspects of Legal Discrimination.* Washington DC: Author.

International Gay and Lesbian Human Rights Commission. (1994, November/December). Lesbians Fired in the Philippines. *Action Alert,* 2-3.

Kannabiran V. & Lalitha, K. (1990). That Magic Time: Women in the Telengana People's Struggle. In K. Sangari & S. Vaid (Eds.), *Recasting Women: Essays in Indian Colonial History* (pp. 180-203). New Brunswick: Rutgers University Press.

Mahmood, M. (1989). *Enforcement of Hudood: Practice and Procedure.* Lahore, Pakistan: Pakistan Law Times Publications.

Moghadam, V. (1992). Revolution, Islam and Women: Sexual Politics in Iran and Afghanistan. In A. Parker, M. Russo, D. Sommer & P. Yaeger (Eds.), *Nationalisms and Sexuality* (pp. 424-446). New York: Routledge.

Musallam, B. F. (1983). *Sex and Society in Islam: Birth Control Before the Nineteenth Century.* Cambridge: Cambridge University Press.

Muzaffar, C. (1992, March). Setting Western Standards for Human Freedom. *Law and Society Trust, II*(34), 1-4.

National Center for Lesbian Rights. (1994, 1995). *Newsletter.*

Ogden, G. (1994, Summer). Women Who Love Sex. *On the Issues,* 44-45.

Programme of Action of the United Nations International Conference on Population and Development. (1994). [U.N. Doc. A/CONF.171/13 (1994)]. New York: ICPD Secretariat, United Nations.

Tambiah, Y. (1993, December). *Decolonization and Third World Lesbian Identities: A South Asian Perspective.* Paper presented at seminar on The History of Alternate Sexualities and the Construction of Gender in South Asia, New Delhi, India.

Thorbek, S. (1994). *Gender and Slum Culture in Urban Asia.* (B. Fredsfod, Trans.). London: Zed.

Chapter 22
Rights and Reproductive Technologies

Gita Sen

Debates about reproductive technology have come a long way since the 1960s when the introduction and rapid proliferation of new methods captured the public imagination. These appeared at the time to foreshadow an expansion of choices, greater control and autonomy over reproductive decision making and liberation for women from a reproductively defined destiny. But challenges by women from countries in the South (and from poor and minority groups everywhere) to coercive fertility control policies and programs and by women from the North to the "medicalization" of women's bodies, have expanded the debate about the real meaning of choices and autonomy.

Recent involvement by women activists in shaping the global human rights agenda has had a strong positive influence in sharpening and clarifying these debates around reproductive technology. At the same time, the debates have become more complex and difficult. In part this is because of the rapid and indeed bewildering proliferation of new reproductive technologies for fertility management and diagnostics, the expansion of systemic, hormonal contraceptives and the impending entry of biotechnologies in contraceptive research. Each cluster of technologies has raised a new set of complex ethical issues (Sen & Snow, 1994). But the debate is also complicated by deteriorating conditions of life and livelihood for many people, which have heightened concern over coercion and the potential for abuse in the research, testing, and promotion of new technologies.

Choices and Conflicts

Does the proliferation of reproductive technologies expand women's choices and enhance their ability to control their lives? Many proponents of mainstream population policies would give an unequivocally affirmative answer. They believe that technological advances have made it possible for women and men to decide whether and when to have children and to greatly reduce the risks of childbirth itself. Providers of new reproductive services such as in-vitro fertilization argue similarly that they are expanding the choices available to both individuals and to couples and are making it possible for those who could not have children otherwise to do so. Fetal diag-nostics is seen by many, both in the medical community and outside, as purely a health measure intended to guarantee against severe ge-netic disorders. By doing so, they argue, technology has opened up the possibility for women to realize their potential outside their re-productive capacity and to lead richer and more fulfilling lives.

Others, including many women's health activists, take a more skeptical stand. Between technology and the women (and men) it is supposed to serve stand a host of social mediations. It is these inter-vening determinants that govern the effects of technology. The re-productive biologist or biomedical researcher deals with an individual suspended, as it were, outside her or his socioeconomic and cultural milieu. But it is the latter that determines whether the availability of a particular technology implies genuine access, free of coercion. Technology, in this view, is not manna from heaven, an unmixed blessing that falls directly into the hands of the user. Social factors govern who comes to control any particular technology and deter-mine under what conditions it becomes available to the user. More fundamentally, perhaps, the social milieu actually shapes what kinds of technologies are developed, and to what end.

This concern with "context" often has been downplayed by the developers and funders of reproductive technology research as a sec-ondary issue, one that needs to be addressed only in particular cir-cumstances. Thus one often hears rebuttals to the effect that the problem is not one of the technology itself but of the context, imply-ing thereby that if the context could be improved then the problem would cease. How valid is such a position for the kinds of reproduc-tive technologies that are currently being tested and promoted? Is the context an issue only in some circumstances and countries and not in others?

The most central aspect of the context which governs the rela-tionship between reproductive technology and its end user is gender compounded by class, ethnic origin, caste or other social relations of power. These include the relationships, beliefs and practices which shape the perspectives and biases of policy makers and implementers, researchers and technology developers, and the field level staff of family planning or other programs. The context also varies across countries and socioeconomic groups.

Context

Key aspects of the context include (1) women's (and men's) poverty, nutrition, health, and work status; (2) the quality of and access to primary and referral health services; (3) access to facilities for clean water and sanitation; (4) access to quality contraceptive services, as well as legal and safe abortion; (5) access to legal protection and redress of technology-related grievances; and (6) a vigilant and interested media, a non-governmental sector and other democratic institutions. Thus the context includes the character of gender relations, economic factors affecting livelihoods and quality of life, social development policies affecting the availability of crucial services, and the strength of the legal and other institutions of civil society.

Each of the above has implications for technology at any or all of three levels: the choice of what technologies are developed or become available; methods of testing and criteria for assessment; and the conditions of distribution and use.

Choice of Technologies

Why are some technologies developed and not others? Where reproductive technologies[1] are concerned, three types of forces appear to determine the answer to this question: (1) potential profits and, more broadly, economic incentives to developers; (2) the professional interests and career advancement or other goals, as well as the gender or other perspectives of researchers who are largely male; and (3) the pressure of population *controlistas* who are concerned to find and support the most efficacious techniques (especially techniques that can most easily be controlled by service providers rather than users).

Although hard evidence is difficult to come by, there is a general belief among those engaged in technology development that private corporations do not view the contraceptive field as profitable enough

---

[1] It is worth bearing in mind that reproductive technologies include methods to prevent or control the timing of birth, methods to promote child-bearing, and a range of diagnostic methods. How particular technologies come to be developed is not the same for all three. For brevity I will focus here mainly on technologies for birth control, while making some passing remarks on the others.

to merit major research and development expenditures (Fathalla, 1994). This view is difficult to assess because reversible contraceptives appear to have a significant and growing demand. The fact that private corporations have, especially of late, spent relatively little on research and development in this field may also reflect risk aversion on their part following some expensive legal battles, e.g., over the Dalkon Shield (Snow, 1994).

Whatever the reason, public funds appear to be critical in supporting research on new methods. According to Fathalla (1994) (based on the only thorough study that has been done to date, viz., Atkinson, Lincoln & Forrest, 1985), private industry spent only about one-third of the total for contraceptive development worldwide in 1980-83. Seven public sector agencies including the Human Reproduction Programme at the World Health Organization spent 41 percent, and the rest came from national governments. "Were it not for the public sector programs committed to contraceptive research and development, the field could have fallen into scientific oblivion" (Fathalla, 1994).

If the above is accurate, then the public sector must take considerable responsibility for the kinds of contraceptive technologies that have been developed in the recent past. If the profit motive has not been the dominant force determining the direction of research in the recent past, then the two forces that have most likely played a central role have been the professional interests and personal predilections of researchers, and the pressures exerted by the population establishment. This is where the context of gender bias and of class, race, or national perspective come to have significant influence.

While there can be little doubt that technology developers have delivered more and more effective methods of birth control and have paid considerable attention to addressing life-threatening risks such as embolisms or diabetic crises (Snow, 1994), they have paid much less attention to side-effects which do not threaten life but which may seriously impair its quality. The most serious of these is abnormal bleeding which is a common side effect of many contraceptive steroids. Indeed, excessive bleeding can be potentially quite risky in malnourished or under-nourished Southern women with a history of iron deficiency anemia. Reduced or irregular bleeding or the absence of regular menstrual periods can be difficult to cope with in social contexts where there is no other easy way of testing for pregnancy, or where cultural practices are closely linked to regular menstrual cycles.

Feminists also are concerned about unknown long-term health risks, particularly for cancer. Fundamental to women's concerns is a continuing disquiet over introducing hormonal steroids on a continuing and long-term basis into their bodies. It is true that drugs are sometimes taken for long periods of time to counter illness, but women tend to object to thinking of their own bodies as "diseased" by definition, and many women feel that the largely male community of contraceptive researchers is only too willing to do so.

In fact relatively little research has gone into the considerable variability among women in their responses to some of the newer steroids (Snow, 1994), feeding women's suspicions that researchers are essentially guided by their own professional interests and by the concern of the population *controlistas* to increase efficacy above all else. While there appears to have been some small shift of resources in the last five years or so towards research and development for barrier methods and microbicides, the bulk of public funds still seem to be dedicated to long-acting, systemic contraceptives or the anti-fertility vaccine.

Testing and its Risks

While the terrain of struggle over the direction of contraceptive research and development thus far has been largely international, contention over contraceptive clinical trials constitutes the heart of national level struggles over technology. Although international developers of contraceptives have become more and more sensitive to the need to build safeguards against abuse in the clinical trial process,[2] many of their guidelines are observed in the breach in Southern countries.

Three aspects of the context are critical here. One is the extent to which the national or local counterparts of international contraceptive developers are free of gender, class or race biases and of a population *controlista* mentality. Prominent researchers in countries such as India and Brazil have been challenged in this regard, and their practices termed unethical. Perhaps even more important, the institutional structures for clinical trials are overly bureaucratic and insensitive. Full and clear information rarely is provided during trials,

---

[2] A good example of this is the detailed guidelines by the Population Council for the testing of Norplant in different countries.

even to middle class and literate or educated participants (Correa, 1994). Women health activists regularly and sometimes success-fully[139] bring to light the abuses in this regard, but this is only possible in countries with functioning democratic institutions and freedom of speech.

A second aspect of the context that is critical here is thus the strength of democratic institutions and the media in preventing or exposing abuse. Norplant has been tested and introduced in countries such as Indonesia, Zaire and Haiti, where it would be an understate-ment to say that the freedom to challenge authority is limited (Cor-rea, 1994). Even in a country such as India with a tradition of a free press and free speech, health activists find it very difficult to success-fully challenge the medical testing bureaucracy.

Perhaps the greatest evidence of the power of the institutions of civil society and a tradition of redressal of grievances is when they function to prevent abuse rather than only expose it when it has oc-curred. A telling example of this is the care with which Norplant has been introduced to the general public (as opposed perhaps to the poor or minority community) in the United States. Two or three page advertisements full of closely-spaced and detailed information on side-effects and contraindications were placed in major weekly magazines and other outlets. Such is the power and importance of the social mediation of technology.

The third aspect of the context that has serious implications for the testing process is the following: to what extent can the results of controlled clinical trials, which explicitly exclude women who are breast feeding, adolescents, and women who are anemic or malnour-ished be extrapolated to a population which includes those groups in very large numbers (Hardon, 1992)? How valid are the results of tri-als conducted in controlled settings in the South where female ane-mia and malnutrition is endemic?

Testing criteria also have come in for considerable scrutiny from women's groups. Three criteria typically have been used: safety, effi-cacy and acceptability. Of these, safety has been challenged because the long term health risks of many systemic contraceptives are essen-tially unknown because clinical trials generally are conducted over three to five years. Testing for acceptability is also suspect since it is

---

[139]Norplant trials were stopped in Brazil when feminists discovered that guidelines had been breached.

conducted in family planning clinics which may have a vested interest in the outcome, and because acceptability often is inferred from method continuation rates (i.e., a method is deemed acceptable to an individual if it has been continued more than one year), rather than through detailed questioning or examination of the person.

Distribution and Use

All the contextual aspects mentioned earlier come together when different contraceptives actually are distributed and used. Many modern contraceptives have serious contraindications that often include hypertension and cardiac problems and require prior medical examinations and continuous monitoring, as well as back-up systems to deal with severe side effects and health dangers. In the South, due to poverty, poor rural infrastructure and abysmal health services (both primary and referral), such conditions are rarely fulfilled. Even worse, in many large countries such as India and Indonesia, contraceptives are administered in camp conditions with little back-up service available.

Much of the literature of the last decade on quality of care in family planning programs has been motivated by concern over the dissemination of technology in highly inappropriate conditions. This is all the more serious because systems for the redressal of grievances or to bring abuses to light are weak in precisely those same contexts.

Another problem is that the field has been so driven by a focus on the risk of pregnancy that almost no attention has been paid to reproductive morbidity and mortality. So little research and program funds and effort have been expended on reproductive tract infections (RTIs) and sexually transmitted diseases (STDs) to date, that their implications for the choice of contraceptive methods has tended to be almost ignored. Certainly they receive short shrift in most field settings.

We are only now beginning to see the tip of the iceberg of reproductive tract infections. If the initial research findings are borne out in larger studies, then there is a major problem on the hands of the health community. Women's health groups often receive complaints about bleeding, pain and discomfort from women using contraceptives. Women who lodge these complaints often are labeled by health workers as neurotics and hypochondriacs. What gender bias has tended to ignore may well be the compounding of an inappropriate fertility regulation method with an RTI or an STD.

Reproductive technologies such as in-vitro fertilization and fetal diagnostics through amniocentesis also raise difficult, if somewhat different, sets of issues. Despite the considerable advertising of the former as a means of solving the problems of the infertile, the procedure has a very low success rate, and puts couples, and women in particular, through considerable physical and mental stress in the process. How much truth there is in the advertising for such techniques is an important issue. More fundamental is the question raised by Bartholet (1994), who argued that while in-vitro fertilization is subject to very few regulatory checks, its non-medical alternative, adoption, is full of barriers and biases.

The most paradoxical set of ethical issues has been raised by fetal diagnostics, amniocentesis in particular. Even if used according to its initial intent, viz., to eliminate serious congenital disorders through an early warning system, it borders too close to eugenics programs to leave sensitive people entirely comfortable. But a more serious problem has arisen from its misuse for sex-selection in societies such as China and India which suffer from a strong preference for male children. What is the best way of dealing with such a technology in societies where population sex-ratios are already adverse to women and reflect deep societal gender biases? While it may be possible to take a clear stand against such misuse, it is not yet clear what course of action either by the state or by civil society would be effective.

Ethical Issues and Human Rights

It should be clear from the above that it is almost entirely impossible to separate a judgment about technology from an assessment of the context. Context is multidimensional and includes not only poverty and the quality of health services, but also gender and other social biases, as well as the strength of civil society's institutions. It determines not only the effect of technology but its very choice.

This does not mean that one can reject all reproductive technologies ipso facto on grounds of race, class or gender bias. Different technologies have different characteristics and hence each should be judged on its own terms. More importantly, the context is not static. Gender and other biases can change, health and service systems do improve, and democratic institutions can be altered. If this were not so, then much of what women's organizations hope to accomplish by their activism would be a lost cause.

An ethical approach to the development, testing and dissemination of reproductive technologies requires transparency on the part of developers, a willingness on the part of the research community to take the concerns of their clients seriously and an honest effort by those implementing population programs to improve the context of service delivery. Only such approaches can be accepted as respectful of the human rights of individual women.

Some of these concerns were part of the Declaration of the International Symposium on "Contraceptive Research and Development for the Year 2000 and Beyond," which was held in Mexico City in March 1993. Participants in the symposium included senior managers of all the international and some national public sector agencies that undertake contraceptive research, as well as program directors and senior staff of other agencies that support or are otherwise engaged in fertility regulation research. This constitutes a very powerful group of those very institutions that influence the direction of reproductive technologies. If their commitment and actions match what they have agreed to in the Declaration, it could mean a significant move in the needed directions for women.

References

Atkinson, L. E., Lincoln, R. & Forrest, J. D. (1985). Worldwide Trends in Funding for Contraceptive Research and Evaluation. *Family Planning Perspectives, 17,* 196-207.

Bartholet, E. (1994). Adoption Rights and Reproductive Wrongs. In G. Sen & R. Snow (Eds.), *Power and Decision: The Social Control of Reproduction.* Cambridge: Harvard Center for Population and Development Studies.

Correa, S. (1994). Norplant in the Nineties: Realities, Dilemmas, Missing Pieces. In G. Sen & R. Snow (Eds.), *Power and Decision: The Social Control of Reproduction.* Cambridge: Harvard Center for Population and Development Studies.

Fathalla, M. (1994). *Mobilization of Resources for a Second Contraceptive Technology Revolution.* Unpublished manuscript.

Hardon, A. (1992). The Needs of Women Versus the Interests of Family Planning Personnel, Policy-makers and Researchers: Conflicting Views on Safety and Acceptability of Contraceptives. *Social Science and Medicine, 35(*6) 753- 766.

Sen, G., & Snow, R. (Eds.). (1994). *Power and Decision: The Social Control of Reproduction.* Cambridge: Harvard Center for Population and Development Studies.

Snow, R. (1994). Each to Her Own: Investigating Women's Response to Contraception. In G. Sen & R. Snow (Eds.), *Power and Decision: The Social Control of Reproduction.* Cambridge: Harvard Center for Population and Development Studies.

Chapter 23
CEDAW, Colombia and Reproductive Rights
Maria Isabel Plata & Adriana de la Espriella

International instruments, such as the UN Convention on the Elimination of All forms of Discrimination against Women (CEDAW), now ratified by more than 115 countries in the world, have succeeded in extracting the concept of the "advancement of women" from the uncertain context derived from each country's national identity. Women's rights can now be considered to belong to the category of fundamental legitimate rights that are based on international law. Under CEDAW, states must guarantee respect for human rights and individual freedoms and they must also ensure access to the conditions that allow the enjoyment of those rights. However, the limitations to women's equal access to rights are due, in part, to lack of sincere political will to improve the social condition of women. According to CEDAW, it is a duty of the states to "take all appropriate measures" to guarantee equal rights and equal opportunities for women.

The new Colombian Constitution, adopted in 1991, incorporated some principles and rights which reflect and strengthen those contained in CEDAW. Such an important legal reform was possible, in part, thanks to lobbying by women's groups which relied on CEDAW's provisions. In 1991, nearly 80 women's groups and organizations formed a network called Women and Constitution aimed at presenting proposals to the Constitutional Assembly that was elected for the drafting of a new Constitution.

There were very different approaches among the women's groups on the issues that were to be presented before the Constitutional Assembly and on the emphasis that should be given to some drafting proposals. The more controversial issues were the inclusion of an article providing for affirmative action for women, the establishment of a mandatory percentage of women participating in the government, the issue of abortion and the issue of divorce for

Catholic marriages. Although the various positions differed a lot, the network was successful in advancing most of the proposals.

The strengths of the proposals advanced by the Women and Constitution network lay not only in their recognized support by the women's organizations but also in the fact that they emphasized that the principles embraced in their proposals were mandates contained in international human rights instruments, such as CEDAW. The proposals won legitimacy by being framed as internationally recognized human rights provisions. In this case, the use of the international human rights language proved to be an effective strategy for introducing women's rights into the Constitution, taking advantage of the fact that Colombia is a country that is constantly scrutinized by the international community for its compliance with human rights principles.

As for the final wording of the Constitution, the text includes the general provision of equality before the law (Article 13), establishing that all persons are born free and equal before the law and will receive the same protection and treatment from the authorities and will enjoy the same rights, liberties and opportunities without any discrimination due to sex, race, national origin, family origin, language, religion, political or philosophical opinions. But, in addition to the general principle, the Constitution establishes that the state will promote the conditions necessary to make equality real and effective and will adopt measures in favor of discriminated groups. Although this last part of the article has not yet had concrete legal developments, it represents a solid constitutional base to promote future affirmative action policies.

Concerning women, the new Constitution explicitly mentions the equality of rights and opportunities that should be granted both to men and women and the prohibition of discrimination on the basis of sex (Article 43). There is also an article providing for the "effective and adequate" participation of women in government (Article 40), though the scope and meaning of this article is yet to be established. Since the adoption of the Constitution, there have been at least three proposals submitted to Congress for the enactment of legislation providing for a mandatory minimum percentage of women participating in government, but none has yet been passed.

Article 42 of the new Constitution defines the family as the fundamental unit of society which can be formed by natural or legal bonds. That is, by the free decision of a man and a woman to marry, or by their responsible decision to establish a family. It also states that within the family, men and women have equal rights and duties, that they both have the right to decide the number and spacing of children, that all forms of violence should be prohibited, and that all marriages, including the Catholic, may end by divorce.

There are also two very important articles, which were not directly lobbied for by the Women's Network but that have definitely served the advancement of women's rights. One is the establishment of the primacy of international human rights treaties and conventions over national legislation, and the other is the introduction of a right to claim legal protection before any court whenever a fundamental right is violated or jeopardized. The legal protection consists of a judicial order to act or to refrain from acting.

Although it is obvious that the simple fact of modifying the Constitution does not in itself guarantee nondiscrimination, equality and empowerment for women, it has indeed given new tools and arguments to defend women's rights in particular cases, and it has served to frame new interpretations of the law that have actually challenged deeply rooted cultural values and attitudes towards women.

To illustrate how these reforms have in fact strengthened the advancement of women in our society, let us mention three examples of decisions by the Constitutional Court. These cases were based on the right to claim legal protection and on the new constitutional articles on women's rights that were discussed earlier and that question traditional interpretations of the law, giving legitimacy to women's claims.

The first case recognizes the need to estimate the monetary value of the woman's domestic work in order to account fairly for the contributions of both parties in a de facto marriage. Although this decision does not yet extend to religious or civil marriages, it might encourage new interpretations regarding joint ownership of property by husband and wife, so that domestic work is included when each party's contributions are listed.

Even though the article on equal rights of men and women is not included in the fundamental rights chapter (it is listed as a social, economic and cultural right, which is not considered to be fundamental), the Court reasoned that a right becomes fundamental whenever its violation precludes the enjoyment of a fundamental right, thus broadening the scope of the chapter on fundamental rights. In the future, fundamental human rights might include the conditions required for their full application.

The second decision has to do with the problem of domestic violence. The Court argued that domestic violence is a violation of the fundamental rights to life and integrity and safety of the person. The Court established the obligation of the state to secure protection for the woman and its duty to intervene to prevent her husband from committing further violence. This decision challenged the traditional view of the role of the state in domestic matters, which were thought to belong exclusively to the private domain of the person.

The third case related to the issue of discrimination on the basis of pregnancy. The Constitutional Court ordered a school to reinstate a girl who had been expelled after becoming pregnant. The Court stated that the fundamental rights contained in the Constitution limited the autonomy that schools and other institutions could exercise in defining their rules.

Finally, it is interesting to mention the language used by the minority of the Constitutional Court in a decision on abortion. Although the majority of the Court reaffirmed the illegality of abortion, the minority opinion reflects a significant change of attitude towards gender issues that is emerging within the judicial system. The minority opinion said, "Pregnancy and maternity greatly affect the identity of women. There is a powerful belief that to become a mother is both natural and desirable. Therefore, when a woman renounces motherhood, it is implied that there is a selfish avoidance of an instinct. Nevertheless, cultural stereotypes have diametrically changed with the involvement of women in the labor market, a reason in itself which equally requires the acceptance of the right of a woman to decide about her reproductive life."

The process of constitutional reform that took place in 1991 gave new life to women's organizations. Women were successful in exercising pressure to include women's rights in the Constitution and in lobbying for governmental programs which included a gender perspective. One of the most important policies that was adopted as a result of this process was called "Health for Women, Women for Health" issued by the Ministry of Public Health.

The document that contains the health policy for women establishes that all women have the right to participate in all decisions related to their health, life, body, and sexuality, whether the impact is on the individual, on the community or on the public institutions. The specific set of rights set forth in the document include:

- The right to a joyful maternity which includes a freely chosen and safe pregnancy.
- The right to a humane medical treatment which treats a woman's body, fears, intimacy and privacy needs with dignity and respect.
- The right to be treated as an integrated person by the health services rather than in terms of one's reproductive capacity.
- The right to have access to integrated health services which respond to women's specific needs taking into consideration special characteristics such as age, activities, economic needs, race and place of origin.
- The right to have access to education that fosters self care and self knowledge of the body and promotes self esteem and empowerment.
- The right to receive information and counseling that promotes the exercise of a free, gratifying and responsible sexuality, not necessarily conditioned to pregnancy.
- The right to have access to sufficient and appropriate information and counseling and to modern and safe contraceptives.
- The right to working and living conditions and an environment that do not affect women's fertility or health.
- The right not to be discriminated against in the workplace or in educational institutions on the basis of pregnancy, number of children or marital status.
- The right to have biological processes such as menstruation, pregnancy, birth, menopause and old age be considered as natural events and not as illness.
- The right to receive value and respect for cultural knowledge and practices related to women's health.
- The right to active participation in the community and governmental decision making levels of the health system.
- The right to access to public health services that treat battered women and victims of all forms of violence.

The document containing this health policy is an interesting official effort to incorporate women as active agents in public health policies and services. It is interesting to note that it considers that social discrimination against women contributes to illness. It also emphasizes that women's health not only includes the biological aspects of reproduction and of the body, but also includes the system of gender roles and functions.

According to the document, there are six basic measures that should be taken to eliminate discrimination against women in the health care system: empowerment of women as a guarantee for the exercise of rights, the right to equal opportunities, respect for pluralism and differences, humanized health care with special emphasis on the right to freedom and privacy, social participation of women in active roles, and integrated health services.

The health policy identified four groups of women whose economic, psychological or social living conditions are precarious and demand special attention. The groups include women who are single heads of family, women between 15 and 49 years (reproductive age), working women and elderly women (over 60 years).

It also established five sub-programs which comprise a comprehensive approach to women's health. These are support and health care in women's health issues, integral services in reproductive health and sexuality, prevention of ill treatment and services to women and minors who have been victims of violence, mental health services and healthy and safe working conditions.

Each sub-program tries to tackle the adverse discriminatory factors which affect women in each case. For example, the new reproductive health and sexuality policy focuses on fertility control but also works to strengthen the self-esteem of women and to guarantee the woman's rights to her body. The Ministry of Public Health ruled that all fertility control programs must help create a collective conscience that accepts the right to a full and responsible exercise of sexuality. The programs also must recognize the right of Colombian women to a desired and planned pregnancy without health risks. The program acknowledges the need to increase the coverage of services to men and women of reproductive age and stresses the importance of working to prevent unwanted pregnancies. The services have expanded to address reproductive tract infections, sexually transmitted diseases, including HIV/AIDS and adolescent pregnancy among others.

The document mandates the need for programs and services which deal with contraception and infertility as inherent in the right of individuals and/or couples to make free and responsible reproductive choices. It also addresses the prevention of unwanted pregnancies, including a special program for adolescents, and it provides for community programs as a means to empower all individuals. The program reaffirms the right to free and voluntary choice of all contraceptive methods, regardless of the marital status of the person, and reinforces the requirement that the program must cover the population between 14 and 49 years. The program also provides for an integrated treatment of incomplete abortions.

In sum, the Health Policy for Women reflects an unprecedented move toward gender sensitivity on the part of the government. It is not possible as yet to give a definitive assessment of the effectiveness of the program during its first three years because there has not been a complete evaluation of its results. However, not all of the Ministers of Public Health who have been in office since 1992 have fully adopted the health policy for women. Still, in the main, the policy and some of the programs have been implemented. Implementation of the policy also has been slowed down by the lack of funds. The resources allocated for the program are not sufficient to cover the vast range of programs and services covered in the policy.

Nevertheless, there are important achievements in three major cities where programs on sexuality and reproduction have been established as well as a network for the prevention of domestic violence. These two programs have been successful in involving local NGOs and in obtaining funding from local health services. The new administration of the Ministry is planning to expand the coverage of these programs to other cities.

Also as a result of the adoption of the health policy for women, a major research project was initiated on the quality of the health services for women in the areas of gynecology and obstetrics and family planning. The results of this research are not yet ready, due to lack of resources to conclude it. However, there are very important findings on the nature of the relationship between doctors and patients and on the medical consultation and treatment of pregnant women.

Among the projects of the Ministry, the present government not only plans the conclusion or expansion of the programs already initiated, but also the elaboration of protocols and models containing criteria and mechanisms that contribute to make all the health services gender responsive. They have also identified the need for further conceptualization and action in the areas of women's mental health and healthy working conditions; in the incorporation of men to programs dealing with fertility and contraception; and in an adequate coordination with the national program of sexual education which was recently launched by the Ministry of Education.

To conclude, this is just an example of a case where the women's right to health has been approached from a human rights perspective, and specifically from the woman's point of view. It has allowed the identification of those areas where the forms of discrimination against women affect their health. But perhaps most importantly, it has forced the service providers who are interested in this approach to start discussing and searching for new strategies and plans to answer another question: how do we improve women's health? Regrettably, it has been an issue neglected in the past.

Chapter 24
Women's Reproductive Rights and HIV/AIDS
Pearl Nwashili

The Idea of Reproductive Rights

What are reproductive rights? Ask as many women as possible, especially from developing countries, to define reproductive rights and one is certain to receive responses that range from total ignorance of such a term to differences in conceptualization based on their level of awareness of women's rights and their location within the country. Answers will include the right to choose sexual partners, access to abortion, the right to choose marriage partners, and the right to be a single mother. The divergent and conflicting conceptions of reproductive rights will reflect the glaring differences in level of education and exposure to other cultures, ethnic origin, religion and class interests of women. One common feature though is that all these "rights" address the general status of women located in the cultural practices that inform societal and state attitudes toward women.

Here we will examine the reproductive rights of the Nigerian woman in the context of HIV/AIDS. The status of women in Nigerian society is central to the societal and state attitude toward women's reproductive rights. What is the worth of a woman? How is she valued in the various "universal" traditions, customs, and practices in Nigeria? There is a "universal" assumption that cuts across cultural boundaries and class levels which makes every woman inferior to men. This assumption of inferiority shapes attitudes towards women's needs, the rights that should be extended to her and the emphasis on her responsibilities to the society. This, of course, shapes state policies.

Thus the concept of reproductive rights under these assumptions accounts for the conspiracy between the society and the state to promote anachronistic values that adversely affect the health of Nigerian women but which the government appears helpless in checking. I will cite a few examples.

Child Marriage and Early Pregnancy

Marriage at its best is a natural social relationship between two consenting adults. But for most Nigerian girls, marriage is a nightmare. On the average, a Nigerian girl is forced to marry much too early, before she has developed physically or psychologically and before she has gained a measure of economic independence. The consequences of early marriage for Nigerian girls include educational underdevelopment, mental incapacitation, vesico-vaginal fistula (VVF), economic and political marginalization and perennial poverty.

The travails of most VVF patients is a clear demonstration of man's inhumanity to woman. A girl who is forced into marriage on her first menstruation is likely to be subject to conjugal rape. Ultimately, she is burdened with pregnancy and because of underdeveloped pelvic bones experiences obstructed labor. She is at risk of delivering a still born baby. If she survives at all, she may end up suffering from severe injuries (a torn bladder or rectum or both) which results in the leaking of urine and sometimes feces. In addition to this physical and psychological suffering, she becomes a social outcast and is divorced by her husband.

Male Preference

There is also the issue of preference for male children. The woman is under undue pressure from her husband and the extended family to have "at least" one male child. This forces her to procreate many times, even to the detriment of her health.

Female Genital Mutilation

Female genital mutilation (FGM) is a practice that involves the surgical removal of part or all of the female external genitalia. Even though this practice is called female circumcision, it is a misnomer. Unlike male circumcision which involves removing the foreskin of the penis but leaves sexual functioning intact, FGM is society's way of reducing women to their reproductive function. The sexual act is for the man's sexual enjoyment and for procreation. The primary purpose of FGM is to curtail women's enjoyment of sexual intercourse so that the society can check "promiscuity" among its female population. In most African countries, Nigeria included, it is believed that an "uncircumcised" female is an abomination and would attract the wrath of the gods on the whole community. FGM is practiced to "purify" the females.

Other cultural practices such as deliberate undernourishment of women from birth, unbridled breeding of children for social and economic reasons, the domestication of women in some countries of the Third World and sexual harassment, all combine to keep women in a subjugated state. As a result, women have internalized a view that they are inferior to men. The subjugation of women prevents them from negotiating sexual practices to protect themselves from contracting HIV and, ultimately, dying of AIDS.

Basic Concepts

Reproductive Health

Based on priciples in the Constitution of the World Health Organization, and the Cairo Program of Action, reproductive health is defined as a condition in which the reproductive process is accomplished in a state of complete physical, mental and social well being. It is not merely the absence of disease or disorders of the reproductive process, but implies that people have the ability to reproduce, to regulate their fertility and to practice and enjoy sexual relationships. Reproductive health also implies that women can go safely through pregnancy and childbirth, that fertility regulation can be achieved without health hazards and that people are safe in having sex. The definition moves beyond the biomedical model, which focuses on disease rather than the whole human being. In this more expansive concept, people become the essence of reproductive health, the subjects rather than the objects.

Rights

Rights are justifications, claims or immunity that one is entitled to by virtue of being human. Human rights are certain privileges defined in international law. These rights are enumerated in the Universal Declaration of Human Rights, the African Charter on Human and People's Rights and the International Convention on Civil and Political Rights. Equal rights addresses unjust differential treatment of persons owing to discrimination, gender, ethnicity, national origin, religion, sexual orientation and disability or illness.

The United Nations Charter affirms equal rights of men and women and recognizes that human beings are born free and equal in dignity and rights. Everyone is entitled to all rights and freedoms set forth therein, without distinction of any kind, including sex. Men and women have equal rights to all economic, social, cultural, civil and political rights.

The African Charter on Human Rights recognizes that women have a right to dignity. The Convention on the Elimination of All Forms of Discrimination Against Women, Article 3, says that state parties shall take all appropriate measures in the political, social, economic and cultural fields, including legislation, to ensure the full development and advancement of women. Article 12 says that state parties shall take appropriate measures to eliminate discrimination against women in the area of health care, including services related to family planning.

I have quoted extensively from these charters and conventions because Nigeria, as well as most African countries and the Third World in general, are signatories and have pledged to respect and implement these rights. In addition, it is worth noting that the 1979 Constitution of the Federal Republic of Nigeria recognizes the individual's right to life, dignity of the human person, personal liberty, fair hearing, private and family life, freedom of expression and freedom from discrimination by reason of sex (Chapter IV, articles 30, 31, 32, 33, 34, 35, 36, 39).

Despite these various instruments, overt discrimination against women continues to exist in Nigeria as it does throughout the world. Because of the weak Nigerian economy and widespread poverty, women have the least access to food, health, education, training and opportunities for employment and other needs. The rights of Nigerian women are infringed in this context. In Nigeria today, 50 percent of women are illiterate and the government continues to use state machinery to pay lip service to the promotion of women rights.

Needs

Needs are constitutional or acquired cravings or wants which are appeased by recurrent satisfaction. Maslow developed a theory of a hierarchy of human needs. These basic needs, in order of their importance, are physiological needs, safety or security, love and the feeling of belonging, self-actualization and self-esteem. The freedom to negotiate one's sexual behavior and maintain reproductive health are basic needs. Women also need security, love and a feeling of belonging to be self-actualized. Meeting the higher order needs leads to understanding of self and environment and to a peak life experience. A strong self-concept leads to creativity and dynamic mental, physical and socioeconomic adaptation to reproductive health stressors. Even though these needs are universal, they are also culturally relative. And this is where the response of the state and the attitude of the society is located in the culture of the people. Nigeria is not an exception.

Responsibility

Responsibility is moral accountability for actions. The individual, community and state are responsible for achieving sexual and reproductive health. A woman is responsible for making choices regarding her reproductive health. The state makes laws and policies and ensures that legislation is enacted. The individual, community and state are responsible for promoting and protecting women's reproductive rights. But sadly, this is not the case in most countries. The whole question of the status of women, state response and half-measure policies shows that responsibility for reproductive health is more often the woman's.

HIV and AIDS

HIV is a slow acting virus. It is carried in blood, seminal, vaginal and cervical fluids. It also has been isolated in breast milk. Low levels may remain quietly in the body for years. But with time, it can get into the blood stream and either destroy the immune system or cause it to destroy itself. HIV is a relatively new virus and its manifestations started unfolding in the late 1970s. Viruses can combine to produce a new one. It has two major strains (HIV I and HIV II) with numerous variations. In Nigeria HIV I is the most prevalent. It is transmitted mainly through unprotected sexual intercourse, both vaginal and anal. More than 80 percent of the cases are transmitted heterosexually in African countries. HIV also is spread through infected blood or blood products transfused into the system; sharing or re-using injection needles; using equipment containing infected fluid without sterilizing it before re-using; antenatal and intranatal transmission from mother to fetus; or use of infected equipment during delivery.

Immune deficiency, in the case of AIDS, means that the immune system is being prevented from functioning. Consequently, some organisms which normally would be controlled by the immune system are given the opportunity to take over. Some HIV-infected persons have lived without signs of illness for as long as 12 years. The majority do get HIV-related illness, sometimes associated with frequent exposure to HIV and other diseases, poor health, lack of treatment and a poor quality of life.

The Nigerian Context

Presently in Nigeria, there is public information about the HIV/AIDS pandemic. However, there is a group of men, especially the urban educated, who respond to HIV/AIDS information with nonchalance and even outright denial of the existence of the disease. Among the grassroots women's groups and the urban poor, reactions to information about HIV/AIDS range from disbelief to helplessness on the part of those among them who desire to protect themselves from infection. Most Nigerian women, especially the urban elites, know that HIV/AIDS is a sexually transmitted disease. They also are aware of the other means of transmission. But what are they doing with this information?

Epidemiologically, the infection rate continues to rise rapidly, especially in Africa. In Nigeria, HIV infection has risen from 0.022 percent in 1987 to 3 percent in 1993. It is estimated that as many as 600,000-700,000 Nigerians may be currently infected. This figure may rise to 1 million by the year 1996. About 128,298 Nigerians will have died of AIDS by 1996. But this is just a tip of the iceberg. Africa bears the brunt of the pandemic, where about 13 million people are infected. Women are hit the worst and are most vulnerable. Infection rates are highest among the reproductive age group of 15 to 47 years.

According to a World Health Organization (WHO) report (from the VIIIth International Conference on AIDS in Africa, December 1993), HIV prevalence among pregnant women attending antenatal clinics is on the increase. In Nigeria, about 5 percent of pregnant women test positive for HIV. Many countries, such as UK and Cuba, carry out mandatory HIV testing on pregnant women. Sero-positive women are therefore "advised" to terminate their pregnancies in order to avoid intra-uterine transmission to the fetus. In the US, 7,000 women with HIV give birth each year. About a quarter of their babies are infected. WHO estimates that since the beginning of the AIDS pandemic, about a million children have been infected worldwide, before or during birth or through breastfeeding.

The vast majority live in developing countries that cannot afford expensive AIDS drugs.

Physiologically, women are especially vulnerable. Younger women are more susceptible because of immature cells of the cervix and exploitation by older men. One risky practice, which appears to be widespread in several African countries, including Ghana, Cameroon, Nigeria, Kenya, Malawi, Zaire, Zambia and Zimbabwe, and has been reported outside Africa in Haiti, Costa Rica, Dominican Republic and Saudi Arabia, is known as dry sex. Dry sex, which involves the use of creams, herbs or other concoctions to ensure a dry, tight vagina, increases the risk of vaginal abrasion and subsequent HIV infection. Dry sex is commonly practiced by both rural and urban women who have had two or more children in an effort to feel more attractive to their partners because all activity is centered around male pleasure. Women's general poor state of health and high incidences of anemia, malaria, malnutrition and untreated STDs increase their risk of HIV infection.

In general Nigerian women remain powerless over the sexual behavior of their male partners. They cannot assert their sexual rights to refuse sex, negotiate safer sex or question the sexual behavior of their partners. They are present to give their men sexual pleasure when the men demand it. Men are reluctant to discuss sexual health even though many men have multiple sex partners and are thus at high risk for HIV infection. Condoms are used mainly for contraception rather than to prevent the transmission of disease. Many couples are either ignorant about the use of condoms or are too poor to purchase them. Sex education for children is limited. Parents tend to discuss sex with their children only in relation to dangers of pregnancy.

The rapid growth of prostitution also is a large factor in the rapid spread of HIV transmission. The rapidly growing need for cash in all areas of society has fueled a rapid growth in various forms of prostitution in developing countries. The STOPAIDS motor park program in Nigeria found that women also exchange sexual favors for food, shelter and even to pay for school fees for children. These findings prompted the STOPAIDS program to design a special reproductive health empowerment program for these women.

Commercial sex work, for many women, is a choice between survival that day or risking HIV infection that day. Many are forced to choose HIV infection. The low-income sex workers are more at risk than higher-income sex workers. However, there is a pattern of commercial sex work among educated and well-to-do women. About 30 percent of sex workers in Nigeria are sero-positive.

Impact of HIV/AIDS on the Reproductive Rights of Women

In Africa, the impact of HIV/AIDS on women is magnified by poverty and underdevelopment. There is greater awareness of the impact on women but scant attention is paid to their needs. The Society for Women of Africa on AIDS (SWAA) describes the impact on women as triple jeopardy in their roles as individuals, mothers and caregivers. Berger and Ray (1993) note that AIDS was killing women all over the world before the disease had a name and before the virus had a name. With more than 80 percent of HIV/AIDS in African heterosexually transmitted, women are in acute danger, but their powerlessness in their sexual relationships compounds their situation.

According to Reid and Bailey (1993), critical realities about the HIV epidemic, which are yet to be grasped, are found in these assertions:

- Women are becoming infected at the rate of one woman every two minutes around the globe. More women than men are becoming infected in developing countries. Of the estimated 30 to 40 million people infected globally, about 13 million are women. The ratio is 6:5 women to men. About 85 percent of the women who are infected worldwide live in Africa.
- Women are becoming infected at a significantly younger age than men, on average five to eight years earlier than men.
- More girls and young women in their teens and early twenties are becoming infected than women in any age group except post-menopausal women. This has been traced to immunological and virological susceptibility in women, which changes with age.

What these trends mean for the African women is that with the male attitude and women's lack of social and physical capacity to insist on safer sex, more women will be infected. For most women, the major risk factor for HIV infection is being married. Most African men practice polygamy and keep one or more mistresses. However, some HIV sero-positive men are bisexual. They engage in homosexual practices, including anal sex, and have female partners too. African women who are knowledgeable about safe sex practices admit they do not always practice it because they lack power in their relationships with men. Reid and Bailey (1993) note that at the current stage of the pandemic, it can be estimated that every day there are 1,500 women who have no sexual partners other than their husbands who are becoming infected. This number will increase as the number of infected men increases.

In African countries even when a woman knows that her partner is infected with STDs or HIV/AIDS, she almost always stays in the relationship because of societal pressure. She is viewed as morally loose where she dares to leave, although the man whom she leaves would be viewed with pity and allowed to replace his wife with another partner.

Women have a shorter survival period than men between incubation and the first signs of illness (Berger & Ray, 1993). In other words, women who contract HIV die more quickly than men. Each day an additional 3,000 women become infected with HIV and 500 infected women die.

Drug treatment with Zidovudine or other palliative AIDS drugs are unaffordable, unavailable and inaccessible in most of Africa. In a situation where most women are poor, the chance that they can afford these drugs is very remote. As care givers, women are always expected to provide home-based care for their ailing relations, including those with HIV/AIDS illness. This, of course, exposes them to danger of infection.

In short, infringements on women's reproductive rights, their inability to enforce safer sex in their relationships and their vulnerability to disease due to the reproductive process all combine to make women more vulnerable to HIV/AIDS infection.

Promotion of Women's Reproductive Rights

Government legislation prohibiting early marriages is not enforced in Nigeria. The half-hearted efforts by NGOs in Nigeria to enlighten the society on the ills of child marriage and early pregnancy have had a minimal effect because most NGOs themselves do not consider this issue a serious threat to women's well-being. The issues of child marriage and early pregnancy are more salient at the international level. Globally, the women's movement continues to gain strength and ideologically the focus is on "quality of life." This concern focuses on reducing inequity and discrimination and has influenced the study of reproductive health and population by highlighting the methodological inadequacy of concentrating on numbers of births without paying equal attention to the well-being of people and to the clear discrimination against women when their status in marriage and in society at large depends on their capacity to bear children.

The need to address the social, cultural, economic and political factors affecting reproductive health cannot be overemphasized. According to Germain and Ordway (1989), women must be able to achieve social status and dignity to manage their own health and sexuality and to exercise their basic rights in society and in partnership with men. This can only be achieved in a country like Nigeria if the state machinery can be used to stop the abuse of women's rights. Women's groups can assist the process by working on changing the conditions of poverty, powerlessness and dependence that women find themselves in and help them to become less vulnerable.

The case of a Nigerian construction worker who was seropositive illustrates the helplessness and vulnerability of women. This man was counseled after testing positive for HIV and advised not to get married. Six months later, he reappeared with a young woman who had been infected by him. The man said that his father convinced him that he did not have AIDS because he (the father) did not have AIDS and could not therefore have transmitted it to his son. The story is representative of the widespread ignorance regarding the primary means of transmitting HIV. The man married this young girl, who now has developed AIDS. Ignorance about the disease of AIDS, the inability to verify the man's sexual health, and her social status all combined to make her a victim.

Clearly the key to successful AIDS prevention campaigns is to mobilize the entire population, as well as policy makers, in long term behavioral change. This involves identifying the target audience, developing and communicating the message to that target audience and developing policy recommendations for encouraging responsible behaviors. Women themselves should be in the forefront of developing strategies to change men's behavior and to forge links between groups of women interested in increasing women's power and assertiveness in sexual relationships with men.

In Nigeria, as in most African countries, public policy on AIDS remains undeveloped. In fact, Nigeria has not yet formulated a full-fledged policy on AIDS. The Federal Ministry of Health has instituted measures to promote and protect the general population from HIV infection. In lieu of a state policy on AIDS, what we have is a program called the National AIDS and STD Control Programme (NASCP).

The objectives of NASCP are to prevent HIV infection, to reduce the personal and social impact for HIV-infected persons and their families, to reduce the impact of the HIV/AIDS epidemic on the society and to unify and mobilize national and international efforts and resources in the fight against AIDS.

As yet, the only special program designed for women is one targeted to commercial sex workers. There are no programs for Nigerian women who are involved in long term relationships with men who have multiple sexual partners. A program is needed which concentrates on women's need to negotiate condom use with their male partners (Gupta, 1993). There are 102 screening centers in Nigeria for women with HIV-related illnesses and for prospective blood donors. STOPAIDS initiated the first reproductive health and HIV program for women at the grassroots level in Nigeria. Few other NGOs are targeting women with HIV prevention programs.

National branches of Society for Women and AIDS in more than 20 countries on the continent are targeting women and AIDS while Women in Law and Development in Africa (WiLDAF) and other groups of women lawyers target women's rights issues, including their reproductive rights. For example, Ugandan women lawyers (FIDA-U) are pushing their government to enact a divorce law that grants equality to women. Immunization against hepatitis and tuberculosis has been stepped up to increase women's immunity during pregnancy. Fortunately there is no mandatory HIV test for pregnant women in Nigeria. Women NGOs are fighting against mandatory testing in many countries where there is such practice. For example, Positively Women in Great Britain has launched a strong campaign against mandatory HIV testing for pregnant women.

Health education strategies in Nigeria are coordinated by the Federal Ministry of Health in the states and implemented by volunteer health workers. The content of the messages is information about the cause, course, mode of transmission and consequences of HIV infection. Safe sex practices are discussed and encouraged. Condoms are distributed mainly to men. Information, Education and Communication (IEC) materials are distributed. Unfortunately, the men who are in the target group are not very accessible. The men often dismiss such programs with chauvinistic arrogance and deny the reality of the HIV scourge. The level of funding for state programs directed towards the epidemic is very insignificant. For instance, individual state governments in Nigeria are allocated only N1 million (about US$40,000) for AIDS programs. In other words, the 30 states in the Federal Republic of Nigeria spend a total of US$1.2 million annually on HIV/AIDS, a figure which is woefully inadequate.

Some progressive policies in the area of health care are reducing the threat of HIV infection. Traditional practices by health workers in agencies have been modified. Disposable syringes are used as much as possible. Those which are re-used are sterilized after each use. More attention is being paid to sterilization of other equipment in hospitals. Traditional birth attendants are being trained to dispose of blood and other body fluids in ways that prevent HIV infection.

FGM, tribal marks and facial scarification are being discouraged by the state to prevent the transmission of HIV infection. The success of these measures is speculative. Breastfeeding is generally encouraged, even though it has been implicated in HIV transmission (10-20 percent), but inexpensive bottle-feeding is available for sero-positive women.

Community Participation

Women's groups at the community level have been very hesitant to defend their rights, especially in the areas of sexuality and reproduction. For the most part there still is not a well organized response to the AIDS crisis at the community level. There is competition among groups for the scarce funds which are available for AIDS prevention. But, in many regions, there is not yet an organized response to AIDS from women at the grassroots level but rather only an uncoordinated and sporadic dialogue focused on women's reproductive health and sexual inequality.

Traditional practices regarding marriage, commercial sex work, female genital mutilation, polygamy and multiple sex partners are far from being modified in relation to the AIDS reality. Child marriage still is being practiced as before, and older men are even more "virulent" today, taking advantage of the deteriorating economy to acquire child brides from poor families.

The Way Forward: The Need for New Strategies

To bring the AIDS epidemic under control it will be necessary to make everyone in the society feel that they are a part of the solution to the problem of AIDS. It will require all people, from national leaders to village residents, to change long established attitudes and traditions that perpetuate the inferior social status and economic power of women. Progress in containing AIDS will depend on reinforcing societal attitudes that encourage relationships based on mutual respect and concern for the health of one's partner.

While women individually may feel that they are powerless to change men's behavior, women collectively can effect extraordinary changes. For example, the women of Maharashtra, India, who decided to tolerate no longer drunkenness from their husbands formed themselves into vigilante groups. As a group they were able to change men's drinking patterns.

Kenyan women, also tired of drunkenness in their husbands, came together to devise strategies for stopping that behavior. Mexican women in the mid-to-late 1970s formed an alliance of women that crossed all social classes to bring down the incidence of rape and sexual assault of women.

There is a need now to look for women's collective action to change entrenched patterns of male sexual behavior. Moreover, women's groups targeting male behavior need the necessary support from NGOs and others to push for change in a short time. Literacy and vocational training can help women achieve economic security, thus enabling them to take charge of their lives and divorce or live independently of men if necessary to protect themselves and unborn children from the ravages of AIDS.

The current focus of AIDS prevention and control programs is inadequate because it fails to deal effectively with issues of gender and economic security for women. Until women are empowered to control their sexuality, HIV and AIDS prevention programs will continue to have limited success. Information campaigns targeted at women should be culturally, linguistically and educationally appropriate. Sexual empowerment is linked to economic empowerment and gender equity. Educational programs (starting in the primary schools) should target gender issues and gender equality as a critical means of equalizing the power relations between men and women.

REFERENCES

African Charter on Human and People's Rights. (1991). London: Amnesty International.

AHRTAG. Human Rights are Everyone's Rights. (1992). *AIDS Action*, 17.

Berger, M. & Ray, S. (1993). *Women and HIV/AIDS: An International Resource Book.* London: Pandora.

Coalition of Nigerian NGOs on Health, Population and Development. (1993). *Position Paper on Health, Population and Development Issues in Nigeria.* Unpublished manuscript.

Germain, A., & Ordway, J. (1989). *Population Control and Women's Health: Balancing the Scales.* New York: Women's Health Coalition.

Gupta, G. R. (1993, April). *Women's Lives and Sex: Implications for AIDS Prevention.* Paper presented at the Conference on International Perspective in Sex Research, Rio De Janeiro, Brazil.

Gupta, J. P. (1993). *AIDS, the Second Decade: A Focus on Youth and Women.* New York: UNICEF.

Hankins, C. (1994, July). *Recognizing and Countering the Psychosocial and Economic Impact on Women of HIV in Developing Countries.* Plenary presentation at the Second International Conference on the Biopsychosocial Aspects of HIV Infection, Brighton, UK.

Ige, T. (1994). *Human Rights Made Easy.* Lagos, Nigeria: Legal Resources Development Centre Publication.

Liquori, A. L. (1993, January). *Reproductive Health and Public Policies.* Paper presented at the Seminar on AIDS, Reproductive Health and Public Policies, Rio De Janeiro, Brazil.

McNamara, R. (1993). *Female Genital Health and the Risk of HIV Transmission.* New York: UNDP.

Nakajima, H. (1994). *Care for AIDS Patients: A New WHO Priority.* No. 3. Lyons, France: Sidalerte International.

National AIDS and STD Control Programme. (1992). Lagos, Nigeria: Federal Ministry of Health and Social Services.

Nwashili, P. (1992, 1993). [Result of Surveys, STOPAIDS Programme, Nigeria]. Unpublished raw data.

Panos Institute. (1990). *Triple Jeopardy: Women and AIDS.* Panos Dossier. London: Author.

Panos Institute. (1994). *World AIDS*, Nos. 33-34. London: Author.

Reid E., & Bailey, M. (1993). *Young Women: Silence, Susceptibility and the HIV Epidemic.* New York: UNDP.

Smith, A. (1994). *AIDS: A Family Disease.* Report on the Conference of the Society of Women and AIDS in Africa (SWAA), Lusaka, Zambia.

World Health Organization. (1991). *AIDS Prevention through Health Promotion: Facing Sensitive Issues.* Geneva: Author.

Chapter 25
Reproductive Technologies and State Policies: Norplant in Bangladesh

Nasreen Huq & Tasneem Azim

Background

Good health is a basic human right. Issues pertaining to health—the human body and services for the human body—encompass respectively, private and public domains. But the two are so interlinked that divisions into separate domains must necessarily break down. In countries such as Bangladesh, where the government has identified population growth rate as the "number one problem" of the country and has developed an extensive population control program targeting women, family planning services are more far-reaching compared to general health services. The family planning program is not integrated with general health care services. Instead it is integrated with maternal and child health services so that women's bodies are defined in terms of reproductive capacity alone.

Such an approach has made family planning programs extremely unpopular with women's movements the world over. There are several problems with an approach that defines women's health in terms of reproduction. First, a woman's right to decide for herself the size of her family is taken away from her and becomes a decision made by the state. Second, the man's role in controlling reproduction is almost entirely ignored and the notion of reproductive responsibility becomes the burden of women alone. As a result, activists have demanded that family planning services for men also be promoted. Third, such an approach does not take into account the whole body but views women only as reproductive beings. This has led to demands that general health services be integrated into family planning services, thus enabling women to take control over their own bodies.

Women activists, in short, have begun to question the entire health system in Bangladesh. From the perspective of activists, health services in Bangladesh, which approach the "whole" human body, are male biased. The services are administered predominantly by men and employ a male perspective of the body. By contrast, health services for females are limited to issues pertaining to the female reproductive system. In effect, female bodies are viewed as male bodies with female reproductive organs, and the function of that body is concentrated around reproduction. By contrast *Naripokkho*, an organization of women activists engaged in advocacy for women's rights and development in Bangladesh, has reiterated a holistic view of women's health. *Naripokkho's* attitude toward Norplant has been that family planning and contraception should provide safe and reliable choices and be placed in the overall context of general health services.

Introduction

The First Five-Year Plan states that, "no civilized measure would be too drastic to keep the population of Bangladesh on the smaller side of 15 crore (150 million) for sheer ecological viability of the nation" (Government of Bangladesh, 1994). This statement summarizes the guiding principle of family planning services in Bangladesh. At the very moment that Bangladesh emerged as a free nation espousing emancipation for all, it undertook a stringent family planning program disregarding the fundamental human rights of all its citizens.

In 1976 the Government of Bangladesh (GOB) recognized population growth as the number one problem of the country and devised a population policy to reduce fertility rates. The Fourth Five-Year Plan (1990-1995) has set goals to reduce the Total Fertility Rate from 4.3 in 1990 to 3.4 in 1995, with the ultimate objective of reaching the Natural Replacement Rate of 1 by the year 2005. The government has set a target for the Contraceptive Prevalence Rate (CPR) in 1995 at 50 percent. The CPR is the percentage of couples in the nation who use contraception. Raising the rate to 50 percent requires an increase of 4.1 million couples over the 1990 figures.

Public policy regarding contraceptive services is to provide a wide range of choices, the so-called "cafeteria system" with a choice of "reliable, modern" methods. The mainstay of the program is oral contraception followed by sterilization, mainly female sterilization. Recently there has been an increase in the promotion of injectable contraceptives and the removal of contraceptive foams from the list of methods available to Bangladeshi couples. Sterilization levels seem to have plateaued at about 30 percent of the total CPR. The emphasis today is on contraceptive methods, such as Norplant, which are long acting and easy to monitor, but also reversible.

Norplant

Norplant is a progestin-based hormonal contraceptive for women. Six tiny silastic capsules containing levonorgestrel are implanted just under the skin, usually in the upper left arm, through a minor surgical procedure. These capsules release the hormone at a low, steady rate of 30 mcg a day into the blood stream. Norplant is effective for five years, after which time it must be removed through another, and this time more complicated, surgical procedure. Norplant becomes effective within hours of insertion and return to fertility following removal of the device is immediate. The most common side effect with Norplant is irregular bleeding. The bleeding varies from woman to woman and ranges from mild spotting to prolonged bleeding. Consultation with a health care provider is recommended only with heavy bleeding. Norplant should not be used by women with active thromboembolic disorders, undiagnosed genital bleeding, acute liver disease, known or suspected breast cancer and should not be used during pregnancy. Women with breast nodules, diabetes, high blood pressure, high cholesterol or triglycerides, migraine or other headaches, epilepsy, depression, gall bladder, or kidney or heart disease can only take Norplant after discussing their condition with their health care providers, and then only if they have regular checkups. This long list of provisos makes Norplant among the most provider-dependent contraceptive methods available. It not only requires trained personnel for insertion and removal but also requires counseling services before insertion and during follow up visits.

Norplant was developed in the United States by the Population Council, which retains the patent for this contraceptive. After a series of trials worldwide, it was accepted as a safe and effective method in 1992 by the Food and Drug Administration of the United States, one of the more stringent drug regulatory bodies in the world. It is used as one of the principal forms of contraception by the Indonesian family planning program. It is manufactured by Leiras Medica of Finland, the first commercial manufacturer of Norplant. It is expected to be produced in other countries in the near future.

Norplant already has been used by several million women in several countries, including the United States, Finland, Indonesia, Chile, the Dominican Republic and China. It was introduced in Bangladesh in 1985 through a Phase III clinical trial conducted by the then Bangladesh Fertility Research Project (BFRP) in three centers. A total of 681 women were recruited in the trial. The success of the clinical trial led to a larger clinical trial in 1988 that included 2,657 women from seven centers, including the three original centers. In 1990 plans were made for a further expansion into a "Norplant Preintroductory Pilot Phase" (NPIPP) to include 32 centers and 24,000 women in small towns close to the rural areas. The NPIPP was designed to "evaluate the possibility of introduction of Norplant in normal programmatic conditions rather than especially equipped clinical facilities" (Kamal, et al., 1991). Based on the results of the trial, GOB purchased 24,000 Norplants with IDA assistance.[1]

Today, Norplant has been incorporated into the Family Planning Program in Bangladesh. Despite protests from women's groups and commitments by the government to include women in policy discussions following the International Conference on Population and Development in Cairo, the government ordered new procurements of Norplant without any consultations with women's groups. A shipment of 5000 Norplants was received in June, 1995, and the government plans to add 36,000 new Norplant users per year.

Norplant has been seen as a panacea for the problem of overpopulation in Bangladesh, especially because safety questions seemed to have been addressed and the product was approved by the Food and Drug Administration of the United States. However, what continues to be overlooked are women's own views concerning their ability to obtain contraceptive services which are critical for the success of any contraceptive method, but especially so for a provider-dependent method such as Norplant.

Naripokkho

Naripokkho is a women's organization established in 1983. Naripokkko was formed by a group of women who felt the need for a space to discuss the status of women and to analyze how development programs in Bangladesh are affecting women. From the outset, it was agreed that Naripokkho's positions on any issue would be

---

[1] International Development Assistance of the World Bank.

based on analysis of our own experiences, which would then lead to campaigns. In 1987, Naripokkho coordinated a year-long discussion on contraception and family planning services following the death of a woman from tetanus after a sterilization operation. Naripokkko came to the conclusion that safe contraception was a basic human right.

The Norplant Campaign

In 1989, Naripokkho started its campaign on Norplant. Naripokkho's concerns regarding Norplant were not so much with the safety and efficacy of Norplant as a contraceptive method but with the service delivery system in place for this very provider-dependant method of contraception. Given the history of family planning policies in Bangladesh and the level of health services available, we were worried that women could be subject to coercion and that their own feelings about their health and symptoms could be disregarded. Naripokkka also worried that women might not be able to get the device removed upon request. It was at this time that the results from the clinical trial were being publicized. Naripokkho had questions regarding the validity of the clinical trial. Examination of the Norplant data worldwide and in Bangladesh revealed different patterns in the side effects reported. Moreover, BFRP, which was conducting the study, reported that women who requested removal of Norplant before the full five years often were asked to take some time to consider their decision. Field reports found that women were asked to wait six months or longer to have Norplant removed. An independent investigation into the quality of services found that of the women who had Norplant removed early, 10 percent reported that it required "a lot" of effort to get the device removed.

In 1990, Naripokkho interviewed five women in a poor Northern district, who had accepted Norplant from a clinic of the Family Planning Association of Bangladesh, an NGO affiliate of IPPF. All five women reported serious problems with Norplant and four requested removal on a variety of occasions but were refused.

Masuda Begum had Norplant inserted December 1988. At the time of the interview in March, 1990, she complained of weakness and continuous bleeding. She reported that she had requested removal twice. But she added, "Every time I asked for removal, they became angry." Romeza Begum had Norplant inserted February,

1989. At the time of the interview, she was suffering from dizziness, weakness, menstrual irregularities and hot flashes. She said when she asked for removal she was told, "Why did you take it? No need to remove it. You will be alright."

Saleha said she started having serious problems with Norplant after the fourth month following insertion. She had problems with irregular bleeding and she blacked out a few times. When she went back to the center, staff members told her the symptoms were related to weakness and gave her iron tablets. But the bleeding continued. By the time of the one-year follow-up, she had become very ill. Her sister took her to the FPAB clinic and asked to have Norplant removed. She said the clinic staff refused to remove the device and showered her and her sister with verbal abuse. Saleha then went to a doctor in her village who removed the Norplant.

Following publicity of these interviews, USAID, the main donor for the Norplant trial, investigated the reports. The USAID investigation corroborated our report. USAID raised questions regarding the record keeping of the trial and initiated a study to examine the quality of Norplant services in the trial. USAID then decided to withdraw its support for the expansion of Norplant in Bangladesh and advised the World Bank to do the same. However, neither the World Bank nor the GOB paid heed to this advice. The plans for the expansion continued.

USAID initiated an independent study to investigate the quality of Norplant services in Bangladesh. They appointed a technical committee to review the design and analyses of the study. The technical committee included Naripokkho and other women health activists. The study thoroughly explored both qualitative and quantitative issues. Results of this study confirmed our initial fears and findings from the interviews of the small group of women. The study showed that only 17 percent of the women who accepted Norplant knew of the possible side effects. Most of the women only knew about menstrual irregularities. Interviews with service providers showed that many physicians and counselors did not know about all the contraindications for the use of Norplant. As far as removal was concerned, only 15 percent of the acceptors were aware that Norplant could be removed on request.

After the study findings were disclosed, the GOB responded with a declaration that removal was a right of the client. Naripokkho continued monitoring Norplant services to see how and whether this "right" was being respected. Interviews with 60 Norplant acceptors in different parts of the country—Dhaka, Bogra, Rajshahi and Rangpur—confirmed an improvement in access to removal. However, major problems with regard to quality of services were revealed. The investigation revealed that:

- Counseling for the acceptors was, at best, cursory.
- Screening procedures which had been used during the clinical trial phase to determine suitable candidates were no longer comprehensive.
- Most of our interviewees were totally uninformed regarding health conditions which contraindicated Norplant use, for example, jaundice, which is quite common in Bangladesh.
- Headaches and blurring of vision, which are very serious side effects, were disregarded as minor problems unrelated to the Norplant.
- Training was inadequate regarding insertions and removal. In several instances incorrect insertion techniques resulted in some of the capsules migrating further up into the arm.
- The quality of health checkups varied from center to center and from woman to woman such that some women did not even get minimal care including having their blood pressure or body weights taken.
- Clinic staff members' response to complaints of side effects was often limited to providing reassurance and nutritional advice. Women who complained of side effects such as dizziness, weakness and, in a few cases, blurring of vision were told their problems would subside after a while. They were advised to eat protein-rich foods, which most could not afford.
- Proper follow-up was further hampered by the attitude of the Norplant providers. Many women complained that service providers were often rude and unsympathetic, which discouraged them from talking freely or approaching them, especially at times other than for scheduled visits. Many women said they were treated as hysterical women and accused of fabricating their health problems.

The problems of the health care system cannot be placed solely at the feet of the Government of Bangladesh. Norplant had been through a clinical trial and a pre-introductory pilot phase in

Bangladesh with international assistance (USAID and the World Bank, respectively). However these trials failed to inculcate any ethos of basic services provision and care. According to the service protocol, body weight, blood pressure, side effects and removal requests are to be recorded. Random examination of client cards by Naripokkho reveal that this is not being done, although records are apparently kept by the service provider. While it is commendable that the service provider has kept this information, possibly for their own use or research purposes, the lack of record keeping on client cards means that if a woman goes to a different health care provider, this information will not be available to assist in her health care.

Conclusion

The service delivery system for Norplant remains poor. The single recent improvement is the recognition of removal of Norplant upon request as a right and refusal to do so as a serious offense. Providers appear to be more accommodating regarding requests for removal. However, providers have not made using Norplant easier. The poor services for follow-up and the reluctance to take side effects seriously are disturbing.

In our advocacy for better services, we must take into account that Norplant is here to stay and that there are women queuing up for it in certain areas. These are facts which cannot be ignored. It reflects women's needs for contraception. The appeal of Norplant is its promise of hassle-free contraception for five years. The desperation that poor women face in Bangladesh is portrayed in the case of a woman in Bogra, who insisted on retaining Norplant when she went to the hospital, even after suffering severe side effects and after doctors advised removal. It is imperative that under these desperate circumstances that efforts be taken to address the issues of general health and contraception together and not as separate entities. Our campaign ultimately is not only for better family planning services but also for the right to good health care in general.

References

Azim, T. & Huq, N. (1990, July 27). Family Planning at the Cost of Women's Health. *Holiday*.

Government of Bangladesh. (1994). *The Bangladesh Country Report submitted to the International Conference on Population and Development.*

Kamal, G. M., Hardee-Cleveland, K., & Barkat-e-Khuda. (1991). *The Quality of Norplant Services in Bangladesh*. Dhaka, Bangladesh: Associates for Community and Population Research.

Population Council. (1990). *Norplant Levonorgestrel Implants: A Summary of Scientific Data*. New York: Author.

Chapter 26

Sex Education and the Religious Hierarchy in Costa Rica

Alda Facio & Laura Queralt

Introduction

During the late 1970s and the early 1980s, Costa Rican feminists began questioning the so-called natural differences between men and women. Feminists held seminars and workshops and wrote, translated and distributed essays on what was defined as the patriarchal socialization process which constructed men from male babies and women from female ones. We talked about how masculinity and femininity are conceived as mirror opposites and how the socialization process works to create and maintain this dichotomy. We analyzed toys and games as gendered. We showed how books, magazines and other publications that children and adolescents read differentiate gender identities even further. We discussed television, radio, films, songs and music. The family, religion and the law were also scrutinized for the role they play in this process which creates so much inequality between men and women.

The educational system also was held responsible for its subordination of women, not only for the sexist materials used in the schools and universities, but also for what transmitted verbally when, for example, girls are scolded for asking questions while boys are praised for doing exactly the same. The educational system also was criticized for omissions: human sexuality was not taught at any level in the schools. Nor was any attention given to how to be happy, healthy, nurturing lovers or how to be responsible, loving parents. Indeed, these were topics which were not even considered as something that could be learned at school.

Essays and articles were published and hand-distributed. Lectures and seminars were offered at the University of Costa Rica, the Supreme Court, the Ministry of Public Education, the Ministry of

Agriculture and the Ministry of Culture as well as in schools, hotels, banks and parks. Many of these workshops, essays, articles and lectures focused on sexuality and reproductive rights.[1] It is interesting to note that although these articles and lectures did not refer specifically to "reproductive rights"—the term was not used in those days—we did understand women's need for full access to a wide range of reproductive health services, which included not only the reduction of maternal mortality and the health risks of illegal and unsafe abortions, but also women's need for a non-sexist sexual education and the right to choose freely when and with whom to be sexual.

In those days we thought that the right to equality and non-discrimination meant that women's needs, including those needs that were particular to us, should be taken into account and be satisfied. Having understood these needs in the context of the right to equality, it was not difficult to move, later on in the nineties, from the concept of sexual and reproductive needs to sexual and reproductive rights as these were defined in Part I in the Introduction and Point 17 of the Final Document of the Regional Caribbean and Latin American Women's Preparatory Satellite Conference on Human Rights, *La Nuestra*, held in San José, Costa Rica, in December, 1992.[2] These read that:

> I. It is necessary, for the recognition of women's human rights to include our diversity as women of distinct ages, races/ethnicities, socio-economic conditions, disabilities, sexual preferences, geographical locations, civil status, etc.

and

> 17. Rights concerning human reproduction should be recognized so that motherhood is for every woman a free and conscious choice. Genetic experimentation without adequate mechanisms of social monitoring in which women are represented should also be considered a violation of the human rights of women.

---

[1] See, for example, the premier issue of the first feminist magazine in Costa Rica, *Ventana*, published in June, 1982.

[2] See, for instance, the nineteen-point petition that the women at this conference drew up in *Memoria de la Reunión Satélite la "Nuestra:" Diagnóstico y estrategias sobre derechos humanos de las mujeres en América Latina y el Caribe.* (1993, October). San José, Costa Rica: Programa Mujer, Justicia y Género, ILANUD and Programa Género y Poder, ILSA.

But back in the early 1980s, although many people listened with interest and displayed respect for these new ideas, many more hurled insults (and, in some instances, rotten eggs) at any woman perceived as feminist. That is why, at the time, we thought that most of the people were not at all convinced that from very early in our childhood we learn the "appropriate" behavior for our sex. On the contrary, we believed that most members of the audience were clinging to the idea that men and women were created unequally by God himself. We thought then that even the women had rejected our belief that if the identities of women and men are constructed by the many patriarchal institutions in society, they can be deconstructed in order to build more egalitarian societies.

Fortunately, we were wrong. Slowly those who attended these seminars, who read the publications or listened to the radio programs that discussed these new ways of perceiving reality from a gender perspective and those who came back to Costa Rica after having studied these theories about the construction of gender identities abroad, started their own quiet revolutions in their fields. One of these many revolutions was and still is happening in the Ministry of Public Education, specifically in the area of education in human sexuality. And, like all revolutions, it is disturbing to those who are opposed to change because they do not want to lose their privileged status.

Unfortunately, we also were wrong in our assessment of the hierarchy of the Catholic Church, which is the representative of the official religion of Costa Rica.[3] The church leadership very definitely understood what we were proposing when we insisted that a different kind of education and, especially a different type of sex education, could produce healthier and freer women and men. The hierarchy of the Church did all it could to combat any efforts to introduce a broad-based and progressive curriculum for sex education into the schools.

The following case study exemplifies how the hierarchy of the Catholic Church tried to stop the introduction of a sex education program into the public education system of Costa Rica. This program was based on the ideals set forth in the Universal Declaration of Human Rights and the Costa Rican Constitution which, among

---

[3] Article 76 of the Political Constitution of the Republic of Costa Rica states: Apostolic Roman Catholicism is the religion of the state, which contributes to its maintenance without impeding the free practice, in the republic, of other cults that oppose neither the universal moral nor good customs.

others, recognizes the need for equality of the sexes in order for women to be able to enjoy their human rights. Although the Church leaders were not successful in halting the program completely, they were able to delay the program for more than four years. During those four years the church leaders held to a conservative philosophy that supported the status quo and the patriarchal views on human sexuality that trap women in a subordinate status.

Information about this process and the intervention of the Catholic hierarchy was given to the authors of this article with the recommendation that the names of the teachers, parents and ministry functionaries who were concerned enough about this not be made public for fear of possible reprisals against them by government or church officials. Although in Costa Rica there are many Catholic priests, nuns and lay persons who have progressive views, their voices are generally silenced by the Catholic hierarchy, which at this moment in history is in the hands of conservative priests, bishops and archbishops. This has not always been so. At other times in the history of Costa Rica, the Catholic hierarchy was crucial in promoting, for example, labor rights and free education for boys and girls.

The Case

Many obstacles were encountered by the Ministry of Public Education of Costa Rica in the process of producing three teacher's manuals on sex education. The church hierarchy and the fundamentalist groups within the church were the constituencies who presented most of the obstacles. The case study reveals the resistance one encounters in trying to introduce a freer, healthier and more egalitarian concept of sexuality in a small country where the Roman Catholic Church is also the state's religion.

The manuals, which contain guidelines for teachers on how to conduct a course on human sexuality for adolescents, were developed by the National Center of Pedagogy (Centro Nacional de Diagnostico e Investigación or CENADI) housed in the Ministry of Public Education under its program Education on Population. This program was created to educate the young on the critical issues affecting the populations of the world from a perspective which transcends the concept of mere population control to one which explains the interconnection among the cultural, social, and economic factors present in these issues.

One of the main areas of the Education on Population Program is the project Education in Human Sexuality. For this program area CE-NADI decided to produce and publish a Teacher's Manual on Sex Education for grades 7, 8 and 9 and, if the project went well, for grades 10 and 11. The guidelines were to help teachers inform and guide their young students on healthy and egalitarian human behavior and sexuality from a wider, more positive and nonsexist approach to human sexuality. The Catholic hierarchy, along with the most conservative and fundamentalist groups within the Catholic Church, intervened in the process of creating these guidelines and interrupted the project at several junctures.

The manuals project began in May, 1987, with the creation of a first draft of each of the three manuals planned by CENADI. Second and third versions followed a few months later after taking into account observations from population and development experts, pedagogues from the Ministry of Public Education and others.

By 1988, the staff of the project was ready to implement some of the activities and workshops proposed in the manuals. A fourth draft of the manuals would include observations from teachers, family members and students who had actually worked with the manuals. At the end of that year, a fourth version of each of those three manuals was ready.

The plan for the program was to submit this fourth version to 13 metropolitan high schools for a validation process during 1989. This did not happen. The Ministry of Public Education suspended the process due to a petition from the Episcopal Conference. The bishops wanted to see the fourth version of the manuals before more students participated in any of the activities the manuals proposed. This was the first time that the Catholic hierarchy intervened in the process of creating the manuals, even though the hierarchy had known earlier that the manuals were being developed with input from the Catholic priesthood.

In order to review these guidelines the Episcopal Conference recommended appointing a committee comprised of lay members of the Ministry of Education and representatives of the Catholic hierarchy. The committee would be appointed by the Episcopal Conference. Because of the powerful influence of the Church hierarchy, the Minister of Education accepted this second intervention. The committee was appointed and worked until February, 1990. The report produced by the committee proposed the creation of a permanent committee to oversee the production of the manuals until a completed final version was accepted by all the parties involved. This permanent mixed committee was established and a fifth version, based on the recommendations of the first committee and on a bibliographic review of the Education on Population program, was created.

Between January and March, 1991, a first printing of the three Teacher's Manuals on Sex Education was produced. The project was set to begin three years after the date originally planned. However, yet another delay was in the offing. This time the Episcopal Conference demanded that these manuals not be distributed to the teachers and argued that they contained "irregular moral standards." Again the Ministry of Public Education complied with the delay. The Episcopal Conference then asked for yet another revision, this time by the bishops themselves. Again the Ministry complied and the revision process continued until July, 1991, when the bishops informed the Ministry that they had not made any specific reforms to the content of the manuals but added the following suggestions:

+ those teachers who were selected to use the manuals were to be given, in addition to the manuals, the Church's doctrinal framework on sexuality and human conduct;
+ Catholic religion teachers should be included among the teachers chosen to apply the guidelines; and
+ teachers should be trained before they are allowed to apply the guidelines.

Even though these suggestions meant that the implementation of the program would be more difficult, more expensive and would be delayed yet again, they were well received by the Minister of Education, who suspended the program until funds could be found.

In November, 1991, the media printed different versions of a story that said that Pope John Paul II himself had criticized the manuals. Rumors circulated that a letter had been sent to the President of Costa Rica by the Pope demanding that the manuals not be used in the schools. Empowered by these stories, the most conservative and fundamentalist groups within the Church started pushing the hierarchy to forbid the use of the manuals. By December 19, 1991, the President of Costa Rica, without consulting those who had been involved in the process of creating the first four versions, announced the creation of still another version.[4] This fifth version would be done by a mixed committee designated by the Catholic hierarchy.

In spite of the President's compliance, several months later the Archbishop of San José declared to the press that a special committee designated by the bishops themselves, without the participation of the state, had done the revising and had now finished a new version of the manuals. The bishops' version, which modified the reforms made by the first mixed committee was handed out in August, 1992. The new reforms eliminated some paragraphs and drawings from the previous versions as well as some of the boxes containing the teachings of the Catholic Church.

By the end of 1992, the Ministry of Public Education had again worked on a final version, which, according to a Ministry informant, took into account only those modifications made by bishops that it felt enriched the content but did not contradict the philosophy and principles of the Education on Population program. The Ministry did not accept some of the recommendations made by the bishops on the grounds that they opposed scientific notions.

In March, 1993, the guidelines finally were distributed to high schools for teachers of home education, religion and science as well as to school orientation departments. These guidelines are designed to be used by these teachers as a supplement to their subject matter and not merely as an extra topic to be discussed at the end of the semester. The manuals offer numerous participatory exercises for use in class. The manuals also promote the establishment of team work to enhance discussion and creativity.

With regard to the content directed at overcoming the sexist power relationships in our culture that discriminate against women, the guidelines make important contributions. For example:

- The 7th grade manual proposes activities that permit students to understand the role of society in shaping feminine and masculine sex roles and allows them to demystify concepts.
- The 8th grade manual presents activities that show, for example, that sexual stereotypes are false social values imposed by society. The manuals also show that it is possible to enjoy sexual experiences with a mature and responsible attitude. The manuals also inform students about the implications of pregnancy for teenagers, the risks for the mother and for the child

---

[4] See the local daily, *La Nacion,* (1995, December 19, p. 1).

and what pregnancy implies for the couple regarding their personal development.

- The 9th grade manual is about the importance of making the right decisions regarding one's own life plan, while taking into account obstacles caused by sexism. It provides a less restrictive concept of human sexuality that allows the young to recognize themselves as sexual beings and to question double standards that give a superior role to men.

Although these manuals are very progressive and non-sexist, they are not an unqualified success because of the repeated interruptions by the church hierarchy. So many delays and so many versions eroded the funds that had been raised to oversee the implementation of these manuals by teachers trained in their use. As a result, neither the training nor the supervision can be done for lack of time and funds. Further, there are no funds available to collect data on how the teachers are using these manuals. The staff member in charge of the project in CENADI indicated that they have isolated data from indirect sources who say that the schools are using the guidelines mainly in home education courses.

The original plan for the manuals project was to oversee and promote the role of teachers as protagonists of the change proposed in the guidelines regarding a new concept and experience of sexuality. It is hard to believe that all teachers will become protagonists of change if they themselves are not even aware of their own sexism and have not begun seriously questioning their own value system in relation to their sexuality. The process of producing the manuals has legitimated, in a way, the influence and power of the Catholic hierarchy over our lives. Within this context, it is difficult for anyone to free himself or herself from his or her own prejudices. But, in the case of teachers, this might be doubly so because they are afraid of losing their jobs if they do anything to antagonize the hierarchy of the Catholic Church.

The good news is that the staff of the Education on Population Program has not been intimidated. This year the staff is working on a teacher's manual for primary schools that includes basic ideas on sexuality. In addition, the staff is finishing the teacher's manual for the 10th and 11th grades. This shows that in their minds, the process itself and the 7th, 8th and 9th grade manuals are successful. In spite of all the controversy and the opposition of the Church, the new manuals include a full range of material on human sexuality, including the connection between love and sex for couples, prostitution, sexually transmitted diseases, heterosexuality, homosexuality and the physiology of the human sexual response.

The students and teachers who will get a chance to work with these manuals likely will have a healthier attitude towards their own sexuality as a result of working with the project. If so, they will have the necessary tools to find solutions to prevent adolescent pregnancy, sexual abuse, discrimination, exploitation and many other problems related to inadequate, abusive or frightening sexual experiences. It is hoped that, over time, a happier, fuller and egalitarian expression of human sexuality will emerge at the societal level.

Part V

Activism to Advance Women's Human Rights

Chapter 27
Organizing for Peace in the Midst of War: Experiences of Women in Sri Lanka[145]

Sunila Abeyesekera

Background

Sri Lanka has been a country in conflict since the late 1970s, when militant youth from the minority Tamil community (which constitutes almost 18 percent of the total population of the island) first took up arms in their struggle for an independent state of Tamil Eelam. In subsequent years, the conflict has escalated with internecine warfare among different Tamil groups and heightened hostility between the Tamil and Muslim communities adding further complexity to the problem. Since the late 1980s, the military conflict has been primarily between the armed forces of the government of Sri Lanka and the cadres of the Liberation Tigers of Tamil Eelam (LTTE).

During the years from 1987 to 1990, the Sri Lankan government also had to deal with an insurgency launched by predominantly Sinhala youth in the south of the island, initially begun as a movement of protest against the signing of a Peace Accord regarding the conflict in the north and east of the country with the Indian government; this insurgency was crushed with the use of massive brute force by the state.

---

[145]In writing this case study on Sri Lanka, I am basing my ideas on my own experiences as someone who has been active in organizing and mobilizing women in Sri Lanka since the 1970s, and as a member of two major women's coalitions in Sri Lanka, the Women's Action Committee and Mothers and Daughters of Lanka, from their very inception. Since there is very little documentation on these coalitions available, and since I am well aware of the subjective nature of my interpretation of events and incidents, I would like to stress the incomplete nature of the reflections that follow, and take full responsibility for *my* opinions as set out below.

The conflict has extracted a heavy toll from all the people of Sri Lanka. Fatalities among the combatant groups, both military and militant, have been in the thousands; thousands of non-combatants have died as well, some of them caught in actual crossfire and others victims of random attacks on civilian targets throughout the island. In the process of "hunting down" alleged militants by members of the security forces, thousands of persons have been detained. The barbaric practice of "disappearance" took root in Sri Lanka in the 1980s, and escalated to a point in which over 40,000 persons are alleged to have "disappeared" in the years from 1987 to 1990. In their report for 1991, the UN Working Group on Enforced and Involuntary Disappearances stated that Sri Lanka is the "worst case ever" on record.

Hundreds of thousands of Sri Lankans have also been displaced from their homes as a consequence of the conflict; many of them have fled abroad, to India and to almost every country in Western Europe and North America. Others have lived in makeshift camps scattered through the north-western, north-central and western provinces for over three years; their lives have been completely disrupted, causing extreme psychological and emotional stress.

Strict regulations controlling the entry of goods to the northern province has created shortages and scarcities of every essential item including food, fuel and drugs for a population that is virtually trapped there by the war. Provision of public services has been severely curtailed: for example, there has been no supply of electricity to the northern province since June 1990. The damage caused to homes and to property, including agriculturally productive land, because of the conflict has been massive. The de-facto division of the island into south (Sinhala-dominated) and north-east (Tamil dominated) has exacerbated the polarization between the two communities.

In this context of civil conflict, Sri Lanka has progressively become an anti-democratic and militaristic state with scant respect for the human and civil rights of its people. Repressive legislation that is counter to international standards and norms was added to the statute books beginning in the early 1980s. The lack of respect for due process by the guardians of law and order coupled with a lack of accountability by state officials contributed to a major crisis of legitimacy in the country. The institutions of civil society, in particular the media, the mechanisms for the administration of justice and the institutes of higher education have been among those that have come most heavily under siege in these circumstances.

As the conflict intensified in the past decade, calling for peace and for a resolution to the conflict that would guarantee dignity and equality for the Tamil people of Sri Lanka became a contentious issue. Sri Lankan society became increasingly polarized in terms of ethnic and religious identities and by the late 1980s, calling for peace and a negotiated end to the war was sufficient for those espousing such views to be labeled as "traitors" by the state as well as by hardline nationalist forces on both sides of the conflict.

Thus, Sri Lanka enters the 21st century with a legacy of political repression and a culture of violence combined with a widespread sense of fear that leads to paralysis and silence among the civilian population; these factors pose a significant threat to any envisioning of a peaceful and democratic Sri Lanka in the years to come. Working for human rights in such a situation has been a dangerous and arduous task; many activists and organizers have paid with their lives for their commitment to principles of justice and equality.

Impact of the Conflict on Women's Organizing

The conflict has had very particular implications for organizing and mobilizing around issues relating to women's rights. The overall situation required an expansion of the parameters for discussing women's rights to include a broader framework of human rights and democratic issues. Simultaneously, building strategic alliances among women's groups, and between women's groups and other actors on the democratic front became a critical factor in determining the survival of any group or organization committed to changing the situation of women.

In Sri Lanka, as in many other countries all over the world, the decade from 1975 to 1985 saw the flourishing of many different forms of organization among women. The older, welfare-oriented women's organizations re-positioned themselves a little from their original agendas, taking into account the new themes of "women and development" and "empowerment" in their considerations of women's needs and concerns, while the women's wings of the political parties became reactivated as well. Among the new, and more "autonomous" women's groups that emerged during this time, some were specific to particular sectors while others located themselves on a regional or provincial basis in the south and north. There were also women's groups that focused more on consciousness-raising, skill-training, research and educational activities with an island-wide focus.

Activity on women's rights in this period focused on what one could identify as the more "traditional" areas. On the one hand, women struggled for gains under the "equal rights" commitment set out in the Constitution of Sri Lanka. In this context, the right to employment and education free of gender-based discrimination, the right to organize, the right to receive equal pay for equal work, the right to protection in the workplace, the right to paid maternity leave were among those which concerned women's groups. On the other hand, women asserted their right to live free from fear of violence, harassment and intimidation in their homes and outside and to control their reproductive functions. This was the basis on which various campaigns against rape, domestic violence, the sexist portrayal of women in the media and the forced use of contraceptives were undertaken.

As Sri Lanka entered the decade of the 1990s, the conflict heightened and the crisis in the country assumed unprecedented proportions, affecting the capacity of women's groups to organize and mobilize. Severe repression of community-based organizing work and a virtual "reign of terror" in many parts of the south of the island and an intensification of the war in the north and east found many women's groups scattered and disintegrated. Agitation on women-specific issues receded to the background, and broader human rights issues came to the fore, such as, the right to freedom from arbitrary arrest and detention, torture and "disappearance," the right to a fair trial, the freedom of opinion, expression and information.

Along with this strategic "retreat" came an increasing awareness of the need to re-think definitions of "human rights" from the perspective of the experiences of tens of thousands of Sri Lankan women; many issues which were affecting women all over the island very deeply were hardly the concern of mainstream human rights organizations within the country. The question of internal displacement and its differential impact on women, the question of the far-reaching and long-lasting consequences of "disappearance" of male family members on the women and children who were left behind, the question of "post-trauma stress syndrome" and how to deal with it, the question of the use of rape as a form of torture of women, the question of special needs of women political detainees, the question of impunity of members of the state security forces who were taking advantage of the existence of a state of emergency to rape and murder women—all these emerged as new areas of concern.

Sri Lankan women who had been involved in organizing and mobilizing around issues of their own in previous years now had to face up to the challenge of taking up issues that were very new to them, and that were dangerous and politically volatile. They had to break down the barriers of silence and mistrust that had grown among women of the different ethnic communities, and try to evolve some common basis for work among all those women who had been the victims of the conflict and of violations of their human rights. They had to move away from relatively "safe" and apolitical words of peace and harmony and take up controversial and dangerous political positions opposing the war.

Some women's groups faced the changes in the Sri Lankan situation by adjusting their regular activities to include more concern for the plight of those women who had been the direct or indirect victims of politically motivated violence. Others launched into more active campaigning against the war, linking the issue of violence against women in the home to violence in the society at large, and also to war.

Among the groups that have worked within this new context are the Mothers' Front and the Organization of Family Members of the Disappeared, both broad-based organizations, which took up the issues around incidents of "disappearance;" Women for Peace, Women in Need, the Family Services Centre, the Family Rehabilitation Centre and several village-based self-help groups, which dealt with economic and psychological problems; and the SURIYA Women's Development Centre, which dealt specifically with the problems of displaced women. In the recent past, the Mothers and Daughters of Lanka (MDSL), a women's coalition, came together in a situation of conflictual diversity for the achievement of common goals. Their experience illustrates something of the limitations, constraints as well as gains of mobilizing women against the war at the actual moment of conflict.

Collective Mobilizing by Women Against the War

In 1982, a solidarity group for women strikers in a garment factory formed an umbrella organization of autonomous Sri Lankan women's groups called the Women's Action Committee (WAC). Membership in this committee was open to women's groups as well as to individual women who were concerned with the socio-political and economic implications of organizing *as* women in the contemporary Sri Lankan context. WAC linked women working in different work sectors as well as in different parts of the country. Involved in this initiative were women factory workers from the industrial zones north of Colombo, peasant women from the north-west and southeast provinces, Tamil women, plantation workers from the central highlands, and community education and media groups with a special focus on women.

The principal aims of WAC were to promote the emancipation of women at all levels of Sri Lankan society, with a particular focus on issues of democracy and respect for human rights. The question of justice and equality for minority communities received high priority. The agenda was clearly political in a broad sense but had no specific party affiliation. With these objectives in mind, WAC organized public meetings and demonstrations, seminars and discussions on women's issues, printed and distributed leaflets, pamphlets and posters, and built up a growing network of contacts among women and women's groups both inside and outside the country.

WAC celebrated three public events each year in the years from 1983 to 1987—March 8, International Women's Day; May 1, International Workers' Day; and December 10, International Human Rights Day. On Women's Day, WAC would organize a public meeting and sometimes a demonstration, inviting all other women's groups and organizations to participate, and have women from diverse sectors and communities speak from the platforms. On May Day and Human Rights Day, WAC would have its representatives speak from platforms arranged by trade unions (for May 1) or human rights groups (for December 10). WAC also lobbied for trade unions and human rights groups to place specific women's demands on their agenda for these meetings and seminars.

From its inception WAC, which was primarily composed of Sinhala women from the southern parts of the island, maintained close contact with Tamil women's groups in the north, in particular, with the Mothers' Front and the Jaffna Women's Study Circle. Although WAC gave priority to working in collaboration with women and women's groups from the minority communities, WAC also attempted to build broad coalitions among the different women's groups and organizations. WAC's distinguishing platform was the call for an end to the war in the north and east, coupled with the demand for a politically negotiated solution to the conflict and for recognition of the rights of Tamil people.

A just peace and an end to the war were the slogans most often reiterated in WAC posters and banners. WAC actively encouraged its members not only to carry on with anti-racist education and campaigning *within* their groups and constituencies but also urged more women to participate in broader public forums, such as those to be found within political parties, human rights groups and trade unions, where the issues of peace and a settlement of the conflict were being raised and discussed. This experience was to have a major influence on organizing for peace in the following years.

In 1984, a group of women calling themselves Women for Peace came together to publish a public call for peace; they were mainly middle-class professionals from all ethnic groups who had a commitment to agitate for an end to the war. Their focus was on public education that would contribute to establishing non-racist attitudes in society. They conducted public seminars, published a series of educational leaflets, and particularly focused on campaigning within schools. However, the heightening of the crisis in the south left even such a group unable to respond to the gravity of the situation.

The worst period of violence in modern Sri Lanka took place in the years from 1987 to 1990 in the south and from 1990 onwards in the north and east. Although tens of thousands of people had been brutally murdered and "disappeared" and many more thousands detained under barbaric conditions, the level of intimidation and terror throughout the island was so high that there were no public protests or condemnations of the violations. During this time, many women's groups had almost ceased to exist, others had severely curtailed their range of activities. The links between the groups had broken down and contacts between the women's groups and other movements were minimal. There was polarization among groups based on ideological and political perceptions of the war and the resolution of the conflict. The WAC became non-functional during this period.

Mothers and Daughters of Lanka

Faced with the paralysis in the south and the worsening situation in the north and east, and confronting the social crisis created by almost 1 million persons (out of a total population of 17 million persons) fleeing from the war zones to the south of the island in a matter of four or five months, in October 1990, some of the members of WAC joined with other women to publish a half-page petition for peace in the daily newspapers. The text was in the form of a poem, and signatures of over eight hundred women, who signed as individuals, were collected. Among the names were those of well-known and respected actresses, singers, writers and public figures.

There was a lot of discussion about who exactly would take the responsibility of publicizing the petition. Although there was no formal structure or organization, it was decided to place a collective name on the petition rather than assign that burden to individuals. Agreeing on a name was a controversial issue; some felt strongly that the word "mother" should be central, others that the use of "mother" would exclude women who were not mothers, yet others that the term "mother" denoted some fallback to biological essentialism. The need was for a name that would denote the concerns of *all* women in this situation, a name that would define the collective identity of the group as females, living on the same soil. The name finally decided on by the group was "Mothers and Daughters of Lanka." Still, this compromise was not without its problems and it led to confusion and a great many jokes even among the signatories.

Obtaining space for the petition in the newspapers proved problematic; editors were concerned about the text, since at this time taking a stand against the war could be construed as being unpatriotic. The prestige of the signatories, a great deal of personal lobbying with editors and newspaper owners and payment of commercial advertising rates however saw the petition appear in print. The impact of this public gesture can only be measured against the total silence of all other groups at the time about the war and the reports of atrocities and hardship in the north that were trickling down to the south very slowly.

Following the publishing of the petition and a fairly enthusiastic response from women, MDSL decided to go ahead with plans for a multi-religious day of prayer for peace in the large park in the center of the capital, Colombo, on December 10. Since this was a time when all public gatherings were forbidden by law, the decision to hold a prayer-meeting was a tactic to get around the prohibition. At the same time, it reflected an understanding among the active members of MDSL that in order to launch a successful public campaign for peace, they would have to build collaborative links with women from a much broader group than those who had been in WAC, including women belonging to various religious denominations.

Posters and banners calling for peace were displayed in the vicinity of the park and over a hundred women gathered there—Buddhist, Christian, Hindu and Muslim—risking their lives in order to share in prayers for peace. This was once again the first public demonstration against the war in Colombo. No political party, no trade union, no broad-based movement had taken such a step up to this point in time.

Since then, MDSL has continued with its public campaign against the war at different levels. It has organized public meetings to celebrate Women's Day, and collaborated in joint meetings for Human Rights Day, carrying its anti-war slogan to every platform. It has supported women in their struggle for rights at every level, but has had a particular focus on the needs and problems of women who are displaced and those who have been the indirect victims of human rights violations because of the arbitrary arrest, detention, torture or "disappearance" of their male family members. MDSL has been actively involved in joint activities with other organizations and initiatives, such as the Coalition of Human Rights Organizations and the Movement for Inter-Racial Justice and Equality. It has also represented women's rights concerns at many public fora, including international meetings.

Any appraisal of these activities must take into consideration the fact that throughout this period, the holding of public meetings and demonstrations, the distributing of leaflets and the putting up of posters are all prohibited under the Emergency Regulations under which the country has been ruled since July 1983. Thus, participating in most events organized by MDSL necessarily involves a certain risk.

Balancing Peace and War: A Difficult Business

From the outset, the task of MDSL has not been an easy one. In an atmosphere in which discrimination and hostility on the basis of ethnic origin had become increasingly institutionalized, MDSL was espousing an unpopular view speaking out against a war that many Sinhala people considered to be a "patriotic" one, and upholding the rights of individuals from all communities and political leanings on the basis of human rights norms and standards that guarantee equality and justice to all alike.

Much of the work of MDSL has involved public campaigns for peace. In particular, MDSL has focused its attention on the majority Sinhala community in the south of the island, since this is where many of its members are based. However, MDSL has always had members from all ethnic communities within its ranks and constantly agitated on behalf of women in the north and east. MDSL has also been involved in a number of support activities for displaced Tamil and Muslim women in the camps. In a context where state and non-state agencies alike engage in war-mongering, it is a difficult and challenging task to carry the message of peace and harmony among the different ethnic groups living on the island, while maintaining a critical attitude towards both the state and the non-state actors in the conflict.

The public campaigns of MDSL are carried out through community-based educational and awareness-raising campaigns supported by the different groups that constitute it. Posters and leaflets, speeches and discussions, meetings and seminars all form a part of this work. The target group is not women alone, and certainly the message is for every citizen, male and female. MDSL has also initiated several mass petitions, one that was signed by thousands of Sri Lankan women from all parts of the island, calling for an end to the war.

Apart from the public awareness-raising campaigns, MDSL has also consistently brought its anti-war opinion to the ears of public servants, policy makers and relevant government authorities, through letters and petitions. At an international level, MDSL has maintained links with women's groups abroad, and, for example, coordinated the collecting of signatures within Sri Lanka on the Violence Against Women campaign for the World Human Rights Conference in Vienna in 1993.

Moving Forward into the 21st Century

Although the activities of MDSL may seem to be on a relatively small scale, by no means have they been insignificant, especially in a situation in which very few voices within Sri Lanka have dared to speak out against the injustice to minority communities or against gross and blatant violations of human rights by the state. The voices of poor urban and rural women in particular are almost never heard in the public space and it is these voices that have strengthened MDSL's endeavors. As the war in Sri Lanka continues, and the toll on the civilian and non-combatant population becomes heavier by the day, it becomes more imperative than ever to have such initiatives taking root, no mater how small.

The experiences of MDSL so far also point to some of the problems that one has had to face in this journey, and perhaps contain some clues as to where the pitfalls in this type of organizing lie, and as to how it may be possible to resolve some of the difficulties.

What follows are some of the points of concern that have emerged in discussions with Sri Lankan women in the past years regarding the possibilities of organizing and mobilizing women around rights issues in the future. These are by no means definitive, and contain many of my personal insights into the situation.

1. Linking Women's Rights with Broader Issues of Rights

One of the main challenges to rights-based organizing posed by the Sri Lankan experiences arises from attempting to separate women's rights from broader civil and human rights, especially in a time of conflict. In tactical terms, such a separation has not been wise, nor even possible. MDSL has had to involve itself in broader human rights organizing work in order to deal with the specific problems faced by women in a situation of gross violations of human rights in general.

The example of "disappearances" is a case in point; mainstream and traditional human rights parameters focus on the person who has "disappeared." There are mechanisms and avenues of redress that can be appealed to in the event of a "disappearance"—even though in a country like Sri Lanka, recourse to such mechanisms and avenues had brought very little relief to those affected. The lack of attention to the plight of the family members of the "disappeared" is a major area of concern; they need a wide range of support services—legal aid and assistance to seek redress through the official and juridical channels; economic support since they had almost all lost a main bread-winner; social and community-based support since the incident of "disappearance" had led to their marginalization from the community; emotional and psychological support to deal with the stress and trauma caused by witnessing the abduction of a loved one and by living for a prolonged period in a state of uncertainty regarding the whereabouts of the "disappeared" person.

Somehow, a more integrated approach needs to be evolved to deal with the very real and human problems of mostly women and children who have been the secondary "victims" of "disappearance," particularly when one is working within a situation where state acknowledgment of responsibility seems still very far away.

2.   Linking Individual and Collective Violence

A particular part of the struggle around issues that has been generated by the Sri Lankan experience has been that of expanding the definition of "violence against women" to mean not only acts of violence against individual women, but to include the differential impact on women of collective and societal violence such as take place in conflicts and wars. This is because the impact has been far more grave on women than on men, in particular due to women's specific vulnerability, their role as caretaker of children and the elderly, and their dependence on support structures integrally linked to geographic location and community networks which disintegrate at a time of conflict. Thus, we have begun to speak of women as both direct and indirect victims of politically-motivated violence in the Sri Lankan context.

3.   Linking Women's Groups and Human Rights Groups

The dynamics of the relationships between women's groups and other human rights and democratic movements has also been a factor that has influenced the effectiveness of the peace campaign. The processes of negotiation and accommodation of divergent interests in a common campaign have been for the most part positive; yet, the need for the few women in the broad fora to constantly struggle to keep women's concerns on the main agenda have exposed the gaps in understanding of women's issues, as well as resistance to foregrounding women's demands that exist within other groups and social movements. In particular, the need to pressure human rights groups to become more sensitive to the specific concerns of women remains a major issue.

4. Rethinking Democracy as a Political Project

A further challenge has been posed by the need to re-think the definitions and dimensions of "democracy" as a political project. In the Sri Lankan case, the demand for the devolution of political power to the regions and decentralization of administrative structures has been a main area of contestation. Thus, women have been forced to enter the arena of discussion on democracy in a broader context than is signified by mere voting practices; women's experiences of oppression and non-representation have been critical in furthering not only their own understanding of the democratic project, but the understanding of others as well.

5. Democratizing Social Movements

The issue of democratizing social movements has also been an area of activity closely linked to the women's movement in the recent years. Through its practice MDSL has, for example, challenged existing forms and structures of organization. MDSL has remained a broad federation of diverse women and women's groups, with a rotating position of coordinator and a principle of discussion and consensus-building on every issue.

6. Linking with Pro-Democracy Institutions

Recent experiences have also led women and women's groups in Sri Lanka to ally themselves more strongly than before on the side of those institutions of civil society which are involved most deeply in the movement for opening up democratic spaces at every level. In particular, women have been closely linked to the Free Media Movement and its campaigns for the rights of freedom of expression, information and opinion.

7. Regional Linkages

The past decade has also seen a closer linking between women at the level of the South Asian region as well as of the Asian region. Sri Lankan women have been active in many regional forums that have focused on rights issues and have participated in meetings and seminars that have attempted to examine the specificities of women's situation within the regional frameworks; among them have been participation in the Asia-Pacific Women, Law and Development (APWLD) network and the Asian Women's Human Rights Commission (AWHRC).

8. Input and Critique at Policy Making Levels

The struggle by Sri Lankan women to affirm their rights within the broader framework of a movement for human rights and democracy has had an impact on policy-making at the national level in several areas. Women from MDSL were involved in a number of consultations summoned by the Ministry for Women's Affairs to draft a Women's Charter. The basic text was based on the Convention on the Elimination of All Forms of Discrimination Against Women (CEDAW); input from women ensured the inclusion of sections on violence against women and on women's reproductive rights into the text of the document. In 1992, several Sri Lankan women, including some from MDSL, drafted a "shadow" report for the CEDAW Committee meeting in New York, when the government of Sri Lanka presented their official report. At the moment, many members of MDSL are also involved in the preparation for Beijing, including a "shadow" report. Although there have been differences of opinion with regard to the efficacy of seeking recourse to international and UN mechanisms for the achievement of women's rights, there is today a definite agreement that there should be an attempt to place the voices of women from base communities firmly at the center of international interventions. Linking with the Women's International league for Peace and Freedom (WILPF), and with the Third World Movement Against the Exploitation of Women (TWMAEW), Sri Lankan women have also put forward their concerns not only about women's rights but about the human rights situation in Sri Lanka in general at the sessions of the UN Human Rights Commission in Geneva in February each year. The specific problems faced by women in the face of torture, "disappearance," arbitrary arrest, detention and execution, and displacement have all been highlighted in this way.

The experiences also led to an affirmation of the need for all development projects and policies to be re-structured taking into consideration the fact that large numbers of families in different parts of the island are now headed by women. This has led to a radical challenge of existing plans and strategies for development and empowerment of women.

9. Involvement in the Global Campaign for Women's Human Rights

The involvement in the Global Campaign for Women's Human Rights and the active campaign to collect signatures to the petition calling for the recognition of violence against women as a human rights abuse at the World Human Rights Conference in Vienna in 1993, which was coordinated by MDSL, made many Sri Lankan women aware of the dimensions of the problem as well as of the need to agitate at both a national and international level to change the situation. Proposals to reform existing legislation, active follow-up of rape cases and cases of domestic abuse and harassment, closer perusal of Personal Laws which permit legal discrimination against women have all been a part of this heightened awareness.

Conclusion

Considering the trends outlined above, it becomes clear that struggling for women's rights in the Sri Lankan context at this stage in time has evolved into a struggle for democratization of the society as a whole and has led to a much wider recognition of the significance and impact of such a struggle on women's lives and daily circum-stances. Mothers and Daughters of Lanka itself stands on the thresh-old of this new and expanded frontier; the challenge of achieving an equilibrium between standing firm on women's demands and making strategic alliances lies ahead.

Chapter 28
The Women's Movement and the Struggle for Rights: The Chilean Experience[1]
Verónica Matus Madrid

Introduction

The institutional changes that took place in the last 30 years in Chile did not take into account discrimination on the basis of sex, race, ethnicity or age, all factors which have obstructed the processes of integration, development and modernization in Chilean society. Rooted in cultural patterns, discrimination against women has been embodied and reinforced by legal and political institutions. Discrimination is a barrier which not only keeps women from fully participating in society but also explains the inequalities that affect them.

The institutional framework rarely records the sustained capability shown by women or the organized actions aimed at securing their rights, more freedoms and equality, and the broadening of their limited citizenship. As a result, women often remain invisible within political, social and economic processes. In Chile, there was a great suffragette movement, a women's party and numerous women's organizations struggling from the beginning of the century for better living conditions, access to education, to health and equal rights.

During the 1960s, Chile began a process of democratization to allow broad sectors of the population living in poverty to reap the fruits of economic and social development. This was a period of great projects for social change, participation and revolution. However, concerns about the status of women were secondary at best or were negated by invoking class differences as the sole cause of discrimination and inequality.

The 1973 coup interrupted Chile's democratic history and reversed the process of integration which had been underway. The

---

[1] This article was completed in July, 1994. Some major changes have occurred in Chile since then. For example, the bill on intra-family violence has been passed.

military and authoritarian government began a gradual process of modernization designed to institute a new economic model based on market supremacy as the regulator of economic life, resulting in profound transformations in Chilean society. During this crisis in Chile's history, women left their habitual spaces and with audacity and creativity expanded their traditional roles as wives and mothers to include caring for others outside the home. This resulted in women leading the fight for human rights, searching for missing relatives detained and persecuted by government agents, cooking for their neighborhood and providing health care to the community when the welfare state stopped providing services.

As women took on these new tasks during the dictatorship and witnessed the closing of traditional channels of expression, they organized themselves and took to the streets to denounce the arbitrary rule of the military government. As a result, the fate of women worsened, their freedoms were restricted even further, and the inequality gap between men and women increased.

The greatest achievement for women during those years was to develop their organizing and managing capabilities, which made their actions visible to society. Under the slogan of "Democracy in the nation and at home," women played a remarkable role in the regaining of democracy and they publicized their concerns about the status of women which up to then had been systematically postponed by Chilean society.

After the democratic elections of March 1990, a transition government came to power, supported by a broad coalition of political parties. Among the first steps taken, a governmental office, the National Women's Office (Servicio Nacional de la Mujer or SERNAM) was created. In 1994, a second democratic government was sworn in, supported by the same coalition.

The Revival of the Women's Movement During the Years of Authoritarian Government

Among the first steps taken by the military government installed in 1973 was the suppression of political parties, unions and citizens' groups. These steps were followed by continuing repression by government agents who systematically violated human rights by intimidating and frightening the population. During the same period, the new economic model imposed by the military government produced high unemployment rates. The closing of traditional political channels allowed for the development of pluralistic and autonomous movements in which broad segments of Chilean society participated: women, professionals, villagers and youth. The goal of these movements was to rebuild the fabric of society which had been destroyed by organizing protests across wide sectors of the national community. These movements also resorted to new themes and forms of action which were different from those traditionally used by the political parties. The Catholic Church also played a crucial role in paving the way to restore democracy, owing to its decisive action in defense of human rights.

The Women's Movement Takes Shape

In their roles as mothers, wives and homemakers women created new spaces to survive under the hard living conditions imposed by the authoritarian government. They formed organizations to defend human rights, to create sources of livelihood and to promote the reemergence and broadening of democracy. Women from different political experiences and social sectors coalesced into a women's movement with political, social and cultural dimensions, where no one dimension represented the whole.

The Defense of Human Rights

The entire period of military government was marked by constant and systematic violations of human, civil and political rights. Torture, disappearances, exile, executions, detentions and banishment, among other abuses, became a sad reality, around which the victims' relatives, mostly women, congregated. Their despair and anguish over the abuse suffered by husbands, fathers or sons was a catalyst for organizing.

Professional women, working women and homemakers coming from different social sectors joined ranks to form the first human rights organizations. They organized to establish procedures to obtain news regarding the status of their relatives. Their main target was the military government which was chiefly responsible for the human rights violations. The women's organizations also established a relationship with the judicial branch through appeals and legal actions, although most requests were denied. They focused on highlighting cases of abuse and the need for justice. The women did not focus on their own rights as women in this early phase of the movement. Instead their mission was to create solidarity for ending human rights abuses by the military government. In pressing their demands for truth and justice, the women's movement created the possibility for other sectors of society to express their own dissatisfaction.

In Search of Livelihood

In addition to working for human rights, women organized to alleviate the consequences of neo-liberal economic policies. As a way of coping with serious issues of subsistence, village women banded together in common soup kitchens, held workshops, engaged in bulk purchasing, organized health care and set up housing groups. Thus, women extended their homemaking roles to the community at large by cooking, taking care of health issues and providing support to neighbors suffering from the same fate. These organizations became a training school and were highly valued by women. It was a new sphere of socialization wherein women shared experiences, built emotional ties and partnerships.

In this collective sphere, women shared secrets buried deep under the cloak of privacy of the family, such as domestic violence and sexual abuse. Meanwhile, this experience provided an opportunity for change in socialization as women left home, broadened their sphere of relationships and created new spheres of shared living.

Women became aware that their individual and daily reality was part of a social problem. However, it would be an exaggeration to imply that women, in these early years, underwent an extensive consciousness-raising process which made them question gender-based discrimination. They did, however, begin a process of personal growth, especially in the areas of self-esteem and empowerment. On the other hand, the collective experience of coming together around one task allowed women to develop a capacity for action and management. The number of women organized at the village level was significant. In 1986, there were 1,383 People's Economic Organizations (Organizaciones Economicas Populares) in Santiago, bringing together a total of 46,759 individuals, mostly women.[2] The makeup of these organizations was homogeneous in that they were mostly

---

[2]   Data taken from Clarisa Hardy. (1987). *Organization to Experience Poverty* (Organizarse para Vivir la Pobreza). PET.

women from urban, working-class sectors who lived in poor neighborhoods. Their main source of support was the church, which encouraged their existence through special programs, and nongovernmental organizations (NGOs) which developed training programs and provided the necessary resources. These groups rarely encountered in their daily activities the power of the municipality or of state agencies. On the contrary, they avoided any dealings with government agencies, which they perceived to be arbitrary and tied to the repression.

Reemergence of Democracy and Its Inclusion of Women

Within the same context, women activists, with links to left-wing parties, formed organizations that questioned the status quo and denounced the economic model that the military government was imposing. One of the main elements of their discourse was the denunciation of human rights violations, around which they organized public actions of solidarity and denunciation. Most of these actions were geared to the working class. Although they were not formally bound by party guidelines, these organizing activities were supported by political parties, sometimes as a tactic to protect themselves from repression.

Their members increasingly noticed the level of discrimination against women practiced within partisan political bodies. The most important of these organizations, Women for Life (Mujeres por la Vida), showed a capacity to reach political agreements in a pluralist setting, in anticipation of the coalition which spearheaded the process of the reemergence of democracy. These organizations maintained ties with women's groups that shared a gender-based and feminist perspective.

Another trend among political women was that of the feminists and other women who linked the authoritarianism of the dictatorship with gender-based oppression. Most of these women belonged to middle-class, professional sectors. Because many of them had been in exile, they had participated in feminist groups and movements in other countries. They organized their actions with a lot of spontaneity and flexibility and they refused to accept mediation from political parties. They nurtured gender-based proposals. Their work with NGOs and women's programs had a great impact.

The Role of Women's NGOs

Although there were not many NGOs and women's programs, they nonetheless provided leadership that gave direction to the initiatives of the women's movement through the coordination of public events which made women visible as an important social force. Moreover, they introduced new concepts and categories pertaining to daily life and sexuality which made it possible to question the sexual division of roles, the basis for discrimination and inequality of women. Other contributions made by the NGO programs were in the field of education, social practices and research on the condition of women. A considerable number of professionals from those NGOs helped design the program of the transitional government.

The Women's Movement During the Dictatorship

Reacting against the dictatorship was a way of life for women and the movement. The women's movement, which was comprised of all social classes and encompassed a broad social agenda, was possible as long as political parties were absent from the political arena. The focus of the women's movement was women's lives. The women were active organizers and participants in the demonstrations against the dictatorship. Women often worked with other sectors to organize specific events, for example the March 8 Celebrations, which were oriented to the re-establishment of democracy. But the women did not establish formal and ongoing alliances with other groups working against the dictatorship.

The reappearance of political parties and the participation of party leadership in the movement which backed the return to democracy highlighted tensions in the women's movement over the priority given to gender-based demands in national politics. As a result of the tensions, the movement divided into groups of broader-based political activists and women who wanted to retain a narrower focus on women's issues. The boundaries of the movement were blurred in this period of transition.

The movement lacked a political strategy to accommodate and legitimate the various women's groups and their leaders which had comprised the women's movement. Moreover, women's discourse during the dictatorship was highly ethical and was not accompanied by a proposal with concrete transformations. It also lacked a common platform that could allow the women from the various sectors to come together as one joint political force. Perhaps the main achievement during these difficult years was making women visible as important players in the political arena.

The New Democratic Scenario

The transition to democracy reopened channels of participation in politics which had been restricted under the dictatorship. For the women in the movement, the scenario became more complex because of a need to define their relationship with central and local government agencies as well as with political parties. When the new, democratically elected government assumed power, women's high expectations of participation clashed with the political parties and the State.

During the transition to democracy, political parties relied upon a process of negotiation and consensus to construct a political agenda for that period. A top priority in these pacts was institutional reform aimed at restoring civil and political rights. This agenda to some extent limited the scope of political concerns that would be addressed and restricted the influence of movements and groups belonging to civil society. The political parties maintained a pragmatic style of mediation oriented toward achieving consensus and relegated the overall needs and topics of interest to women and other interest groups to a secondary plane. The women's movement, during the transition to democracy, was so fractured as to deny the political logic underlying consensus. The women's movement and other movements that emerged under the authoritarian government ended up being displaced into an invisible realm within civil society.

The Women's Movement Within the New Framework

During the first years of the transitional government, the women in the women's movement were confused and unable to find a common identity. Together with the rapid fragmentation of the movement was the atomization of women's social presence. In addition, the women's movement, and other groups in civil society, existed in the shadow of government entities, such as the newly created National Women's Office (Servicio Nacional de la Mujer), and political parties. Both downplayed any reference and/or leadership from civil society. Human rights organizations were displaced first, since the justice issue was one of the most difficult factors in the transition.

Tensions among the various sectors of the women's movement persisted. Some groups proposed autonomy and refused the mediation of parties. Others groups, including the political activists, postponed specific items of interest to women because they exceeded the boundaries set for negotiations by the political parties.

In addition NGOs abandoned their role as political referees in the women's movement in order to concentrate on professional and technical support. Each NGO carried out its programs and established priorities in accordance with its own specific criteria, without regard for generating strategies to influence the political process. The NGOs also confronted financial constraints because of sharp reductions from international sources which had provided greater support during the dictatorship.

The drop in financial aid resulted in the reduction of support and training programs for women's organizations in working-class sectors which eroded the close ties that had been established among those groups. Grassroots organizations in general were affected because the NGO programs had sustained most of their activities. Although the women's organizations had to begin relying on their own financial initiatives, they continued to be well organized and active. Still there was nostalgia for the more visible position and recognition they had enjoyed in previous years.

The Women's Movement and New Institutions

The strides made in rebuilding democratic institutions were important for women and for all of society. But the restoration of public freedoms and the exercise of sovereignty did not mean that the relations of power had changed between the State and civil society. The problems of coordination, leadership and representation of the various social and political sectors which comprised the women's movement in the previous period were not easily resolved. The creation of channels that facilitated open debate and allowed for an expression of differences and the drawing up of platforms for joint action, subsumed the development of new abilities, such as negotiation and the capacity to set up alliances within the movement and with other social and political players. The experience of NGOs, whose initiatives were intended to provide a public presence for women, showed the need for change. In 1993, during the parliamentary election campaign, women carried out public actions in Santiago to collect signatures around the slogan "More women in Parliament." There also were protests by women demanding justice for cases of human rights violations. In both instances, the women revived the organizing practices they had used during the years of dictatorship.

During the first years of democratic government, many working-class organizations placed special hopes for support and recognition in SERNAM. But their disenchantment soon followed because they received no answers to their needs. The absence of mechanisms for dialogue between government agencies and the women's movement was a primary problem. Relations between the State and social organizations, in general, and those of women, in particular, were ambiguous, given the absence of a policy aimed at fostering participation. SERNAM did not develop initiatives designed to support the consolidation of women's social organizations.

A new form of coordination that offered a path for the future emerged from the networks of women shaped by the NGO programs and, in some cases, by grassroots organizations. The networks explored new ways of ending the isolation and making it possible to establish links with other organizations. The networks developed into a lobby targeted at parliamentarians and political parties. The actions of the Chilean Network Against Domestic and Sexual Violence were relevant with respect to the proposed Intra-Family Violence Bill. The network supplied technical support and organized the women's organizations that belonged to the network for a systematic campaign aimed at passing the bill. During the campaign the women in the network sent letters to parliamentarians urging them to vote for the bill.

Other networks included the Women and Labor Network and the Reproductive Rights Network, each of which developed actions directed at both the State and civil society. The networks also joined international networks involved in the women's movement based in Latin America and around the world.

The State and Its Policies Toward Women

SERNAM was established in 1991 to push for the improvement of the condition of Chilean women. This specialized cabinet-level agency was created by Law Nx 19.023. Its director became part of the Cabinet and was the first and only woman minister of the democratic government. The office was given a ministerial ranking, subordinate to the Ministry of Planning.

The law states that SERNAM is the agency responsible for working with the Executive Branch to study and propose general plans and measures for women to enjoy equal rights and the same opportunities as men in the political, social, economic and cultural development of the country, while respecting the nature and specificity of women and their role in the family. The process of legitimizing SERNAM within the State apparatus has not been easy, especially given the fact that it was treated by other State institutions as an agency which specialized in women's issues which are difficult to incorporate into public policies.

Since SERNAM was established, no strategies have been developed that lend coherence to the many programs developed in different areas of the government. Priority programs were aimed at low-income women and at carrying out legal reforms that would lead to greater equality. In selecting these programs as priority concerns, the government took up topics of interest to the women's movement and focused on the poorest sectors.

SERNAM has carried out many programs and pilot projects. Two programs are especially noteworthy. The Information Center on Women Rights provides guidance and legal and psychological advice which is accessible in all parts of the nation. The Intra-Family Violence Prevention Program has centers which provide care in select communities. One of the most important contributions of the violence prevention program during this period was to highlight intra-family violence as a social problem and to include it in the public agenda.

Since SERNAM began, several public campaigns have been carried out in the mass media to foster awareness about discrimination that affects women. The campaign which had the greatest impact was the mass media campaign denouncing intrafamily violence.

Legislation Proposed by the Government

The lack of strategies in the Executive Branch and SERNAM for dealing with the legal status of women is notorious. The adoption of equality for women at the constitutional level was not approved by the Parliament when it was sent by the Executive Branch, in conjunction with a package of highly controversial constitutional reforms, including the removal of the Commander in Chief of the Army.

The only laws in the package that was approved by Parliament was the law creating SERNAM and two labor laws designed to improve the rights of working women. One of those laws requires employers to grant an indemnification to domestic workers. The second law requires amendments to individual labor contracts which deal with improvements in working conditions for part-time employees. The amendments include requirements for setting of schedules, minimum salary, working conditions for women workers in agribusiness, commerce, hotels and private homes and the possibility for parental leave in the event of the birth or illness of a child.

Two other important laws affecting women which must be mentioned and have taken more than four years to enact are: (1) The bill amending the laws governing married couples' estates which created the legal concept of the family asset. These assets cannot be taxed or sold without the consent of both spouses. The bill allows a magistrate to grant the use of the couple's assets to the spouse who is in charge of the children's care in the event of an annulment, separation or the death of one of the spouses. The bill also reformed the law with respect to adultery so that both men and women can be charged with adultery for having a sexual relationship outside the marriage.

(2) The bill dealing with intra-family violence and child abuse was a joint initiative of the SERNAM and a group of parliamentarians. This bill characterized intrafamily violence as any ill treatment leading to actions or omissions that affect the physical or mental health of a relative, spouse, live-in partner or disabled minors who are dependent upon the aggressor. The bill established a special, timely and expeditious response to violence. It authorizes the magistrate to prohibit the aggressor from entering the shared home or place of work or study of the victim. In addition the magistrate can order a delivery of personal effects to the victim of an act of aggression who has had to leave home, may establish a temporary allocation for food and may order that tuition be paid for school age children. Finally, the bill provides that the magistrate may order the aggressor to attend therapy or family guidance meetings or to perform ad honorem tasks for the municipality in which his/her domicile is located.

Parliament

When they are up for election, legislators always show great interest in obtaining the women's vote, which in Chile accounts for

51.73 percent of the voting population.[3] However, in practice, laws dealing with women usually take a long time to be enacted. From 1990 to 1994, only one law was enacted that dealt with improving the lot of women: the creation of SERNAM. The other two laws that were passed, as stated earlier, dealt with the specific condition of working women in two areas: domestic employees and seasonal workers.

In these last four years, more than 30 bills were submitted by the Executive Branch and Parliament on questions related to women and the family. Among the most important projects still pending are binding divorce, reinstating therapeutic abortions and reform of the criminal laws in the areas of rape, sexual harassment and sexual abuse.

At the end of the four years of transition, during the second Government of Reconciliation (Gobierno de la Concertación), the intra-family violence bill and the modification bill of the laws governing married couples' estates are expected to be finalized.

The Restricted Citizenship Rights of Women

In Chile women have citizenship rights which are restricted to the act of voting. Demanding a broader set of rights is not common among Chilean citizens. Citizens typically demand rights only in the judicial setting. But even there the legal resolution of conflicts is slow and bears the imprint of class bias. Overall, Chilean laws treat women as objects to be regulated and laws tend to reinforce traditional roles. In Latin America in general and Chile in particular, the Catholic Church and the law have contributed to naturalize conduct prescribed in the Napoleonic Codes relegating women to a subordinate status.

Most Chilean women are socialized into traditional family roles. Hence, education and training in women's rights require a civic education to be effective. In Chile, during the dictatorship, many educational programs were aimed at the growth of women's awareness. Few programs dealt with the issue of civic education and women's rights. The participation of women and their actions appealed to dignity, justice and solidarity, not to the demand of their rights. For Chilean women to exercise their full share of power requires both an

---

[3] Data taken from the Electoral Service of 1993.

expansion of the meaning of citizenship as well as an expansion of women's rights.

The International Agenda and International Legal Tools

In 1975 the International Year of the Woman was celebrated and a Plan of Action adopted which included recommendations to the States and the international community. In those years, the nascent women's movement in Chile was breaking new ground in denouncing the military government. Little if any information reached the movement from outside the country. The military government gave no importance to the strides made by the international community. When the United Nations passed the Convention on the Elimination of All Forms of Discrimination Against Women (CEDAW) in 1979, the convention was ignored by the military government (although the government eventually did ratify CEDAW in 1989). The Nairobi strategies of 1985 also were ignored by the government.

Although the Chilean government is by no means in compliance with CEDAW, there have been some gains since ratification. Legislation creating SERNAM stated that it was enacted to comply with the Convention. There also have been some gains regarding constitutional equality and reform of civil and criminal legislation, although some provisions that are discriminatory against women have not been repealed.

On the other hand, CEDAW's requirement that States press for social policies that promote equality for women have not been met. Women have remained in a precarious position in the areas of work, education, health and access to credit. The drop in social spending and the privatization of health services has diminished the quality of care and made services more expensive, leaving women who have fewer resources unprotected.

Information regarding the appointment of a Special Rapporteur on Violence Against Women following The Vienna Declaration on Human Rights, in June 1993, has been widely disseminated in Chile by the Network on Violence Against Women. Generally speaking, however, international instruments have not been widely disseminated. NGOs have done the most work to create awareness of international instruments inside the country. More recently some law schools have incorporated them into their curricula.

In Chile international instruments relating to women's rights are mainly invoked by the women's movement to put pressure on State agencies. Other movements, like those working for the rights of children or of indigenous people, also have disseminated pertinent international instruments. International instruments also are being widely used as an important source of information in anticipation of the enactment of the law against domestic violence and its application by civil judges. Yet despite the passage of the domestic violence law, the Chilean government has not signed the Inter-American Convention to Prevent, Punish and Eradicate Violence Against Women, recently enacted by the Organization of American States in Brazil.

The Future of the Women's Movement

The focus of the Chilean women's movement in the future must be on moving from broad declarations of principles and global ideological statements to specific gender-based proposals at the level of the State and of civil society. The movement must concentrate on setting up alliances between the women's movement and other groups in civil society where there is an overlap of interests and the possibility of strengthening the pressure on government to enact laws and social policies that benefit women.

Another priority is to strengthen relationships with government agencies, especially SERNAM. Specifically, there is a need to open up a sphere of discussion that allows for the expression of differences among groups of Chilean women but, at the same time, fosters joint action on specific campaigns where solidarity is necessary to produce gains for women. The implementation of a Plan for Equal Opportunity for Women, produced by SERNAM, should elicit support from women's organizations once it is adequately disseminated.

There also is a need for concentrated work at the community level which will lead to legitimizing grassroots organizations and their proposals. The implementation of programs on Education for Democracy would be a positive step toward developing political leaders among women and providing women with the training to negotiate with other leaders in government and civil society regarding proposals to advance the women's right agenda.

The international agenda for women's rights is an important point of reference and tool for the work of the women's movement in Chile. The dissemination of international instruments within

Chilean society must be followed by consistent pressure to incorporate the principles of international law into national law. The women's networks must maintain close ties with the international women's movement and take advantage of strategies for influencing State agencies, civil society and the Chilean women's movement itself.

Of all the tasks facing the Chilean women's movement, the most important one continues to be coordination of support among women's groups in the movement. The challenge is for the groups to legitimize one another by recognizing one another as "subjects" who embody the right to expression and association. Women must participate in order to influence policy at the local or national level in the women's movement, in unions, in political parties and in government. The expansion of rights for women depends, in the long run, on women exercising their power to act on their own behalf to create a society that recognizes women as full citizens.

Chapter 29
Women in Russia: Building a Movement

Irina Jürna

Only by examining the history and cultural context of the women's movement in Russia can we begin to understand why feminism and a culture of women's rights remain undeveloped in the post-communist era. The early women's movement was coopted by the Bolshevik revolution which pledged equal rights to women as a part of communist ideology. But the hardship that women endured under the Soviet system of "equality" has left a legacy that defines equality with men as an undesirable goal for many Russian women.

The absence of a culture of women's rights renders Russia, and the post-communist region, as a whole, out of step with the rest of the world. A fledging women's movement is developing now in Russia but it lacks organization, resources and clear goals. To catch up the women's movement must begin to define the concrete interests of Russian women and then build solid linkages to Russian society as a whole. Above all, it is necessary to draw Russian women, who are now mostly isolated from public life, into the political process where they can begin to define their economic and political rights. This can only be achieved by opening up the small, closed circle of women's groups to a much wider audience by using media to break down antiquated stereotypes regarding women's roles and to build a mass movement which can endure.

Understanding the contemporary status of women in Russia requires an understanding of the general characteristics of Russian society. Yet nothing about these characteristics is clear cut. Nor is there a consensus among either theoreticians or leaders of social movements in Russia on the character of Russia. Most attempts to interpret contemporary Russia are hindered by various kinds of stereotypes which, as a rule, depend upon the political biases of a particular analyst or public figure.

In Russia today, development usually is described as chaotic and unpredictable. Development is indeed an extremely complex process and the long term outcome still is unknown. Yet, at the same time, the degrees of chaos and unpredictability often are exaggerated by Western observers because the actual trajectory of development in Russia does not fit the largely idealized stereotypes that many westerners deploy in their attempt to interpret modern Russian reality.

In order to evaluate what is happening in Russia with respect to the position of women and their reflection in the public consciousness, it is essential to reject stereotypes. This requires a knowledge of Russian history because the socio-cultural situation in Russia today is a product of a fairly long historical development. It also is essential to take into account two historical perspectives: long-term and short-term.

The long-term perspective spans several centuries and reveals that, despite several attempts to modernize during the last 300 years, some traits of traditional Russian society have proved to be extremely stable and even capable of regenerating themselves after having almost disappeared or having been repressed. A list of enduring Russian traits would include the structure of family relations, the sex roles, relations between generations, the hierarchy of socio-cultural values and the image of the ideal woman.

By contrast, the short-term perspective focuses on those changes which were reflected in Russian society during the Soviet era and which directly affect the events of the post-Soviet period. Analyzing the Soviet period is made more complicated by a multitude of ideological stereotypes both in Russia itself and beyond its borders.

The Soviet Woman

It is not easy to describe the Soviet woman because the Soviet period, despite its brevity, was extremely dynamic. The Soviet period was characterized by abrupt turning points that alternated with periods of relative stability. At some junctures multiple products of the planned society were instituted in tandem and effected simultaneous changes in society. The situation was complicated by the constant presence of "double think." In some situations it was clear to everyone that the official text either did not correspond to reality or that it corresponded only partially. The official text represented a kind of "quasi-reality," which no one confused with genuine reality, but which nevertheless could not be disregarded. Thus, the formal equality established by the Soviet Constitution helped to undergird the myth of the emancipated Soviet woman. The strength of the myth was responsible, in large part, for preventing the growth of a women's movement of the sort that exists in the West. Such a movement could not exist in a country in which all of women's problems already had been resolved at the state level. Issues that concerned the women's movement in the West occasionally found their way into the Soviet media and tended to provoke smiles or irritation from cynical Soviet women. The fight for the right to vote: we have that and what difference does it make to us, living under a communist regime? The fight for equal rights in choice of work: theoretically we have this as well. ("Let them come to this country and haul heavy sleepers for railway repair works in a place where there's no mechanization of any kind.") The fight for legalization of abortion: in a country where abortion was the sole practical means of contraception, where the average woman has had several abortions, without anesthetic, and where women seeking abortions are humiliated by the medical personnel, could legalizing abortion be perceived as something good?[1]

On January 23, 1981, the Supreme Soviet of the USSR ratified the United Nations Convention on the Elimination of All Forms of Discrimination Against Women by a Declaration, and at the same time, admitted that the idea of constitutional equality of the sexes had not been realized in practice.

A History of the Russian Women's Movement

The women's movement in Russia began to take shape toward the middle of the 19th Century and drew many of its ideas from the

---

[1] According to the official statistics, which include only those abortions registered by medical establishments, the number of abortions per 1,000 women aged 15-49 were as follows: 1985 - 116; 1986 - 119; 1987 - 114; 1988 - 121; 1989 - 118; 1990 - 109; 1991 - 95. In 1989 in the Russian Soviet Federate Socialist Republic 32,133 official abortions were carried out on women under the age of 17. (There are no data on illegal abortions, many of which are carried out in medical establishments, where women illegally pay for the procedure). Eighty percent of women coming in for abortions had previously tried to terminate their pregnancies by themselves according to data from a survey carried out by the clinical diagnostic reproductive center, Yuventa ("All People are Sisters," 1993, p. 70).

French Revolution and Russian literature. In the 19th Century the essays of Nikolai Dobrolyubov and Peter Lavrov and the novel by Nikolai Chernyshevsky, *What is to be Done?*, had a major influence on the formation of the early women's movement. At the beginning of the 20th Century, Russian feminist journals began to be published along with special research on the theme of women's position in society. Women's associations, women's publishing houses and voluntary societies were set up. In the opinion of several researchers, the Bolshevik revolution in 1917 coopted the women's movement. In the words of one writer, "the October revolution put an historical end to the development of feminism in Russia" (Kuchkina, 1990). According to this theory, the fact that revolutionary decrees granted Soviet women equal rights with men stifled the free women's movement. All the forces that were not pro-Communist were excluded from the debate. As a result of lively discussions on the role and place of woman in society, the winner was, as always, Soviet communist ideology. In this frame, women were seen as participants in the laboring process. As one writer saw it, "The Workers' Republic approaches women primarily as it would a laboring unit, a unit of living labor" (Kollontai, 1991, p. 105).

If we examine the transformation of the early notion of feminism in Russia into a notion of pseudo-equality that characterized the early Soviet period, we see an attempt to realize a fairly radical modernist program in the larger sociopolitical context (and also in the areas of art and literature, the social sciences and pedagogy). The next phase of Soviet development, however, which affected many areas of life, was characterized by a rejection of radical modernization. The modernist program was succeeded by a fairly distinctive symbiosis of modernist and traditional (patriarchal) components. The elements of modernist programs that were retained were those that either met the practical (primarily economic) needs of the regime or were those that matched the traditional structures of the social and political hierarchy.

Forced industrialization, carried out at the expense of the population, required a lot of cheap labor including female labor. The image of the toiling woman, therefore, occupied an important place in the system of Stalinist propaganda. The following is a typical sample:

> The USSR is the first country in the world to have emancipated women from a legal point of view and to continue emancipating them in actuality.

Accordingly, the role of women in productive labor in this country is also enormous. In connection with the industrialization of the country and the reconstruction of agriculture, the significance of female labor in the economic life of the USSR is growing irrepressibly. The USSR has millions of female workers, collective farm laborers, workers promoted to administrative posts, shock-workers, genuine heroes of labor, and builders of a new life (Album, 1931).

From then on this image of the Soviet female laborer remained an important component of Soviet ideology because the need for cheap labor was a constant characteristic of the Soviet planned economy.

At the same time, the hierarchical system of the totalitarian society succeeded in making use of elements of traditional culture, whereby women, as the most dependent and obedient members of society, constituted the foundation of the hierarchy. The society as a whole reflected hierarchical structures and patriarchal attitudes. The distribution of material wealth and decision making was carried out from above. The cinema critic Maiya Turovskaya, analyzing the image of the Soviet woman in film from the 1920s-1950s, notes that the traditions of free love favored by Aleksandra Kollontai, a well-known revolutionary and feminist, came to an abrupt end in the 1920s, while the perception of woman as a laboring unit remained for the duration of the Soviet period. There are examples of women with important careers during the Soviet period. But those careers took place within the patriarchal system of relations. And the patriarchal role in this context is occupied not by the woman's husband, lover, or family, but by the party, and the party leader, who lead her to the summit of power.

In the Soviet system, family relations were destroyed and patriarchal relations took their place. Women were not perceived as sexual objects because "the party and the leader did not need her as a body" (Turovskaya, 1992). This probably explains, in large part, the unwillingness of the majority of modern Russian women to protest about the representation of women as sexual objects in the Soviet system. Their striving, through the clothes they wear and their behavior, to underline their sexuality, often shocks representatives of Western women's movements.

The position of the Soviet woman was bipartite. On the one hand she was heavily involved in the sphere of production and had a fairly high level of education. So by these parameters she could be considered fairly emancipated. On the other hand, in the sphere of family and daily life she occupied a clearly subordinate position. The feminist Irina Sandomirskaya reduces the whole history of the Soviet Union as the history of "the complete physical destruction of the male and painful training of the female population." In her opinion, the "resolution" of the woman question in the USSR occurred in practice at the expense of the extermination of men and the forced involvement in the economy of those women who remained alive, through their taking over jobs previously held by the men (Sandomirskaya, 1992, pp. 54-59). Furthermore, if one takes into account that in their professional activity women, as a rule, remained on the lower rungs of the ladder (key positions were occupied by men) and were obliged to carry the burden of virtually all housework, then one can say that the real and full emancipation of women in Soviet society was not achieved. As always in the Soviet state, it was difficult to actually get a hearing on the large gap between state declarations of equality and the real situation. Any claims or complaints by women about the excessive double burden provoked aggression: "You wanted equality. Now you've got it. You only have yourself to blame." This legally consolidated but unrealized equality, in its own way, drove the women's movement into a blind alley. The women themselves who suffered daily hardships and excessive burdens, in many cases, were (and, sadly enough still are today) convinced that their lives are the real result of full emancipation. In the post-Soviet era, however, the contradiction between formal equality and the concrete reality of women's lives has entered into the public consciousness.

The End of the Soviet System: From Stagnation to *Perestroika*

The gradual increase in crisis phenomena, characteristic of the last years of Soviet society, was accompanied by several changes in the situation of women as well. Those traits of modernization, which in the public consciousness were most firmly linked with socialism as a political system (that is, actively involving women in productive and social activity) were regarded increasingly negatively and were seized upon both by women themselves and by men. Some critics of the Soviet system questioned whether women should work in manufacturing. There was more emphasis placed on a professional career.

At the same time, the press, radio and television began to reflect an increase in traditional attitudes to the effect that a woman's place is in the kitchen. The party propaganda reflected the same twin developments. The party strove increasingly to create an "elevated" image of woman, seen not only fulfilling her professional duties but also becoming a splendid housewife.

Simultaneously, the social structures in Soviet society were characterized by a growth in paternalistic tendencies. The final years of Soviet power were increasingly oriented to values characteristic of a traditional society, such as emphasis on age, size of family, etc. As a result, in many cases women were compelled to devote less attention to work (where the effectiveness of individual labor played an ever less important role) and to refocus their energies toward household activities (because, for example, the only way for the majority of families to get an apartment was to have several children). Soviet women had a high educational level (in 1987, out of 1,000 women occupied in the national economy, 888 had a secondary education and some higher education). The corresponding figure for men with a secondary education plus some higher education was 890. But women often occupied positions that did not correspond to their qualifications. Figures from 1988 showed that among women who had been married for 10 years or longer, around one quarter were employed outside their specialization (Rimashevskaya, 1992, p. 16).

Gorbachev and the other reformers in the Communist Party of the Soviet Union, having launched in the mid 1980s the attempt to reconstruct the Soviet system from within, included in their plans a specific program for women. They proposed to create public associations of women, women's councils, which, in the opinion of the official reformers were to have played an important role in the democratization of society. However this attempt at a new mobilization of women failed. The women's councils that had been formally set up did not last very long and did not make any significant contribution to public life. The official reformers did not manage to find a point of contact between their political plans and the concrete interests of women. On the contrary, the initiatives handed down from above inflicted the usual casualties, and thus contributed to a negative image of the Soviet women's movement.

The Contemporary Women's "Movement" in Russia

The question of whether a women's movement exists in Russia today (which crops up at virtually every conference or discussion about women's issues) and, if it does exist, then what its main features are, is fairly complicated. In order to answer it, we must define the parameters that define a women's movement and its existence in the social and political life of society. These parameters are conditional upon the general socio-cultural situation, which in present-day Russia is fairly distinctive.

Russia, together with the Soviet Union as a whole, formed the basis of the so-called second world, that is, the socialist world. And this special position retains a certain significance up to the present day when real socialism as a social and political system has ceased to exist. Researchers sometimes attempt to evaluate the Russian situation, including the position of women, according to Western standards. At other times the vantage point is that of third world countries. In both cases an inadequate picture emerges. In the first case it is inadequate in so far as neither the economic situation nor the social structures can be directly compared with the situation in the post-industrial world. Modernization in Russia was not complete and consistent enough. In the second case, the inadequacy has to do with the fact that along with the whole inconsistency of modernization in Russian society in the twentieth century, individual elements of modern industrial and even post-industrial society were created (albeit living side by side and even overlapping with traditional social and cultural structures in strange ways). Thus, modern Russian society is to a very high degree urbanized and characterized by a large pool of qualified workers with a high level of education. This directly concerns women whose educational level is higher than average. According to figures from the State Statistics Committee for November, 15, 1989, 12 million women employed in the Russian national economy had higher and secondary specialist training, which accounted for 62 percent of the overall number of professionally qualified specialists.

Those enterprising women's groups which have appeared in Russia in the last few years and are usually regarded as the manifestation of the women's movement in Russia are associated with various social impulses. The first impulse was the reaction to the official "women's movement" of the Soviet regime. In the Soviet Union there was a network of women's organizations directed by a central body, the Committee of Soviet Women, a sort of women's branch of the Communist Party of the Soviet Union. Their task, as in the case of other "public organizations" in the Soviet Union (children's, young people's, professional, etc.) was to implement control over other women's groups by imitating the initiatives coming from those groups. The hypocrisy of the leaders of the Committee of Soviet Women and their policies aroused the hostility of a significant section of the population a long time ago, and so, as soon as the instruments of force weakened, there were immediate attempts to create real public organizations. This was the case, for example, with the trade unions when, alongside the old and official unions, there began to appear new, unofficial unions created by informal labor leaders. A similar situation occurred in the women's sphere.

Alternative women's groups can be divided into two categories, depending upon the basis of their formation. The first category comprises groups of women from the academic and intellectual sphere. (For example, the Laboratory for Gender Studies at the Institute of Social and Economic Problems of Population of the Russian Academy of Sciences, the Association of University Women, the Federation of Women Writers, and others). These groups were fairly informed about the situation of women in the West and about feminism. Their activity can be generalized as an attempt to reform Russian society according to a certain Western image. In this sense they constitute the wholly organic part of the overall reform movement of modern Russia, i.e. fairly mixed impulses handed down "from above" by various elites and presupposing the possibility of a fairly complete mastering of the Western experience for the progressive reformation of Russian society. (The tradition of "reform from above" is fairly characteristic for Russia, at least in the course of the last three centuries, beginning with Peter the Great.) The dependence of these groups on contact with the West is associated not only with the supply of information, which makes up the intellectual foundation of their activity, but also with the fairly heavy material help which several groups and their individual representatives receive from Western funding bodies and parent organizations (including various types of grants, financing of trips to conferences and a supply of modern technology). Help of this kind is extremely important because, in Russia itself, social groupings capable of supporting the reforming women's movement do not yet exist.

The second category is the grassroots movement of representatives of various women's groups attempting to fight for the realization of citizen's rights or even just elementary human rights. Such movements include the Mothers of Soldiers (which originally united women whose sons had died in the army during peacetime), women's ecology groups, the Committee of Mothers and Widows of Soldiers Who Died in Afghanistan, Women Against Chernobyl and others. These women's groups tend not to articulate their own interests as women and as sovereign individuals. Instead their focus is on those individuals closest to the women, first and foremost their children and, to a significant degree, their husbands. In some cases they also can identify themselves with the community as a whole as, for example, in the case of the women's associations that represent the interests of ethnic groups in national conflicts.

As a rule, the grassroots women's movement has a weak informational base. Its contacts beyond the borders of Russia (except in the case of Russians who live in the territory of the former USSR) are extremely weak and the participants are not especially interested in developing such contacts. They do not usually have intellectual leaders capable of working out detailed programs of action and formulating clear-cut goals except immediate, concrete ones. But then, in the grassroots movement, it is the moral position of the group that is extremely important, not strategy.

As in the case of other social movements, one of the main problems lies in the fact that there is virtually no contact between elite and grassroots movements. Moreover, in several cases, the women's movements regard one another as rivals, a situation that has produced alienation and even hostility among the groups. (It should be mentioned that Russians still do not regard competition as normal.) Many Russians either try to avoid competition altogether or, if that is not possible, strive to exclude the competitor from the game. As a result, there are women's programs in Russia which have been developed in elite circles that do not find support beyond the boundaries of the elite, and the elemental need of women to take part in the resolution of social and political problems is not provided for by such programs.

Independent women's groups, lacking coordination and competing among themselves, were not able to unite. There were several attempts at unity including, for example, at the time of the Second Women's Independent Forum in 1993, in Dubna. The attempt to create a Women's Party failed. First of all, the representatives of various women's groups do not want a rigid organization, headed by someone else's leaders and demanding inner-party discipline. Apart from this, the majority of participants have concluded that it is perhaps unreasonable to create a party that unites people on the basis of their sex, given that the women who attended the forum were of totally different political persuasions.

The second, and possibly the main, reason for the lack of success of independent women's groups in the Duma (Russian parliament) elections was their caste exclusivity. There also is a certain feminist snobbery towards the media. Over the past several years, feminists have rejected links with representatives of the Russian press on grounds that the press, in previous experiences, had distorted ideas and facts in covering the feminist movement. As a result, the serious and energetic activities of the feminist movement are virtually unknown to the larger Russian public.

What is a Social Movement in Modern Russia?

The organizational difficulties of the women's movement in Russia also are connected with several general ideas about the definition of a social movement. It is assumed that an influential social movement must closely resemble a mass political party and have a fairly rigid structure. This idea can be explained, on the one hand, by traditional Soviet society, in which the majority of public organizations were built on a totalitarian model. On the other hand, women's leaders have witnessed that in the period of transfer from the Soviet regime to the post-Soviet state in Russia and other republics of the former Soviet Union, a key role was played by mass democratic movements of the patriotic front type (for example, "Democratic Russia"). These democratic movements have shown that neither a large scale organization nor a rigid structure is an essential condition for the success of a political or social movement. There are other factors which are far more critical to success including a good financial base, connections with influential business and political circles and the ability to make effective use of the mass media. A political or social campaign can have a much greater effect on the public life of modern Russia than the work of mass organizations that lack material resources and links with the mass media. Judged by these standards, Russia is making steady progress toward developing democratic

structures. Russia has been quick to incorporate important democratic features into its social and political life that bring it more
closely into line with countries that have a much longer democratic
tradition. At the same time, however, the structure of Russian society remains amorphous and unstable. As a result, public opinion in
Russia is malleable and wide open to the danger of manipulation by a
variety of demagogues and populists.

A women's movement is taking shape in Russia in the context of
the larger and rapidly evolving society. The difficulties which the
women's movement is encountering—the lack of outstanding public
leaders or clearly defined programs supported by fairly numerous social groups, the lack of coordination and the inconsistency of
actions—are not specific to the women's movement but are characteristic of most spheres of Russian public life in the post-Soviet period. The women's movement also is hampered by the continuing
presence of older, traditional elements in Russian society which nar-
rows the field of imagination for what it means to be female in post-
Soviet Russia.

Is the Russian Women's Movement Politicized?

A fairly serious and little studied issue is the participation of
women in the life of the political party. When studying party documents it is impossible not to notice how little attention is devoted to
overcoming discrimination between the sexes. This is particularly
striking in the documents of democratic parties. There is reference to
the need to achieve equality without dependence on creed or on
national and party membership. But gender is not mentioned. Russian democrats do not believe the problem of gender discrimination
exists.

In private discussions the leaders of "Democratic Russia" and
other democratic parties are sincerely surprised about the need to include the "women's question" in their programs. Even the Russian
Committee for Human Rights does not consider the issue of
women's rights a pressing issue. Communist and nationalist parties
include the women's issues in their programs, although they connect
it principally with the strengthening of patriarchal relations in the
family, promising women that they will put a brake on the influence
of the market economy. The "Women of Russia" movement, in its
pre-election programs, synthesized a traditional and patriarchal view

of Russian women, appealing to them as wives and mothers to avert wars and conflicts and to help men lead Russia out of the crisis with a fully feminist program of equal rights and opportunities. Many women who voted for "Women of Russia" may have done so because it was the only movement to appeal to personal rather than political feelings. In the contemporary Russian situation, a personal orientation is probably the most successful, given that the majority of the population declares itself apolitical, apathetic and disenchanted with public life.

What are the political reference points of the independent women's groups which were supported in the elections by participants in the women's movement? This question was first addressed at the conference on "The Women's Movement and the Contemporary Political Situation in Russia: To Participate or to Observe?" conducted by the Association of Women Journalists in July 1994. About 60 representatives of women's groups and journalists took part in the discussions. Summing up the results of this extraordinary meeting, one can single out several principal trends.

1. Representatives of the women's movement, with rare exceptions (including, for example, the Women's Liberal Fund, led by Duma Deputy Irina Khakamadaya), avoided discussing the contemporary political situation and refused to articulate their political leanings.

2. Those who stood as deputies in the elections explained their participation in a particular bloc as an opportunity to enter the Duma, rather than as support for the programs of the parties or for the candidates that the parties stood for election.

Several women participants in the pre-election campaign transferred from one party to another, in some cases switching between parties with diametrically opposed political orientations. These women argued that it does not matter how a candidate gets into parliament. Rather, in their view, what is important is to be where decisions are made and to have the opportunity to influence the position of women in the country. Some of the women's groups recoil from politics on a grand scale and label the unpleasantness of contemporary politics as something "dirty" or "male." These groups are satisfied to confine themselves to the "politics of small matters."

Stereotypes and Self-appraisal

This article began with the statement that the myth about the Soviet woman being equal to the Soviet man had little in common with reality. The argument is that the idea of women's equality, introduced by socialist ideologists into patriarchal Russian society, existed only in the form of a myth and only at the ideological level, not descending to the level of everyday consciousness. The people, who were accustomed to a double consciousness, did not see a serious contradiction in the declaration of equality and the preservation of patriarchal relations within the family.

The theme of real equality for women, the overcoming of discrimination, which usually manifests itself strikingly in periods of serious social change, completely fell out of the public view during the period of *perestroika*. The absence of orders for serious research on women's issues was an indicator of the fact that the social status of women's problems in society was extremely low. The weak research base is one of the reasons why such issues are not being developed further and why their status in the public consciousness remains unaltered.

In this paper I have, therefore, leaned to a significant degree on my own observations of the press, on interviews I have carried out, on practical seminar work, and on conferences which give a certain picture of public opinion.

Mirrored Stereotypes

The disappearance of Soviet ideology happened so quickly that it resulted in a major ideological vacuum and became for many a severe ordeal. The loss of the accustomed stability, closely connected with Soviet ideological postulates, demanded a very rapid compensation. Thus, in place of the old stereotypes there appeared, like lightning, new ones that had just as little in common with reality as their predecessors. The new stereotypes, built on a simple rejection of the old ones, became their mirror images.

If in Soviet times a woman was a "laboring unit," an asexual public figure, then in the post-Soviet period it became acceptable to speak and write about the woman only in connection with the family or with sex. Working women became a symbol of the unproductive Soviet economy. And the idea itself of equality between men and women provokes aggressive annoyance, regarded as an element of

Soviet ideology. The distinctiveness of the Russian situation is that the "woman issue" is considered unprestigious, unworthy of discussion not only at the level of everyday consciousness, but also in intellectual and artistic circles. Contemptuous references to other nationalities are also a fairly widespread phenomenon in Russia, yet the person making such references marks himself socially and politically, whereas anyone who wishes to can permit himself insulting references on the subject of women, whether he be a minister or a film director.

Here are some examples:

The world famous film director, Nikita Mikhalkov, said in an interview with a journalist from the largest of the country's women's magazines, *Rabotnitsa* (Working Woman): "In my soul I am Asiatic and consider woman to be a lesser being." This phrase is calmly put into print and arouses no objections from the journalist, from the women editors, or from the magazine's one million readers. Most importantly, it does not lessen people's love for the famous actor and cinema director. The most shocking thing is that this example is absolutely typical. Practically any publication can contain utterances of this sort. The illustrated magazine *Ona-On* (She-He), for example, published an interview with two well-known Russian writers, Aleksandr Kabakov and Viktoria Takareva. Kabakov said, "I usually don't associate much with women when I am abroad. It's hard to be friendly with them. In the West there is feminism." Later, Kabakov added, "Unfortunately, our women also, as if by a virus, have begun to be infected with the idea of feminism. The negative consequences of the life of society in our country are ensuing sooner than the positive ones." (Pleshakova, 1993, p. 8.) About Viktoria Takareva, the editor of the magazine (a woman), writes: "Her profession is a male one. She is a writer." Viktoria Tokareva herself said, "In general women who are not very interested in men, but who are focused on themselves or on some imagined women's problem or other, provoke me to wild irritation. By the way, I should say, you have probably already understood that I am an active antifeminist, although I write a great deal about women. When I encountered this phenomenon in the West, I saw that feminism is the ugliest thing" (Plotnikova, 1993, p. 100-102.)

Conclusions and Perspectives

The women's movement in Russia is encountering a series of serious problems. The fundamental problem, that leads to many others, is the extremely low level of awareness among women of their own interests and rights. The extremely poor self appraisal typical of the majority of Russian women—irrespective of the social affiliation, profession and level of education—is the major obstacle to women's rights in Russia today. A related problem is the misguided sociopolitical orientation of many women's groups and organizations and an absence of clarity regarding the actual position of women in society. Women's groups can declare (and many do) a rejection of political orientation in general (which reflects the disenchantment with politics on the part of society as a whole).

At the same time, there is a pressing, though little recognized, need for public representation of women's interests, position and rights in ·the new Russia. This was shown by the conservative women's political association "Women of Russia" at the last parliamentary elections in December 1993. The limited success of "Women of Russia" in fielding candidates suggests that the failure of the reformers to address the interests of women leads to a situation in which some sectors of the women electorate could be attracted to antireformist or extremist powers.

The Russian women's movement is drawn largely from the professional ranks. Among its active participants are no small number of specialists in women's issues with a background in theories and ideas, but without direct contacts with women in various spheres of practical life. There are women who are ready to play leading roles in the women's movement. But they do not reflect the interests of the average Russian woman who would need to form the base of any large scale women's movement. In Russia there is no real feminism as yet (if we do not count the declarations of small, elite groups). But feminist elitism does exist and this could discredit the women's movement before it has a chance to gain momentum. The result could be the strengthening of conservative and even fundamentalist tendencies in society.

In order to strengthen the fledging women's movement, it is essential to carry out serious practical work. What is required is a departure from the sphere of speculative theory and borrowed slogans. It is critical that the leaders of the women's movement study the concrete interests and needs of women drawn from various sectors of Russian society. Careful attention must be paid to their traditional ideas and customs. In connection with this, the women's movement needs to work actively and systematically with the media, which is critical to the formation of public opinion. Conferences for narrow and almost unchanging circles of participants, as well as specialized publications with a small print run, cannot effect a radical change. There is a special need to work with journalists, especially women journalists, who cover women's issues. Journalists can begin to dismantle both traditional and new stereotypes which distort the interests of and limit the possibilities for Russian women. These stereotypes present a serious obstacle to the growth of a women's movement in Russia.

The principal task is to overcome the gap that exists between the qualified and active, but fairly closed, circle of women's groups and organizations, and Russian society as a whole. Only when we have overcome this isolation can we speak of the existence of an actual women's movement in Russia in the sense in which the term is used by our colleagues in other countries. For the time being, our women's movement can be described only in the context of its "specific Russian character."

References

Album. (1931). *Voprosy pola polovogo vospitanija, braka i sem'i* [Issues of Sex, Sexual Education, Marriage and Family]. Moscow: Prometei.

Bogdanova, L. (1992). Na zolotom kryl'ce sideli [Sitting on the Golden Porch]. *Rabotnica,* No. 3-4, 10-11.

Kollontai, A. (1991). Revolucija byta [The Revolution in Everyday Life]. *Iskusstvo Kino,* No. 6, 105-109.

Kuchkina, O. (1990, March 7). Muzcina i zenscina [Man and Woman]. *Komsomol'skaja Pravda,* p. 4.

Pleshakova, A. (1993). Truslivyj nesoversenen v l'ubvi [The Coward Is Not Perfect in Love]. *Ona-On,* No. 2, 100-102.

Plotnikova, T. (1993, Autumn). *Byt' vsegda vljublennoj, chot' cutocku* [To Be Always in Love, At Least a Little Bit].

Rimashevskaya, N., (Ed.). (1992). *Koncepcija gosudarstvennoj programmy ulucsenija polozenija zensciny, sem'i, ochrany materistva i detstva* [Conception of the State Program to Improve Women's Position, Family, Patronizing of Motherhood and Childhood]. Moscow: Institut Problem Narodonaselenija.

Sandomirskaya, I. (1992). Vokrugz: vlast' i magija bukvy [Around: The Power and Magic of the Letter]. *Idioma,* 54-59.

Turovskaya, M. (1992, November 15). *Zenscina-ubijca v sovremennom kino* [The Woman Killer in Contemporary Cinema]. Paper presented at the seminar on Women in the Russian Socio-Cultural Context, Foreign Policy Association, Moscow.

Zabadykina, Y. (1993). Zensciny v sovremennoj Rossii [Women in Contemporary Russia]. *Vse Iljudi Sestry,* No. 1-2, 60-72.

Chapter 30
Immigrant Women's Rights Organizing[1]
Deeana Jang and Leni Marin

The United States is predominantly a country of immigrants. Everyone, with the exception of Native Americans, is an immigrant or a descendent of an immigrant. Yet since the 1880s, the United States has instituted exclusionary immigration policies based, in large part, on race and national origin. Historically, immigrants were welcomed with open arms when the country needed a cheap and exploitable pool of labor to build the economy. However, in times of economic hardship, immigrants have been scapegoated and anti-immigrant sentiment, followed by exclusionary policies and violence against immigrants, has been the norm.

There are a number of underlying themes in the history of women's immigration to the United States. In the past, women were discouraged from immigrating because the United States preferred and recruited male laborers only. Furthermore, when immigrant labor was needed during times of economic hardship in the United States, immigrants often were not allowed to bring families with them to ensure that they could easily be deported when their labor was no longer needed. Prior to 1930, men comprised between 60 to 70 percent of the newly arrived immigrants.

Since 1930, it is estimated that women and children comprise approximately two-thirds of all documented immigrants to the United States (Houston and Mackin Barrett, 1984). The rise in women immigrating independently today can be seen as a reflection of the changing labor needs of the United States (from an industrial economy to a service economy) creating low-paid, low-skilled jobs for which immigrant women are explicitly recruited; the escalation of violence against women in areas of the world where there are

---

[1] The authors gratefully acknowledge Rachel Kahn of the Coalition for Immigrant and Refugee Rights and Services in San Francisco, CA, for her comments and editing.

repressive regimes, civil wars and other internal political conflict; and the increasing burden on women as principal breadwinners for their families in economically depressed areas of the world. For example, Filipina women who came to the United States in the 1940s were predominantly brought over as "War Brides" by Filipino men living in the United States, who at that time were not allowed to marry Caucasian women under United States laws (Osumi, n.d.). However, many Filipina women who started immigrating in the 1960s until the present are single professionals (nurses, doctors, medical technicians, etc.), low-skilled workers or part of a family unit. Likewise, the war in Central America caused huge numbers of immigrants and refugees in the 1980s to flee atrocious human rights abuses including the rape of women by the military. As these immigrants settled, they forged distinct communities reflecting not only their cultural heritage but the political context that shaped their migration.

In the most recent period, the United States in the last 15 years has changed from the largest creditor nation to the largest debtor nation. The United States Congress, in response to growing anti-immigrant sentiment especially heightened during economic recession, made sweeping changes in immigration policy in 1986 and for the first time criminalized undocumented immigrants (Immigration Reform and Control Act, 1986). The Coalition for Immigrant and Refugee Rights and Services (CIRRS) was one of the many organizations which sprang up throughout the United States during this time to defend all immigrants, regardless of their status. Women activists in CIRRS found that particular issues affecting women under the new law were not being addressed by immigrant rights, women's rights, or other civil rights organizations or policy makers. In response, they formed the Immigrant Women's Task Force (IWTF) of CIRRS. An element critical to the success and effectiveness of this group has been the racial and ethnic diversity of its membership. Immigrant women play a central role in defining the work of IWTF.

The IWTF describes itself as a coalition of individuals and organizations including immigrant women, advocates, lawyers, service providers, community activists, students and educators. Our purpose at IWTF is to promote and defend the rights of all immigrant and refugee women regardless of immigration status with the goal of eliminating all social, political, economic, legal, and institutional barriers to full participation in society. We undertake policy reform, public education, outreach networking, and coalition building, training, and litigation, and provide support for immigrant leadership development and community-based initiatives.

IWTF has engaged in a variety of organizing strategies to bring attention to the public about the plight of immigrant women in the United States, to promote policies supporting the rights of immigrant women and to encourage organizing of immigrant women themselves. These organizing strategies are utilized on all levels from local and state to national and international and address the need for women's rights organizations, immigrants' rights organizations and other civil rights groups to take on the issue of immigrant women's rights within the broader civil rights movement. The organizing strategy of the IWTF encompasses four main elements reflecting a multi-level approach:

- working with other movements in coalition;
- strengthening the capacity of grassroots immigrant and refugee women themselves;
- setting concrete and realistic goals for change; and
- holding state, private sector and institutions and other agencies accountable.

Dreams Lost, Dreams Found: Immigrant Women Speak

The first major step in shaping IWTF's organizing work was to hear from the immigrant women themselves. In February 1991, IWTF released *Dreams Lost, Dreams Found: Undocumented Women in the Land of Opportunity,* a pioneering study and needs assessment survey of undocumented immigrant women in the San Francisco Bay Area. Four hundred undocumented Chinese, Latina and Filipina women in San Mateo, San Francisco, and Alameda counties talked to peer interviewers about the problems and the social service needs of this growing and neglected population.

In conducting the study, IWTF sought not only to highlight the problems and conditions of undocumented women but also to work with the women to develop realistic ways to address their needs. Thus, one of IWTF's first goals was to identify representatives and leaders of the communities and establish their trust. As a result, gaining the confidence of community members helped IWTF to gain access to undocumented women, a task many said would be virtually impossible. In fact a unique aspect of the survey was that the majority of the project interviewers were immigrant women, many of whom were undocumented themselves. Both survey interviewers and participants were recruited through personal contacts such as house meetings, friendship and service provider networks, and individual communications.

The survey revealed the severe economic deprivation and vulnerability of undocumented women and their families. It examined the factors causing increased migration by women to the United States and how these factors influence women's lives once they are here. The study covered such areas as family planning, domestic violence, employment, women's fears in seeking public assistance, and lack of knowledge about services and community resources and made recommendations (Coalition for Immigrant and Refugee Rights and Services, 1991).

The study and its resulting report were substantial accomplishments in and of themselves. However, interviewers and participants sought to ensure that the research project did not become a mere academic exercise, but helped to transform it into a vehicle for educating and organizing undocumented women to address the problems identified by the survey.

Mujeres Unidas Y Activas: Training for Leadership

Dreams Lost, Dreams Found resulted in the creation of *Mujeres Unidas Y Activas* (Women United and Active). Under the auspices of *Mujeres*, former survey interviewers are working with IWTF to organize other newly arrived Latina immigrant women around issues of domestic violence, economic independence, access to health services, family planning, AIDS and safe sex, job opportunities and employment rights. Although many of the organizers do not have "official" experience as community outreach workers, they have assumed this role, though unrecognized and unpaid by any institution. IWTF provides financial resources, coordination, training, back-up advice and technical support for *Mujeres*.

Mujeres meets once a week with more than 150 women from diverse cultural and class backgrounds. Child care is available and ensures that all women can participate fully in the meetings. The relaxed and social atmosphere of the meetings helps women learn about their rights, breaks down their isolation by introducing them to others with similar hardships and fosters a spirit of trust and cooperative problem solving. For some, the group provides the support necessary to leave a battering relationship; for others it has given them valuable community connections and social resources, enabling them to better provide for themselves and their families. In effect, *Mujeres* provides the only link between the women and the much needed and often times critical services.

Mujeres has implemented several strategies to organize and inform newly arrived Latinas about the organization, including the use of interviews broadcast through Latino media outlets and on public affairs radio talk shows. *Mujeres* has distributed educational materials in the form of comic books and "fotonovelas" to churches and English language classes, at cultural events and ethnic markets, on street corners and door-to-door. *Mujeres* also works to provide skills and training opportunities for its members to gain better access to employment. For example, the group provides English as a Second Language (ESL) training and has implemented a project to train women as home health care providers. Furthermore, it formed a food preparation cooperative (*Manos Sabrosas*) to supplement members' incomes.

With membership steadily increasing, *Mujeres* organizers started a leadership training program to help women develop skills in initiating and leading other support groups and in becoming effective advocates for basic rights through public speaking and communication. More importantly, the organizers hope that by disseminating information about their experience, they will inspire others to adapt the *Mujeres* model to their own ethnic communities.

Diversity and Commonality

Perhaps the most difficult challenge in organizing immigrant women in the United States is addressing the differences between and within the immigrant groups themselves. While the majority of immigrants in the United States are from Asia or Latin America, there are many differences between those who are considered refugees and immigrants; documented and undocumented; those who have been in the United States for a significant period of time versus those who are more recently arrived; and between national groups and minorities within those national groups. With the focus on the U.S.-Mexico border, immigrant rights in the United States have been primarily perceived as a Latino issue. IWTF has struggled with this issue along with the rest of the immigrant rights movement. IWTF's connections to other women of color organizations has served to help bridge some of the barriers between groups.

However, striking a balance between diversity and commonality is a formidable task. At the core of it is the need to bridge these numerous gaps and to enable immigrant communities to appreciate each others unique conditions and value system and, at the same time, to strengthen the common interests that collectively bind all immigrant communities together. This was the impetus in calling for "Dreams Lost, Dreams Found: Women's Organizing for Justice," a national conference on immigrant and refugee women held in Berkeley, California, in the Fall of 1991.

The successful conference was attended by 350 immigrant and refugee women from around the United States, representing 25 nationalities from Africa, Asia, Latin America, the Middle East and Eastern Europe. The participants represented a wide range of professions and activities, from grassroots community organizers, labor union activists, lawyers, domestic violence counselors, social workers, health care providers, teachers, volunteers and more. Each one brought a wealth of experience stemming from their expertise and knowledge of the issues to which they have chosen to devote their personal and professional lives. To reflect the multitude of issues that face immigrant and refugee women on a daily basis, the conference provided workshops on a wide range of interests that included: (a) labor rights and remedies; (b) working conditions of urban-based workers and rural-based farm workers; (c) self-employment; (d) community organizing; (e) violence against women during migration; (f) strategies to end violence in the home; (g) health care issues including mental health, HIV/AIDS and maternal and child care.

The conference was an important beginning to the very complex process of uniting immigrant women in their common struggles to assert their rights. The conference broke down the isolation felt by immigrant women providers around the country and provided a forum for networking and long-term collaboration.

Organizing for Public Policy Change

The Conference set the basis for immigrant and refugee women to develop strategies collectively and to collaborate on plans of action to seek remedies for the problems faced by immigrant and refugee women. One example is within the arena of organizing and developing policy initiatives. Advocates for the rights of battered immigrant women targeted the need for public policy reform in the United States immigration laws to effectively respond to those who are victims of domestic violence. Under the Immigration and Nationality Act, United States citizens and permanent residents can, but are not required to, file relative visa petitions so that their spouses can obtain legal permanent residency through the marriage and legally reside in the United States.[2] Citizen and resident spouses choose when and whether to file visa petitions and they can revoke those petitions at any time prior to the issuance of permanent residency to their spouse.[3] The power to keep a spouse in a permanent state of risk of deportation provides batterers who are citizens and legal permanent residents with a coercive tool to hold battered immigrant women and family members in abusive relationships. Many immigrant women live in extremely dangerous situations fearing for their lives because their batterer spouses threaten them and their children with deportation if they seek assistance from the police or report their abusive behavior (*Untold Stories*, n.d.). For example, if a woman chose to run away to find safety in a domestic violence shelter, the batterer spouse may go to the immigration authorities to withdraw his petition for her documentation and have her deported instead. In this way, he also escapes being prosecuted for criminal offenses related to the physical abuse of his wife.

Because of the high incidence of domestic violence in immigrant communities,[4] the Immigrant Women's Task Force decided to take on reform of United States immigration law to protect the lives of battered immigrant women and their children. IWTF collaborated with groups such as the Family Violence Prevention Fund (FUND) and AYUDA, Inc. as well as with feminist rights groups in the United States such as National Organization of Women (NOW) Legal Defense and Education Fund, in developing and crafting effective new

---

[2] See 8 U.S.C., Section 1186a.

[3] See 8 C.R.F., Section 205.1(a)(1).

[4] A survey of over 400 undocumented women in the San Francisco Bay Area, conducted by the Immigrant Women's Task Force of the Coalition for Immigrant and Refugee Rights and Services, revealed that 20% of Filipina participants and 34% of Latina participants had experienced some form of domestic violence with the partner, either in their country of origin, in the United States, or in both (Hogeland and Rosen, 1990).

policy to enable battered immigrant women married to citizens or permanent residents to be able to file residency petitions on their own. Hence, these battered immigrant women are no longer fully dependent on their batterer spouses for their legal residency status. Furthermore, if a battered immigrant woman is placed in deportation proceedings by authorities, she can now apply for a waiver of deportation upon proof of being subjected to physical abuse or extreme cruelty by her U.S. spouse. The waiver gives her basis to apply for her legal permanent residency. The passage of this policy was a major victory, demonstrating that immigrant women can work together for effective and critical policy change. This pro-active campaign will save hundreds, if not thousands, of battered immigrant women's lives.

Unfortunately, much of the work of IWTF has been to help mobilize the fight against anti-immigrant initiatives. The work of IWTF has resulted in national and local women's organizations joining in the movement to defend immigrants' rights. This is critical because in the last few years, anti-immigrant sentiment has become even stronger. Elected officials from every political spectrum are calling for stronger border enforcement, more restrictive asylum regulations, and greater restrictions on immigrants' rights to public services, education and health. IWTF has been mobilizing its broad membership of service providers from community-based organizations to join the fight against these dangerous measures and to broaden the movement for immigrant rights. The most frightening example is the "Save Our State" (SOS) Initiative or Proposition 187. Anti-immigrant groups gathered enough signatures from California voters to place Proposition 187 on the November 1994 ballot. Proposition 187, which was passed by the voters, is a measure designed to deny health, education and other social services to undocumented immigrants. It also would force health providers, educators, social service providers and law enforcement personnel into becoming agents of the Immigration and Naturalization Service (INS) by requiring them to report "suspected" undocumented aliens to INS and the State Attorney General. The initiative is having a national impact by giving politicians the green-light to promote more restrictive immigration policies in order to further their political careers. IWTF mobilized to publicize the dangers of this initiative on women and children and educated domestic violence advocates and others to organize against the initiative.

Holding the United States Accountable

The American public incorrectly perceives that human rights abuses are only committed outside the borders of the United States and sees the main role of the United States as maintaining and protecting human rights in other countries. In fact, the human rights of immigrant women are violated every day in the United States. To illustrate this fact, the IWTF organized the first ever hearing documenting human rights abuses against immigrant and refugee women in the United States. The hearing's objectives included introducing the concept of female human rights as a tool for immigrant and refugee rights advocacy, providing evidence for necessary changes in United States immigration policy and other public policy arenas negatively impacting immigrant and refugee women and drawing public attention to the gender-based human rights violations experienced by immigrant and refugee women in the United States.

Personal testimonies were given by women who would not otherwise have had the courage to come forward with their stories if not for the IWTF hearing. Testimonies were given by an HIV-positive Haitian refugee detained in Guantanamo camp by the United States government, a legal resident beaten by the United States border patrol when crossing lawfully into the United States and a domestic worker enslaved by her employers. Making the issues more visible through a human rights framework lends a compelling call for urgent action and holds accountable the state and actors that perpetuates and tolerates these abuses.

Relationships with Other Movements

The work is not without its challenges. The women's movement in the United States has been primarily focused on equality for Caucasian women, with questions of race, class and sexual orientation rarely addressed. At the same time, the civil rights movement has not historically addressed women's rights as a civil rights issue. To add to the complexity, the civil rights movement also has focused narrowly on racial conflict and discrimination between blacks and whites. Immigrant groups, the largest being Latino and Asian, have struggled to be included on the civil rights agenda in recent years (Tamayo, 1987-1988).

The labor movement in the United States also has had a history of racism and anti-immigrant sentiment. The Working Man's Party, which was the precursor to the American Federation of Labor (AFL), led the charge for the passage of the Chinese Exclusion Act in the 1880s. More recently, the AFL-CIO supported the discriminatory employer sanctions provisions of the Immigration Reform and Control Act of 1986. Progress has been made in getting individual unions of the AFL-CIO which have significant immigrant membership to change their positions on immigrants' rights.

There is a history of immigrant women workers' struggles playing a key role in the development of the labor movement and the women's movement. Immigrant women make up a major portion of the service and garment industries. Immigrant women workers have formed their own groups organized to challenge the labor movement. For example, Asian Immigrant Women's Advocates (AIWA) in Oakland, California, has been involved in a campaign to bring the issues of garment industry abuse to the public's attention. AIWA's Garment Workers' Justice Campaign has focused on a well-known garment manufacturer Jessica McClintock, Inc. to pay back wages, and guarantee safe working conditions, decent wages, and job security to the workers. *La Mujer Obrera* in El Paso, Texas, an organization of immigrants, women and workers, does similar work at the U.S.-Mexico border and also addresses the impact of the North American Free Trade Agreement on women workers and on the environment.

The environmental movement also has ignored immigrants' rights, blaming immigrants for environmental problems and failing to take up issues such as toxic dumping in immigrant communities. In the United States, there are various environmental groups ranging from the Sierra Club to Zero Population Growth which have been active in calling for greater control of our borders. More recently, there is a growing "environmental justice" movement which is challenging these groups for their lack of inclusion of environmental issues affecting poor and minority communities, lack of people of color in their leadership and their positions against immigrants. Immigrant women have been taking leadership in the environmental justice movement in terms of organizing their communities around toxic waste and other environmental hazards which have a particular impact on immigrant women and children's health.

Conclusion

The task of organizing for immigrant and refugee women's rights in the United States is a complex one. A multilevel approach is necessary in order to build the movement for immigrant and refugee women's rights. IWTF has been able to utilize this approach to place immigrant women's rights on the agenda for women's and civil rights on a local, national and international level.

REFERENCES

Coalition for Immigrant and Refugee Rights and Services. (1991). *Dreams Lost, Dreams Found: Undocumented Women in the Land of Opportunity*. San Francisco, CA: Author.

Hogeland, C. & Rosen, K. (1990, March). *A Needs Assessment of Undocumented Women*. San Francisco, CA: Coalition for Immigrant and Refugee Rights and Services.

Houston, K. & Mackin Barrett, J. (1984, Winter). Female Predominance in Immigration Since 1930: A First Look. *International Migration Review, 18*(4).

Immigration Reform and Control Act. (1986). Pub. L. No. 99-603, 100 Stat. 3359.

Osumi, M. (n.d.). Asians and California's Anti-Miscegenation Laws. In N. Tsuchida (Ed.), *Asian and Pacific American Experiences: Women's perspectives*. Minneapolis, MN: University of Minnesota, Asian/Pacific American Learning Resource Center and General College.

Tamayo, W. (1987-1988). Defending the Rights of the Undocumented: A Challenge to the Civil Rights Movement and Local Governments. *Review of Law and Social Change, 16*(1).

Untold Stories: Cases Documenting Abuse by U.S. Citizens and Lawful Residents on Immigrant Spouses. (n.d.). San Francisco, CA: Coalition for Immigrant and Refugee Rights and Services.

Chapter 31
Rape as a War Crime : A Continuing Injustice
Lourdes Indai Sajor

After 50 years of silence about crimes committed against the women in Asia by the Japanese Imperial Army during World War II, the victims of gross human rights violations have finally started to speak of their anguish.

Of all human rights violations, violence against women in armed conflict situations is one of the most massive in scale, given the nature of the atrocities committed and the number of persons affected. Yet history has rarely recorded war crimes committed against women and its occurrence has been repeatedly denied. One of the most painful reasons for this denial is that these are violations perpetrated against women.

It is only now that war crimes against women are receiving attention at national and international levels, mainly because the women victims have decided to come out and tell the stories which they once tried to forget. Most importantly, their coming forward has given the issue of rape a political significance.

Mass rape, which has been committed against women in war and conflict situations for hundreds of years, has been accepted as a normal part of the violence of war. During the early period of colonization, the colonizers—generally all men—would ravage countries, cities, towns and villages, rape the women, kill the men and steal domestic animals. This happened during the World Wars and it is still happening today, both in international wars and in internal armed conflicts.

Rape as a strategy of war is a terrible manifestation of the historic treatment of women as objects. The logic of war targets women of the enemy as objects of aggression. They are raped in order to destroy their dignity as women and to demoralize and humiliate the male enemy. The sufferings of the women are never a concern. Past war settlements never came to the defense of women or saw the need for rehabilitating the lost dignity and integrity of the women who have been raped. The world has come to speak of rape as an inevitable fact of war—as part of the reality of the behavior of armed forces. Rape and other human rights violations are blamed on the enemy and used as war propaganda. But the origins of the systematic practice of rape, and why it is rampant in armed conflict situations, is never discussed.

The violence of the culture of war and the use of rape as a weapon of war has its roots in patriarchal systems. Women as victims are not heroes; they are merely by-products of the war. On those occasions where rape cases have been brought to public awareness, the women are recognized as victims, but their injury or death does not lead to the prosecution of the perpetrators or the war criminals; nor is their demand for justice, compensation and reparation ever considered.

It is only recently, as in the case of the Asian "comfort women" and the women of former Yugoslavia, that victims of rape in war have come out to demand justice and compensation. Yet despite the validity of their claims, the cases remain either pending in court or have been reduced to an investigative report by the United Nations.

Case Study: Military Sexual Slavery by Japan

This is a case of the comfort women of Asia, whose demand for justice has been totally negated by Japan, whose war crimes and crimes against humanity remain in the shadows of their conscience as a people. The case of the Asian Comfort Women of the Japanese Imperial Army during World War II is unparalleled in that the government itself, using the entire army apparatus, systematically planned, ordered, conscripted, established and controlled army brothels and forcibly abducted women from the occupied territories and countries to serve in the brothels.

The abduction, detention and mass rape of a large number of women in Asia during World War II should be understood as part of the war strategy to annihilate the enemy by demoralizing and terrorizing the population. When the Japanese Imperial Army invaded the continent of Asia at the beginning of the 1930's, it immediately started to build army brothels as part of its garrisons.

The tragedy of this action is that most of these women were young girls between 11 to 20 years old, forcibly detained and repeatedly raped. Testimonies proved that many of these women were kidnapped while washing clothes at the river, working in the fields, walking towards the market. Others were induced by officials of the colonial government to be employed in factories with promises of good pay.

In the brothels the comfort women usually had to service 10 to 50 soldiers a day and generally more on weekends. Many who were infected by venereal diseases were treated with large doses of harmful drugs while others had to undergo forced abortions. Most of the women who were injured in the process of torture and rape were never given any medical treatment and such abuses resulted in many deaths.

It is estimated that some 200,000 women from all over Asia were conscripted officially as sex slaves for the Japanese Imperial Army. Historians estimate that fewer than 30% survived the ordeal by the close of the war. After the war, the soldiers abandoned the comfort women, some were summarily executed, others were ordered to commit suicide along with the Japanese soldiers. The women who survived had to return home to their countries or villages with great difficulties.

Upon returning home, many of these comfort women carried the burden of shame. Because of their traumatic experiences, many could not marry or failed in their marriages. Their sense of guilt, sickness, or the isolation they suffered in their own community or society affected their human relations. For those women who came from poor or deprived backgrounds, the conditions they returned to were even harder, because they had been comfort women.

Based on the testimonies given by the Asian comfort women, it is evident that more than one crime has been committed against one woman. Evidence points to crimes of rape, murder, forced labor, kidnapping, sexual slavery, torture, racial discrimination, massacre and genocide. Never before in Asian history have so many crimes been perpetrated against individual women on such a massive and systematic scale.

Breaking the Silence

History has placed a mantle of silence over the atrocities committed against the women. This silence has a fundamental cultural significance: It denies the historical meaning of rape and its structural importance in gender relations. To suppress and ignore that female experience means to privatize it and make it invisible, and therefore to deny its political face.

Men wish exclusively to have their experience with the female body interpreted according to criteria that leave their social position of power unquestioned. This hegemonic position defines their power over the discourse, allowing them to define experience, to determine limits and values, to assign each experience its place and qualities, and to determine what can and cannot be expressed.

As long as the women remain silent, the perpetrators will remain free and the violence justified. Bringing the violence into cultural consciousness and making it public are requisite for change. Only when sexual violence is perceived as a political issue, when it is publicly discussed and analyzed, will it be possible to establish the causes and to envisage strategies to stop it.

To recognize sexual violence as a war crime, to develop a new discourse that allows these women to articulate their experience publicly in a way that preserves their dignity—these are prerequisites for bringing rape in war and rape as a military strategy to the center of the historical and political discourse, so that these crimes can be addressed and ultimately prevented and the perpetrators punished.

Organizing for the Victims of Rape in War.

On April 2, 1993, the Filipino comfort women of the Lila Pilipina - Task Force for Filipino Victims of Military Sexual Slavery by Japan joined the Korean comfort women belonging to the Association of Pacific War Victims and Bereaved Families and filed a class suit against the Japanese Government at the Tokyo District Court, demanding post-war responsibility, compensation and reparations for the crimes against humanity it committed during World War II.

How these women's organization reached the stage of bringing the case to the Tokyo District Court and to the United Nations started with the victims. When the women slowly started to come out and tell their horrifying stories during the war, the world cried with them. Several women's non-governmental organizations and human rights groups took the issue to the streets, called for a press conference, picketed the Japanese embassy in their countries, signed petitions and protest letters urging Japan to apologize and pay compensation to the victims and finally brought the issue to the United Nations.

In 1992 several women's organizations in Asia took the issue of the comfort women in their countries into their own hands. In most cases they collaborated with women's human rights organizations in their countries and with human rights lawyers and NGOs in Japan. In the Philippines, the Task Force for Filipina Victims of Military Sexual Slavery by Japan was initiated and founded by the leaders of the Asian Women's Human Rights Council. In South Korea, we have the Korean Council for Women Drafted for Military Sexual Slavery by Japan and the Association of Pacific War Victims and Bereaved Families. The Taipei Women Rescue Foundation took a lead role in organizing the comfort women in Taiwan. In Malaysia, the AWAM has taken the initiative in looking for the women.

In the Democratic People's Republic of Korea, a Committee for Measures on Compensation to Comfort Women for the Army and Victims of the Pacific War was set up by the government to address the issue. The Association of former Prisoners of War in Netherlands has produced several Dutch women who were drafted as sex slaves in Indonesia. In Indonesia, the comfort women's organization was initiated by human rights lawyers. In China, lawyers from Japan initiated fact finding missions to bring out the women victims of war.

More important is the support groups in Japan composed of scholars, lawyers, academicians, businessmen, students, workers and women who are supporting the demands of the Asian comfort women. They play a major role in bringing the issue to the Japanese Diet and forging alliances with members of the Parliament. Organizations like the Japan Committee for the Filipino Comfort Women (JCFCW), Executive Committee Concerning Post War Compensation of Japan, and many others have pursued the case in Japanese courts together with other war crime issues.

In August of 1992, the first regional meeting of all these organizations handling comfort women in Asia met in Seoul, Korea to strengthen solidarity and unify their demands. By the same year, an International Public Hearing on Post War Compensation in Tokyo was organized by Japanese lawyers and academicians. They invited Rapporteurs of the UN Commission on Human Rights. It was the first time that testimonies from the victims and advocates in different countries came together to pressure the Japanese government to face its war responsibility.

In October of 1993, a second regional meeting in Tokyo was organized as a follow up to the 1992 meeting, to discuss concerted efforts to be undertaken in their demands to the Japanese government. An official meeting with the representatives of then Prime Minister Miyazawa met with the group and heard the testimonies of some of the victims. They promised to forward the demand to the Prime Minister and the Foreign Affairs Minister, who is now taking a lead role in the issue of the comfort women.

The women's organizations' pledged to continue their demands through mass campaigns in the form of marches in the streets, pickets, petition signing, filing the lawsuit in Japanese courts and bringing the issue to the United Nations and international fora. Linkages were established with the women victims of the former Yugoslavia and solidarity activities and campaigns are being initiated along the lines of rape as a war crime and a crime against humanity. Considering that the UN has set up a war Tribunal to hear the cases of women in former Yugoslavia, everyone awaits its implementation.

Activist organizations share strategies about how to organize and counsel the women victims and empower them through full knowledge and control of their demands against the Japanese government. They also continue to search for survivors or their kin and women are bravely coming out to tell their stories. Several actions were initiated by the women victims themselves, with the advocates playing a supportive role.

Negotiations with their respective governments in order to pressure the Japanese government to adhere to demands of the comfort women has been quite frustrating. One reason for this is that Japan is the biggest international development donor in Asia, and being recipients of such aid weakens the demand for full war reparations, including the prosecution of the war criminals, for most of the affected countries.

Due to the initiatives of the women's human rights organizations and the international human rights NGOs, the issue of the comfort women has gained extensive recognition in the United Nations. The moral grounds in organizing the women victims of war, and naming rape as a war crime, is a victory for the women's movement. So is bringing up the issue around the world and encouraging other women victims to speak out so that this kind of crime will not be repeated.

The Japanese government's defensive response is a measure of the campaign's success, which has extended as far as opposing Japan's membership in the UN Security Council. The issue of the comfort women has become a diplomatic irritant in the relationship between the Japanese government and its neighboring Asian countries. Unfortunately, this relationship is easily compromised by donor/recipient agreements.

From the point of identifying the comfort women in the villages and communities to setting up national organizations to directly handle the cases of the former comfort women and building coalitions of women's human rights groups to advocate for comfort women's issues, to implementing regional level consultations, conferences, campaigns and alliances—the issue of the comfort women has gained enormous national and international support and awareness. Never before in history has such an issue gained such media mileage internationally.

But it is the bravery of these old women that allows one to recognize the impact of openly vocalizing rape as a war crime. The crime becomes real, and the issue is recognized by the international community. The most important factor in this case is the continuing struggle of the comfort women for justice, compensation and reparation for their dignity, in their fervent hope that this instance of violation against the human rights of women would never be repeated in future generations. Indeed, it is a lesson learned at too high a price.

References

Convention on Non-applicability of Statutory Limitations to War Crimes and Crimes Against Humanity, in force Nov. 11, 1970, 754 U.N.T.S. 73

International Commission of Jurists. (1993). *Comfort Women: The Unfinished Ordeal* (Preliminary Mission Report). Geneva: Author.

Parker, K. (1992). *Compensation for Japan's World War II Victims*. San Francisco: International Educational Development.

Philippine Comfort Women Compensation Suit. (1993). Tokyo: Task Force for Filipina Victims of Military Sexual Slavery by Japan & The Japanese Committee for the Filipino Comfort Women.

The Issue of Korean Human Rights During and After the Pacific War. (1993). Seoul, Korea: The Association of Pacific War Victims and Bereaved Families.

U.N. Commission on Human Rights. (1993). *Statement of the Republic of Korea* (U.N. Doc. E/CN.4/1993/SR.27).

Van Boven, T. (1993). *Study Concerning the Right to Restitution, Compensation and Rehabilitation for Victims of Gross Violations of Human Rights and Fundamental Freedoms.* (Special Rapporteur's Final Report. UN Doc. E/CN.4/Sub.2/1993/8).

War Crimes on Asian Women: Military Sexual Slavery by Japan During World War II: The Case of the Filipino Comfort Women. (1993). Manila, Philippines: Task Force for Filipina Victims of Military Sexual Slavery by Japan and Asian Women Human Rights Council - Philippine Section.

War, Victimization and Japan: International Public Hearing Report. (1993). Osaka, Japan: Toho Shuppan Inc.

Working Group on Contemporary Forms of Slavery. (1992). *Report* (U.N. Doc. E/CN./Sub.2/1992/34).

World Council of Churches. (1992). *Rape of Women in War* (Report of the Ecumenical Women's Team Visit - Zagreb). Geneva: Author.

Yoshiaki. Y. (1992). *Historical Understanding on the "Military Comfort Women" Issue.* Tokyo: Chuo University.

Chapter 32
Organizing at the Regional Level: The Case of WiLDAF

Akua Kuenyehia

Introduction

The seeds for the formation of a regional network in Africa to promote and enhance the rights and status of women were sown at the Third World Forum on Women, Law and Development which was held in Nairobi, Kenya, during the World Conference on Women in 1985. The Forum brought together a number of women from all walks of life who had recognized that law is a potential tool for the improvement of the situation of women in the Third World. At the Forum, participants sought to find out what strategies have been used in pursuit of the improvement of the situation of women and to discuss how those strategies could be improved upon and what practical steps could be taken to use law as a tool for raising women's legal, social, economic and political status.

The Forum provided a unique opportunity for the participants to examine in a systematic way how law, both formal or statutory and customary, affects women and their development, to begin to devise strategies that will overcome some of the constraints identified and, thus, enhance the participation of women in their own development. This helped to articulate effective action-oriented strategies using both the law and new innovative methodologies geared towards the improvement of the situation of women.

One of the most important outcomes of the Third World Forum on Women, Law and Development was the realization by the participants that because they all were fighting similar obstacles, combining efforts was an important step towards overcoming those obstacles which women face everywhere. One of the recommendations, therefore, was the implementation of regional conferences to bring together women's organizations to exchange information, share strategies addressing women's rights issues, and develop mechanisms to coordinate research and action at the regional level (Schuler, 1986).

Origins of WiLDAF

As noted earlier, WiLDAF originated from the Third World Forum on Women, Law and Development in Nairobi, Kenya in 1985. The establishment of WiLDAF represented the final step of the Women, Law and Development project of OEF International under which regional networks had been established in Latin America and Asia. The establishment of WiLDAF started with a meeting of 13 women's rights advocates from nine African countries. This meeting reaffirmed the recommendations of the WLD Forum in Nairobi, Kenya, in 1985, and participants made a commitment to build a regional network with the principal objective of promoting strategies that link law and development to empower women.

At this meeting issues of common concern to women all over Africa were identified and discussed. Some of the most important issues identified related to women's role in the family, especially maintenance and custody of children, divorce and issues of both testate and intestate succession. Economic rights such as ownership of and access to land, credit and property were also highlighted, as well as formal and informal employment and domestic and other forms of violence.

At the meeting, it was also discovered that there were a lot of similarities among programs designed to combat some of the identified problems. Law reform and legal aid were the most prevalent approaches used for the improvement of women's rights.

The WLD team embarked upon a process of consultation, in the form of country workshops, during which these issues were further explored and refined and a number of strategies for confronting some of the issues tested. In the course of these workshops, which took place in almost all the countries which originally made up the network, the various issues of concern to women were further clarified and strategies explored and prioritized. As noted in Schuler (1990), "The country workshops laid the groundwork for the regional conference in two important ways: (1) by clarifying the needs and obstacles of women's legal rights programs; and (2) by facilitating a systematic analysis of the most critical problems facing women." The dialogue and strategy-building initiated by the workshops stimulated the participants' interest in learning from the programmatic experiences of women in other African countries. In addition to the above, the various workshops also afforded individual women working on various issues an opportunity to network and exchange ideas. A regional conference at which participants from 14 African countries met to discuss and exchange ideas, provided the forum for building a consensus at the regional level around issues of common concern. This then was how WiLDAF, a network of individual professional women from varied backgrounds and from various institutions, was brought into being in February 1990.

WiLDAF - The Organization

WiLDAF was established on the explicit beliefs that law plays a pivotal role in the process of empowerment and that if appropriate strategies could be found to link law and development, women who were exposed to the various programs would be empowered sufficiently to participate effectively in the developmental process. The regional conference, held in Harare, Zimbabwe, in February 1990, which established the network, had as its theme: "Networking for Empowerment in Africa." As noted above, the participants envisaged the primary goal of WiLDAF as empowering women in Africa in the use of law as an instrument of social change for equality and development. It was envisaged that women would be able to use law and legal institutions to promote their rights and also promote the basic concept of human rights in Africa as enshrined in the Universal Declaration of Human Rights.

To fulfill the goals of WiLDAF, the conference formulated the following specific objectives.

(1) To establish and facilitate communication among network members in order to:

(a) learn from one another's experiences, success and challenges in the area of legal education, law and policy reform and legal services; and

(b) promote effective ways of using law as an organizing and educational tool at the local, national and regional levels;

(2) To help strengthen legal rights programs for women at the local, national and regional levels;

(3) To provide assistance and training to groups for the development and improvement of legal literacy programs, by the production

of simple educational materials, lobbying, mobilization and networking strategies;

(4) To establish and maintain a regional emergency response system to respond quickly and effectively to violations of women's rights, regionally and internationally; and

(5) To exchange and coordinate activities with other African and international human and women's rights networks.

WiLDAF was set up as a Pan-African nongovernmental, non-profit organization. It has a flexible membership policy. Membership is open to individuals of any profession involved in women's rights initiatives and governmental and nongovernmental organizations or institutions working in the area of women, law and development.

The network is governed by a 15-member Executive Committee which sets policy and oversees the implementation of the objectives and policies. The Executive Committee met immediately after the establishment of the network and set its programmatic priorities as: (a) providing training for resource persons in skills which will enable them to carry out legal literacy and rights awareness among grass-roots women; (b) setting up an information exchange system; and (c) creating an emergency response system to respond to serious violations of women's rights within the region.

WiLDAF Programs

(1) The first priority established by the Executive Committee was training for legal literacy and rights awareness. It was envisaged that WiLDAF would be involved in the training of resource persons in skills such as popular legal education methods and techniques, developing simple legal education and literacy materials, leadership building and organization strengthening, program design, planning and implementation, law reform techniques and lobbying and human rights mechanisms. The purpose of this training program was, among other things, to develop among the network members, a clear understanding of the concepts, issues and effective strategies for carrying out legal literacy and rights awareness for women and also equipping them with the skills to carry out the education. It was hoped that by developing a corps of highly trained resource persons in this area, the network would be able to respond to the training needs of members, thus helping to strengthening the various organizations in their training programs.

(2) The second program area identified by the Executive Committee was the development and dissemination of legal rights education materials. These materials were to be produced in response to the specific needs of the network members. The materials range from posters for use as resource materials during training, as well as for promotional purposes, to pamphlets giving simplified information on women's rights and development issues and training manuals for both lawyer and non-lawyer legal advocacy groups[1].

By producing these resource materials, especially in response to the expressed needs of network members, the network would be helping in no small way to address the perennial problem of lack of resources that most NGOs, especially women's rights groups, face on the continent. The training manuals, especially, will help to realize the objective of helping to strengthen and improve legal literacy programs by assisting in the proper training of the personnel who carry out these programs and also helping them to use the proper educational methodologies in carrying out this programs. Because the internal situation of network members vary, each group is expected to adapt the materials to suit their own particular situations and needs.

(3) The third program area is the development of an emergency response system within the region which will respond quickly and effectively to violations of women's human rights by bringing the full force of the network to bear on the offending government or institution. It also would involve the network mobilizing pressure both regionally and internationally in order to put a stop to violations of women's rights.

So far, this program area is the least developed. The network has yet to clearly articulate the procedures for the emergency response and to put up the structures that will ensure an effective utilization of the system. Nevertheless, in the few cases in which the network has had to use such an emergency response, it has proved quite successful. The notable example is in the Unity Dow case in Botswana. When it was learned that the Botswana government intended to put the issue of the citizenship of the children of a Botswana woman

---

[1] So far WiLDAF has produced a number of posters on issues of inheritance, maintenance of children, etc. In Zimbabwe, WiLDAF has produced a small explanatory pamphlet on inheritance to inform the current debate on inheritance. WiLDAF also has published its training manual for non-lawyer advocates. The manual for lawyers is soon to be published.

married to a foreigner to a referendum, the network mobilized protest letters from the whole of the membership to the Botswana government. It is likely that this contributed to the referendum being
shelved for the moment. Notably, the Botswana government has yet
to implement the court's decision in that case.

This program area is one of the priority areas of the network at
the moment. This is because the development of an efficient and
effective emergency response system to deal with violations of
women's human rights is one of the ways in which a network such as
WiLDAF can help to promote respect for women's human rights
within the continent.

WiLDAF - Three Years On

In view of its objectives, how has the network fared in the three
years that it has been operating? At the meeting which established the
network in 1990, there were members from 14 countries. Three
years later, membership has increased to 16 countries with four more
countries about to join. The original members of the network were
Ghana, Nigeria, Senegal, Cote d'Ivoire, Kenya, Uganda, Tanzania,
Sudan, Mozambique, Lesotho, Swaziland, Botswana, Zambia and
Zimbabwe. Since then, Mali and Cameroon have joined and Angola,
Namibia, Malawi and South Africa are all about to join.

The greatest challenge has been the coordination of membership
from the French speaking African countries and also West African
countries. At its inception, a decision was taken to make the network
a truly Pan-African one and, therefore, to aim at having members
throughout the continent. This, of course, has its own peculiar problems, one of the most important of which is language. Thus far a satisfactory solution has not been found to the problem of bridging the
language barrier in such a way as to make real inroads into the French
speaking countries. In the three years during which the network has
been operating, it has faced some real difficulties in terms of reaching
out to its members in the various parts of the continent. Its activities
have centered mainly around the southern subregion thus creating an
impression, albeit an erroneous one, that it is a southern network.
The fact that the regional secretariat is located in Harare, Zimbabwe,
is a factor contributing to this impression. But it seems that mainly
donor conditionalities and idiosyncrasies are to blame. Most donors
who have funded the network so far seem to be interested mainly in

the southern subregion and to some extent the eastern subregion. For the most part, they specify that their moneys, especially moneys given for projects and allied support, be used in specific countries within the southern subregion. Needless to say, this has created a situation of serious imbalance in the manner in which the network responds to the needs of the various subregions. Thus in the three years of operation, it has not been able to provide any meaningful assistance to the West African subregional members of the network. This is in spite of the fact that the programs that are presented for funding from the regional secretariat have been global in nature covering all member countries. As mentioned earlier, the problem so far has been with donor selectivity.

The network has however been able to establish country offices in Botswana, Zimbabwe, Zambia, Mozambique and Lesotho. These country offices are designed to coordinate the networking between NGOs in the various countries and to support those activities like legal literacy, rights awareness and others which fall within the mandate of the network. At the moment, it is not possible to assess the efficacy of these country offices because they have not operated long enough. It may, however, be necessary to revisit the idea in the near future so as to improve and strengthen the work of WiLDAF within member countries.

It will be noted from what has been said so far that no country offices have been established in East Africa or West Africa. The idea of country offices is a flexible one under the WiLDAF Constitution. Consultations carried out in East Africa prior to the establishment of country offices indicated that a lot more work needs to be done to encourage membership within the network before offices could be set up. Luckily, a donor has provided a substantial sum of money for the necessary ground work to be carried out and it may be that at the end of the consultation, a subregional office rather than country offices would be recommended. Whatever the outcome, the idea is to have the subregional as well as country structures that would enhance participation of members in the network as well as make the network responsive and an active participant in the drive to empower women on the continent.

The Potential Influence of WiLDAF at the Regional and International Level

At the regional level, WiLDAF has secured an observer status with the African Commission on Human and Peoples' Rights. This is an important step towards realizing the objective of using the network as a leverage in securing the observance of the rights of women. Making meaningful contributions to the work of the Commission will go a long way in the process of empowering women on the continent. Among the mandates of the Commission is the interpretation of the African Charter as well as the undertaking of studies and research on African problems in the field of human and people's rights and to make recommendations to governments. Because the issue of women's human rights in Africa is a priority issue, there is a role that WiLDAF can play in moving the work of the Commission forward. At the moment, due to structural weaknesses at the Secretariat of the African Commission, the Commission is not in a position to undertake any studies on any problem. Because research is a major objective of WiLDAF, it should be possible to find a collaborative way in which the findings of research done by WiLDAF in member countries, on issues of women's human rights, can be made available to the Commission to enable the Commission to make relevant recommendations to the affected governments.

The Commission has potential that can be exploited by WiLDAF so as to secure the effective promotion of the human rights of women on the Continent. So far WiLDAF has participated meaningfully in the last three sessions of the Commission and there are plans for the Commission in collaboration with WiLDAF to hold a training workshop for members of women's organizations from all the member states of the Organization of African Unity (OAU).

As the Secretariat of the African Commission becomes strengthened by the acquisition of the resources that will enable it to function effectively, it should be possible for WiLDAF to utilize its influence as a Pan-African network to use the potential of the Commission for the betterment of the lot of women within the continent.

Apart from the African Commission, WiLDAF has the potential, through a proper development of its emergency response system, to exert pressure on African governments. Thus WiLDAF can combine its lobbying efforts within the African Commission on Human and Peoples' Rights and also the OAU with its emergency response system and, working in collaboration with other regional organizations, it can effectively promote and defend women's human rights within the continent and beyond.

At the international level, the experience of WiLDAF's participation in the World Conference on Human Rights in Vienna in June 1993 shows that, if it organizes itself properly, WiLDAF has the potential to be a major player within the international NGO community. WiLDAF saw the World Conference as an opportunity for its member organizations and individuals to assess the status of women's rights in their respective countries and bring the shortcomings to the attention of the world community. It was therefore imperative to play a major role in the preparatory activities leading to the Conference itself.

WiLDAF thus participated in the Preparatory meeting for Africa held in Tunis November, 2-6, 1992, and the NGO Forum held just before that. Together with other participating women's NGOs, WiLDAF sought to lobby government delegates to call for the inclusion of women's human rights in the agenda of the World Conference. At the Tunis meeting, the NGOs present resolved to involve more women in the organizing before and also during the Vienna Conference. WiLDAF and a Moroccan NGO were mandated to facilitate those meetings.

WiLDAF was able to hold subregional meetings for Southern, Eastern and Western African countries in preparation for the Vienna Conference. It also held a Pan-African meeting, attended by members from 10 African countries, to agree on a common agenda or priority issues and strategies.

The purpose of the subregional meetings was to bring together women's rights activists and organizations in each subregion. It was also to identify women's priority human rights issues and the strategies to adopt at the national, subregional and Vienna Conference.

The recommendations from the subregional meetings formed the basis of the WiLDAF statement adopted at the Pan-African meeting in Accra. The meeting in Accra was attended by 38 participants from 10 African countries. Immediately after that meeting, WiLDAF sent three representatives to the 4th and final preparatory meeting of the World Conference held in Geneva, Switzerland, in April 1993. In an effort to ensure that women's concerns were reflected in the draft declaration which was being prepared by government delegates at this meeting for adoption at the Vienna Conference, Geneva involved lobbying other women's rights advocacy groups as well as government delegates. This was in order to ensure that the identified concerns of African women were not left out (Butegwa, 1993).

As observed earlier, WiLDAF's participation at the World Conference on Human Rights in Vienna was a learning process and it demonstrated one important point: that WiLDAF can be a leading network on women's rights in Africa. Fortunately, WiLDAF is seriously pursuing a consultative status with ECOSOC to enable it to pursue better its lobbying efforts within the UN system.

WiLDAF'S Role at the Local/National Level

The experiences of WiLDAF in the last three years have shown that even though it has great potential to play a leadership role at both the national as well as regional and international level, its role will be much more enhanced and relevant if it is organized in such a way as to be responsive to the expressed needs of grassroots women's organizations at the national level. This requires that at the local and national level WiLDAF has to be so organized as to be in a position to promptly respond to the needs of members. The ability to bring within the network at the national level all individuals and organizations working in the area of women's rights is a big step in this direction. The process of coordination at the national level is at various stages of development in the various member countries and it is for the secretariat to provide ongoing assistance to help clarify the role of WiLDAF within the context of women's rights so as to foster a better understanding among individuals and organizations. With this kind of understanding, networking can proceed smoothly, avoiding duplication of efforts and utilizing effectively resources for the pursuit and betterment of women's rights at the national level.

It is important to build up networking and better coordination of efforts and utilization of resources at the national level because it is obvious that when this is done, then the efforts of the network at the regional and international level will be of direct benefit to the membership at the national level.

Challenges Ahead and Prospects for the Future

The last few years have witnessed a tremendous change in women's rights activities and an environment that is constantly changing, giving rise to new opportunities for tackling existing problems and also creating new concerns and issues. Thus one of the biggest challenges facing WiLDAF as an organization is its ability to take on board these new issues and to play the leadership role in women's rights expected of it in Africa. The appointment of the United Nations Special Rapporteur on Violence Against Women during the 50th session of the United Nations Commission on Human Rights in March 1994 offers WiLDAF a unique opportunity to determine ways of working with the rapporteur to strengthen initiatives on violence against women and girl children on the continent of Africa.

The problem of violence against women is an all pervasive one of the African continent and yet in many ways it is a hidden menace. This is because there are no statistics to illustrate the extent of the problem and very little has been done by either governments or nongovernmental organizations to carry out empirical studies on the extent of the problem of violence against women.

WiLDAF, therefore, has an opportunity not only to initiate studies within member countries, aimed at eliciting information and statistics on the extent of the problem, but also to explore ways of working with the special rapporteur to find lasting solutions to the problem.

One of the negative impacts on the rights of women in the last 10 years has been Economic Structural Adjustment programs. These programs, imposed on African governments by the International Financial Institutions in an effort to revamp ailing economies, have further impoverished women and other vulnerable groups. As a women's rights organization, a challenge in this area is to document the negative effects that these Structural Adjustment Programs have on the rights of women and to demonstrate the connection between these effects and human rights so that yet another "voice" can be added to those already out there calling for "a human face" to these Adjustment Programs in order to protect the rights of women as well as other vulnerable groups.

Another new challenge facing WiLDAF is the issue of women in conflict situations. As at the time of writing, there is conflict in one form or another in many African countries and 28 countries are either producing or receiving refugees. There also are large scale internal displacements within many African countries as a result of conflict, drought or poverty and, in all these situations, women are subjected to many abuses, several of them gender specific. Some of these abuses are rape by warring armies and militia, sexual harassment and exploitation. What can WiLDAF, as a women's rights organization, do to publicize the plight of these women and also to demand that both national governments as well as the African Commission on Human and Peoples' Rights, the Organization of African Unity and the international community respond to these abuses and take steps to alleviate them? Internally, WiLDAF will have to pursue efforts at enhancing the participation of all individuals and organizations that work on women's rights issues so as to be able to coordinate programs and strategies developed to resolve problems. In addition, the newsletter produced by the secretariat, which serves as the communication channel among the members, will have to be used more and more not just to inform on issues but as the medium for the exchange of experiences and strategies. Each member of the network has a role to play in order to make the newsletter a true and effective medium of communication between members.

Conclusion

The prospects ahead for WiLDAF are very bright. At its recent General Assembly (1994) to review the past three years and to set goals for the next three years, the whole of the activities of WiLDAF was critically and objectively reviewed. The shortcomings and various options for remedying the problems were considered. All in all, the verdict was positive as to the role of WiLDAF in the promotion and protection of women's rights in Africa. The gathering renewed the mandate of the network in virtually the same terms with emphasis on the need to initiate research on the emerging areas which pose challenges to the women's rights movement in Africa including economic Structural Adjustment Programs, conflict situations, internal displacement and the consequent trauma that women suffer, among other things.

As WiLDAF forges ahead with its preparation towards the Women's Conference in Beijing in 1995, it is doing so in the full realization of its role as a women's rights organization in Africa with a distinct advocacy emphasis. It is hoped that the problems that have been identified will be rectified with time and resources, and WiLDAF will play the leadership role that has already been ascribed to it in Africa on women's rights issues.

References

Butegwa, F. (Ed.). (1993). *The World Conference on Human Rights: The WiLDAF Experience*. Harare, Zimbabwe.

Schuler, M. (Ed.). (1986). *Empowerment and the Law: Strategies of Third World Women*. Washington, DC: OEF International.

Schuler, M. (Ed.). (1990). *Women, Law and Development in Africa. WiLDAF: Origins and Issues*. Series on Women, Law and Development: Issues and Strategies for Change, No. 4 (Africa). Washington DC: OEF International.

Chapter 33
The Global Campaign: Violence Against Women Violates Human Rights[1]
Charlotte Bunch and Niamh Reilly

Introduction

The United Nations *Universal Declaration of Human Rights* proclaimed in 1948 states unconditionally that it applies to all human beings "without distinction of any kind such as race, colour, sex, language . . . or other status" (Article 2). Nevertheless, many violations of women's human rights continue to be ignored, condoned, and perpetrated by societies and governments in every region of the world. A particularly clear example is gender-based violence against women, which has not until quite recently been understood as a human rights issue much less as one requiring attention from the international human rights community.

Over the past decade, a movement around women's human rights has emerged to challenge such limited notions of human rights. It has focused particularly on violence against women as a prime example of the bias against women in human rights practice and theory. This movement seeks to demonstrate both how traditionally accepted human rights abuses are specifically affected by gender, and how many other violations against women have remained invisible within prevailing approaches to human rights.

As women's activities and projects have developed globally during and following the United Nations Decade for Women (1976-1985), more and more women have raised the question of why "women's rights" and women's lives have been deemed secondary to the "human rights" and lives of men. Declaring that "women's rights are human rights," women have sought to make clear that

---

[1] This article is adapted from Bunch, C. & Reilly, N. (1994). *Demanding Accountability: The Global Campaign and Vienna Tribunal for Women's Human Rights.* New York: Center for Women's Global Leadership , UNIFEM, & Women Ink.

widespread gender-based discrimination and abuse of women is a devastating reality as urgently in need of redress as other human rights violations. More women die each day from various forms of gender-based violence than from any other type of human rights abuse. This ranges from female infanticide and the disproportionate malnutrition of girl children, to the multiple forms of coercion, battery, mutilation, sexual assault and murder that many women face in every region of the world, throughout their lives, simply because they are female.

Origins of the Global Campaign

While such questions have been raised for a long time, a coordinated effort to change this attitude using a human rights framework has gained momentum in the past five years. Various international, regional and local women's groups have been strategizing about how to make women's human rights perspectives more visible. For our part, the Center for Women's Global Leadership (Global Center) convened such a group in 1991 in the New York/New Jersey area which works on women's human rights. It is composed of women from many countries working in human rights and in women's NGOs, as well as at UN agencies and area universities.

The Global Center's first Women's Global Leadership Institute held in 1991 was also devoted to linking women, violence, and human rights. At that time, participants from 23 countries developed many strategies but the most unifying was launching an annual campaign of *16 Days of Activism Against Gender Violence*, linking November 25, International Day Against Violence Against Women, to December 10, International Human Rights Day.[2] The *16 Days* campaign has grown steadily since then, involving women's groups in dozens of countries who have organized hundreds of events, including petition drives, hearings, demonstrations, lobbying, media campaigns, street theater, cultural festivals, radio programs, panels, and

---

[2]　November 25 was declared the International Day Against Violence Against Women by the first Feminist Encuentro for Latin America and the Caribbean in 1981, Bogota, Colombia. The day commemorates the Mirabal sisters who were brutally murdered by the Trujillo dictatorship in the Dominican Republic in 1960. December 10 celebrates the anniversary of the Universal Declaration of Human Rights proclaimed in 1948. The period also includes World AIDS Day (December 1), and the anniversary of the Montreal massacre (December 6) when a man gunned down 14 female engineering students for being "feminists."

the production of buttons, t-shirts and posters. Groups participating in the campaign select their own objectives for the activities they organize locally but all are done with a sense of being part of a larger global operation. Many of the events are aimed at promoting greater public awareness and gaining media attention for the issue of gender violence as it occurs locally. Others have used the 16 Days period as a time to lobby for national legislation around violence against women or to challenge human rights organizations to recognize this fundamental abuse of women as a human rights violation. Many marked the 16 Days in l991 and 1992 by mobilizing women to participate in the preparatory process for the 1993 UN World Conference on Human Rights.

The United Nations World Conference on Human Rights (the first one since l968) became a natural vehicle for many women's groups to highlight the new visions of human rights thinking and practice being developed. Its initial call did not mention women or recognize any gender-specific aspects of human rights in its proposed agenda. Therefore it became the unifying public focus of the first *16 Days of Activism Against Gender Violence* campaign in 1991, during which a petition drive was initiated which called upon the World Conference "to comprehensively address women's human rights at every level of its proceedings" and to recognize "gender violence, a universal phenomenon which takes many forms across culture, race, and class . . . as a violation of human rights requiring immediate action." The petition, originally sponsored by the Center for Women's Global Leadership and the International Women's Tribune Centre (IWTC), was distributed in English, Spanish, and French through dozens of women's networks. It was subsequently translated into 23 languages and used by women in many different ways at the local, national, and regional levels. It served to inform women about the World Conference and, more importantly, as a way to begin discussions of why women's rights and gender violence in particular were traditionally left out of human rights considerations. By the time of the World Conference, over 1000 sponsoring groups had gathered almost a half million signatures from 124 countries.

After gathering signatures, many of those involved in the petition drive began asking, what next? How do we show more clearly how violence affects women and what it means for women's perspectives to be incorporated into human rights? In response to this need, grassroots hearings were launched as part of the second *16 Days of*

Activism campaign in 1992. A call was sent with suggestions for how to hold such hearings and a revised UN documentation form for receiving complaints that took more account of women was distributed. The hearings were aimed at giving voice to gender-based human rights violations, articulating more precisely the spectrum of issues behind the global petition drive.

From November 1992 on, women began holding public hearings and speak-outs to document individual complaints and group cases of violations of women's human rights. The resulting testimonials were recorded, and the documentation sent to the UN Centre for Human Rights, providing concrete evidence of the need for human rights mechanisms that are more responsive to women's lives. Many who could not hold hearings gathered information and documented female human rights abuses and these records informed submissions to the World Conference.

At the same time, regional women's groups also began to focus on the World Conference, and at the regional preparatory meetings held in Tunis, San José, and Bangkok, women demanded that the human rights of women be discussed. Women in Latin America organized a women's human rights conference called *La Nuestra (Ours)* prior to the regional meeting in San José (Feminist International Radio Endeavor, 1992). They prepared a *19 Point Agenda* to be presented there which women from other regions also utilized. Women were also an active presence at various national preparatory meetings, and held non-governmental events aimed at influencing the World Conference agenda. For example, Women in Law and Development in Africa (WiLDAF) organized a series of sub-regional meetings where women defined their own human rights concerns and drew up a regional women's paper which was presented at preparatory meetings for the World Conference (Butegwa, 1993). The Asian regional meeting was held late in the preparatory process, so Asian women drew upon other regional and international efforts as well as their own specific initiatives to integrate women's perspectives into the final Asian NGO statement. In all of these documents, violence against women emerged as one of the key questions to be addressed as a human rights concern.

In February 1993, the Center for Women's Global Leadership convened a Strategic Planning Institute to plan how to influence most effectively events at the Vienna conference and to place violence against women squarely on the agenda (Center for Women's Global

Leadership, 1993). This meeting of women from around the world who had been active in working for women's human rights regionally gave definition to the emerging Global Campaign for Women's Human Rights. It focused on two levels: 1) lobbying strategies for the UN intergovernmental Conference, which included further development of a set of recommendations on women's human rights to be used at the final international preparatory meeting in Geneva and in Vienna itself; and 2) planning women's non-governmental activities for Vienna and, in particular, a global tribunal on women's human rights to bring greater media visibility to women's demands.

In addition to those mentioned above, several regional networks, such as the Asian Women's Human Rights Council, CLADEM (Latin American Committee for Women's Rights) and other international organizations were also mobilizing to put women's concerns on the agenda for Vienna. By the final meeting of the international preparatory committee held in Geneva in April 1993, which was to draft the conference document for Vienna, women were prepared with demands to present to the governments.

Yet, there was still uncertainty about whether the conference would even be held. In two prior preparatory committee meetings, the governments had not been able to agree on the conference agenda nor to start drafting the document for it. These meetings had split, primarily along North-South lines, over the questions of which human rights issues had priority (socio-economic versus civil and political) and what rights should be considered universal. Thus, at the opening of the final Geneva preparatory meeting there was no agreed-upon text to serve as a basis for the agenda for the World Conference. This provided an opportunity for women who had focused on building coalitions across North-South lines and addressing socio-economic as well as civil and political rights, to get their ideas included in the Conference agenda.

The women's caucus at the final meeting of the preparatory committee included representatives of international women's and human rights NGOs that are often present at such gatherings, as well as Third World women active in their regional processes, many of whom were organized to attend through the United Nations Development Fund for Women (UNIFEM). This coalition crossed long-time divisions, not only along North-South lines, but also between women working in government, in non-governmental organizations, and in United Nations agencies. This caucus succeeded in two critical areas. First, it effectively pressured for the inclusion of text on women in the draft document which was accepted by governments at the Geneva meeting with few 'bracketed' reservations—a process which virtually assured its passage later in Vienna; and second, it formed the basis for many women to continue working together across these lines in Vienna.

The Global Campaign for Women's Human Rights in Vienna

In spite of women's invisibility in its original mandate, when the World Conference ended in June 1993, gender-based violence and women's human rights emerged as the most talked-about subjects, and women were recognized as a well-organized constituency. The final statement issued by the 171 participating governments at the conference—the Vienna Declaration—devotes several pages to treating the "equal status and human rights of women" as a priority for governments and the United Nations; further, it sounds an historic call to recognize the elimination of "violence against women in public and private life" as a human rights obligation. The Conference also supported the appointment of a special rapporteur on violence against women by the UN Commission on Human Rights, called upon the General Assembly to adopt the *Draft Declaration on Violence Against Women*, and urged States to "combat violence against women according to its provisions." This progress on women's human rights was the product of women's organizing locally and globally both before and during Vienna.

Throughout the Conference a Women's NGO Caucus convened on a regular basis in order to assess the Conference proceedings and their implications for women. A lobby group from the caucus met daily to keep track of the drafting process in the government conference and many women were actively involved in learning to lobby their national delegations to ensure that the gains that had been made in Geneva were not lost. They responded to threats of new clauses inimical to women's human rights in addition to drafting new text for delegates to introduce. The Caucus also debated substantive issues raised by women who wanted more out of the *Vienna Declaration*. A tension existed between the fuller human rights demands that women wanted addressed and the gains that seemed possible at this particular conference. Those who had been involved in the process prior to Vienna tended to feel that the proposed text represented substantial progress for women. But many women new to the process felt left out of defining what issues were most important and saw the draft declaration as much too limited in its commitment to women. While the caucus debates were often difficult, they helped to expand women's understanding of both the usefulness and the limitations of UN world conferences and they helped to develop women's leadership for the future.

Another daily women's caucus was organized by UNIFEM (United Nations Development Fund for Women) at the intergovernmental conference which brought together women governmental delegates and women from NGOs and UN agencies to explore collaborative ways to advance women's human rights at the Conference as well as afterwards. These sessions not only addressed the *Vienna Declaration*, but also went beyond it to look at how to integrate gender perspectives and women's human rights into the regular operations of the United Nations. At the UNIFEM-sponsored women's caucus, meetings were held with staff from the UN Centre for Human Rights, with members of the monitoring committees for various Treaty Bodies, and with some of the thematic and country rapporteurs in order to examine how gender consciousness would affect work in their areas.

As part of the non-governmental activities in Vienna, a wide range of women's groups and human rights NGOs organized dozens of panels, workshops and events which addressed violations of women's human rights and supported women's efforts to be on the agenda of the World Conference. Women's visibility was ensured further by the organizing of this presence around an area called *The Rights Place for Women*. The Rights Place consisted of a large room used for office work, meetings, and information dissemination and a portion of the corridor outside the room, which was set up with displays of women's literature, posters on the walls and T-shirts telling women's stories hanging from a clothes line, and small tables and chairs for informal gatherings. Located in a central spot on the floor where the NGOs were based, it was almost impossible for anyone moving around in the NGO space to miss seeing that women were there in large numbers. The Rights Place thus established a visible sense of women's organized presence and their determination to be a recognized part of the human rights scene.

The major media strategy of the Global Campaign was *The Global Tribunal on Violations of Women's Human Rights*, which took place on June 15, 1993. It gave vivid expression to the life and death consequences of women's human rights violations by providing graphic demonstration of how being female can be life threatening, subjecting women to torture, terrorism and slavery daily. The Tribunal consisted of testimony from women who had been victimized and from women advocates in five inter-connected thematic sessions: Human Rights Abuse in the Family, War Crimes Against Women, Violations of Women's Bodily Integrity, Socioeconomic Violations of Women's Human Rights, and Gender-based Political Persecution and Discrimination.

The Tribunal was held on the second day of the conference so that it would immediately call attention to the demand to address gender-specific human rights concerns. It was also understood as a way to utilize the media present, not only to reach the delegates in Vienna, but also to bring greater mainstream attention to female human rights abuses and violence against women generally.

The over-arching objective of The Tribunal was to provide a global forum in which to demonstrate the failure of existing human rights mechanisms to promote and protect the human rights of women. (This placed it in the context of the UN World Conference agenda, which was to review and appraise the effectiveness of human rights machinery internationally.) The testimonies were symbolic of the situation of many thousands of women, and they documented and made visible violations of women which the current conceptualization and practice of human rights has not adequately addressed. By bringing patterns of gender-based human rights violations to the foreground, the Tribunal speakers made concrete women's challenges to the international human rights community. The Tribunal posed key challenges to the United Nations, national governments, and the international human rights community in several areas. In particular, it sought to: 1) demonstrate obstacles to women's enjoyment of human rights that stem from the distinction between public and private, especially around violence against women; 2) expose the often ignored violations of female human rights in war and conflict situations; 3) reassert that women's human rights are indivisible and universal, and highlight the ways in which some claims to cultural and religious rights impede the universality of human rights with respect to women; 4) illustrate the gender-specific dimensions of already recognized international human rights violations; 5) underscore the implications for women of the secondary status of social, economic and cultural rights relative to political and civil rights; and 6) evaluate the effectiveness of human rights instruments, procedures, bodies and agencies, including non-governmental human rights organizations, in protecting and advocating for the human rights of women.

The impact of the Global Tribunal on Violations of Women's Human Rights in Vienna was considerable. Women who testified there or as part of ongoing hearings elsewhere have helped to dismantle the wall of silence that has long surrounded gender-based human rights abuse. This is a critical part of creating the political climate necessary for the realization of women's rights as human rights.

Implementing Women's Human Rights After Vienna

Through the focus on the World Conference, women were successful in raising the profile of women's human rights and calling attention to gender based violence against women in particular. The challenge now is to translate that experience into long term advances in the implementation of women's human rights on an everyday basis, from the local to the global level.

In its early stages, the Global Campaign made the strategic decision to emphasize issues of gender-based violence as ones which best illustrate how traditional human rights concepts and practice are gender-biased and exclude a large spectrum of women's human rights abuse. Since different forms of violence against women clearly parallel other types of human rights violation that the international community has condemned, such as torture, enslavement, and terrorism, they were a useful starting point for demonstrating a gender perspective on human rights. Unfortunately, some interpreted this strategy as lack of concern for other types of human rights abuse. This was complicated by the media, which reported on the violence aspects of the Global Tribunal and almost universally ignored the testimonies of socio-economic violations that were given there. The challenge now is to work simultaneously to implement the promises made to women in Vienna around gender-based violence and at the same time to build an understanding that women's human rights includes other issues as well, such as health, socio-economic rights, and racial justice. As part of this effort, the *16 Days of Activism Against Gender Violence* campaigns for 1994 and 1995 seek to demonstrate how violence is linked to other aspects of women's human rights abuse in areas like migration, poverty, and reproductive health. The first post-Vienna action by the Global Campaign for Women's Human Rights, announced at a press briefing sponsored by UNIFEM on the last day of the conference, was to demand that the United Nations report on progress made toward implementing the Vienna Declaration at the time of the UN Fourth World Conference on Women (WCW) to be held in Beijing in September 1995. Toward that end, the petition campaign continues with a new version which calls upon the UN to report in Beijing on concrete efforts to implement women's human rights. The petition is meant to keep the UN and governments aware that women are watching to see how they will deliver on the promises they have made. It is also intended, as the initial petition did, to serve as a local organizing and educational tool to inform women about the *Vienna Declaration* and other international human rights instruments so that they will know more about their rights and utilize international human rights language and documents in their organizing.

The Global Campaign is also continuing to encourage local hearings and tribunals to expose and document the human rights abuse that females suffer. The Asian Women's Human Rights Council is sponsoring a series of public hearings over the next two years as are many other national and regional groups. In collaboration with several organizations active in the Global Campaign, the Center for Women's Global Leadership held a hearing at the International Conference on Population and Development in Cairo in September 1994 and another at the World Summit on Social Development in Copenhagen, March 1995. These were aimed at increasing recognition of the women's human rights dimensions of reproductive health and socio-economic rights. A global tribunal in Beijing will seek to hold the UN and its member states accountable for the promises that they made to women not only at the Human Rights Conference, but also in the *Forward Looking Strategies* document at the end of the UN Decade for Women in Nairobi in 1985, and in other documents like the *Convention on the Elimination of All Forms of Discrimination Against Women*. The Beijing Tribunal will form the basis for a report on women's human rights to be presented to the UN WCW in Beijing as well as to the UN on the occasion of its 50th anniversary celebration in October 1995.

Much that was learned from the Tribunal held in Vienna can be applied to other hearings women are planning. The Global Tribunal on Violations of Women's Human Rights was effective on a variety of levels: 1) it provided legitimacy in an international arena for women to articulate and record violations of their human rights that were symbolic of the experiences of hundreds of thousands of women; 2) it deepened the analysis of what constitutes women's human rights, and fostered greater consciousness of gender-based human rights abuse; 3) it brought women's human rights issues to wider attention through the media and therefore created more pressure on the UN and governments to listen to women's demands; 4) it provided a powerful focal event to which diverse women could point in support of their varying claims, and was an empowering occasion for many who testified as well as for those who listened or heard about it later; and 5) the Tribunal became a symbol or metaphor for the long neglected abuses of women and their growing determination to demand accountability for these violations.

However, there are limits to what a nongovernmental or popular tribunal can achieve. As a tool to promote public awareness of issues and to invoke political and moral pressure, it is not a legal process and does not produce recommendations that are enforceable. Those who testify must understand this, because for some people a tribunal represents a last hope for justice. Popular tribunals should strive to present cases which are being actively pursued, legally and/or politically, by local or regional groups. In this way, participation can contribute to the political momentum of a social movement without raising false expectations for an individual testifier.

Further, while exposing women's victimization in this manner is a critical step toward eliminating violations, it is equally important not to represent women only as victims. Therefore, the testimonies also need to highlight efforts organizations are making to counter the human rights abuse described in their accounts. This dimension of a hearing can be enhanced if it is systematically linked to subsequent workshops, events or actions. In doing so, those who testify and listen can strategize more concretely about how to transform existing human rights practice so that female human rights abuse is considered.

The promotion and protection of human rights involve both political and legal strategies. Much of the Global Campaign for Women's Human Rights has been focused on the political—developing a conceptual understanding of how gender affects human rights, exposing the neglect of violations against women, and creating the political will to do something about them. As a greater understanding of the human rights of women develops and the political pressure to address them grows, there is increasing need for more work on the legal aspects of these issues.

Documentation is a critical component to pursuing legal redress for women's human rights abuses and to giving definition to violations previously ignored. Documentation of individual cases can and should be gathered as part of the process of holding hearings or tribunals. This documentation process can also reveal patterns of violations which affect women across social, economic, cultural and geographic boundaries, thereby strengthening women's demands for their human rights as a group.

Even though gathering documentation and achieving legal accountability are difficult, there are many avenues within the UN and regional human rights machineries through which human rights policy can be influenced, and particular incidents of human rights abuse condemned. The realization of women's human rights requires not only that the Convention on the Elimination of all Forms of Discrimination Against Women (CEDAW) and gender-specific mechanisms be implemented but that, in addition, other treaties on political rights, torture, etc. are utilized to benefit women. One of the most important aspects of the *Vienna Declaration*, therefore, is the recognition that "The equal status of women and the human rights of women should be integrated into the mainstream of United Nations system-wide activity. These issues should be regularly and systematically addressed throughout relevant United Nations bodies and mechanisms" (Para. 37). This call for the integration of women and gender perspectives into United Nations human rights machinery will not happen automatically. It requires special attention. Specific measures to achieve such integration are suggested in the Declaration, for example, treaty-monitoring bodies should use "gender-specific data," states should "supply information on the situation of women de jure and de facto in their reports," and the UN should provide training for its "human rights and humanitarian relief personnel to assist them to recognize and deal with human rights abuses particular to women and to carry out their work without gender bias" (Para. 42).

If these objectives are to be met, women must not only keep up the political pressure on both governments and the UN, but also develop documentation, guidelines, and case studies that demonstrate what it means to integrate gender into all areas of human rights. Such a full integration will require changes in human rights theory and application of concepts as well as in human rights practice. Many human rights documents state non-discrimination as a principle, but the interpretation of their basic tenets is usually shaped by the experiences of the males who have traditionally dominated this field. For example, the *Universal Declaration of Human Rights* asserts that everyone has the right to "security of person" and the right not to be subjected to "cruel, inhuman or degrading treatment." Read from the perspective of women's lives, it seems clear that an issue like violence against women should be included under such a concept. Yet, it has taken over 40 years for such a woman-centered reading to begin to be understood. Such is the depth of the hidden gender-bias that has affected the definitions of which human rights will be promoted and protected. Only as more women become fully involved in defining and documenting the variety of female experiences of human rights abuse will this imbalance be corrected and the full range of both female and male human rights abuses be addressed.

References

Butegwa, F. (Ed.). (1993). *The World Conference on Human Rights: The WiLDAF Experience*. Harare, Zimbabwe: Women in Law and Development in Africa.

Center for Women's Global Leadership. (1993). *International Campaign for Women's Human Rights 1992-93*. Report. New Brunswick, NJ: Author

Feminist International Radio Endeavor. (1992). *Satellite Meeting "La Nuestra."* San José, Costa Rica: Author.

Chapter 34

On Surrendering Privilege: Diversity in a Feminist Redefinition of Human Rights Law

Celina Romany

The feminist discourse that has successfully challenged human rights law exclusions has had, up to now, a Northern face. But in spite of strategic successes, failure to critically examine lessons of invisibility that Northern feminism has brought to Southern women[1] will only continue to reinforce the sophisticated and intricate hegemonic patterns of feminist international human rights law.

Challenges to international human rights law brought about by feminist human rights scholars and activists have gained international attention, particularly in the area of violence against women. The 1993 Vienna World Conference on Human Rights represented for women the most successful attempt to raise these issues in the field of human rights. The Vienna Conference was a significant introduction to global efforts of women to redefine the social contract that legitimizes international society and its government. The Conference was the culmination of preparatory efforts to insert women into a transition process that will usher human rights protections into the 21st century, a century that must respond to the realities of a radical restructuring of global politics as the post Cold War world traces new routes of interdependency.

The Vienna Conference was also a microcosm of the world-wide power differentials present in feminist social redefinitions and practices. The Vienna experience was full of lessons to be learned in order to develop a diverse feminist challenge of the international structure, a key turn on the road to the 1995 Beijing Women's Conference.

---

[1] Far from describing a geographical location the term South/North is used in this essay to name countries which, in the post cold war era, remain at the periphery of full development and which many still call the "Third World".

International society is a highly bureaucratized and specialized world, mostly populated by men and informed by male views of international law and relations. The task of breaking ground in the human rights field requires an interdisciplinary effort incorporating a feminist agenda into the net world of international law and practice. In so doing, women must challenge both official and unofficial actors who, consistently, trivialize and marginalize women's issues.

International human rights conferences have historically been beyond the expertise of most women's organizations which devote their work to equality issues at the domestic level. However, that expertise has increasingly been acquired at meetings of nongovernmental organization (NGOs). Those meetings have been opportunities for women's human rights strategizing for United Nations consumption.

Transitions are rarely smooth, particularly when they require a restructuring of patriarchal power relations. Women's organizations, many of which are adept in challenging male hegemony at national levels, have confronted a familiar set of obstacles, from official and unofficial sources, in the international sphere. Affiliations with national grassroots movements do not necessarily guarantee non-sexist platforms. As national experiences show, women often confront the same pattern of hierarchical entrenchments within domestic NGO frameworks which often replicates governmental actions in international society.

The Vienna Conference was a scenario where women tested global/patriarchal waters at every level. For the first time women organized globally with a definite agenda of reconceptualization. Violence against women became the banner that summarized and conveyed the brutal face of male subordination of women operating across race, class and ethnicities. The road was rocky, but passable, full of lessons and valuable experiences for future agendas that aim to fully incorporate women within the protection and guarantees of international human rights law and practice.

Dealing with non-governmental organizations, our unofficial peers, was not an easy task by itself. It was a crucial experience in the women's global project. More so since NGOs can be gatekeepers, allies and/or rivals influencing official hierarchies within the UN system. Consequently, women's organizations not familiar with the system had to lift the veil from NGOs' human rights rhetoric dressed as substance. Despite their progressive agenda, NGOs still relegate women's issues to the sidelines.

At the preparatory meeting towards the Vienna World Conference on Human Rights held in Geneva, we soon learned how the consultative status granted to NGOs by the United Nations Economic and Social Council (ECOSOC), generates a coziness with UN structures (status and privileges included) leading to territorial disputes with "outsiders." NGOs with ECOSOC status were threatened by 'outsider' women NGOs which, although unseasoned in UN practice, brought a challenging substantive agenda to this arena. They also brought with them a wealth of national organizational experience.

Status divisions among NGOs also reared their heads at the Geneva Preparatory Meeting. Geneva-based NGOs controlled the overall planning of the Vienna NGO parallel conference,[2] an important forum for strategy, denunciation, networking and the exchange of valuable information. A militant coalition of NGOs (primarily from the grassroots South) challenged the planning committee's composition and, after hard negotiations, achieved some measure of success. These last-minute maneuvers (only a few months before Vienna), however, left the original planning committee with most of its original power intact, resulting in the control of invitations and travel funds for the Vienna conference, a major factor in assuring a diverse constituency at these conferences. This control allowed those from the original planning committee to gather a significant number of regular participants who, by virtue of their familiarity with the human rights network, created a ready-made domination of the process.

Notwithstanding our long-standing presence in the world, women are still newcomers in international society. Thus we are adversely affected by the control of information and resources that a history of network contacts ensures. Newcomer grassroots NGOs soon encountered at Vienna the unholy alliances which international politics generate and nurture. They quickly perceived that, compared to NGOs whose work life is primarily spent in the halls of the Palais des Nations, their access was limited.

A rule forbidding working groups to make explicit country-specific statements on human rights violations was received by many of the "non-professional NGOs" at Vienna with indignation. That rule raised doubts as to the "parallel" nature of a parallel NGO conference

---

[2] A parallel conference held alongside the official event, organized by NGOs, which gave the latter an opportunity to strategize and design lobbying agendas.

intended to articulate a comprehensive reexamination of the current status of human rights to be presented to the official governmental delegates meeting upstairs.

Women's organizations with grassroots connections were quickly exposed to unholy alliances and co-optation of UN based NGOs. But they also saw how both grassroots and UN based NGOs joined camps in their sexist behavior. Under the banner of regional, political and cultural allegiances, many grassroots organizations were equally dismissive of women's rights issues. Grassroots NGOs kept insisting on traditional formulations of human rights which prioritize political and economic power issues while obscuring their patriarchal component and ignoring the so called "private" social sphere.

The organizational structure of UN conferences present complex conceptual, strategic and organizational barriers to those women's organizations that advance a human rights agenda. The thematic and regional grouping of issues present daunting hurdles for a feminist human rights agenda that attempts to walk the tightrope of women's commonalities and differences across cultures and regions.[3]

Women's organizations grappled with conflicts generated by a division of labor that puts thematic and regional organizing in different camps. The conflicts among regions and groups that organize themselves across-regions, (such as women, racial and ethnic minorities and indigenous people) present significant obstacles to women who try to advance a feminist agenda that properly intersects with these fragmented realities and which attempts to break the traditional assignment of women's issues to "special interest" working groups.

At the Vienna World Conference, violence against women, (which conceptually allowed for more common denominators than differences) was the tapestry woven as a banner for a universal critique of a gender biased human rights law and practice.

The staging of a Tribunal, coordinated by the Center for Women's Global Leadership, coupled with an intense and focused

---

[3] As Marysia Zalewski points out:

[W]hat makes these views fundamentally different from mere competing perspectives inhabiting the world of the liberal pluralist is that a most crucial part of feminist standpoint is the word "feminist". The implication of a theory of oppression and exclusion which is held within the word feminist will lead us away from the untheorized position of mere perspectives. And as there are multiple ways of being feminist, there will be multiple feminist standpoints (Zalewski, 1993, pp.13-32).

lobbying effort, concretized in a dramatic way the systematic yet invisible pervasive problem of violence against women. The Tribunal was instrumental in publicizing and recording in the official Vienna Declaration the recognition that human rights of women are "an inalienable, integral and indivisible part of universal human rights." The Declaration and Programme of Action "urge[d] the eradication of all forms of discrimination" and condemned "gender-based violence and all forms of sexual harassment and exploitation" while welcoming the decision of the Commission on Human Rights to consider the appointment of a special rapporteur on violence against women" (Programme of Action, Pars. 18, 39, 40).

Such a strategic and substantive priority was not immune to the pulls and tensions brought about by diversity and difference. Hierarchies within women's organizations were highly visible at Vienna. The financial and informational resources of the Northern NGOs determined their leadership role in the feminist reconceptualization of human rights and dictated, in turn, the dynamics of their control of this issue at the Conference. A hierarchical division of labor flowing from these structural components revealed a scenario of lopsided strategizing around the issue of violence. Only a core of women at Vienna were privy to strategy agendas that were bounced off at women's caucuses or, given the organizational chaos, in the hallways.

The planned agenda of working groups at Vienna, although necessary for this historic event, weakened and often suppressed important insights of women who did not possess the luxury of rehearsed dialogues. On the very first day of the women's working group meeting, many participants sat and listened with disbelief how a well-traveled working document which had been discussed in different regional preparatory meetings failed to address the intersection of race, gender, class and ethnic subordination in its definition of discrimination

Women used to combating inequality against governments felt more included in regional caucuses full of familiar male faces than in the women's working group. On more than one occasion I was told by some women from Asia, Africa and Latin America not to waste my time with the "Ms." working group. They were alluding to the self-absorbed gender character of women's discussions at the Women's Working Group. What a debilitating situation and waste of resources it was, given the key role that empowered Southern women have to play in the feminization of traditional human rights organization, to place women's issues at the bottom of the priority ladder.

Many women felt objectified by Northern women who conveyed a romanticized solidarity reminiscent of the similar constructions of class and racial struggles of the white or elite left. Press and public relations, the public face of women's efforts at this conference, were controlled by a minority. Most women were left to feel like power-less clients re-presented to the world by the enlightened advocates of the North. Women were once again cast as sinners for the redemption script of missionaries.

Lack of diversity among women's organizations with the re-sources and expertise to participate in these conferences clashes with the strategy to democratize UN structures, the prevalent insider-NGO framework and progressive human rights organizations. The empowerment of women who represent diverse social, economic and cultural sectors is essential. The conceptualization of a women's human rights agenda which fails to intersect with the realities of the woman of the South sabotages the goal of making the NGO network more responsive to grassroots needs and aspirations.

Not only can Southern women offer a more complete conceptual picture to the feminist redefinition of human rights, but they can also play leading roles in building alliances and coalitions among these di-verse groups.

At Vienna, many of us worked together with groups that repre-sented our integrated realities as members of exploited regions or colonized minorities. On a daily basis we met with regional caucuses and with coalitions of regions strategizing around a myriad of human rights issues, where we consistently underscored the ways these is-sues uniquely impact women. For many of us, to be a woman from the South meant advocating for a women's agenda not totally ab-sorbed by an exclusive gender axis.

Conceptual and Strategic Presence

To position women at the center of a reconceptualization dia-logue is to address the need to view human rights from an integrated perspective. For those women privileged enough to understand the sources and ramifications of gender oppression and who have in-serted themselves into new social movements struggling for mini-mum conditions of dignity and justice, the maintenance of universal standards for the characterization and implementation of human rights is extremely important. Yet the presence of inequities in global politics and international relations also point towards an understanding of that universality through a filter of historical realities which expose the implementation of Northern values alongside colonial and neocolonial exploitation, as well as cultural hegemonic practices that devalue Southern identities.[4] Northern feminist legal scholars and activists still reenact the "orientalist" dichotomy coined by Edward Said (in which the Orient is defined in opposition to the Occident through an imperialist lens) where the Southern world is "shackled to brutal chaos" while the North embodies democracy and the rule of law (Nesiah, 1993, p. 201).

The presence of Southern women in the reconceptualization of a human rights dialogue refines and deepens an understanding of multiple oppressions and puts on the table the discourse of differences. To engage the discourse of differences not only mirrors the diversity of the world but also raises significant questions about the voices that get to be heard. It also raises the critical issue as to what power structures need to be in place to facilitate the required dialogue in building an agenda that problematizes gender subordination. To signal differences is to raise questions about the ways in which an essentialist feminist discourse replicates hierarchical and exclusionary theories and practices (Romany, 1991, 1993). It raises questions about the implication of women in the oppression of other women. It raises questions about the legitimacy of the paradigm-making nature a feminist discourse of human rights law assumes for national constitutional processes and legal reform in general. It illuminates dark boundaries between ontology and strategy, it brings a long silenced perspective on the theoretical and practical value of standpoints as well as on the elusive quest for foundational interdisciplinary knowledge that anchors legal reform and social transformation.

The inclusion of women from the South allows for the cognizance of integrated realities which are not mathematical formulas

---

[4] As Vasuki Nesiah notes:

By invoking experience as if it somehow captured the lived realities of all women at some basic level, theorists begin to take gendered individuals for granted. When the experience of gendered oppression is given the authority simply to assume a feminist alliance, it not only obscures other structures of oppression but also renders the operation of gendered oppression too neat, ahistorical and fixed (Nesiah, 1993, p. 201).

which add gender to race, class or ethnicity (Romany, 1991) but complex identities that both describe and provide normative world views for a human rights critique. The insertion of women with specific social locations allows for the negotiation of the multiple ramifications of power such as colonial, ethnic, religious, economic and, of course, gender (Nesiah, 1993, p. 206). This insertion rectifies an incomplete picture of gender subordination, with a picture of social citizenship that intersects with the realities of underdevelopment, structural adjustment, foreign occupations, homophobia and race and ethnic discrimination.[5] As the Vienna conference showed, violence against women requires more than a descriptive approach which does not expose the structural foundations that an intersectional approach unveils, such as the insertion of the systematic violent behavior within the broader social, economic and political picture (Mertus & Goldberg, 1994).

As Chandra Mohanty notes:

[T]o define feminism purely in gendered terms assumes that our consciousness of being "women has nothing to do with race, class, nation or sexuality, just with gender....Ideologies of womanhood have as much to do with class and race as they have to do with sex....It is the intersections of the various systemic networks of class, race (hetero)sexuality, and nation, then, that position us as "women"....(Mohanty, 1991, p. 13).

The inclusion of women from the South also helps to raise important questions about the division of labor embedded in the feminist methodology used to critique human rights law and practices. A division of labor that recreates the hierarchies of patriarchal societies fails to politicize theoretical critiques, and contaminates findings which claim to articulate diverse women's voices.[6] As Maria Lugones

---

[5] As Julie Mertus and Pam Goldberg correctly point out exclusionary dynamics present a limited range of participants whose inquiry tend to be on the discriminatory "act" itself, overprivileges gender and generates an organizing strategy that is single focused. The issue of violence can move "beyond the description of acts" (Mertus & Goldberg, 1994).

[6] In the context of Black women in the United States, Nancy Caraway talks about a division of labor that recreates the hierarchies: "The politicization of the criteria for theoretical knowledge becomes one of the most significant achievements of Black feminist discourse. The question of who is 'authorized' to create theory, in what voice and from what spaces of life, become powerful interventions enabling Black feminists to reject the policing authority of both the feminist and the phallocratic establishments" (Caraway, 1993, p. 35).

points out, there is a big difference between developing ideas together in a "pretheoretical" stage engaged as equals in joint inquiry and

> . . . one group developing—on the basis of their own experience, a set of criteria for good change for women and then reluctantly making revisions in the criteria at the insistence of women to whom such criteria seem ethnocentric and arrogant (Lugones, 1983, p. 579).

Inclusion generates a praxis and a methodology of "oppositional consciousness." Although Southern women do not form a monolithic group, their common experiences vis-a-vis Northern hegemonic practices germinates an oppositional knowledge which allows for "incoherences and contradictions" within a Southern location and gives voice to those who powerfully speak "coloredly" and who do not always speak with one voice (Caraway, 1993).

This oppositional consciousness allows one to see gender specific solutions as short term, and generates a "gendered framework for thinking about oppressions,...drawing connections between oppressions and communities without ranking them or minimizing them but emphasizing their inter-relations" (Mertus & Goldberg, 1994).

Since inclusion sheds as much light on the reality of the excluders, it is a consciousness that operates in many directions. It unveils the ways that a Northern world view is constructed for Northern women, unveils the specificity of the production of narratives that serve as a platform for the feminist critique of human rights. To be inclusive is to expand Northern women's understandings of their own social constructions.

Strategy profits too from an inclusive dialogue. In the realm of strategy where political constituencies (not biological or sociological ones) are represented (Nesiah, 1993, p. 203), differences and commonalities tend to blend, common panoramas tend to emerge. The legitimating power of strategic alliances derives from procedural fairness, from democratic processes where those key formulations of the common picture are authored by egalitarian forces.

Women leaders from the North, if genuinely interested in avoiding the divisions that often occur within their respective countries, must develop a protocol for surrendering privileges. That protocol, far from utopian, must be developed incrementally and with contours shaped by mutual respect and a genuine commitment to view feminism as a liberation project, as essential to the eradication of all types of oppression (Romany, 1991).

At the top of the protocol agenda lies an understanding of our shifting positionalities as women who belong to a world besieged by conflict and domination, as women committed to a peaceful world, where disagreements are discussed without missiles. Right at the top must be a space where we can agree to disagree.

The fulfillment of such aspirations requires credibility as a crucial enabling condition. Spaces for open dialogues without hidden agendas are basic for trust and for developing empowering conditions. Credibility requires more than rhetoric. It is produced by the ability to engage openly in self-criticism and with practicing new approaches stemming from lessons learned. In the human rights field this means the commitment and will to attack one's country's record of human rights violations, one's country record of discrimination, broadly defined. It is common to see how women from the Northern regions fail to deal with the compounded discrimination suffered by migrant women or women of color, how often they fail to acknowledge their implication in such subordination in their countries. Call it the invisible South within the North.

The surrendering-protocol must deal with accountability, with processes, hierarchies, and resources facilitating the exercise of leadership. A key question for discussion is the role of donors in maintaining such division of labor and an exploration of the avenues for making these leader-organizations (favored by donors) responsive and accountable for a more democratic framework.

The democratization of the women's NGO effort has to combat elitism and careerism. Oftentimes women leaders from North and South are so invested in their leadership because their professional careers and the trimmings of power are at stake.

Women NGOs doing international work must devise ways for opening national lines of communication. Ways must be developed for disseminating the international experience domestically and for doing coalition work with national women's organizations which can provide fresh approaches to the international dialogue.

The flow of information around international conferences is crucial. While it is important to maintain cores of experienced women in international meetings, it is equally important to give visibility to new faces (and new generations). Similarly, systems must be in place for keeping domestic organizations abreast of new developments around these conferences, while stimulating attendance at preparatory meetings of a broader audience.

Consultations are also important, particularly those which can gather experts and grassroots activists who mutually profit from their respective experiences and which take place in diverse regions, primarily in areas which experience the brunt of women's human rights violations.

The task of educating progressive human rights NGOs—national and international—must not be underestimated. The absence of ideological rallying points, brought about by the end of the Cold War, makes it more urgent than ever to build progressive agendas from coalition work, and this requires the identification and education of potential allies.

International human rights law and practice will be oppressive to many women to the extent that the essentialist feminist critique overprivileges gender subordination, and as long as that critique holds the orchestra seats in the performances which challenge the gender biased nature of international human rights law.

A new definition of sisterhood awaits us at Beijing to lead feminist redefinitions into the 21st century.

References

Caraway, N. (1993). *Segregated Sisterhood: Racism and the Politics of American Feminism.* Knoxville, TN: University of Tennessee Press.

Fuss, D. (1989). *Essentially Speaking: Feminism, Nature & Difference.* New York: Routledge.

Harris, A. (1990). Race and Essentialism in Feminist Legal Theory. *Stanford Law Review ,42,* 581-616.

Gunning, I. (1992). Arrogant Perception, World-Travelling and Multicultural Feminism: The Case of Female Genital Surgeries. *Columbia Human Rights Law Review, 23,* 189-225.

Lugones, M. & Spelman, E. (1983). Have We Got a Theory for You! Feminist Theory, Cultural Imperialism and the Demand for 'the Woman's Voice.' *Women's Studies International Forum, 6*(6), 573-581.

Mertus, J. & Goldberg, P. A. (1994). Perspective on Women and International Human Rights: The Inside/Outside Construct, *New York University Journal on International Law and Politics, 26,* 201-234.

Mohanty, C., Russo, L. & Torres, C. (1991). *Third World Women and the Politics of Feminism.* Bloomington, IN: Indiana University Press.

Nesiah, V. (1993). Toward a Feminist Internationality: A Critique of US Feminist Legal Scholarship. *Harvard Women's Law Journal, 16,* 189-210.

Romany, C. (1991). Ain't I a Feminist. *Yale Journal of Law and Feminism, 4,* 23-33.

Romany, C. (1993). Women as Aliens: A Feminist Critique of the Public/Private Distinction in International Human Rights Law. *Harvard Human Rights Journal, 6,* 87-125.

Spelman, E. (1988). *Inessential Woman: Problems of Exclusion in Feminist Thought.* Boston: Beacon Press.

Zalewski, M. (1993, Summer). Feminist Standpoint Theory Meets International Relations Theory: A Feminist Version of David and Goliath? *The Fletcher Forum,* 13-32.

Major Human Rights Treaties & Conventions

International Instruments

- The UN Charter (1945)
- Universal Declaration of Human Rights (1948)
- International Covenant on Economic, Social and Cultural Rights (ICESCR)
- International Covenant on Civil and Political Rights (ICCPR)
- Optional Protocol to the International Covenant on Civil and Political Rights
- International Convention on the Elimination of all Forms of Racial Discrimination
- Convention on the Prevention and Punishment of the Crime of Genocide
- Convention on the Elimination of all Forms of Discrimination Against Women (CEDAW)
- Convention Relating to the Status of Refugees
- Protocol Relating to the Status of Refugees
- Convention Against Torture and Other Cruel, Inhuman and Degrading Treatment or Punishment
- Convention on the Rights of the Child
- Declaration on the Elimination of all Forms of Intolerance and of Discrimination Based on Religion or Belief
- ILO Convention Concerning Indigenous and Tribal Peoples in Independent Countries

Regional Instruments

- African Charter on Human and People's Rights
- American Convention on Human Rights
- European Convention for the Protection of Human Rights and Fundamental Freedoms and Its Five Protocols
- European Social Charter.
- The Cairo Declaration of Human Rights in Islam.
- The American Declaration on the Rights and Duties of Man
- Conference on Security and Cooperation in Europe; Final Act 1975, Expert, Part 1
- Charter of Paris for a New Europe: A New Era of Democracy, Peace and Unity

A Women's Rights Agenda for the 90's and Beyond

From October 24 to 28, 1994, more than 100 women human rights activists from 42 countries met together in an strategy meeting in Kuala Lumpur, Malaysia, to assess recent gains and to plan future strategies for the protection and promotion of the human rights of women. The analysis and recommendations from the meeting form the core of a women's rights agenda presented here as a guide for future action.

Preamble

1. The World Conference on Women held in Nairobi in 1985 recommended state actions necessary to eliminate the wide range of discriminatory practices that maintain the pervasive subordination of women worldwide. In subsequent years, women successfully mobilized to intervene in all contemporary debates on major global issues, including development, human rights, democracy, population, peace and the environment at national, regional and international levels. Their efforts brought gender to the center of these deliberations and expanded the frontiers of the debate as a whole.

2. At the major UN World Conferences on Environment and Development (UNCED/"Earth Summit," Rio de Janeiro, 1992), Human Rights (WCHR, Vienna, 1993), and Population and Development (ICPD, Cairo, 1994), women made significant gains in addressing global issues from the point of view of women's lives and experiences, and in integrating a gender perspective into policy-making processes at the regional and international level.

3. Women's growing impact on global issues is especially evident in the area of human rights. The worldwide mobilization of women to claim their rights as human rights transformed the human rights agenda in a fundamental way.

4. Women's involvement in the human rights discourse has contributed to the expansion of the parameters of human rights as a concept, focusing on its dynamic character and transformative potential. This has resulted in a more integrated approach to human rights, which emphasizes the indivisibility and interdependence of rights as well as the universality of their applicability on the basis of the fundamental principle of non-discrimination.

5. As a result of the global mobilization of women, the World Conference on Human Rights held in Vienna in 1993 recognized that "the human rights of women and of the girl child are an inalienable, integral
   and indivisible part of universal human rights" and urged "the full and
   equal enjoyment by women of all human rights and that this be a priority for governments and for the United Nations". The Vienna Declaration and Programme of Action also calls for the elimination of
   "violence against women in public and private life" as a human rights
   obligation.

6. The Programme of Action adopted at the International Conference on
   Population and Development (Cairo, 1994) reaffirmed these developments and cited the applicability of universally recognized and indivisible human rights and ethical standards to the field of reproductive and
   sexual health. The Programme of Action recognizes the physical integrity of the human being and equality in relations between men and
   women. It broadens the concept of women's empowerment to include
   the elimination of all forms of violence against women. Advancing gender equality and equity and ensuring women's ability to control their
   fertility are seen as the cornerstones of population and development
   programs.

7. On the basis of these achievements, women have won recognition as a
   specific and significant constituency and it has become imperative for
   all international, inter-governmental agencies to integrate a gender
   perspective in their work.

8. Despite, or perhaps because of these accomplishments, it is critical for
   women's human rights activists to understand the challenges that remain at this juncture. Women's rights advocates are waging the struggle for women's human rights at a time when adherence to human
   rights is emerging as an important norm in governing international relations in the post cold war era.

9. At the same time, the complex economic and political forces at play in
   the international arena are creating an environment that is adverse to
   the full and effective realization of women's human rights and poses a
   major challenge.

10. The globalization of the economy, the interventions of multilateral in-
    stitutions and the processes of structural adjustment programs have
    meant the withdrawal of state responsibility from provision of basic
    services for their people and an erosion of state accountability to citi-
    zens. However, this global trend does not absolve the state from pri-
    mary responsibility and accountability for the protection of
    fundamental human rights.

11. The pursuit of free market development models and strategies by states, international financial institutions and transnational corporations which emphasize consumption and indiscriminate exploitation of natural resources—and are thereby unsustainable—has eroded the material conditions necessary to improve the quality of life.

12. The impact of structural adjustments has been particularly adverse to women who are burdened with meeting the essential needs of family and community in the face of increasing economic hardship. At the same time, structural adjustment programs rely on the devaluation of labor in both the formal and informal sectors to lower production costs. Women workers are the most harshly affected by these programs.

13. The growth of religious fundamentalism, identity-based politics and chauvinistic nationalism based on ethnic and other differences is also exacerbating social polarization in many societies. In many parts of the world, issues of cultural, religious, ethnic and other forms of identity have become highly politicized. Movements based on identity are acquiring increasing importance. In many instances, the ideologies of these movements demand control over women's sexuality and reproduction and keep women confined to roles that reinforce and perpetuate their subordination and prevent them from full enjoyment of their human rights.

14. The high levels of militarization worldwide, as manifested in military and arms expenditure, the upsurge of armed conflicts, and the channeling of investments/expenditures into defense and "national security" systems, contributes to an imbalance of power not only between states, but also between the state and its citizens. These trends undermine democratic processes by reinforcing authoritarian and repressive forms of government and draining scarce economic resources away from social development. Women are disproportionately affected by this situation.

15. The socio-economic and political climate within which the world's women struggle for the full realization of their rights is therefore profoundly insecure. Considering both the gains we have made, as well as the environment within which we operate today, the need for assessment and self-reflection and planning for future action is paramount.

Framing a Rights Platform: Themes and concerns

In response to the factors affecting women's rights today, the *From Basic Needs to Basic Rights* Conference brought together women's rights advocates, activists and scholars from all regions of the world to evaluate the progress of the women's rights movement over the past decade and to formulate a rights platform that can serve as a guide to future action. Following are the conclusions of the Conference deliberations, with recommendations and action strategies to tackle some of the most pressing issues facing the women's rights movement today: a) achieving human rights accountability to women and the elimination of gender violence, b) integrating social and economic rights, c) overcoming the conflicts between women's enjoyment of their rights and their ethnic, religious and cultural identities, and d) advancing the reproductive and sexual human rights of women.

Civil, Political, Economic and Social Rights

a.   The challenges facing the international women's rights movement, and the human rights movement in general, are threefold: a) to ensure the full realization of women's civil and political rights; b) to strengthen, promote and ensure the realization of economic, social and cultural rights; and c) to defend and advance the fundamental principles of the universality and indivisibility of all human rights.

b.   Women continue to face routine denial of these rights throughout the world today. This denial takes many forms, from the outright violation of women's fundamental rights to the failure by governments and the international community to recognize and remedy such violations when they occur. The world community's persistent failure to respect and guarantee civil, political, economic and social rights for women not only prevents women from fully participating in the economic, social, political and civil life of their countries, but also compromises the principles of universality and indivisibility on which the entire human rights system is based.

c.   The worldwide mobilization of women to claim their human rights has not only exposed the systematic and widespread denial of rights to women but also has pointed to the need to reinterpret and fully expand these rights to encompass the reality of women's lives. Women's groups have drawn attention to the relationship between gender discrimination and unequal power relations between men and women in both the private and public spheres.

d.   The realization of women's civil and political rights is linked indivisibly to the fulfillment of their economic, social and cultural rights. The existing documentation of gender-based human rights violations repeatedly demonstrates that the prevalence of violence against women throughout the world is intimately related to their lack of social and economic power. Discrimination based on gender as well as other socio-economic and demographic variables such as class, ethnicity, race, rurality/urbanity, age and region create particular obstacles for women to access and enjoy their human rights. Moreover, women's responsibilities at home limit the exercise of their rights in the public arena. Hence, ensuring state compliance with national and international norms related to social, economic, civil and political rights is an imperative.

Violence Against Women

a. The contemporary women's movement has made significant progress in highlighting the pervasiveness of violence against women and girls in all its forms globally. Their efforts have yielded, among other developments, the recognition by the United Nations that violence against women is a human rights violation and that the state has a responsibility to end gender-based abuses even where the violence is perpetrated by non-state actors (Vienna Declaration, 1993). Subsequently, the UN General Assembly adopted the Declaration on the Elimination of Violence Against Women (1993).

b. The appointment by the UN Human Rights Commission of a Special Rapporteur on Violence Against Women (1994) was a significant result of the pressure exerted by women on governments and the international system itself. The challenge for women's organizations now, however, is to support the work of the Special Rapporteur in such a way that this new commission significantly contributes to the underlying goal of ending violence against women in all its manifestations. The women's movement, a critical and natural constituency of the Special Rapporteur, is now called upon to play a significant role in making the mandate effective.

Cultural, Religious and Ethnic Identities

a. Although women are considered the custodians of culture in the majority of societies, most religious, cultural and traditional practices are defined on the basis of patriarchal norms that limit women's human rights. The growing power of religious fundamentalism, which emphasizes the role of culture, religion and the family, reinforces patriarchal notions about women's roles within and outside the family that deny women their rights.

b. Increasingly, women are coming forward to challenge the ways in which they have been, and are being, defined by religion, culture and tradition, and to claim their right to define and interpret religious, cultural and traditional norms and practices according to their individual and collective needs and experiences. It is imperative that women play an active role in the transformation of culture, by calling attention to oppressive practices and interpretations that violate their human rights.

Sexual and Reproductive Rights

a. Bodily integrity and self-determination are at the core of women's fundamental rights. They include the right to express one's sexuality and to exercise one's reproductive rights. The protection of bodily integrity and self-determination are inseparable from enabling conditions of social, economic, civil, political and cultural rights.

b. Different historical, cultural, social and economic experiences inform the relationships of women to their bodies, and consequently to sexual and reproductive health.

c. The construction of heterosexual norms within the framework of patriarchal gender relations--reinforced by state laws, policies, and cultural norms--limits sexual, reproductive, and life options for women and men, irrespective of sexual orientation. Patriarchal laws, institutions, and attitudes limit women's ability to express and enjoy their sexuality both within and outside marriage, to choose their partners, to shape their sexual identities, to make decisions whether and when to bear children, to protect themselves from disease (STD's, HIV/AIDS) and violence, and to participate equally in all aspects of economic and social life.

d. In patriarchal religions and cultures, including modernized societies, women are frequently unaware that they can view experiences, especially those affecting their bodies, in ways other than the ones into which they have been socialized. This constructed ignorance has serious ramifications for the exercise of choice in sexual and reproductive matters.

e. The attempt by Eastern and Western fundamentalist religious groups to dominate the International Conference on Population and Development in Cairo illustrates the political use of controversial issues, such as abortion and homosexuality, to intimidate people and to obstruct women's empowerment and exercise of their fundamental rights.

f. Violence against women in all its forms is a major obstacle to the attainment of sexual and reproductive rights. This has been reiterated and emphasized in various UN declarations including CEDAW's Recommendation No. 19, the UN Declaration on the Elimination of Violence Against Women, the Vienna Declaration and Programme of Action, and the ICPD Declaration and Programme of Action.

g. The HIV/AIDS pandemic affects women's sexual and reproductive health in gender-specific and particularly devastating ways. Policies and programs should be formulated at national and international levels to protect women living with HIV/AIDS, from discrimination in housing, employment, international travel, and access to quality health services.

Recommendations

The full implementation of civil, political, economic, social and cultural rights must be supported by the following strategies and commitments at the international and national levels:

International

Civil, Political, Social and Economic Rights

1. All human rights organizations and UN human rights bodies (including treaty-based bodies, the specialized agencies and the Special Rapporteurs) responsible for monitoring and advocating state compliance with the international human rights standards should, within the context of the gains made in the Vienna Declaration, integrate into their work and mandates the analysis of human rights violations informed by gender. Methods of such integration should include the results of discussions with women at all social and economic levels so that women themselves may articulate the consequences of these gender-sensitive policies on their lives;

2. Human rights organizations should take appropriate action at the international level to call into question:
    a. State ratifications that are accompanied by reservations and declarations inimical to the spirit of the international conventions, and
    b. States that ratify international human rights conventions without implementing substantive national laws and policies that give effect to the international instruments;

3. The CEDAW Committee should work together with all other treaty-based bodies and specialized agencies within the UN in monitoring the realization of women's rights under all international human rights instruments;

4. International financial institutions must be called upon to undertake gender specific impact studies in regard to the implementation of economic and social rights as an integral component of their prescribed programs prior to and during implementation at the national level. These studies must be made available and disseminated in order to ensure transparency.

5. Documents from the Beijing Women's Conference and the Copenhagen Social Summit should address the complex issue of the impact of different trade regimes on women's lives including their participation in the workforce;

Violence Against Women

1. The UN Conference on Women should be used as a special opportunity for initiating a process to evaluate the observance of the Declaration on the Elimination of Violence Against Women;

2. The Special Rapporteur on Violence Against Women should be allotted sufficient resources to establish a network for receiving and exchanging information on violence against women in all member States of the UN;

3. UN agencies, national governments and NGOs should sponsor and undertake campaigns, regionally and internationally, to combat and terminate trafficking in women;

Cultural, Religious and Ethnic Identities

1. In a global context marked by the rapid expansion of religious fundamentalism and chauvinist nationalist movements, measures should be taken to support and strengthen democratization processes that provide women the space to assert their cultural, religious or ethnic identities without fear of reprisal.

2. International human rights organizations should, on a global basis, investigate violations of women's human rights as a result of fundamentalist and nationalist interventions.

Sexuality and Reproductive Rights

1. States should implement the commitments of the ICPD Programme of Action that focus on education and awareness as key elements that enable people to broaden their understanding of sexuality and reproductive rights and possibilities for self-determination, in particular the commitments to provide:
   a. access to quality education for women and girls with a priority to eliminate gender disparities in educational attainment;
   b. comprehensive sex and gender education for people of all ages;
   c. education and awareness programs on HIV/AIDS prevention and management particularly addressed to women, and to counter societal discrimination and neglect;
   d. education and awareness regarding sexual abuse, exploitation, trafficking and violence;

2. States should implement the commitments of the ICPD Programme of Action, in order to ensure:

   a. the provision of family planning and pregnancy-related care in the context of sexual and reproductive health care and, in turn, as an aspect of universal, quality primary health care;

   b. the eradication of all forms of coercion, including incentives and disincentives to achieve population targets, in sexual and reproductive health programs;

   c. that all women should have full access to the highest available standards of health care regardless of their class, caste, race or ethnicity, age, sexual orientation, disability, marital, rural/urban or citizenship status, or geographical location;

   d. that health care is provided respectful of the needs and self-determination of indigenous women, and of women's diverse cultures and healing traditions;

   e. that safe, effective and available fertility regulation and disease prevention methods be available and developed, including methods for men;

   f. that women's perspectives inform, and NGOs be involved in, the planning, implementation and evaluation of research and development of new reproductive methods, and of policies and programs for the provision of sexual and reproductive health care, and sex education;

   g. that enabling conditions for sexual and reproductive health be ensured by national and international action; these include adequate nutrition, sanitation (including safe water supply) and a safe, toxin-free work and living environment, and women's education and empowerment, all of which are encompassed in an indivisible concept of human rights;

3. All intergovernmental and non-governmental organizations, including the international and regional human rights bodies (especially those charged with enforcement of relevant treaties), and the specialized agencies must take immediate steps to implement and monitor implementation of the ICPD Programme of Action and develop accountability mechanisms.

4. The Secretariat of the World Conference on Women should call upon the States and intergovernmental organizations at every level to report on progress in and obstacles to the implementation, monitoring and enforcement of the ICPD Programme of Action.

5. The Economic and Social Summit and the World Conference on Women should explicitly reaffirm the ICPD Programme as well as recognize the issues that were sidestepped in Cairo.

6. The status of all religious institutions to enjoy the observer state privileges in the processes of the United Nations, must be re-examined under international standards, and new strategies must be developed to overcome their undue influence in matters of sexuality and reproductive rights and health.

7. New technologies should be developed in collaboration with women. Technologies should be responsive to women's needs and tested in strict accordance with informed consent and ethical standards. Ethical testing must include women (as well as men) as subjects and must not extrapolate generalizations from studies on women whose economic, social and health conditions are not comparable to those of the anticipated users. An orientation that is sensitive to the needs and choices of women must inform scientists involved in the development of reproductive technologies.

National

Civil, Political, Social and Economic Rights

1. States should comply with their obligations according to the International Covenant on Civil and Political Rights and adopt the legislation necessary for the promotion and protection of women's civil and political rights;

2. States should comply with the interpretation of the Economic Covenant to the effect that regressive economic and social policies are inconsistent with social and economic rights;

3. States should elaborate and adopt Optional Protocols to the Women's Convention and to the International Covenant on Social, Economic and Cultural Rights which would allow individual complaints of violations under these conventions to be given due process;

4. States must ensure that documents emerging from the Beijing Women's Conference and the Copenhagen Social Summit Conference address the complex issue of the impact of social and economic policies on women's lives. Women's participation in both the formal and the informal sectors should also be addressed;

5. States must ensure women's access to and enjoyment of social and economic rights. They must guarantee access to education and training according to women's needs, and educate them on state obligations with respect to women's rights;

6. When appropriate, states must take the required actions to ensure that social, economic, civil and political rights are built into constitutions and made enforceable;

7. Because legal reform can only be meaningful within the context of real independence of the judiciary, states should ensure such independence;

Violence Against Women

1. All States should be guided by the provisions of the Declaration on the Elimination of Violence Against Women and implement laws and policies aimed at guaranteeing women and girl children protection from and remedies for gender-based violence and discrimination;

2. The State and relevant international agencies should ensure the safety of particularly vulnerable sectors of women: women living in areas of armed conflict, under occupation and economic sanctions; refugee and displaced women; returnee women; migrant and immigrant women; indigenous women; lesbians; disabled women; and women prisoners;

Cultural, Religious and Ethnic Identities

1. National laws should specify and reflect strict separation between the State and religion and religious institutions.

2. States (and communities) should not compel women to choose between their cultural, religious and ethnic identities and the exercise of their fundamental rights. Nor should women be prohibited from choosing an alternate ethical paradigm or pursuing a secular existence.

3. States should assure that women be given opportunities to exercise their rights as citizens and to participate in decision-making processes at all levels.

4. In order to assure that women can exercise their rights as full citizens, states should not differentially apply democratic principles (such as the rights to vote) to women.

5. In states where there is constitutional protection of minorities, states should not compromise women's rights in the interests of fulfilling constitutional provisions for minority groups.

Sexuality and Reproductive Rights

1. State, multinational and national bodies should be accountable for provision of health services for women. An international code that protects individuals and national groups from activities that are harmful to health is required in order to adequately monitor state compliance;

2. All national governments, both recipients and donors, must immediately take steps to implement the ICPD Programme of Action and

thereby ensure its commitments to all women without discrimination based on class, caste, race, ethnicity, sexual orientation, disability, marital, urban-rural or citizenship status, and with particular respect for indigenous women's self-determination and women's diverse cultures and healing traditions.

3. Women should be provided with a free choice of all contraceptive technologies and birthing options available by giving them full information and appropriate and safe health services.

Women's Advocacy Strategies

Civil, Political, Social and Economic Rights

Ensuring Accountability

1. Women's organizations should participate in the development of a regional and international jurisprudence that promotes the indivisible understanding of human rights, the full realization of civil and political rights and the concretization of economic, social and cultural rights through state accountability ensured by legal means;

2. Women's rights networks should lobby for the formulation of Optional Protocols to the Women's Convention and to the International Covenant on Social, Economic and Cultural Rights

3. Women's organizations should become familiar with the international instruments and in particular with the Vienna and Cairo Declarations in order to effectively pressure governments to implement policies contained in those declarations;

4. Women's NGO's and other human rights organizations should continue to monitor national compliance with international instruments;

5. Women's NGO's and human rights organizations should report to other national women's organizations on the evaluations, by relevant treaty-bodies, of state compliance with international instruments;

6. Women's organizations and human rights organizations must use the existing treaty review process to monitor government compliance with international norms and standards through national publicity and, if necessary, the development of alternative reports;

7. Women's organizations should act as pressure groups to ensure State conformity of national legislation with international human rights standards;

8. Women's organizations and human rights organizations should make sure that Governments report periodically to their national parliaments

on human rights implementation, paying special attention to the implementation of women's rights;

9. Women should demand of governments annual reports in parliament on their compliance with social and economic rights as well as regular reporting to CEDAW and other international treaty-based bodies;

Integrating Social and Economic Rights

1. Women's organizations should continue to establish alliances locally and internationally to critically analyze the proposed mandate and structure of the new World Trade Organization and demand that research be pursued in order to identify the actual and expected consequences on women's economic and social rights of new trade regimes and dispute resolution mechanisms. Research also should be encouraged in order to determine the best mechanisms to guarantee respect for women's rights in the context of economic globalization;

2. Women's organizations should pursue efforts to guarantee the existence and operation of women's advocacy networks capable of influencing the most powerful economic institutions on behalf of the world's women, and particularly on behalf of those without any effective access to those centers of power;

3. International organizations must also be lobbied, either through national delegates where these exist or directly, in order to ensure that:
   a. economic policy reforms do not violate the provisions of the international human rights instruments;
   b. programs of all international development organizations improve women's social and economic rights and position; and
   c. programs of bi-lateral donors do the same;

4. National women's organizations should increase research on the gender impact of macro-economic policies and on the impact of these policies on various sectors of the population. Adequate funding must be made available for that purpose;

5. National women's organizations and human rights organizations should monitor the expenditure patterns of national budgets in order to understand what these patterns mean for women. This understanding will, over time, allow for a more precise definition of workable policy agendas which reinforce social and economic rights. Adequate funding must be made available for that purpose;

6. Women's organizations must lobby their governments to ensure that the programs of international financial institutions implemented at the

national level respect the norms and standards of international human rights instruments;

7. Women's organizations should give special attention and support to the organization of women workers, especially the most vulnerable groups of women workers, e.g. domestic workers; migrant workers; workers in export processing zones;

8. Because women's organizations continue to be central to the articulation of violations of women's rights, they need to strengthen their capacity to lobby, monitor, conduct research and formulate policy with respect to implementation and enforcement of social and economic rights. Women's organizations must also develop the capacity to critique the policies of the international financial institutions and to articulate alternative economic models.

Religious and Ethnic Identities and Rights

1. Women's groups should equip themselves in order to engage in theological debate and participate in the re-interpretation of religious doctrine and practice.

2. Women's groups should evolve strategies to work with parliamentary bodies and juridical institutions on issues concerning the re-interpretation of religious doctrine and practice. They also should formulate strategies that enable women to choose the ethical framework within which they want to live, whether secular or religious.

3. Women's groups should enlist the cooperation of the media in gaining public support and raising awareness on women's issues.

4. Women's groups should link with interfaith coalitions across the globe in order to contend with the consequences of religious fundamentalism.

Violence Against Women

1. Women's groups and NGOs should form a network to ensure the international observance of the Declaration on the Elimination of Violence Against Women;

2. Women's NGOs should assist the work of the Special Rapporteur by:
    a. expanding the base of skilled documentors and monitors within women's NGOs;
    b. identifying cases of violence and detecting emerging issues that are as yet unrecognized under the rubric of violence;
    c. providing specific and accurate documentation and statistics on violations;

d. contributing to new ways of conceptualizing violence against girls and women;

e. providing pressure at local, national and regional levels to ensure that states comply with UN recommendations to eliminate violence;

f. publicizing information on the mandate of the Special Rapporteur;

g. implementing rights education programs, so that women can better understand the violations of their rights and bring them to the attention of the Special Rapporteur;

h. monitoring compliance at state levels and reporting findings to the Special Rapporteur or other appropriate offices.

Sexuality and Reproductive Rights

1. Women's organizations should generate appropriate discourse and discussion about health, sexuality and reproduction among women and in the larger society, using popularization and empowerment methodologies to build self-determination and solidarity;

2. Women's organizations and other human rights organizations should oppose the regulation of female sexuality conducted by methods such as electro-shock and "corrective" therapy, whether such physical and mental treatment is administered to girls and women by private individuals or by the State;

3. Women's organizations should use the media to promote discussion of sexuality and reproductive issues, and to publicize relevant provisions of international human rights instruments;

4. Women's organizations should critique the media's role in perpetuating gender violence and stereotypes as well as hold the media responsible for advancing open discussions of sexual and reproductive issues and producing programs that are free of gender and other biases;

5. In working to accomplish the goals of the ICPD Programme of Action, women's organizations must vigorously pursue the reconceptualization and reform of medicine, healing and health from the perspectives of women, taking into account women's health over the entire life cycle and not simply in the context of maternity, and injecting a gender perspective into medical education, training and service;

6. Women's organizations also should oppose the worldwide trend toward privatization of health services and cutbacks in the public sector, which often result in inequities of access, higher prices and, for all but the most privileged, declining quality of care.

Conclusion:

The Fourth World Conference on Women represents a historic moment for the international community and women's movements worldwide. It will be the time to assess progress towards the achievement of the goals outlined in the Forward Looking Strategies of Nairobi, which focused on Equality, Development and Peace. It also will be the moment to formulate plans and programs of action for the advancement of women in the coming decade.

1. For UN member states:

    a. The Beijing Conference will be an opportunity for member states to take stock of their record concerning the implementation of their international commitments to the protection and promotion of women's human rights and to transform the promise of international recognition of these rights into their full realization of these rights at local, national, regional and international levels.

    b. States must act with absolute urgency to realize the commitments made in Agenda 21 of the Rio Conference, the Vienna Declaration and the International Conference of Population and Development Programme of Action. The UN World Conference on Women must give efficacy to the international community's commitment to the protection and promotion of women's human rights by recommending the adoption of an optional protocol to CEDAW.

2. For women's human rights advocates:

    a. Advocates should use the Beijing Conference as an opportunity to reaffirm and consolidate the gains made thus far in articulating and advancing women's human rights.

    b. Women's movements need to articulate and adopt new strategies to secure women's full realization of their rights. Chief among these is the continued struggle to refine human rights theory and practice to reflect women's experiences and interests, and to address the global economic trends that constrain the realization of human rights. In particular, women's groups must emphasize the principle of indivisibility and interdependence of all categories of rights, while simultaneously strengthening mechanisms to ensure women's full enjoyment of their human rights.

In order to achieve these ends, it is imperative that we build on our existing and evolving networks and alliances to strengthen linkages between women across regions, classes, ethnicity and other differences in a way that acknowledges diversity. Only by continuing to mobilize and organize at local, national, regional and international levels will we overcome the systemic global oppression and subordination of women and ensure every woman's ability to fully and equally participate in all spheres of life.

Contributors

Asma Abdel Halim is a lawyer and a member of the Steering Committee of Women in Law and Development in Africa (WiLDAF). She practiced law in the Sudan and was a member of the Committee on the Status of Sudanese Women. She was active in the legal literacy programs of the Sudanese Women's Union before it was forcibly dissolved, and has spoken widely on women's rights and human rights in the Sudan.

Sunila Abeyesekera has been a political activist since 1976, with a focus on women. A trained actress and singer, she is committed to using theater and music as a means to organizing within social movements. She is a founder member of several women's groups, including the Women's Media Forum. She is also a founder of INFORM, a human rights documentation group, and has been active in the Sri Lanka lobby group at the UN Human Rights Commission.

Gladys Acosta Vargas is a lawyer and head of the program on Women and Power at the Instituto Latinoamericano de Servicios Legales Alternativos (ILSA) in Bogotá. She was formerly at Flora Tristan in Lima, and is a long-time women's rights and human rights activist.

Mahnaz Afkhami is Executive Director of the Sisterhood is Global Institute and the Foundation for Iranian Studies, based in Bethesda, Maryland. She has been active in the women's movement, both in Iran and internationally, for a number of years. She founded the Association of University Women in Iran in 1968, and was Minister of State for Women's Affairs, 1976-1978. She is the author of several papers on women's rights and human rights.

Tasneem Azim is an immunologist and a member of Naripokkho, an organization that focuses on advocacy for women's rights and development in Bangladesh. She is active in the area of women's health and empowerment, and has worked extensively at the national and international levels.

Charlotte Bunch is the Director and founder of the Center for Women's Global Leadership at Rutgers University, New Jersey. She has been an activist in the women's and civil rights movements for over two decades, and has been working on global feminism with a variety of organizations since the 1980s. She has edited seven anthologies and authored *Demanding Accountability: The Global Campaign and Vienna Tribunal for Women's Human Rights.*

Florence Butegwa is Regional Coordinator for Women, Law and Development in Africa (WiLDAF), and a leading human rights lawyer. She has played a key role in ensuring that the regional human rights agenda includes women's rights, and has been very active in the international human rights field. She has taught law at Makerere University in Kampala and the Kenya Polytechnic in Nairobi, and has written several articles on women's rights and human rights.

Barbara Cameron teaches public policy at York University, Toronto, where she is Assistant Professor of Political Science. Her research interests center on women and public policy, particularly trade, employment and labor market policy. She has held research and policy positions with trade unions in Ontario, and works closely with the Canadian National Action Committee on the Status of Women.

Roberta Clarke is a lawyer practicing in Port of Spain. She is a consultant to the Gender and Human Rights Program of the Caribbean Association for Feminist Research and Action (CAFRA). She has worked extensively on legal literacy and legal aid for women in the Caribbean.

Radhika Coomaraswamy is Director of the International Centre for Ethnic Studies in Colombo, and the United Nations Special Rapporteur on Violence Against Women. She has written and edited a number of books and articles that focus on women, ethnicity and human rights; violence against women; women and the law; democratic traditions and conflict resolution.

Rhonda Copelon is Professor of Law at the City University of New York and Co-Director of CUNY's International Women's Human Rights Law Clinic. She has been a consultant to the Inter-American Institute of Human Rights and as well as the United

Nations Latin American Institute for the Prevention of Crime and the Treatment of Delinquency (ILANUD). She has been very active in the international women's reproductive rights movement.

Lisa Crooms is Visiting Associate Professor of Law at Howard University Law School in Washington D.C. Formerly, she practiced employment and labor law in Oakland, California.

Adriana de la Espriella is a lawyer providing legal services for women at PROFAMILIA, an NGO which deals mainly with reproductive health matters, in Bogotá. She has worked as a private attorney and at the office for Youth, Women and the Family at the Presidency of Colombia.

Alda Facio is a feminist jurist and writer. She is currently the Director of the Women, Gender and Justice Program of the United Nations Latin American Institute for the Prevention of Crime and the Treatment of Delinquency (ILANUD). Since 1988, she has been the Costa Rican correspondent for *Mujer/Fempress* based in Santiago, Chile. Her recent book describes an original methodology for the incorporation of gender analysis into legal texts and contexts.

Joan French has been an activist in the women's movement for over 20 years, as well as in the teachers' trade union movement. She works extensively on the issue of socio-economic development and is associated with the SISTREN Theatre Collective and CAFRA. Currently she is Coordinator of the Caribbean Policy Development Center based in Barbados.

Sharon Hom is Professor of Law at the City University of New York. Her work focuses on international human rights and women's rights, and gender issues and law in the People's Republic of China. She has taught American legal methods and administrative law at several Chinese universities, and has written and spoken extensively on women, law and legal education in China.

Nasreen Huq is a nutritionist and a member of Naripokkho, an organization that focuses on advocacy for women's rights and development in Bangladesh. She has been very active in the area of women's rights and health, and has participated in several national and international fora on women's health.

Deeana Jang is an attorney at the Asian Law Caucus in San Francisco, California. She was staff attorney at the San Francisco

Neighborhood Legal Assistance Foundation. She is co-editor of *Domestic Violence in Immigrant and Refugee Communities: Asserting the Rights of Battered Women*, and has authored several articles on immigrant women and domestic violence.

Rani Jethmalani is an attorney at the Supreme Court of India. She was the founding director of the organization Women's Action Research and Legal Action for Women (WARLAW) in New Delhi. She has long been active in the field of women's rights, and was one of the earliest legal activists to focus on dowry deaths in India and bring cases before the Indian courts.

Irina Jurna is Press Secretary of the Foreign Policy Association and the director of its Women's Center. She is also co-director of the Association of Women Journalists in Russia. She was editor-in-chief of *Vestnik*, a magazine that was published by the Soviet Ministry of Foreign Affairs until 1991, and thereafter by the Foreign Policy Association. She was also editor of the newsletter *Women's Movement in Russia.*

Akua Kuenyehia is a Senior Lecturer in Law at the University of Ghana. She has worked extensively on women's issues in Ghana and in Africa in general, and has authored several articles on women's rights issues and the law. She is a founding member of WiLDAF, and a member of its Steering Committee.

Lucie Lamarche is Professor of Law at the University of Quebec. She has authored a number of articles and reports on social and economic rights, including women's rights. Her most recent book is *Les Programmes d'accès à l'égalité en emploi.* She has also been active in community and women's groups in Quebec.

Leni Marin is a Senior Program Specialist at the Family Violence Prevention Fund in San Francisco. She coordinates the Fund's Battered Immigrant and Refugee Women's Rights Project, and played an active role in realizing the landmark Violence Against Women Act. An immigrant to the US from the Philippines, she has been an advocate for the rights of battered women for over ten years.

Verónica Matus Madrid is a lawyer in charge of the women's program of the Chilean Commission on Human Rights. She has been active in the human rights movement in Chile since the 1973 coup. She worked extensively with women whose family members had disappeared, and later with women's groups on several community initiatives. More recently she has worked to incorporate human rights, especially for women, in democratic governance.

Sharon McIvor is a lawyer and the Justice Coordinator of the Native Women's Association of Canada. She was Constitutional Advisor of the NWAC, has worked extensively for native women's empowerment in Canada, and authored several papers on native women's rights and aboriginal self government. She is a member of the Lower Nicola Indian Band, Merritt, British Columbia.

Pearl Nwashili is the founder and Executive Director of STOPAIDS Organization in Lagos. She is also a member of the National AIDS Committee of Nigeria, and has developed educational programs on HIV/AIDS and STDs for grassroots women and other populations .

Maureen O'Neil is a Partner at the Institute of Governance in Ottawa. She was President of the North-South Institute, and has held senior positions in the Canadian federal and provincial governments. Internationally she has represented Canada on the UN Status of Women Commission, and has been on Canadian delegations to the UN Conferences on the Status of Women.

Rosalind Pollack Petchesky is Professor of Political Science and Women's Studies at Hunter College of the City University of New York as well as International Coordinator of the International Reproductive Rights Research Action Group (IRRRAG). She is the author of *Abortion and Women's Choice: The State, Sexuality and Reproductive Freedom,* and of many published articles on reproductive rights and feminist theory and movements. She was recently awarded a MacArthur Fellowship.

Maria Isabel Plata is a lawyer and Deputy Director of PROFAMILIA in Bogotá. She has conducted research on the law and the status of Colombian women, domestic violence and human rights. She has authored several case studies, the most recent of which is "Reproductive Rights as Human Rights: The Colombian Case."

Laura Queralt is a feminist psychologist whose personal experiences as a young woman living in a sexist society led her to become an activist for the human rights of women. She has worked in the Women, Gender and Justice Program at ILANUD in Costa Rica. She has also worked at the National Television Channel producing one-minute spots on women's rights.

Darini Rajasingham is the Research and Project Coordinator at the International Centre for Ethnic Studies, Colombo, Sri Lanka. She has taught at Princeton University and the University of Birmingham. She is the author of a number of papers on ethnicity, colonialism and ethnic conflict.

Niamh Reilly coordinated the Global Tribunal on Violation of Women's Human Rights (Vienna, 1993) and is responsible for the international campaigns at the Center for Women's Global Leadership at Rutgers University, where she is a Senior Program Associate. She co-authored *Demanding Accountability: The Global Campaign and Vienna Tribunal for Women's Human Rights* with Charlotte Bunch, and is writing her Ph.D. dissertation on Gender, Human Rights and Political Transformation.

Celina Romany is Professor of Law, and former Co-Director of the Women's International Human Rights Program at City University of New York Law School. She has written extensively about feminist theory, human rights, international law, critical race theory and labor and employment law. She is also a representative of the American Association of Jurists at the United Nations.

Indai Lourdes Sajor is the coordinator of the Asian Women's Human Rights Council (AWHRC) and the Asia-Pacific Women's Action Network (APWAN). She is currently working with Filipino Comfort Women who filed a class action suit against the Japanese government. She was a political prisoner during the martial law years of the Marcos regime in the Philippines, and has been an energetic women's human rights activist for many years.

Margaret Schuler is Executive Director of the Institute for Women, Law and Development and has worked internationally in the area of women's rights for over 15 years. She was instrumental in developing networks of women's rights advocates in Asia, Africa and Latin America, and has extensive experience in legal literacy and leadership development. She has authored or edited six books including *Empowerment and the Law: Strategies of Third World Women* and *Legal Literacy: A Tool for Women's Empowerment, and Freedom From Violence.*

Gita Sen is Professor of Economics at the Indian Institute of Management, Bangalore, and Adjunct Professor in Development Economics at Harvard University. She is a founding member of DAWN, Development Alternatives for Women in a New Era.

Widely known for her work on women and development, she also conducts policy research on environment, health and population.

Rebecca Sewall, a cultural anthropologist, explores the impact of macro-economic policies on the quality of employment opportunities for women. She is the founder of the Development and Employment Policy Project, an organization designed to raise awareness of gender-biased labor practices as an international development concern. She is currently a Senior Program Associate at the Health and Development Policy Project based in Washington D.C.

Farida Shaheed is a sociologist working at Shirkat Gah, a women's resource center in Karachi and Lahore that integrates research, development and advocacy. She is a founder member of the national women's lobby, Women's Action Forum, and is one of the coordinators of the international network, Women Living Under Muslim Laws. Her publications include *One Step Forward, Two Steps Back? Women of Pakistan,* co-authored with Khawar Mumtaz.

Jirina Siklova promoted human rights in Czechoslovakia under communism. She was a participant in Prague Spring, a signer of Charter '77, and a dissident who was imprisoned. She is a sociologist and chair of the Department of Social Work at Charles University in Prague. Her published works in English include "Backlash." She is also a founder of the Gender Studies and Curriculum Center, and was elected "Woman of the Year 1995" for the Czech Republic.

Yasmin Tambiah is a Senior Program Associate at the Institute for Women, Law and Development. She was a researcher at the International Centre for Ethnic Studies in Colombo, and has taught in the Women's Studies Program at Yale University. She has authored papers on violence against women and female sexuality, and is working on her doctoral dissertation which focuses on the organization of sexuality in medieval Jewish, Muslim and Christian communities.

Dorothy Q. Thomas is Director of the Human Rights Watch/Women's Rights Project based in Washington D.C. She was recently a fellow at the Bunting Institute at Radcliffe College, and is currently working on a book that examines the application of international human rights to the struggle for women's rights in the USA. She is the author of several reports and articles on international women's human rights, among which are *Criminal Injustice: Violence Against Women in Brazil* and *Double Jeopardy: Police Abuse of Women in Pakistan.*

Sima Wali is President and CEO of Refugee Women in Development (RefWID) Inc., an international organization supporting refugee and displaced women's organizational development efforts, based in Washington D.C. She serves on the boards and advisory committees of several refugee and women's national and international organizations, and has received awards for leadership in the field of refugee women in development.

Noeleen Heyzer is Director of UNIFEM, the United Nations Development Fund for Women. A former head of the Gender and Development Programme of the Asia Pacific Development Centre (APDC), she has authored ten books and many articles and papers on women and development issues. Ms. Heyzer is also a founding member of Development Alternatives with Women for a New Era (DAWN), a network of women leaders from the South.

Index

H

I